JOHN KEATS

The Making of a Poet

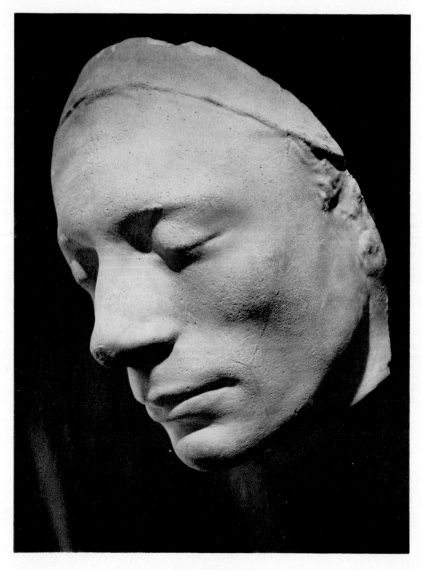

1 JOHN KEATS

From the life mask by B. R. Haydon, 1816,
Keats Memorial House, Hampstead

JOHN KEATS

The Making of a Poet

BY AILEEN WARD

THE VIKING PRESS

NEW YORK

First published in 1963 by The Viking Press, Inc.
625 Madison Avenue, New York 22, N.Y.

Published simultaneously in Canada by The Macmillan Company of Canada Limited

Library of Congress catalog card number: 63-15218

M B G
Set in Baskerville and Bulmer types
Printed in the U.S.A. by Vail-Ballou Press, Inc.

To Marjorie Hope Nicolson

and the memory of

Victoria Louise Schrager

Contents

Plates

Plates I and VII are photographs by Christopher Oxford from the collection in Keats Memorial House, reproduced by permission of the Hampstead Borough Council. The source of each of the other plates appears with the plate.

Preface

A NEW LIFE OF KEATS requires a word of explanation. The story has been told many times before and will be told again, as new facts about his life continue to be brought to light and critical revaluation clarifies and redefines his place in English poetry. But a new biography of Keats should attempt more than to present new information or synthesize recent criticism: it should try to convey a new sense of the meaning of his life. Keats's life has in fact meant something new to each generation that has reflected on it, for it was an extraordinary life, both in the intensity with which he lived it and in the unconscious eloquence with which he recorded it. Indeed, it has that representative quality, that fullness of significance, of which Keats himself was thinking when he wrote, "Shakespeare led a life of Allegory: his works are the comments on it." As Lionel Trilling has suggested, it was a life cast in the heroic mould. A close reading of Keats's poems and letters reveals the allegory that he himself sensed in it; his recurrent image for his own endeavour in poetry is a voyage of exploration across uncharted seas. He died thinking he had not reached his goal; yet in spite of the interruption of his work just as he attained maturity, his life shows a significant completion—the achievement of identity, the self-making which, according to Otto Rank, is the most important act of any artist's career. Keats's own remark on Milton may then be applied to him: "There was working in him as it were that same sort of thing as operates in the great world to the end of a Prophecy's being accomplished."

In our time Keats has been regarded increasingly as the man of his letters: so much so that F. R. Leavis has had to remind us sharply that our final concern must be with his poetry. In my view of Keats his greatness as a man is something distinct from, yet at the same time significantly related to, his greatness as a poet; his life was essentially a process of integrating these two aspects of his nature. The profound and delighted and ultimately tragic insight into human life which Keats communicated so immediately and directly in his letters was something he learned only slowly to express in his poetry as he re-shaped his poetic medium to convey it. Slowly—that is, in three years of the most concentrated effort in our literature. My account of his life, therefore, is concerned primarily with the development of his character as a poet—that audacious act of self-creation which he de-scribed in connection with the writing of *Endymion*. Where his previ-ous biographers have viewed him against the long tradition of English poetry or his day-to-day study of the poets from whom he learned his art, or against the wide backdrop of Regency society or the minutiae of his daily existence, I have tried to convey something of the inner drama of his creative life as it is recorded in his poems and letters. Inevitably this has limited my critical focus. The interpretation of Keats's poetry in the following pages is offered not as the detailed and rounded criticism which can alone do justice to the individual poem, but as a study, chiefly through his imagery, of the process by which his goal in poetry became clear to him, in that miraculous unfolding which John Middleton Murry has called the mystery of Keats. The mystery remains beyond analysis in the end, and fortunately so: for it is the compelling reason for us to continue reading Keats.

It is a pleasure to record the obligations incurred in writing this book. My first thanks are due to Elizabeth Ames and the Yaddo Cor-poration, for hospitality of the most constructive sort in the early stages of my work. I am also grateful to the American Association of University Women for the award of a Shirley Farr Fellowship which helped me to continue it.

The staffs of the New York Public Library, the Pierpont Morgan Library, the Skidmore College Library, the Harvard University Li-brary, the Cambridge University Library, the British Museum, and the Keats Memorial Library of the Hampstead Borough Council have extended me many courtesies. For permission to examine manuscripts and other documents relating to Keats, I owe especial thanks to Signora Vera Cacciatore, Curator of the Keats-Shelley Memorial House in Rome; Mr. J. H. Preston, former Curator of the Keats Memorial House and Museum in Hampstead; and most of all to Miss Mabel A. E. Steele, Curator of the Keats Collection of the Harvard University Library, who has generously and knowledgeably answered countless questions about the Keats documents in her charge. I am also grateful to all the present owners and custodians of Keats's letters for answering my in-quiries regarding them.

The Keats Memorial Library of the Hampstead Borough Council has kindly granted permission to use on the title page a drawing after that by Joseph Severn, found in Charles Brown's copy of *Endymion*, of the

Greek lyre which Keats asked to have engraved on his tombstone. For permission to reproduce the illustrations in this book I am grateful to the Houghton Library of Harvard University, the Keats Memorial House in Hampstead, the Keats-Shelley Memorial House in Rome, the Radio Times Hulton Picture Library of London, the Victoria and Albert Museum, and the National Portrait Gallery, London.

In my effort to work as completely as possible from Keats's own writings and those of his friends, I am profoundly indebted to Keats's editors—Harry Buxton Forman, Maurice Buxton Forman, H. W. Garrod, and Hyder Edward Rollins. I am also keenly aware of what I owe to the researches of many scholars in the field of Keats and his circle, especially to Keats's previous biographers, Sir Sidney Colvin, Miss Amy Lowell, Miss Dorothy Hewlett, and Mr. Robert Gittings. On several earlier occasions I have expressed my disagreement with certain aspects of Mr. Gittings' interpretation of Keats's life, particularly Keats's relations with Isabella Jones and the influence of Burton's *Anatomy of Melancholy* on his work. I would like to take this opportunity to record my admiration of many other aspects of Mr. Gittings' research and of the manner in which he has set it forth.

In the interest of general readability, I have kept the documentation of this book to a minimum. It is assumed that students of Keats will be familiar with his poems and letters in the editions of H. W. Garrod and H. E. Rollins and with the documents collected by Professor Rollins in *The Keats Circle* and *More Letters and Papers of the Keats Circle*. Therefore, except where a reference is obscure or a point controverted, I have not given notes to these primary sources in the life of Keats. I hope that my general indebtedness to the previous biographers of Keats and his friends will also be immediately apparent to students of the period and will be sufficiently acknowledged in the bibliography. Again for the sake of a readable narrative, I have quoted freely from Keats's letters without indicating omissions and have sometimes transposed the order of sentences; I have taken care, however, not to distort Keats's meaning in the process, and I trust that the close reader of Keats will recognize and accept these occasional condensations of the text. Wherever I have departed from the established text in my quotations, the emendations are indicated in detail.

Miss Dorothy Hewlett graciously answered a number of questions I asked her concerning Keats's life, and Mr. A. J. Liebling provided some valuable information about boxing in the nineteenth century. For other information I am indebted to Mr. W. R. LeFanu, Librarian of the Royal Society of Surgeons of England; Mr. William Lichtenwanger, Assistant Head of the Reference Section, Library of Congress; Mr. Cyril E. R. Platten, Town Clerk of the Borough of Enfield; Miss

Ellen Shafer, Librarian of the Rare Book Department, Free Library of Philadelphia; Mr. Lawrence E. Tanner, Keeper of the Muniments and Sub-Librarian, Westminster Abbey; and Mr. A. W. Wheen, Keeper of the Library of the Victoria and Albert Museum. I wish also to thank Professor Willard Bissell Pope, of the University of Vermont, and Professor Charles W. Hagelman, Jr., of the Lamar State College of Technology, for permission to cite from their unpublished doctoral dissertations. I am especially grateful to Dr. Erik H. Erikson for sending me a copy of his monograph, "The Problem of Ego Identity," prior to its publication in the *Journal of the American Psychoanalytic Association;* and to Dr. Frederick Wyatt for reading and commenting on the early chapters of my manuscript.

My greatest thanks are due to my editors, Marshall A. Best, Malcolm Cowley, and especially Catharine Carver, whose patience and skill have contributed immeasurably to the final form of this book.

It is a pleasure also to record the names of friends who have helped in many different ways during the course of my work: First, Kirsten Scott, for invaluable assistance in typing my manuscript; Mary Jane Holmes Baillie, Sylvia Berkman, Daphne Wilson Ercoli, Emma M. E. Hess, Mrs. Searle F. Holmes, Carter Harman, Kenneth Lewars, Lawrence Lieberfeld, Helen Drusilla Lockwood, Jean Baker Read, my colleague Robert Wagner, my student Elizabeth Caffrey, and last but not least, my parents, Aline Coursen and Waldron Merry Ward.

A. W.

New York City
April 1963

JOHN KEATS

The Making of a Poet

Chapter One

Close to the Source

IN the summer of 1803 the threat of invasion hung over England like a thunder-cloud. All along the shores of Kent and Sussex red-coated troops were pitching camp. A chain of Martello towers was being thrown over the hills of the southeast coast, and a defence canal dug across Romney Marsh; even the fishing boats were arming for conflict. In the coastal towns nervous civilians refused to undress at night, and petitions for deliverance from the foe were read aloud in every church of the land. Out at sea the squadrons of the Royal Navy stalked up and down before the French naval ports of Brest and Rochefort and Toulon, while a detachment of cruisers patrolled the Channel; on the cliffs of Dover sentries stood watch around the clock. Twenty miles across the strait the chalk cliffs of the French coast gleamed quietly in the summer sun; but in the crowded harbor of Boulogne the air rang with the sound of shipwrights' hammers. On the beaches the "Army of England," a hundred and fifty thousand veterans of the Revolutionary Wars, practised landing manœuvres and waited for their commander's orders. Napoleon Bonaparte had broken the Treaty of Amiens, signed with England only the year before. First Consul in France and virtual master of the Continent, he needed only to bring the British to their knees to rule unchallenged over Europe.

London meanwhile seethed with activity. On intercepting Bonaparte's plans for invasion, the Government had declared war in March, calling up the militia and setting the press gangs to work to man the fleet. Government agents slipped out of Whitehall, bound for France with plots against the First Consul's life. George

III, autocratic as ever though now only intermittently sane, had
dismissed the great Tory leader Pitt in 1801 and brought in the
ineffectual Addington as Prime Minister, thus making it easier to
play the Tory factions off against each other. The Prince of Wales,
who had broken with Princess Caroline several years before to
return to his first but illegal wife, Mrs. Fitzherbert, was now on
the point of finally breaking with her. Fat, silly, extravagant, universally unpopular, he dabbled in Whig politics mainly, it was said,
to annoy his father.

Yet the nation as a whole was united by the menace of invasion
as it had not been since the days of the Armada. The Army might
be corrupt and inefficient—a collection of dissipated young blue-
bloods commanding troops drawn from the scum of society, who
were kept in line mainly by the lash—but the citizens of England
rallied proudly to her defence. When nearly half a million recruits
answered the call for volunteers, the Government was so short of
muskets that it had to issue pikes instead. There was hardly an
able-bodied man in the whole country who did not join some
military unit or other. Up in Westmoreland, William Wordsworth, who had been carried away by republican ardor in the
early years of the French Revolution, now marched in a red coat
with the Grasmere volunteers and poured out sonnets calling
England to "Victory or Death!" In London a young whippersnap-
per named Leigh Hunt paraded gaily in the fashionable St. James
Regiment at Burlington House, then pranced off to wine-parties
or the theatre afterward. The wave of patriotic fervor reached its
height that summer with a grand muster of twenty-seven thousand
volunteers in Hyde Park.

All this while, in a quiet northern suburb of London off City
Road, a small boy was playing with his brothers—John Keats,
seven and a half years old. No more than any boy of the time could
he have escaped the tide of military excitement that was sweeping
over England. Beside their hoops and tops and kites, English lads
of 1803 had toy guillotines to play with, toy cannons to fire with
real gunpowder, and great English victories to act out in their
games. Their hero was Nelson, who had whipped the Spanish off
Cape Saint Vincent, the French at the Nile, and the Danes in the
Baltic; "Boney" was the ogre who, they were told, would carry
them off if they misbehaved. Parades became commonplace in
London that summer, but small boys were always ready to cheer

a line of soldiers marching by to drums and trumpets, led by officers with white plumes and drawn swords on prancing chargers. The Clerkenwell Volunteers drilled in a field near Keats's home in Craven Street; the Honourable Artillery Company practised on their grounds close to his father's stable on Finsbury Pavement. Keats's father, an accomplished horseman, most likely joined a cavalry unit, perhaps the Clerkenwell cavalry, which rode out in smart leather breeches and magnificent bearskin helmets.[1] * Keats's uncle, Midgley John Jennings, was a lieutenant in the Marines and had fought in the battle against the Dutch off Camperdown in 1797. In his old school at Enfield it was a legend that his tallness had made him a special mark for enemy fire, which he coolly ignored, and that the Dutch commander had afterward remarked on his courage to Admiral Duncan.

In this time of mobilization and suspense, John Keats confronted an anxious future of his own—the traditional first trial of manhood in England. He was to be sent away to his uncle's old school, the Clarke academy at Enfield. What he felt at leaving the safe haven of family and home is not a matter of record. But years later, when he faced the last separation of his life—leaving the country and the girl he loved, to die in a foreign land—these days stirred in his memory. With the thought of the journey waking him up each morning at dawn, he nerved himself to leave England, he wrote, "as a soldier marches up to a battery." The image is significant. From the time of his first encounter with the world, life was to seem a test of whatever fortitude he could bring to it.

In later years Keats almost never mentioned his boyhood. Indeed, for the first twenty of his twenty-five years, there is no personal record except for a handful of short poems of uncertain date. Beside these remain a few bare facts, some of them disputed, about his parentage and schooling, and the fragmentary and often conflicting impressions of four or five of his contemporaries, mostly recalled a quarter-century after his death and distorted by bias or clouded by sentiment. Nevertheless most of his biographers have assumed—perhaps on the analogy with nations that have no history—that his boyhood was a happy one. Keats's silence on this

* Superior numbers refer to Notes, pp. 416–440.

point may raise a doubt; yet his first seven or eight years do seem to have been remarkably happy, though in an unremarkable way.

His father, Thomas Keats, had come up as a boy from the west of England to make his way in London. From the little that is known of him, he was a likeable young man, energetic, intelligent, short but strongly built and good-looking—"a man much above his station in life," as he was later described. He had sprung from humble people and first worked as a groom in the London stables. By twenty he had become head ostler at the Swan and Hoop, a prosperous livery establishment in Moorfields owned by one John Jennings; and there, like the industrious apprentice of legend, he won the love of his master's daughter. Frances Jennings was a headstrong girl of nineteen, with a fine figure and a pretty face a little spoiled by too wide a mouth. She was evidently a flirt; one of her neighbours remembered her habit of picking up her skirts in crossing a muddy street to show off her good-looking legs, and another—an unsympathetic witness—reported "her passions were so ardent that it was dangerous to be alone with her." [2] If she risked her parents' disapproval in marrying her father's foreman, she was not one to be deterred. In October 1794 she and Thomas Keats were married at St. George's in Hanover Square, a fashionable West End church several miles from her own parish. Neither of her parents was present to sign the register; but whether they merely refused to indulge her whim of a Mayfair wedding, or whether she needed to keep the marriage a secret till after the event, remains a mystery. There is some uncertainty about the exact birth date of her oldest son, and some reason for thinking it occurred only seven or eight months after her marriage.[3] But her parents cannot have greatly disapproved of the match, for the young couple returned to the parental roof and the family business, and their first child, John, was born in their rooms over the stable. At his baptism the following December, the date of his birth was given as October 31, 1795, and this apparently is the date Keats regarded as his birthday—though, we are told, he always disliked having it celebrated. Three brothers followed him—George in February 1797, Thomas in November 1799, and Edward in April 1801; then a sister, Frances Mary, in June 1803.

From the little evidence we have, it was a lively and affectionate family to grow up in. John Jennings was all a grandfather should be. Hearty and confident like most self-made men, he was riding the great wave of English prosperity in the later eighteenth century. Road transport, shipping, commerce, agriculture, and industry—all were expanding at an unprecedented rate. It was the great age of coaching, between the surfacing of the turnpikes and the advent of the railway; the new crack coaches cut travelling time to a quarter of what it had been in the mid-century. A stable such as the Swan and Hoop, well located near the center of the city, could make a small fortune for its owner. Yet for all his business acumen, John Jennings had a generous nature—too generous and gullible, according to his grandson George Keats, for him to become really rich. He loved good food and drink; it was said that the women of his household spent four days out of the week roasting and baking for Sunday dinner—though this may only reflect the fact that he was an innkeeper or "victualler" as well as a stable-keeper.[4] Alice Jennings, his wife, was a more sober character, sensible, kindly, and warm-hearted, well liked by her neighbours and adored by her grandchildren. She was the kind of woman to whom people instinctively turn in distress, one to take care of orphans and befriend country girls in the city. In the family background there were a few shadowy cousins and aunts and uncles, most of them apparently small merchants in London; in the foreground a crowd of little boys laughed and tumbled and scrapped, watched with indulgent eyes by their parents.

Frances Jennings had been an ardent young girl in love; as a mother she poured out affection unrestrainedly. Like her father, she had a great gusto for life. It is said she was "passionately fond of amusement" and paid no attention to hours or seasons or even pregnancies in pursuing it.[5] Her son George remembered her chiefly for her "doting fondness" and her recklessness with money —a trait which her sons inherited. According to George, John, the firstborn, was her favourite child, the one most like her in appearance and temperament, whom she humoured in all his whims. As Freud (a favourite son himself) once remarked, "A man who has been the indisputable favourite of his mother keeps for life the feeling of a conqueror, that confidence of success which frequently induces real success." From the beginning John seems to have been a boy of intense feelings and a vivid imagination, fiercely devoted to his mother. Once, it is told, when she fell ill and absolute quiet was ordered, John found an old sword and took up his post outside her door with the blade bared, forbidding anyone to enter. The family atmosphere was one of warmth and freedom, in which the brothers grew up knit by unusually close bonds of loyalty; and for his young sister Keats was to develop an almost fatherly tenderness. Perhaps their first experience of loss, when Edward, the youngest boy, died in infancy, drew them still closer together.

Not long after his daughter's marriage, John Jennings, already ailing with gout, retired from active control of his business and moved with his wife to the country. Thomas Keats was then left in charge of the Swan and Hoop, which became his property in 1803. By about 1800 he had prospered enough to move his growing family from the rooms over the stables to a house in Craven Street, half a mile to the north in Shoreditch. Still it was the Swan and Hoop that gave John Keats his first glimpse of the world, and the colour and clamour of those earliest impressions must have sunk deep in his memory. The stableyard was the scene of constant comings and goings, of shouts and neighs and clattering hoofs, of jingling harness and gleaming horseflesh, of strong smells and swift movement that would fill a small boy with delight. Thomas Keats, though he was described as an unostentatious man, loved good horses and kept a remarkably fine one for his own use; he cut a handsome figure when he rode out on Sundays to the meets at Highgate and Highbury. Among the tall men astride their powerful horses who were Keats's first image of splendour and mastery, his own father must have seemed the most magnificent.

Their new home in Craven Street, a backwater of neat brick houses not far from Charles Square, marked a step up in the world. The Keatses were prospering, and their sons must have felt the force of their parents' ambitions for them. When it came time to think of the boys' schooling, there was talk of sending them to Harrow. It was an impractical idea, though not impossible. The lines that divided one class from another in England were as sharply drawn as ever at that time, and the public schools were far fewer in number and less open to middle-class pupils than they later became. The son of a tailor in the Strand is remembered as the one boy whom Shelley fought and whipped at Eton; there was a place in that world for the sons of the owner of the Swan and Hoop, but they would have had to fight for it. At Harrow, Keats would probably have missed making the acquaintance of the young Lord Byron, who was seven years his senior; he would have gained a perfunctory training in Latin and Greek and a more thorough one in cricket and fives, but little else. Studies in the public schools then were narrow and poorly directed; games took more of the boys' time than work; discipline was brutal, bullying and dissoluteness common. However, the question of Harrow did not have to be answered till Keats reached twelve or thirteen. His parents decided to start his education at Mr. Clarke's academy at Enfield, and they chose better than they knew.

-»»-«-

John Clarke had started out in the law but soon found teaching more congenial. After a few years as classics master in the famous Dissenting academy in Northampton then headed by the eminent Baptist minister John Collett Ryland, he married Ryland's daughter and moved to Enfield to set up a school of his own. A stocky, square-headed man of liberal convictions, he remained unshaken in his beliefs when public opinion turned toward reaction in the 1790s. He was a friend of John Cartwright, the Parliamentary reformer, and of Joseph Priestley, the great scientist, Unitarian minister, and radical, whose house and laboratory were wrecked by the Birmingham mob in 1791. Through these men Clarke was aligned with a small but significant minority who, even after England went to war with France in 1793, continued to uphold the principles of political democracy and religious freedom which had triumphed in America and inspired the early days of the French Revolution. In 1794 twelve of the leading Reformers were indicted for high treason in a wave of anti-Jacobin hysteria; but though the Government failed to win a conviction, it managed to stifle effective protest for many years afterward, and it was a brave man who openly maintained his faith in the principles of reform in those oppressive years.

Clarke had enlightened theories of education, which, like his liberal stand in politics, were rare in schoolmasters of his day. He thought that a school should bring out the good in boys, not merely hold the bad in check. Instead of caning his pupils into learning their lessons, he set up rules enforced by rewards rather than by punishments and encouraged voluntary extra work with special prizes. The school was evidently modelled on the Dissenting academies of the time, which offered a much more modern and rounded curriculum than the public schools, including history, science, and modern languages as well as the classics. Keats later complained that French had been crammed down his throat as though he were a young jackdaw, but he never regretted his ability to read Voltaire or Ronsard in the original. Mr. Clarke also encouraged hobbies; he provided garden plots, for instance, for the boys who wanted to work in them. His system left the pupils far freer to develop in their own directions and at their own rates than most schools of the day; it was a good soil for John Keats to take root and grow in.

The village of Enfield lay about twelve miles north of London, among rolling fields and shady woods, the remains of the old Enfield Chase. It was a pleasant countryside for half-holiday rambles, and the New River provided good swimming for the boys. The schoolhouse was a handsome, airy residence, with a classical façade garlanded with flowers and fruits and heads of cherubim. Behind it lay the playground, bordered with poplars, and gardens and a pasture. A fine pear tree stood in the playground, and a morello cherry tree grew against the courtyard wall; strawberry beds were planted beside the pond, and the boys who watered them were given the berries when they were ripe. Here Keats must have sampled his first "antiquated cherries full of sugar cracks" and acquired the weakness for "pear-tasting—plum-judging —apricot nibbling—peach scrunching—Nectarine-sucking and Melon-carving" to which he later confessed. Probably he too had his garden plot to tend, for he developed a close and loving knowledge of flowers, to judge from the drawings of pinks and violets scattered up and down the margins of one of his lecture notebooks. Beyond the school the meadows stretched away to the dark edges of the forest, from which the song of nightingales unfurled endlessly in the still May nights.

Here Keats arrived in the summer of 1803. Cowden Clarke, the fifteen-year-old son of the headmaster, remembered him only dimly in his first year as the smallest of the seventy or eighty pupils, still wearing the frilled dress of a little boy. His brother George either came with him or followed not long afterward, and they were later joined by Tom, the youngest. From the beginning there was some confusion about the brothers' ages. Even as a boy John was unusually short, and George soon outgrew him; as a result, Cowden Clarke, who later became his close friend, always took

Keats as George's junior and thought him a year younger than he actually was.

Whatever the ordeal of separation from home, Keats must have soon surmounted it, for he rapidly became popular with his schoolmates and a favourite of Mrs. Clarke. Cowden Clarke's first clear recollection of Keats was "his brisk, winning face"—a mobility of expression that was to become striking in his young manhood. There was every reason for him to be happy at Enfield. His grandparents lived only a few miles away in Ponders End; his uncle occasionally returned to his old school to dine with the headmaster; and his father and mother often drove out for a Sunday visit. Thomas Keats impressed John Clarke as a man of "fine commonsense and native respectability," unaffected by his rapid rise to prosperity. It is true that Cowden Clarke, who reported this verdict, was eager to prove that Keats's family was not merely respectable but "estimable." Yet his own recollection of Thomas Keats's "lively and energetic countenance, when seated in his gig and preparing to drive his wife home," gives a glimpse of a forceful and attractive man, one whose image must have sunk deep into his young son's mind.

The family's future looked bright; then disaster struck out of a clear sky. On April 15, 1804, Thomas Keats, riding home late at night from Southgate, was thrown when his horse slipped on the pavement in City Road, and fractured his skull against the railings. He was alive but speechless when the watchman found him and carried him home; the next morning he died. A week later he was buried at St. Stephen's Church in Coleman Street.

Frances Keats was now left alone in London with four young children to support and a busy livery stable to manage. Her parents were a dozen miles away in Middlesex, her father past seventy and ill. As an attractive young widow with a thriving business, she was a desirable match, especially under the law of those times by which a woman's property became her husband's at marriage. It is not difficult to see why a suitor presented himself almost immediately, but it is hard to understand her acceptance of him barely two months after Thomas Keats's death. Neither loneliness nor a sense of helplessness, nor even her passionate nature, can quite account for the haste of this remarriage; and her motive in being married a second time in St. George's Church, on June 27, 1804, is still harder to fathom. But most obscure of all is her

reason for choosing William Rawlings as her second husband.
A bank clerk in the City, with no property of his own, he seems
to have taken a far keener interest in the Swan and Hoop than in
his new wife and family.

The marriage did not last. Frances Rawlings soon found life
with her new husband so intolerable that she left him, even
though, under the law of the time, she thereby lost all claim to her
property and all legal control of her children. Alice Jennings, who
had disapproved of the marriage from the start, then took the
grandchildren to live with her—whether on Rawlings' insistence
or her own initiative does not matter. Rawlings sold the stable
at the beginning of 1806 and thereupon dropped out of Keats's
life for good; [6] while his mother, according to the only account
of her life, disappeared for several years, taking to brandy, it is
hinted, and living "as the wife of a Jew at Enfield, named Abra-
ham." [7]

Keats's biographers have usually mentioned this story of his
mother only to deny it and maintain that she went to live with her
mother and her children on leaving Rawlings, but the evidence
is against them. In a jingle describing his boyhood which he later
wrote to amuse his sister, Keats mentioned their "Granny good"
but, significantly, not their mother; indeed, he never referred to
her in all his letters to Fanny. Once, however, he guardedly told
a close friend that "his greatest misfortune" since childhood was
that "he had no mother." [8] George Keats recalled his mother only
dimly, while Fanny hardly ever mentioned her in all her later
voluminous writings about her childhood. And the fact that for
four years Mrs. Rawlings did not collect an annuity of fifty pounds
bequeathed her by her father in 1805 [9] strongly implies that she
was estranged from her family after leaving her second husband,
if not also living on the support of another man. None of the
children ever spoke of their stepfather, though Keats may have
had him in mind in his cryptic mention, years later, of "earlier
Misfortunes" preceding his mother's death. So complete was his
silence on the events of his early life that his later friends were
astonished to learn of them after his death.[10] His reserve has been
laid to his diffidence about being born over a livery stable, but
it was far more probably due to an insoluble conflict of emotions
about his mother.

His father's death and his mother's remarriage would be staggering blows to any boy of eight or nine; their effect on John Keats can hardly be exaggerated. In two short months the very foundations of his security had been knocked out from under him. Some writers have taken these losses as mere "unpropitious occurrences," brief interruptions in the happy course of Keats's boyhood; [11] but it is worth recalling another tragedy very similar to his. "But two months dead!" The parallel with Hamlet's situation is startling, and it helps illuminate the welter of incommunicable emotion which young John Keats felt against his faithless mother and his father's usurper. The timing of these two blows was also particularly unfortunate. Keats lost his father at the stage in a boy's development when his earlier jealous rivalry begins to yield to proud identification with his male parent; as a result, he was to search for an idealized father in one older man after another throughout his life. He had also barely reached the end of the period of intense possessiveness about his mother—marked dramatically for an English boy by his being sent off to school— when his former rival disappeared and a new and hateful one took his place. But still harder for Keats to accept must have been his mother's subsequent disappearance and mysterious disgrace. The idealized woman of his crucial early experience, beautiful and recklessly affectionate, had betrayed and abandoned him in a manner beyond his understanding, and forever afterward he was haunted by the fear that any woman he loved would play him false and then leave him. The boy began to develop a wariness in his dealings with others, beneath his instinctive openness and spontaneity. "All my life I have suspected every Body," Keats later wrote; and though his biographers have discounted this statement, he had good reason for making it.

Yet the immediate effect of this tragedy was not to plunge Keats into a Hamlet-like paralysis: quite the reverse. Almost overnight, it seems, he changed from an affectionate child into a rebellious schoolboy, protesting against the world by the only means he had —his fists. Fifteen years later Keats still remembered the glory of winning his first battle—like being "lifted from the tribe of Manessah"; and in spite of his small size he soon established himself as the pluckiest and scrappiest fighter in the school. Fighting was "meat and drink to him," as Edward Holmes, one of his first friends, recalled; "he would fight anyone, morning, noon or night." Such pugnacity must have had a driving force deeper than mere ambition to win a place in the schoolboy world. Some of it must have sprung from half-conscious rage against his stepfather and his errant mother. Some of it came more consciously from another source: identification with his heroic uncle, Lieutenant (later Captain) Midgley Jennings of the Royal Marines. "Their sailor relation was always in the thoughts of the brothers," Holmes remembered, "and they determined to keep up a family reputation for courage." Regrettably it appears that the story of Jennings' intrepidity under fire at Camperdown was mostly invented [12]— perhaps by his own nephews. Yet the fact that Cowden Clarke believed it suggests that Keats had more than the average small boy's talent for boasting. With the death of his father he desperately needed an image of manhood on which to pattern himself; and in an England whose Navy had saved it from Napoleon and whose national idol was Nelson, Keats's choice of his uncle as hero was inevitable.

Less than a year after his father's death one more link with his childhood snapped when his grandfather died in March 1805. The old man had laboured well for his family. John Jennings left more than £13,000—a respectable estate in those days—to be divided among his wife, his sister Mary Sweetingburgh, his son Midgley, his daughter Frances Rawlings, and his four Keats grandchildren. The will was badly drawn, and as a result much of the estate was later entangled in Chancery proceedings; but for the present the family was comfortably provided for. Mrs. Jennings received a moderate income of £200, and Mrs. Rawlings the annuity of £50 mentioned earlier. The grandchildren inherited £250 each in trust, and much more of the estate was eventually to come to them. With the breakdown of their mother's second marriage soon afterward, however, they were left less well off than John Jennings could have foreseen. When Rawlings sold the Swan and Hoop, pocketed the money, and disappeared, all the dreams of a Harrow education for the Keats boys vanished with him.

But Alice Jennings immediately picked up the broken pieces of their lives. Soon after her husband's death she took a house in Edmonton, a village about four miles from Enfield, and here Keats found a second home. Mrs. Jennings became a second mother to him, winning from him a devotion very different from the love he had felt for his mother, yet almost as deep. The fact that Keats had two mothers during his boyhood—one young, beau-

tiful and unreliable, the other much older, equable and affectionate—is worth noting. It helps explain a division in his nature
which appeared later in many forms, one being a tendency to be
drawn toward two quite different types of women—flirtatious
young beauties and serious young ladies, sexually much less challenging, often several years older than himself.

No doubt the new home lacked some of the warmth of the old
one, but it gave the Keats children a stability they needed. Here
Fanny grew up into a shy little girl, quiet and well behaved—
her grandmother's child rather than her mother's, and the pet of
her three older brothers. And here no doubt Keats enjoyed himself in all the ways that boys did at that time: "played cricket," as
his friend Haydon described his own boyhood, "rode a black pony
about the neighbourhood; pinned ladies' gowns together on market days and waited to see them split; knocked at doors by night
and ran away; swam and bathed, heated myself, worried my parents, and at last was laid on my back by the measles." [13] From
Keats's later poems and letters we catch glimpses of him in those
years at home or on half-holidays at school, roaming the meadows,
climbing trees, watching the clouds overhead drift into fantastic
figures, sailing homemade boats on the ponds, and thus becoming
acquainted with "the whole tribe of the Bushes and the Brooks"—
"Gold-finches, Tomtits, Minnows, Mice, Ticklebacks, Dace, and
Cock-salmons." The "Song About Myself" he later wrote for his
sister recalls his habit of bringing fish home to keep in the washing-
tubs—"In spite Of the might Of the Maid"—

> O he made
> 'Twas his trade
> Of Fish a pretty Kettle
> A Kettle—A Kettle
> Of Fish a pretty Kettle
> A Kettle!

At school there was little to mark him off from the other boys
except the very intensity of his boyishness. From all accounts he
was as thoughtless, impulsive, boastful, and self-centred as any
growing lad. Years later Keats wrote, "The most unhappy hours
in our lives are those in which we recollect times past to our own
blushing," and singled out his schooldays as those he would like
most to forget. From the first—or from the time he acquired a
stepfather—he cared conspicuously little for the good opinion of

the masters but scrambled through his lessons with no visible effort. He took all a boy's usual delight in jokes and pranks, and in sports he was outstanding. Like any schoolboy of his age he learned to ride, swim, box, row, and play cricket—a game he was still keen on a dozen years later. But it was as a fighter that he made his name. The older boys came to look on him as a kind of pet gamecock, while the younger boys who wanted to win his friendship had to prove themselves in battle. Apparently there was a histrionic streak in him—some more than usually vivid sense of playing a noble part. Cowden Clarke reports that when his fighting temper was up Keats resembled no one so much as the great Shakespearean actor Edmund Kean in one of his dramatic transports. Once, Clarke recalled, when Tom Keats spoke saucily to one of the junior teachers and was cuffed for it, John rushed up to the defence of his frail young brother and struck out in a fury at the astonished usher, who was twice his size. Mr. Clarke was so touched by this bravado that he could not bring himself to punish Keats when the boy was haled up before him.

Yet under these gestures appears a certain nervous instability, evidence of the emotional conflict still latent. Keats was plagued by violent swings of mood; Holmes remembered him as always between "outrageous fits of laughter" and "passions of tears," and Clarke recalled that his temper was sometimes almost uncontrollable. In his dark moments he used to lash out savagely at his younger brother. George, a far more even-natured lad, seems to have inherited their father's self-assurance and stability, while John took after their mother, and it was also George, the taller and heavier, who usually won their battles. Clarke reports that George used to pin John down by main force and laugh while John raged against him—a humiliating defeat to take from one's younger brother. Nevertheless George remained the closest companion of his boyhood. According to Holmes, Keats made few of the warm attachments that most schoolboys form at this age; evidently the mysterious disgrace hanging over his family life made friendship difficult. Yet he was an attractive lad, with his curly reddish-gold hair, large hazel-coloured eyes, and trim athletic build; and, with his daring and generosity of character, he was universally liked. Holmes summed him up forty years later as "a boy whom anyone from his extraordinary vivacity & personal beauty might easily have fancied would become great—but," he added significantly, "rather in some military capacity than in literature."

For Keats's schooldays were played out against a steadily darkening background of war. For two long years after 1803 England remained poised to meet the French invasion, while Napoleon crowned himself Emperor, reorganized his government, and revised his strategy. In the summer of 1805 the French fleet slipped out of its blockade at Toulon, then was cornered by the British off Cape Trafalgar. There, with Nelson's death, England won decisive command of the seas; yet war on the Continent was to drag on for another decade. On hearing of the defeat of the Third Coalition at Austerlitz in December, 1805, the ailing Pitt cried, "Roll up that map of Europe—we shall not need it these twenty years." A few weeks later he died, followed shortly by Charles James Fox, the great Whig leader and the last liberal spokesman in Parliament. After Austerlitz came more disasters at Jena and Wagram; by 1810 Napoleon's empire extended from the Baltic to the Straits of Messina, from the Niemen River to Cape Finisterre. The war simmered down to a struggle between rival blockades and endless skirmishing in Spain. Under the blockade English landowners' fortunes rose as food prices soared, and the enterprising new factory owners prospered with them; but the wages of the workers on the farms and in the mills sank to the starvation level. To muffle their discontent the Government outlawed trade unions and political societies, prosecuted its critics for sedition, and forbade meetings of protest. In 1811, Keats's last year at school, George III became hopelessly insane and his dissolute and unstable son was appointed Prince Regent.

Keats's own life grew darker during these years. At the end of 1807 his uncle Midgley, whom he worshipped, was stricken with consumption. The following year he died at Huntington at the age of thirty-one,[14] leaving Keats, at thirteen, the oldest male member of his family. Far more disturbing was his mother's reappearance not long afterward. At last she returned to her family in Edmonton, an ill woman, bedridden in her early thirties, evidently broken in both body and spirit. To Keats, on the threshold of adolescence, the sight of her faded beauty and dimming vitality must have been a deeply troubling experience. Then in 1809 her illness changed disastrously for the worse: she too developed signs of consumption.

This was merely the last stage in an illness that must have been advancing unchecked for several years. Tuberculosis * was epidemic in England at that time, taking the life of one person out of every four in London,[15] yet almost nothing was understood about its cause or cure. It was thought to be hereditary, and there was no way of diagnosing it with certainty till its final symptoms appeared, when it was too late. First came a low fever, barely detectable, alternating with periods of good health and spirits; then lassitude, pallor, and loss of weight; later a persistent cough with blood-spitting; then finally a sudden decline and wasting of the body. This was the change Keats had to watch taking place in his mother, and it shook him to the depths. All the devotion he had felt to her as a child came surging back, redoubled by the passion of early adolescence. During his holidays at home he insisted on taking over the whole task of nursing her. He cooked her meals and administered her medicine; he read novels to her by day and sat up nights in an armchair, watching by her bed.[16] On returning to Enfield he must have cheered himself along with dreams of her recovery, for when the news of her death came, in March 1810, it was a sudden and staggering blow. On March 20 he followed one more coffin out of St. Stephen's and stood by one more grave in the churchyard at Coleman Street. Back at school, he was overcome by the loss for weeks afterward. Attacks of grief used to seize him during study hours; then he would hide behind the master's desk to fight it out alone, while the schoolroom was hushed in sympathy.

-》》《《-

Poetry, Cyril Connolly has said, comes from the ferment of an unhappy childhood working through a noble imagination. Keats is no exception to this rule, though the painful experience of his childhood took a special form—intense happiness suddenly shattered by his father's death and his mother's defection. The tragedy of his mother's death not only upset whatever equilibrium he had managed to recover in his schooldays but added a far more complicated experience of bereavement to the earlier one. Just as he

---

* This term was not used till the end of the nineteenth century. In Keats's time the disease was called phthisis or, in its final stages, consumption.

lost his father at the age when he needed him most keenly, he found and then lost his mother again at the time of his sexual reawakening, when the unusual physical intimacy with her would have been especially disturbing. These losses did not, of course, make Keats a poet, but they laid a burden of emotion on him which would later seek an outlet, and they shaped the ways in which he received and interpreted his later experience just as surely as Byron's humiliating deformity and Calvinistic upbringing and Shelley's persecution at school formed their sensibility. By comparison with them, Keats seems to have reacted more straightforwardly to his experience, much as any healthy child would have done; so, rather than distorting his view of life, his bereavement appears at first only to have given it precocious depth and clarity. The line seems to run straight from his early experience to his later vision of

> Beauty that must die;
> And Joy, whose hand is ever at his lips
> Bidding adieu; and aching Pleasure nigh,
> Turning to poison while the bee-mouth sips. . . .

The intensity of the beauty, the joy, the pleasure, and the bitterness of their loss: this "knowledge of contrast, feeling for light and shade," which he spoke of in the last letter he ever wrote as "necessary for a poem," was the lesson of his boyhood. The experience of his adolescence, however, was to shape his later life in ways more obscure than this, which would become apparent only with the passing of the years.

His mother's death seems to have transformed Keats even more dramatically than his father's death six years before. All at once the aggressive and irresponsible boy who had taken such delight in jokes and brawls became a silent adolescent, concentrated, aloof, passionately absorbed in reading. Before this time he had shown no interest in books; now he would be up and at work before seven in the morning. Driven out by the masters to play cricket, he would walk up and down the garden with a book; at supper he ate with a folio propped between him and the table. Almost overnight he seems to have lost his taste for fighting; his battle with the world appears to have turned in on himself. George testified that from this time on he and John "never passed an opposing word" [17]—surely an exaggeration, but still some sign of change. The fiery spirit portrayed by Holmes turned melancholy and fretful, given, according to his brother, to "bitter fits of hypochondriasm."

This was apparently not the usual melancholy moodiness of early adolescence but a deep and prolonged depression in which the experience of death was compounded, as it often is for sensitive children, with a feeling of guilt. For Keats's absorption in his studies, at first a way of withdrawing from a world which had become too painful to deal with, soon became an endeavour to win the adult approval he had scorned before, and thus perhaps to fend off an obscure sense of responsibility for his mother's suffering. Life suddenly became a serious affair. Already he had to face the question of his future career, for only one more year of school lay ahead. Then, probably within a few months of his mother's death, he was confirmed.[18] This experience must have raised large issues of human nature and destiny at a time when they would have been most troubling to him. Behind all these questions lay the greatest riddle of all—his mother. She had not been a good woman; yet he had loved her. She had betrayed him, then, betrayed herself, had returned to him; he had devoted himself to caring for her, then she had died. The dilemma of her nature, the irony of his failure, the meaning of death itself—all were problems that he could neither solve nor keep from posing themselves.

Keats may have retreated into books as a refuge from painful reality, but they soon became an imaginary world that almost made up for the one he had lost. He went headlong through the school library, devouring everything from *Robinson Crusoe* and *The Arabian Nights* to Captain Cook's voyages and Robertson's histories of Scotland and the reign of Charles V. Some of his pocket money went on the thrillers popular with schoolboys of his time, such as Beckford's *Vathek* and the novels of Monk Lewis and Mrs. Radcliffe. Shakespeare, on first reading, appealed to the same thirst for excitement, for Holmes recalled Keats's saying of *Macbeth* that no one would dare read it alone in a house at two o'clock in the morning. History satisfied another deep need, for heroes to worship. "The memory of great men" was to be a constant theme of Keats's early poems, especially the champions of freedom such as Brutus and Milton, William Tell and William Wallace, and King Alfred, whose portrait appears on the

seals of many of his early letters.[19] Years later this hero-worship-
ping tendency led Keats on an out-of-the-way expedition to copy
a letter of Nelson's—"very much to his honor"—to show his
friends.

Something else drew him to the world of mythology and the
wanderings of Aeneas—the first stirrings of a sense of beauty and
pathos. Years later Cowden Clarke recalled Keats at this time as
poring over a handbook of classical mythology till he knew it by
heart; but this picture appears to be an elderly schoolmaster's
sentimental exaggeration—unless Keats was fascinated, as was
Leigh Hunt at the same age, by the alluring illustrations of the
goddesses.[20] Yet as a voluntary task in his last year at school he
undertook a prose translation of the entire *Aeneid.* Books now
became a new world to conquer, and he threw himself into his
studies with the same energy he had given to games and fighting.
In his last two or three terms at school he won first place for voluntary work each time, emerging with a miscellaneous assortment
of prizes—Kauffman's *Dictionary of Merchandise,* Robertson's
History of America, and Bonnycastle's *Introduction to Astron-
omy.* The first made no impression on him, but the other two
were to send his imagination on distant journeys.

In discovering this new world Keats also found the first and
most important friend of his youth. Cowden Clarke, the headmaster's son, was eight years his senior and had tutored him in his
first lessons at Enfield. But with Keats's sudden intellectual development the gap between their ages began to narrow, and Clarke
took an increasingly warm interest in his pupil. He was a born
teacher, enthusiastic and generous, with a keen feeling for poetry
and a gift for bringing the past to life; years later he was to make
his name as a lecturer and writer on Chaucer and Shakespeare.
Tall, sturdy, with bristly hair and a hearty laugh, he was also a
first-rate cricketer and subsequently wrote a popular book on the
game. He loved music and played the piano well; in the dormitory
upstairs Keats used to lie awake nights listening to him practise
Mozart and Handel. One evening Clarke found young Edward
Holmes listening to him on the stairs, and on learning of the
boy's passion for music agreed to give him lessons; Holmes grew
up to be an accomplished pianist and to write the first biography
of Mozart in English. Clarke encouraged Keats by lending him
books from his own shelves and discussing his interests, in politics

as well as literature, with him. Bishop Burnet's *History of My Own Time,* the folio volume which Clarke remembered Keats reading at supper, gave the boy his first glimpse of the long struggle for freedom in England. Keats also started borrowing *The Examiner,* the leading liberal magazine of the day, from Mr. Clarke, and from it he began to form a vivid picture of the contradictions and injustices of the world around him.

Soon enough he would have to come to grips with that world, in one of its more uncompromising aspects. Mrs. Jennings, who was now nearly seventy-five, realized she needed help in providing for her grandchildren's future. Shortly after her daughter's death she appointed two London merchants, John Rowland Sandell and Richard Abbey, to be their guardians and made over to them the money left her by her husband to hold in trust for the children. Sandell played a minor part in this responsibility; six years later he got into financial difficulties and fled from his creditors to Holland, where he later died. But Abbey, who had come from the same Yorkshire village as Mrs. Jennings and had known her family in London, readily assumed the role of authority in the Keats children's lives.

In all England it would have been hard to find a more solid pillar of the established order than Abbey—prosperous tea broker in Pancras Lane, landowner and churchwarden in Walthamstow, member of the Port of London Committee and the Honourable Company of Girdlers, Steward of the City of London National Schools Examinations, and twice Master of the Honourable Company of Patten Makers. Stout, conscientious, unimaginative, he was as old-fashioned in his dress as in his opinions and kept on wearing the white cotton stockings, breeches, and half-boots of the mid-eighteenth century for years after they had gone out of style. The prudence one looks for in a trustee took some strange forms with Abbey, however. The Sunday School Committee in Walthamstow, of which he was a member, awarded a guinea to every poor pupil who, after leaving the school, remained for a year in his first employment. But when Abbey became chairman he required that, in order to receive their guineas, the pupils produce the Bibles and prayer books they had been given on leaving school, to prove they had not sold them.[21] As Master of the Patten Makers, Abbey cut down on the Company's dinners, which had been noted for their conviviality, and outlawed the serving of wine. It was Abbey who disapprovingly described Frances Jennings as a flirtatious young girl and dissolute young widow. He thought she had married beneath her and suspected there was bad blood in the family; but he resolved to do his duty, as he saw it, by his four charges.

On becoming their guardian, Abbey must have discussed the question of careers with John and George at some length. With their limited resources, it was important they get off to a good start. At fourteen or fifteen, it would seem, a boy hardly knows who he is, much less what he wants to do with his life; yet this was the usual age for middle-class lads to leave school and start work. George apparently had no trouble making up his mind; Abbey offered to take him into his counting-house and, as far as can be known, he accepted without hesitation. But the tea brokerage, or any other business, had little appeal for John. His record at Mr. Clarke's suggested a professional career, but in what? He could have entered the law by way of an apprenticeship, or have followed the example of Cowden Clarke and gone into teaching; but evidently neither of these possibilities tempted him. Advancement in the Army required wealth and social position; as for a naval career like his uncle's, he came three inches short of the height required of an officer.[22] If Keats felt any disappointment at giving up what may well have been the ambition of his boyhood, there is no record of it. The change which his mother's illness and death had made in him reached deep, for it is the only explanation of his final choice of career. He decided to become a doctor.

This decision has astonished so many of Keats's later readers that it is often assumed that his guardian forced it on him. But Cowden Clarke, his closest friend at the time, always understood it was "his own selection" and not Abbey's.[23] Certainly from Abbey's point of view a medical career was a sensible choice. The boy could not hope to become a physician—the topmost rank of the profession, which required years of advanced study; but he could easily qualify as an apothecary or surgeon, the equivalent at that time of a general practitioner. This involved a shorter and less expensive course of training, quite within John's reach—an apprenticeship of some years to a local doctor, perhaps followed by a year's study in a London hospital to qualify for the Surgeons' Examination. Moreover, Mr. Thomas Hammond, the surgeon

of Edmonton, needed an apprentice in the summer of 1811. Hammond lived in Church Street, not far from Keats's own home, and
often paid calls at the Clarke school; Mrs. Jennings must have
known him, and it is probable that he tended Mrs. Rawlings in
her last illness. He was the inevitable choice for Keats's master.

What Keats felt at the transfer of authority from John Clarke
to Thomas Hammond is not known. Hammond was respected in
the neighbourhood; he is said to have kept two apprentices, which
suggests that his practice was large. Over and above the usual
apprenticeship fee of £40, he charged a premium, as was customary—but of £200, a fairly high figure for a country doctor.[24] For
this sum he provided his apprentice with room and board as well
as training. Keats on his part had to promise in the traditional
indentures not to "waste the goods of his said Master nor lend
them unlawfully to any," or "commit fornication nor contract
Matrimony within the said Term," or "play at Cards or Dice
Tables or any other unlawful Games," or "haunt Taverns or
Playhouses nor absent himself from his said Master's service day
or night unlawfully," but to obey his master faithfully in everything he commanded.[25] The indentures were duly signed and the
fees duly paid. The long, irresponsible years of boyhood were
over. At the end of the summer term in 1811, not yet sixteen,
Keats left Mr. Clarke's to serve as bound apprentice to Hammond
for five years.

Chapter Two

The Widening Stream

MR. Hammond lived in a square-built, three-storied brick house on Church Street, standing back from the road in a front garden enclosed by a brick wall. A gate at the side led to the surgery, a small building in the back garden, where the doctor received his patients. Keats took his meals in the house; he studied and slept in a little room above the surgery with two narrow windows set under the roof. It was a cramped, airless place. On summer afternoons, with the sun beating down on the roof, he thought longingly of the half-holidays he had spent swimming in the New River or chasing the fish in the shady ponds at Enfield. Winter evenings, sitting in front of his fire with a book, he was sometimes overwhelmed by the "blue devils," the melancholy fits that used to plague him at school. Yet at first his new work left little time for moodiness or ruminations. His tasks were menial to start with: driving Hammond on his rounds, running errands, sweeping out the shop, keeping accounts, and helping with patients in the surgery. At the same time he was beginning his study of anatomy and physiology and the *materia medica*. Later he would make up pills and potions, and, under Hammond's direction, learn how to bleed and vaccinate, dress wounds, set bones, pull teeth, and apply leeches and cups and poultices—the sum of the accomplishments of most country doctors of that time.

Keats's choice of medicine as a career seems a puzzle only if one reads his life backward, from the standpoint of his later poetry, not forward; considering the possibilities that were open to him at fifteen, it was a good choice he made. Medicine in his day was being slowly revolutionized, like English society as a whole, by middle-class energy breaking through the traditional system. For centuries the practice of medicine had been divided among three distinct groups—physicians, surgeons, and apothecaries. In Keats's time the field was still dominated by the physicians, a small and conservative group trained at the universities, who alone took the title of "Doctor" and charged fees that only the wealthy could pay. They did little to meet the growing demand for medical care, however; as late as the beginning of Victoria's reign there were fewer than three hundred licensed physicians in all Britain, as compared with eight thousand surgeons.[1] It was the surgeons who tended most of the country's sick, consulting the physicians only in special cases; and their development of new medical techniques helped immeasurably to raise the general level of health, and with it the population, in the later eighteenth century. Before that time medicine was hardly a profession in the modern sense, and surgery was hardly a science; quacks were everywhere, and surgeons were not considered gentlemen. Not until 1745 did the surgeons break away from the medieval guild of the Barbers and Surgeons and begin to establish professional standards and qualifications of their own; not until 1800 were they granted a charter for their own Royal College. The apothecaries, the lowest rank in the medical hierarchy, soon followed suit. In the eighteenth century they were still classed as tradesmen and were forbidden by the physicians to dispense medical advice along with their drugs; in actuality they were the doctors of the poor. Only in 1815 did they finally win their independence of the physicians by an act of Parliament empowering the Society of Apothecaries to license candidates for general medical practice. By this time it was becoming customary for apothecaries also to qualify as surgeons by a year of "walking the hospitals" after the usual apprenticeship. Thus the modern system of medical training began to emerge and the various practices to draw together in a single profession.[2]

Keats could look forward, then, to a comfortable and respectable existence as a small-town doctor. But a boy of his talents does not choose his career for practical reasons alone; other important though more obscure motives must also have been at work. There was a strong admixture of idealism in his nature. Years later he confessed—not once but several times—that he was "ambitious of doing the world some good." Medicine must have first appealed to him, as it does to many medical students, as an opportunity to relieve suffering. But it is still more significant that he chose medicine of all careers in the year after the deeply affecting experience of his mother's death. His taking on the responsibilities for her care during her illness is a touching reminder of the possessive little boy guarding her sickroom with a sword; but it was also an experience which helped transform Keats from a thoughtless, brawling schoolboy into a sober and purposeful youth. In nursing his mother Keats seems to have been making amends for the rage he had felt at her remarriage; perhaps in taking up medicine after her death he was trying to relieve an unconscious sense of guilt for having failed to save her. On a more conscious level, his decision expressed the same sturdy resolution to face and subdue the harsh realities of the world, rather than retreat from them, that he had shown as a belligerent schoolboy at the time of his father's death. Whatever the reasons for his choice, Clarke tells us that he felt a deep satisfaction in his new work and that his apprenticeship was "the most placid period of his painful life."

Yet Clarke's picture of Keats as the industrious apprentice is, like his recollection of the prize-winning student, a little too schoolmasterish to be the whole truth. Keats was never placid by nature; his brother George described him at this time as "nervous" and "morbid." He appears to have been lonely in Edmonton. George, still his closest friend, was now working a dozen miles away in London. His schoolboy world seems to have broken up almost at once, for none of his Enfield acquaintances figured in his later life, and evidently he made no real friends for several years. As for girls, they remained remote and magical beings, glimpsed from afar and endlessly dreamed over, but never approached. Yet for all his shyness Keats was a healthy lad, with the sap of adolescence rising in his veins; this isolation, apparently self-imposed, is a sign that he had not really made his peace with the world.

In his loneliness he turned increasingly to his books or went rambling in the woods and fields around Edmonton. The sense of beauty was growing in him, and from his later writings it is plain how great a weight of emotion displaced from its lost human objects was now transferred to the natural world around him. The imagery of his later poems and letters suggests that what moved him most deeply in this world was its very apartness, the

wild secret life which he sensed going on far from human awareness. The birds singing without a thought of being heard, the
small bright-eyed animals running their errands through the
underbrush, "fruit ripening in stillness,"

> the birth, life, death
> Of unseen flowers in heavy peacefulness, . . .

offered him a world in which he could forget his own isolation.
He would lie for hours stretched out in a thicket or a nest of tall
grass, close to the moist and fertile earth, listening to the "little
noiseless noises" that betrayed the life stirring all around him.
Yet from this refuge close to the ground he was constantly looking
upward "into the fair and open face of heaven." The sky was the
field of freedom, where larks soared or pigeons tumbled in the
clear summer air; but he also imagined that it held mysterious
presences in its depths, angels and departed spirits. The blueness
of noon seemed to smile down on him, and the faces of the dead
peered out of the clouds at sunset; he lay awake at night, staring
up at the stars, which seemed to gaze unblinkingly down on the
earth below. With this sense of a mysteriously animated world
his solitude became an element in which he could escape from the
emptiness of the world around him.

Another refuge from loneliness was the world of books which
Cowden Clarke had opened up to him. On leaving Enfield, Keats
realized that his schooling was still far from complete, and both
the Clarkes, father and son, encouraged him to continue. As quick
a student as ever, he soon found he had plenty of time to spare
from his medical studies. During his first year with Hammond
he completed the prose translation of the *Aeneid* he had begun at
school, and perhaps it was to reward him for this effort that Mr.
Clarke gave him a scholarly edition of Ovid's *Metamorphoses*,
which Keats signed with a flourish, "John Keats emer [itus] 1812."
The same sprawling signature appears in a large, handsomely
illustrated edition of *Paradise Lost* which he had acquired two
years earlier: [3] already he was building up a small library. After
the *Aeneid*, Keats rounded out his knowledge of classical poetry
with Vergil's *Eclogues* and Ovid and Terence and Horace—all
of whom he could quote with effect years later—and continued
his reading of the French historians and philosophers, among

whom Voltaire became his favourite. Clarke recalled that he "translated and copied an immense quantity" during his time at Hammond's; he "devoured" books rather than read them. Naturally he was also reading the great English authors—Bacon and Addison and Swift and Locke, Shakespeare and Milton and Pope, Fielding and Smollett and Sterne. Though Pope's translation of Homer made a lasting impression on him,[4] most of Milton and Shakespeare was evidently still above him, as Leigh Hunt tells us they were for him at this time.[5] History was still Keats's absorbing interest, a field in which he "made himself learned for his age," according to his later friend Charles Brown.

Only one story survives from the early years of his apprenticeship, and it is probably apocryphal. One winter day Keats went with Hammond on a call at Mr. Clarke's in Enfield. As he waited outside with the horse, word went round the schoolyard that John Keats, the famous fighter, was sitting out front in the doctor's gig. Keats was deep in a book and did not notice the knot of younger boys that gathered to see him. Then one lad whispered a dare to another, and a snowball hit Keats square in the back. He whirled around to see his attacker take to his heels, leaped up to give the boy a thrashing, then—to the disappointment of the others—thought better of it and went back to his book. Somehow, they must have felt, he had changed.

Soon Keats began slipping out of the surgery once or twice every week with a book under his arm, to trudge four miles across the fields for an afternoon of talk with Cowden Clarke at Enfield. His old tutor was a link with the past and a guide to the future. He gave Keats the intellectual direction he needed; at the same time his humour and energy must have been a healthy counterpoise to Keats's spells of gloom. Keats still addressed him deferentially as "sir," but the constant sharing of interests drew them close together. Clarke was a keen theatre-goer and used to walk fifteen miles into London to see John Kemble or Mrs. Siddons—the sun already setting on her magnificence—play Shakespeare at Covent Garden. His enthusiasm was infectious. On summer afternoons the two young men used to sit in an arbour on the far side of the school grounds reading the plays aloud, or wander through the shaded lanes of Enfield debating some point of literature or history. Often their talk ran on after supper, when Clarke would play a Mozart sonata or two and Keats would pick out another book from his shelves; then they would walk halfway to Edmonton together, to part with a handshake in the middle of the fields.

"Nothing is finer for the purposes of great productions," Keats later wrote, "than a very gradual ripening of the intellectual powers." It is striking that he did not show any real interest in poetry till late adolescence—till nearly eighteen, in fact. All the elements were there—the sensitivity to language, the intensity of feeling, the sensuous response to the natural world; but they did not fuse in one great moment of discovery till Clarke introduced him to Spenser. One afternoon, probably in the summer of 1813, Clarke read the "Epithalamion" aloud and looked up to see Keats's face transfigured with pleasure. This was poetry of a kind he had never heard before: all the joyous bustle of the wedding morning, the noisy procession to the church, the bride blushing with downcast eyes, the feasting and dancing, the wine splashing the walls, the bells clanging through the town, then at last nightfall and the silent consummation, recalling the love of Cynthia and Endymion, of Jupiter and Alcmena, and of Maia, the mother of Hermes,

> whenas Jove her took
> In Tempe, lying on the flowery grass
> Twixt sleep and wake, after she weary was
> With bathing in the Acidalian brook.

This encounter with Spenser was a turning point. Up to this time Keats had never borrowed a book of poetry from Clarke; that night he went home with the first volume of *The Faerie Queene*. Clarke thought it was "mere boyish ambition" that led him to ask for it; but the next time they met he found that Keats had gone through the book "like a young horse through a spring meadow—ramping."

The Faerie Queene led Keats into a new world of bright colour and honied language, of romantic adventure and chivalric devotion far above the level of actual life. He never quite recovered from this first discovery; the most significant poetry he later wrote was an attempt to set this world of imagination in clear perspective against the world of sober experience. But for Keats at eighteen, with the best of life lying before him, the boundaries between dream and reality were still unclear, and Spenser's poetry was a trumpet call to rouse the sleeping figures of his own imagination. Such a discovery is no more, or less, mysterious than falling in love; the only question is why one poet and not another should touch it off. The supple music of Spenser's verse had a strong appeal to him, and the painterly effects of his description. But Clarke specifically mentioned Keats's "ecstatic" expression as he listened to "the more passionate passages" of the "Epithalamion"; apparently the innocent yet exuberant sensuality of Spenser's wedding song opened up a realm of poetic experience which had previously existed for Keats only in dream. His narrow life at Hammond's had dammed up all his longings for an ideal beauty, bright and sweet and soft and fair; now they burst out into this new channel. Almost overnight his life acquired a direction it had lacked before.

John Clarke was surprised and even amused to hear of Keats's new enthusiasm, but Cowden Clarke, a versifier himself, did all he could to encourage it. His tastes in poetry were typical of a well-read young schoolmaster of his time, broad but not revolutionary; it is doubtful, for instance, that he yet knew the work of Wordsworth, who was still unrecognized and largely unread in 1813.[6] He introduced Keats to the principles of poetry held by the eighteenth century, with its carefully distinguished styles and clearly defined forms and moralizing bias, and, except for Spenser and Shakespeare, their reading at first kept to the standard authors, from Milton to Gray—the limits established by Johnson's *Lives of the English Poets*. From Spenser it was an easy move to Spenser's eighteenth-century imitators, Thomson and Shenstone and Beattie, and then to Milton's early poems and the more introspective and elegiac poets of the mid-century, Gray and Collins and Cowper. Yet despite the great deal of uninspired poetry Keats read at the start, he rapidly developed a fresh and perceptive taste of his own. The passages he marked in his copy of *The Faerie Queene* show a love of precisely observed colour and light and sound and movement, and an image compressed into a single explosive epithet filled him with an almost physical delight. One day he and Clarke read together a passage of Spenser describing the monsters of a magic sea-storm:

> All dreadful portraits of deformity,
> Bright Scolopendraes, arm'd with silver scales,

> Great whirlpools, which all fishes make to flee,
> Spring-headed Hydras, and sea-shouldering whales. . . .*

As Clarke recalled, Keats "hoisted himself up, and looked burly and dominant, as he said, 'What an image that is—sea-shouldering whales!'" For a moment he was himself shaking the weight of oceans from his back. From the beginning poetry was an intensely physical experience for him, felt almost literally in every nerve and along every fibre of his body.

Spenser did more than open Keats's eyes to poetry: he led him to write his first poem. From our vantage point we can see all his past and future converging on this act; to Keats himself it must have seemed a miracle, an event lifted out of time. The "Imitation of Spenser" is a strangely unpromising first performance, full of clumsy syntax and overblown imagery, written in a worn-out eighteenth-century idiom. But though Keats later destroyed much of his early poetry, he included the "Imitation" in his first volume and acknowledged it as his first poem: somehow it meant a great deal to him. If it is true that a writer often reveals himself more directly in his first work than he ever does again, this poem may offer a clue not merely to Keats's idea of poetry at the start of his career, but also to his deeper reasons for writing it. At first glance the "Imitation" recalls one of Keats's favourite passages from *The Faerie Queene,* the description of the Bower of Bliss, a Circean paradise of crystal streams and laurel groves. Yet a closer reading reveals something very different from mere imitation. Spenser's landscape is a clear-cut allegory of sensual temptation to be overcome; Keats's is a vision of almost indescribable beauty, transfigured with inexpressible meaning like a dream.

But what is he dreaming of? It is a morning in spring; the rising sun lights up flower-spangled hills surrounding a placid lake. An island overgrown with roses lies in its midst, golden-scaled fish circle in its depths, and on its surface floats a single swan. The scene is a romantic stage-set; and yet Keats insists it is far more than this:

> Ah! could I tell the wonders of an isle
> That in that fairest lake had placed been,
> I could e'en Dido of her grief beguile;
> Or rob from aged Lear his bitter teen:

---

* *Faerie Queene,* II.xii.23. I take the liberty of transposing the second and fourth lines of the quatrain.

> For sure so fair a place was never seen,
> Of all that ever charm'd romantic eye:
> It seem'd an emerald in the silver sheen
> Of the bright waters; or as when on high,
> Through clouds of fleecy white, laughs the cœrulean sky.

It is a scene strikingly similar to his first view of Lake Windermere, some four years later, which stunned him into silence. But why did it move him so? A dream cannot be pressed too far for its meaning, yet a meaning is always there. For all the staleness of its phrasing, the freshness of the morning in this poem evokes the wonder of another dawn—the new-created world of early childhood. It is significant that the swan at the centre of the scene, floating proudly on the bosom of the lake, appears in several of Keats's other early poems as an explicit symbol for the poet— Bryon, his friend Mathew, himself. If this swan represents—below the level of conscious intention—Keats himself in his dawning consciousness, the lake on which he floats, ringed about with hills and arched over by a sky smiling with light, seems a dreamlike re-creation of the child's first horizons, the circle of his mother's arms and the meridian of his father's gaze. It is curious how this swan encircled by sky and water—two primordial symbols for male and female—calls up another image from Keats's earliest memories: the painted sign of a swan in a hoop that no doubt hung outside his grandfather's stable.[7]

Another interesting cluster of images is the trio of flower, fish, and swan, for Keats used these same three images a year later as explicit symbols of the spiritual growth of a young poet, in a passage which strikingly suggests the processes of conception and embryonic development he had learned in his medical texts:

> For thou wast once a flowret blooming wild,
> Close to the source, bright, pure, and undefil'd,
> Whence gush the streams of song: in happy hour
> Came chaste Diana from her shady bower,
> Just as the sun was from the east uprising;
> And, as for him some gift she was devising,
> Beheld thee, pluck'd thee, cast thee in the stream
> To meet her glorious brother's greeting beam.
> I marvel much that thou hast never told
> How, from a flower, into a fish of gold
> Apollo chang'd thee; how thou next didst seem
> A black-eyed swan upon the widening stream;

And when thou first didst in that mirror trace
The placid features of a human face. . . .

Perhaps it is significant, then, that the swan in the first poem still
has sole possession of the lake, while in the last stanza the water
rippling in delight up the side of the rose-strewn island evokes
a contentment still closer to the oceanic consciousness of the infant.

This does not mean that Keats intended even half-consciously
to describe the child's first inexpressible felicity in these stanzas.
Rather it appears that, in trying to paint the most beautiful scene
he could imagine, he drew on certain unconscious images of his
own childhood experience and thus cast over the landscape an
aura of feeling derived from his earliest memories—the serenity
of the swan at the center of the scene, the happy unity of water
and earth and sky around him, and the beauty of the flowers
drenched by stream or tide in the kind of joyous intermingling
which Keats was later to describe as "moistened and bedewed
with Pleasures." Clearly this landscape was no Bower of Bliss to
be destroyed, but a paradise to be regained. Keats seems to have
regarded even the Bower of Bliss in this spirit, for he later repeated to a friend in love the very advice which Spenser intended
his hero to refuse:

> "So passeth, in the passing of a day,
> Of mortal life the leaf, the bud, the flower;
> Ne more doth flourish after first decay,
> That erst was sought to deck both bed and bower
> Of many a lady, and many a paramour.
> Gather therefore the rose, whilst yet is prime,
> For soon comes age, that will her pride deflower:
> Gather the rose of love, whilst yet is time,
> Whilst loving thou mayst loved be with equal crime."

For Keats at eighteen the passing of beauty "in the passing of a day"
was all too vivid a recollection. His first poem suggests not only
how deep the experience of childhood happiness, once enjoyed to
overflowing and then suddenly snatched away, had sunk into his
mind; it also suggests that the discovery of poetry was so momentous an event to him because it pointed out a road back to
that lost paradise of sensuous and emotional delight.

≫≪

Between work and study and his new absorption in poetry, Keats's life may well have seemed placid to Cowden Clarke. But Clarke did not know the whole truth: Keats did not tell him of his first efforts to write poetry, nor did he mention his growing restiveness in his work. For reasons which are not clear, Keats began to rebel against his master. "Seven years ago," he wrote in 1819, thinking of the constant renewal of the body's tissues, "it was not this hand that clench'd itself against Hammond." This gesture seems to have been no mere flare-up of temper but a settled antipathy. In later years Keats was almost as silent about his apprenticeship as about his boyhood; when he did mention his days with Hammond, it was to regret he had undergone "a one of them." Clearly Hammond was no John Clarke; perhaps he was a neglectful master. It was not uncommon for masters to collect large fees from apprentices and give them little training in return; and even Abbey came to think that Hammond "did not conduct himself as he ought to have done to his young pupil." Perhaps Keats also struck Hammond as an unsatisfactory pupil, with his habit of slipping off on afternoons and returning late with a book under his arm. A nameless fellow apprentice described him as "an idle loafing fellow," and this may well have echoed Hammond's own opinion. But the real trouble seems to have been a conflict of personalities or opinions. Hammond and his pupil did not agree, Clarke later recalled rather vaguely; "Keats's tastes [were] totally opposed to his master's." [8]

One wonders what subjects were discussed around Hammond's dinner table. It is improbable that Hammond would have had any opinions on poetry, for few surgeons at that time had any literary education; a much likelier topic is politics. Keats's rebellion against Hammond may have been only one phase of his growing quarrel with the established order, on which the evidence is clear. The temperature of political debate was rising in England as the war drew to an end. The year 1812 marked the turning point, with Napoleon's retreat from Moscow; with his abdication after the fall of Paris in April 1814, it seemed that peace had come at last. Yet England was more bitterly divided than it had been for over a century. The gap between the rich and poor had steadily widened under the pressures of twenty years of war. The average worker paid out over half of his meagre earnings in in-

direct taxation, but under a corrupt and antiquated voting system neither he nor the middle-class citizen had any real voice in
Parliament. Factory hands in the Midlands, driven out of work
by the new cotton-spinning machines, began smashing them in
despair; Parliament replied with a Frame-Breaking Bill which
punished these acts with hanging. In protesting against the bill
in his maiden speech in the House of Lords, young Lord Byron
described the wretchedness of the factory towns as worse than the
most squalid provinces he had seen in his travels in Turkey. But
the countryman's lot was no better. Cut off from the land by
enclosures, pauperized by the parish dole, the farm worker faced
starvation as food prices rose; but if he went poaching to feed his
children, he risked being transported to the colonies. Yet all this
while the gentry were living more comfortably than ever in their
fine country houses; and in London the fashionable world was
entering a new era of extravagance and dissoluteness centered at
Carlton House. Here the Prince Regent squabbled publicly with
his wife, whom he had accused of bearing an illegitimate child
while living abroad, and managed in 1813 to deprive her of the
custody of the young princess. Small wonder that he was hissed
by a London mob in 1814 as he led a procession of the Allied
sovereigns at the celebrations for the Peace of Paris.

It is easy to guess how a quick-witted and idealistic lad of
seventeen or eighteen would react to these events, and it is not
surprising that of the nine or ten poems Keats wrote during his
apprenticeship at Hammond's, four dealt with political themes.
Injustice and autocracy ruled in England no less than in Europe;
in the end, there seemed little to choose between the tyranny of
Napoleon and that of the despots who opposed him. Such, at
least, was the view which Keats absorbed from his regular reading
of *The Examiner,* the most articulate liberal voice of the time.
This magazine was a red rag to the John Bulls of the day. When
Abbey learned that Keats had begun reading it at Mr. Clarke's,
he swore that "if he had fifty children he would not send one of
them to that school." [9] Keats laughed when he told the story to
Cowden Clarke, but it shows him already in secret revolt against
his guardian. It was a time for taking sides—between conservative
or liberal, faith in the Thirty-Nine Articles or in human perfectibility, the complacencies of the aristocracy or the reforming
zeal of the middle-class intellectuals. In the front ranks of the

struggle was the youthful editor of *The Examiner*, Leigh Hunt, who was leading an attack on Tory oppression that drew the attention of all England at this time.

Here was a man to turn any young idealist's head: poet, critic, polemicist, wit, and something of a dandy to boot. Born in 1784, the son of a fashionable London preacher from Barbados, Hunt was a precocious lad who at sixteen published a facile little volume of verse which went through four editions in as many years. From this he turned to more original work in theatre criticism while clerking in the War Office, then joined his older brother to set up *The Examiner* in 1808. John Hunt was a sober and courageous journalist, dedicated to upholding traditional English liberty against government encroachment. He acted as manager and news editor of the new weekly, giving his mercurial brother most of the political commentary as well as the reviews of art and music and literature to write. At once the paper was attacked as pro-Bonapartist, and soon it ran afoul of the Tory censorship. Three times in its first three years the Hunts were haled into court for discussing such touchy subjects as the sale of army promotions by the Duke of York's mistress, the unpopularity of George III's ministers, and the flogging of soldiers; but all three prosecutions were dismissed. The trials succeeded merely in raising *The Examiner*'s circulation and adding glitter to Leigh Hunt's reputation.

So when, in March 1812, *The Morning Post* hailed the Regent on his fiftieth birthday as the "Glory of the People" and an "Adonis in Loveliness," Hunt rose gaily to the challenge. "Now no one can accuse me of not writing a libel," he remarked to Charles Lamb, and a few days later his article on "Princely Qualities" appeared. No Adonis but "a corpulent man of fifty," the Regent was described as "a violator of his word, a libertine over head and ears in disgrace, a despiser of domestic ties, and the companion of gamblers and demireps." A fourth indictment was promptly issued against the Hunts; eight months went by while the Regent tried to buy them off; then at last they were tried before a jury packed with Government officials. Public interest was unprecedented: ten thousand copies of *The Examiner* were sold in the hour after the verdict was published. It was, of course, Guilty. On February 3, 1813, the sentence was pronounced. It was a stiff one: each of the brothers was to serve two years in a separate prison, pay a fine of £500, and provide £500 security for good behaviour for the five years following. Undaunted, Leigh Hunt rolled off in a hackney coach to the Horsemonger Lane Gaol with his head still high, dressed in his natty best, and carrying a slim volume of the neo-Latin poet Erycius Puteanus.

Imprisonment made Hunt's name as a martyr to the liberal cause. Tom Moore wrote him verses of glowing tribute, and young Percy Shelley sent him £20 to help meet the fine. A repentant juror later offered him £500, which Hunt refused—a quixotic gesture he could hardly afford, since he was already deep in debt. Nevertheless he borrowed several hundred pounds with which to turn his two prison rooms into a snug apartment papered with trellised roses and furnished with bookcases, busts of his favourite poets, and a piano. Nothing was overlooked that could disguise the reality of the situation. Venetian blinds hid the bars of his windows, the prison yard outside was planted with pansies and sweetbriar, and the ceiling of his living room was painted with a blue sky and fleecy clouds. While his brother John served his term quietly at Coldbath Fields, Leigh Hunt moved his wife and children into his apartment and began receiving his admirers—James Mill and Jeremy Bentham, Henry Brougham the great Whig lawyer and his defence counsel, Thomas Barnes of *The Times,* Benjamin Haydon the historical painter, William Godwin the radical philosopher, Maria Edgeworth the novelist, William Hazlitt, Charles and Mary Lamb, and many others. The guests were allowed to stay till ten in the evening. Tom Moore brought Byron with him, who was so taken with "the wit in the dungeon" that he gave a dinner party in the cell. So Hunt's evenings were spent in pleasant conversation on Elizabethan literature and Italian poetry, which he had begun to translate; the days sped by in reading and writing, strumming on the piano, playing battledore and shuttlecock with his children, and dashing off political commentary for *The Examiner,* which he continued to edit through his term. In fact, his imprisonment only brought new lustre to the paper, since Barnes and Hazlitt were now regular contributors, with Lamb and Haydon occasionally joining in.

Echoes of this excitement arrived in Edmonton with every Saturday's *Examiner;* but Keats was beginning to follow Hunt's adventures at closer range. Cowden Clarke had met Hunt at a musical party in London in 1812 and had been dazzled by his jaunty charm. Now he went each week to visit Hunt in jail, bringing him fruit and eggs from Enfield and joining in the discussions around the fireside. His reports of these expeditions crystallized Keats's political loyalties. Hunt supplied him with just the example of bravado he needed in his smouldering rebellion against Hammond and Abbey. The distant glories of Camperdown and Trafalgar faded from his mind. Now the Government itself became the enemy, backed up by its red-coated troops and the machinery of Church and State; and the hero of his time was an elegant young man discoursing on Spenser and writing ironic editorials from a prison cell. Hunt's poetry gave Keats a new model for his own, while *The Examiner* continued to guide his opinions. In the second poem of Keats that has come down to us, a stilted sonnet "On Peace," we find him closely following *The Examiner*'s editorial line of the spring of 1814. At that time Hunt hoped that the Peace of Paris might bring about constitutional monarchy in Europe, and so Keats echoed him: [10]

> O Europe! let not sceptred tyrants see
>   That thou must shelter in thy former state;
> Keep thy chains burst, and boldly say thou art free;
>   Give thy kings law—leave not uncurbed the great;
>   So with the horrors past thou'lt win thy happier fate!

Though these hopes were soon to be dashed, for a few months it seemed that the liberal cause, at home as well as abroad, might carry the day.

All this while another current was beginning to run under the surface of Keats's existence, one still less visible to Clarke than his rebellion against Hammond. The opposite sex was beginning to exert its tidal pull on Keats's life, even though he seems to have long resisted its force. Evidently his deep-seated reserve and the half-monastic isolation of his life at Hammond's made him shy and awkward on his first ventures into society. Keats later confessed that he had made almost all his friends through his brother George, who, it appears, lost no time in forming a circle of new acquaintances in London after leaving school. Most of these friends—Briggs, Peachey, Kirkman, Archer, Squibb, Frith, Parker, Beilby—remain mere names. But a few—William Haslam, a young law clerk, and Henry and Charles Wylie, two spruce young lads with a warmhearted mother, the widow of an infantry officer, and a shy but charming younger sister—were to play im-

portant parts in both brothers' lives. On his occasional visits to
town Keats began to slip into this circle; but here he found a
new difficulty. George was turning into a handsome young fellow
who could bring a smile and a blush to a pretty girl's face; but
John was often taken for George's younger brother, just as in
his schooldays. For this his height was chiefly to blame. At his
full growth he reached not quite five foot one—not remarkably
short in those days, when five foot six was the average and five
foot ten was tall, but still about ten inches shorter than George,
who was growing nearly as tall as their famous uncle. So on his
first meetings with young ladies Keats had to struggle against a
feeling of physical insignificance, even though, from all accounts,
he was a good-looking young man. Yet all his self-consciousness
could not stifle his susceptibility to beauty; rather his stand-
offishness only encouraged his boyish tendency to idealize women.
"When I was a Schoolboy," he wrote some years later, "I thought
a fair Woman a pure Goddess, my mind was a soft nest in which
some one of them slept though she knew it not." Now, at closer
contact, he scented danger—the risk both of rebuff and of disillusionment. If he must fall in love—and at his age it was inevitable—far safer to choose some unattainable beauty whom he
could worship from a safe distance in secret.

This is a common adventure at seventeen or eighteen; what
was uncommon in Keats's experience was both the distance and
the duration of the involvement. It began casually one summer
evening in 1814 during the riotous Peace celebrations in London,
when he went for a fling at Vauxhall, the public gardens in
Southwark, which were then at the height of their popularity.
And there a chance encounter with a nameless young woman fired
what seems to have been the first real passion of his life. The
meeting itself was nothing: for half an hour or so he watched her
as she talked with friends over a table, enthralled by her every
gesture, waiting for a smile of recognition she never quite gave
him. The verses he wrote afterward—"Fill for me a brimming
bowl"—seem lighthearted enough, mere conventional protesta-
tions of longing and despair. Yet the emotion which the experience kindled somehow survived and grew to a talismanic significance in Keats's mind. For, he maintained in two sonnets of
1818, it still haunted him four years later:

Time's sea hath been five years at its slow ebb;
　　Long hours have to and fro let creep the sand;
Since I was tangled in thy beauty's web,
　　And snared by the ungloving of thine hand. . . .*

The remembrance of her beauty, he claimed, had stood between him and every other woman he had met in those years; still more, her power over him had come to mean a fulfilment in love which at twenty-two he feared he would die without attaining:

And when I feel, fair creature of an hour!
　　That I shall never look upon thee more,
　　Never have relish in the faery power
Of unreflecting love!—then on the shore
Of the wide world I stand alone, and think
Till love and fame to nothingness do sink.

It is always a delicate task to gauge the weight of biographical implication in a poem, though it may be said that Keats's poems in general have a more direct relation to his life than the work of most poets. Yet even if in these sonnets he was more interested in working out a theme than in expressing an emotion, still they imply that the casual experience of 1814 had become a refuge from troubling actuality for him—whether he understood the exact nature of his feelings or not. And the early lyric already hints at a recurrent theme of his later work: beauty as a rare and unearthly visitant, who appears and then departs as suddenly as she came, leaving a chill of premonition in the air behind her.

➤➤➤ ⫷⫷

As 1814 drew on, Keats's life darkened again. His grandmother, Alice Jennings, now seventy-eight, fell ill; in the middle of December she died. Nothing is known of her illness; but however she died, it was a painful loss for Keats. For ten years she had been a second mother to him and an example of gentle selflessness he could never forget. About a week after her death he wrote a sonnet to her memory ("As from the darkening gloom a silver dove"), fervently asserting his faith in her soul's reward in heaven. So deep were his feelings about her that he apparently never showed the

---

* Keats in 1818 had either forgotten the precise date of the encounter or preferred the euphony of "five" to "four" in the first line.

poem to anyone till two years later and then would not tell even
his brothers to whom he had written it.[11] He kept his grief, as
he did his other emotions, to himself. Besides, he was now head
of the family, to whom the younger ones would look for support.
With Mrs. Jennings' death the pattern of their life together was
finally broken up. Fanny, now eleven years old, was taken off to
live in the stale respectability of the Abbey household in Walthamstow. A letter which George wrote her that winter from Pancras
Lane, asking her to make him an eyeshade to wear at work, gives
a glimpse of her as a shy and dutiful little girl struggling to improve in her music and skipping rope in the cold weather to
stave off chilblains. Tom was taken out of school and set up beside
George on a stool in Abbey's counting-house; Keats was left
alone in Edmonton.

A deep depression now overtook him, from which he could
escape only through poetry. A few stilted stanzas addressed "To
Hope" express the mood of numb despair, all too familiar at
nineteen, in which the world appears too large and indifferent
even to struggle against. Grief for his parents, anxiety about his
future, doubts of his ability to win a woman's love, misgivings for
the cause of freedom—these evidently were the thoughts that assailed him as he sat before his solitary fire or wandered through
the woods in the early winter evenings. He found companionship
only in the verse of two young poets—Byron, the pale mysterious
exile of *Childe Harold,* nursing his secret sorrow, and Chatterton,
"the marvellous boy" who, rather than face failure, poisoned himself in a London garret at seventeen. With them, at least in imagination, Keats could share his moods. In the poems he wrote during
these dark months the world seemed a prison, and death at times
the only release; poetry itself was a kind of communication with
the immortal dead, or of the dead with one another, and the poet
a birdlike figure who escapes the bonds of earth to join them.
These are the outpourings of an unhappy adolescent; yet they
sound two central motives of Keats's later work—a sense of the
constant hovering regard of the dead, and the attempt to reach a
transcendent realm of the spirit through poetry. By some healthy
instinct, Keats seems to have kept these melancholy poems to
himself; [12] but, locked within his own gloom, he could not have
found his loneliness easier to bear.

At last this spell was broken, by a real release from a real prison.

Leigh Hunt's two-year term was to expire on February 2, 1815. This was a glorious event, a vindication of both the liberal spirit and the poetic mind; and Keats decided to commemorate it in verse. The resulting sonnet was a tame echo of Tom Moore's lines to Hunt; yet it expressed something of Keats's sense of vicarious liberation. For, he asserted, even in prison a spirit like Hunt's was far freer than the "minion of grandeur" who bolted him in:

> In Spenser's halls he strayed, and bowers fair,
>   Culling enchanted flowers; and he flew
> With daring Milton through the fields of air:
>   To regions of his own his genius true
> Took happy flights. Who shall his fame impair
>   When thou are dead, and all thy wretched crew?

Imprisoned at Hammond's, Keats caught a glimpse through Hunt of a liberty of the imagination that only poets know, and an immortality of fame more triumphant even than that of the soul.

In his enthusiasm, he decided that the time had come for him to speak out as clearly as Hunt had done. Cowden Clarke, he knew, was going up to London to congratulate Hunt on his release; Keats met him in the fields and walked with him a good part of the way. At the last gate he stopped to say good-bye to Clarke, hesitated, then handed him the sonnet to Hunt. Clarke was surprised: this was the first he knew of Keats's writing poetry. Yet he sensed at once the significance of the moment. He would never forget—or so he said years later—the "conscious look" with which Keats gave him the poem. In the excitement of his release, the sonnet evidently made no impression on Hunt; [13] but it represented an important step forward for Keats. He had declared himself a poet to the man who was his one link with the world of poets, and committed himself to Hunt's side in politics —an act with more consequences than he could yet glimpse.

At about the time he worked up his courage to show his sonnet to Clarke, Keats found another friend to share his interest in poetry. George Felton Mathew, one of the young men Keats met through George in London, seems at first an unlikely companion. Mathew later described himself as "of a serious and tender nature," "thoughtful beyond his years," and "diffident to the last degree." The son of a prosperous textile dealer with a home in the fashionable new Regent's Park, he was then clerking in the

firm of a West India merchant, "a secular and uncongenial employment" which he found a trial to his "weak nerves and trembling feelings." Mathew's enthusiasms in poetry ran to long-
winded romantic epics such as *Ossian* and Wieland's *Oberon*,
and saccharine lady versifiers such as Mary Tighe. A few years
later Keats found it almost impossible to believe that he had once
enjoyed such stuff; but now, in the pleasure of finding a "genius-
loving heart" like his own, he identified his tastes with Mathew's
and exalted their friendship into a "brotherhood in song" like
that of Beaumont and Fletcher. The evenings they spent reading
their verses to each other must have been a decided change from
his sessions with Clarke; but Mathew gave Keats what his old
tutor could not—the admiration of a contemporary and the
stimulus of a fellow craftsman.

Mathew belonged to a large family, and Keats was soon drawn
into this circle. Mathew's sister Mary took an interest in her
brother's "poetical friend" and copied his verses in the album
which, like most young ladies of the day, she kept for her friends'
literary efforts. So did her cousins Ann and Caroline Mathew, at
whose house in Goswell Street George Keats had first introduced
his brother to the set. They were not a lively clan, the Mathews.
Both families were earnestly evangelical, and one of their cousins
became a famous "apostle of temperance." Neither Ann nor
Caroline ever married; instead, they grew into sour spinsters, full
of pious horror at their youthful frivolities. These were innocent
enough—"little domestic concerts and dances," as Mathew described them, at which the young ladies tinkled on the pianoforte
and attempted arias from *Don Giovanni* and the young gentlemen
perspired through the quadrille. If Keats did not shine in this
part, his talent for writing new words to the young ladies' favourite
tunes was highly appreciated. He soon learned to string together
the clichés of the most popular poets of the times in graceful little
lyrics; at the same time, it appears, some of his shyness began to
wear off.

It is hard to imagine Ann or Caroline Mathew as one of the
goddesses who slumbered in Keats's mind during his lonely years
at Edmonton; but there was a dark-haired bright-eyed beauty in
this little circle who evidently filled the place. Mary Frogley held
the center of the stage at the Mathews' parties; all the young men
flirted with her in turn, including George Keats and even Mathew

himself. If three sonnets "On Woman" which Keats wrote at about this time [14] were inspired by her, as many of his early poems were said to be, Keats was struck almost speechless by her beauty:

> Light feet, dark violet eyes, and parted hair;
>   Soft dimpled hands, white neck, and creamy breast,
>   Are things on which the dazzled senses rest
> Till the fond, fixed eyes forget they stare. . . .

Yet this dazzling apparition, he at once realized, could also be "flippant, vain, Inconstant, childish, proud, and full of fancies." In her impulsive gaiety, which offered to release him from the constrictions of his own shyness, a woman like Mary elated him yet disturbed him profoundly. Torn between longing and timidity, he felt far safer with young ladies like the Mathew sisters, of "lovely modesty and virtues rare," who combined "dove-like" innocence and "mild intelligence."

> Ah! who can e'er forget so fair a being?
>   Who can forget her half retiring sweets?
>   God! she is like a milk-white lamb that bleats
> For man's protection, . . .

he exclaimed, in lines which, it is astonishing to learn, moved him to tears at the time he wrote them.[15] This division within his feelings—the belle matched against the bluestocking—clearly echoes the earlier and deeper one between the two very different women who had dominated his boyhood—his mother and his grandmother. In the fascination of a vivacious and unpredictable beauty like Mary he must also fear rejection or even betrayal; evidently he could trust himself only in a non-sexual relationship. So Ann and Caroline became the first of several pairs of sisters, usually older than himself, with whom Keats was to carry on a kind of semi-serious platonic affair, safe in the company of one of his brothers.

This friendship with the Mathew sisters inspired what are certainly the feeblest of all his early poems. In the summer of 1815 Keats wrote two sets of verses to thank them for sending him "a beautiful dome-shaped shell" from the seaside. Cast in the jingling measures of Tom Moore, they mix nightingales and cherubs, sylphs and moonbeams and dewy flowers with platonic compliments to the sisters' "elegant, pure, and aerial minds." Keats drew on their favourite poem, Wieland's *Oberon,* to describe the shell as "the work of a fay," a magic canopy under which the fairy king crept, when deserted by Titania, to strum sad songs on his lute:

> In this little dome, all those melodies strange,
>   Soft, plaintive, and melting, for ever will sigh;
> Nor e'er will the notes from their tenderness change;
> Nor e'er will the music of Oberon die. . . .

In style and sentiment, these poems are atrocious; yet they merely show Keats following the worst poetic fashions of his day. It was not an easy time to be a young poet. After the great achievement of Dryden and Pope, English poetry had long since run dry in the sandy flats of didactic verse or settled in the marshes of sentimentalism. The poets who appeared at the end of the eighteenth century to give it a new voice and new substance had hardly yet won a hearing. Meanwhile the lilting sentimentalities of Moore, the patriotic flutings of Campbell, and the elegant inanities of Rogers held the stage, along with the tireless chivalrics of Scott and the melancholy posturings of the young Byron.

It should be no surprise, then, that at nineteen Keats had not surmounted the mediocre poetry that was in him and all around him. He was not one of those rare poets who are born, not made. He lacked the endowments or opportunities with which the other great poets of his time started—Blake's unerring ear for word-music, for instance, or Wordsworth's experience of the French Revolution, or Byron's exotic adventures in the Mediterranean, or Shelley's wide knowledge of the classics. As Carlyle said of Burns, "Every genius is an impossibility till he appear"; but Keats seems one of the greatest impossibilities of all. He was to rise above his own narrow background by stubborn ambition and hard work, making himself a poet by studying the best examples of poetry he could find and absorbing what he could from them, one after another; but as yet he had hardly begun. His verses to the Mathew sisters merely mark the depth from which his climb upward must be measured.

With his new friendships in London, Keats had still more reason to chafe against the narrow limits of his life at Hammond's; but the excitement of the spring of 1815 was enough to make any young man restless. The news that Napoleon had escaped from Elba burst like a thunderclap on the Congress of Vienna at the beginning of March. The Hundred Days had begun. While Louis XVIII scurried to Belgium for refuge, the Emperor swept triumphantly up from Cannes to Paris, welcomed by his people on every side. England at once despatched Wellington to the Low Countries while the Allies regrouped their forces. With the odds mounting against him, Napoleon struck out in mid-June, and at last the game ended at Waterloo. But for many English liberals this was no real victory. William Hazlitt described it as "the sacred triumph of kings over mankind." [16] Even Leigh Hunt, an advocate of constitutional monarchy, had come out for Napoleon that spring, disillusioned by the sovereigns' betrayal of their promises to their peoples at Vienna.[17] When the Emperor arrived at Plymouth to seek political asylum with the English, huge crowds gathered on the shore to cheer him. Keats's reaction to these events may be gathered from a little poem which he wrote at the height of the Hundred Days, when the bells were rung all over England on May 29 to commemorate Charles II's restoration.[18] "Infatuate Britons," he burst out angrily—why should they celebrate their "direst, foulest shame" and forget the martyrs of freedom, the heroes of his schoolboy reading of Bishop Burnet, whom Charles had put to death?

> Ah! while I hear each traitorous lying bell,
> 'Tis gallant Sydney's, Russel's, Vane's sad knell,
> That pains my wounded ear.

Keats's protest against the rule of mere legitimacy sprang from deep conviction but also from his growing awareness of the resistance which a man of talent would meet in trying to rise above the level of his birth and education in the society of that day. He was no warm admirer of Napoleon, but the triumph of "the divine right gentlemen" whom he despised must have sharpened his own sense of oppression.

Revolt was in the air; and in the summer of 1815 Keats saw his chance to escape from Hammond's authority. After a year of wrangling between the Society of Apothecaries and the Royal College of Physicians, Parliament finally passed the Apothecaries Act. Under its regulations no one could now practise as an apothecary without attending a prescribed course of lectures in a London hospital and then passing an examination set by the Society.[19] At first it appeared that this would merely add an extra year of training to his five-year apprenticeship, but Keats wondered. Could he not cut his term short and try for the Apothecaries' Examination in another year? It was not unheard of to break one's indentures, and evidently he felt he had learned all that Hammond could teach him. He would have to win Abbey over, but it should be easy to persuade him to any plan for avoiding the extra expense. So Keats must have thought, and so he acted. Somehow he won both his guardian's and his master's consent. Hammond wrote out a statement that Keats had satisfactorily completed his apprenticeship, and Keats, armed with this certificate of good behaviour, packed his belongings in the middle of September and went up to London to enter the United Hospitals of Guy's and St. Thomas's.

Chapter Three

The Dark City

THE United Hospitals stood on the edge of the Borough of Southwark, a jumble of narrow streets, sunless alleys, and tenements swarming with the poorest of London's million inhabitants. To reach the hospital from the City, one had to cross London Bridge, dodging the long whips of the draymen coming up from Kent with their wagon-loads of vegetables, then pick one's way through the filth of Borough High Street and turn left into St. Thomas's Street. Here stood the ancient foundation of St. Thomas's Hospital, surrounded by a few fine houses left above the rising tide of the slums. A new wing had been added to the hospital in 1814, containing an anatomical museum, a large dissecting room, and a handsome lecture theatre. Guy's Hospital, founded a century before by an enterprising publisher of Bibles, stood across the street—a group of well-proportioned Georgian buildings facing on a central courtyard behind an imposing iron gate. Here Keats presented himself on October 1, 1815, signed the register of Surgeons' Pupils, and paid a matriculation fee of £1.2. The next day, according to the register, he paid his tuition of twenty-four guineas for a twelve-month term; then work started in earnest.

It must have been a busy and exciting time, that first week or two—the beginning of a year of new friends, new experience, new and demanding work. A full-fledged medical student, he was free at last from the surveillance of Hammond and on his own in the greatest city in the world. In a few weeks he would be twenty, and by the end of the next summer he would be ready to practise medicine for himself. Almost at once he made his first new friend, a younger student named John Spurgin who, after two years at St. Thomas's, was about to enter Cambridge to train as a physician.[1] Spurgin, an odd, enthusiastic young man, was a fanatical Swedenborgian, and he may have fastened on Keats at first with the idea of converting him. He was to lend Keats books and write him long letters from Cambridge in the months ahead; and evidently he was glad to show him around the Borough in the first few days. He may also have helped Keats find lodgings near the hospital. Once settled, Keats bought himself the necessary equipment—a collection of medical texts, a case of surgical instruments, and a supply of two-shilling notebooks, whose pages he neatly numbered. Then he plunged into his new routine.

The day began early, with a lecture on midwifery at seven-thirty in the morning. From that time on there was a steady round of lectures to attend, operations to watch, hospital wards to visit, dissections to perform. His first day in the dissecting room must have been an ordeal, even with the two pints of beer which, by tradition, each new student had to supply. Here, in a clutter of macerating tubs and jars of anatomical specimens, pipkins and syringes, sawdust underfoot and formaldehyde in the air, he faced the fact of death in its most literal form. The subjects were stolen from nearby graveyards, doubled up stark naked in sacks, and smuggled in at the dead of night by body-snatchers—"resurrection men," as they were called—who were paid three or four guineas for each corpse. Their silent company did not keep the students from using the place as their common room, where they cooked their suppers over the grate, played dice or cards in their spare hours, and drank and joked together. Sometimes their jokes turned into horseplay up and down the rows of dissecting tables; but this ghoulish humour must have helped nerve them against the living horrors of the operating theatre.

Keats apparently met the test of initiation as well as the next man. Yet after the first week or two, when Spurgin left for Cambridge, he found himself lonely and depressed in his new surroundings—to judge from a sonnet he wrote at the time.[2]

> O Solitude! if I must with thee dwell,
>   Let it not be among the jumbled heap
>   Of murky buildings; climb with me the steep,—
> Nature's observatory—whence the dell,

> Its flowery slopes, its river's crystal swell,
>   May seem a span; let me thy vigils keep
>   'Mongst boughs pavillion'd, where the deer's swift leap
> Startles the wild bee from the fox-glove bell. . . .

Imprisoned in the Borough, he was suddenly homesick for the summer woods and fields of Edmonton. Keats was no real Londoner, and the noisome streets and smoky skies of the city must have oppressed him more as autumn drew on and the days grew shorter. Most of all he missed "the sweet converse of an elegant mind," * as his sonnet unhappily put it, which was not to be found in the dissecting room. Who the "kindred spirit" was with whom he longed to share his solitude we can only guess—perhaps Spurgin, or Cowden Clarke sixteen miles away in Enfield, or Mathew, to whom he sent a copy of the sonnet; perhaps some ideal companion he had not yet discovered.

But just as he had done five years before at school, Keats conquered his depression by throwing himself into his work. His ability must have soon caught the notice of his superiors, for within four weeks he won a real distinction. An assistantship under one of the surgeons, a Mr. William Lucas, became vacant; Keats applied and was appointed—the first man in his group of students to be assigned to such a post. In the register of Guy's it was noted on October 29 that six guineas were returned to John Keats, "he becoming a dresser," and beside the October 2 entry of his name was added "6 Mo." Since on starting his work as a dresser in the spring term Keats would pay his fee directly to Mr. Lucas, the difference between the full-year tuition and the half-year fee of eighteen guineas was refunded to him, and in the following March his name was entered under "Dressers to the Surgeons" for a twelve-month term.[3] The dressers were a group apart from the ordinary students, with special privileges and responsibilities. Each of the three staff surgeons at Guy's had four dressers serving under him, along with one or two apprentices or private pupils—young men destined for outstanding careers. Besides the honour, the position also represented a heavier financial commitment for Keats. The dresser's fee would be fifty pounds; in addition he would have to pay an extra half-year's living expenses before he would be ready to take the Surgeons'

---

* The reading of the autograph version (*The Poetical Works of John Keats*, ed. H. W. Garrod, 2nd ed. [1958], p. 43).

Examination a year from the following spring. The change of plan shows a serious ambition on Keats's part, for Abbey probably objected to the added drain on his inheritance.

It is not known how Keats came to apply for the dressership, but it seems likely that he was recommended by Astley Cooper, the distinguished surgeon who was his professor of anatomy and physiology. Cooper was at any rate interested enough in Keats early in the term to ask two of his young assistants to look after him. Immediately they invited Keats to move into their lodgings at 28 St. Thomas's Street—a welcome change from his previous solitude. Keats now had two of the most serious and promising students at Guy's for company: Frederick Tyrrell, Cooper's apprentice and later a staff surgeon at St. Thomas's; and George Cooper (apparently no relation), his dresser. Tyrrell had spent the previous summer in the army hospitals at Brussels, tending the wounded from the battle of Waterloo,[4] and his stories of this adventure must have stirred Keats to a new sense of dedication to his work.

All this left little time for poetry, at least for a while. It was not often he could spend an evening or a Sunday with Mathew, and when he did his friend sensed a change in him. For one thing, Keats's new independence, his new friends, the new experiences of medical school, all seem to have plunged him from adolescence into manhood in a matter of weeks—such is the difference between his poems of the summer and of the fall of 1815. For another, Keats had recently discovered some poets of the early seventeenth century—Michael Drayton and William Browne—beside whom Mathew's enthusiasms began to seem pallid indeed. Evidently troubled by the gap opening between them,[5] Mathew wrote some "Lines to a Poetical Friend," urging Keats not to let his medical studies interfere with his writing or turn him from the poetry they had enjoyed together—Wieland's romantic "tales of the elf and the fay" and "captures and rescues and wonderful loves." He could not have guessed that "the music of Oberon" was indeed fading for Keats. The very poem in which Keats answered Mathew's "Lines" shows him shaking off his friend's influence and practising a sober masculine style patterned on Drayton's verse-letters. Already Keats realized that their "brotherhood in song" would have to yield to his new responsibilities, and hinted at this as gracefully as he could. Not only was he too busy to write; he was also becoming aware of the contrast between his own experience of life and Mathew's poetic version of it:

> Too partial friend! fain would I follow thee
> Past each horizon of fine poesy; . . .
> But 'tis impossible; far different cares
> Beckon me sternly from soft "Lydian airs", . . .
> [And] might I now each passing moment give
> To the coy muse, with me she would not live
> In this dark city, nor would condescend
> 'Mid contradictions her delights to lend.

The contradictions were all too clear: the stark realities of the dissecting room set against the fairy rings and moonlit groves of Mathew's verse. Yet Keats still believed with him that writing poetry required the inspiration of "some flowery spot, sequester'd, wild, romantic," and the stimulus of a sympathetic friend; lacking these, he could only be silent.

So he buckled to the serious business of lecture hall and hospital ward. Day after day, dressed in a dirty linen gown, Keats worked at one of the tables in the dissecting room, following his outline of anatomy from chapter to chapter—bones, muscles, joints, internal organs, blood vessels, nerves. A pleasant change from this work came with the weekly lectures in *materia medica* or medical botany at the Herb Gardens of the Apothecaries' Society in Chelsea. This course was sometimes supplemented by trips to the meadows outside London to gather specimens—a real holiday. Gradually Keats's brown leather-covered notebooks, one of which has survived, filled up with close-packed summaries of lectures, with here and there a few drawings of skulls and fruits and flowers in the margins. At times, it appears, Keats found note-taking tedious—as well he might, since it was the custom to repeat each statement three times for the benefit of the slower students. Compared with the careful notes which a fellow student, Joshua Waddington, kept in three thick volumes now in the library at Guy's, Keats's are sketchy and disjointed. This may mean that Keats was quicker-witted and more retentive than Waddington, or simply that his detailed transcription of his lecture notes— which every student was expected to make [6]—has not survived.

The lecturers at the United Hospitals were for the most part the leading men in their fields; their lectures would have been thoroughgoing but rarely dull. Astley Cooper was the most bril-

liant of the lot, a fashionable surgeon whose practice earned him
about £20,000 a year and, eventually, a baronetcy. A handsome,
energetic man of great charm and warmth, something of a fop but
also a hero to his students, Cooper was a daring innovator in
operative technique. In the spring of 1816 he was to perform the
first ligation of the aorta for aneurysm—an astonishing surgical
feat. Every Tuesday and Friday, when he visited his surgical patients in the ward at Guy's, the students swarmed around him,
hanging on every remark, then jammed into his lectures at St.
Thomas's. Speaking in a broad Norfolk twang and giving an odd
snort of appreciation at his own jokes, Cooper enlivened his talk
with observations from his own surgical experience and anecdotes
from the affairs of the day. Once Keats noted with curious interest
"Mr. C's" sarcastic remark on physicians, that "in disease medical
men guess; if they cannot ascertain a disease, they call it nervous."
Another time he recorded Cooper's account of the division of the
sciatic nerve in a wound suffered by Kosciusko, the champion of
Polish independence who had fought under Napoleon and whom
Keats later commemorated in a sonnet.

Cooper was not only a great doctor who more than anyone
else in his time made surgery an esteemed profession; he was also
a well-read man with a taste for poetry and liberal leanings in
politics. Like other adventurous young Englishmen in 1792,
including William Wordsworth, he had been drawn to France
and become involved in the Revolution, though he had had to
give up his Jacobin connections when he was appointed staff
surgeon at Guy's in 1800. A number of other members of the
staff at Guy's had liberal or unorthodox convictions, and the
intellectual atmosphere must have encouraged freethinking among
the students as well as a sturdy belief in scientific progress.
Mathew, a timid conservative, was alarmed to find Keats becoming
a more and more outspoken advocate of reform and "a fault-
finder with everything established," and their discussions evidently became heated.

His new friend Spurgin was also distressed by Keats's growing
scepticism about religion. In answer to one of his theological
harangues, Keats had confessed that he was in a "mazy Mist" of
doubt about Christian belief. Thereupon Spurgin, who had in
the meantime gone up to Cambridge, wrote him a long letter
expounding the principles of Swedenborg, from the purpose of

Creation to the imminence of Christ's coming, laying special stress on the doctrine of the Trinity. "In every page of the Bible," he pleaded, "we may find that there is One God in Essence and in Person, in whom is a divine Trinity, the same as may be seen in a Glass (as it were) in Man: (viz) Soul, Body, and Operation, the whole of which I will prove from Passages out of the Bible. . . . Dear Keats," he added several closely written pages later, "I FEEL, I PERCEIVE, and acknowledge thereby the Truth and Sanctity of these Writings, and . . . the Love which I am led and taught to bear to my Fellow Creatures, leads me to wish you as a Part thereof a Partaker of those Blessings and Sound and lasting Felicity which an Obedience to the Laws of God can and does most liberally bestow." [7]

Yet Spurgin's exhortations had no apparent effect. Perhaps by way of reaction Keats, who had taken to scribbling doggerel verses in the notebooks of his fellow students to amuse them during lectures, dashed off the following irreverent lines in the syllabus of his friend Henry Stephens:

> Give me women, wine and snuff
> Until I cry out 'hold, enough!'
> You may do so sans objection
> Till the day of resurrection;
> For bless my beard they aye shall be
> My beloved Trinity.

From this it would seem that Keats was fitting comfortably into the life of the average medical student. His friends at Guy's, if they ran true to type, were tough-skinned, level-headed young men, hardened against the physical and mental rigours of their work. Probably it was in their company that Keats acquired his taste for claret and snuff and cigars, learned to play billiards and whist and brag, a kind of poker, and began going to boxing matches, cockfights, and even the bear-baitings at Southwark— the amusements London offered to young men with shillings to jingle in their pockets but not guineas to squander over the tables at White's or Boodle's. No doubt Vauxhall drew him back on other visits. Even the pious Spurgin missed the freedom of the Borough and complained there was "no female Society" in Cambridge.

What kind of female society the Borough offered can only be guessed. In a scrap of would-be Middle English prose cataloguing

the charms of a sleeping maiden which Walter Cooper Dendy, another medical-school acquaintance, tells us Keats tossed off during
an evening lecture, we see him at least posing as a gay dog. Yet,
looked at more closely, these scrawls suggest not a change so much
as a conflict between two aspects of his nature which he could not
yet resolve: his aspirations in poetry and his struggle to come to
terms with the realities of life around him. Keats kept up his
friendship with Mathew through the winter but never introduced
him to his friends at Guy's; [8] he must have sensed that the two
worlds could not be joined. Perhaps the rowdy lines he scribbled
for his fellow students were, like the strained and sentimental
verses he wrote to the Mathew sisters, merely efforts to break out
of the isolation he still felt in his inmost self from the world outside.

᠁

With the start of his second term, in March 1816, Keats's load
of work grew heavier. He began attending Cooper's evening lectures in surgery, in addition to his other courses; [9] and as dresser
to Mr. Lucas he had many new responsibilities at the hospital.
Every Wednesday, which was "taking-in day" at Guy's, he went
round the wards with his master, carrying the tin plaster-box
which was the badge of his rank and noting Lucas's instructions
for each new case. After their first visit the surgeons rarely saw
their patients again but left the dressers in charge. The nurses
gave them little help, for they were illiterate handywomen who
kept busy scrubbing floors, emptying pans, and making up linseed
poultices when they were not boiling mutton for broth in the
middle of the wards. Cleanliness was rudimentary; one of the
highest-paid members of the hospital staff was the bug-catcher.
Since antiseptic techniques were still unknown, wounds constantly festered and dressings had to be changed at least once a
day. Besides his daily rounds, each dresser took his turn every few
months at living in the hospital for a week as dresser-in-charge,
a kind of resident intern. During this time he supervised all the
wards, attended to accident cases, drew teeth, and dressed out-
patients in the surgery, calling on his superior only in emer-
gencies. It was hard work, but valuable training for a committed
student. It must also have tested a young man's emotional endur-

ance. Guy's had been established as a charity hospital for incurables—patients who were too poor and too ill to be taken in elsewhere.[10] There was no better place to learn the limitations of medical science in those days—the mystery that still surrounded most forms of disease and the helplessness of doctors to deal with it most of the time.

If Keats could have served under Cooper, he might have become a great surgeon, but Mr. William Lucas, Jr.—"Billy," the students called him—was not a man to encourage a brilliant pupil. Tall, stooped, shuffling, deaf, he was good-natured and undemanding but dull as an instructor and evidently several generations behind Cooper in surgical technique. Faulty diagnoses and even worse blunders on the operating table were attributed to him, and one of the favourite stories circulated at Guy's told that once he forgot from which direction he was amputating a leg and neatly finished off the discarded end while leaving the raw bone projecting from the stump.[11] Lucas must have put Keats's interest in surgery to a severe test. Since the dressers assisted at operations, they saw at close range what was a nerve-shaking spectacle for many of the students packed in the operating theatre behind them. Ether was not to be introduced for another thirty years; so the patient was usually carried in half-stupefied with drink and strapped down on the table while the operation was performed as rapidly as possible. As Cooper put it, the surgeon needed "an eagle's eye, a lady's hand, and a lion's heart" for his work.[12] Yet even with as skilled an operator as he, the strain was gruelling. Every now and then one of the students would be overcome and stagger out into the corridor, half fainting from the foul air and the groans of the patient under the knife. Perhaps a scene from these days flashed through Keats's memory several years later when he described the anguish of the fallen Titans in *Hyperion:* [13]

> Next Cottus: prone he lay, chin uppermost,
> As though in pain; for still upon the flint
> He ground severe his skull, with open mouth
> And eyes at horrid working. . . .

No matter how well he may have acquitted himself under Lucas, these experiences of helpless agony seared his memory.

At the start of his appointment as dresser, his room-mates Tyrrell and George Cooper finished their course at Guy's and left —Cooper to enter practice near London and Tyrrell to go to

Edinburgh for further study. Keats then gave up their set of rooms and moved in with Henry Stephens and his friend George Wilson Mackereth, who had an apartment in the same house on St. Thomas's Street. His new companions were a decided change from Cooper and Tyrrell, for Mackereth was to fail his examinations at Guy's, and Stephens later turned from medicine to the manufacture of ink. Stephens had a mild interest in poetry and the theatre, however, and soon became Keats's closest friend at the hospital. Yet they were never intimate; Keats told him nothing of his family life, and Stephens later recalled only vaguely that he was an orphan.

Nevertheless, his new room-mate left a revealing picture of Keats at this time, taken at close range and from an unflattering angle. Stephens himself was a practical and self-possessed young man of conventional tastes; he admired Pope, whom Keats was learning to despise, and found Keats's enthusiasm for Spenser slightly ridiculous. When they read their own poems to each other, Keats let him know that he thought little of Stephens' efforts. This was galling; but Stephens was still more nettled by George and Tom Keats, who on their visits to St. Thomas's Street boasted that their brother would "exalt the family name." Stephens had his revenge, however, when Henry Newmarch, an old acquaintance of Keats training at St. Bartholomew's, dropped in for an evening. Newmarch was a good classical scholar as well as a lighthearted, bantering fellow, and he and Keats often discussed Latin poetry together; but when Keats showed him his verses, Newmarch gave them rough critical treatment, which set off violent quarrels. In Stephens' eyes, Keats had too much the air of "one of the Gods mingling with mortals," and some occasional ridicule was required to bring him down to the level of "mere Medical students." Yet apparently it succeeded only in driving Keats back on himself. With Stephens he became quiet and "unsocial"; in their rooms he would often sit abstractedly by the window, staring out into space. Once off the subject of poetry, Stephens conceded, he could be "agreeable and intelligent," and was always "gentlemanly in his manners." Yet when Stephens took him on a visit to some of his friends in the country, the occasion was not a success. Keats could not easily unbend, Stephens noted, "unless he was among those who were of his own tastes, and who would flatter him."

Some of the "pride and conceit" which irritated Stephens may have been only the impact of a first-rate mind on a second-rate one. But there was more to it than that. From many signs it appears that Keats was torn that spring by a division within himself that he could not understand, an estrangement from himself that estranged him from everyone else. Each of the accounts of him at this time describes him differently, agreeing only on the point of his alienation. Mathew, the serious and sentimental, began to find him too readily amused with "the frivolities of life" and indifferent to the true pathos of poetry. He noted disapprovingly that Keats's eye never filled, his voice never broke as they read together; rather he seemed pleased only with "external decorations" such as imagery. Stephens, representing the average medical student, found him standoffish and conceited. Dendy, an older student who stayed on at the hospital as a junior demonstrator, was struck by Keats's growing inattention at lectures. It would seem that Keats was entering a crisis encountered by many young men at his age: a deep uncertainty about his own nature and purposes at the very moment of undertaking his role in life.

The fact that his friends' impressions of him were blurred suggests that Keats himself was uncertain of his own identity—a term which, it is interesting to note, he later used many times in a sense strikingly close to its present-day meaning, to describe the firm sense of selfhood which he now began to realize he lacked.[14] Normally by the age of twenty the individual is ready at last to come to terms with himself, to weld all his previous aspirations and conflicting impulses and various potentialities into enduring decisions for work and marriage, and to achieve a settled character or identity underwriting these commitments. But at just this crucial point in Keats's development the effect of the hidden psychic damage he had suffered in the deaths of his father and mother began to be manifest. Under the strain of his life at Guy's he became increasingly unsure of who he was or what he might become. Wherever he looked for an image of himself— in the eyes of a woman, at the medical students around him, even within his own inner self—the reflection that returned seems to have filled him with doubt and anxiety.

Evidently he had reached a crisis in his relations with women. It is significant that after writing some shyly amorous lyrics in the early months of 1816, Keats suddenly stopped and, except for one brief interlude, wrote no more real love poetry for almost three years.[15] In a man of twenty, responsive as Keats was to a woman's charm—and few English poets seem to have been so deeply affected by the sheer physical beauty of women as Keats—this about-face needs explaining. There may be a clue in the fact that apparently the last of these love poems was a valentine addressed to Mary Frogley,[16] the belle of the Mathews' balls, praising her bright eyes and graceful gait and dark luxuriant hair. Years later it was said that she had been "an old flame" of his; at some time, it appears, and most probably this winter, a romance flickered up between them and was suddenly snuffed out. Keats did not even send the valentine himself; instead his brother George copied it out and sent it to Mary in his own name. Whether this represents one more battle which Keats fought and lost to his enterprising younger brother cannot be known for sure, any more than whether it was a rebuff from Mary Frogley that silenced his love poetry. But something happened at this time that drove him to the sidelines and left him brooding over his dream of a perfect woman. Whatever it was, it still rankled two and a half years later, when Keats confided to a close friend that he had been "disappointed since Boyhood" in his affairs with women. Years of humiliation lie behind the savage remark with which he then attempted to dismiss the subject: "I do think better of Womankind than to suppose they care whether Mister John Keats five feet high likes them or not." Perhaps an echo of this experience may be caught in a wistful sonnet he wrote that winter at Guy's, beginning "Had I a man's fair form." [17] As Henry Stephens, who chose to call him "little Keats," dryly noted, "He would have been pleased to find himself admired by the Fair Sex, for his Genius, but not for his person." In his physical self, Keats had become convinced he could never win the love of a woman he desired; as for his genius, he had written nothing yet that proved it.

The transition from boyhood to manhood is especially uncomfortable for a young man convinced that he has great abilities but aware that the world is not convinced of them. Bernard Shaw has described his own uneasy sense at this age of living under false pretences till at last he began to realize his potentialities and forced the world to acknowledge them. Till then, he noted, young men of talent are "tormented by a shortcoming in themselves; yet they irritate others by a continual overweening." [18] Besides irritating Stephens and his friends, Keats was also beginning to wonder how much scope for his potentialities he would find in the career he had chosen. Suddenly that spring his dedication to medicine began to flag. He started cutting lectures for several weeks at a time and, when present, sat lost in abstraction or working out a sonnet instead of taking notes. Once he told Stephens that he thought medicine at best merely a way "to live in a workaday world." [19] This is a remarkable change from the energy and ambition Keats had shown in the fall. One cause must have been his disillusionment with Lucas; perhaps another was his feeling of superiority to most of his fellow students, destined for the prosaic existence of small-town surgeons. Surely life held more than this!

Yet it also appears that Keats's overweening, like Shaw's, concealed a gnawing suspicion of shortcoming. He confided to Stephens that he was not sure whether he could "keep up the strain" of surgery. Apparently he was encountering a difficulty which is a frequent cause of failure in medical school—an excessive identification with the patient, arising from the student's inability to develop a sense of detachment from suffering early in his career.[20] Several years later Keats admitted he was often disturbed by profound and unconquerable anxiety in close contact with an invalid, especially when alone with him.[21] Probably this vulnerability to suffering began to trouble him when he started assisting Lucas at operations and serving as dresser in the wards. Here he would have encountered one hopeless case of consumption after another—a daily reminder of his mother's last illness. Try as he might to struggle against it, the memory of that time was returning to haunt him. This seems the only meaning, at any rate, of some strangely revealing lines describing a sickroom which he wrote later in 1816. This passage, which occurs near the end of a long poem eventually entitled "I Stood Tiptoe on a Little Hill," has no logical connection with the rest of the poem; in fact its very irrelevance suggests that it sprang from one of the deepest levels of his mind:

> The breezes were ethereal, and pure,
> And crept through half closed lattices to cure
> The languid sick; it cool'd their fever'd sleep,
> And soothed them into slumbers full and deep.
> Soon they awoke clear eyed: nor burnt with thirsting,
> Nor with hot fingers, nor with temples bursting:
> And springing up, they met the wond'ring sight
> Of their dear friends, nigh foolish with delight;

Who feel their arms, and breasts, and kiss and stare,
And on their placid foreheads part the hair.

Taken in itself, the passage may seem insignificant; but this scene
is only the first of several such scenes in Keats's poetry, which acquire a greater weight of meaning with each recurrence. It is a
vision of a return to life from a deathlike sleep, the kind of dream
which one often dreams after the death of a beloved person, and
which may well have been the recurrent dream of a boy who had
watched at his dying mother's bedside but not witnessed her death.
In dream language it states the vain hope of her miraculous recovery, which, it now appears, was probably another deep though
unrecognized motive in Keats's original choice of a medical career.
As a level-headed medical student of twenty, he should have been
able to dismiss the fantasy as absurd; but the need to cling to it
in the face of his daily experience of death must have been a strong
motive in his growing revulsion from a medical career. The growing hold which the fantasy seems to have taken over him suggests
something of his reasons for withdrawing from his friends to stare
gloomily out the window on St. Thomas's Street.

Alienated from the part he was playing in the outer world, Keats
looked inward; and here again he must have felt a stranger to himself. Not only was he disturbed by the discrepancy between "little
Keats," whom Stephens and Newmarch found so easy to ridicule,
and his own proud sense of himself; it would seem that he had
no clear image of the self he struggled to assert. There were more
sides to his nature than could be contained within any single personality. The disasters of his early experience apparently had produced discontinuities in his development which he could not
bridge. The sober, withdrawn adolescent, dedicated to serving
the world as a doctor, was very different from the high-spirited
rebellious boy who appeared destined for military greatness, like
his uncle, and each seemed unrelated to the happily indulged
child he had been, the favourite of his doting mother. A few years
later Keats became acutely aware of this inner division and described it in various terms: as the alternation of what he called energy and indolence, or the active and passive sides of his nature; as
his vacillation between "a Life of Sensations" and "of Thoughts";
or as the battle of the claims that love, ambition, and poetry made
on him, as he felt one with Troilus longing for Cressida, Achilles
shouting in the trenches, or Theocritus singing in the vales of

Sicily. These doubts and conflicts assail many young men as they face the transition from the freedom of youth to the commitments of adulthood; but for Keats, lacking the support of parents or other enduring patterns of maturity, the conflicts reached deeper and the resolution was more difficult than for most. At the threshold of manhood, he halted in uncertainty.

From this uncertainty there was one refuge—a character deliberately assumed to cover up the lack of identity he felt. He would become a poet. It was a part into which he had been drifting all through the year, and it is impossible to tell at what point the resolve became conscious. Not that it implied giving up medicine, for obviously he needed his profession as a livelihood. Yet however slowly or suddenly it appeared, the resolution transformed Keats from the lonely youth who "sighed out sonnets to the midnight air," into a man dedicated to the task of asserting his own being to the world through his poems and of measuring himself against the great poets of the past. It is significant that, from the spring of 1816 on, Keats's poetry is addressed primarily to men, deals with masculine preoccupations—chiefly, for a year at least, the writing of poetry itself—and challenges comparison with the most serious poets of the day. So overpowering did this ambition become that he reportedly told his brothers at about this time that if he did not succeed he would kill himself.[22] Poetry was already becoming what he later called his "only life." Otto Rank has described the psychological mainspring of creative achievement as the "will to self-immortalization" arising from the universal fear of death—a fear which the average man meets by immersing himself in life through his family and his work.[23] But Keats at twenty found himself blocked in his first strivings toward sexual love and increasingly disturbed in his work by its daily reminders of illness and death. Just as six years before he had escaped from painful reality by retreating into study, now he threw himself into his other life of poetry with the energy almost of despair.

Again it was Henry Stephens who marked the change. Keats informed him that poetry was "the only thing worthy the attention of superior minds," and that to rank among the poets was "the chief object of his ambition." At first this involved striking a pose; as Auden has remarked, we are all actors who cannot become something before we have first pretended to be it. So, Stephens noted,

Keats began to appear "with his neck nearly bare à la Byron," his shirt collar turned down and tied with a black ribbon instead of trussed up to his chin with the customary neckerchief. Sometime during 1816 he also took to wearing a kind of loose trousers like a sailor's and a short seaman's jacket, which Byron had affected in protest against the dandiacal fashion of the times; he let his own thick curls grow even longer than Byron's, and experimented with a set of moustaches. There was nothing remarkable in Keats's behaviour, though it was intended to appear remarkable. He was only following the usual course of the young artist, who, before any real act of creation, must appoint himself an artist and create his own creative personality by patterning himself on the stereotype of the artist in his society.[24] The parts most men play are slipped on as easily and attract as little attention as a ready-made suit of clothes. But the young artist in assuming his role hurls a challenge at the world, which he is then obliged to justify by exceptional achievement. Before he makes good his claim, he can only appear ridiculous to prosaic young men like Henry Stephens. Even George Keats, who bragged that his brother would "exalt the family name," later admitted that John had been "a little infected" with the "cockney affectations" of Leigh Hunt at this time.

For Hunt, still more than Byron, was Keats's exemplar of the poet. Sometime that spring Keats decided he must take the crucial step of submitting a poem for publication, and this meant, inevitably, sending one in to *The Examiner*. No doubt he looked over his poems with much anxious deliberation before finally choosing his sonnet "To Solitude." He mailed it in signed only with his initials, then waited. On May 5 the new *Examiner* arrived, and there, at the bottom of an inside page full of miscellaneous foreign despatches, he found it—his own poem published. In all his twenty years he could have felt no more glorious moment than this recognition by Hunt, the champion of freedom, the spokesman of the new poetry. It was the first tangible proof that he might fulfil his claim to being a poet, and a long stride toward his goal. He showed the paper to Stephens, not bothering to hide his delight, and Stephens was impressed. He must also have shown it to Mathew. But to Mathew, who disapproved of everything *The Examiner* stood for, Keats's achievement can have seemed only one more sign of the distance growing between them.

Happily Keats made a new friend this spring who was eager to accept him on his own terms, if his other friends were not. Joseph Severn, an acquaintance of his school friend Edward Holmes,[25] was a struggling young painter whose father, a tyrannical music-master, had bitterly opposed his choice of career and apprenticed him to a copper-engraver. Severn detested this occupation and held stubbornly to his ambition, attending night classes at the Royal Academy while making water-colour portraits at half a guinea each to buy the oils he needed. A good-looking young man, thin with delicately chiselled features, fair hair which he wore in straggling curls, and a mouth almost girlish in its beauty, he was still rather unsure of himself, but he had a natural good humour that opened out in congenial company. Meeting Keats raised Severn "to the third heaven," as he later wrote, and filled him with new hope for his own career. It appears that from the start Severn set more store on their friendship than Keats; he did not become one of Keats's intimates until over four years later. Yet each had much to give the other. From his father Severn had acquired some skill as a pianist, and he introduced Keats to the world of painting. Together they began to visit the British Institution, where Severn pointed out his favourite Titians and Poussins and Claudes; on other holidays they talked of books, for which Severn had little time in the long drudgery of his apprenticeship. He was not only a gay companion but an appreciative one. Evidently he matched Keats's mood that spring far better than the melancholy Mathew, and his admiration must have reflected back to Keats the image he sought of the rising young poet.

As spring turned into summer they began to go for long walks together on Hampstead Heath. Once away from the city and out in the fields, Keats's spirits always soared, and Severn was struck by his vivid response to every sight and sound. Nothing escaped him, Severn later recalled—the distant note of a thrush answering its mate in a nearby hedge, the rustle of a stoat in the underbrush, the foxlike expression of a passing tramp, the sway of meadow flowers in the breeze. His greatest delight was the sight of the wind rippling over a field of wheat and the sound it made like rushing water as it surged through the branches of oaks and chestnuts. Evidently his boyhood absorption in the hidden life of nature had only been intensified by his training in close observation as a medical student. Severn on his side was studying Keats with the eye of a portrait-painter, noting the trim but muscular body with its narrow hips, long trunk, and small skull poised above broad shoulders, watching the play of emotion across his face. He was puzzled when he saw Keats fall into one of his taciturn moods, gripped by "a profound disquiet which he could not or would not explain." Then he noted how in his outgoing moods Keats seemed taller than his real height, partly because of his erect bearing and a characteristic backward toss of the head, but still more because of "a peculiarly dauntless expression, such as may be seen on the face of some seamen." [26] It was a significant resemblance that he caught.

Evidently, with the end of the term at Guy's, Keats found more time for tramping on the heath with Severn, swimming in the New River with Stephens, or, best of all, spending a whole afternoon by himself, reading in the tall grass or working out a sonnet. Writing still did not come easily to him: his early drafts are full of false starts and stops, of wrenched syntax and misplaced accents and bad rhymes,[27] of painful searching for the right word and angry scratching out of lines at a time. Still he kept at it, driven by an unconquerable determination to struggle through awkwardness and inexactness and inanity to some perfect utterance which he dimly sensed as his goal. His worst difficulty was still a tendency toward mawkishness and verbosity: only here and there in his sonnets did he achieve the noble chiselled line toward which he was groping.

Another difficulty, revealed in his sonnet "How many bards gild the lapses of time," was the echoes of other poets' work that began chiming in his head whenever he started a poem of his own. This June he was full of a new discovery, *The Story of Rimini,* which Leigh Hunt had published that spring, retelling the episode of Paolo and Francesca from the *Inferno.* Though Hunt had turned Dante's noble and laconic tragedy into a long-winded sentimental romance, the poem scored an instant success with the poetry-reading public. The Tory critics could sneer, but ladies wept over it; Byron, to whom it was dedicated, called it "devilish good," while Haydon the painter thought it "the sweetest thing of our time." Keats was swept off his feet by it. Hunt's easy conversational tone and his lush descriptions of woods and gardens and secret bowers brought the knights and ladies of romance down to a recognizable earth and present. At once Keats wondered—

could he not do the same? Starting a long poem was taking a great dare, but his appearance in *The Examiner* had given him the courage. He took a subject from Spenser—the youth of Calidore, one of the heroes of *The Faerie Queene*—and began: "Lo! I must tell a tale of chivalry." [28] At once he was overwhelmed by his own presumption. Interrupting his tale to write a preliminary "Induction," he apologized to Spenser for daring to follow in his footsteps and begged Hunt, his "lov'd Libertas," to intercede for Spenser's favour.

But with July this project was cut short. The Apothecaries' Examination was coming up, and Stephens, for one, was sure that Keats would not pass. Only a few weeks were left in which to make up for the hours dreamed away in the lecture room. But, as Stephens admitted, Keats was "quick and apt at learning, when he chose to give his attention to any subject." The examination stressed the terminology of medicine, and here Keats's knowledge of Latin gave him an edge. When he and Stephens and Mackereth went up to the Apothecaries Hall on July 25, Mackereth was "ploughed" and Keats, to everyone's surprise, passed. As his certificate recorded, John Keats, "of full age," having served as apprentice to Thomas Hammond and attended the required courses of lectures at the United Hospitals, was examined by Mr. Brande of the Worshipful Masters and found qualified "to practise as an Apothecary in the Country"—that is, throughout England and Wales though not in London. It erred in stating that he was twenty-one—unless, of course, his baptismal record was mistaken—and that he had completed a five-year term with Hammond; but these errors merely underscore his achievement. For all the doubts and distractions of his first year at Guy's, Keats had successfully qualified as an apothecary in the shortest possible time and at the earliest possible age.[29]

→»·«←

Two months now lay ahead before the start of the fall term. Keats had earned a carefree holiday for himself, but he was worried about his younger brother. Apparently Tom had not been well for some time. He had grown into a tall, narrow-shouldered, high-strung lad of sixteen, with a build that doctors then described as "consumptive." From the time he began clerking for

Abbey his health had suffered from the long hours and the smoke and fog of London. Sometime during the previous winter he had been sent to Lyons for its milder climate and perhaps also to learn the hat trade, in which Abbey had an interest. Now back in London, he still looked pale and thin, and Keats decided that a vacation by the sea would do him good. So they packed up and went off to Margate, a popular resort on the Kentish coast, complete with the usual ballrooms and cardrooms, a sandy beach for swimming, and a promenade from which to watch the yacht races.

The two brothers were good company for each other. The four-year gap between their ages made little difference now, and Tom, gifted, as Keats later said, with "an exquisite love of life," was developing as great an appetite for books as his older brother. According to George, Tom understood Keats better than anyone else. While George was in most ways John's antithesis, practical, gregarious, a steady balance-wheel to his wide swings of mood, Tom had much of Keats's own delicacy of feeling and playful imagination, as his few surviving letters show. Tom had his moods too, and this summer it appears that he was unhappily in love with a mysterious young Frenchwoman named Amena, an acquaintance of his school friend Charles Wells, with whom he was carrying on a long sentimental correspondence. Wells, a precocious red-haired fellow and a great joker, now a junior clerk in a solicitor's office, was also vacationing at Margate. He had already developed an interest in the theatre which in a few years was to lead him into playwriting; now he was eager to cultivate Keats's acquaintance. His company must have livened up their holiday, besides making it possible for Keats to spend some longed-for time by himself.

For he had come on this vacation primarily to write, to see what he could do in a month or more away from the responsibilities of the hospital. Day after day he went tramping along the coast with a book or a half-finished poem in hand, drinking in every new sight and sound. Apparently this was his first visit to the seaside, and it seemed he could never tire of watching the line of a gull's flight, the slow curve and crash of a wave, the shadows stretching across the fields at evening, the flash of a falling star across the night sky. Almost at once the vast openness of the scene, with its endless motion and glimmer, entered into his poetry, adding a new dimension to the earthy, enclosed, overshadowed world of his earlier poems. But these "wonders of the sea and sky," as he called them in a sonnet he sent to George shortly after arriving, did more:

> The ocean with its vastness, its blue green,
>   Its ships, its rocks, its caves, its hopes, its fears,—
>   Its voice mysterious, which who so hears
> Must think on what will be, and what has been, . . .

sank deep into his consciousness and merged there with the unanswered question of the winter. What was his life to be? What place could he find in it for poetry? As yet he could not glimpse an answer; but as he stood on the cliff at Margate, staring at the wide plain of water beneath him, an image began to take form in his mind. His future seemed to lie spread before him like an uncharted sea. Where was he going? When would he set out? The question made him restless. But for the present he could put it out of his mind by stretching out in the oat fields along the cliff's edge, now bright with poppies, to read or work on his poems.

It was here that he picked up the long verse-narrative of Calidore's boyhood which he had started in the spring. For about a hundred lines all seemed to go well; then he ran into difficulties. He could not make anything happen. His young hero rows across a lake in the evening to welcome two knights and ladies who have ridden up to his castle; he helps the ladies off their horses, embraces them with delight, escorts his guests to a chamber—and there the story breaks off. Much of the poem merely describes the same scenery of lake and island as the "Imitation of Spenser"; yet a comparison with the early poem suggests a reason for Keats's failure to finish it. It is significant that Calidore crosses the lake to emerge from the maternal element of water into real human life. The guests whom he meets in the castle constitute a small society, an older and a young couple.[30] The older knight is Calidore's lord and generous benefactor; the younger knight is a visitor, almost a stranger, whose exploits the boy longs to hear recounted and perhaps to emulate. He is the mighty horseman who appears in several other of Keats's early poems, wielding a stout lance, proud in the possession of a beautiful lady, admired from a distance by the boy-poet. The reminders of Keats's father and grandfather are striking; even the castle courtyard, with the horses "slanting out their necks with loosened rein" as their riders dismount, seems a recollection of his childhood home. Whatever Keats's original intention for his narrative, it has apparently been drawn into the orbit of boyish fantasy. This may explain the excessive emotion which Calidore feels on greeting his guests, and perhaps also account for Keats's sudden faltering at the end, when the knights retire with their ladies to bed. Though "Calidore" is a fantasy of rebirth, of emergence into a masculine world, not of mere retreat as was the "Imitation of Spenser," it shows Keats still closely tied to half-remembered early experience, not yet ready for the full freedom of mature creation.

Keats himself was aware that "Calidore" was not going right, and in July he wrote a long verse-letter to George describing his discouragement. This artless confession suggests another reason for his failure: Keats was looking for a vision. Lying in the grass, staring up into the sky at sunset, he was listening for a "spherey strain," striving "to think divinely." He still clung to a notion which he attributed to Spenser and Hunt, that poetry was a kind of supernatural insight into some transcendental realm, a matter of seeing knights on white coursers in the clouds and the clash of their combat in the sheet-lightning along the horizon at dusk. If writing poetry was as mysterious a process as this, then what marvellous beings poets were, and what folly for him to hope to become one! Yet still more awe-inspiring was the poet's responsibility to society, his power to move men to noble deeds or instruct them in true wisdom, which won him the reward of an immortal name after death. The more Keats thought about becoming a poet, the more exalted the role came to seem—one that would absorb his whole being and require all his energies, not merely what he could give it after his daily work was done. But this was madness. For all the pleasure his poems might give, or even the good he might do in speaking out for freedom and justice, he had been trained for another part. "Ah, my dear friend and brother," he burst out,

> Could I, at once, my mad ambition smother,
> For tasting joys like these, sure I should be
> Happier, and dearer to society.

The world needed good doctors, and he needed a livelihood. And why should he delude himself for a moment that he would ever join the ranks of the great poets whose faces he seemed to glimpse in the feathery clouds of sunset?

His verses limped; the promise in the sunset faded; but he did not quite give up. For even as he wrote, his purposes began to clarify. He had brought with him on vacation two small volumes of poetry by Wordsworth,[31] whom, it appears, he had not heard of till Hunt printed a few of his sonnets in *The Examiner* that winter. This was one of the significant discoveries of Keats's career. Almost at once he recognized Wordsworth as the greatest of the living poets, and the one who had most to teach him. It was to take Keats another year or more to grasp Wordsworth's full meaning; but already this summer echoes of the older poet's sonnets began to appear in his own lines—especially Wordsworth's magnificent images of the sea and the night sky. And already he found in "Tintern Abbey" and the ode on "Intimations of Immortality" an eloquent expression of his own response to the beauty of the natural world. As Wordsworth described the poet, he was no romantic visionary but "a man speaking to men" of their own most deeply felt experience; a man "who rejoices more than other men in the spirit of life that is in him" and "in the goings-on of the Universe around him," where he finds a life like his own, sharing his own "passions and volitions." The deep organic bond between the poet and the world of nature, the slow, plantlike unfolding of the poet's mind, the mysterious ebb and flow of his imagination: these were the doctrines that Keats absorbed with each rereading of Wordsworth and which were soon to transform his whole conception of poetry.

As "Calidore" began to sound hollow to his ears he turned back to another poem he had started in June, a long and wandering description of the sights and sounds of a summer's day he had observed from a little hill on Hampstead Heath. The poem had no name, no theme when he began it, not even a clear sense of direction; but that seemed not to matter. He let it run on from morning to evening, double back on itself to round out the cycle of the hours, then run on again, full of his delight in the blossoming world around him. For the earth had never seemed more beautiful than it did that summer, nor the sweep of the heavens above the plain of the sea, nor—most of all—the moon, which he watched starting her climb as he walked along the Margate cliff after sunset. Now the moon became a presence in his poetry as though he had never seen it before, lighting up a field of broken clouds like white bean-blossoms, gliding from behind a dark cloud like a swimmer into water, or

> Floating through space with ever loving eye
> The night crowned queen of ocean and the sky.[32]

Why should this beauty move him so deeply? He did not quite know. But as he read and walked and pondered, he began to see more clearly what he was trying to say. There was more to it than listing all the sights and sounds of a summer's day, however beautiful. The ocean spoke with a "voice mysterious," the moon gazed down on the earth with an "ever loving eye"; everywhere in nature the poet looked, he found, as Wordsworth had said, "relationship and love"; and this, Keats now began to see, was the stuff of poetry, not the fancied visions of his sunset musings. The poem which he had started so simply on a June morning on Hampstead Heath began to move in a new direction, though he still could not quite see his goal.

The August sunlight thinned into September, and Keats's vacation was drawing to a close. Then a piece of welcome news arrived. George wrote that Cowden Clarke had moved to the city. His father was about to retire from the Enfield school, and Clarke had decided to try his luck in publishing. Keats had been out of touch with his old tutor during his year at Guy's, though he had evidently gone out to Enfield to see him early in the summer. That must have been a pleasant reunion, with Keats's appearance in *The Examiner* and Clarke's growing friendship with Hunt to talk over. Now as he looked forward and then back on their friendship, Keats was struck by how much he owed to the older man for opening up the world of poetry to him. Yet he had never expressed his gratitude, just as he had not yet dared show Clarke most of his poems. He decided to write him a verse letter of thanks; yet no sooner than he began he was overcome by the same discouragement as he had felt in writing George. The distance between his present achievement and his ambition as a poet was so vast that he hardly had the courage to start:

> Whene'er I venture on the stream of rhyme,
> With shatter'd boat, oar snapt, and canvass rent,
> I slowly sail, scarce knowing my intent. . . .

But his sails filled as the poem moved on, swelling out in praise of Clarke, of poetry, of freedom, of friendship, of Leigh Hunt, whom Keats shyly hinted he would like to meet—Hunt

> who elegantly chats, and talks—
> The wrong'd Libertas,—who has told you stories
> Of laurel chaplets, and Apollo's glories;
> Of troops chivalrous prancing through a city,
> And tearful ladies made for love, and pity:
> With many else which I have never known.

The tribute was sincere, but the tone of slack-limbed sentimentality unerringly caught from *Rimini* suggests that closer acquaintance with Hunt might not be all for the good.

Soon after he finished this epistle to Clarke it was time for Keats to return to London—his two long poems still incomplete, his questions about the future still unanswered. He and Tom took rooms together in Dean Street near the hospital,[33] for Keats had decided that Tom was still not well enough to go back to work for Abbey. He picked up his own tasks at Guy's again, but most of the time his thoughts were elsewhere. At the first chance he had to slip off, he went to look up Clarke at his sister's in Clerkenwell, two miles away on the other side of the city, and took him the poetry he had written over the last few months. Clarke was delighted to see him and impressed by his poems. He asked Keats about his work at the hospital and was surprised to hear him speak of it with dislike, as though he had to keep at it against his will.[34] Then Clarke made a suggestion which must have sent the blood rushing to Keats's forehead. He would take the poems to show to Leigh Hunt on his next visit and see whether an invitation could be arranged.

Not long after his release from prison Hunt had moved from London to the Vale of Health, just outside of Hampstead. At that time Hampstead was a pleasant country village, four miles from the northernmost suburbs of London, famous for its clear air and mineral springs and the view of half a dozen counties from the top of its hill. In his cottage on the edge of the Heath, Hunt held a kind of literary court while editing *The Examiner* and turning out gossipy essays and poems on the pleasures of rural life. Cowden Clarke was one of the company invited out for conversational evenings around the fire or family picnics on the Heath or those "sweet forest walks" which Keats had heard about with a touch of envy. Knowing Hunt's enthusiastic spirit, Clarke was sure Keats's poems would be well received. But he was taken by surprise when Hunt, after reading for only a minute, burst out in genuine admiration. This was real poetry, he exclaimed—immature, perhaps, but was the man only twenty? Horace Smith, a fashionable writer and wit who happened to be visiting Hunt that morning, was equally impressed. He read aloud to Hunt the sonnet "How many bards gild the lapses of time," repeating the next-to-last line, which struck him as especially well turned for so young a writer. Hunt quizzed Clarke about his protégé, then asked him to bring Keats along on his next visit. Back in London, Clarke forwarded the invitation at once, and Keats replied in jubilation. "The busy time has just gone by," he wrote on October 9, shortly after the beginning of the term, "and I can now devote any time you may mention to the pleasure of seeing Mr Hunt— 't will be an Era in my existence." He began copying out some of his poems, then in a moment of despair tossed half of them into the fire. The verse-letter to Mathew was perhaps good enough to show Hunt, but nothing he had written earlier.

The appointed day came. As they started out early on their walk to Hampstead, Keats was in such high spirits that his expression caught the attention of the passers-by. He fell silent as they started up the long hill together, but did not slacken his pace. At the porch of his white-painted cottage, Hunt met them with a warm grasp of the hand—a tall, slender, good-looking man in his early thirties, his dark eyes shining with the liquidity of shortsightedness, and a full-lipped smile lighting up his pale and rather softly moulded features. His welcome had all the grace of a man who had rarely if ever doubted his own charm, his talents, or the rightness of his convictions. Hunt led them into the parlour, which also served as his study, a small neat room hung with prints of mythological scenes and lined with bookcases and busts of his heroes, with a pianoforte in one corner and a baize-topped desk with a small vase of flowers in the other. Clarke watched him putting Keats immediately at his ease—the great man deferring to the young one, drawing out his opinions, dazzling him with a burst of eloquence, then dissolving the effect in a joke. But Clarke also saw that Keats was holding his own, and that Hunt warmed to his enthusiasm. The two were hitting it off perfectly. Their visit stretched out to three times the length of a proper call and ended with Hunt's inviting Keats to come again, and often.

As Keats foresaw, this meeting opened a new era in his life. Hunt urged him to bring out more of his poetry and praised it almost to extravagance. At once his friend the painter Haydon, who was taking a fortnight's holiday in Hampstead, begged to be introduced and was so delighted with Keats on their first meeting that he immediately invited him for Sunday dinner in his Hampstead lodgings. Keats agreed—though it may be with some embarrassment when he learned that Hunt was not to be included. Haydon, however, wished to introduce him to a protégé of his own, the poet John Hamilton Reynolds. Only a year older than Keats, Reynolds had just published his third volume of verse, *The Naiad,* a romantic tale in the style of Hunt, and dedicated it to Haydon. Sworn to secrecy about the dinner, Reynolds may have come with some misgivings mingled with curiosity

> To meet John Keats, who soon will shine
> The greatest, of this Splendid time,
> That e'er has wooed the Muses nine—

as Haydon put it in his rhymed invitation. Reynolds must have scented a rival, and perhaps Keats was overawed by the young poet whose work had won the attention of Wordsworth and the praise of Byron, and who was dramatic critic of *The Champion* and man about town as well. The two young men had much in common; but since they met as respective disciples of Hunt and Haydon, their friendship proceeded rather cautiously at first.[35] Yet this acquaintance was one more sign to Keats of the glorious world that was opening up before him.

The air was still electric with adventure when, one evening later in October, Clarke invited him up to Warner Street to share a discovery. A friend of Hunt's had loaned him a 1616 folio of George Chapman's translation of Homer, a treasure in the days when much Elizabethan literature had not been reprinted and was hard to come by. Both Keats and Clarke knew Homer only through Pope's translation, which tailored the long, swinging hexameters of the Greek to the neat proportions of the balanced couplet. As they searched Chapman for some of the great passages —Helen's conversation with Priam on the walls of Troy, the descriptions of the shield of Diomed, the chariot of Neptune—they

found a free-striding verse that matched Homer's own, and a hard
masculine strength of phrase that made Pope's elegant abstractions
seem thin and bloodless. Where Pope had described the ship-
wrecked Ulysses as he staggered up on the Phaeacian shore, streaming with salt water:

>   his knees no more
> Perform'd their office, or his weight upheld:
> His swoln heart heav'd, his bloated body swell'd:
> From mouth to nose the briny torrent ran,
> And lost in lassitude lay all the man,
> Deprived of voice, of motion, and of breath,
> The soul scarce waking in the arms of death, . . .

Chapman showed him

>   both knees falt'ring, both
> His strong hands hanging down, and all with froth
> His cheeks and nostrils flowing, voice and breath
> Spent to all use, and down he sank to death.
> The sea had soak'd his heart through. . . .

As Clarke recalled, Keats shouted with delight at this last line.
This was what it was to lead a band of heroes against Troy and
voyage homeward through long years of misadventure and lie half
drowned on a lonely beach; this was what Homer had been saying
all along—or so he thought; * this was poetry of a kind that had
not been written in England for two hundred years.

All night they turned the pages of the great calf-bound book
together. When Keats tore himself away at last it was almost six.
He walked home through the empty streets under the fading
planets, with the lines of a sonnet beating in his head. The storm
of that night's excitement had stirred up the very depths of his
mind; things he had seen and felt and read in the last few months
and six or eight years ago were washing up together on the shores
of his consciousness. The sea which he had stared at from the cliffs
of Margate, the stars he had watched and the moon

>   lifting her silver rim
> Above a cloud, and with a gradual swim
> Coming into the blue with all her light, . . .

the Mediterranean islands and the new vistas of poetry which he
had glimpsed that evening with Clarke: all these were jostling in

---

* The line that especially pleased Keats was an interpolation of Chapman's: see the
literal translation by A. T. Murray in the Loeb Classical Library *Odyssey*, p. 203.

his mind with phrases from Shakespeare and Wordsworth and recollections more distant still—passages from Bonnycastle and Robertson describing Herschel's discovery of the planet Uranus and Balboa's discovery of the Pacific and Cortez's first view of Mexico City, which recalled a painting by Titian which Severn may have pointed out to him that summer. When he reached Dean Street at dawn he took a piece of paper, marked lines down the right-hand margin to guide him in his rhymes, and wrote out the poem that had been taking shape in his head.* When it was done, he made a copy and sent it off by messenger to Clarke, who found it on his breakfast table when he came down that morning:

ON THE FIRST LOOKING INTO CHAPMAN'S HOMER

Much have I travell'd in the Realms of Gold,
   And many goodly states and kingdoms seen,
   Round many Western islands have I been
Which bards in fealty to Apollo hold.
Oft of one wide expanse had I been told,
         deep
   Which ~~low~~-brow'd Homer ruled as his Demesne:
   Yet could I never judge what Men could mean,
Till I heard Chapman speak out loud and bold.

Then felt I like some Watcher of the Skies
   When a new Planet swims into his Ken,
Or like stout Cortez, when with wond'ring eyes
   He star'd at the Pacific, and all his Men
Look'd at each other with a wild surmise—
   Silent upon a peak in Darien.[36]

It is not hard to imagine Clarke's amazement as he read the sonnet over. The poem was a miracle; not simply because of its mastery of form, or because Keats was only twenty when he wrote it, or because he wrote it in the space of an hour or two after a night without sleep. Rather because nothing in his earlier poetry gave any promise of this achievement: the gap between this poem and his summer work could be leaped only by genius. He had still to rework a phrase here and there before he was quite satisfied; he overlooked a false rhyme in the sixth line and a historical slip in the eleventh which went unnoticed till Tennyson pointed it out years later. But the unity of form and feeling that begins in the first line and swells in one crescendo of excitement to the final crashing silence was instantaneous and unimprovable. After the

---

* This draft is reproduced as Plate X.

reverberation of that ending has died away, something new appears to our eyes. The sonnet, we realize, is not about Chapman, or Homer, or even Keats's reading of Chapman's translation. It is about something much larger, more universal, the rapture of discovery itself—of a new star in the vast heavens, of a sea where none was known before. Cortez standing on his peak is Keats himself on the cliff at Margate, staring at the sea and thinking "on what will be, and what has been"; the poem as a whole expresses his rising excitement of the previous weeks, from the moment Clarke promised to introduce him to Hunt. Saluted by Hunt and his friends, his eyes opened to new kingdoms of poetry, Keats felt the horizons of his world expanding beyond all expectation. It was the limitless possibilities of his own future that he saw spread out before him that morning, shining with the promise of El Dorado.

Chapter Four

The Green Shore

A W E E K or two later Keats turned twenty-one. The event seems to have gone unmarked, perhaps because of his queer dislike of having his birthday celebrated, perhaps because he was too busy at the hospital. Apparently he did not even receive his inheritance at this time, for it was found necessary to look up an old servant who could testify to the exact date of his birth.[1] Yet in the most important sense he had already come into his own: in writing the Chapman sonnet he had proved his title as poet. Though nothing that he wrote for months afterward was to sound quite the same note, in this sonnet he had spoken out at last in his own poetic voice. Leigh Hunt at once caught the unmistakable accent. He must have stared with at least a moment's wonder at this work of his new protégé, but he lost no time in praising it to his friends. Hazlitt and Godwin, dining at Hampstead not long afterward, were shown the sonnet and agreed it was as extraordinary as he had thought, a work which "announced the new poet taking possession." Hunt could not have put it better. For almost a year the idea of becoming a poet had been the stuff of Keats's dreams, the object of his most determined efforts, even the subject of much of his writing; now he had done the actual deed. From this time on Hunt began to introduce him in his circle as the young man to watch.

It was an interesting and often brilliant group that gathered at Hunt's, all men who had made their mark in one way or another. They included Horace Smith, the stockbroker, a minor novelist and master parodist; Thomas Barnes, the *Times'* dramatic critic and soon its editor-in-chief; John Scott, the editor of the new liberal weekly *The Champion;* Vincent Novello, a distinguished conductor and organist who introduced Haydn's and Mozart's religious music to England; William Godwin, the ageing author of the once notorious *Political Justice,* the Bible of the radicals of the 1790s; Haydon, Hazlitt, Lamb, and many lesser names from the compact London world of letters, affairs, the theatre, and the arts. Hunt's genius for hospitality and his eager interest in everyone and everything attracted men of many different temperaments and abilities. Yet he also had a wit that could cut both ways—against his friends as well as his enemies. He was especially fond of quizzing Haydon, a stout believer in the Bible as the literal Word of God and the Duke of Wellington as the defender of civilization; and eventually they had to agree never to argue on religion or Napoleon. Because of his airy manners and unorthodox opinions, Hunt's opponents found it easy to sneer at his "vulgarity." Yet Barry Cornwall, the poet, a man who set great store by politeness, declared Hunt was "essentially a gentleman." [2] Perhaps the point needed stressing, for Hunt was something of a Bohemian before his time, and his style as a writer is marred by a misplaced informality which, then as now, many readers found distasteful who did not know his charm as a man.

Few men have displayed the defects of their virtues more flamboyantly. Things always seemed to come easily to Hunt. As he once gracefully remarked, he found it as delightful to be obliged to a friend as to oblige him; but, having no head for finances, he usually ended up on the debit side. Generous in paying tribute to others, he was shamelessly fond of praise himself—especially from the ladies, to the distress of his bachelor friends. Hunt had ideas about freer relations between the sexes that few men of his time could accept; [3] and, between his literary sister-in-law Elizabeth Kent and his pretty but scatterbrained wife Marianne, his household was a queer mixture of the bluestocking and the sentimentalist. His friendliness was irresistible, but, as his son Thornton later said, "he invested his personal friends with ideal attributes"—a risky business—and thus "seldom viewed anything as it really was." Even while serving his prison term for speaking unpopular truths, he had begun to narrow his gaze more and more to what he called "the sunny side of things." On leaving his rose-trellised cell he went through some kind of nervous crisis;

London life seemed so "hideous" that he fled to Hampstead to escape it. His political enthusiasms were cooling, his literary tastes becoming more dilettantish; and *The Champion* was beginning to challenge the popularity of *The Examiner*. In fact, though no one yet suspected it, by 1816 Hunt had passed his peak. The fate of the child prodigy, the early fading of an early-blooming talent, was overtaking him.

If none of Hunt's friends could see this change, still less could Keats. Meeting Hunt was the great turning point of his life. As Severn said, it "intoxicated him with an excess of enthusiasm" for months afterward.[4] Hunt's friendship was a dream come true, Hunt's interest in his work the proof of his wildest ambition. He began to steal more and more time away from the hospital for what Hunt called his "evenings joco-serio-musico-pictorio-poetical," when his friends gathered at the cottage and the wine went round. The talk ranged in all directions—from Wordsworth's merits to the principles of punning, from the life of Petrarch to the latest *Political Register;* then it would break off as Hunt went to the piano and accompanied himself in an aria of Mozart's or played a flute sonata with one of his guests. If it turned to art, Hunt would take down one of his portfolios and "read" a painting, as he called it, scanning a print of Titian or Raphael or Poussin for its mythological implications. All this was Keats's first taste of good conversation, and it left him almost drunk with delight. Even the eight-mile walk back to the Borough, across the Heath under the frosty stars, seemed nothing after such an evening.

As Hunt's protégé, he was content at first to sit on the sidelines and listen. Clarke pictured him in a characteristic pose at these debates, sitting with one leg crossed over the other while absent-mindedly smoothing his ankle with his hand. He impressed the modish Horace Smith as "a loose, slack, not well-dressed youth," his manner "shy and embarrassed, as of one unused to society." [5] In England then, even more than now, dress and diction were unmistakable badges of class; and for Keats, who spoke with a trace of a Cockney accent,[6] his first acquaintance with such men as Smith may well have heightened his natural diffidence. Only with Clarke and Hunt could he feel quite at ease. Hunt began calling him "Junkets," a nickname which he apparently accepted in good humour, along with Hunt's other whimsicalities. These

ranged from birthday celebrations for men of genius, alive or
departed, to sonnet-writing contests, often with a time limit of
fifteen minutes. At these Keats made his mark with one of his
most successful poems that winter. One snug evening when a
cricket began chirping on the hearth, Hunt proposed they match
wits on the subject of "The Grasshopper and the Cricket." They
set to, and Keats finished first, under the time limit and in top
form. As he read out his first line, "The poetry of earth is never
dead," Hunt exclaimed over the promising start, then interrupted
with "Bravo Keats!" at his modulation from the drowsiness of
summer to the silence of frost near the end. Not to be outdone,
Keats insisted to Clarke on their way home that Hunt's sonnet
was much better than his own, and Clarke smiled to himself at
each man's eagerness to find everything admirable in the other.

Keats's adulation of Hunt could not last, of course, and while
it did it had some regrettable effects. With the publication of
Rimini, Hunt had become the leader of a kind of "New Poetry"
movement which aimed at breaking the lingering hold of Dryden
and Pope over English verse while it also managed to trivialize
Wordsworth's revolutionary attempt to make poetry out of the
real experience and language of men. So Hunt encouraged Keats's
own tendency to think of poetry as a kind of exquisite indulgence
in poetic sensations, a matter of almond blossoms, nightingales,
and white-handed nymphs; he also sanctioned all the qualities
Keats most needed to discipline in his work—vagueness of thought,
looseness of language, extravagance of sentiment. Yet, for all his
dilettantism, Hunt had the widest range of taste of any critic of
his day, and the keenest ear for the new talent of his time. To his
credit, he pointed out to Keats many poets of the past who were
to contribute significantly to his work, and convinced him that
English poetry was entering on a great new age. Still better, he
introduced Keats to an audience worthy of his gifts, and helped
turn his imagination in a significant new direction.

In the fall of 1816 Hunt was pursuing a new enthusiasm for
Greek mythology, fired by Wordsworth's discussion of myth in
The Excursion which, Hunt felt, had rescued the myths from the
inanities of neo-classic verse and restored them to their true esti-
mation. Hunt now planned to write a series of poems retelling the
Greek legends in the style of *Rimini* and was already at work on
the story of Hero and Leander.[7] At this, it seems, Keats's scattered

intentions suddenly came to a focus. In the myths, Hunt told him, the early poets were attempting to express their sense of the beauty of the natural world through some equally beautiful human form. For Hunt, they were mere "lovely tales" and nothing more, and for Keats at this point that was all the justification they needed. The old stories which he had mused over in his schoolbooks now sprang to new life, especially when Hunt showed them transmuted into poetry by the Elizabethans—Spenser and Chapman and Fletcher and Sandys, whose translation of Ovid was a treasure-house of classical legend. Now at last he glimpsed his goal in the long poem he had started in June, standing "tiptoe upon a little hill." The beauty of the myths sprang from no mere fancy but from something as real as what he experienced rambling over the Heath—all the shifting moods of nature, from the springlike joy of the story of Psyche to the desolation of Pan baffled by the fleeing Syrinx. So he would retell these stories: best of all, he would recount the legend of Cynthia and Endymion. This myth explaining the mysterious disappearance and reappearance of the moon—"Peace ho! the moon sleeps with Endymion And would not be awaked"—had always moved him more deeply than he could explain. No other tale could better convey the sense of unearthly loveliness he had felt in his moonlit walks at Margate, the lingering notion of a realm of transcendent joy achieved by the poet, or, perhaps, the still uncommunicated vision of the "fair goddess" sleeping in his mind. It was an idea which Hunt must have approved wholeheartedly.[8]

Yet just as the future began to take new shape the past tugged unexpectedly at his sleeve. In October, George Felton Mathew's "Lines to a Poetical Friend" were published in *The European Magazine*. This gesture, probably intended to revive their failing friendship, could only have reminded Keats of enthusiasms he could no longer share. The cruel truth was that he was moving ahead at a pace that his friend could not follow. If Mathew opposed everything that Leigh Hunt stood for, it was Hunt's world that Keats had cast his lot with. Sometime that fall they apparently had an argument in which Keats's "sceptical and republican" convictions flared up, and which left Mathew shocked and hurt. "I respected Keats's opinions, because they were sincere," he later wrote, "and only asked him to concede with me the fallibility of human judgment; while he, on his part, expressed regret on finding that he had given pain or annoyance by opposing with ridicule or asperity the opinions of others." Evidently Keats was tactless in talking Mathew down, though he did not consider their friendship broken. But Mathew withdrew, salving his vanity with the conviction of his own righteousness.

Mathew blamed Hunt for Keats's irreligious notions, but this was no passing phase. Keats's scepticism had troubled his friend Spurgin a year before, and later friends were to find his religious opinions "extraordinary and revolting." [9] He had evidently emerged from his year at Guy's a thoroughgoing deist, believing in a Supreme Power who created the world but denying the divinity of Christ and all the other supernatural aspects of the Christian faith. Keats's rejection of Christianity was rooted deep in his past, however, as appears from an angry sonnet "In Disgust of Vulgar Superstition" which he wrote one Sunday morning this winter. The church bells which broke in on his reading of the poets—"converse high of those with glory crown'd"—sent "a chill as from a tomb" down his back, wakening the memory of bells tolling at five funerals within his own family. Yet there was more to his protest than mere bitter association. The Church of England at that time was a hollow shell of form without real belief, of dogma unsupported by reason, to which few intelligent men could wholeheartedly subscribe; it was also a pillar of the established order which Keats hated, venal, complacent and reactionary. His private image of orthodoxy may well have been Richard Abbey, the prosperous churchwarden haggling with his Sunday-school pupils over their rightful guinea.

Hunt gave Keats a glimpse of another kind of religion, which he insisted was true Christianity as distinct from "Christianism," or the faith of the Thirty-Nine Articles. From his father, a Unitarian minister, Hunt had derived a kind of aesthetic Unitarianism, which opposed the church and its doctrines with all the fervor of Voltaire, while affirming the human goodness of Christ and the benevolence of the Creator,

> Who we know, from things that bless,
> Must delight in loveliness,
> And who, therefore, we believe,
> Means us well in things that grieve, . . .

as he wrote that spring in a hymn that soon became famous, "To the Spirit Great and Good." Keats seems to have had some such religion in mind when he ended his sonnet with the prophecy of a happier faith in time to come, when

> . . . fresh flowers will grow,
> And many glories of immortal stamp.

Yet by "glories" he may also have meant the poetry which, half a century later, Matthew Arnold thought would replace religion as an interpretation of life. As Keats put it a few months later, at the end of an argument on religion, "Shakspeare is enough for us." At twenty-one, full of hope for the future and delight in the world around him, he demanded no more explanation of existence than Hunt's easy tribute to its "loveliness."

Yet, from the beginning of Keats's friendship with Hunt, a powerful force was drawing him in another direction. Benjamin Haydon had been greatly impressed by Keats on their first meeting in Hampstead. Soon after returning to London early in November he invited Cowden Clarke to bring him for Sunday breakfast in his studio. Keats was exultant. "Very glad am I at the thoughts of seeing so soon this glorious Haydon and all his Creation," he exclaimed in his reply to Clarke. His first glimpse of Haydon's painting-room at 41 Great Marlborough Street was a revelation. It was a small room, crowded with casts and sketches of heads and torsos, with the half-finished canvas of "Christ's Triumphal Entry into Jerusalem" blocking one entire wall. Haydon had been working on this picture, which he counted on to make his fortune, for over two years, but still only four or five characters in the foreground were completed, and the central figure of Christ on a donkey was being repainted in one of these repeated transformations which, his friends uneasily noticed, only heightened its uncanny resemblance to Haydon himself.[10]

More chaos than creation, the place must have seemed, but Haydon was the indisputable god at work. Short-legged, bull-throated, broad-browed, his hair worn long like Raphael's, he looked the very embodiment of the energy and determination which, he believed, were the chief requisites of greatness. With his loud voice and a laugh like the trumpet of Jericho, he radiated confidence; nothing in his appearance betrayed the occasional flashes of misery and doubt which he confided only to his diary. Haydon had had to make his way against poverty, parental opposition, and a nagging physical handicap of weak eyesight. Other handicaps were his fiery temper and his unmitigable egotism. What he described in his journals as "irresistible, perpetual, continued urgings of future greatness" used to shoot through him with such intensity that he could only "lift up his heart and thank God" for these assurances of divine favour. Taste was turning against the outsized heroic paintings which Haydon believed were the highest form of art; yet he not only continued to paint one huge canvas after another, but quarrelled with his patrons and even the Royal Academy. Turner, Constable, Blake: these are the names in the English art of his time that live today. But Haydon had only scorn for landscape painting—"Think what *I* am doing," he once remarked to Constable—and evidently knew nothing of Blake's work.[11]

By the sheer force of his enthusiasm, Haydon persuaded most of his contemporaries to take him at his own estimate as a great painter; he also persuaded them that it was he who prevailed on the British Government to purchase the Elgin Marbles. These sculptures, which Lord Elgin had salvaged from the Parthenon for his private collection, had left Haydon thunderstruck on his first view in 1808. Official taste of the time took the effeminate Belvedere Apollo and the insipid Medici Venus as the high points of classical art; by contrast, the Parthenon statues seemed mere "Phidian freaks." It is forever to Haydon's credit that he immediately grasped the difference between the imitation and the original. From his long study of anatomy he recognized at once the profound knowledge underlying the effortless nobility of the sculptures, from the articulation of the wrist of Cecrops' daughter to the ripple of muscle across Theseus' back.[12] He spent months sketching the Marbles, though never quite capturing the secret of their strength; then, when Elgin offered to sell them to the British Government in 1811, he hurled himself into the resulting controversy. Hellenophiles such as Byron protested that Elgin was no better than a thief; connoisseurs insisted that the works were not Greek at all but late Roman copies. Haydon wrote, wrangled, buttonholed, bullied; but not until 1815, when the archaeologist Visconti and the sculptor Canova declared the Marbles genuine, did the tide of opinion turn. Early in 1816 a Government committee heard the recommendations of seven leading British painters that the sculptures be purchased. Haydon, who had played a very minor part in the hearings, was determined to get his word in; accordingly he published a stinging attack in *The Examiner* on Payne Knight, a director of the British Institution, who had testified against the authenticity of the Marbles. When the committee at last decided for the purchase, Haydon was convinced—and convinced his friends—that his article had won the case, and extravagant tributes to his victory, including sonnets from Wordsworth and Hunt, poured in from all sides.[13]

Keats had met Haydon in the very week that Hunt was hailing him in *The Examiner* as the successor of Michelangelo and Raphael, and his first impression of Haydon as the champion of the Marbles struck deep. At once he wrote a sonnet praising Haydon but also—and this is noteworthy—congratulating all those who had shared his belief:

> How glorious this affection for the cause
> Of stedfast genius, toiling gallantly! . . .
> Unnumber'd souls breathe out a still applause,
> Proud to behold him in his country's eye.

This shows a remarkable sense of proportion in a man of twenty-one, which Keats maintained on closer acquaintance. On November 19 he visited Haydon in his studio again. It was a memorable evening, full of Haydon's discoursings on art and literature, past and present; but it seems they also talked of Keats's future, and Haydon made a sketch of Keats in profile. From the start he had been struck as much by the modelling of Keats's head as by his poetry, and now he proposed to paint Keats as one of the spectators in "Christ's Entry," along with Wordsworth and Hazlitt, Newton and Voltaire. The next day Keats wrote him tersely: "Last Evening wrought me up, and I cannot forbear sending you the following." It was another sonnet, "Great spirits now on earth are sojourning," praising his heroes Wordsworth and Hunt along with Haydon,

> whose stedfastness would never take
> A meaner sound than Raphael's whispering, . . .

then soaring into a prophecy of the future of English poetry:

> And other spirits there are standing apart
> Upon the forehead of the age to come;
> These, these will give the world another heart,
> And other pulses. Hear ye not the hum

> Of mighty workings in a distant mart?
> Listen awhile ye nations, and be dumb.

Haydon answered at once, suggesting that Keats shorten the
next-to-last line, then announcing he would send the sonnet to
Wordsworth. To Wordsworth! "The Idea," Keats replied, "put
me out of breath—you know with what Reverence—I would send
my Wellwishes to him." What Haydon did, however, was to take
the sonnet around to show to his young friend Reynolds, who
replied the next morning with one of his own in praise of Haydon
—fourteen fulsome lines to Keats's two:

> Haydon!—Thou'rt born to Immortality!—
> I look full on;—And Fame's eternal star
> Shines out o'er Ages which are yet afar;—
> It hangs in all its radiance over thee! . . .

Weak though it was in comparison to Keats's, Haydon had Reynolds' tribute printed two days later in *The Champion*. Six weeks
passed, however, before he sent Keats's sonnet to Wordsworth,
who wrote back at the end of January that it "appears to be of
good promise." [14]
  Keats may well have smiled wryly when he saw Reynolds' sonnet in print. Yet—as he wrote a year later to a friend who had
been wounded by another display of Haydon's egotism—"As soon
as I had known Haydon three days I had got enough of his character not to have been surprised at such a Letter as he has hurt
you with." This may be the wisdom of hindsight; yet both Keats's
sonnets to Haydon present him in clearer perspective than either
Hunt's or Reynolds', and they give the painter his due in twice
describing him as "stedfast." Divided as he still was between two
vocations, Keats found in Haydon an example of hard-working
devotion to art very different from Hunt's dilettantism. "I begin
to fix my eye upon one horizon," he announced to Haydon on
November 21, while thanking him for his praise of the second
sonnet.
  This remark has been taken to indicate some kind of break
in Keats's work at Guy's, since he and Tom had left Dean Street
only a few days earlier to move into lodgings with George at
76 Cheapside, over a mile from the hospital. Yet the record shows
that Keats continued to attend lectures and perform his duties at
Guy's all through the winter.[15] The reason for the move to Cheap-

side seems to be quite simply that the three brothers wanted to live together after their five-year separation. They found rooms over the archway of Bird-in-Hand Court, a few steps from the Mermaid Tavern and Bow Church of the immemorial bells, and around two corners from Abbey's counting-house in Pancras Lane, where George still worked. It was a pleasant arrangement, as appears from a sonnet Keats wrote on the evening of Tom's seventeenth birthday, November 18, while listening to the crackling of coals in the grate and watching Tom absorbed in a book. This was the nearest thing to a home of their own they had had for years, and at this point in his life Keats could not imagine a happier existence.

Still it is clear that poetry was the "one horizon" on which Keats told Haydon he was fixing his gaze; and two weeks later it lit up with a portent. On the first of December, Hunt published an article praising Keats's poetry to the world. Under the title of "Young Poets," he welcomed three recruits to the "new school" of poetry championed by *The Examiner*. The first of these was Percy Bysshe Shelley, a virtually unknown young writer who in 1813 had privately printed a long philosophical poem, *Queen Mab,* which no one had read, and then early in 1816 had published an allegorical poem, *Alastor,* which had been dismissed by two or three of the reviews as "sublime obscurity" and "delightful nonsense." In October, Shelley had sent his "Hymn to Intellectual Beauty" in to *The Examiner* under the pseudonym "Elfin Knight"; then, when a month went by and nothing happened, he evidently wrote Hunt again to ask about it. Hunt, who had mislaid the manuscript, made his amends by praising Shelley in his review as "a very striking and original thinker." It is one of the ironies of criticism that, next to encouraging Keats, Hunt did no better service to poetry than calling attention to Shelley's talent in this roundabout fashion. After discussing Reynolds' *Naiad* at greater length, Hunt then gave Keats pride of place at the end of the article, as the youngest of the three aspirants and the most promising. "He has not yet published anything except in a newspaper," Hunt remarked, "but a set of his manuscripts was handed us the other day, and fairly surprised us with the truth of their ambition and ardent grappling with Nature." Then he concluded, with unerring effect, by quoting the sonnet on Chapman's Homer. The article was all that a young writer needed

to send his hopes soaring. Its effect on Keats was succinctly described by Henry Stephens: "This seald his fate."

For shortly afterward he nerved himself to an important resolve.
Urged by Hunt, encouraged by his brothers, he decided to bring
out a book of his poems. It was a gamble on which he risked his
whole sense of himself as a poet, but the stakes for which he was
playing were high, and his chances seemed good. There was a
large audience for poetry in those days. Fashionable poets such as
Sir Walter Scott and Tom Moore could ask, and get, three thous-
and pounds or more for a long verse narrative; Byron's *Corsair*
sold ten thousand copies the day it appeared, in a London of about
one-eighth its present population. Keats had enough poetry on
hand—sonnets, lyrics, epistles, and several fragments of longer
poems—to work up into a little book like Hunt's and Byron's
first volumes, and Hunt already had a publisher for him. His
friend Charles Ollier, an amateur musician and poet, had just
decided to enter publishing with his older brother, James, and
was eager to take Keats on as one of his first authors.[16] Keats's
own reasons for the decision went deeper. With each step he had
already taken toward becoming a poet, he saw more clearly what
he wanted. Not fame alone, though he dreamed of it as much as
any man of twenty-one; not money either, though the wild hope
had already crossed his mind that his books might earn him a
release from medicine; but rather to join the ranks of the great
poets, the finest of human beings—so he believed—who somehow
served the highest of human purposes. Publishing was a decisive
act of commitment and a necessary step toward his goal.

In these last months of 1816 Keats was "standing on the top of
golden hours," at that extraordinary moment in life when all the
dreamed-of future begins to become actual. Two portraits made
of him at this time catch him in the flush of decision. As Hunt
once described Keats's face, it showed "energy and sensibility
remarkably mixed up"; and these two sides of his nature, the
dream of achievement and the determination to realize it, were
captured in striking contrast by Severn and Haydon. Severn's
pencil sketch of Keats in three-quarter profile, made one evening at his rooms in Cheapside, presents the young disciple of
Hunt, with his hair worn long and curling, his throat bare above
the turned-down collar. It is Keats seen through the eyes of a
sentimental miniature-painter, the features softened to effeminacy,

the nose lengthened, the chin shortened, the lips almost quivering. The portrait is a falsification except where, by some magic about the eyes, it suggests the dazzling mobility of Keats's expression, which all his friends mentioned at one time or another. But sometime early in December, Haydon made a cast of Keats's face, as he did with the other friends whom he was putting into "Christ's Entry," and this life mask gives the enduring truth of Keats's appearance. The wet plaster slowly hardening over his features stilled their intense expressiveness; but it recorded all the lean masculine strength of the low brow and the hollow cheeks, the compact nose, the stubborn jaw, and the wide mouth which Hunt found too pugnacious for his taste. The energy seems poised, purposeful; the sensuousness hinted at in the long curve of the lips is controlled.*

But Keats left his own record of the moment when his purpose finally crystallized—that long, rambling, ecstatic poem called "Sleep and Poetry." One evening at Hampstead the conversation ran on so late that Hunt offered to put him up overnight on the sofa in his study. Keats was too excited to sleep, and as he lay there, conscious of the great names surrounding him on Hunt's crowded shelves, he had a kind of waking dream of his own destiny. It was a moment such as Shelley had experienced as an unhappy school-boy, when he walked out into the fields one May morning and vowed to struggle all his life against tyranny; or such as Words-worth had known, when, near thirty, he revisited the countryside around Tintern Abbey and came to understand the change which the years had worked in him. For Keats that night his sense of the all-engrossing present expanded to a vision not only of his own future but also of the past of English poetry and their inter-section in the moment at which he stood. He thought of the great-ness of Chaucer and Shakespeare and Milton and the triviality, as he felt it, of Pope and his successors; then of Chatterton and the new poets, led by Wordsworth, in whose ranks Hunt had told him—Keats's blood raced at the recollection—he would be num-bered. Thought crowded on thought, and a poem began to take shape in his mind.

As he gazed into the darkness, a painting which he and Hunt may have studied that very evening—Poussin's "Empire of Flora" —flashed on the screen of his imagination.[17] In the foreground

---

* These portraits are reproduced as Plates VIII and I.

lay the garden of Flora, thronged with nymphs and lovers of classical legend; high above them Apollo in his golden chariot lashed his horses across the skies. The painting became an image of his own career: the poetry which he was writing at present, full of the "o'erwhelming sweets" of youth, which he now saw he must leave behind for a goal which still lay out of sight—a poetry that dealt with "the events of the wide world," that faced "the agonies, the strife of human hearts" and wrested another kind of beauty from them. As yet he could envisage this poetry only in the dimmest fashion, as "shapes of delight, of mystery, and fear"; but someday, somehow, he knew he would write it. As he lay on his narrow bed between sleep and waking, line followed on line with the miraculous ease of dream, and when the light began to glimmer at the window he could not believe morning had come so soon. He rose up, full of the energy of a man with a task which he is eager to start.

"Sleep and Poetry" inevitably fell short of Keats's experience that night. Built on the very movement of his mind between fatigue and excitement, hope and despair, much of it is a jumble of confused images and wildly shifting moods. In essence, the poem was a challenge to the conservative tradition symbolized by Pope and a proclamation of Hunt's notion of poetry—that

> they shall be accounted poet kings
> Who simply tell the most heart-easing things.

Yet at the same time Keats was groping toward a more arduous and significant ideal—a poetry that took on itself the Wordsworthian "burthen of the mystery." "Sleep and Poetry" has been called "an attempt to express in the style of *Rimini* something of the spirit of 'Tintern Abbey' ";[18] but in some ways it comes closer to another far greater poem of dedication—Milton's "Lycidas." In each the young poet hesitates between the joys of the senses, which other young men seize without a thought, and the uncertain rewards of "the thankless Muse":

> Were it not better done as others use,
> To sport with Amaryllis in the shade,
> Or withe the tangles of Neaera's hair? *

---

* "Withe" (*NED, with, withe:* to twist or plait) seems to have been Milton's intended meaning in this line.

For Milton, however, the decision "to shun delights and lead laborious days" raised no troubling doubts; for Keats it was much more of a problem. Sleep and poetry, the rather odd set of contrasts on which he built his poem, were, as he saw, not an antithesis but a necessary ebb and flow of poetic power, the alternation of what he later described as "indolence" and "energy." Time after time the poet must surrender to the health-giving delights of the body, give rein to its hungers and draw new strength from their satisfactions in order to rise again to the discipline of art. More than this, Keats was also beginning to grasp something which words hardly yet existed to describe—the creative activity of the unconscious mind in dream, as it fashions

> many a verse from so strange influence
> That we must ever wonder how, and whence
> It came. . . .

Yet Keats had as strenuous a notion as Milton of a great purpose to be achieved through poetry, a goal higher even than individual fame. Like most young men, they could define their purpose best in terms of what they were opposed to—the outworn tradition of eighteenth-century poetry for Keats, the corruptions of the English Church for Milton. And for each the sense of his mission took on an unexpected urgency from the thought of death. While in his earlier poems death was a mere abstract possibility for Keats, a fact of someone else's life, he now refers to it repeatedly as something that will happen to him. It seems that to fully admit his ambition raised a haunting fear that life would not be long enough to achieve it.

> O for ten years, that I may overwhelm
> Myself in poesy; so I may do the deed
> That my own soul has to itself decreed. . . .

Life was a precarious matter, as he knew all too well; his father had died at thirty, his mother at thirty-six. At twenty-one, he could not think a decade was too much to ask.

-»»-«««-

In deciding to publish his poems, Keats tapped a new spring of creative energy. In the four or five weeks that followed, he wrote half a dozen new sonnets, completed "Sleep and Poetry," and turned back to his long poem on nature and myth, which he now called "Endymion." He was reaching the climax of the poem, a retelling of the moon goddess's love for the young shepherd whom she visited nightly in his sleep. Yet here unexpectedly he ran into trouble. As he started to describe the hushed beauty of their bridal night another scene unaccountably interposed itself —the miraculous recovery of a sick woman, waking "clear-eyed" and feverless from a deep sleep, and her reunion with the anxious watchers by her bedside, "nigh foolish with delight." This is the dream which, as was suggested, had haunted his imagination for years and returned to trouble him at Guy's; and only the wild logic of dream can relate this episode to the scene of erotic fulfilment which follows. Yet, as he went on to recount the final episode of Cynthia's wedding, Keats faltered and broke off with four lines of apology for his inadequacy. He could only hint at some deeper significance in these events:

> Cynthia! I cannot tell the greater blisses,
> That follow'd thine, and thy dear shepherd's kisses:
> Was there a Poet born?—but now no more,
> My wand'ring spirit must no further soar.—

Around the original core of his myth were gathering meanings which he was still struggling to formulate to himself: the birth of the poetic consciousness, now somehow linked with a dream of fulfilment in sexual love.

At the end of these four lines Keats stopped in indecision, added a dash, then wrote the date, "Decr. 16," in the margin. The poem was incomplete, but for the time being he did not know quite what to do with it.[19] The next day he wrote in discouragement to Clarke: "I have done little to Endymion lately—I hope to finish it in one more attack." Clarke, who was to visit him that very evening, was evidently following his progress with the book almost from day to day. There was much to be done. After assembling his poems from his jumbled copies, Keats had to decide which to leave out and which to include, then polish off their rough edges. Tom began copying the poems into a notebook as he revised them, and Hunt later went through this copy and suggested some corrections.[20] Reworking a poem in cold blood Keats found a tiresome task. While the revisions in the manuscripts of his later poems show an assured craftsman at work, in these early poems he was often merely saving himself from blunders. Yet he was also learning how to sharpen an image or tighten a phrase or cut out an internal rhyme. He spotted the one lame line in his Chapman sonnet—"Yet could I never judge what Men could mean," which struck him as "bald and too simply wondering"— and with a sure hand changed it to its present form, "Yet did I never breathe its pure serene." Slowly Tom's copy-book filled up and the volume began to take actual shape before Keats's eyes.

In the meantime a new character made a dramatic entrance on the Hampstead scene. Shelley, touched by Hunt's tribute to him in *The Examiner,* wrote him from Bath a glowing letter of thanks. As "an outcast from human society," he confessed, he had become discouraged in his attempts "to interest or improve mankind" through his poetry. But now his faith was restored: "With you, and perhaps some others (though in a less degree I fear) my gentleness and sincerity find favour, because they are themselves gentle and sincere." Shelley had indeed been an outcast for most of his twenty-four years—as a tormented schoolboy at Syon House, as "The Atheist" at Eton, as the author of a pamphlet on *The Necessity of Atheism* which got him expelled from Oxford, and now as the rebellious heir to a baronetcy and a fortune who had eloped at nineteen with the daughter of a tavern-keeper and then run off to Switzerland three years later with Mary Godwin, the daughter of the philosopher. Far more radical than Hunt in his political and religious opinions, Shelley had a correspondingly greater capacity for idealizing his friends and then becoming disillusioned with them. But the friendship that began on December 12, when he presented himself at Hunt's cottage, was to become central in both men's lives. On the thirteenth Hunt invited several of his friends, including Keats and Horace Smith, to meet the newest member of the circle. The stockbroker immediately noted Shelley's Etonian manners and well-cut clothes, which he wore with an air of abstracted untidiness, and was impressed by his conversation on Plato.[21] Here, he realized, was a gentleman and a scholar. From this pleasant introduction to the Vale of Health, Shelley returned to Bath the next day to learn that Harriet, the young wife he had deserted two years before, had drowned herself in the Serpentine. He immediately returned to Hunt's to straighten out his affairs in London. A letter he wrote to Mary Godwin on the sixteenth makes uncomfortable reading. Immediately accepting a slanderous account of the circumstances of Harriet's suicide, Shelley found "little to regret" in her death beyond "the mere shock of so hideous a catastrophe having fallen on a human being once so nearly connected with me." Everyone, he added, "bears testimony to the upright spirit and liberality of my conduct to her," while Hunt sustained him in his painful contemplation of the "vice and folly and hard-heartedness" of Harriet and her family.[22]

All during the last two weeks of December, while Shelley began the battle to gain legal possession of his two children, he and Mary —whom he married on the twenty-ninth—stayed with Hunt. The friendship so tragically interrupted at its start was now cemented. Though Shelley was already carrying the financial burdens of his friend the novelist Thomas Love Peacock and his new father-in-law, William Godwin, he immediately offered Hunt assistance, which Hunt, deeper in debt than ever, agreed at once to take. A year later, in fact, as he was "proud to relate" in his *Autobiography*, Hunt received £1400 from Shelley to settle his debts. But though Hunt came to regard Shelley as the finest character he had ever met, few of his friends shared his admiration. Lamb, Hazlitt, Haydon, Reynolds, Crabb Robinson the diarist, even Godwin, all found reasons for distrust or even dislike. It is true that Shelley was under great emotional stress this winter; it is also true that for years he had suffered from delusions bordering on paranoia that put a severe strain on his friendships. With Hunt he lived on a level of radiant idealism; to Hazlitt, he had "a fire in his eye, a fever in his blood, a maggot in his brain, a hectic flutter in his speech, which mark out the philosophic fanatic." Shelley loved to set up questions for debate that had more than merely philosophic interest for most men. With his high-pitched voice, girlish complexion, narrow shoulders, and nervous mannerisms, he appeared a harmless adversary; but, after advancing the most outrageous opinions with studied casualness, he would fall on his unsuspecting opponents with crushing logic.

Keats managed to avoid tangling with him except on one occasion, which he did not forget. While at Hunt's in December, Shelley read over Keats's poems, then took him for a walk on the Heath and advised him not to publish. Perhaps this was wise counsel, for Shelley's first poems had been drubbed by the Tory critics, but Keats could hardly be expected to agree. He politely declined Shelley's advice, and thereafter kept his distance in a manner that Shelley could not quite understand. The reasons are plain: the clash of Shelley's unconscious patronizing with Keats's fierce pride; a profound difference of temperament; most important of all, perhaps, a disagreement about poetry itself. The didacticism of much of Shelley's work was becoming more and more alien to Keats. As Shelley admitted, he hoped to create the world anew by "familiarizing the highly refined imaginations of the more select classes of poetical readers with beautiful idealisms of moral excellence." Keats, as Hunt remarked, could not follow him in these "Archimedean endeavors to move the globe with his own hands" [23]—nor did he care to. He was still feeling his way toward the kind of poetry he wanted to write; but disagreement with Shelley, it appears, helped sharpen his sense of direction.

Shelley, it was later said, also offered Keats help, presumably financial, in getting his first volume published. This is very doubtful,[24] but if he did the offer could only have stiffened Keats's new-won sense of independence. He very soon became aware that Hunt was accepting Shelley's largesse, and though he was in no position to impress Shelley as being well off himself, that is precisely what he managed to do. Half a year later Shelley, in writing Hunt to explain that he could send him no more money at the time, suggested, "But there is Keats, who certainly can." Keats certainly could not. It is almost impossible to untangle the truth of his financial affairs from the conflicting figures and contradictory statements which he and his friends left behind. The one sure fact is that money matters depressed him so much that he never looked closely into his own accounts, with the result that he usually assumed he had more money than he actually did. Curiously, however, there was some truth in this assumption. Under the terms of his grandfather's will, Keats should have received by reversion or direct bequest about three thousand pounds on reaching twenty-one.[25] But Abbey, for reasons of his own, apparently told him that he had inherited only a fifteen-hundred-pound legacy from his grandmother, a sum which his medical training had reduced to a thousand pounds or less. It was not much, though for a while it allowed Keats to feel that he had money both to spend and to lend: so much so that within the next two or three years he loaned nearly two hundred pounds to

various friends, and a larger figure to his brothers. Tom was in
poor health and earning nothing; George was an extravagant
spender, especially on clothes; and, so long as they were under
age, they had only their older brother to turn to when they ran
over their incomes. After he came of age Keats managed to keep
his own expenses down to nearly a hundred pounds a year [26]—a
very "moderate subsistence" for a young bachelor; even so, he
was constantly dipping into his principal. But at twenty-one, full
of confidence in the future, he must have felt that his money
would last as long as he needed it.

The early months of 1817 were filled with hopeful work and
mounting excitement. After his poems were sent off to the printer,
there was the task of proofreading—no task at all but the heady
delight of seeing page after page of his poetry in print for the
first time. Keats was too busy in January and February to write
more than a few new sonnets, but Hunt printed two of these in
The Examiner during February to whet his readers' interest in
the forthcoming volume. Probably about this time Haydon got
him a ticket to the British Museum Reading Room, where he
might continue what he called his "study"—his intense and eager
reading of the older English poets from whom he was learning
his craft, noting with an increasingly expert eye the fine points of
diction and versification, structure and imagery. But Keats did not
make much use of this ticket—perhaps because he had already
discovered the Abbey Library at Westminster, formerly the chief
public library of London and now a half-forgotten treasure-house
of old books where he could browse in cloistered solitude.[27] All
this while he was finding his way around a new London, a city
of bookstores and printshops, galleries and theatres. This winter
he became a regular theatregoer with Clarke and Reynolds, and
for the best of all reasons: Edmund Kean was now appearing regularly at Drury Lane, electrifying the London audience with his
new style of acting, natural, intimate, full of Elizabethan fire—
"like reading Shakespeare by flashes of lightning," as Coleridge
described it.

We catch echoes of evening parties in Keats's rooms off Cheapside, lively with wine and wit and disputation, at which Keats
once dumfounded Severn by maintaining that Milton was not a
great poet. He was developing a habit of what his friends called

rodomontade—upholding the worse side of an argument for the sake of the intellectual drama that ensued. The shyness which Horace Smith had noticed disappeared with his growing confidence in his abilities and among friends of his own choosing. He was rapidly becoming good friends with Reynolds, who now introduced him to his own family: his father, the mathematics and writing master at Christ's Hospital; his mother, a writer of sorts and a conversationalist who could hold her own with Charles Lamb; and his four sisters. Keats at once struck up a brotherly chaffing relationship with Jane, the eldest, four years his senior, a rather humourless young lady on the verge of spinsterdom. Mariane Reynolds, two years younger than he, seems to have shone for a while in the eyes of his brother George—but not dazzlingly, for George was already more than half in love with Georgiana Wylie, the young sister of his friends Henry and Charles, the "nymph of the downward smile and sidelong glance" to whom Keats wrote a sonnet of praise that winter. Keats was also going with Clarke and his old schoolmate Edward Holmes to the famous musical evenings at Novello's, the organist and friend of Lamb and Hunt. In his rose-painted living room overlooking Hyde Park, writers and musicians and painters gathered from all over London to drink "Lutheran beer" and listen to Novello playing Bach and Purcell on his chamber organ. Holmes remembered Keats on one of these occasions joking with Hunt about Bach fugues, that they were like nothing so much as two dogs chasing each other through the dust.[28]

But a still more memorable experience for Keats this winter was meeting William Hazlitt at Hunt's—an enigmatic, many-talented, much disappointed man, an unreconstructed Bonapartist and a great but still unrecognized critic whose trenchant articles on politics and the theatre Keats had long admired in *The Examiner*. One wonders if he was also at Hunt's on February 9, when, as Mary Shelley noted in her diary, the guests stayed on for "a discussion until three in the morning with Hazlitt concerning Monarchy and Republicanism." For Shelley was usually to be found at Hunt's now, arguing on every conceivable topic from vegetarianism to the national debt. Keats also spent many evenings at Haydon's studio, talking about painting and poetry and reading Shakespeare aloud—whom, Haydon once said, he enjoyed more with Keats than with any other man. Yet despite his fervent

admiration for Haydon, Keats's opinions struck the older man as
dangerously wrongheaded. One evening, evidently after an argument on religion, he walked over to the canvas of "Christ's Entry,"
where, next to Wordsworth bowing in reverence before Christ,
Haydon had painted Voltaire as a smiling scoffer. Before this portrait, whose hideous sneer Hunt had bitterly criticized, Keats put
his hand on his heart, bowed, and said, "There's the being I will
bend to!"

Haydon had his reasons, then, for being troubled by Hunt's
hold over Keats. With Shelley's appearance, a curious four-cor-
nered battle of friends and disciples was joined. It is revealing
to note that Hunt, in his sonnets at least, immediately began ad-
dressing Shelley as "Percy"—a rare intimacy in those days—while
Keats remained "Young Keats" or, conversationally, "Junkets."
On his side Keats, who was scrupulous about these matters, continued to call him "Mr. Hunt," though he dropped this formality
with Haydon a few weeks after their meeting. The first open
skirmish in the battle took place at Horace Smith's one afternoon
in January. As Haydon came in late to dinner, Shelley, carving
a piece of broccoli with elaborate care, remarked in a gentle tone,
"As to that detestable religion the Christian—" Haydon, not having met Shelley before, looked around in astonishment and saw
Hunt and his wife and sister-in-law smiling in anticipation; he
then pitched in and at once found himself cornered. Shelley,
backed by Hunt, maintained that the moral code of the Old
Testament was inconsistent with the New; Haydon flatly con-
tradicted them. The question shifted to whether Shakespeare had
believed in Christianity; Shelley and Hunt asserted he had not,
while Haydon shouted them down by quoting passage after passage from the plays. Logic evaporated in the heat of the argument,
and argument gave way to insult. Meanwhile Keats sat silent with
Smith and the other guests. Haydon finally retired into the next
room to cool off, and the discussion ended; but Hunt could not
keep from making one last dig. When the ladies went to get their
cloaks, he asked, "Are these creatures to be damned, Haydon?"
What a morbid view of Christianity, Haydon retorted, but decided then and there to avoid Hunt and his arguments in the future.

Keats kept up his acquaintance with the Shelleys until they left
London in the middle of March, but the afternoon at Smith's

must have set him thinking. Intellectually he stood with Hunt against Haydon, on the liberal and sceptical side of most questions. But he had seen enough of life already to sense that the truth was more complicated than it appeared from Shelley's black-and-white view of the universe, and more serious than Hunt's largely aesthetic interest in ideas would admit. Nor was he willing to risk a friendship for mere argument's sake, as Hunt did so blithely. When at their first meeting he saw Shelley drawing Severn into a debate on the Christian miracles, Keats stepped in to take Severn's side. A year later he was to admit, "I shall never be a Reasoner because I care not to be in the right." One wonders how much Shelley's obsession with being in the right fostered this scepticism, or whether Keats had heard enough disputations at Hunt's that winter to begin to doubt the power of reason to settle every issue.

Keats was beginning to look on Hunt with more detachment than in the first days of their friendship; yet he still realized how much he owed to Hunt's encouragement. One evening in February, when a last-minute note came from Ollier, asking if his book was to have a dedication, Keats sat down in the middle of a party in his Cheapside rooms and wrote a sonnet "To Leigh Hunt, Esq.," which he sent off to the printer with the final proof-sheets. "Glory and loveliness have passed away," it began; the early-morning walker finds no nymphs on Hampstead Heath, no incense rising from pagan altars. Yet Hunt could offer his friends "delights as high as these," Keats averred, and

> in a time, when under pleasant trees
> Pan is no longer sought, I feel a free
> A leafy luxury, seeing I could please
> With these poor offerings, a man like thee.

The apology in the last line is conventional enough; but at the last minute Keats added a real one. In a prefatory note he let it be known that "the Short Pieces in the middle of the Book, as well as some of the Sonnets, were written at an earlier period than the rest of the Poems." Why he had decided to include some of his earliest and poorest poems, dating back to his friendship with Mathew, we can only guess; the fact is that at the last moment he had some misgivings.

This dissatisfaction with poems he had written a year and a

half before is one more sign of Keats's extraordinary development
since the previous fall. But the final revisions of his recent poems,
in which he tried to prune the lusher sentimentalism of his style,[29]
also suggest that he was becoming aware of something he could
not yet openly admit—that he was outgrowing Hunt's influence
as surely as he had outgrown Mathew's. Almost from the beginning of their friendship Hunt's idea of the poet and of poetry
satisfied only one part of Keats's double nature—that curious
mixture of energy and sensibility which Hunt himself had noted.
Now he felt increasingly drawn toward Haydon's conception of
art. Haydon stood for the heroic manner and the grand scale,
where Hunt represented the sentimental and intimate; Haydon
worshipped Shakespeare, while Hunt preferred Spenser; Haydon
gloried in Homer's virile Greek, while Hunt—who had had little
taste for Homer from the time an irate schoolmaster knocked out
one of his teeth with a copy of the *Iliad*—delighted in the romantic
fantasies of Tasso and Ariosto.

All through this fall and winter Keats tried to keep these two
allegiances in balance, but the conflict between them may be read
in the poems he wrote at this time. His earliest notion of poetry
as a return to the idyllic world of childhood or a release from
hated imprisonment and a flight to some supernal realm soon gave
way to a set of images describing it as a retreat to some delightful
and quite earthy refuge—a bower, a pavilion of boughs, a lair of
wavy grass, the bosom of a leafy world. This was the direction in
which Hunt's verse pulled him, with its "places of nestling green,
for Poets made" *—the realm of Flora, which, even as he described it in "Sleep and Poetry," Keats knew he must leave behind. Toward the end of 1816 his conception of poetry began to
take a very different metaphorical colour. One is struck by the
many images of height scattered through the poems of this period:
Cortez on his peak in Darien, for instance, Endymion on Latmos's
top, Wordsworth on the summit of Helvellyn, or Keats himself
standing more modestly "upon a little hill." "For what a height my
spirit is contending!" he exclaimed of the dizzy excitement he felt
on the first evenings at Hunt's cottage. This upward aspiration,
reflected in a whole vocabulary of compounds—"upborne," "up-
cast," "upcurl'd," "upflown," and so forth—suggests that Keats

---

* A quotation from Hunt which Keats later used as the epigraph for "I Stood
Tiptoe upon a Little Hill."

was unconsciously finding in poetry a compensation for his small stature.

Yet the height he sought was only a vantage-point from which to survey the task before him, the great poetry he must some day write. The image in which he conveyed this idea is significant. The boy who devoured stories of exploration and identified with his uncle in the Marines, who seemed to give promise of greatness "in some military capacity," re-emerged in the young poet who imagined his life work as a sea voyage. Earlier, in his epistles to Mathew and Clarke, Keats had described poetry in terms of sailing; it was by the sea at Margate, standing on the cliff and listening to the ocean's "voice mysterious," that he began to think of devoting his life to poetry; and the Chapman sonnet started with a voyage to the Spanish Main and reached its climax with the discovery of the Pacific, in an image recalling Keats himself on the cliff at Margate. In "Sleep and Poetry," where he finally committed himself to his vocation, the sea is the metaphorical warp of the entire poem. Poetry is "the grand sea," to whose "mighty winds" and "gathering waves" he gives himself; "a vast idea" of his future "rolls" before him, "an ocean dim" whose "widenesses" he must explore through "many days" and "desperate turmoil." The appearance of this imagery at this time suggests a subtle psychological transformation taking place. Not merely was Keats's sense of the poet's nature, derived from his earlier identification with Hunt, beginning to change and enlarge as he came to see Hunt in clearer perspective. All the events of the winter—his acceptance into Hunt's circle, his decision to publish, his meeting with Shelley—were turning him away from merely playing the part of the young poet, toward a new awareness of the unique creative individual he might become. In this search for his own identity he began half consciously to draw on the resources of his early experience, to see his life again in terms of the first image he had formed of himself in his battle with the world—the naval hero.

The call to action came sooner than he perhaps expected. Ever since the end of December he had been mulling over plans for his next effort in poetry. In spite of his dissatisfaction with "Endymion," he had finally sent it off to the printers unfinished as it was, for he had decided to write another and longer poem on the legend. Accordingly he dropped the title of "Endymion" and, unable to think of another, substituted an epigraph from *Rimini* instead—with the awkward result that the poem has been called by its first line, "I stood tiptoe upon a little hill," ever since. Then Shelley, sometime before leaving London in March, announced his plans for his next work, a long narrative poem on an imaginary revolution in the Middle East, and suggested to Keats that they write their poems in a friendly competition over the summer.[30] Each poem was to run to four thousand lines and be finished in six months' time. It was a breath-taking proposal. The new *Endymion* would be twice the length of Hunt's *Rimini,* over ten times the length of his *Hero and Leander.* Nothing Keats had written so far showed the strength for such an effort. But his mettle was up, and he accepted Shelley's challenge.

The time of decision had come at last, the point toward which he had been moving irreversibly for almost a year. He would give up medicine. *Endymion* would require all his time, all his powers; there was no other way to achieve his goal. When the Surgeons' Examination was held on February 7 and his friends Stephens and Newmarch went up and passed, Keats was not with them.[31] One reason may have been the fact that, though he had already completed his term with Lucas, he still lacked eight months of the age of twenty-two required to qualify as a surgeon. But far more important were his overpowering ambition in poetry and his steadily growing revulsion from surgery. At last the strain of operating became too much for him. One day at the hospital as he was opening a man's temporal artery he found himself overwhelmed by the thought of the disaster that would result from a possible slip of his lancet. With a great effort he went on and performed the ligation neatly, but all the while he seemed to be standing outside himself and watching his own dexterity with disbelief. The conflict between the cool scientific detachment required of a surgeon and the sensibility and warmth of feeling instinctive to him as a poet had reached its crisis. When he laid down his instruments at the end he realized he could never operate again.

On the face of it, throwing up a secure profession to risk everything on his still unproved abilities as a poet was sheer foolhardiness, as at least one of his friends privately declared. But a man with a daemon like Keats's does not listen to mere prudent advice. With all writers the compulsion toward achievement remains a mystery in the end, and its motives are many and obscure. The longing for fame that will outlive death is certainly one of them; the desire for love, which seemingly cannot be won any other way; or even, it has been suggested, the need to expiate some imaginary guilt deep in the unconscious. Of these possible motives, Keats had already clearly expressed the first; the second he seems not yet to have admitted to himself; the third was a force whose existence he could not even suspect. Yet it appears that, on a conscious and realistic level, he had calculated the risks in his decision. If he made a name with his *Poems,* he might begin to make a fortune with *Endymion.* Surely it was possible to earn a living by writing if one had the talent and the determination. Reynolds had given up a dull job clerking in an insurance office the year before to write articles and reviews, and was turning out a book of poetry a year. Perhaps when Keats called for "ten years" to devote himself to poetry he had also figured how long his money would last in the effort to prove his powers.

Once he had made his decision, he had to tell his guardian. Abbey, meanwhile, had been laying plans for his future. Partly to spite Hammond, partly because Mrs. Jennings was still remembered in the neighbourhood, he had arranged to set Keats up in practice in Tottenham, only two miles from Edmonton. Keats's reply to this proposal left him fuming with astonishment. Not intend to be a surgeon! What in the world did he plan to do? When Keats answered that he intended to make his career in poetry, Abbey retorted that he was either a fool or a madman to throw over five years' study for such an absurd idea. As calmly as he could, Keats told him he believed that his abilities were greater than most men's, and that he could earn his living by writing. A long argument ensued. Keats held his ground, and Abbey's rage sputtered out at last in calling Keats "a silly boy" and assuring him he would fail. Keats swallowed his anger; Abbey was still the figure of authority, who, though he could no longer legally control his actions, still administered his inheritance. But opposition only hardened his purpose. "In no period of my life have I acted with any self will, but in throwing up the apothecary-profession," he wrote three years later. "That I do not repent of."

Two friends at least cheered him in this decision. A young lady —Jane Reynolds, perhaps—sent him congratulations in the form of a laurel crown, a gesture not unheard of in Hunt's circle. Keats thanked her in the usual sonnet, breathing defiance of Abbey's tyranny and devotion to her gentleness. Haydon also endorsed the plan for *Endymion,* an undertaking much to his mind, on the heroic scale and in the Greek spirit. As a token of his approval, he presented Keats at about this time with a copy of Goldsmith's *History of Greece,* inscribed "from his ardent friend B. R. Haydon." [32] But he did much more: he took Keats at the beginning of March to see the Elgin Marbles, which were now on public view in the British Museum. Like his meeting with Hunt six months before, this marked a new era in Keats's existence. He had a notion of Greek art based, as was then inevitable, on eighteenth-century prints of Roman copies of Hellenistic statues; he had seen Haydon's drawings of the Marbles and perhaps worked a few images from them into his poems; but none of this prepared him for the shock of the reality. He was struck almost at once by the contemporaneousness of the sculpture—the freshness and vitality which made all copies look ancient and lifeless by contrast. Like Haydon, Keats immediately recognized the profound knowledge of anatomy shaping bone and muscle and tendon in these forms. But he was far more deeply moved by the surging energy of the young horsemen, the robust grace of the maidens, the magnificent serenity of the gods and goddesses. This was the Greek spirit made flesh, "the religion of joy," he once called it, an embodiment of a religious attitude which he now realized more clearly than ever was his own. A few months later, on one of his many trips back to the museum, he told Severn, "I never cease to wonder at all that incarnate delight." [33]

His immediate reaction, however, was not delight but speechless astonishment. Somehow he felt that Haydon expected a more vocal response, and on his return home he wrote him a sonnet apologizing for his failure to express what he had felt. It is curious to note that for the moment he lapsed into Haydon's own extravagant rhetoric, borrowing phrases—for lack of any of his own—from Haydon's essay on the Marbles.[34] In a second sonnet, a day or two later, he came much closer to expressing the contrast between his previous notion of greatness and his new vision. In the unassertive strength of Phidias's sculpture, so different from the overwrought effeminacy of the verse he had written under Hunt's influence, he sensed the possibility of a new accent for poetry, embodying the weight, the density of marble itself:

My spirit is too weak—mortality
 Weighs heavily on me like unwilling sleep,
 And each imagin'd pinnacle and steep
Of godlike hardship tells me I must die
Like a sick Eagle looking at the sky. . . .
Such dim-conceived glories of the brain
 Bring round the heart an undescribable feud;
So do these wonders a most dizzy pain,
 That mingles Grecian grandeur with the rude
Wasting of old Time—with a billowy main—
 A sun—a shadow of a magnitude.

The "godlike hardship" of creation, which he had barely glimpsed before—the seas to cross, the pinnacles to scale, the shadowy magnitude to measure and define—now appeared to him in palpable form, with the force almost of a command. Would he be equal to the work he had set himself?

—»» «««—

On Monday, March 3, 1817—a year to the day from the beginning of his term as dresser at Guy's—Keats's first book appeared at last. It was a neat pocket-sized volume, bound in gray boards backed with a white label announcing "Keats' Poems: Price 6s." The title page was embellished with a portrait of Spenser under a Spenserian motto that struck the keynote of "delight with liberty" for the poems that followed—some hundred and twenty crisply printed pages of them, fresh as a new coin. It is not hard to imagine Keats's sensations when he held the first copy in his hands. This was probably an advance copy which Charles Ollier sent him on Sunday, inscribed with a sonnet of congratulation, "Keats, I admire thine upward-daring soul." It is rare for publishers to pay tribute in verse to their own poets, but Ollier was a versifier before he turned publisher, and he was confident that his first publication would win laurels for its author and success for the new firm as well. Ollier was also generous with presentation copies, for Keats had nearly twenty to give away. Almost his first act was to go out to Hampstead with a copy for Hunt. He found him walking in Milfield Lane, on the edge of the Heath; and Hunt, who recalled this meeting vividly a dozen years later, must have accepted the gift as gladly as Keats gave it. In reply to the dedication, he wrote Keats another congratulatory sonnet, foreseeing with Ollier "a flowering laurel" on his brow.[35] On Monday evening the publication was celebrated at a party in Haydon's studio, to which Clarke and Reynolds were invited. Their spirits must have run high. Haydon, who had received Keats's sonnets on the Elgin Marbles that very morning, thanked him with characteristic enthusiasm: "You filled me with fury for an hour, and with admiration forever." A day or two later, on reading "Sleep and Poetry," he wrote Keats in a burst of prophecy: "It is a flash of lightening that will rouse men from their occupations, and keep them trembling for the crash of thunder that *will* follow."

The first peal of recognition came a week later with his fellow poet Reynolds' review in *The Champion*. To the readers of that magazine, who had never heard of Keats before, it proclaimed that he would eclipse the greatest names of the day—Byron, Moore, Samuel Rogers, Thomas Campbell—and compared him with Shakespeare and Chaucer. Reynolds conceded that the earliest poems in the volume fell short of this standard; but the sonnets, he maintained, ranked with Milton's and Wordsworth's. This was audacious praise, of a kind which only one very young man can give to another; yet Reynolds unerringly singled out the very qualities in Keats's early work which later became his distinctive excellences. Keats was dazzled by the review but not blinded. He sat down at once to write Reynolds a few "mono-sentences" of thanks: "Your Criticism only makes me extremely anxious that I sho^d not deceive you. It's the finest thing by God— as Hazlitt wo^d say However I hope I may not deceive you." Then, realizing that very few of Reynolds' readers would agree with his estimate, he rounded off his thanks with a joke: "There are some acquaintances of mine who will scratch their Beards and although I have, I hope, some Charity, I wish their Nails may be long."

Whoever these acquaintances may have been, Reynolds was becoming one of Keats's most valued friends. A young poet of promise who had gone through three styles in his first three books —the early Byron, Wordsworth, and Hunt—Reynolds was only beginning to find his own voice, that of a dandified romantic who turns away from nature for his inspiration to the green-room, the Garrick Club, and the prize ring. A good-looking young man, with dark eyes, thick lashes, and dark hair combed smooth over his forehead like a fighter's, he had a mobile and intelligent face with a curiously arch smile. A streak of the sardonic was appearing in him, which was rapidly to turn against himself. Even if he sensed that his new friend might displace him as the coming talent, he was still drawn to Keats, and Keats to him, by a similar zest for life and sense of humour. They shared enthusiasms for the theatre and boxing; and Reynolds, as a member of the sporting set known as "The Fancy," probably took Keats on some of his visits to Jack Randall's in Chancery Lane to watch the sparring. In the feud that Shelley stirred up that winter, Reynolds naturally sided with Haydon and thus heightened the strain on Keats's loyalty to Hunt. Meanwhile Reynolds was introducing Keats to his own set, where he found congenial company untrammelled by the claims of discipleship. James Rice, a young solicitor; Benjamin Bailey, a divinity student at Oxford; Charles Wentworth Dilke, an official at the Navy Pay Office with an active interest in literature; John Martin, Reynolds' first publisher; John Taylor, his present publisher, with his partner James Augustus Hessey; and Richard Woodhouse, an old Etonian and barrister who acted as reader in Taylor's firm—these were to be the friends of Keats's lifetime. It is not hard to see why. In Reynolds' circle Keats was no longer a protégé but a man to be met on his own terms, with one promising book already to his credit. In becoming the poet he wanted to be, he found the friends he had sought but never made for himself before.

Yet for all their expectations, the crash of thunder which Haydon predicted remained a mere rumble on the horizon. Three weeks went by after Reynolds' review till another appeared, a short but favourable notice in the *Monthly Magazine;* then silence. The sale of the book slowed to a halt. As Cowden Clarke admitted, it might have been published in Timbuctoo for all the attention it received. Hunt printed three of Keats's new sonnets in *The Examiner* during March to try to rouse some interest in the book, but this failed. Indeed, Shelley's friend Peacock told Mary he was so scandalized by the badness of the sonnet on "The Floure and the Lefe" that he would petition Hunt not to publish any more. Keats sent a copy of the book to Mathew, inscribed with a friendly greeting, but evidently heard nothing in reply. He also took Abbey a copy, by way of proving his boast of a month before. His guardian agreed to read it, but only because Keats had written it. On their next meeting he commented, "Well,

John, I have read your book, and it reminds me of the Quaker's horse—hard to catch and good for nothing when he was caught." The joke stung. Even as Abbey chuckled over it, he sensed that Keats would never forgive him, though he pretended not to notice it. There was nothing for Keats to do but swallow his pride and go back to work—pondering the plan of *Endymion* and extending his close study of the Elizabethan poets. The leading reviews sometimes took months to get around to a book by a new author; in the meantime he would keep his spirits up.

Yet it appears that he was getting restless in London. Now that his responsibilities at the hospital were over, there was nothing to hold him in the city. His rooms in Cheapside were hardly the place for study and work, and the life of literary London, which had seemed so pleasant all winter, was beginning to pall. Around the middle of March he suddenly decided to leave town for a while. Haydon advised him to live alone to concentrate on his work, and Tom and George agreed, though reluctantly. Keats himself was ready to admit that he had had an overdose of City air and late hours. "Banish money—Banish sofas—Banish Wine —Banish Music," he wrote Reynolds in a Falstaffian vein, "But right Jack Health—honest Jack Health, true Jack Health—banish health and banish all the world." Hampstead was the inevitable choice.[36] Keats found rooms near the Heath in the house of the postmaster, Benjamin Bentley, on Well Walk, a pleasant lime-bordered avenue leading to the springs which had been fashionable in the eighteenth century. From here it was only a five-minute stroll to the Vale of Health, where Hunt could read him the latest lines of his new poem or play over his new hymn, "To the Spirit Great and Good." From a letter which Keats wrote to Clarke on March 25, relaying an invitation to take a part in the hymn at Novello's the next evening, it appears that his relations with "Mr. Hunt" were as cordial as ever. Hunt, he reported, had "got a great way" into his new poem, *The Nymphs*, and "said a number of beautiful things"; while he himself had "written a few Lines and a Sonnet on Rimini." Hunt was revising *Rimini* for a second edition, and Keats, on reading it again, had been struck anew by its charm. A few phrases in his sonnet, as well as his mention of writing "a few lines," make it sound as though he was already at work on the opening of *Endymion* and had reread *Rimini* with his own long poem in mind.

Yet this tranquillity was too poetic to last. Unluckily one day Hunt took it into his head to turn his prophecy of a laurel wreath for Keats into a reality.[37] As they sat drinking their wine after dinner, he proposed to Keats that they crown themselves with laurel and ivy "after the fashion of the elder Bards" and write sonnets on their "sensations." Keats agreed but, once the wreaths were produced, found he had nothing to say. While Hunt, delighted with his own whim, dashed off one sonnet and then started on another, Keats sat blankly searching for an idea, then limped through fourteen lines describing his lack of inspiration. At this point three callers were announced. Hunt snatched off his crown before the ladies entered, but not Keats. He refused to disown so abjectly what the laurels stood for. Instead, "in his mad enthusiastic way," he wore his wreath without explanation all through the visit, to the callers' amusement, and when they left he succeeded in writing a second sonnet "To the Ladies Who Saw Me Crown'd." His bravado was more than a match for Hunt's; but soon afterward he began to regret the pretentiousness of the gesture and did what he could to prevent the sonnets from getting into circulation.

For slowly but surely Keats was breaking out of Hunt's orbit. Early in April an invitation came from Shelley, suggesting that he come down with Hunt and his family on a long visit to Marlow, where the Shelleys had taken a house overlooking the Thames. At once Keats realized this would not do. He needed his own "unfetterd scope," as he later put it, to work on *Endymion;* he could not write with Hunt looking over his shoulder and Shelley, who had already made a good start on his poem, pulling ahead of him day after day. Besides, he was increasingly troubled by Hunt's cheerful acceptance of his position as one of Shelley's pensioners —"a Situation which I should be less eager after than that of a galley Slave," as he later remarked to Haydon.

Keats declined Shelley's invitation as gracefully as he could; but meanwhile another awkward situation arose when he and Hunt began talking over their new poems together. *The Nymphs* was turning into a pretty little treatise on the Greek demigoddesses, written with much the same feeling as that with which Hunt had studied the engravings in his schoolbooks of mythology. But Keats's idea of the Greek spirit was rapidly changing, and evidently he now had confidence enough in his own judgment to question a few of Hunt's phrases. Hunt retorted by casting doubts on Keats's whole project of *Endymion*. "Why endeavour after a long poem?" he asked. Perhaps it was a sensible question, now that the failure of Keats's first volume was apparent, but for Keats it meant the end of his discipleship. "There is no greater Sin after the 7 deadly than to flatter oneself into an idea of being a great Poet," he exploded in a letter to Haydon not long afterward. If Hunt had flattered him as well as himself into such an idea, Keats was now undeceived; but if Hunt refused to encourage him with *Endymion,* Keats refused to be discouraged. As Haydon noted in his diary at this time, Hunt deprecated any undertaking on the epic scale because he was too lazy to attempt one himself; but Keats realized that there was no way to discover whether he could write a long poem—to him the test of the great poet—but to try, even at the risk of failure. And, as he later wrote, "I would sooner fail than not be among the greatest."

Yet he did not make an open declaration of independence. When Hunt went off to Marlow on April 6, he left Keats with two commissions which show that he still thought of him as one of those friends to whom he was glad to be obliged. He asked Keats to read the proofs of the new edition of *Rimini* when they came back from the printer, and to go through his study destroying papers connected with some obscure financial matter. Since Hunt was over a thousand pounds in debt at this time, it seems likely that "old Wood," whom Keats in his letter reporting on the affair described as "a very Varmant—sharded in Covetousness," was a bailiff with a search warrant whom Hunt was trying to forestall.[38] Keats, who was clearly embarrassed by the request, decided to lock the papers up in a trunk instead of destroying them; and perhaps it was this shabby episode that completed his disillusionment with Hunt. However this may be, a few days later he made a decisive move: he broke with Hunt's friends the Olliers and went over to Reynolds' publishers, Taylor and Hessey—an interesting switch, since Hunt had just transferred from Taylor and Hessey to the Olliers with the second edition of *Rimini*.

This charge was an important decision for Keats and one which he never had cause to regret. Taylor promised to keep him in funds in exchange for "the refusal of his future works." The agreement shows great faith in Keats's talent on Taylor's part, for the Olliers had understandably become dismayed at the number of unsold copies of the *Poems* left on their shelves. On April 15 Taylor wrote to his father, a bookseller in Bath, about his new author: "I cannot fail to think that he will become a great Poet, though I agree with you in finding much fault with the Dedication &c. These are not likely to appear in any other of his Productions." Taylor had reasons other than political for regretting the dedication of the *Poems* to Hunt. Six months before, he had advanced him twenty guineas for the collection of mythological poems which Hunt had started with *Hero and Leander;* but though the book was advertised, Hunt never finished it and put off repaying the advance for over a year.[39] Taylor, a man of the world some fourteen years older than Keats, was almost as much amused as impressed by the young poet when he met him in March, for he described his "singular style of dress" in some detail in a letter to his brother. Yet besides his faith in Keats's ability he soon came to feel a very real warmth toward him—"a strange personal interest in all that concerns him," as he once half apologetically put it.

Perhaps Taylor's encouragement helped Keats to make one more decision that week—to get completely away from London in order to work on *Endymion*. He had not found the solitude he needed in his new lodgings. It was not warm enough yet to spend days on the Heath reading and writing, and at Well Walk he was plagued by the Bentleys' carrot-haired children, who filled the house with "horrid rows" and the smell of worsted stockings. Then George and Tom evidently decided sometime in early April to give up their rooms in Cheapside and join him in Hampstead. Perhaps they moved for economy's sake, or to find a better air for Tom; or perhaps it was at this time that George quarrelled with Abbey's junior partner Hodgkinson and left his job in Pancras Lane. Haydon's advice that Keats try living alone in the country was now more to the point than ever. After all the excitements and disappointments and contradictions of the winter he needed to get away—most of all, it would seem, to escape from Hampstead, where his hopes for poetry had soared so high and then collapsed. As he looked back on the events of the winter and spring, Keats was suddenly overcome with consternation and disbelief. How could he have been duped into thinking himself a great poet—even worse, how could he have joined Hunt in the masquerade of the laurel crowning? What an affront to the god of poetry, however he could be imagined to exist! Half in mock-ery, half in earnest, Keats wrote a "Hymn to Apollo" by way of apology and promised to "put on no Laurels" till he finished *Endymion*. The next six months would tell whether he could claim them in the end. On April 14 he packed up and started out for the Isle of Wight, not to return, so he promised himself, till his poem was done.

Chapter Five

A Leap into the Sea

L A T E that afternoon Keats climbed up on an outside seat in the Southampton coach and felt the excitement surging up in him as they clattered out of the Holborn innyard. He had said good-bye to friends and brothers, to congratulatory sonnets and laudatory reviews; he was going into self-imposed exile with a great work to be done. Soon after clearing the toll-gate at Hyde Park Corner they reached the open road, speeding south and west between dusty hedges and empty fields in the fading light. The outside seats, cheaper than those within, were usually occupied by smart young gentlemen who cared little about changes in the weather; Keats sat up, trying to look unconcerned, drawing his plaid around him as the evening air grew cold. But after three stages he was glad to take an empty seat inside for the rest of the journey. Here he dozed by fits and starts as they rattled through nameless little towns, where stone fountains and barber poles loomed up and fell away again in the dim light of their lamps. When he looked out again the sun was rising, and yellow furze was ablaze along the roadside. The unaccustomed hour, the brightness, the promise of warmth in the chilly air, sent his spirits soaring with the larks.

Soon they reached Southampton, rolled through an old gate flanked by two lions, and drew up in front of their last inn. Keats climbed down a little stiffly, ordered breakfast, then suddenly felt so lonely that he unpacked a volume of Shakespeare to read with his meal. He found that the boat to the Isle of Wight would not sail till three. The tide was out; the harbor was dank. He spent the morning walking up and down the Southampton streets, noting that the men and women looked no different from those in London; then, beginning to feel a little muzzy, he returned to the inn to dine on a chop and write a letter to George and Tom.

A good sleep at Newport that night and a trip around the island on Wednesday restored his spirits. Spring came early to the Isle of Wight; the fields were already green with young wheat, and the hedges were thick with cowslips and primroses. On the coach from Cowes to Newport they passed a huge army barracks, "a Nest of Debauchery," a fellow passenger told him, which had quite spoiled the people of the island, especially the women. But, said Keats in a letter to Reynolds, "I must in honesty confess that I did not feel very sorry at the idea of the Women being a little profligate." Wondering where to stay, he looked at Shanklin, a fishing village popular with summer visitors, perched over the great wooded cleft of the Chine; but he finally chose Carisbrooke, a hamlet outside Newport in the center of the island. Though less picturesque, it was cheaper, and somehow he felt cheered to see the coast of England from a hill nearby. His landlady, Mrs. Cook, was unexpectedly amiable, for she did not object when he exchanged the print of a French ambassador hanging in his room for one of Shakespeare which had caught his eye in the hallway. After pinning up the Shakespeare with three pictures of his own, Keats arranged his books in a row underneath and told himself he had done a good morning's work. He felt unaccountably restless. After clambering around the ruins of Carisbrooke Castle, he went for a walk by the sea, then began a letter to Reynolds, begging for news of his brothers and Reynolds' sisters and all their friends.

For some reason he could not bring himself to start work yet, though he was all in a tremble, as he told Reynolds, from not having written anything for so long. Instead he turned to his books and began rereading Shakespeare. As he went headlong through his favourite plays he discovered new meaning in line after line that had never struck him before. "I find that I cannot exist without poetry," he wrote Reynolds, "half the day will not do—the whole of it—I began with a little, but habit has made me a Leviathan." Then there was the sea, even vaster and more mysterious than the summer before. As he walked along the

shore, scanning the horizon, listening to the ceaseless whisper of
the tide, the noise and confusion of London faded from his mind.
Thursday evening, haunted by a passage from *King Lear* on the
view from the Dover cliffs, he worked out a sonnet "On the Sea."
It was the last he was to write for nine months. The sonnet form
came almost too easily now; he wanted to say something greater
than could be contained in its limits. Yet writing it somehow
steadied his nerves, just as, it seems, his walk by the sea renewed
the sense of his symbolic journey that had come to him at Margate.* He stood like a diver poised for a moment, then plunged
into the timeless world of *Endymion*.

As he first conceived his poem, it was to be a test of his powers
of invention—to "make 4000 Lines of one bare circumstance and
fill them with Poetry." [1] The legend of Endymion's winning immortal youth through the love of the moon goddess was only the
beginning, or rather the ending; he had to fill up his four books
with living characters, set them moving in a world of their own,
and breathe new meaning into the old legend. The meaning, as
he phrased it in his first lines, was quite simple:

> A thing of beauty is a joy for ever:
> Its loveliness increases; it will never
> Pass into nothingness; but still will keep
> A bower quiet for us, and a sleep
> Full of sweet dreams, and health, and quiet breathing.

Such things of beauty are the sun, the moon, daffodils, and clear
streams

> That for themselves a cooling covert make
> 'Gainst the hot season; . .

but also the memory of "the mighty dead"—the great names of
history he kept constantly before him—and "All lovely tales that
we have heard or read." Essentially he still held, with Hunt,
that a poet should "simply tell the most heart-easing things." It
was the sheer beauty of the story of Endymion, its association with
the moon, and its theme of endless youth and love that first appealed to him—both to his worship of nature and to the idealism
which still regarded a fair woman as a pure goddess. His head
was filled with "lovely tales" from his winter's reading of Eliza-

---

* The image of poetry as sailing recurs in the introductory lines of *Endymion*.

bethan poetry, which had set him an example for retelling the Greek myths with a wealth of description and adventure and amorous encounter and an admixture of allegorical significance. Some idea of a spiritual development to be undergone by his hero in winning immortal love was also taking shape in his mind, an expression of the "religion of joy" he had found given tangible form in the Elgin Marbles. All the varied experiences of the last year, hope and discovery and discouragement, all the arguments on poetry and art and religion he had heard at Hunt's and Haydon's, all his own aspirations toward some dimly sensed goal, were stirring in his mind and gathering around the centre of Endymion's quest.

This ferment of ideas and impressions kept him in "continual burning of thought," as he called it, in his first week at Carisbrooke and made it difficult to begin. Furthermore, he had no clear sense of the direction of his story. A year later he confessed, "Before I began I had no inward feel of being able to finish; and as I proceeded my steps were all uncertain." But still he struck out. His plan was to send Endymion on a journey through the elements in search of his goddess, describing the strange worlds through which he passes and telling other myths along the way. "Do not the Lovers of Poetry like to have a little Region to wander in," he wrote George, "where the images are so numerous that many are forgotten and found new in a second Reading: which may be food for a Week's stroll in the Summer?" This is a formless design for a long poem, no doubt, the result of starting with a predetermined length rather than a clearly conceived action. Yet marvellous adventures and exotic scenery were all to the taste of the romance-readers of the time: and what better place to start his poem than the Isle of Wight in mid-April?

> . . . so I will begin
> Now while I cannot hear the city's din;
> Now while the early budders are just new,
> And run in mazes of the youngest hue
> About old forests; while the willow trails
> Its delicate amber; and the dairy pails
> Bring home increase of milk. . . .

He looked ahead, not to the ending of his poem, which was still unclear, but to the autumn which must come, and laid his plans:

> O may no wintry season, bare and hoary,
> See it half finished: but let Autumn bold,
> With universal tinge of sober gold,
> Be all about me when I make an end.

For a few days all seemed to go well. The first book opened in a forest on the sides of Mount Latmos, and he filled almost a hundred lines with description of the "copse-clad vallies" all around him, the sunrise he had seen on his journey, the murmurings of the sea on his evening walks. Yet after a week, just as he was getting started, he faltered and broke off. The loneliness of Carisbrooke together with the excitement of his work was too much for him. He found himself losing his appetite and unable to sleep at night for thinking of his poem hour after solitary hour. Suddenly he decided he could work better in the familiar surroundings of Margate and wrote Tom to meet him there, then astonished Mrs. Cook by telling her he must leave at once. But as he was packing up she insisted he take the portrait of Shakespeare he had liked so much. It struck him as a good omen.

At Margate Tom's company was a steadying influence. They walked and talked together as they had the summer before, and Keats returned to *Endymion* on a schedule of eight hours of reading and writing a day. Tom, who was deep in Plutarch's *Lives,* sometimes read aloud passages of Pope's Homer from the translation he was reading, and Keats thought Pope's lines seemed "like Mice" compared to his. As he picked up the first book again with his head still full of the lavish beauty of the Isle of Wight, he composed a long "Hymn to Pan" in which the shepherds give thanks to their god for the abundance of their lives:

> O thou, whose mighty palace roof doth hang
> From jagged trunks, and overshadoweth
> Eternal whispers, glooms, the birth, life, death
> Of unseen flowers in heavy peacefulness;
> Who lov'st to see the hamadryads dress
> Their ruffled locks where meeting hazels darken;
> And through whole solemn hours dost sit, and hearken
> The dreary melody of bedded reeds—
> In desolate places, where dank moisture breeds
> The pipy hemlock to strange overgrowth;
> Bethinking thee, how melancholy loth
> Thou wast to lose fair Syrinx—do thou now,

> By thy love's milky brow!
> By all the trembling mazes that she ran,
> Hear us, great Pan! . . .

They were triumphant lines, full of the riches of the earth and touched with the mystery of the vital force binding all living things together. Yet as Keats moved on into the narrative portion of his poem, the most difficult part for him, his old doubts returned. "The high Idea I have of poetical fame makes me think I see it towering to high * above me," he wrote George in a fit of dejection. He was discovering the anxieties of labouring day after day to bring into being a work conceived on a grand scale. He read his lines over; they seemed worthless. His ambitions for *Endymion* were soaring so high, he confessed to Hunt, that he feared he would overreach himself and "drop into a Phæton." Why, he asked, should he think himself a poet more than other men?

Perhaps the first adverse criticism of his *Poems,* which appeared in the *European Magazine* for May, contributed to this mood. Damning the volume with very faint praise, the reviewer found a few promising poems outweighed by "feeble and false thoughts" and a "redundance of poetical decoration." He criticized the Chapman sonnet as "unseemly hyperbole," and predicted that the attack on Pope in "Sleep and Poetry" would bring "ridicule and rebuke" down on the young author. Curiously enough, the only poems he approved were those addressed to the Mathew girls and the sonnets "On Woman," which Reynolds in his review had called "very inferior to the rest." This critic scoffed at Reynolds' praise of Keats and deplored the influence of Hunt. As he warned Keats in conclusion, "the mere luxuries of imagination" can only "inculcate the falsest and most dangerous ideas and refine us into the degeneracy of butterflies that perish in the deceitful glories of a destructive taper." The review was signed simply "G.F.M." [2]

Keats must have been staggered by this obituary notice of his friendship with Mathew, though he never mentioned it beyond remarking offhandedly in a letter to Haydon that "Envy and detraction" were mere "stimulants to further exertion." Evidently it

---

* Keats apparently intended "too high," as appears from an image that haunted him at the time, of trying to scale the Dover cliff—"the Cliff of Poesy": "I am 'one that gathers Samphire, fearful trade'" (see *The Letters of John Keats,* ed. H. E. Rollins [1958], I, 131, 139, 141, 169).

reached him around the same time as a gloomy letter from George on May 11 about money matters. What these were is impossible to guess exactly. The country was going through a postwar period of depression and unemployment, and George was having a hard time finding work. Shortly after leaving Abbey, it seems, he became involved in a business venture with a friend named Wilkinson—probably one Thomas Wilkinson, an auctioneer and agent on Bread Street, off Cheapside.[3] George evidently had to put up some capital for the project, and Keats had contributed £40 or £50 of his own. Now, it seems, the plan was heading toward disaster. To make matters worse, George had written a rash note to the Olliers late in April, reproaching them for the slow sale of the *Poems* and asking how many copies were left on hand—perhaps with the idea of buying them out. The Olliers wrote a stinging reply to thank him for relieving them of "any further connection" with the volume and to report that many of their customers considered it "no better than a take in." This news was enough to bring Keats to a complete halt somewhere near the middle of his first book. His cash was running low, and unpaid bills were nagging at him; evidently before leaving London he had run up an account for some new and more presentable clothes. When Taylor and Hessey came to his rescue with an advance of £20, he thanked them in a note of embarrassed jocosity. Was he going to end up like Hunt, sponging on his publishers' confidence?

His uneasiness about Hunt continued. A letter came from Marlow, asking about the commissions Hunt had left him with, but Keats put off answering it for two weeks. He finally replied as best he could in their old easygoing style, commenting on the latest *Examiner* and citing two new passages on the still-vexed question of Shakespeare's Christianity—one for, one against. After asking how *The Nymphs* was progressing and offering a little guarded advice, he admitted his discouragement with *Endymion,* then immediately made a joke about it: "Does Shelley go on telling strange Stories of the Death of kings? Tell him there are strange Stories of the death of Poets—some have died before they were conceived. Does Mrs Hunt tear linen in half as straight as ever? Tell her to tear from the book of Life all blank Leaves." He signed himself "John Keats alias Junkets," but the familiarity was forced. He could write Haydon about his hopes and fears without self-mockery, but to Hunt no longer.

Yet Haydon presented another difficulty. He had written Keats one of his fiery letters, warning him against the "delusions & sophistications" that were ruining Hunt's talent and prescribing his own remedy for discouragement—prayer. From this refuge, he said, "I always arose, with a refreshed fury—an iron clenched firmness, and chrystal piety of feeling, that sent me streaming on with a repulsive power against the troubles of life, as if I were a cannon shot, darting through feathers." Keats replied that Hunt's "self delusions" about being a great poet were "very lamentable," but added uneasily that he hoped he was not deceiving himself in the same manner. Haydon, he felt, was the one person who understood the "turmoil and anxiety" of creation, "the readiness to Measure time by what is done and to die in 6 hours could plans be brought to conclusions." Yet Keats could not "trust in God" in his moments of doubt as Haydon urged him to do. "I never quite despair and I read Shakspeare," he confessed. "I am very near Agreeing with Hazlit that Shakspeare is enough for us." Then, realizing this might lead them into another argument on religion, he desisted.

This casual echo of Hazlitt's remark is a clue to a silent but momentous change that was taking place in Keats's mind that spring. He was discovering in Shakespeare the poet of all poets for him, who not only replaced Spenser and Hunt as his exemplars in poetry but was also bringing to focus his convictions on human experience. All through 1817 Keats's letters echo with Shakespeare's lines, whether he is making a joke or describing his profoundest aspirations. Even his poetry was beginning to show the influence of the dense thinginess of Shakespeare's style, concentrated where his own early verse was diffuse, tough in its sensuousness rather than luxurious. Yet more than this, Keats was drawn to Shakespeare by that most elusive of essences, his outlook on life—the honesty, the saneness, the depth of his humanity in confronting the whole range of human experience. Perhaps Keats first became aware of these qualities in that futile argument at Horace Smith's over Shakespeare's Christianity, for what evidently impressed him then was that neither Haydon nor Shelley could prove his point—that indeed Shakespeare had no point to prove beyond the inexhaustible richness of human character. The portrait of Shakespeare which he had brought from Carisbrooke now hung over his books at Margate, as it was to hang over his writing desk ever afterward. Looking up at it one day after reading over some lines which struck him as better than he had thought at the time he wrote them, he recalled Haydon's belief that a good genius presided over his painting. Could it be, he asked him, that he too had a good genius? "Is it too daring to Fancy Shakspeare this Presider?"

Yet, in spite of these flashes of encouragement, Keats found he had written himself out after three weeks at Margate. The first book was barely half finished, but his nerves were on edge and his head swam as though he had been on "a Mental Debauch." Suddenly tired of Margate—"this treeless affair"—he decided to move again, this time to Canterbury. There the thought of Chaucer, he wrote Taylor, would "set [him] forward like a Billiard-Ball." Canterbury itself, evidently the first cathedral town he had seen, gave him a glimpse of the Middle Ages that sank deep into his memory. With Tom he must have wandered for hours through the narrow streets and strolled up and down the aisles of the cathedral, marvelling at the royal tombs, the stone tracery, the soaring arches, the stained glass of the great window. After this breathing space he set to work again, and by the beginning of June, it seems, he had completed the draft of the first book—over a thousand lines. It was an achievement. Already he was learning to fill in a large-scale plan line by line, episode by episode. Still more, he was beginning to find he could work without the constant encouragement of an older friend. He refused to copy out a passage for Hunt's approval, and even told Haydon he could say nothing about his poem till it was half done. However far the first book fell short of his intentions— and it was to undergo much agonized rewriting—he had battled through to the end of his first round.

Now he decided to take a holiday. While Tom returned to London, Keats went off to a seaside village near Hastings with the improbable name of Bo-Peep, where Haydon occasionally went on vacation. And here he had an adventure. For years Keats had stood in the shadow of his handsome and enterprising brother George so far as women were concerned; now all on his own he met an attractive woman several years older than himself and struck up a flirtation. The affair is shrouded in mystery for us, and even to Keats the lady remained "an enigma." He referred to her in several later letters to George merely as "the lady from Hastings," not because he did not know her name but because she imposed secrecy on him. Nevertheless her identity can be gathered from scattered references to her by Keats's friends and

from several of her own letters to Keats's new publisher, John
Taylor, with whom she was on friendly terms. She was Isabella
Jones, the "beautiful Mrs. Jones," as John Reynolds wistfully
recalled her years later.[4] A member of semi-fashionable literary
society in London, she was attached in some undefined manner
to an elderly Irishman of a titled family named O'Callaghan, with
whom she spent summers in Hastings. Intelligent and sophisti-
cated, she was perceptive enough to take an interest in this young
protégé of Taylor's. As for Keats, she was apparently just the
woman he needed to break the bonds of his shyness. If, as seems
possible, the song "Hush, hush! tread softly" was his recollection
of this episode some months later,[5] she had to steal secretly out
of the inn late at night, away from her "jealous old bald-pate," to
meet him in the garden below. How far the affair went in those
few days—Keats said merely that he had "warmed with her"—
can never be known. It may have been only a holiday romance of
strolls along the shore, tea in the garden, and evenings of whist;
it may have been his sexual initiation. They parted after a week,
but Keats must have returned to London with a sense of greater
triumph than he had anticipated. And when he went back to
Endymion he began the second book with a hymn to the "sover-
eign power of love."

--->>> <<<---

The summer now slipped by, leaving almost no trace beyond a
few ripples in the widening circle of his friendships. After Carisbrooke, Keats had quietly dropped his plan not to return to London till the end of the year. Back in Hampstead with George
and Tom, in close touch with his friends in town, he had no
need to write letters, and thus only two short notes survive to
document the summer. In the first, still hard-pressed by duns, he
asked Taylor and Hessey for another loan, this time of £30.
Perhaps it is significant that in this letter he jokingly spoke twice
of losing his virginity—"with respect to money Matters." In the
second note, near the end of August, he told Haydon he had just
finished the second book of *Endymion*. This does not seem like
much to show for ten weeks, but probably much time went in
reworking the first book [6] and in reading. During this summer
he formed the habit of borrowing books from the well-stocked

shelves of Taylor and Hessey's shop. Taylor, one of the most generous and sympathetic of publishers, loaned his young author whatever caught his eye and seems not to have murmured when Keats kept some of his books for over a year. A slight man with a fine intellectual head, Taylor looked more like a scholar than a businessman and had in fact already published several volumes on the authorship of the Junius letters. Hessey, his younger partner, was a round-faced, gregarious, good-humoured man who lived with his wife and young family in rooms over the bookshop at 93 Fleet Street and looked after the firm's business affairs. Taylor and Hessey published some of the best writers of the time— Coleridge, De Quincey, Landor, and Hazlitt among others—and through them Keats's acquaintance in literary London steadily widened. Soon the house in Fleet Street became a kind of club for him, a good place to drop in for an hour of literary or political talk, to browse among the old books in the back room, or occasionally to dine with his publishers and their authors.

The walk into London was a pleasant one in the long afternoons. Keats must have gone many times to visit the Wylies in Romney Street with George, whose interest in Georgiana was now something to speculate about, or to call on the Reynoldses in Little Britain. Here he would match wits with Mrs. Reynolds, listen to Charlotte playing the piano, or tease Jane and Mariane a little; or he would go off with Reynolds and his Oxford friend Benjamin Bailey, who was visiting him that summer, for walks on the Heath or a look at the theatre. On Sundays, Clarke and Severn often came out to Hampstead, and Clarke remembered Keats's once reading them the "Hymn to Pan" with evident pleasure. Severn was getting on well in his work, for his first large oil painting—on a subject from Shakespeare which Keats had suggested to him—had been shown and praised in a review. But this summer Keats's long friendship with his old tutor was cut short when Clarke moved with his parents to the farthest end of Kent. With this break Keats's strongest link with Hunt was snapped. Evidently, of all his friends, Hunt was the one Keats saw least this summer. Hunt returned from Marlow in mid-June and moved from Hampstead to a smaller house in Paddington, on the western edge of London. Early in July he wrote to Clarke rather crossly, "What has become of Junkets I know not. I suppose Queen Mab has eaten him."

This was not far from the truth: Junkets had disappeared for good. The break with Hunt was a painful neccessity for Keats and impossible to explain to the older man. Though he was finding Hunt's influence on his poetry no easy burden to shake off, he was determined to prove his independence in *Endymion*. Perhaps Hunt's review of his *Poems*, which appeared in *The Examiner* in erratic instalments through June and July, had something to do with his resolution. Hunt began his review with a lengthy discussion of the revolt against the school of Pope; when he got around to Keats, a month later, he first examined his faults— those very qualities of superabundant imagery and careless versification which Keats had caught from Hunt himself—reserving the "beauties" of the volume for a final notice. By and large, Hunt's criticism was just; but one or two readers, at least, thought it "done with an air of patronage, not with heart." So Caroline Scott, the wife of the editor of *The Champion*, wrote Haydon, adding a word of caution to Keats against Hunt's undue influence.[7] What Keats thought of the review is not known. But it was about this time that he sent his sonnet "On the Sea" to *The Champion*, where it appeared in the middle of August—his first poem to be printed in a magazine other than *The Examiner*.

Of Keats's other activities this summer we know only indirectly. At about this time, in a flare-up of his schoolboy spirit, he fought and trimmed a great lubber of a butcher-boy whom he found torturing a cat in an alley, and earned a name for himself in Hampstead as a result. Probably also during these months he wrote a little group of love lyrics which express all the moods of a summer romance—excited anticipation ("Hither, hither love"), tender farewell ("Unfelt, unheard, unseen"), dissuasions against remorse ("Think not of it, sweet one, so"), reproaches for coldness ("You say you love").[8] Yet, more than with his other poems, it is difficult to decide how closely, if at all, these verses reflect the moods and events of the time they were written. Even the lady's identity is only a guess, for Keats gave copies of one of these poems to both Isabella Jones and Jane Reynolds.

We can be certain, however, about his growing friendship this summer with Reynolds' friend Dilke, who lived halfway down Hampstead Hill in Wentworth Place, the pleasant double house which he had built on the edge of the Heath. Charles Wentworth Dilke was a man of good family; among his knighted forebears were a distinguished jurist and a leader of the Puritan opposition under Elizabeth. His post at the Navy Pay Office gave him enough leisure to edit early English plays, cultivate an interest—rare for his time—in William Blake, and contribute to the liberal magazines. Dilke was something of a doctrinaire; the theories of William Godwin, Shelley's philosophical father-in-law, provided him with an explanation for almost everything. Yet he was an interesting conversationalist, a keen sportsman, a connoisseur of snuff— and he had a charming wife. Maria Dilke was a close friend of the Reynolds girls and later took a warm interest in young Fanny Keats. Dark-haired, vivacious, unpunctual, and plump, the mother of a badly spoiled seven-year-old boy, she was still something of a flirt and loved an evening of dancing and banter. Keats and his brothers were welcomed at Wentworth Place at all hours and soon were drawn into her Hampstead set.

And always there was the Heath close at hand for long walks through Caen Wood and out into the open fields. Mile after mile they stretched away through meadow and marshland, hawthorn and holly, heather and fern, past willow groves where gipsies sat outside their vans, laughing and chattering in the sun. Keats found that Reynolds shared his taste for reading in the open air, and they used to spend hours on the Heath with Keats's new treasure, a facsimile Folio of Shakespeare.[9] No doubt they also read their own new verses to each other and talked about the future. Reynolds was deep in love with Eliza Drewe, a young lady he had met in Exeter the summer before, and was already thinking of marriage. With this in view, he was planning to give up journalism to enter the law, even though this would leave him far less time for writing than before. Keats opposed the idea; once or twice he even argued with Reynolds against the whole idea of marriage, and this question must have clouded some hours of their talk. Still, it was summer, they were both young and full of plans, the Heath was still fragrant with clover and honeysuckle, and butterflies fluttered through the sunlit afternoons; it was still time for poetry.

The second book of *Endymion* begins in this summer setting of heath and woodland. Keats had barely got his story under way in the first book, where Endymion confides to his young sister Peona that he has fallen in love with a mysterious bright being— the goddess of the moon, though he does not suspect it. Three times she has appeared to him in his dreams: from the sky, from a well, and in a cave. Now he is bidden to search for her through the regions of earth, water, and air, and he starts by plunging into the depths of the earth. Here he wanders through "one faint eternal eventide of gems," like the interior of a cathedral—Canterbury, perhaps?—on a bright day. This lifeless world miraculously springs into leaf and flower as he approaches the bower of Adonis, where he discovers Venus waking her lover from his winter sleep. Venus then guides him to a mossy bower, where he meets the love of his dreams in a brief but rapturous encounter. Yet she steals away without revealing her identity, and he wanders on forlorn. After meeting two more lovers—Alpheus, the river-god, pursuing the stream-changed Arethusa—and praying for their happiness, Endymion looks up to find "the giant sea above his head": he has completed the first stage of his journey.

In the third book Endymion makes his way across the floor of the sea, past sharks and skeletons and forgotten wrecks. Here he meets Glaucus, a terrifyingly old man who begs Endymion to free him from the doom of endless age by performing a magic rite. Thereupon Endymion changes Glaucus back to his youthful self and not only reunites him with his beloved nymph Scylla but restores to life all the drowned lovers of ten centuries past. In the celebration which follows, Venus promises Endymion that his love will soon be revealed to him and his devotion rewarded in "endless heaven." He faints with joy, then wakes to find himself back on earth again.

By the time Keats had reached the third book, however, the summer was running out and he was left stranded in Hampstead. Haydon, the Reynolds girls, even the Dilkes had all gone off on visits; George and Tom, their finances temporarily recovered, had left for a trip to France, where, it seems, Tom had hopes of meeting his mysterious young lady-friend Amena.[10] Luckily for Keats, Bailey, who had returned to Oxford to read for Schools a month before the start of term, asked him up for a visit at the beginning of September. Oxford, spacious and serene in the first golden days of fall, struck Keats as "the finest City in the world," as he wrote to his sister Fanny, with its "old Gothic buildings—Spires—towers —Quadrangles—Cloisters Groves &c" and "more Clear streams than ever I saw together." Though the university was almost deserted over the long vacation, the sleepy magnificence of the colleges stirred Keats's imagination to a new sense of the past. The air swarmed with bells on the hour; deer nibbled the lawns of the park behind Magdalen, and squirrels darted through the shadows of its oaks. In Bailey's rooms in Magdalen Hall he found snuff and cigars and cordials, a sofa to lounge on with a book, and shelves lined with authors whose names he had never heard before. Under a grim-faced portrait of Jeremy Taylor the two young men worked for four or five hours every morning. Keats had set himself a stint of fifty lines a day, and he astonished Bailey by the ease with which he turned them out. None of the doubts of the spring assailed him; he was now an assured and disciplined writer. Sometimes he finished his task before the morning was up, and read or wrote letters till Bailey was through; then at two they knocked off, dined, and went for a long talkative stroll along the Cherwell.

Bailey opened the door to a new intellectual world. Four years older than Keats, with one year of divinity at Oxford to his credit, he took himself with great seriousness. He impressed Keats as being immensely learned. Plato and Aristotle, medieval commentary and seventeenth-century poetry, Milton's theology and Coleridge's metaphysics, "the relative state of man and woman," "the unity of nature," "the insufficiency of language"—titles of projected essays he hoped to get Taylor to publish—these were the topics revolving in Bailey's mind. "I have seen, from my first glances, an analogy, conformity, & unity in all things," he wrote Taylor that winter, "or, to speak intelligibly perhaps, the two last are perceptible *by* analogy. I have thought that this principle is the governing one of the universe, and that I have equally perceived it in nature, external & internal—in the minds of men as reflected through the best authors—and (as far as we can glimpse) in the eternal mind—of which every thing that exists, it seems to my apprehension, is but the image of the Decree—the word, the Logos. Now all this (which were I to indulge myself I could write on to the end of time almost)—all this, I say, *to me is clear as noonday.*"

Alas for the insufficiency of language! The essays were to remain mostly unwritten; Bailey left Oxford the following spring without a degree and eked out a narrow life as a country parson, colonial chaplain, and finally archdeacon in Ceylon. But in 1817 he represented, however imperfectly, a new and vastly exciting idea to Keats: philosophy. It was the attraction of opposites, for, as Keats

confessed, he could never be convinced of a truth by "consequitive reasoning" but only by "a clear perception of its Beauty."
Understandably, then, the book on Bailey's shelves which made
the most lasting impresson on him was Madame Dacier's *Works
of Plato Abridg'd,* which contained several of the early dialogues
and the *Phaedo,* that beautiful demonstration of immortality by
Socrates on the afternoon of his death. This introduction to Plato
added the name of Socrates to Keats's roll of great men; it also
posed the questions of knowledge and virtue and happiness in
new terms and turned his thought in a new direction—inward,
on the activity of the mind itself. Bailey, who had first been drawn
to Keats by his "naturalness and simplicity of character," was evidently delighted to play the role of mentor. He has left us an odd
image of himself with his hand placed on Keats's head, noting that
"the silken curls felt like the rich plumage of a bird." Of his
own he had little to teach Keats, but he provided the intellectual companionship which Keats needed most at this time. From
Keats's letters a month or two later, we can see a remarkable intellectual flowering has already taken place. In these conversations
with Bailey, it seems, his own ideas began to unfold; all that he
had read and heard and pondered in the last few years became
articulate, fluent, thought linking up with thought.

As the weeks slipped by in an unbroken spell of fine weather,
they took a boat out on the Isis every afternoon. Drifting with the
stream, they talked of a hundred things—Syriac etymologies and
Newton's theory of light, for instance, Coleridge's ideas on the
imagination, Hazlitt's essays, Reynolds' decision to enter the law,
and their dislike of literary ladies. Love and marriage surely came
in for discussion too, for Bailey was giving them much thought.
Keats, unaware that he had already started courting Mariane Reynolds, believed that Bailey was suffering the pangs of unrequited
love for Thomasine Leigh, a close friend of Reynolds' fiancée.
A month later, when he guessed the situation at the Reynoldses',
he wrote Bailey circumspectly, wishing him all the happiness of
"a little Pæona Wife." This young-sisterly kind of love was not
at all what he wanted for himself, for as he later said of the Reynolds sisters, "They do not know what a Woman is." Indeed Bailey
was troubled by the importance which Keats attached to physical
love. Later he was to accuse Keats of loose moral principles and
to lament the "indelicacy" of *Endymion,* though now he had only

praise for it. But, as a parson-to-be, he was still more disturbed
by Keats's doubts about Christian belief. To Bailey, Christianity
could explain all the bitter dilemmas of existence, but Keats was
not easily convinced. "Why should Woman suffer?" was one question that vexed these young idealists—innocent and helpless as
they believed women to be—and to Keats the third chapter of
Genesis was no answer. Bailey later insisted that Keats was "no
infidel," but he had to admit that their notions of divinity were
very different. He got Keats to promise to give up scoffing at religion, but that was all.

But mostly they talked about poetry, the enthusiasm that had
first brought them together, and their pleasantest hours on the
river were spent drawn up in a cove of rushes reading aloud to
each other. Bailey wrote poetry himself, in a melancholy Wordsworthian vein, which survives in the albums of the Leigh sisters.[11]
Together they discussed the metaphysical poets whom Keats had
discovered on Bailey's shelves, and Bailey's favourites, Milton and
Dante and Wordsworth. Bailey, who had filled his edition of Milton with scholarly annotations, told Keats that he could not claim
to be a poet with his sketchy knowledge of *Paradise Lost;* and
Keats, evidently convinced, resolved to make a close study of Milton that winter—a decision of consequence. Poetry to Bailey was
a matter not of luxuriant description or exquisite sentiment but
of moral and philosophic truth. Hunt might think Milton the
poet of "love for gentle Lycid drown'd"; to Bailey he was the supreme example of the great poet who "ought himself to be a true
poem." So also with Wordsworth: Bailey turned Keats's interest
from his early work to the philosophic and religious vein of *The
Excursion.*

Keats had evidently been rereading this long meditative poem
on nature and the imagination more thoughtfully during his work
on *Endymion* that summer and had been more deeply impressed
than ever by the discussion of the origin of myth in the fourth
book. Here Wordsworth traced the poet's sense of an inward
meaning in nature back through the divinities with which the
Greeks had peopled their world to the angelic visitations which
Adam had received at the beginning of Creation, when he heard
"borne on the wind, the articulate voice of God." To Keats the
story of Genesis was a myth with no more special claim to belief
than the Greek legends; but, discounting Wordsworth's Christian

bias, he was profoundly convinced by his theory that the myths were not mere "lovely tales" expressing the changeful beauties of nature, but embodiments of enduring truths of existence. So midway through *Endymion* he tried to convey his own sense of how the Presence brooding over nature spoke with voices that echoed on the wind from cavern to forest to lake and, when caught by the first poets, gave rise at last to myth.[12] A fancy, perhaps; yet the myth, he claimed with increasing conviction, revealed a kind of truth, "the best music in a first-born song." A new sense of the significance of his own legend was growing in his mind as he went on with his poem, a sense which must have deepened in his long afternoon discussions with Bailey on the nature of imagination.

Yet Keats could not keep to Bailey's level of high seriousness indefinitely. In a letter to Reynolds he knocked off a waggish parody of one of Wordsworth's poems, suggested by a prominent feature of Oxford life—"There are forty feeding like one"—which ends:

> There are plenty of trees,
> And plenty of ease,
> And plenty of fat deer for Parsons;
> And when it is venison,
> Short is the benison,—
> Then each on a leg or thigh fastens.

His high spirits spilled over into a series of letters to Jane Reynolds at the seashore, in which he made fun both of himself holding his own in conversation at Magdalen and of Jane trying to make sense out of his foolery, or argued with her about Shakespeare's finest heroine—Juliet, of course—or the best time of day for a walk by the sea. Perhaps without realizing it, Keats was drifting into a kind of platonic flirtation with Jane. With her, as the older sister of his closest friend, he must have thought he was on safe ground, and his inveterate teasing seems clearly intended as a defence against any closer meeting between them.

There was no teasing in the letter he wrote to his own sister from Oxford, however, but a great deal of brotherly tenderness. Fanny's life with the Abbeys was evidently turning her into a sad and spiritless young girl. "Do you ever laugh?" George once asked her, swearing he had not seen her "so undignified" since the age of six—since the time, that is, of her mother's death.[13] Keats quizzed her a little on her reading, gave her a summary of *Endymion,* then

added news of George and Tom in France. They had seen "Cathe-
drals Manuscripts. Fountains, Pictures, Tragedy Comedy," he reported, "with other things you may by chance meet with in this
Country such as Washerwomen, Lamplighters, Turnpikemen Fish
kettles, Dancing Masters, kettle drums, Sentry Boxes, Rocking
Horses &c and, now they have taken them over a set of boxing
gloves."

But high spirits and fine weather could not last forever. On September 21 he reported to Reynolds, "I am getting on famous with
my third Book—Bailey likes what I have done very much." Five
days later, when he reached the end, his mood had changed completely. In exactly three weeks he had written one thousand and
thirty-odd lines, day after day without flagging; yet as he looked
them over he was profoundly discouraged. Perhaps he had written
them too much in the spirit of cramming for an exam—like Bailey,
studying his theology across the table; perhaps he now realized
how far they fell below his growing sense of the significance of
myth. For a moment he thought of tearing up all three books and
starting over again, then realized this would not do. "I am tired of
it and think the time would be better spent in writing a new
Romance which I have in my eye for next summer," he wrote Haydon dejectedly on the twenty-eighth. Already another poem, on
a subject much more to Bailey's liking, was taking shape in his
mind—the story of Endymion's "lute-voiced brother" Apollo, the
god of poetry, in his struggle with Hyperion and the overthrow of
the Titans: a theme of almost the scope of Milton's epic of the
revolt of the angels and the fall of man. Meantime autumn was
setting in and he did not want to face Hunt and Shelley with *Endymion* unfinished. Yet, as he confessed to Haydon, "My Ideas
with respect to it I assure you are very low." As he approached the
climax of his story, where Endymion was at last to win "immortal
bliss" with his goddess, his invention began to flag.

The Oxford long vacation was nearly over, and Keats and Bailey
decided to take a holiday before parting. Stratford was forty miles
away, and Keats was eager to see Shakespeare's birthplace—Shakespeare whose birthday he had marked alone in Carisbrooke that
spring, whose portrait had watched enigmatically over every line
of *Endymion*. They approached Stratford with expectations high
and were met by what Keats later called "the flummery of a birth
place." They visited the half-timbered house in Henley Street,

now divided between an inn and a butcher's shop; [14] climbed the
narrow stairs and added their names to the thousands of others
on the blackened walls of the low attic room where, they were
told, Shakespeare was born. When they went to look at his grave
in Holy Trinity Church, they were pestered by a custodian who
would not let them see it for themselves. Keats was struck by the
painted statue in the elaborate sculptured frame over the gravestone. A bald, plump man, his lips slightly parted, stiffly holding
his pen and staring blankly ahead: yet this, he realized, was the
most authentic of all the likenesses of Shakespeare. Keats said little,
Bailey recalled. It was a great moment, but still the gap between
expectation and reality must have yawned wide.

⋙ ⋘

The day after his return to Hampstead Keats plunged into the
riptide of London life once again. He went into town to call first
at the Reynoldses', then on Haydon, who had just moved into a
new studio in Paddington, not far from Hunt's. "Every Body
seems at Loggerheads," he reported to Bailey. "There's Hunt infatuated"—Shelley was there with Hunt, his long poem *Laon
and Cythna* finished within the six-month limit—"theres Haydon's Picture in statu quo. There's Hunt walks up and down his
painting room criticising every head most unmercifully—There's
Horace Smith tired of Hunt. 'The web of our Life is of mingled
Yarn.'" During his absence at Oxford, Hunt had reprinted his
"Grasshopper and Cricket" sonnet in *The Examiner,* perhaps as
a gesture of reconciliation after Keats's appearance in *The Champion* in August. Now Haydon drew him aside and said, "Keats,
don't show your lines to Hunt on any account, or he will have
done half of it for you"; while Reynolds told him that on meeting
Hunt at the theatre a week before he had reported that Keats was
near the end of his four thousand lines and Hunt had replied, "Ah
—had it not been for me, they would have been seven thousand!"
"Now is not all this a most paultry thing to think about?" Keats
exclaimed to Bailey. His independence of Hunt had cost him a
struggle; yet for all this, he wrote Bailey, "I shall have the Reputation of Hunt's elevé— His corrections and amputations will by
the knowing ones be trased in the Poem." He longed for Oxford
again. "I am quite disgusted with literary Men and will never

know another." Except Wordsworth, he added; perhaps he had learned from Haydon that Wordsworth was planning to visit London that winter.

With Haydon another storm was blowing up. In September he had written Keats asking him to look up a talented young painter named Charles Cripps whom Haydon had met in Oxford that summer, and whom he now offered to take as an apprentice for a year without the usual fee, if money could be found for his living expenses. Keats and Bailey, delighted with the idea, volunteered to raise a fund by subscription. Back in London, however, Keats found Haydon less interested in the young painter than he had at first seemed. Thereupon Bailey wrote him a reproachful letter; Haydon sent a stinging reply; Bailey then determined to end their acquaintance. At this point Keats stepped in to try to patch things up. He knew that Haydon liked to make generous promises and then hedge on them; but he could not think this was a reason for dropping him, though he also saw why Bailey should. "The best of Men have but a portion of good in them," he pleaded in a later letter. Keeping a friend like Haydon was far more important than being in the right; and the true test of friendship was to recognize a man's faults and then see whether the bond still held. Keats was as convinced as ever of Haydon's greatness as an artist, even while aware that this greatness did not include the "probity and disinterestedness" which he admired in Bailey. He must also have begun to realize that Haydon could be as irresponsible in money matters as Hunt. But how did one balance the claims of genius against ordinary uprightness? Keats was not sure; he only knew that Cripps must not be disappointed, and he set to work on his own to raise the promised funds.

At home there were still more worries. George and Tom had come back from Paris with empty pockets or worse. At the Palais Royal they had discovered the *rouge et noir* tables, plunged, and lost—an unspecified amount, but more than they could afford.[15] George had not yet found a job to his liking. Abbey was trying to persuade him to go into the hat business, but this did not work out. And Tom, in spite of his summer holiday, was looking ill and miserable. After a few weeks Keats became thoroughly alarmed. His trained eye must have noted symptoms that reminded him all too well of his mother's illness—pallor, feverishness, a recurrent cough. For a while he thought of shipping Tom off to Lisbon for the climate; but in another few weeks he seemed well enough so that they decided he should winter in Devon instead. One of the most troublesome aspects of consumption was its unpredictable ups and downs. There was no way of knowing whether Tom was really infected—indeed, the disease was not then thought to be infectious; and, if he was ill, there was no telling when or even whether his condition might become serious. And Keats had his own health to worry about. Toward the end of his stay at Oxford he had picked up a mysterious illness which hung on all through October and which he mentioned a number of times in his letters to Bailey in carefully guarded terms.

The truth seems to be that during his visit with Bailey Keats had contracted a venereal infection, probably syphilis. This point has been hotly denied ever since the story was first told, fifty years later, by a doctor who had it from Keats's friend Henry Stephens, whom he still saw occasionally this fall; [16] but there are several references in Keats's letters at this time which can be explained no other way. He had confided his fears to Bailey before leaving Oxford and wrote him a few days after his return to assure him that the mercury—the specific remedy for syphilis at that time—which he had taken had "corrected the Poison"; though, he added gloomily, he felt he would "never be again secure in Robustness." Apparently on doctor's orders, he spent the next fortnight—a period in which his infection would have been acutely contagious—confined to Hampstead, suffering, as he put it, "for vicious beastliness." And the doctor whom he consulted at this time was evidently not the Hampstead surgeon but one Mr. Solomon Sawrey in London, who in addition to his general practice was a specialist in venereal diseases.[17] By the end of October, Keats felt he was safely over the infection, but he was still troubled enough to keep discussing it with Bailey. The Reynolds sisters had become concerned about his health and wondered whether he was showing signs of consumption like Tom; as Keats wryly remarked, they had a better opinion of him than he deserved. It was a narrow scrape, and one which no doubt affected him more deeply than he could admit. More than any other experience of this year, it must have rubbed the bloom off his idealism and opened his eyes to the unpredictabilities and incongruities of human experience. "Lord! a man should have the fine point of his soul taken off to become fit for this world," he wrote Reynolds a month later, when he had regained his balance. This bravado may express his relief at his escape; it conceals the anxiety which he must have felt about possible after-effects, as well as an inevitable pang of guilt. The immediate effect of this adventure, however, was to plunge him into a numbing depression. For several weeks he could not bring himself even to write Bailey again. A kind of deadness settled over him, in which he began to doubt the genuineness of what he now could only remember feeling.

This was hardly the mood for following Endymion on his quest of "immortal bliss." By the end of October it was clear he had lost his wager with Shelley, for he had written a bare three hundred lines of the fourth book—the equivalent of a single week's work at Oxford. These lines begin with a dejected tribute to the Muse of English poetry, in which he admits his own unworthiness as a poet; they go on with a "Song to Sorrow" sung by a mysterious Indian maiden who makes her entry at this point. Her song builds up into a frenzied hymn to Bacchus, then dies away in the mournful reflection that pleasure cannot lighten the load of sorrow. The first day that Keats was well enough to go to town he had spent the evening with Reynolds' lawyer friend James Rice, in whose rooms a little club was beginning to gather every Saturday to drink and play whist and *vingt-et-un* and crack jokes hardly worth repeating. This gaiety hauled him out of the doldrums for a few evenings, but no more. November came, and in three weeks he dragged out only two hundred more lines.

Perhaps one reason for his despondency was a new worry added to all the others. *Blackwood's,* a magazine recently founded in Edinburgh by three young Tory wits who were determined to outslash even the formidable *Quarterly Review,* came out at the end of October with the first of a series of articles "On the Cockney School of Poetry." It was "a flaming attack" on Hunt, as Keats described it to Bailey, "depreciating his Wife his Poetry—his Habits —his company, his Conversation." Today it is hard to believe the bitterness of the political warfare that raged in the literary reviews of that time, or the absolute power they wielded over writers' reputations. But in the reactionary years after Waterloo, when any kind of intellectual nonconformity was suspect, a man's literary preferences were usually taken as a badge of his political opinions and vice versa. So *Blackwood's,* after proclaiming that only "men of some rank" could qualify as real poets, assailed Hunt's liberal views by describing his poetry as "glittering and rancid obscenities," his style that of "a tea-sipping milliner's girl" who "speaks unclean things from perfect inanition," and so on and so on. This outburst, which was signed only "Z.," hinted that Keats would be the subject of the next instalment. Hunt demanded in *The Examiner* that "Z." reveal his identity, and Keats resolved to send him a challenge. At this Reynolds became concerned and arranged for Keats to meet his friend Jonathan Christie, *Blackwood's* London agent, in the hope of fending off the attack. When the second instalment appeared later in November, "Z." was still pursuing Hunt, and Reynolds must have breathed easier. But Keats could not have been much heartened. Two final reviews of his *Poems* appeared this fall in two of the more influential magazines, *Constable's* and the *Eclectic,* which warned him against the "uncleannesses" of Hunt's poetry and the "affectations" of his style. At last Keats realized that his tributes to Hunt in his *Poems* had succeeded only in damning the book with the general public. But quixotically he felt drawn toward Hunt again, now that a battle was in prospect. He admitted to Haydon that his tributes had been impolitic, but insisted that Hunt had been generous to him and he would stand by him in trouble.[18] Within the next few months he called on and dined with Hunt a number of times and even joined in their old game of versifying on a set subject.

But in November, amid his worries, his glooms, and his "little two penny errands" to raise funds for Cripps, he was being driven farther and farther off course. The "wintry season" was fast coming on, and the fourth book of *Endymion* was still half finished. There was only one remedy—to get away from London again. This time he chose Burford Bridge in Surrey, where he had heard of a pleasant inn at the foot of Box Hill. From the top of this steep chalk scarp, shagged with boxwood and juniper and yew, a magnificent view of the downs stretched away to the Channel, thirty miles distant. At its foot a little weed-choked river, spanned by the three stone arches of Burford Bridge, crept along between the cliff and a deep forest, where the last flames of autumn were swathed in mist. It was a landscape after his own mood. The solitude which had weighed on him at the Isle of Wight was now a miraculous restorative. His first morning there, November 22, he wrote a long and richly reflective letter to Bailey; that evening he climbed Box Hill, watched the moon rise, came down, and added some lines to

Endymion—a hundred, more or less [19]—then wrote another letter, to Reynolds. He was himself again.

In this calm the disturbing events of the last two months fell into a new perspective. The passage he added to *Endymion* that evening describes a curious psychological experience which marks a turning point in Endymion's progress and, perhaps, in Keats's own life. Endymion, faced with seeming failure in his quest, enters the "Cave of Quietude," a retreat "of remotest glooms" in the dark depths of consciousness. Here the spirit that has moved beyond all hope of happiness, beyond even the sensation of despair, falls into a dreamless sleep and awakes mysteriously renewed, the fever of self-absorption past, to find the world full of blessings. So, it appears, Keats woke from his own depression at last. The experiences of the fall—Tom's illness and his own, disillusionment with friends and with himself, discouragement about his poetry—had finally shattered his faith in what most young men instinctively assume: that life holds out the promise of happiness to be gained, and sorrow avoided, by one's own efforts. He had learned at last that this was impossible; yet beyond this he had found that life was still good, that indeed there was a kind of beauty revealed through sorrow—the beauty of "light and shade," as he later called it—more intense than mere sunlit delight. "I have the same Idea of all our Passions as of Love," he told Bailey, "they are all in their sublime, creative of essential Beauty." What he had discovered between writing the first and the last books of *Endymion* was a whole new dimension of experience, to be grasped only by surrendering to the wayward and endless richness of the immediate moment. "You perhaps at one time thought there was such a thing as Worldly Happiness to be arrived at, at certain periods of time marked out," he remarked to Bailey. "I look not for it if it be not in the present hour—nothing startles me beyond the Moment. The setting sun will always set me to rights—or if a Sparrow come before my Window I take part in its existince and pick about the Gravel."

This taking part in the existence—or, as he later called it, the identity—of other beings was one of Keats's most important insights as a poet. What he called "essential Beauty" was a sudden realization of the innermost character of a person or thing, won by imaginative identification with it; and through this insight a new universe was revealed to him. So he could become one with the intense absorption of the sparrow picking for its food in the dirt, or with the loneliness of the oyster asleep in its shell at the bottom of the sea; he could even feel his way, as he once said, into a billiard ball delighted with its own smooth motion and perfect roundness.[20] What he described to Bailey was, of course, a quality which he had often achieved in his poetry without being quite aware of it, when his focus shifted from his own response to an object to the imagined inner life of the object itself: the sensations not only of the astronomer discovering a new planet, but of the star itself gazing down on the earth, or of the lazy power of a breaking wave and the delight of the rock weed swirled about in its foam. This ability to enter into the identities of other beings was, he found, not only the source of a great secret joy and the wellspring of his poetry but also the one thing sure among the uncertainy and incompleteness of experience, a faith to replace his earlier longing for some transcendental fulfilment. As he put it to Bailey, "I am certain of nothing but of the holiness of the Heart's affections and the truth of Imagination—What the imagination seizes as Beauty must be truth—whether it existed before or not." By grasping the essence of a thing through identifying with it, the imagination discovers a beauty in it which lies hidden to the outer gaze; and these essences were to Keats the ultimate reality of existence. "The Imagination," he wrote, in one of those very flashes of perception which he was trying to define, "may be compared to Adam's dream—he awoke and found it truth."

But this new insight into essential beauty and the truth of imagination implied a new idea of poetry, even of the poet himself, very different from the one he had held so long. Poetry was to be found everywhere, not merely in the special experience of luxurious beauty which Hunt cultivated; and to discover it required "Humility and capability of submission" before experience, not the assertion of a special character with special privileges such as Haydon represented. Men of talent who impose their "proper selves" on what they create should be termed "Men of Power," he wrote Bailey, in contrast to the true "Men of Genius," who "are great as certain ethereal Chemicals operating on the Mass of neutral intellect—but they have not any individuality, any determined Character." This receptivity to all experience, sorrow as well as joy, the commonplace as well as the heroic or the exquisite, together with the most self-effacing fidelity of expression, im-

pressed him more and more forcibly as the essence of Shakespeare's greatness. Now in rereading Shakespeare's *Poems*—a copy
of which he had just borrowed from Reynolds—he was struck as
never before by the poetry of real things which Shakespeare scattered so lavishly through his lines. "He has left nothing to say
about nothing or any thing," he wrote to Reynolds; "for look at
Snails, you know what he says about Snails," and then, after a little
thumbing of the pages, he found the stanza in *Venus and Adonis*
describing Venus's eyes rolling upward in her anguish over her
wounded lover:

> Or, as the snail, whose tender horns being hit,
> Shrinks backward in his shelly cave with pain
> And there all smothered up in shade doth sit,
> Long after fearing to creep forth again. . . .

This he thought a superb example of "fine things said uninten-
tionally—in the intensity of working out conceits." It was the kind
of poetry which he himself was aiming at, that "does not startle
the soul or amaze it with itself but with its subject."

So with Shakespeare again his presider, he rediscovered his former spontaneous joy in writing, as proved by the hundred lines
he added to *Endymion* on his first day at Burford Bridge. In writing Bailey it occurred to him that this disembodied delight of creation, the "empyreal reflection" of his moments of imaginative
identification with other essences, was a kind of immortality
achieved in life itself. If there is a hereafter, he mused, it must consist of this "happiness on Earth repeated in a finer tone," in which
"the simple imaginative Mind may have its rewards in the repetition of its own silent Working coming continually on the spirit
with a fine suddenness." So Shakespeare's image of the snail was
to return to him a few months later when he described these "silent workings" as "the innumerable compositions and decompositions which take place between the intellect and its thousand materials before it arrives at that trembling delicate and snail-horn
perception of Beauty." In a great burst of energy he raced through
the last five hundred lines of his poem in seven days and signed
the manuscript "Burford Bridge, Nov. 28, 1817" to mark the end.
His task was done.

>»⋙⋘«<

Though he finished *Endymion* with extraordinary speed, it may be wondered whether Keats clearly saw the ending of the poem until he had almost reached it. For in the fourth book the action takes a most unexpected turn, just as the tone changes from joyous idealism to melancholy. Endymion emerged from his adventure under the sea tested in courage and humanity and ready to continue his journey through the region of air to win his promised "immortality of passion." Yet just at this point he meets the dark-haired Indian maid who sings the "Song to Sorrow"; and while reproaching himself for infidelity, he falls passionately in love with her. Together they ascend, dreaming, into the heavens; then Endymion wakes to find Cynthia, the goddess of the moon, bending over him, and realizes at last that she is the love of his visions. But she fades, weeping, from his sight as he turns back to the Indian maid; then she too fades from him in the cold light of the rising moon. In despair, Endymion enters the Cave of Quietude, sleeps, and awakes renewed in spirit on earth again, to find the maiden at his side. At once he decides to renounce his hopeless love for Cynthia:

> I have clung
> To nothing, lov'd a nothing, nothing seen
> Or felt but a great dream! O I have been
> Presumptuous against love. . . .

Then, describing the autumnal beauty of Latmos in lines which Keats might have written on top of Box Hill, Endymion asks the maid to share his life of simple human pleasure in the forest: "Say, is not bliss within our perfect seizure?" But she refuses, mysteriously forbidden to love him on these terms. Endymion then resolves to become a hermit, while the Indian maid reluctantly vows to dedicate herself to Diana, the goddess of chastity. By the end of the day, however, Endymion has found none of the higher pleasures of contemplation he had expected in his solitude, only blank sluggish despair. Now he realizes that his earlier notion of happiness in human love was a trivial one, a thing of "flowers, garlands, love-knots, silly posies"; and the melancholy beauty of the autumn sunset moves him so deeply that he is content to accept his mortal lot and die with the death of the season. Then the will to live and love surges up again. "I did wed Myself to things of light from infancy!" he cries; and when he meets the Indian maid coming to the temple of Diana with his sister to take her vows, he grasps her hand and defies the fate which has separated them. At this a miracle occurs: the dark maiden is transformed into the bright-haired goddess before his very eyes. The love of his dreams has become real at last, and they vanish into the forest together, leaving Peona lost in wonder.

This miraculous ending to a miraculous tale has left many readers as bewildered as Peona herself. Unwilling to take the poem as meaning what it seems to say, most of Keats's critics have moralized it into an allegory of a kind of supersexual love for a supersensuous beauty. Thus Endymion's wanderings become the quest of the poetic soul for "communion with the ideal," and his agonized vacillation between the maiden and the goddess, and the final change of the one into the other, are taken to indicate the seeming conflict and ultimate harmony of the actual beauties of this world with ideal Beauty.[21] Yet this interpretation is hardly convincing. The texture of the poem itself, so richly sensuous and unabashedly sensual, not merely obscures such a meaning, it contradicts it. Moreover, Keats at twenty-one, with his distrust of "consequitive reasoning" and his hunger for "a life of Sensations rather than of Thoughts," was not the kind of young man to prefer abstractions to realities, or the kind of poet to contrive an allegorical system. Indeed, as he later admitted, the development of his tale was "uncertain," lacking a clear plan from the start.

Just as Keats never mentioned an allegory in discussing *Endymion* with his friends, so none of his first readers found any hint of allegory in the poem—not surprisingly, for the allegorical tradition was dead in Keats's time, even for readers of Spenser. Those who enjoyed the poem praised it chiefly for the imagery and accepted the metamorphosis of the Indian maid as the proper fairy-tale ending of a romance.[22] Only Jeffrey in *The Edinburgh Review* sensed Keats's real innovation—to have given the familiar mythological figures "an original character and distinct individuality," that is, a human significance; only Bailey suspected a hidden meaning in the action, which he could not believe Keats really intended: its approach "to that abominable principle of *Shelley's* —that *Sensual Love* is the principle of *things*." This suggests why, in the increasingly literal-minded and prudish age of Tennyson, when the fairy-tale ending was no longer readily accepted, a Victorian lady critic found it necessary to invent the moralistic al-

legory to disguise Keats's naked meaning.[23] For the poem is about
sensual love, like most poems by men of twenty-one. Endymion
represents not the poetic soul but the ideal lover; his adventures
are an assertion of "the holiness of the Heart's affections," and it
is only because the poem expresses such an exalted idea of sexual
love that the Victorian critics felt his quest must have another
goal.

But if there is no allegory in *Endymion,* there is clearly a symbolic significance, one inherent in the events themselves, not imposed on them from without, which might be defined simply as
the young man's discovery of the true nature of love. Keats himself seems to have discovered his full meaning only gradually, in
the very act of writing. He started with "a thing of beauty," and,
like Adam in his dream, "awoke to find it truth." Sexual love, as
Endymion describes it near the end of the first book, is the highest reach of happiness, the richest form of "blending pleasurable," [24] that most completely annuls the division between the self
and the world outside; as such, it is the crown of all other values
and the worthiest goal of our strivings. But even as Endymion set
out on his quest of "endless bliss," Keats's own ideas on the nature of love were changing. His new-won independence of Hunt,
his deepened understanding of Shakespeare, his friendship with
Bailey, his growing sense of tender responsibility for his young
sister, his adventure—whatever it amounted to—with Isabella
Jones, the disillusionments of the autumn, all these profoundly
altered the naïve idealism with which he had begun. By the time
he reached the fourth book, he had come to see the "immortality
of passion" which Endymion pursues as the hollow unreality that
it is. And so an astonishing inversion of the legend takes place.
The hero, on the point of winning his goddess, apparently betrays
her; he wins her in the end only after renouncing her, and not
in her own identity but by discovering her in a mortal maiden.
It is hard not to believe that this unexpected turn of plot was
deeply influenced by Keats's own emotional reversals of the fall.
For up till the very end Endymion's progress parallels Keats's own
feelings as he recorded them in his letters of October and November—disillusionment, depression, recovery; his loss of faith in the
certainty of happiness, his renunciation of idealism, his discovery
that the setting sun could put him to rights.

What of the ending, then? Is it a mere contrivance, a wrenching of the psychological narrative back to the foregone mythological conclusion? Partly so; or rather, the dénouement is presented in highly ambiguous terms and can be read in two quite different ways.[25] On the first, or mythological level, the maid is merely the goddess in a disguise which she has adopted to test Endymion's fidelity—a familiar fairy-tale device which Keats may have borrowed from a version of the legend in one of his Elizabethan poets.[26] So when Endymion seems to renounce human love in reasserting his devotion to "things of light," the maiden turns back into the goddess and rewards him with the "immortality of passion" promised in the myth. On the second, the psychological or symbolic level, the maid represents a new conception of human love, far higher than Endymion's adolescent dream of "endless bliss." So when he finally realizes that to renounce the maid is to deny life itself, he is rewarded by the maid's transformation into the goddess; that is, real love, when accepted for the good it contains, leads to the fulfilment Endymion has sought all along. The ambiguity is inescapable; Keats's legend pulled him in one direction, his experience in another. As between the two interpretations, however, it seems clear that he gravitated toward the second, the human rather than the magical meaning. The last lines of the poem announce that Endymion has been "spiritualiz'd" by "some unlook'd for change" in his final adventure;[27] and—what is not usually noticed—Cynthia herself has changed during the course of the story. She has surmounted her "foolish fear" of yielding to a mortal lover and defied the "decrees of fate" that doomed her to eternal chastity; she has been humanized, has learned to "throw the goddess off," as Keats put it in a later poem, and "play the woman's part." Endymion meanwhile has been spiritualized in a most unexpected fashion by his encounter with the maid, for he wins his goddess at last not through his earlier acts of valour or disinterested sympathy but by learning to love another human being.

Keats's implication, taken in the context of his time, is audacious. He is saying that a man is spiritualized not by self-denial but by self-fulfilment; that a lover becomes perfect in love not by chastity but by the gradual realization of his passionate nature. He gives a hint of this in the first book, in his praise of sexual love as "the chief intensity," the most "self-destroying" of entanglements. This outgoing of the spirit into the identities of others is first experienced in response to the beauties of nature—the intense but ethereal pleasures of boyhood, when

> every sense
> Of mine was once made perfect in these woods.
> Fresh breezes, bowery lawns, and innocent floods,
> Ripe fruits, and lonely couch, contentment gave.

But with the advent of sexual longing this emotional self-sufficiency breaks down. Endymion's simple delights give way to troubled dreams, his boyish ambitions are forgotten in "ardent listlessness." Significantly, he begins his ascent toward love by plunging into the depths of the earth and exploring its "silent mysteries" alone and in darkness. The meaning of his new need becomes clearer to him as he observes other lovers and learns to give of himself in friendship. But his rapturous dreams of an ideal love are followed by desolate awakenings, and often he longs to return to "the old garden-ground of boyish days." His first actual experience of love with the Indian maid seems a betrayal of his dreams; thus he can love her with only "half [his] soul," and discovers in this conflict his painful lack of "identity." When at last he gives up the dream for the reality and acknowledges the fact of human incompleteness, he finds the "self-destroying" completion through another that lies beyond it. So by loving first in guilt and confusion, then with greater understanding and self-acceptance, he is at last "spiritualized" and wins his goddess as the legend promised.

Keats's search for a truth underlying "the bare circumstance" of his legend is the real significance of *Endymion*. He was the first English poet to sense the possibility of a human meaning implicit in the myths themselves, rather than to fit them into a preconceived allegorical pattern, as in general the Elizabethans did, or merely to use them for decorative effect, like the eighteenth-century poets. His revolutionary attempt—if not his actual achievement—was, as Jeffrey implied, to suggest that the Greek myths were as relevant to our inner experience as the Christian myth was to Milton in an age when the pagan gods had lost their hold on men's imaginations. *Endymion* is a "Song of Innocence and Experience" transposed into the mythic mode. Through Endymion's adventures Keats attempted to state, however gropingly, his belief in the necessity of growth, the value of the progression into experience, the impossibility of regression into innocence, the goal of a more complex harmony of being. The originality of his attempt becomes clear if *Endymion* is viewed against the literary conventions of his time. In romantic fiction, it has been pointed out, the polarities of sexual experience—lawful and lustful, tender and sensual, familial and alien—were usually represented by two heroines, a fair and a dark lady; and the hero, when forced to choose between them, invariably renounced his dark and passionate mistress for his innocent fair-haired love. Keats from the beginning blends these opposites: the bright-haired goddess appears to Endymion by night, the dark maiden by day; and in the end, by ambiguously wedding himself "to things of light," Endymion chooses both women, as one is transformed into the other. In bringing the two parts of his own nature together, he becomes "whole in love" and finds the object of his love has become whole for him.

Still the conflict between Keats's first and final intentions remains embedded within *Endymion,* and he apparently soon became aware of this. The doubts he expressed in September grew deeper. The following January, in the midst of revising the poem, he described it ironically to Haydon as "deep and sentimental"; in February he told Taylor, "I am anxious to get Endymion printed that I may forget it and proceed." By April this weariness had turned into profound dissatisfaction. As he admitted with fanatical candour in the preface he wrote at this time, "There is not a fiercer hell than the failure in a great object." The chief fault of the poem, he realized, was the inexperience of life underlying the original conception. "The imagination of a boy is healthy," he wrote, "and the mature imagination of a man is healthy; but there is a space of life between, in which the soul is in a ferment, the character undecided, the way of life uncertain, the ambition thick-sighted"—and from this sprang the "mawkishness" which he castigated in what is surely the most extraordinary preface any author has written to any poem.

Yet for all its obvious faults of immaturity, *Endymion* is a uniquely interesting work, a Lucretian hymn to the vital force that creates beauty and heroism and love along with life itself, a young man's poem about a central experience of young manhood. Inevitably, and from the very time it was published, it has been compared to Shakespeare's *Venus and Adonis. Endymion* lacks the verbal control and dramatic power of the earlier work; but Shakespeare was twenty-eight when he wrote his first long poem, Keats was twenty-one. He was handicapped not only by his youth but by the sentimental tradition of his time, which left him no acceptable idiom for dealing forthrightly, as Shakespeare could, with physical love, at the same time that it led him to set a much more complex valuation on it. For better, for worse, *Endymion* is a work of romantic art.

And the final value of the poem is a peculiarly romantic one—its value to the poet himself. *Endymion* represents almost half of the poetry Keats published in his lifetime, and occupied him through nearly one-fourth of his poetic career; writing it was a major factor in his creative development. Keats himself was the first to value the poem in this fashion, and this was all the value he eventually allowed it. "It is as good as I had power to make it —by myself," he wrote Hessey a year later. "Had I been nervous about its being a perfect piece, & with that view asked advice, & trembled over every page, it would not have been written." In the end, he saw, his having written it mattered more than what he had written, and for a significant reason: "That which is creative must create itself.—In Endymion," he added, "I leaped headlong into the Sea, and thereby have become better acquainted with the Soundings, the quicksands, & the rocks, than if I had stayed upon the green shore, and piped a silly pipe, and took tea & comfortable advice." *Endymion* made Keats a poet, whatever Keats made of *Endymion*. In the very experience of failure he discovered the truth of achievement: "That which is creative must create itself."

Chapter Six

Soundings and Quicksands

K E A T S spent another solitary week in Burford Bridge, putting the final touches on *Endymion,* then returned to town early in December to see George and Tom off for Devonshire and turn his manuscript in to Taylor for approval.[1] There was still much work ahead, recopying his four thousand lines and seeing the book through the press. But for a while it was off his hands, and time lay like a path of gold before him. He was just twenty-two and alone in London; he had completed a long poem which, he still believed, made a confident bid for fame. After months of lonely struggling with *Endymion,* it was pleasant to find himself sought after as the coming young poet. Invitations began flooding in; his cavalier days, as he later called them, had begun.

For the first five or six weeks, it was a rare day that Keats spent at home. In London he was making dozens of new acquaintances in the worlds of literature and art and the theatre. Now (if not before) he caught the eye of William Godwin, the erstwhile leader of London radical intellectual society. There were always old friends in town to pass an evening with, and he now had a standing invitation to Sunday dinner at Haydon's, where he often met Hazlitt. In January he began attending Hazlitt's new course of lectures on "The English Poets," where he usually met the whole circle of his London friends. In Hampstead he dropped in at Wentworth Place almost every day to see Dilke, with whom he began a close reading of *Paradise Lost,* or occasionally to call on Dilke's neighbor Charles Brown, a literary-minded bachelor who occupied the other half of the double house. One Sunday he entertained Severn and Tom's old friend Charles Wells at Well Walk—an occasion for letting off steam. "I pitched upon another bottle of claret—Port," Keats wrote to his brothers. "We were all very witty and full of Rhyme—we played a Concert from 4 o'clock till 10." Claret and high spirits called for music, but the only music they had was what they made themselves. This led to a noisy habit among Keats's friends of making up little bands in which each man imitated a different instrument—Keats usually taking the bassoon. "I said on that day the only good thing I was ever guilty of," he added in his letter. They were talking about the theatre and Henry Stephens's preference for the top gallery— "and I wondered that careful Folks would go there for although it was but a Shilling still you had to pay through the Nose."

Saturday nights he turned up regularly at Jem Rice's now for whist and brag and gin-and-water. Rice, despite chronic poor health, had an irrepressible sense of humour, and Keats livened his letters to George and Tom with some of his bawdy puns. He was picking up some new slang at Rice's too: "They call good Wine a pretty tipple, and call getting a Child knocking out an apple, stopping at a Tavern they call hanging out—Where do you sup? is where do you hang out?" Keats had an ear for lingo of all kinds—the jargon of the boxing ring and the cockpit, the small talk of London drawing rooms, and, later, the short e's of the Devonshire girls—"the prettiest ees in the Language"—and the lilt of the Scots. The slang of his Saturday-night set soon found its way into a song he wrote for Reynolds' amusement called "Sharing Eve's Apple," a deft little piece of *double entendre* addressed to an equivocal young lady and ending with the plea:

> There's a sigh for yes, and a sigh for no,
>   And a sigh for I can't bear it!
> O what can be done, shall we stay or run?
>   O cut the sweet apple and share it!

Undoubtedly there was talk better worth reporting at Horace Smith's, the stockbroker's, where he was invited to dine in the middle of December. This was a change from Smith's rather condescending notice of Keats as Hunt's protégé the winter before. Smith's set were men who had earned a position in the fashionable literary world or cultivated those who had; and Keats evidently held his own with them, for the evening resulted in a series of invitations. Smith himself had made his name as a wit five years

before with a volume of *Rejected Addresses,* parodies of the leading poets of the day so good that Walter Scott, on reading the
burlesque of his own verse, exclaimed he must have written it
himself. In an age which regarded parody as a fine art, the book
earned Smith a thousand pounds and an entrée into the drawing
rooms of countesses.² One topic that must have been discussed
around his table on Keats's visit was the case of William Hone,
the radical journalist, who was being tried that same week for his
Biblical parodies attacking the Ministry. This trial was only the
climax of a year of mounting political and social unrest, which
the Government tried to quell by reviving and extending the
wartime policies of anti-Jacobin repression—suspending habeas
corpus, piling a tax of fourpence on penny newspapers, and prose-
cuting its critics for seditious libel. After a brilliant and witty
self-defence, Hone was found not guilty, and twenty thousand
Londoners cheered him as he emerged from the courtroom. Apparently Keats's elation at his acquittal, and possibly the example
of Smith himself, moved him to write a parody of his own mocking
the Tories—that cryptic sonnet called "Nebuchadnezzar's Dream,"
which echoes some political criticism he had managed to slip into
*Endymion.*³ Yet his evening with Smith's friends left him bored—
or so he told his brothers. For all their brilliance, "they only served
to convince me, how superior humour is to wit in respect to enjoyment," he wrote, echoing a favorite distinction of Hazlitt's.
They "say things which make one start, without making one feel."
They were all alike; they even had the same style in handling a
decanter. "They talked of Kean & his low company—Would I
were with that company instead of yours said I to myself!"

This remark shows which way his attention was turning. The
week he dined at Smith's he also made his debut as a dramatic
critic for *The Champion,* replacing Reynolds, who was going off
for a Christmas visit with the Drewes. This could not have come
at a better time, for on December 15 Edmund Kean returned in
triumph to Drury Lane after a severe illness. That night Keats
saw him play his greatest role, Shakespeare's Richard III, in top
form, and another deep-dyed villain from Massinger several nights
later. His first review brimmed over with his long-standing admiration of Kean's interpretation of Shakespeare. Kean's greatness
was almost an anachronism in these shabby days of 1817—"Habeas
Corpus'd as we are out of all wonder, curiosity, and fear," Keats

wrote, slashing irrelevantly at the Government; Kean "is a relict of Romance." This tribute suggests the curious temperamental affinity between the two men which Cowden Clarke had noticed in Keats's schoolboy bravado, and which was to grow on Keats himself as the years went by. Kean, like Keats, was very short, but by sheer intensity managed to convey an effect of heroism on a grand scale; as Keats said, "he always seems just arrived from the camp of Charlemagne." What struck Keats most was the gusto or vital force of Kean's art by which he conveyed a character's whole past and future in the present moment. "When he says in Othello 'Put up your bright swords, for the dew will rust them,'" Keats exclaimed, "we feel that his throat had commanded where swords were thick as reeds." [4]

His assignments the following week were very different—a review of a fifth-rate new tragedy, *Retribution,* a fair sample of the wretched melodrama being turned out by the playwrights of his time; and a notice of the inevitable Christmas pantomime, which Keats turned into a parody of some well-known dramatic critics of the day. Standing in the wings at Covent Garden and having some "curious chat" with one of the managers, Keats got his first real smell of greasepaint. Not long afterward Tom's friend Charles Wells took him to one of the small private playhouses that mushroomed in the dank neighbourhood of Covent Garden and smuggled him behind the scenes. Here Keats revelled in the unconscious comedy of the performance as seen from backstage. The musicians had to play the overture three times over and more before the curtain went up. One of the actors was routed by a gibe from the gallery, and another, who stood beside them sweating with anxiety, never got on stage at all when the evening dragged on too long for the third piece in the bill to be played. After being sworn at by grimy stagehands Keats managed to squeeze his way into the green-room with Wells, where they chatted with "a little painted Trollop" dressed in the part of a Quaker and got caught in a quarrel among the actors.

It was a great spectacle, as Keats described it to his brothers. The theatre was in his blood—the lively, lusty, noisy, showy theatre world of the Regency—and was stirring up a new ambition in him. He would write plays. Perhaps in time he could bring the English stage to life again and give Kean some better parts to play than the miserable stuff now provided him. He knew this would be the work of years, but he decided at once to try his hand. So he began rereading Shakespeare with a new eye for the details of dramatic construction—stage directions, characterization, "bye-writing"—and sketched out a satirical verse-drama called "The Castle Builder" and some lyrics for an opera. Nothing came of these two projects, but the ambition took root and grew; and the ambition itself was significant. It is as though in finishing *Endymion* Keats had begun to be released from the preoccupation of proving himself a poet. Now he could turn his gaze outward to the world of other characters, and start to write the more objective and Shakespearean poetry he had glimpsed while reading Shakespeare at Burford Bridge in November.

The Christmas season brought the usual round of parties and visits. Fanny was in town, on vacation from boarding-school, and Keats went to see her as often as he could. Mrs. Abbey, a stupid and querulous woman, always cast a gloom over their meetings, and Abbey himself had decided that Keats was a bad influence on his sister and hinted he was not welcome at Pancras Lane. Christmas Day Keats evidently spent, rather uncomfortably, at the Reynoldses'. The friendship between the Keats brothers and the Reynolds sisters was beginning to cool. George had done something to put himself in their bad books, and Jane Reynolds, her tongue growing a little sharper as she moved, still unmarried, from twenty-five to twenty-six, was beginning to make Keats uneasy in the part of the younger brother which he had chosen to play. But Keats enjoyed himself thoroughly at several dances during the holidays. One especially, at some old friends', the Redhalls', he described in detail in a letter to Devon. Old Mr. Redhall—an innocent well-powdered little man with a lisp, a single topic of conversation, and two outsized nieces—was not used to giving parties and had no idea of how much wine would be consumed. Halfway through the evening his guests discovered he had set out eight dozen bottles on the kitchen stairs, and things thereafter got rather out of hand. They became still livelier when the ladies retired after supper. "On proceeding to the Pot in the Cupboard," Keats reported, "it soon became full on which the Court door was opened Frank Floodgate bawls out, Hoollo! here's an opposition pot—Ay, says Rice in one you have a Yard for your pot, and in the other a pot for your Yard." Keats danced little that evening, perhaps finding himself at a disadvantage with the two large nieces; instead he drank deep and spent most of his time cutting for half-guineas, ending up one to the good. "Rice said he cared less about the hour than any one," he reported to Tom and George, "and the proof is his dancing—he cares not for time, dancing as if he was deaf. Here a happy twelveth days to you," he concluded, "and may we pass the next together."

This greeting, so gaily confident—was Keats whistling to keep their courage up? For Tom was not mending in Devon as he should. New symptoms were appearing—palpitations and spitting of blood. This news must have struck Keats with a chill of foreboding: there could be no doubt now that Tom had consumption. He immediately conferred with Sawrey, the London surgeon he had consulted in October; but Sawrey merely asked that Tom send him a full report of his progress. It is hard to tell whether Keats was reassured by the surgeon's unconcern or was putting up a show of confidence for his brothers' sake. Tom's condition was not yet critical, and in any case there was little to do but keep him in Devon till summer, build up his strength and his spirits, and hope for the best. Meanwhile Keats had his own life to live —a life which he now tried to share with Tom as much as possible through his letters.

One piece of news he did not send. Taylor had evidently read *Endymion* and returned the manuscript to him before the end of December with carefully qualified praise. Though he probably did not tell Keats as much, he was disappointed in the poem as a whole, despite many strikingly beautiful passages; he was puzzled by the ending and downright alarmed by the more passionate episodes.[5] Evidently he spoke firmly to Keats about the need of not offending the ladies, and indicated some lines, especially in the second book, where straightforward references to breasts, legs, "milky toes," "blending pleasurable," and other delights could be toned down. Keats, momentarily taken aback, agreed; he told Taylor he was sorry "that any one should have to overcome Prejudices" in reading his verses. Nevertheless he was irked, as may be gathered from his later sarcastic references to "meretricious romance verse" written to please ladies rather than men; and some of Taylor's suggestions about rewording certain passages he flatly refused to accept.[6] But these disagreements were nothing compared to the troubles which he heard Shelley was now having with his publishers over his long poem. After *Laon and Cythna* had appeared early in December, the Olliers suddenly became alarmed over its atheistic and incestuous aspects. They recalled all the copies they could and made Shelley delete some offending passages and completely change the relationship of the hero and heroine. The revised poem finally appeared late in January as *The Revolt of Islam*. "Poor Shelley I think he has his Quota of good qualities, in sooth la!!" Keats remarked in reporting the blow-up to his brothers, but it may have sobered him into taking at least some of Taylor's advice. So he began recopying *Endymion* on the fifth of January, revising as he went along.

But the news which Keats should have taken the greatest pleasure in sharing with Tom and George was his long-anticipated meeting with Wordsworth, who was in town on one of his rare visits that winter. On December 28 Haydon invited Keats, along with Charles Lamb and Thomas Monkhouse, a relative of Wordsworth, to a small dinner in the poet's honour. Keats found himself introduced to a tall parsonish gentleman near fifty, with eyes like two smouldering coals, a deep rough voice, and the bearing of an Old Testament prophet. They dined in Haydon's studio with the canvas of "Christ's Entry" looming up behind them in the firelight. Wordsworth was at his most oracular, Lamb at his most roguish. The talk began with a debate on Homer, Shakespeare, Vergil, and Milton; but with Lamb getting tipsy, as he usually did, it soon descended from this level. Lamb assailed Wordsworth for condemning Voltaire in *The Excursion;* then turned on Haydon for putting Newton into his picture. Keats joined Lamb in attacking Newton, whom he accused of destroying the poetry of the rainbow by reducing it to a prism. Lamb seized on this as the occasion for another toast, and they drank to "the confusion of mathematics." Haydon, delighted with his own party, thought it was like nothing so much as a scene from Shakespeare, with each man freely expressing his own nature.

After dinner they moved into the sitting room, and other friends began dropping in—John Landseer, the painter; Joseph Ritchie, a young surgeon and African explorer; and John Kingston, a minor dignitary with intellectual pretensions whom Keats had met at Horace Smith's. At Kingston's entrance the evening took a new tack. As Haydon described it, "Into this company a little heated with wine, a Comptroller of the Stamp Office walked frilled, dressed, and official, with a due awe of the powers above him, and a due contempt for those beneath." In Kingston's view, all of the company fell into the latter category except Wordsworth—whose position was ambiguous. Wordsworth held a sinecure in the Stamp Office; as a mere Collector he stood below a Comptroller. Kingston introduced himself in his official capacity, which, according to Haydon, had "a visible effect" on Wordsworth. Then the Comptroller began plying the Collector with observations: "Pray, Sir, don't you think Newton a great genius?" "Don't you think, Sir, that Milton was a very great genius?" Lamb, who had been dozing off by the fire, found this too idiotic to get by. He made Kingston repeat his questions, then seized a candle and staggered across the room on his spindly legs to examine the Comptroller's phrenology and see "Wha-a-at-sort-fello-he-waas." Kingston laughed uncomfortably while Wordsworth tried to smooth things over and Keats and Ritchie struggled to keep a straight face. Finally Haydon had to take Lamb into his studio to sober up, where every now and then he could be heard roaring nonsense rhymes as the Comptroller continued making observations. Keats took refuge in drink, astonishing Kingston at supper, so he told his brothers, by "keeping my two glasses at work in a knowing way." With Ritchie he immediately became friends. Ritchie had already read and admired Keats's poems, and Keats listened with interest to his plans for exploring the Sahara. When they parted, Keats promised to send him a copy of *Endymion* to take and fling into the middle of the desert.

Three days later Keats met Wordsworth walking on Hampstead Heath and was invited to call on him in town. Flattered by the kindness, Keats presented himself on the indicated day, but was kept waiting an uncomfortable while. At last Wordsworth appeared in full dress, knee breeches, silk stockings, and stiff collar, in a hurry to be off. "The thing, Kingston," had invited him to dinner, and Wordsworth had evidently forgotten his young caller. Keats swallowed his anger and accepted Wordsworth's invitation to dine two days later, and this meeting was followed by several others during January. Yet in his letters to his brothers and Bailey, who must have been eager to hear of them, Keats was strangely silent about these occasions. Writing to Haydon on January 10, he affirmed his belief that *The Excursion* was the finest poem of the age; but of Wordsworth himself he was having a bitter revelation.

The great poet of the revolutionary vision was turning into a dog-matic reactionary, driven by repressed hatred of what he had loved before. At home in Westmoreland he could play the role of prophet unchallenged; in London it was a different matter. One afternoon in January, while Wordsworth was dealing out critical judgments in his usual pose, with left hand thrust in his waistcoat, Keats started to make a remark of his own. To his astonishment, Mrs. Wordsworth put her hand on his arm and said, "Mr. Wordsworth is never interrupted." Keats may have remembered this snub when he wrote to Haydon two months later, "He cannot expect his fireside Divan to be infallible he cannot expect but that every Man of worth is as proud as himself." But he may have been re-calling other incidents of the winter. One evening at Lamb's, Coleridge had expressed his admiration of Wordsworth's poetry by reciting it at length; Wordsworth responded by quoting not Coleridge's poetry but more of his own. Another time, hearing that Scott was about to publish his novel *Rob Roy,* Wordsworth read aloud his own ballad of the same name and remarked, "I do not know what more Mr. Scott can have to say on the subject." Luckily Keats could not have known that the copy of his *Poems* which he gave Wordsworth this winter inscribed "With the Author's sin-cerest Reverence," stood uncut and unread thereafter on Words-worth's shelves.[7]

By mid-January Keats had to confess he had been "racketing too much." He had written almost nothing for a month and had not yet finished revising the first book of *Endymion.* All at once he was tired of dining out, even almost of good talk. Several feuds had broken out in his set—Hunt and Taylor disagreeing about the profits of *Rimini,* Haydon and Reynolds falling out over an un-answered invitation, Hunt and Haydon bickering over some bor-rowed silver which Mrs. Hunt had failed to return. "Uproar's your only musick," Keats commented ruefully to his brothers. He felt it was somehow his responsibility to bring his friends together again, but this was perplexing, as he saw, when the point of dispute often mattered much less than the disposition to quarrel. At the same time, perhaps without quite realizing it, he was developing a vivid sense of the human comedy with its many-sided clash of differing natures, which he now began watching with the same detached pleasure as he would a play; and this too made intervention difficult.

"The commonest Man shows a grace in his quarrel," he later noted. Two very different outlooks were balancing in his mind—that of the sober moralist and that of the budding dramatist, who, as he later wrote, takes as much delight in Iago as in Imogen.[8] By now he clearly saw the egotism inseparable from the creative temperament such as Haydon's; yet he continued to admire Haydon even while he was coming to value more highly than ever the "probity & disinterestedness" he found in Bailey. Haydon's interest in the young painter Cripps had finally collapsed, though Keats had not yet given up trying to raise the money for his expenses. Haydon had also offered to sketch a head of Keats as frontispiece for *Endymion*, then let the weeks slip by and forgot his promise—just as he had forgotten a similar one to Hunt the year before, and another promise to Bailey to make him copies of his life masks of Keats and Wordsworth.

As for Hunt, the clash of their natures was still something he could not be quite objective about. When, around January 20, Taylor finally approved the revised first book of *Endymion*, Keats took it round to Hunt's before sending it off to the printer. To his surprise, both Hunt and Shelley were a good deal less than enthusiastic. They seemed all too ready to catch him up on small slips, and Hunt, after skimming the book through, objected especially to the "high-flown" conversations between Endymion and his sister. Keats was angry, even though he knew Hunt was wrong: the story of a mortal loved by a goddess could not be written in the style of *Rimini*. At the same time he realized that Hunt and Shelley were hurt, and perhaps justly, because he had not shown them any of the poem before—though they could hardly be expected to understand why he had found this necessary. Keats tried to make amends by staying on that evening and writing an impromptu ode on a lock of Milton's hair which Hunt had just acquired. But this effort merely betrayed his anxiety. For all his "burning and strife," he wrote, his poetry was still bound by "childish fashion"; not for many years, till he had grown "high-rife With Old Philosophy" like Milton himself, would he be able to pay Milton a tribute worthy of his greatness.

This admission reveals Keats's restlessness as well. Already he was impatient to turn his full attention to his next poem, the Miltonic epic on the fall of Hyperion which had occurred to him during his visit with Bailey, and for which he was beginning to prepare himself in his close study of *Paradise Lost.* It also appears that Hunt's criticism of *Endymion* caused him a sudden twinge of dissatisfaction with it. Two days later, writing to Haydon, Keats half-mockingly contrasted the "deep and sentimental cast" of *Endymion* with the "more naked and grecian Manner" he hoped to achieve in *Hyperion.* And shortly afterward he began tinkering with the text of *Endymion,* even though it was already being set up in print. From the first six hundred lines he finally cut about forty—thereby involving Taylor in some extensive charges for resetting. It is significant that all these cuts were aimed at removing as much of the Hunt-like "sentimental cast" of the poem as Keats could at this late stage.[9] Clearly the thought of adverse criticism was beginning to trouble him. "But whose afraid?" he exclaimed. "Ay! Tom! demme if I am."

But a still more sobering experience was in store for him. At a gathering at Haydon's studio one afternoon late in January the painter asked him to recite some lines from *Endymion* for Wordsworth. Keats replied with the "Hymn to Pan"—of all the poetry he had written, the most Wordsworthian in feeling—and repeated it in his characteristic half-chant, walking up and down the room. At the end there was an expectant silence; then the older poet dryly remarked, "A very pretty piece of paganism." Keats was stunned; the party soon broke up.[10] As Haydon savagely commented, "Wordsworth's puling Christian feelings were annoyed"; he rightly blamed Wordsworth both for the lack of tact in his remark and for his literal-mindedness in taking the hymn as "paganism." Keats himself never mentioned the episode in his letters. He suddenly stopped seeing Wordsworth in the last week of January, however, and a month later he told his brothers that he was "sorry that Wordsworth has left a bad impression where-ever he visited in Town—by his egotism, Vanity and bigotry." "Yet," he immediately added, "he is a great Poet if not a Philosopher." The truth was that the Christian philosopher in Wordsworth was slowly strangling the poet—the man who fifteen years before had written in his concern for the England of his day,

> Great God! I'd rather be
> A pagan suckled in a creed outworn;
> So might I, standing on this pleasant lea,

Have glimpses that would make me less forlorn;
Have sight of Proteus rising from the sea;
Or hear old Triton blow his wreathed horn.

Keats, of course, could know nothing of the bitter spiritual struggle that had brought Wordsworth to this point; he did know by a kind of instinct, however, what his own life as a poet required. His disillusionment with Wordsworth was a staggering blow to his conception of poetry itself, and to recover from it he was driven back for the time being on his own deepest resources of poetic vitality.

⇛⇚

On January 22, before turning back to *Endymion* to revise the second book, he decided to read *King Lear* again; and on opening his Folio he was overcome as never before by the disparity between his own achievement and Shakespeare's tragic stature—the "Cliff of Poesy" which towered as high above him as it had nine months before. It was a moment to take his bearings and make a new start. "The thing appeared to demand the prologue of a Sonnet," he told his brothers—the first serious sonnet he had written since the day before starting *Endymion*. Looking back and then forward, he took his leave of "golden tongued Romance, with serene lute" to submit himself to the purgatorial sufferings of Lear:

once again, the fierce dispute
Betwixt damnation and impassion'd clay
Must I burn through; once more humbly assay
The bitter-sweet of this Shakespearian fruit. . . .

As he looked ahead to *Hyperion,* he wondered whether he was yet ready to meet this test of tragic and heroic power; and once again he called on Shakespeare to be his "Presider":

When through the old oak Forest I am gone,
Let me not wander in a barren dream,
But, when I am consumed in the fire
Give me new Phœnix wings to fly at my desire.

This sonnet broke the spell. "I think a little change has taken place in my intellect lately," he wrote his brothers shortly afterward, "I cannot bear to be uninterested or unemployed, I, who for so long a time, have been addicted to passiveness." In the next few weeks songs and sonnets came pouring out in exuberant vari-

ety—tributes to Mrs. Reynolds' cat and to the Mermaid Tavern,
a joking attack on a fellow poet and lines in praise of Robin Hood.
He made his first trials of the Shakespearean sonnet—debating
with Reynolds in one whether blue or brown eyes were more beautiful, recalling in two others the mysterious lady "seen for a few
moments at Vauxhall." In the first ("Time's sea hath been five
years at its slow ebb") he testified to the sway she still held over
him:

> Thou dost eclipse
> Every delight with sweet remembering,
> And grief unto my darling joys dost bring.

What had called her back? If the sonnet is more than a mere exercise, it would seem that his sexual disillusionment in the fall had
paradoxically revived his dream of a perfect love. A more sombre
note is struck in his second sonnet. Written only a few days after
rereading *King Lear*, it shows his dedicatory mood heightened by
a new anxiety:

> When I have fears that I may cease to be
>   Before my pen has glean'd my teeming brain,
> Before high-piled books, in charact'ry,
>   Hold like rich garners the full-ripen'd grain;
> When I behold, upon the night's starr'd face,
>   Huge cloudy symbols of a high romance,
> And think that I may never live to trace
>   Their shadows, with the magic hand of chance;
> And when I feel, fair creature of an hour!
>   That I shall never look upon thee more,
> Never have relish in the faery power
>   Of unreflecting love!—then on the shore
> Of the wide world I stand alone, and think
> Till love and fame to nothingness do sink.

Tom's illness, it seems, had revived the half-repressed sense of his
own mortality that had broken through in "Sleep and Poetry."
Once again, but far more urgently, the thought of all that he hoped
to achieve called up the fear that life would not be long enough.

In this mood he began looking at *Endymion* again more crit-
ically. Wordsworth's brusque dismissal of the "Hymn to Pan"
as merely "pretty" seems to have jarred him into rethinking the
poem's meaning as a whole. One of the passages in the first book
which he had let Taylor emasculate was a statement of his faith
in the value of love—that "blending pleasurable" which is the

most "self-destroying" of all feelings. Now he saw how necessary these lines were as a preface to his account of Endymion's gradual ascent toward perfect love. Accordingly he rewrote the passage and asked Taylor to have it reinserted:

> Wherein lies happiness? In that which becks
> Our ready minds to fellowship divine,
> A fellowship with essence; till we shine,
> Full alchemiz'd, and free of space. . . .[11]

Apparently his conversations with Bailey in the fall had deepened his sense of what he had tried to express the preceding spring, for the "fellowship with essence" which he now described as the eventual result and justification of sexual love is clearly related to the idea of "essential beauty" discovered through "taking part in the existence" of other identities which he had discussed with Bailey in November. Only the week before he had written his brothers that he believed "a very gradual ripening of the intellectual powers" is the best. It is a striking example of such ripening that the final meaning of his myth became clear to him only several months after he had finished his poem.

Keats's experience with Wordsworth seems also to have led him into new speculations on poetry in general. For a few weeks, indeed, his resentment of his remark on the "Hymn to Pan" led him to doubt Wordsworth's greatness as a poet, especially when measured against Shakespeare's. As he asked Reynolds early in February, "For the sake of a few fine imaginative or domestic * passages, are we to be bullied into a certain Philosophy engendered in the whims of an Egotist—We hate poetry that has a palpable design upon us—and if we do not agree, seems to put its hand in its breeches pocket." There are echoes here of a comment on Wordsworth in one of Hazlitt's lectures which Keats had heard a few days earlier, but the criticism of what he later called "the wordsworthian or egotistical sublime" reaches farther back into Keats's own thought. Six weeks before, while walking into town with his Hampstead neighbour Dilke to see the Christmas pantomime, he had listened to Dilke hold forth in his dogmatic fashion on various subjects. "Several things dovetailed in my mind," Keats wrote his brothers, "& at once it struck me, what quality

---

* Perhaps this word is miscopied from Keats's own term "dramatic," which describes Wordsworth's early poetry far better than "domestic."

went to form a Man of Achievement especially in Literature & which Shakespeare posessed so enormously—I mean *Negative Capability,* that is when man is capable of being in uncertainties, Mysteries, doubts, without any irritable reaching after fact & reason." This ability to "remain content with half knowledge"— what today is called "tolerance for ambiguity"—was, as Keats saw it, essential to the poet insofar as he above all men explores the frontiers of human experience and struggles with its endless diversity and contradictions in an effort to extend the limits of human awareness. The lesser poet, such as Coleridge, "would let go by a fine isolated verisimilitude caught from the Penetralium of mystery" because he insists on imposing his own limited interpretation on reality.

But this capacity for suspending judgment in order to report faithfully on experience also involves the "capability of submission," the capacity for "annulling self" and thereby entering into other identities which Keats had previously described to Bailey. As Keats later realized, the ability to "annul self" depended on a very firm sense of self: Dilke, for instance, he came to see was "a Man who cannot feel he has a personal identity unless he has made up his Mind about every thing." [12] At this stage, however, Keats's belief in negative capability seems to have sprung partly at least from his awareness of his own mental growth. His bewildering shifts of allegiance from one poetic influence or intellectual position to another, sometimes in the space of a few weeks, were not contradictions so much as necessary steps in his ever more inclusive development. Still young, still experimenting, he had not yet reached the point where the mind pauses, then begins to exclude, concentrate, harden. He must then have been deeply moved to hear Hazlitt in his January 27 lecture characterize Shakespeare in the very terms which he himself had already set up as his own guidelines in poetry. "He was nothing in himself," Hazlitt remarked; "but he was all that others were, or that they could become." This, of course, was a definition of Shakespeare's dramatic genius; and it is significant that three days later Keats confided to Taylor his new ambition to make his "chief Attempt in the Drama."

For several weeks now he was glad to be mostly alone in Hampstead, revising *Endymion,* studying Milton, and being lazy when he liked. London was full of new people to meet: Peacock, the novelist; Benjamin West, the painter; Peter Moore, a manager of

Drury Lane; Peter Patmore, the journalist; Peter Pindar, the political satirist; Mrs. Opie, a fashionable authoress; and Caroline Scott
"con occhi neri," the beautiful Italian wife of the publisher of *The
Champion* and an especial admirer of Keats's poetry. Crabb Robinson, the friend of Coleridge, a diarist famous for the famous men he
became acquainted with, came out to Hampstead to call. Even
Keats's former publisher was making amends. As he dryly remarked
to George and Tom, honours were rushing thick upon him: "What
think you, am I to be crowned in the Capitol, am I to be made
a Mandarin—No! I am to be invited to a party at Ollier's to keep
Shakespeares birthday Shakespeare would stare to see me there."
But he was learning how to refuse invitations. All through February
his only regular trips to town were to hear Hazlitt lecture each
Tuesday evening.

    Hazlitt by now had become, and was to remain, the chief living
intellectual influence on Keats. Hunt's and then Wordsworth's
influence had waned; his discipleship to Haydon had sobered into
friendly respect; from now on his only masters in poetry were "the
mighty dead." With Hazlitt, Keats never became intimate, despite
the affinity of their outlooks; but again and again his critical remarks provided the spark that set off Keats's own most searching
speculations on poetry. Intimacy in any case was not one of Hazlitt's
talents. A shy, unkempt, blunt-spoken man, "brow-hanging, shoe-
contemplative, strange," as Coleridge described him,[13] he carried
with him a heavy load of unhappiness—poverty, ill success, an uncongenial marriage, alienation from his early friends, and the
failure of his political ideals. Hazlitt was one of the few men of his
generation in England to remain outspokenly loyal to the principles of the French Revolution through the wars with Napoleon
and the years after Waterloo. This uncompromising liberalism was
one thing that drew Keats to him; another was his enthusiasm for
the acting of Kean. Hazlitt's first appearance as dramatic critic had
coincided with Kean's debut at Drury Lane in 1814; brilliance
had called forth brilliance, and Hazlitt made his own name as
well as Kean's with reviews of his Shylock and Iago and Hamlet.
Along with his hatred of injustice and cant, Hazlitt had a great
capacity for enjoyment: "gusto," one of his favourite words, he
made a critical term. He admired a great variety of things, from
the painting of Titian to the racquets-playing of the famous John
Cavanagh. Charles Lamb found his conversation the best in Lon-

don, and Reynolds described his *Characters of Shakespeare's Plays*
as the only criticism of Shakespeare that was worthy of him. This
book, which Keats began reading in the spring of 1817, did much
to deepen his understanding of Shakespeare and led him at the
beginning of 1818 to class Hazlitt's criticism with Wordsworth's
Excursion and Haydon's painting as the "three things to rejoice
at in this Age."

The audience at the lectures on the English poets was a mixed
lot—Quakers, Dissenters, and mind-improvers, along with Keats's
set and a sprinkling of Hazlitt's enemies. They gave him an assortment of prejudices to set on edge with his inimitable skill. As a
result the lectures were punctuated by murmurs and laughter, irrelevant applause, and shouts of disapproval. Crabb Robinson, one
of Hazlitt's detractors, noted in this diary that he quoted "unseemly verses" (John Gay's) to "a congregation of saints" and "even
eulogized the modern infidel, so indiscreet and reckless is the
man!" [14] The modern infidel was, of course, Voltaire; the eulogy
set Keats to rereading him a few days later. When Hazlitt came
around to criticizing Wordsworth, Robinson felt called upon to
hiss. Hazlitt looked calmly in the direction of the hissing, then
turned back his page and repeated the entire passage. Despite their
contentiousness, the lectures contained some "fine discriminating
criticism," which Keats was to mull over for months afterward.[15]
Only one thing disappointed him—the discussion of Chatterton.
To Hazlitt he was only "the marvellous boy" of uncertain promise,
"the sleepless soul who perished in his pride" when the poems
which he tried to pass off as the work of a fifteenth-century monk
were found to have been written by himself. Keats apparently
protested afterward, and the next week Hazlitt took time to explain his opinion at some length because it had "given dissatisfaction to some persons with whom I would willingly agree on all
such matters."

Hazlitt's taking a cue from Keats suggests that their respect was
at least partly mutual. A cue which Keats took from one of the
earlier lectures was to have more significant results. On February
3, in commenting on Dryden's translations of Boccaccio, Hazlitt
had remarked that a rendering of some of his other tales "could
not fail to succeed in the present day." Keats at once dug up an
old prose translation of *The Decameron,* and in the first tale which
Hazlitt had suggested he found what he was looking for. The tragic

story of Isabella and her lover murdered by her own brothers—
here was a subject full of dramatic possibilities, and one which he
could easily turn into another romance while preparing himself
for the much more ambitious *Hyperion*. He roughed out some
stanzas, then mentioned the idea to Reynolds, who was so enthusiastic that they decided to work on a volume of tales from
Boccaccio together.

Keats's friendship with Reynolds was now at its height. In his
new-won independence of Hunt and Haydon, the friendly give-and-
take of rivalry with a man of his own age was just what Keats
needed. In November he promised to send Reynolds a new poem
with every letter he wrote, and from this time on his letters to
Reynolds contain his most thoughtful reflections on poets and
poetry. Reynolds himself was riding high these months. In January his theatre reviews for *The Champion* had earned him a
handsome offer—ten guineas per sheet of sixteen pages—from
Constable, the publisher of the *Edinburgh Magazine,* one of the
best of the literary journals. He turned it down in order to become the mainstay of a new weekly, *The Yellow Dwarf,* which
Hazlitt and John Hunt were starting up. He was already at work
on a long verse narrative when Keats suggested the Boccaccio
project, and eventually he completed two of these tales. His creative outburst that winter must have been partly a consequence of
his engagement to Eliza Drewe. But she had exacted a price: he
must give up writing and become established in the law before
they married. Reynolds agreed only halfway: he entered his uncle's
law office in November and relegated his writing to his spare time,
of which he managed still to find a good amount. On February 14,
probably as a valentine to his fiancée, he wrote a semi-wistful sonnet
of "Farewell to the Muses," which he later gave to Keats—only the
first of many farewells. Three years later he was still unmarried and
still promising

> as time increases
> To give up drawling verse for drawing leases.[16]

In mid-February, however—perhaps as a sign of the strain of this
conflict—Reynolds came down with a rheumatic fever which kept
him house-ridden for three months. To cheer him up, Keats started
a letter to his friend one sunny morning a few days after he fell
ill. The first hint of spring was in the air; thrushes and blackbirds
were beginning to sing in the bare-branched trees. He had picked

up his regular reading that morning but soon let his book drop and his mind wander. "When Man has arrived at a certain ripeness in intellect," he observed, "any one grand and spiritual passage serves him as a starting post towards all 'the two-and thirty Pallaces.' How happy is such a 'voyage of conception,' what delicious diligent Indolence!" His thoughts circled around the conflicting impressions of the last few months—all the clashes of character he had witnessed, the arguments about poetry, the efforts to win a dispute; then he took a new tack. "Many have original Minds who do not think it—they are led away by Custom—Now it appears to me that almost any Man may like the Spider spin from his own inwards his own airy Citadel—the points of leaves and twigs on which the Spider begins her work are few and she fills the Air with a beautiful circuiting." This required that each man trust to his own "isolated verisimilitudes" but something more: "Man should not dispute or assert but whisper results to his neighbour, and thus by every germ of Spirit sucking the Sap from mould ethereal every human might become great, and Humanity instead of being a wide heath of Furse and Briars with here and there a remote Oak or Pine, would become a grand democracy of Forest Trees." Was he still thinking of Wordsworth, or of his own disagreement with Hazlitt two days before?

A moment later his mind veered back to the mystery of the creative power which he felt growing stronger within him; the old adage of the bee gathering honey came to his mind, and he turned it upside down. "The flower I doubt not receives a fair guerdon from the Bee—its leaves blush deeper in the next spring—and who shall say between Man and Woman which is the most delighted? Let us not therefore go hurrying about and collecting honey, bee-like * buzzing here and there impatiently from a knowledge of what is to be arrived at," he added, thinking of Reynolds fretting on his sickbed, "but let us open our leaves like a flower and be passive and receptive—sap will be given us for Meat and dew for drink—I was led into these thoughts, my dear Reynolds, by the beauty of the morning operating on a sense of Idleness—I had no Idea but of the Morning and the Thrush said I was right." And here Keats broke into a blank-verse sonnet which, like the thrush's song, turns back on its own cadence as its thought moves forward.

---

* Following M. B. Forman's punctuation (*The Letters of John Keats*, 2nd ed., revised [1935], p. 104).

> O fret not after knowledge—I have none,
>   And yet my song comes native with the warmth.
> O fret not after knowledge—I have none
>   And yet the Evening listens. He who saddens
> At thought of idleness cannot be idle,
> And he's awake who thinks himself asleep.

"Now I am sensible all this is a mere sophistication, however it may neighbour to any truths, to excuse my own indolence," he ended. "It is no matter whether I am right or wrong either one way or another, if there is sufficient to lift a little time from your Shoulders."

This letter deserves comment, for, though Keats apparently wrote it off without forethought, it conveys one of his most characteristic beliefs. His letters at the time he began writing *Endymion* express all the young writer's sensations as he struggles with his work; but now he could stand back from the struggle and speculate on it. Just as he had begun to observe the interplay of temperament and cross-purpose among his friends with the absorbed detachment of the dramatist, he was learning to watch the ebb and flow of his own creative power with the objectivity of the critic. With no preconceptions about how poetry should be written—"it is no matter whether I am right or wrong"—he realized that for himself at least it required long stretches of drifting with the tide. Perhaps he had come to see this more clearly from silently comparing himself with Shelley—Shelley the indefatigable, full of a dozen political and literary projects at a time; Shelley, who seemed able to turn out a poem in twelve cantos at will. Keats was beginning to recognize in himself a rhythm of energy and indolence, of alternation between the masculine imposition of self upon experience and the feminine surrender to it. This indolence could be a delight, as when he gave himself up to the beauty of an early spring morning; at other times it took the form of a paralysing blankness of feeling and thought, as in the autumn before, when he had wondered whether there was something "radically wrong" with his nature. But now he was beginning to accept these swings of mood, as he did his shifts of intellectual position, as not only inevitable but fruitful in the end. A few weeks later he was to develop this idea in one of his most characteristic metaphors, in a sonnet on "The Human Seasons." Recognizing this fact of his nature, he could now wait more patiently for the "very gradual ripening" of intellect which he realized would be necessary for *Hyperion*—a longer period of "sucking the Sap from mould ethereal." A year or two earlier, he had described the writing of poetry in terms of a journey, a battle, a cliff to be scaled, a vast sea to be explored: now he saw it in images of grain ripening, of wine ageing, of the sun rising and setting, of the flower which

> must drink the nature of the soil
> Before it can put forth its blossoming.[17]

As he wrote to Taylor at this time, "If Poetry comes not as naturally as the Leaves to a tree it had better not come at all."

Yet the indolent fit of the morning of February 19, when he wrote to Reynolds, turned to energy by afternoon. Horace Smith had invited him to dinner; Keats wrote, begging off with the excuse that his brothers were expecting him shortly in Devonshire and he had many days' work still to do. He was recopying the third book of *Endymion* while reading the proofs of the first, and he was increasingly anxious to be done with it. He was restless to get on with *Isabella* and to have more time to read for *Hyperion*. In Devon it appeared that George too was restless. A letter from Georgiana Wylie came addressed to him at Well Walk; it struck Keats that he must have told her he was soon returning to town. By the end of the month George arrived. On February 28 he came of age at last—an occasion, no doubt, for a serious interview with Abbey and a visit to the Wylies. The two brothers spent a few days together in Hampstead, probably discussing George's future, still uncertain, and the family finances, more tangled than ever. Then Tom wrote from Teignmouth that he was feeling much better and might come up to London himself. This could not be allowed to happen. Keats immediately packed up a few books and the remains of his manuscript and boarded the Exeter coach.

Luckily, however, he found time the evening before he left to hear Hazlitt's last lecture—one on "The Living Poets," to which he must have looked forward eagerly. Hazlitt began with a sober reminder that current popularity is no true test of a poet's worth, and that "those minds which are the most entitled to expect it can best put up with the postponement of their claims to lasting fame." After briefly dismissing some lady poets and fashionable rhymesters, he went on to a critique of Wordsworth, Southey, and Coleridge—the poets whose acquaintance he had made in the days of their revolutionary ardour and who had since disavowed him, in private and in print, in the ardour of their reaction. Hazlitt balanced some just praise of Wordsworth's and Coleridge's early poetry against a composite portrait of the Lake Poet of 1818: "He hates all greatness and all pretensions to it, whether well or ill-founded. He hates all science and all art; he hates chemistry, he hates conchology; he hates Voltaire; he hates Sir Isaac Newton; he hates wisdom; he hates wit; he hates prose; he hates all poetry but his own; he hates the dialogues in Shakespeare; he hates music, dancing and painting; he hates Raphael, he hates Titian; he hates the Apollo Belvidere; he hates the Venus of Medicis. This is the reason that so few people take an interest in his writings, because he takes an interest in nothing that others do!" This peroration must have brought the house down, and it was still reverberating in Keats's mind in a letter he wrote to Haydon over two weeks later: "It is a great Pity that People should by associating themselves with the finest things, spoil them—Hunt has damned Hampstead and Masks and Sonnets and italian tales— Wordsworth has damned the lakes—Millman has damned the old drama—West has damned—wholesale—Peacock has damned sattire Ollier has damn'd Music—Hazlitt has damned the bigotted and the blue-stockined how durst the Man?! he is your only good damner and if ever I am damn'd—damn me if I shoul'nt like him to damn me." [18] Hazlitt's critical explosion had evidently cleared the air. More plainly than before, Keats now saw where his own business lay. So with this as postscript to the last two months and a half, he brought his cavalier days to a close and turned his eyes in another direction.

➤➤➤◄◄◄

He left London on the night of a gale. Trees were blown down and coaches overturned on the way, and Keats, riding outside as usual, got drenched. This was his first, and prophetic, impression of Devon; his second was a "middle-siz'd Devonshire girl of about 15" waiting at an inn door with "a quartern of brandy." A year and a half later he remembered that "the very thought of her kept me warm a whole stage—and a 16 miler too." This was not enough to keep him from catching cold, however, and he arrived in Teignmouth with a bad sore throat.[19] Tom seemed to be benefiting from the care of Dr. Turton, a Teignmouth physician to whom he had taken a fancy, but the Devon climate which was supposed to cure him had taken a turn for the worse. It rained for a week after Keats arrived, let up for a day or two, then started again; and it rained at this rate for most of March and April. Haydon, a Devonshire man, and Reynolds, in love with a Devonshire girl, had made him eager to see the place; but the weather kept him penned up indoors for almost two weeks. Their lodgings also were less than satisfactory—a small airless apartment facing north on a narrow alley, an unhealthy location for a tubercular patient, and still more so for anyone shut in at close quarters with him. One night they went out to the theatre, and Keats—for what reason he never said—was insulted. Evidently they had ladies with them, for Keats kept his temper and did not fight, but he was angry that he could not get redress afterward. In this mood he went doggedly ahead putting the final touches on *Endymion* and amused himself in his letters to London by blasting Devon for its "urinal qualifications" and its inhabitants as a race of "dwindled englishmen."

Teignmouth itself offered as few diversions as any seaside resort in a cold and rainy spring—a deserted promenade, an empty bandstand, sailboats anchored under tarpaulins. There were a theatre, where Keats met with his insult, and a ballroom, where waltzing was banned. But George and Tom had already made some pleasant acquaintances among the townspeople, especially Mrs. Jeffrey, their landlady, and her three daughters. With the two elder ones, "laughing thoughtless Sarah" and "steady quiet Marianne," George and Tom had struck up a four-sided flirtation. George as usual seized the initiative and carried off the prize—a lock of Sarah's hair, which he took back to London with him. Marianne evidently withstood his charms, but when John arrived, she seems to have fallen in love with him at once. Together they all strolled along the shore and read poetry; and when Keats left Devon in May, Marianne poured out her feelings in some sentimental verses of farewell, which were published along with her other poems years later. Keats was too preoccupied with Tom to reciprocate, and perhaps the fact that she wrote poetry counted against her. Young ladies who asked to be taken seriously put him on his guard. Jane Reynolds sent him a little Tassie seal at this time, showing Leander swimming the Hellespont in a storm—perhaps as a joking reference to the weather; but Keats never used the seal on any of his

letters, though he thanked her politely in a sonnet. Still dissatisfied with himself as a poet, he evidently could not quite yet accept
himself in the cavalier's role. So he kept the Jeffrey sisters at arm's
length with the same brotherly teasing he used toward the Reynolds girls, and went his own way.

He had other things on his mind at this time besides Tom's
health and his own work—the beginning of a disagreement with
Bailey. Keats had come a long way since his visit to Oxford the
previous fall. Closer contact with Hazlitt's incisive mind and the
sombre realization of Tom's illness made him more sceptical than
before of Bailey's easy assumption that all was well with the world.
Bailey had turned an important point in his career that winter;
he had preached and published his first sermon. This was something of an embarrassment to his friends—to Taylor, who brought
it out, for it did not sell, and to Dilke, who reviewed it in *The
Champion* and found it pedantic and high-flown.[20] Evidently
Keats loaned his copy of the sermon to Wordsworth, who did not
return it, and had to borrow another from Dilke a while later.
When he finally came to comment on it, he must have strength-
ened Bailey's doubts about his principles. "You know my ideas
about Religion," he wrote rather awkwardly. "I do not think
myself more in the right than other people and [I think] that
nothing in this world is proveable.[21] I wish I could give you a
Page or two to your liking," he added. "I am sometimes so very
sceptical as to think Poetry itself a mere Jack a lanthern to amuse
whoever may chance to be struck with its brillance." What Bailey
replied to this we do not know, for Keats was not in the habit
of keeping his friends' letters. We do not even know what Keats
said in answer to his reply, in a letter he wrote at the end of April
that has not survived—which is curious, for Bailey carefully preserved his other letters from Keats. A slight constraint appears in
Keats's next letter, in May, which he closed with the enigmatic
remark that at their next meeting they would "discover whether
a little more knowledge has not made us more ignorant."

Just as Keats finished his letter commenting on Bailey's sermon,
Tom began to cough a little blood. Then, to Keats's alarm, he
had a severe haemorrhage a day or two later, which seemed to
undo all the good of the last three months. After a few nerve-
shaking days he was out of danger, thanks to Dr. Turton, and

began to mend slowly. Keats put on a cheerful front before the invalid, like the high fooling he kept up in his letters to his friends; but secretly he was caught in a terrible conflict between anxiety for Tom and the depression that overtook him in close contact with illness, which made him almost angry with himself. A week later, as Tom's health picked up, the weather relented a little, and Keats seized the chance to escape on some long walks. He clambered along the rocky coast, explored the villages on the Teign and sampled their cockles and cream, then struck inland through fields already thick with daisies. The first days of the Devonshire spring swept the gloom from his mind. In a letter spilling over with verse, he told Haydon that he would stay all summer:

> Then who would go
> Into dark soho
> And chatter with dack'd hair'd critics
> When he can stay
> For the new mown hay
> And startle the dappled Prickets?

He soon discovered another of the beauties of Devon—the middle-sized, delicate girls, with their lilting salute, "Well, where be ye going?" So he added to the doggerel verses he sent to Haydon some bantering stanzas of "b———hrel"—"Where be ye going, you Devon maid?"

> I love your Hills and I love your dales
> And I love your flocks a bleating—
> But O on the hether to lie together
> With both our hearts a beating.
>
> I'll put your Basket all safe in a nook
> And your shawl I hang up on this willow
> And we will sigh in the daisy's eye
> And kiss on a grass green pillow.

Devon was a good field for sowing wild oats, and this was apparently the only relief Keats found from the constant tension of worry over Tom. For a month or so dairymaids and barmaids, the girls at the bonnet shop across the way, and the wild young things at Dawlish Fair all figure in a season of pulling apron strings and rumpling meadows of fern. But it could not last. Some weeks later he told Reynolds he was "sick of Venery," and it was in a verse-letter to Reynolds at the end of March that he gave a hint of an experience that made all such pleasure seem unreal as a daydream.

He had walked down to the shore one evening and sat on a weed-covered rock. The sea at this hour usually brought him peace; but this time he glimpsed it in something he had never seen before:

> 'Twas a quiet Eve;
> The rocks were silent—the wide sea did weave
> An untumultuous fringe of silver foam
> Along the flat brown sand. I was at home,
> And should have been most happy—but I saw
> Too far into the sea; where every maw
> The greater on the less feeds evermore:—
> But I saw too distinct into the core
> Of an eternal fierce destruction. . . .

An abyss suddenly opened up before him. Now at last, it appears, he realized that Tom would not recover; for all his exquisite love of life, nothing could save him in the end. The quiet, unconcerned beauty of nature, which had always been Keats's refuge against unhappiness, now seemed to hold no assurance of any triumph over suffering, or even of any meaning in pain and death:

> Things cannot to the will
> Be settled, but they tease us out of thought.
> Or is it that Imagination brought
> Beyond its proper bound, yet still confined,—
> Lost in a sort of Purgatory blind,
> Cannot refer to any standard law
> Of either earth or heaven?

Neither Bailey's theological explanation of evil nor Hunt's sentimental insistence that evil was unreal, nor even the faith he had absorbed from Wordsworth of some benevolent Power presiding over nature, was proof against this vision of "eternal fierce destruction." The shark and the hawk at prey, even the robin "ravening a worm" in mindless savagery, were as real as the sea and the stars that peaceful evening. Nature itself offered no clue to the riddle of existence: it meant only what the individual himself glimpsed in it. For a moment the whole world reeled in his imagination. Then with an effort Keats wrenched his gaze away from the nothingness he had stared into, turned back to thoughts of Reynolds' recovery and the new poem he had begun writing.

Yet try as he might to forget it, he could not quite blot this glimpse of "Purgatory blind" from his memory.

Keats picked up *Isabella* at this time, it appears, in a deliberate effort to escape from these "detested moods" which he momentarily confided to Reynolds. It was to be, like *Endymion,* a "Romance"—"a fine thing notwithstanding the circulating Libraries," as Keats still felt: a tale combining supernatural plot and essential human emotion, a pair of star-crossed lovers and a *Hamlet*-like ghost who recounts his own murder. Much of Keats's immature sentimentality lingers on in the opening picture of the young lovers; yet as the poem moves ahead, it begins to show a striking new sense of the dramatic at work. Already Keats was learning to submerge himself in the character and feelings of his hero and heroine and to tell his story in flashes of visualized action—the jealous brothers biting their lips in silence, the murderers dipping their swords in the stream, Isabella tossing back her hair as she digs in Lorenzo's grave. Boccaccio set him a good example of concise, straightforward narrative; but even more significant are Keats's additions, where a new note begins to sound in his poetry. In Boccaccio's tale the brothers murder Lorenzo merely because of his illicit passion for their sister; Keats added an economic motive with the brothers' greedy ambition to marry Isabella to a wealthy noble.

> With her two brothers this fair lady dwelt,
>   Enriched from ancestral merchandize,
> And for them many a weary hand did swelt
>   In torched mines and noisy factories,
> And many once proud-quiver'd loins did melt
>   In blood from stinging whip;—with hollow eyes
> Many all day in dazzling river stood,
> To take the rich-ored driftings of the flood.
>
> For them the Ceylon diver held his breath,
>   And went all naked to the hungry shark;
> For them his ears gush'd blood; for them in death
>   The seal on the cold ice with piteous bark
> Lay full of darts; for them alone did seethe
>   A thousand men in troubles wide and dark:
> Half-ignorant, they turn'd an easy wheel,
> That set sharp racks at work, to pinch and peel.

Bernard Shaw once claimed that these stanzas "contain all the Factory Commission Reports that Marx read, and that Keats did not read because they were not yet written in his time." [22] Extravagant, perhaps; but Keats had been reading *The Examiner* for years, he had a stingy guardian, and, as he once said, "you must allow for imagination." Another contrast with Boccaccio comes out in the conclusion. Boccaccio had tried to mute the horror of his story by describing Lorenzo's body as miraculously uncorrupted when Isabella dug it up and reburied his head in her pot of basil; Keats calmly presented the fact of its physical decay in order to heighten the pathos of Isabella weeping over it in her madness.

Perhaps he was aiming at the quality he had praised in *King Lear* a few months before—that intensity which makes "all disagreeables evaporate, from their being in close relationship with Beauty & Truth." But a closer look at the means by which he achieved his effect reveals something still more striking. A string of images of medicine and disease runs through the poem like a dark vein through marble—a description of Isabella as thin and pale as a young mother with a sick child; accounts of stifling and pulsing and hallucinations and fever; pharmaceutical lore of distilling and compounding, of poisonous flowers and strong potions; observations of haemorrhage, psychological shock, and consumption; a metaphor of amputation; and, finally, a detailed picture of a freshly exhumed corpse, perhaps recalled from the dissecting room at Guy's two and a half years before. This imagery implies a more direct confrontation of reality than Keats had yet made in his poetry; and its sudden appearance at this time is strangely significant. The previous spring Keats had told George, "I have forgotten all surgery." Now, it seems, the experience of nursing Tom was bringing this buried self to life again. The doctor he had started to become at the time of his mother's illness and then repudiated, now returned to question the poet he had chosen to be instead. During his months in Devon, Keats spoke repeatedly of his ambition to do some constructive service for the world, even—as he remarked in a sombre moment—of "dying for a great human purpose." In the face of Tom's suffering, poetry began to seem "a mere Jack a lanthern." He told Reynolds he was glad he had kept his medical books and resolved to read them again; even if he made no practical use of it, this study would strengthen his grasp on realities which up to this time he had tried deliberately to exclude from his poetry. Just as, a year or two before, his sense of identity as a poet had widened to include his boyhood vision of life as a

heroic struggle, now it began deepening to include his later awareness as a surgeon of the extent of human suffering and his resolution to relieve it.

But the first effect of Tom's relapse in mid-March was to pre-
cipitate all the dissatisfactions Keats felt over *Endymion*. On
March 19 he wound up his labours by drafting a preface that
slashed recklessly at his failure in the poem, admitting all the uncertainties he had felt in writing it and the distance it fell short
of his hopes, and daring his critics to think worse of it than he. "In
duty to the Public I should have kept it back for a year or two,
knowing it to be so faulty," he confessed; "but I really cannot do
so:—by repetition my favorite Passages sound vapid in my ears."
It was an impossible preface. Taylor gave the task of telling Keats
this to Reynolds, who wrote tactfully suggesting that there was
too much of Hunt in its style. "I am not aware there is any thing
like Hunt in it," Keats retorted, "(and if there is, it is my natural
way, and I have something in common with Hunt)." But, he went
on, "a Preface is written to the Public; a thing I cannot help looking upon as an Enemy." He had not laboured for "the thousand
jabberers about Pictures and Books," and he would not humble
himself to them—"or to any thing in existence,—but the eternal
Being, the Principle of Beauty,—and the Memory of great Men. I
never wrote one single Line of Poetry with the least Shadow of
public thought," he added, forgetting for the moment how the idea
of fame had haunted him when he began *Endymion*. Yet even then
he had thought of fame not as the applause of his own time but
as "a light thrown to posterity." Now he had discovered that between him and posterity stood the public—the commonplace people who "read the Edinburgh and the Quarterly and think as they
do," and who would find fault with *Endymion* to prove their own
importance. Kingston criticism! This he had not bargained for.

As he finished his letter to Reynolds it stopped raining
for an hour, and he went out for a walk to let his temper
cool. The lane was banked with primroses on either side,
and he noticed that the hedges were beginning to leaf. Perhaps he remembered the first primroses in the Isle of Wight, the
April before, and the mood in which he had begun *Endymion*. The
next morning he sat down and rewrote the preface. In this second
version he made essentially the same points as in the first, but in a
far different spirit. Again he admitted that the poem was merely

"a feverish attempt, rather than a deed accomplished," and that he regretted publishing it as it stood. But this time he spoke not to the hateful public but to men "who look with a zealous eye, to the honour of English literature." This was what mattered in the end, not the scorn or applause he might win himself; and with this thought he was already plotting and fitting himself, he confessed, "for verses fit to live." With the greater object of *Hyperion* before him, Keats could now accept his failure in *Endymion* with some equanimity. His last act was to dedicate the poem "To the Memory of Thomas Chatterton." The deed was accomplished, the feverish attempt was over.

Now there was the future to deal with. Keats must have spent many hours talking this over with Tom, for his plans were becoming more closely linked all the time to his brother's needs. Tom's illness made another winter in England something to be avoided if at all possible, and George, who still had not found work to his liking, was increasingly restless in London. But there was also Keats's own work to consider. Already his conception of *Hyperion* seemed to be outstripping his power to execute it, even further than his ideas for *Endymion* the year before. He had planned to write the poem in a vein of epic loftiness patterned on Milton; now he felt he must learn Homer and even Dante in the original to master this style. More than this, he realized, the theme of the poem as he envisaged it would require the philosophic mind which, Wordsworth had said, only the years can bring. "I know nothing I have read nothing," he told Taylor, "and I mean to follow Solomon's directions of 'get Wisdom—get understanding.'" Hazlitt would be his guide here, yet Keats felt he needed at least a year's study before he could intelligently ask Hazlitt "the best metaphysical road" to take. But he also realized that he needed something more than "continual drinking of Knowledge" to fit him for the poetry he dreamed of—some actual experience of the world's grandeurs. Slowly his plans took shape. Dilke's neighbour Charles Brown had written from Hampstead suggesting that Keats accompany him on a walking trip through the north of England and Scotland that summer—where, he realized, he would see Wordsworth's own lakes and mountains. Tom must spend the next winter in Italy, and Keats would make the voyage with him in the autumn. Once in Europe, there were "the Kingdoms of the Earth and the glory of them"—"stupendous recollections" to gather for his poetry. He would climb Ben Nevis this summer, Mont Blanc the next. "I will clamber through the Clouds and exist," he wrote Haydon, already drunk with the idea. A life of study and travel, living in Europe at the lowest cost, with his poems bringing in a little money—for the moment Keats forgot the Devonshire rain beating against the window. So at the end of April he announced to Taylor—who had just sent him a copy of the newly published *Endymion*—that he planned to take his books and "retire from the World," meaning London, for some years.

What Keats apparently intended was a period of retirement such as Milton had undertaken after leaving Cambridge with the deliberate purpose of preparing himself for great poetry. Within the last month or two it seems that Milton had begun to take a place beside Shakespeare in Keats's mind, not only as an example of a certain style of poetry but also as a model of the poet himself. It was Milton who first raised the troublesome question of what good a poet could do for the world. From a wildly joking letter to James Rice toward the end of March it appears that Keats was then reading Milton's prose works, in which he had turned from poetry in mid-career to enter the battle between Royalist and Puritan on the side of freedom. "He was an active friend to Man all his Life and has been since his death," Keats commented soberly. In a number of Keats's other remarks this spring there are echoes of Milton's defence of his so far unproductive career in the *Reason of Church Government*. Milton himself had wondered whether he could be "anything worth to his country," and the idea that a poet could serve society in his work, pursue not his own fame or self-fulfilment but what Keats called "the glory of making his country happier," began to take firm root in Keats's mind at this time and grow there. Among the many notes he penned into his copy of *Paradise Lost,* he observed that, like himself, Milton had "an exquisite passion for poetical Luxury," and with this he would have been content "if he could, so doing, have preserved his self-respect and feel of duty performed; but there was working in him as it were that same sort of thing as operates in the great world to the end of a Prophecy's being accomplished." [23] That Milton should have completed his career by writing *Paradise Lost*—one of the works which, Keats thought, "benefit the 'Spirit and pulse of good' by their mere passive existence"—suggested an answer at last to the troubling question that Tom's illness had raised. "I find there is no worthy pursuit but the idea of doing some good for the world," he confided to Taylor. "Some do it with their society—some with their wit—some with their benevolence—there is but one way for me—the road lies through application study and thought."

So, after two months of reading and thinking in Devon, his ideas were beginning to fall into place around a new center. If he could retell the myth of Hyperion to convey the new understanding of things that was taking shape in his mind, he would be serving mankind in the best way he could. On May 3 Keats started a long letter to Reynolds which, along with the usual jokes and new verses, gives hints of what was turning over in his mind as he pondered his theme. Reynolds was now well enough to return to his law studies, and he seemed convinced that this would be the end of poetry for him. Keats tried to persuade him it would not. His own study of medicine had not hindered him in his poetry; he was beginning to see that it had helped. "An extensive knowledge is needful to thinking people," he argued; "it takes away the heat and fever; and helps, by widening speculation, to ease the Burden of the Mystery. The difference of high Sensations with and without knowledge appears to me this," he added, "in the latter case we are falling continually ten thousand fathoms deep and being blown up again without wings and with all the horror of a bare shoulderd Creature—in the former case, our shoulders are fledged, and we go thro' the same air and space without fear."

The echoes of *Tintern Abbey* along with *Paradise Lost* are significant. By now Keats had moved far enough beyond his experience of Wordsworth as a man to reconsider him as a poet, which at this point involved measuring him against Milton's genius. In February he had dismissed Wordsworth as "not a philosopher," at the same time that he was coming to admire Milton for his vast learning and philosophic grasp of the problem of good and evil. By May, Keats was beginning to see an equal value in Wordsworth's more intuitive but perhaps more profound awareness of life, because he himself had begun to explore some of the shadowed depths of experience from which this awareness had sprung. Turning from *The Excursion,* with its lofty philosophizing, back to Wordsworth's early poems of beggars and gipsies, of girls abandoned by their lovers and fathers by their sons, Keats saw where Wordsworth's genius lay—in "thinking into the human heart."

Beside this gift, Milton, for all his brilliance, showed "less anxiety for Humanity." Milton's theology, it struck him, was something that could be learned, and by one "not much advanced in years"; Wordsworth's insight, by contrast, could be gained only by undergoing a similar experience. "Axioms in philosophy are not axioms until they are proved upon our pulses," Keats remarked. He was beginning to understand Wordsworth's central perception—that the nature of the world changes as the individual's growing capacity to experience it changes; and this led him to describe the change as he himself had felt it.

"I compare human life to a large Mansion of Many Apartments," he wrote Reynolds, "two of which I can only describe, the doors of the rest being as yet shut upon me." In the first, "the infant or thoughtless Chamber," we remain "as long as we do not think"; but at length, "impelled by the awakening of the thinking principle—within us," we move into "the Chamber of Maiden-Thought," where "we see nothing but pleasant wonders, and think of delaying there for ever in delight"—the period in Keats's life, we may guess, from his discovery of poetry to the writing of *Endymion*. Yet the awakening of thought has the effect in time "of sharpening one's vision into the heart and nature of Man—of convincing ones nerves that the World is full of Misery and Heartbreak, Pain, Sickness and oppression—whereby This Chamber of Maiden Thought becomes gradually darken'd and at the same time on all sides of it many doors are set open—but all dark—all leading to dark passages—We see not the ballance of good and evil. We are in a Mist—*We* are now in that state," he added, returning to Reynolds. "We feel the 'burden of the Mystery.' " Wordsworth's greatness was in exploring these dark passages: "he is a Genius in so far as he can make discoveries, and shed a light in them." These hidden reaches of the mind, Keats now saw, were the intellectual problem posed by their own times, far more complex than the theological questions with which Milton was absorbed. So Wordsworth was "deeper than Milton," he concluded, though more because of "the general and gregarious advance of intellect, than individual greatness of Mind"—thanks to that "mighty providence" which "subdues the mightiest Minds to the service of the time being."

In sketching this picture of spiritual growth, Keats was not merely measuring Wordsworth's greatness against Milton's; he was stating in a different key one of the meanings he glimpsed in his own myth of Hyperion—mankind's long struggle toward greater understanding. As a child of his age he had almost unconsciously accepted the belief that the spread of enlightenment —the forward thrust of scientific knowledge, the extension of political responsibility, the deepening insight into the mind itself— —must effect "a continual change for the better": [24] the ascent he now saw symbolized in the Olympians' victory over the Titans. It was no mere abstract faith in reason he was trying to express, however, but the great revolutionary struggle of his age against the irrational repressive forces of the old order, in society as well as thought; nor was it an easy faith in progress he held. In his glimpse of "Purgatory blind" that evening in March he had for a moment doubted there was any real goal to the struggle; now he was beginning to sense what the struggle would cost. So, he suggested to Reynolds, if they were to continue as poets, or even to go on living and thinking, they too must explore Wordsworth's dark passages. But, not to leave his friend with too gloomy a picture of the future, Keats ended his letter with the promise, "Your third Chamber of Life shall be a lucky and a gentle one—stored with the wine of love—and the Bread of Friendship."

The lines of verse which he sent in this letter were the beginning of an ode to Maia, the mother of Hermes, which he had started on the first of May. They are different from anything he had written before: they ring with a new resonance, a new maturity. Keats, who had been longing to learn Greek poetry, comes far closer in these lines than anywhere in *Endymion* to the spirit of those

> bards who died content on pleasant sward,
> Leaving great verse unto a little clan.

The sense of a new balance struck, a new peace with himself, and a calm delight in the new season emerges from his prayer:

> O, give me their old vigour, and unheard
> Save of the quiet Primrose, and the span
> Of heaven and few ears,
> Rounded by thee, my song should die away
> Content as theirs,
> Rich in the simple worship of a day.

In these lines Keats had gone far toward closing the gap between his real nature as it is revealed in his letters—masculine, energetic, straightforward—and the over-intense, half-effeminate idiom into which his early poetry had been lured by the example of Hunt and his contemporaries. At last he was beginning to shake free of the style of other poets and work out his own. Yet it is worth noting that the last line of the ode, so rich in multifold meaning for all its simplicity, echoes the last line of a memorable passage prefacing *The Excursion*—"A simple produce of the common day." Keats had burned through the experience of disillusionment to discover what remained essential and meaningful to him in Wordsworth.

But the ode remained a fragment. The day after Keats sent it off to Reynolds, unexpected news came from London. George had decided to marry and leave England. All at once it was time to return home.[25] Tom had spat a little blood the day before, but seemed well enough to make the trip. They packed hastily, borrowing some money from Mrs. Jeffrey for the journey.[26] Sarah Jeffrey offered to go with them on the first stage, and Tom, under doctor's orders to avoid emotional scenes, made a brief farewell to Marianne and her mother. Then the two brothers climbed into the post chaise with Sarah, to make a dash to Honiton for the Exeter coach which would carry them back to London.

>>>————————————————————<<<

Chapter Seven

Mist and Crag

A T Honiton they bade Sarah an affectionate farewell, and Keats sent back a note to Mrs. Jeffrey telling her that Tom had borne the first leg of their journey remarkably well. But twenty miles farther on, at Bridport in Dorset, the worst happened. Tom had another severe haemorrhage. For two or three days they rested in the little coastal town, with Keats in a sweat of anxiety whether to stay or go on. When Tom got some of his strength back they moved on in easy stages and reached London a week after setting out. Here Tom picked up again in one of his unexpected returns of good health and spirits. He insisted he felt better than he had when they left Devon, and his friends managed to cheer him into believing that his illness was "mistaken Fancy." Even Sawrey seemed to find him improved by his winter in Teignmouth and told him that "confinement and low spirits" were his chief worries. Though Sawrey may have suspected, as did Keats, that Tom was "in a lingering state," his advice was to the point, for the emotional condition of a tubercular patient has a considerable effect on his progress. So Tom was encouraged to lay plans for a trip to Italy in the fall. As he wrote to the Jeffrey girls in high good humour, he was thinking of spending the winter in the fine old Lombard town of Pavia, with its ancient university, where he hoped to acquire "a stock of knowledge and strength which will better enable me to bustle through the world."

But both John's and Tom's plans were overshadowed by George's. For months he had been thinking he might emigrate to America, and now at last he had won Mrs. Wylie's consent to marry

Georgiana and take her with him. With a thousand-odd pounds of his inheritance he would buy a farm and strike out on his own. Morris Birkbeck, an enterprising Quaker who had found several large settlements on the frontier, had recently published an account of the opportunities of life in Illinois that aroused great interest in England that year. Yet for George to join Birkbeck's pioneers—knowing nothing of farming and no climate more rigorous than London's—seemed more reckless than enterprising to most of their friends. As Keats told the Jeffrey girls, "They say we are all mad." But George would not be daunted. In a year or two, he believed, he would be earning enough money to support both his brothers and the Wylies. Then they all should follow him to America, with George's old friend Haslam, and Dilke too—the only member of the Hampstead set who approved of his project—and make their fortunes together in the new country.[1]

Keats admitted that this was the best course for George to take, for he saw that his brother was too independent and high-spirited to be happy as a small London merchant. Nevertheless it plunged him ten thousand fathoms deep into gloom again. "I am in that temper that if I were under Water I would scarcely kick to come to the top," he told Bailey in announcing the news. He did not know when he might lose Tom; but now, within a month, he would lose George—his first and in most ways still his closest friend. In the last few years George, who had always appeared to be his older brother, had taken on the major burden of their practical affairs as well; now Keats realized that he must shoulder it himself at the very time that Tom's illness was adding a new load of worry. As for the marriage itself, he told Bailey, he felt almost stony-hearted about it. Beneath his natural but unutterable jealousy of George's happiness were stirring up all his half-forgotten sexual anxieties. This was enough to break through—for the only time in all his letters—his close-guarded reticence about his boyhood. To Bailey he confided that "My Love for my Brothers from the early loss of our parents and even for earlier Misfortunes has grown into a affection 'passing the Love of Women'—I have been ill temper'd with them, I have vex'd them—but the thought of them has always stifled the impression that any woman might otherwise have made upon me."

Writing to Bailey a few months later, Keats was to mock his habit of carrying matters to extremes—"so that any little vexation

grows in five Minutes into a theme for Sophocles." Nevertheless
there were real enough reasons for this lethargy which now
weighed on him like lead. One evidently was the discovery that
his inheritance was dwindling more rapidly than he had thought.
On overhauling his accounts after his return, he decided to transfer
five hundred pounds—most of his remaining resources—to a cash
account at Abbey's, probably to draw on for Tom's extra expenses.
Besides this sobering realization, there were ominous rumblings
from the reviews. The first two notices of *Endymion,* at the end of
May and the beginning of June, were fair-minded and even enthusiastic. But then *The British Critic,* one of the leading Tory magazines, printed a slashing burlesque of a review, which made the
poem out to be both nonsensical and immoral; and meanwhile
Blackwood's and the *Quarterly* seemed to be swinging their guns
into position. *Blackwood's* had found a priceless opportunity for
renewing its campaign against Hunt when his new collection of
verse, entitled *Foliage,* appeared early that spring. This contained,
among other things, four sonnets addressed to Keats, two of them
recording the unlucky occasion, a year before, when he and Keats
had crowned themselves with ivy and laurel. So in the May issue
of *Blackwood's* Hunt was set up as "the King of the Cockneys,"
surrounded by a court of would-be poets and crowned with ivy
by "the delicate hand of young Mister Keats—an amiable but infatuated bardling." A few weeks later, the *Quarterly* delivered a
stunning broadside against both *Foliage* and Hazlitt's *Characters,*
along with a clear warning that Keats and Shelley would be their
next targets.[2]

Keats joked about this to Bailey—"I have more than a Laurel
from the Quarterly Reviewers for they have *smothered* me in
'Foliage' "—but the remark was edged with irony. Just when he
wanted to win a hearing for *Endymion* on its own merits, Hunt's
volume had appeared, linking their names more closely than ever.
So he was going to have the reputation of being Hunt's *élève* after
all! In such a mood a fulsome tribute which Bailey published in
an Oxford paper, comparing him to Shakespeare and Milton while
twice mis-citing "Lycidas," [3] could only exacerbate him—"because
the world is malignant enough to chuckle at the most honorable
Simplicity. Yes on my Soul my dear Bailey," he wrote in thanking
him, "you are too simple for the World—and that Idea makes me
sick of it. Were it in my choice," he added, "I would reject a

petrarchal coronation—on account of my dying day, and because women have Cancers."

A savage remark—what had happened to make him lash out at Bailey like this? Not simply his apprehensions about *Endymion* or a momentary impatience with Bailey's plodding appreciation. Even Tom's illness, which no one but himself would admit was hopeless, would not have weighed so heavily on him had he not also been ill himself. His appearance on returning from Devon evidently gave concern to several of his friends. For most of May and June he was not well enough to risk a walk to town in the night air; early in June, in fact, Sawrey ordered him to keep to the house till he got better. What the matter was, Keats did not say. It may have been only a return of the sore throat he had caught in March—which, however, he must have known can be a secondary symptom of syphilis—or he may have noticed symptoms still more disturbing, which with his usual secretiveness he kept to himself. But at this time a strange premonition took hold of Keats. It was unreasonable, and no doubt he told himself so and tried to shake it off. Still it is the kind of idea which, once it gets into a man's mind, is not easy to dislodge. For some reason or other, Keats became convinced that he had only three more years to live. This was an obsession very different from the fear that had gripped him in January, when "the family disease" had reappeared unmistakably in Tom and he realized that his own life might also be cut short before he reached his goal in poetry. Now the thought seems to have shaped itself with a chilling precision: he had three years—a little more than a thousand days—to live. He knew it was unreasonable; he also knew it was possible. Though he made no explicit mention of his foreboding, he let slip half a dozen references to the possibility of his early death in his letters during the next two months.[4] So he must have listened to George's and Georgiana's plans for him to follow them to America with a sense of unreality. Outwardly he agreed to a year's visit; to himself he added the proviso, "If I live to the completion of the three next." "Life must be undergone," he wrote despondently to Bailey; his one consolation was "the thought of writing one or two more Poems before it ceases."

To shake off this mood Keats tried his usual remedy: a few of the old Saturday nights, getting "a little so-so" with Rice and Reynolds; a few Sunday dinners at Haydon's, playing the bassoon

in another boisterous "concert" or getting into a political debate
with Hazlitt; a few calls at the Reynoldses'—but there the old gaiety
was lacking. Mrs. Reynolds openly disapproved of George's plans
to emigrate,[5] perhaps regarding his engagement as a defection from
Mariane, and conversation with the sisters was growing steadily
less enjoyable. Keats found it was more of a pleasure to drop in at
Wentworth Place, close at hand, where he could always count on
Mrs. Dilke's good humour or the solid masculine talk of Dilke
and Brown. One evening in June, Keats went with George and
probably Reynolds to the Lyceum, where Charles Mathews, London's favourite comedian and ventriloquist, was holding one of his
noisy "At Homes." On the way they unexpectedly met Isabella
Jones.[6] One wonders whom she was with or where she was going,
and what happened in the sequel. Keats introduced his companions
to her, and the meeting may have been extended into a supper
party, for at one time, he later noted, the four of them were all in
a room together. Whatever the meeting became, it ended as casually
as it began, for they parted with no thought of renewing the
occasion.

In the end it was another woman who succeeded in lifting Keats
out of his depression—unexpectedly, his new sister-in-law. He had
liked Georgiana Wylie ever since their first acquaintance, and in
their new intimacy he found himself growing fonder of her than
he had thought possible. From a sweet but elusive girl of fourteen
she had grown in two years into a witty, spirited, and intelligent
young woman. She was evidently not pretty and lacked the style
conferred by a fashionable upbringing; but she possessed the virtue which counted most with Keats—what he called disinterestedness. She seems to have been the first woman of his age to whom
he attributed any kind of moral identity. Up till now, Keats had
evidently subscribed to the prevailing masculine belief that "Most
women have no character at all"—an attitude which does not,
however, preclude idealizing them, but arises from it. Now, on
closer knowledge, he discovered that a girl of sixteen could show
courage and enterprise. That Georgiana could leave family and
friends and the comfortable life of London for a backwoods farm
in America, and all for the love of his brother George—he had to
admit he was puzzled. "To see an entirely disinterrested Girl quite
happy is the most pleasant and extraordinary thing in the world,"
he wrote Bailey. "Women must want Imagination and they may

thank God for it—and so may we that a delicate being can feel happy without any sense of crime." It was the first marriage he had observed from close hand since he was eight, and it gave him much to ponder.

For the time being, however, there were too many other things to occupy him. There had been the wedding itself at the end of May—"I never rejoiced more than at my Brother's Marriage," Keats wrote two months later—and celebrations before and after the event. Now there was the summer ahead to think of. For some reason—perhaps Tom's health, perhaps the state of the family finances—the plans for a winter in Italy were shelved around the beginning of June. For a while Keats wondered whether he should also give up his trip to Scotland. But to confess his worries about his brother would seriously alarm Tom himself, and evidently Tom insisted that he go, since the trip was part of the program for *Hyperion.* "I should not have consented to myself these four Months tramping in the highlands," he wrote Bailey in July, "but that I thought it would give me more experience, rub off more Prejudice, use me to more hardship, identify finer scenes load me with grander Mountains, and strengthen more my reach in Poetry, than would stopping at home among Books even though I should reach Homer." They had neighbours in Hampstead to keep Tom company, and Mrs. Bentley, their landlady, was a kindly woman who could help if needed.

So Keats went ahead with his plans. George and Georgiana were to sail for Philadelphia at the end of June; he and Brown would travel by stagecoach with them up to Liverpool, then from there to the Lakes. Brown, whom Keats had known up till now merely as Dilke's old friend and neighbour,[7] promised to be an excellent companion for the trip—energetic, practical, cheerful, and an experienced traveller. Scottish by ancestry, nine years older than Keats, he was also a writer of sorts and had seen a good deal of the world. On his advice, Keats bought himself a knapsack, then assembled old clothes and new socks, packed up pens, paper and ink, and the manuscript of *Isabella* to mull over. For his summer's reading he chose "a Book Full of vowels," as he described it to Fanny—Carey's translation of *The Divine Comedy,* just published by Taylor and Hessey in three minute volumes which fitted neatly into the remaining inches of space.

The two or three days before leaving were full of the usual last-minute errands. One of these was a financial settling with George. The brothers' accounts had become badly tangled over the last few years, and George had not kept as careful account of his many borrowings from John as he had promised. According to a later statement of Brown's, the sum he finally repaid his brother was less than Keats had expected, and Keats found the settlement less than satisfactory.[8] Money worries were not allowed to spoil their farewell, however. There must have been a flurry of parties at Brunswick Square, where the young couple were spending their honeymoon. To one of these, three days before leaving, George invited Taylor, an amateur phrenologist, to "discover if the lines of [Mrs. Keats's] face answer to her spirit." Abbey's parting words were to call them all Don Quixotes, much to Keats's amusement. He was too busy at the end to say good-bye to many of his friends but swept them all up in a final hurried note to Taylor the night before leaving. Still worried that Tom might be lonely, he asked Taylor to keep him well supplied with books, then to do something he had unaccountably forgotten—send a copy of *Endymion* to Mrs. Reynolds. Signing himself jokingly "John O' Grots," he was ready at last to be off.

At noon on June 22 they boarded the Liverpool coach at the Swan with Two Necks in Lad Lane, near the Guildhall: George, with his thousand pounds of credit; Georgiana, wearing a pretty bonnet; and Keats and Brown with their knapsacks, already dressed for the road. Twenty-five miles from London they stopped for dinner at Redbourn, where, Keats remembered, his medical-school friend Henry Stephens had set up in practice. Keats sent him a note, and Stephens joined them at the inn. If Stephens noticed a change in Keats since his last days at medical school, he did not mention it in recalling the meeting years later; his attention was caught by Georgiana. She was an "original" in his eyes—"not what might be called strictly handsome," "somewhat singular in her attire," but "with an imaginative poetical cast." A man of sensibility might easily fall in love with her, he decided to himself, and observed that Keats introduced his sister-in-law with great satisfaction.

Dinner over, they said their good-byes, and the coach started north again through the long golden afternoon. Almost two hundred miles to their destination—over the Chiltern hills and across the Ouse at Stony-Stratford, through Northamptonshire and Warwickshire in the brief summer night, and into the quiet cathedral city of Coventry at dawn; along the borders of Shropshire as the sun swung high and down into the plains of Cheshire with the mountains of Wales showing blue toward the west; then across the Mersey and into Liverpool at last in the early evening.[9] They were met by a smell of salt and tar, the rumble of drays through streets lined with tall warehouses, and a forest of masts in the harbour. George and Georgiana took rooms at the Crown Inn to wait for the next sailing, and Keats said his last good-byes that evening. Early the next morning he and Brown were to take coach for Lancaster, the starting point of their tour. His brother and sister-in-law were still asleep when he left at dawn, with their farewells and their promises of a reunion in America still fresh in his ears. He was never to see Georgiana again.

-»»·«««-

The walking trip began with bad weather and an unpleasant surprise. When Keats and Brown reached Lancaster late that afternoon they found the city in an uproar. It was the eve of a parliamentary election in which Henry Brougham, the great Whig lawyer who had defended Hunt in his second trial, was challenging the Tory incumbent, Lord Lowther. Alarmed by the seething discontent of the industrial population, Lowther had persuaded the Government to send troops into the district to keep order. The city was crowded; drink flowed freely while votes were bought and sold. Keats and Brown had to wait two hours for their dinner, for the inns were full, then walk the narrow streets looking for lodgings.[10] Here Keats heard, probably for the first time, "that most disgusting of all noises," as he described it, the shuttles of the spinning mills. Lancaster was the first industrial city that he had seen at close hand, and whatever he glimpsed of the poverty of the cotton-spinners set him thinking. During the next months, in the midst of the stupendous scenery he had travelled northward to see, the image of poverty was to haunt him like an unanswered question: was all this ugliness and misery necessary? One wonders whether his outburst against the greedy Florentine merchants who battened on this misery was added to *Isabella* after his view of Lancaster.[11]

After putting up for the night in a private house, Keats and

Brown rose early next morning to find it raining hard. For three hours they waited for it to clear, while Brown read aloud from *Samson Agonistes* by way of recommending patience; then at last they strapped on their packs, took their sticks, and set out in a Scotch mist. As they left Lancaster a factory worker jeered at them—gentlemen with nothing better to do than make work for themselves. Perhaps it was at this point that they were struck by the appearance they presented: two nondescript travellers, one tall, heavy-set, and bewhiskered, the other short and lithe, looking like pedlars or sportsmen or neither. Keats was dressed reasonably enough in an old jacket with leather buttons and belt, stout shoes, and the great plaid he usually took on his travels slung over one shoulder—to which he subsequently added a fur cap that caught everyone's eye. Brown had outfitted himself more philosophically in "the best possible dress, as Dr. Pangloss would say": a suit of tartan for warmth, an oilskin cape to keep off the rain, a white hat to protect his bald head from the sun, a plaid over his shoulders, and spectacles on his nose. Keats nicknamed him the Red Cross Knight. Since there was no room in their packs for a change of clothes, they were not taken for gentlemen after their first day's tramp. For it started raining again after their four-mile walk to breakfast, and they walked seventeen miles that day through wet and dry. At the first place they stopped for dinner they were turned away; and twice when they asked for a bed for the night they were refused because the inns were full of Lowther's soldiers. On their third try the landlady took them in grudgingly, and after supper in her whitewashed kitchen a man who had been drinking in the corner staggered toward them and hiccupped at Brown, "Do you—u sell spectacles?" These were still enough of a novelty that Brown's pair was taken as a sign of his trade.

The second day's walk brought them into the Lake Country at last. The morning was fair, though muted by haze, and the larks were singing as they started out on their fourteen miles to Windermere. The road wound upward through fern and furze, and the air grew cool. The Fells of Furness began to show over the hilltops; then suddenly the view opened out, and Windermere lay below them, the Cumbrian Mountains beyond. Keats stopped, wonderstruck. It was a scene which he had described in imagination over and over again in his early poems—the shining lake edged with feathery trees, a green island floating in its midst; the mountains a sombre blue behind, with a silver cloud resting on the lower hills. Now it rose before him, suspended in the strange unreality which scenes long dreamed of wear on their first view, and for a moment blotted out all sense of time and space. "How can I believe in that?" he exclaimed, then, recovering, asserted to Brown that it must beat anything in Italy.

At last they turned down the path to Bowness. Here they found a first-rate inn by the side of the lake, really too luxurious for their tastes, but promising an excellent meal. While waiting for dinner, they rowed out to the island with a man to get trout from wooden cages moored at its edge, then took a swim while the fish were cooking. After dinner they walked five miles up the lake to Ambleside, along a wooded path bordered with fern and purple foxglove, with the water gleaming through the trees and the mountains growing darker behind. That evening Keats wrote to Tom: "The two views we have had [of Windermere] are of the most noble tenderness—they can never fade away—they make one forget the divisions of life; age, youth, poverty and riches; and refine one's sensual vision into a sort of north star which can never cease to be open lidded and stedfast over the wonders of the great Power." He had found what he had come to see.

The next morning he and Brown rose at six and climbed the steep hill behind Ambleside to view the falls, which drop for nearly a hundred feet from a crevice in the rocks. They lost their way in the woods and had to find it by following the roar of the stream. Suddenly the waterfall sprang into sight ahead; they were near the top of the highest fall. Approaching, they watched it plunge like an arrow into a slate-lined pool fifty feet below; then, as they climbed down to the second fall-head, they saw the stream spread out like a fan at their feet and, as it shot over the edge of the third fall, dash itself into a mist. The thunder of the water rang in their ears; its freshness cooled their cheeks. "I cannot think with Hazlitt that these scenes make man appear little," Keats wrote to Tom. "I never forgot my stature so completely—I live in the eye; and my imagination, surpassed, is at rest." They clambered down over moss-covered boulders, grasping at the slender birch and ash trees which grew out of crevices in the rocks, Keats surefooted, Brown following heavily with a nervous glance at the rapids below; then saw the whole fall from a distance, "streaming silverly through the trees," as Keats described it. "What astonishes me more than any thing is the tone, the coloring, the slate, the stone, the moss, the rock-weed; or, if I may so say, the intellect, the countenance of such places. I shall learn poetry here, and shall henceforth write, more than ever, for the abstract endeavor of being able to add a mite to that mass of beauty which is harvested from these grand materials by the finest spirits and put into etherial existence for the relish of one's fellows." *

This, of course, was the great purpose for which he was making the trip—to "identify finer scenes" and strengthen his reach in poetry. It is significant that in describing it Keats unconsciously echoed one of his favourite passages from Wordsworth:

> Beauty—a living Presence of the earth,
> Surpassing the most fair ideal Forms
> Which craft of delicate Spirits hath composed
> From earth's materials—waits upon my steps. . . .

Even more, his sense of the "countenance or intellectual tone" of Ambleside suggests Wordsworth's description, published years later, of the "workings of one mind, the features Of the same face" he once glimpsed in the Simplon Pass.[12] For the time being, at least, Keats had forgotten his look "too far into the sea" at Teignmouth, when he had caught sight of a nature uninformed by any divine principle, indifferent to any human values. At Windermere and Ambleside it was impossible not to believe in what he once called "the poetry of earth," that mysterious sense of a meaning in nature, or in "the great Power" who expresses His nature through these wonders. Nor could he doubt that somehow from his experience of this sublimity great poetry would be born. A few weeks later, at his first sight of Burns's native countryside of Ayr, with the sea and the black hills of Arran beyond the green valley, Keats wondered, "How is it they did not beckon Burns to some grand attempt at Epic?" Feeling as he did, he found exclaiming over scenery in the usual picturesque terms as distasteful as "jabbering about Pictures and Books." After describing the Ambleside waterfall in his letter to Tom, he apologized—"but how can I help it?" —and promised to send no more descriptions. And after the shock of the first two or three tremendous adventures, his letters contain none of the rhapsodies which Brown, the nearsighted romantic traveller, added to his journal day after day. Keats did not miss

---

* Letters, ed. Rollins, I, 301. The last sentence is repunctuated in order to make Keats's meaning clear.

a shade or colour or echo of the wild magnificence all around them, but the true journal of his trip to the north is *Hyperion*.

After Ambleside, their next stop was Rydal, where Keats was to pay a long-planned call on Wordsworth. When he inquired at Bowness about the way to Wordsworth's house, he learned that it was one of the chief landmarks for the fashionable visitors, and that Wordsworth had been in Bowness a few days before, canvassing for Lord Lowther. Wordsworth versus Brougham! This was a jolt, though it might have been less of one had Keats known that Wordsworth was electioneering for Lowther during his London visit the winter before.[13] Nevertheless he kept to his plan and hiked on that morning with Brown to Rydal Mount, at the head of Windermere. Wordsworth was not at home, they were informed, nor any of his family. There was nothing for Keats to do but write a note and leave it on the mantelpiece, propped against what he recognized as a portrait of Dorothy Wordsworth. As he turned dejectedly to go, his eye was caught by the view from the parlour window. Before them Windermere lay at full length, shining under the open sky, reaching ten miles into the silent hills. What a window to sit and read in, or stare out of hour by hour! Keats only half noted it in his hurry to be gone, but the image dropped like a seed into his mind.

Again they set out north, tramping along Rydal Water and Grasmere, then on to Thirlmere at the foot of Helvellyn. Around them on every side rose the green and purple-shadowed mountains whose names Keats had first learned in Wordsworth's poems: Loughrigg, Skiddaw, Scafell, Kirkstone, Silver How, Hammer-Scar, and Helm Crag. He and Brown had planned to climb Helvellyn, the grandest of them all, but the next morning they woke to find it raining. So they started out again, walking eight wet miles to Keswick for breakfast, then tramping ten miles around Derwent Water to climb the Falls of Lodore, then, after returning to Keswick for dinner, trudging another three miles, uphill and down, to see the Druid Temple near the Vale of Saint John. They went to bed "rather fatigued" that night, but not too tired to rise at five the next morning to climb Skiddaw before breakfast. For once the weather promised to be fair, but after they hauled their way nearly to the top, a mist fell over the valleys below. Still they could see beyond the clouds the hills of Lancashire to the south and the coast of Galloway beyond the Solway Firth to the north and west, with the highest peaks of the Cumbrian range all around them. Snow lingered in the crevices of the mountain, and it grew colder and colder as they climbed. "We were glad at about three parts of the way," Keats wrote to Tom, "to taste a little rum which the Guide brought with him, mixed, mind ye with mountain water, I took two glasses going & one returning. We went up with two others, very good sort of fellows, All felt on arising into the cold air, that same elevation, which a cold bath gives one—I felt as if I were going to a Tournament."

The exhilaration of new experience countered any sense of fatigue the first week or two; Keats found that fourteen miles in the Lakes seemed less than the four between Hampstead and London. But even after the first excitement wore off, he and Brown kept to the same routine. Twenty miles a day was their usual stint. The long summer evenings they spent poring over the map and figuring distances, playing cards, reading Milton and Dante, or writing up their journals. Brown kept a diary full of minute details about the scenery and people they passed, with an eye to publishing it later. Keats was more inclined after a long day to sit with his feet up on a chair and laugh at Brown's methodicalness as, evening after evening, he pulled out of his knapsack first, paper; second, pens; and third, ink. Why not vary it a bit? Keats asked— try taking out the pens first. "But I might as well tell a hen to hold up her head before she drinks instead of afterwards." His own journal took the form of long letters to Tom, to which he added a page almost every day. He kept another diary besides this prose one—poems which he wrote, as Wordsworth had done on a similar tour in 1803, to commemorate the places they visited. These sonnets all show a sense of strain, however; writing poetry to order was not one of his real talents, especially when his mood conflicted with what the occasion seemed to demand.

For, in the unpredictable way that all trips do, the journey was turning out different from what he envisaged. He had counted on meeting hardship, fatigue, even hunger, though the actual form of these discomforts—blisters, drenchings, fleas, gadflies, dirty food, a sickening monotony of eggs and oatcake when they reached the Highlands—could not be imagined beforehand. He managed to joke about them all and even to write poetry about some—the gadflies, for instance, that plagued him when he swam in Loch

Fine. But even before the excitement of mountains and lakes and ruins began to wear off, he found an unexpected source of interest in the people they met along the way—a soldier who had fought Napoleon up and down Europe for seventeen years, a Scottish gentleman who cautiously admitted to being a Deist, a pretty Irish chambermaid, a drunken Irish weaver, a provincial playgoer, an Argyllshire innkeeper's family, a schoolmaster in the Hebrides, the shepherds in the Isle of Mull. His first encounter with northern ways was delightful. At the village inn where they stopped in Ireby he and Brown discovered a dancing class in full swing. Half amused, half admiring, they watched the fresh-cheeked boys and girls weaving through the intricate patterns of strathspey and reel. With Burns's "Tam o' Shanter" running through his head, Keats described it to Tom: "They kickit & jumpit with mettle extraordinary, & whiskit, & friskit, & toed it, & go'd it, & twirld it, & whirl'd it, & stamp't it, & sweated it, tattooing the floor like mad.* I was extremely gratified," he added, "to think, that if I had pleasures they knew nothing of. they had also some into which I could not possibly enter I hope I shall not return without having got the Highland fling."

Scotland was in fact still a foreign country to the Englishman of that time. Keats was immediately struck by the broad Lowlands accent—"how is it a' wi' yoursel'?"—and, as in Devon, he tried a poem in the dialect. His eye too was caught by the barefoot Scottish girls, a crowd of whom they passed walking to a horse-fair with their shoes and stockings in hand to put on at the edge of town. Brown was dismayed by their large feet, but Keats noted, with an anatomist's eye, the beauty of the human foot that had been allowed to develop naturally. Yet the farther north they journeyed, the more he was struck by the poverty of the Scottish peasants. Smoke-blackened cottages with no chimneys and often no floors, thatched with turf, picturesque, perhaps, as Brown thought, but very primitive; barefoot girls driving cattle across stony pastures or standing by cowsheds up to their ankles in dirt —he could not look at them as merely part of the landscape. The solemnity of the Scots also began to oppress him. An expressionless

---

* Following F. W. Page's emendation of this sentence from John Jeffrey's transcript of the original letter (*Letters of John Keats*, Oxford World's Classics [1954], p. 133; cf. *Letters*, ed. Rollins, I, 307).

stare usually greeted the two travellers on entering a village; the children played in silence, and even the pretty girls they called out to on the road rarely ventured to smile. Poor little Susannahs, Keats thought, so terrified by the elders of the Scottish Church. "The kirk is greatly to be damn'd," he burst out to Tom. "These kirkmen have done scotland good (Query?) they have made Men, Women, Old Men Young Men old Women, young women boys, girls and infants all careful—so that they are formed into regular Phalanges of savers and gainers—such a thrifty army cannot fail to enrich their Country." Yet also "these kirkmen have done Scotland harm—they have banished puns and laughing and kissing (except in cases where the very danger and crime must make it very fine and gustful)."

When, a few days later, they crossed from Portpatrick to Ireland, the first chambermaid they met in the inn at Donaghadee—"fair, kind and ready to laugh"—proved the difference between the two nations. Yet at the same time the appalling raggedness and dirt of the Irish, cutting peat in bogs or penned up in mills in Belfast, filled Keats with despair. One old woman in a sedan chair whom they encountered near Belfast struck him as the image of Ireland's misery. "The Duchess of Dunghill," he called her, a squalid old woman in a dog kennel, "looking out with a round-eyed skinny lidded, inanity," like "an ape half starved from a scarcity of Buiscuit in its passage from Madagascar to the cape," smoking a pipe with her head nodding like an idiot's while two wretched ragged girls staggered along with their burden. The lot of the Irish seemed far worse than the Scots', but what was there to do about it? According to Malthus, the only economist of the age whom Keats ever mentioned, such poverty was inevitable. "The present state of society demands this," Keats mused, "and this convinces me that the world is very young and in a verry ignorant state—We live in a barbarous age."

He and Brown had expected to spend a week tramping through Antrim and Down. But after their first day's walk though bogs and slums, they found they had miscalculated. Forty-eight Irish miles to the Giant's Causeway came to seventy English ones; worse, the Irish inns charged three times as much as those in Scotland. So they returned to Donaghadee and sailed back to Portpatrick the next day and continued their tramp northward. Reporting this

foray to Tom gave Keats an opportunity to speculate on the differences of national character, a favourite pastime of the traveller.
Yet in the midst of spinning his theories he shrewdly noted that
both the Irish and the Scots are "sensible of the Character they hold
in England and act accordingly to Englishmen." The last thing
an inexperienced traveller expects to find in another land is a
new awareness of himself and his own country, but Keats was making this discovery even while he described travelling to Reynolds
as "one of the pleasantest means of annulling self." Most of the time,
of course, he and Brown might have been traveling incognito; they
were mistaken for "Spectacle venders, Razor sellers, Jewellers,
linnen-drapers and Spies," Frenchmen in Ireland, English soldiers
in the post office at Portpatrick, and excise men in whisky country.
This escape from one's habitual character is one of the pleasures of
travelling; but there comes a time on every journey when a
familiar image glints off the novel surfaces of things and the
traveller is suddenly confronted with himself again.

Keats had caught a glimpse of that image in Dumfries, their
first stop in Scotland, which they reached early in July. Here Burns
was buried, and a visit to the grave of this early hero of Keats was
one of the goals of his pilgrimage. The visit inspired Brown to
make the predictable observations on the value of memorials to
great men; but to Keats it brought something absolutely different
and unexpected, that unsettling sense of dislocation known as
déjà vu:

> The Town, the churchyard, and the setting sun,
>   The clouds, the trees, the rounded hills all seem,
>   Though beautiful, cold—strange—as in a dream
> I dreamed long ago, now new begun.

If it is true that in such moments one does in fact dimly recall a
scene already witnessed and repressed, Keats may have been struggling with the memory of another graveyard—St. Stephen's in
London, where his parents lay buried. Or was it that, standing in
this northern churchyard, staring at the large white-painted, iron-
railed mausoleum, overwhelmed by its ugliness—"anti Grecian &
anti Charlemagnish"—and its incongruity with Burns, he had a
vision of still another grave? He had expected to be moved by the
thought of Burns himself—Burns whom Hazlitt had called "as
much of a man, though not a twentieth part as much of a poet, as

Shakespeare." Instead Keats felt only a familiar numbness—"the feel of not to feel it"; and the poetry that came to his mind was not Burns but Shakespeare:

> For who has mind to relish, Minos-wise,
>   The real of Beauty, free from that dead hue
>   Sickly imagination and sick pride
>   Cast wan upon it?

The echo of Hamlet's meditation on death is significant. In May, when Keats told Reynolds, "We read fine—things but never feel them to the full until we have gone the same steps as the Author," he had added, "Now I shall relish Hamlet more than I ever have done." Now as he stood beside the grave of a poet who had died with his promise still unfulfilled, he felt, like Hamlet in the graveyard, that death makes all great endeavour meaningless; and at the same moment, again like Hamlet, he bitterly reproached himself:

> Burns! with honour due
> I oft have honour'd thee. Great shadow, hide
> Thy face; I sin against thy native skies.

Like Hamlet, he had sinned with the pride of the imagination: instead of "annulling" himself in the occasion, he had let it be sicklied over by his fancy that, for the moment, he stood not by Burns's grave but by his own.

After their tramp westward through Galloway and their hasty trip to Ireland and back, Keats and Brown turned northward again toward Ayr and the birthplace of Burns. These days were full of enough adventure to lighten the burden of the mystery for Keats for a while. He tasted his first whisky—"very smart stuff it is"— and learned how to make a toddy, "very pretty drink, & much praised by Burns." On the boat to Donaghadee he had listened to two old men singing ballads—one on the Battle of the Boyne, another on "Robin Huid" with the refrain "Before the King you shall go, go, go." He even made a joke out of his troubling experience at Dumfries in the "Song About Myself" which he wrote two days later to amuse his sister:

> So he stood in
>   His shoes and he wonder'd,
>   He wonder'd,
> He stood in his
>   Shoes and he wonder'd.

Nevertheless the thought of Burns's misery kept haunting him. "Poor unfortunate fellow," he remarked to Tom in the midst of his speculations on the Scottish character, "his disposition was southern—how sad it is when a luxurious imagination is obliged to deaden its delicacy in vulgarity, and riot in things attainable that it may not have leisure to go mad after things which are not." But as they approached Burns's native town he made an effort to put all such thoughts out of his mind.

The first view of Ayr late in the afternoon overwhelmed him with its beauty—the valley rich in every imaginable shade of green, and the silver Doon flowing to the sea, spanned by its famous bridges. He and Brown lingered on the bridge which Tam o' Shanter crossed, then walked on to Burns's cottage in the nearby village of Alloway, which they found turned into a whisky shop. Here something went extraordinarily wrong. An old man who had known Burns was there ready to spin anecdotes and drink a glass with any visitor who happened by, and he filled Keats with unaccountable rage. "He is a mahogany faced old Jackass who knew Burns— He ought to be kicked for having spoken to him," he burst out to Reynolds. "O the flummery of a birth place! Cant! Cant! Cant! It is enough to give a spirit the guts-ache." Part of the reason for his rage was that "the flat dog made me write a flat sonnet." The poem he had intended to write here took still more of an effort than the one at Burns's tomb, and he told Reynolds and Bailey and Tom that it was too wretched to copy for them. Apparently he was so overcome by its badness that he destroyed it several days later—though fortunately not before Brown had made a transcript.

Yet the sonnet is not as bad as all that; and if it were, its badness would not account for the anger and then despair Keats felt at the time. Furthermore, he wrote many poorer poems, both before and after this one, which he let stand; this is the only poem, to our knowledge, that he took the trouble to destroy after burning some of his earliest verses two years before. Why did he single this sonnet out? Perhaps because his own unhappiness and "sick pride" obtruded still more openly here than in his sonnet at Burns's grave:

> This mortal body of a thousand days
>   Now fills, O Burns, a space in thine own room,
> Where thou didst dream alone on budded bays,
>   Happy and thoughtless of thy day of doom!

It struck Keats with a terrible irony that he should be sitting there in Burns's own house, drinking the whisky Burns loved, looking out on the hills of his beloved Ayshire—that on this summer evening he should be alive and Burns dead.

> Yet can I stamp my foot upon thy floor,
>   Yet can I ope thy window-sash to find
> The meadow thou hast tramped o'er and o'er,—
>   Yet can I think of thee till thought is blind,—
> Yet can I gulp a bumper to thy name,—
> O smile among the shades, for this is fame!

The irony of the poem is summed up in the last line; but the terror is in the first. "This mortal body of a thousand days": again Keats found himself staring at the prospect of his own death, less than three years ahead. The thought he meant never to express had slipped out, and as soon as he regained his balance he tried to expunge it.

This is the only way of accounting for his extraordinary act of destroying his own poem; it is also the only way of bridging a strange hiatus in his letter to Reynolds describing the visit. "I cannot write about scenery and visitings," he went on. "His Misery is a dead weight upon the nimbleness of one's quill—I tried to forget it—to drink Toddy without any Care—to write a merry Sonnet—it wont do—he talked with Bitches—he drank with Blackguards, he was miserable—We can see horribly clear in the works of such a man his whole life, as if we were God's spies.— I should not speak so to you—yet why not—you are not in the same case—you are in the right path, and you shall not be deceived," he continued with a curious emphasis. "I have spoken to you against Marriage, but it was general—the Prospect in those matters has been to me so blank, that I have not been unwilling to die." The thought had been torn from him—that he would go Tom's way and not George's. But immediately he recovered himself: "I would not now, for I have inducements to Life— I must see my little Nephews in America, and I must see you marry your lovely Wife. Believe me," he added, "I have more than once yearne'd for the time of your happiness to come, as much as I could for myself after the lips of Juliet. One of the first pleasures I look to is your happy Marriage—the more, since I have felt the pleasure of loving a sister in Law." He had righted himself by now, and closed his letter with a message to the *vingt-et-un* players. "Tell my friends I do all I can for them, that is drink their healths in Toddy."

⤜⤛

The visit to Burns's cottage marks the turning point in Keats's journey. Here for the first time he allowed himself to express the fear that he had been trying to forget ever since leaving England; at the same time he found himself admitting to a desire which he had tried for several years to deny—for the love which is the best human defence against death. The idea that he should ever wish to marry was a revelation, unexpected and deeply troubling. Perhaps it had come over him only three days earlier, when a wedding party rode past them in Galloway and he found the tears springing to his eyes. Now as he wrote Reynolds he recalled with a pang all the times he had "rodomontaded" against marriage. Some of his reasons for trying to avoid it were fairly clear to him. His devotion to his brothers, deeper for the losses they had suffered together; his warm friendships with a circle of men who shared his interests and ambitions; the opportunities for easy sexual adventures all around him, combined with the general deprecating attitude toward women he caught from his society— that they were for the most part "children to whom I would rather give a Sugar Plum than my time"—all these had left little room of any importance in his life so far for a woman to fill. But there were stronger reasons than the mere absence of need. There were the demands of his work for solitude and for freedom to extend his experience, a freedom which marriage would circumscribe. There was the passionate sensuousness of his nature, which demanded a richer satisfaction than he found, for example, in the Reynoldses' drawing room; there was his own deep-rooted conviction of his physical insignificance. And deeper still, probably far below the level of his awareness, was the fear that to love a woman wholeheartedly meant only to risk betrayal and loss—the legacy of his attachment to his mother.

But in the last half-year he was being forced to wonder whether the challenge of marriage could be argued away. Reynolds' engagement to Eliza Drewe, for whose sake he was almost willing to give up his literary career; George's marriage to a lighthearted girl who was also a disinterested character; even Bailey's heavy-footed pursuit of Mariane Reynolds "with the Bible and Jeremy Taylor under his arm" [14]—all these suggested to Keats that marriage could be the most significant relationship in a man's life. His circle of bachelor friends was beginning to break up; and with George in America and Tom so ill, he was beginning to glimpse the loneliness in prospect for him. Yet at the same time he found himself more and more uncomfortable in the presence of women, especially the young women to whom he was still closest, the Reynolds sisters. Bailey, on learning at Little Britain that Keats had given up his regular calls there before setting out for Scotland, took it on himself to regret this in a letter of July. Keats replied with some asperity. After all, he was a man with "Books to read and subjects to think upon," and moreover he had been able to go out very little in June. But he realized that the truth lay deeper than this, and he went on to give Bailey an extraordinary piece of self-analysis, almost a century before the very idea of such analysis had been conceived:

"I am certain I have not a right feeling towards Women—at this moment I am striving to be just to them but I cannot—Is it because they fall so far beneath my Boyish imagination? I have no right to expect more than their reality." These "pure Goddesses" of his schoolboy dreams were human beings after all; he was also discovering some very human failings in his own reactions to them—that he was "thinking insults in a Lady's Company" which he realized were unjustified. "One who is tender of being insulted does not like to think an insult against another— When among Men I have no evil thoughts, no malice, no spleen —I feel free to speak or to be silent—I can listen and from every one I can learn—my hands are in my pockets I am free from all suspicion and comfortable. When I am among Women I have evil thoughts, malice spleen—I cannot speak or be silent—I am full of Suspicions and therefore listen to nothing—I am in a hurry to be gone—You must be charitable and put all this perversity to my being disappointed since Boyhood," he added. "Mister John Keats five feet high"—how could he expect a woman to take him seriously? Yet in recognizing the cause of his anxiety he still refused to leave it at that. "I must absolutely get over this —but how? The only way is to find the root of evil, and so cure it 'with backward mutters of dissevering Power' That is a difficult thing; for an obstinate Prejudice can seldom be produced but from a gordian complication of feelings, which must take time to unravell and care to keep unravelled."

This admission of a hostility which till now he had successfully concealed suggests that Keats was beginning to look to women for something he had not sought before—the fulfilment not of a single need but of his whole self. Apparently he also felt that, for some reason, he was being unfairly sceptical about their capacity to meet such a demand. The reason was close at hand, whether he realized it or not. Charles Brown, whose company he was sharing hour by hour during these months, must have acted as a solvent of whatever adolescent idealism Keats still preserved. Brown was an enigmatic character, a mixture of Scottish strictness in money matters and Rabelaisian gusto in others; a lover of broad jokes and good poetry; a misogynist who liked to tease pretty young women; a freethinker full of passionate prejudices, who requested before his death to be given a pauper's burial or —to save all funeral expenses—to be consigned to a medical school for dissection.[15] He had lived a far more adventurous life than any of Keats's other friends. After starting work at fourteen in a London merchant's office, he was sent to St. Petersburg at eighteen to manage a branch of the business there. Five years later the firm failed and Brown returned to London, penniless. For another five years he scraped along as a journalist, at one time so poor that he ate at fourpenny ordinaries where the knives and forks were chained to the table. An unexpected inheritance from his brother and the success of his comic opera *Narensky* at Drury Lane put him back on his feet again; a year later he and Dilke, a schoolfellow, built Wentworth Place together. Here Brown settled into a comfortable bachelor existence, living tidily on his small income and continuing to write mainly for his own amusement, his masculine needs satisfied by occasional visits to the shabby side streets off Covent Garden.

Though at first sight they seemed an ill-assorted pair, Brown was eventually to become Keats's closest friend. Better than anyone else he could offer Keats both the brotherly companionship which George had always given him and the fatherly support of an older man which he had sought from Hunt and Haydon. But what Keats seems to have valued in him was that Brown liked him as a man rather than as a poet. Brown's humour was a refuge from his own black moods; his common sense also seemed the antithesis both of Hunt's sentimental falsification of life and Haydon's egocentrical distortions of it. That Brown was, in his own way, as much of an egotist as Hunt or Haydon, incapable of understanding an outlook different from his own, indifferent to the pain his bluntness might cause,[16] Keats had as yet had no time to discover. How far at this point he could share the older man's attitude toward women is another question. Brown's cynicism dated from a romantic setback he had suffered in St. Petersburg in his early twenties. There he had become engaged to an English lady who then turned him down for a compatriot whose business prospects seemed brighter. This gentleman went bankrupt and died shortly afterward, and years later it was hinted to Brown at Hampstead that the widow would be glad to resume their acquaintance.[17] Brown declined the offer, evidently with satisfaction; it certainly confirmed him in his jaundiced view of the sex. Yet the affair kept rankling long enough for him to start an autobiographical novel, thirty years after the event, in which this early defeat is translated into an imaginary victory. The lady is punished for her faithlessness, while Brown himself, in the character of his hero, is both rewarded and vindicated when the lady returns to him, abandoned and ill, and he deserts his wife to live with her, "enduring every slander that the world can heap upon [him]." [18] No better proof could be found of the theory that the cynic is only an inverted sentimentalist.

It is difficult to imagine Keats ever sharing Brown's belief that women are mere sexual objects and no more, though it is clear from his letters on the trip that he enjoyed Brown's bawdy humour. Whether he was aware of a less obvious aspect of his friend's nature is not clear. All the while this sturdy masculine figure was tramping through the Highlands with Keats he was evidently cherishing the image of a fresh-faced boy at Eton—Henry Snook, the thirteen-year-old nephew of his friend Dilke. A few sentences from one of Brown's long letters to Henry reveal a "complication of feelings" equal to if different from Keats's own: "I have thought of you, and your brother, and my two nephews, every day on my walk," Brown wrote. "To have left you all, after so long having been your companion, sometimes comes across my mind in a painful manner, and the farther I have travelled away the stronger has been the feeling. There may be many who cannot understand why I should think of you so much, but my dear boys know how much I have loved them. But let the proof of this remain till some future day, for in the meanwhile I can have nothing to offer but assurances of affection. God keep you well, my dear Boy," he ended, "and believe me your more than brother-friend." [19] Whatever the actual nature of Brown's attachment to the young Snooks, it seems clear that the older man's deep-grained dislike of women helped to bring to the surface all Keats's ambivalent feelings toward them this summer. Yet there was nothing to do about the problem for the time being but to postpone it. So Keats wrote to Tom at the end of July to describe the snug life they would lead together at Well Walk next winter, studying hard, visiting Fanny, going to the theatre every now and then, and added, rather cryptically, "With respect to Women I think I shall be able to conquer my passions hereafter better than I have yet done."

The thought of Tom alone in Hampstead kept troubling Keats, the more so because, after receiving one letter from him at Portpatrick, he could not expect another till he reached Inverness a month later. Uncertainty about his brother's health and a nagging sense of guilt about going off on his adventure added to his uneasiness, and the thought of Hampstead kept coming to his mind more often as the excitement of the trip began to wear off. "I assure you I often long for a seat and a Cup o' tea at well Walk— especially now that mountains, castles and Lakes are becoming common to me," he confessed to Tom. "Yet I would rather summer it out for on the whole I am happier than when I have time to be glum." This mood reflects more fatigue than boredom, however. Day after day, with Brown checking off the distances on the map, they trudged twenty miles, sometimes more, between sunrise and late afternoon; only a hard rain was allowed to slow them down.

From Ayr they walked north to Glasgow, then headed northwest into the Highlands. Loch Lomond on a bright summer evening was "grand in excess," yet they were disappointed to find it, like Windermere, overspread with "the miasma of London." "Steam Boats and Barouches take a little from the Pleasure of such romantic chaps as Brown and I," Keats remarked wryly to Tom. They had looked forward to climbing Ben Lomond but found the guides too expensive. The wild country farther west, around Loch Fyne and Loch Awe, was more to their liking. Here they could walk for miles through the heather and hear no sound

but mountain streams, or see no living thing but a few sheep on
the hills or an eagle soaring overhead. The Highlanders spoke
Gaelic, the first foreign language Keats had heard; they were intelligent and friendly, with nothing of the Lowlanders' suspicion of
the English, but their living conditions were still more primitive.
At Newton Stuart early in July, Keats found a sofa and some hair-
bottomed chairs worth mentioning in his journal; evidently they
were the last he encountered for over a month. The Highland
fare—eggs and oatcake, meal after meal, washed down with water
and a gill of whisky—became sickening. "Sometimes when I am
rather tired," Keats wrote Mrs. Wylie, "I lean rather languish-
ingly on a Rock, & long for some famous Beauty to get down from
her Palfrey in passing; approach me with—her saddle bags—&
give me—a dozen or two capital roast beef sandwiches."

One of the goals of their journey was a visit to Staffa in the Inner
Hebrides, a tiny island built on pillars of basalt rising sheer out
of the sea. At Oban, finding that the boat fare to Staffa was an ex-
orbitant seven guineas, they almost decided to give the visit up
when an obliging fellow offered to take them at a bargain. This
involved walking thirty-seven miles across the Isle of Mull instead
of sailing around it. They agreed; then, as they started on their
tramp through the island, the weather turned bad, and the track
through the mountains proved as good as none at all. For two
weary days they climbed up hill and down, in wind and rain,
jumping from boulder to boulder, fording streams with their
breeches tucked up and their shoes in hand, wading ankle-deep
through bogs a mile long. They spent the night in a shepherd's
hut with no floor or chimney, the air thick with peat smoke; and
here, sleeping on the ground in damp clothes, Keats caught a
violent cold. At the far end of Mull, however, an adventure waited
them: a visit to Iona. Keats had heard nothing of this fabled
island, where, thirteen centuries before, Saint Columba had
founded the first Christian settlement in Great Britain and where
through the Dark Ages all the Kings of Scotland were buried. A
stunted little old schoolmaster showed them over the ruins of the
cathedral and cloisters. Keats was most stirred by the narrow rows
of royal graves in the churchyard, and the moss-covered tombs of
Highland chieftains with their effigies in armour lying at full
length on top.

From Iona they took a boat to Staffa. As they approached it on a gently swelling sea, the honeycomb of purple-black columns on which the island is based seemed to rise out of pure crystal. The rare good weather allowed them to land and explore Fingal's Cave at the head of the island—a stupendous work of natural architecture which immediately struck Keats as the setting for a scene from *Hyperion*. "Suppose now," he wrote to Tom, "the Giants who rebelled against Jove had taken a whole Mass of black Columns and bound them together like bunches of matches—and then with immense Axes had made a cavern in the body of these columns—of course the roof and floor must be composed of the broken ends of the Columns—such is fingal's Cave except that the Sea has done the work of excavations and is continually dashing there—the roof is arched somewhat gothic wise and the view into the sea through the large Arch at the entrance for solemnity and grandeur far surpasses the finest Cathedrall."

After Staffa and Iona, Scotland could hold few wonders more. They rested a few days in Oban, then started north again with the rain dogging them; and when they reached Fort William on the first of August, Keats's cold had turned into a flaming sore throat. But he was determined to climb Ben Nevis with Brown—the more so for having missed both Helvellyn and Ben Lomond. Ben Nevis, the highest mountain in Great Britain, rose nearly four and a half thousand feet from sea level at Loch Linnhe, where they started —as much as climbing "10 Saint Pauls without the convenience of Stair cases," Keats figured. They set out at five on a grey morning with a guide in tartan, a dog, and a good supply of whisky. Rise after rise they climbed through the mist, with the head of the mountain still hidden behind the next ascent; heath soon gave way to loose stones and patches of snow; then chasms a thousand feet deep, filled with clouds, opened suddenly before them. On one of their brief stops they amused themselves by tumbling rocks into the chasms and setting the echoes at work; then, after a glass of whisky apiece, they started on again. Over the loose stones the going was very rough—"sometimes on two sometimes on three, sometimes four legs, ringing changes on foot, hand, Stick, jump boggle, stumble, foot, hand, foot, (very gingerly) stick again, and then again a game at all fours." Near the top the fog lifted and they were surrounded by swirling clouds, which parted every now and then to give them a burst of sunshine or a glimpse of the crags below. On they crawled, through sun and mist and cold wind;

then at last they reached the summit. Keats found himself standing on a stony plain, which appeared to be low ground but
dropped off into nothing at the edge; at a great distance, the tops
of other mountains rose below. Some artillerymen had piled the
stones near the summit into a neat pyramid; Keats climbed this
mound and thus, to his delight, "got a little higher than old Ben
himself." Then he sat down to write a sonnet.

It was the peak of the summer's adventure, and suddenly there
was nothing to say. Looking out into the clouded emptiness ahead,
he forced this nothingness into a poem—one of the lamest of the
five lame sonnets he wrote on the trip, yet significant as summing
up the summer's meaning:

> Read me a lesson, Muse, and speak it loud
>   Upon the top of Nevis, blind in mist!
> I look into the chasms, and a shroud
>   Vaporous doth hide them,—just so much I wist
> Mankind do know of hell; I look o'erhead
>   And there is sullen mist,—even so much
> Mankind can tell of heaven; mist is spread
>   Before the earth, beneath me,—even such,
> Even so vague is man's sight of himself!
>   Here are the craggy stones beneath my feet,—
> Thus much I know that, a poor witless elf,
>   I tread on them,—that all my eye doth meet
> Is mist and crag, not only on this height,
> But in the world of thought and mental might!

He had come all this way to discover that adventure is not life;
that the finest scenes and the grandest mountains do not of themselves make poetry; and that at the farthest reach of his journey
the familiar spectre of his own impotent bewilderment stood facing him. At the top of Ben Nevis lay the "Purgatory blind," the
vision of the meaninglessness of existence which he had first confronted on the shore at Teignmouth and that was waiting for him
at Hampstead. From now on the road lay downward and backward.

" 'T was the most vile descent—shook me all to pieces." But
once again they shouldered their packs and struck out, through
Glen More and the Great Glen, seventy miles along Loch Lochy
and Loch Ness. When they reached Inverness four days later,
Keats had a burning fever. The doctor whom Brown summoned
looked grave; Keats's throat was ulcerated, and he was too thin

and worn to keep on with the journey. Reluctantly he agreed to return home. It was a blow, but only to Keats's pride; Brown decided at once to complete the trip alone. The two men stumped on for two more days to Cromarty, where they said good-bye and Keats boarded the smack to London.

A nine days' trip—his first sea-voyage—was marred by rough weather and poor food and a toothache at the end; but he reached Hampstead in good humour, glad to be home at last. Stopping in at Wentworth Place before climbing the hill to Well Walk, he startled Mrs. Dilke half out of her wits. She noted in her diary on August 19: "John Keats arrived here last night, as brown and as shabby as you can imagine; scarcely any shoes left, his jacket all torn at the back, a fur cap, a great plaid, and his knapsack." He must have heaved this off his shoulders with relief before dropping into a comfortable stuffed chair—the first since Newton Stuart—and exclaiming with a grin, "Bless thee, Bottom! bless thee! thou art translated!" [20] Then he learned the news they had to tell him.

Chapter Eight

The Shores of Darkness

T o m was not better but much worse. Early in August he had had a relapse so serious that Sawrey asked Dilke to send for Keats at once. Dilke's letter reached Inverness after Keats had already sailed, and its news had to be broken that night at Wentworth Place. With a sinking heart Keats climbed the hill to Well Walk, where Tom lay waiting—pale, feeble, pitiably thin, and seized now by the uncontrollable nervousness of the last stages of consumption. All the brave pretences of the months before were shattered. Neither one could now deny the truth to the other: Tom was dying. Keats had known this would come in time; he can hardly have guessed how soon. His first act the next morning was to write to Fanny. His toothache still throbbed; his throat still burned with fever. A letter she had written him at Inverness called for answers on half a dozen irrelevant topics—the death of her canary, the pebbles she had asked him to bring from Scotland, the flageolet she wanted him to buy for her. But she must be told the news, and, still more, Abbey must be talked into allowing her to come to see Tom. His letter was as tender as ever but distracted, and he cut it short with a promise to visit her soon.

But this meeting did not take place for two weeks. His own sore throat kept hanging on, and, a few days after his homecoming, Tom took another turn for the worse. Keats was now left almost entirely alone to take care of his brother. Tom became so agitated by visitors that when the Reynolds sisters offered their help Keats had to refuse it as politely as he could. His close friends seemed to have vanished. Brown was still in Scotland; Dilke, who fell ill himself in August, went off to Brighton to convalesce; Haydon and Rice and Reynolds and Taylor were all off in the country. Severn came down with an attack of typhus later in September; only George's faithful friend Haslam stood by week after week. Keats's regular company now consisted almost entirely of his landlady, Mrs. Bentley, Mrs. Dilke, and old Mr. Lewis, a Hampstead neighbour who had called on Tom daily during the summer with presents of fruit. To add to his sense of isolation, day after day went by with no letter from George. Uncertain of where to address him, Keats held off writing for weeks, then could not bring himself to start a letter because of the news of Tom he must send. Fanny was grudgingly allowed to visit Well Walk once or twice in September; but Tom found it so hard to let her go at the end of the day that Keats wondered whether she should come again. Abbey soon took this matter out of his hands, however. On one of these visits, Keats took Fanny to see Mrs. Dilke without thinking to ask Mrs. Abbey's permission in advance.[1] When she learned of this infraction of the rules, Fanny was forbidden to come again for several months.

So Keats returned to his long watch by Tom's beside, nursing him through chills and coughing fits, trying to calm him in spells of despair, reading to him in his comfortable hours, and keeping up as cheerful a front as he could. One Sunday evening, while rereading *King Lear* as his brother lay asleep, his eye was caught by the words "poor Tom"; suddenly overcome, he underlined them and added the date in the margin of his Folio. Once or twice he tried to surmount his anxieties by writing, but found himself plagued by an uneasy feeling of guilt about his brother. "If I think of fame of poetry it seems a crime," he confessed in a letter to Dilke. "Yet I must do so or suffer." Caught between his desire to ease Tom's suffering and his instinct somehow to escape from it, he felt a "hateful siege of contraries" burning in him like a fever. Then something happened that made all writing impossible for several weeks. Early in September the storm of criticism that had been threatening ever since June broke at last. *Blackwood's* came out with the fourth of its "Cockney School" articles, this one devoted to *Endymion*.

It was a blow aimed squarely below the belt. The reviewer began by gibing at the poetry-writing mania which had turned footmen and retired governesses to scribbling verses in imitation of

Robert Burns and Joanna Baillie. The latest victim of this malady, he continued, was a young man who had been destined by his friends for a useful career as apothecary but who had fallen under the unfortunate influence of Leigh Hunt—"the most worthless and affected of all the versifiers of our time." Encouraged by Hunt, this "Johnny Keats" has deserted his gallipots and written a long poem on the subject of Endymion, which can only be described as "calm, settled, imperturbable drivelling idiocy." After sneering at Keats's education and slashing at Hunt's politics, the review quoted some of the poem's weakest passages, then wound up with this advice: "It is a better and a wiser thing to be a starved apothecary than a starved poet; so back to the shop, Mr. John, back to the 'plasters, pills, and ointment boxes,' &c. But, for Heaven's sake, young Sangrado, be a little more sparing of extenuatives and soporifics in your practice than you have been in your poetry."

All this was in "Z.'s" usual style of insult, especially bitter to a man as proud and reserved as Keats. To be dubbed "apothecary's boy" and classed with governesses and footmen had an added sting. It was, after all, not a trade he had been trained to but a profession; and in the circle of his friends, he was counted a gentleman among gentlemen. Yet at the same time Keats had "a fierce hatred of rank," as Haydon tells us, of the arrogance with which the aristocracy flaunted its privileges during the bitter years after Waterloo. It has been said that Keats was ashamed of his background— the livery stable, the Clarke school, the apprenticeship to a village apothecary. But this seems to have been not Keats's attitude so much as that of his more class-conscious friends, including even Brown and Hunt; [2] Keats's reticence about his boyhood had other, very different causes. Yet he could do nothing about the *Blackwood's* affront, not even challenge the reviewer to a duel as he had once resolved, for "Z." still refused to reveal himself, despite all the efforts to force him into the open.

In the middle of September an invitation came from Taylor's partner, Hessey, to dine at Fleet Street, along with Woodhouse, the firm's literary and legal adviser, Hazlitt, and some other friends. It was almost the first break in Keats's long exile in Hampstead, and he mustered up what good spirits he could for the occasion. He must have been especially glad to see Hazlitt, for *Blackwood's* had opened a campaign against him in the same issue as the review of *Endymion*. After sneering at him as "pimpled

Hazlitt," a slander too pointless to refute, "Z." had launched into a long outrageous assault on his education and critical opinions, which Hazlitt promptly answered by initiating a suit for libel. But at the time of Hessey's dinner Hazlitt was more aroused by his treatment in the *Quarterly,* an older and far more influential review than *Blackwood's.* The second edition of his immensely successful *Characters of Shakespeare's Plays* had not sold a single copy for the last three months. For this only one thing was responsible—William Gifford's review in June in the *Quarterly,* jeering at Hazlitt's style as borrowed from washerwomen, and attacking him for "senseless and wicked sophistry" and even "sedition." [3] A year ago it seemed that the *Characters* had earned Hazlitt his fame as a critic at last; now the *Quarterly* had blasted it.

Hazlitt's fighting spirit was up, as Keats knew; but he said nothing about the reviews that evening, and Keats followed his example. Still he could not keep from dropping a bombshell of his own. He announced that he had given up poetry. To the astonishment of most of his listeners he began arguing that there was nothing new or valuable left to be done in poetry; all its riches had long since been exploited, and he for one would write no more. Woodhouse, who was a logical man as well as a warm admirer of Keats's work, tried to dispute his point and left at the end of the evening still disturbed by the conversation. Hessey, more practical and less argumentative, also more familiar than Woodhouse with Keats's "rodomontade," did not take him so seriously. A day or two later he reported to Taylor, who was still on vacation in Bath, that their young author was "studying closely, recovering his Latin, going to learn Greek, and seems altogether more rational than usual." For all of Keats's fits and starts, Hessey was still convinced that "sometime or other he will do something valuable." [4]

As for the *Blackwood's* review, if Hessey had told Keats what Taylor already knew about it, he would only have deepened his discouragement. Keats must have wondered how the account of his early years had reached the enemy camp; for a while he and his friends suspected Ollier of being somehow responsible. Not until some time later is it likely that he connected the article with a curious letter he had received from Bailey during his trip in Scotland. Bailey was now a country curate near Carlisle, where, he told Taylor, he was "endeavoring to *humanize* a set of boors." [5] Through a Cambridge friend, George Robert Gleig, he had been meeting the *Blackwood's* set in Edinburgh that summer and thus had an opportunity to forward to Keats an invitation from Mr. Blackwood himself. The editor, who had been impressed by his friend Christie's favourable report on Keats the winter before, had asked him to call when he reached Edinburgh, and Bailey advised Keats that he would do well to conciliate the Tories by accepting. According to Brown, Keats indignantly refused; whereupon Bailey at the end of August wrote not Keats but Taylor a carefully censored account of what followed.

On a visit to Gleig at Stirling, Bailey had met John Gibson Lockhart, a dark, good-looking young Oxford graduate and contributor to *Blackwood's*. After listening to him abuse Keats at dinner, along with Hunt and his set, Bailey put in a word or two on his friend's behalf. Lockhart then talked the slow-witted Bailey into telling him what he knew of Keats's early life—the "respectable family," "the small but independent patrimony," the apprenticeship to Hammond, and all.[6] Once the story was out, Bailey had a sudden misgiving, but as he looked up and down the table he must have realized he was in an awkward spot. His friend Gleig was now working for Blackwood himself; Gleig had a sister who had already caught Bailey's eye; and at the head of the table sat Gleig's father, the Bishop of Brechin, Primus of the Scots Episcopal Church. It was not the moment for an ambitious curate to rise to the defence of a young poet of obscure origins and disreputable connections who had just published a long poem in praise of physical love. Bailey did what Bailey could. He begged Lockhart not to use his information against Keats, and Lockhart sardonically agreed that it would not be used "by *him*." Bailey, taking alarm, then wrote Taylor warning him that *Endymion* might be "dreadfully cut up in *Blackwood's*," recounting Lockhart's abuse of Keats but saying nothing of his own share in the discussion.

Taylor, who had been taking steps of his own to win Keats a fair hearing in the Tory reviews, must have been thunderstruck. One wonders also how much that sharp-eyed scholar read of Bailey's real part in the conversation between the lines of his letter. For Bailey, who three months earlier had praised the "beauty and power" of *Endymion* in an Oxford review, now found its "indelicacy" indefensible—especially in its implication that *"Sensual Love* is the principle of *things."* Bailey then spoke of Tom's relapse. "I do not know well what to think, whether good or bad, of the death of this young man, if it happen. It looks harsh to say it is happy; and yet from his character he must have lived a life of discomfort to himself and those with whom he was connected, if the character I have heard of him be just. Happen as it will, I am *religiously* persuaded, all *is* for the best." So, after a change of heart, does one find oneself on the right side once again. Bailey's next letter to Taylor in October, inquiring about some theological works recommended by Bishop Gleig, was noticeably cooler; and his correspondence with Keats came to a sudden halt at this time. But from several mentions of the conversation in his letters to Taylor, it is clear that it still lay on his conscience—so much so that three years later he wrote Taylor a guarded memorandum defending his part in it, supplemented by a fuller account some thirty years afterward, trying to prove that the use of his information in the review was merely a coincidence.[7]

Taylor can hardly have repeated Bailey's words on Tom to Keats, and it is uncertain how much he told Keats of his friend's unlucky conversation with Lockhart. Keats himself never mentioned Bailey in connection with the *Blackwood's* article; yet it is significant that by the end of 1818 "parson" had become a term of contempt with him. By this time Hazlitt's suit against *Blackwood's* had had the indirect effect of forcing his assailant to identify himself, and so at last the world learned that the infamous "Z." was none other than Bailey's dinner companion, Lockhart himself. In September, however, Keats could have guessed none of this. A week or two after "Z.'s" attack appeared, he spoke of Bailey in a letter to Dilke merely to say that he had heard Bailey was in better spirits than usual, and to note also that his name was not often mentioned at the Reynoldses' now.

His own calls at Little Britain were of course less frequent than ever, with Reynolds in Devon and Tom still too weak to be left for long; and Keats was probably glad enough to be relieved of this obligation. Wentworth Place was much nearer, and Mrs. Dilke was not only a helpful neighbour but a good-humoured companion as well. Keats was a frequent caller at the Dilkes' during the first month or two after his return from Scotland, and it was most probably at this time that he met the family who had taken Brown's half of the house for the summer—a widow with a young son and two daughters. Mrs. Brawne, he wrote to

George in December, "is a very nice woman—and her daughter senior is I think beautiful and elegant, graceful, silly, fashionable and strange we have a little tiff now and then." Thus casually, and three months or more after the event,[8] Keats recorded a meeting which at the time threatened to throw him completely off balance. Fanny Brawne, just eighteen, graceful, silly, and strange, had walked into the Dilkes' drawing room and with a word, a gesture, a glance of her blue eyes, assailed his entire being as no woman had ever done before. As he later wrote her, "If you should ever feel for Man at the first sight what I did for you, I am lost." Clearly, then, his laconic introduction of the Brawnes to George in December was an elaborate camouflage of his real feelings. He confessed a little more of them in a letter to Reynolds in September, not long after the encounter: "I never was in love—Yet the voice and the shape of a woman has haunted me these two days— at such a time when the relief, the feverous relief of Poetry seems a much less crime—This morning Poetry has conquered—I feel escaped from a new strange and threatening sorrow—And I am thankful for it—There is an awful warmth about my heart like a load of Immortality." [9]

It was a narrow escape, so he must have thought. Several days after meeting Fanny, Keats had written her an impetuous letter declaring himself her "vassal"; but a few days later he burned the letter instead of sending it because, at their next encounter, he felt she had taken a dislike to him. This was probably the time that he took Severn with him to the Dilkes'—Severn, whom Fanny Brawne remembered as never serious for ten minutes together.[10] Perhaps his friend's good looks and high spirits made a visible impression on Fanny; perhaps Fanny herself, who had a reputation as a flirt, set out to impress Severn. Whatever happened, Keats, who had been roused to new anxiety by their first encounter, felt rebuffed and withdrew. Fanny's beauty was a threat, his response to it a "crime"; in relief he turned back to the activity in which he could assert the identity she threatened. "Poetry has conquered," he told Reynolds. That morning he copied out the first poem he had written since the day he stood on Ben Nevis—a free translation of a sonnet by Ronsard—and enclosed it in his letter with an apology for leaving off the last two lines, which he had forgotten:

Nature withheld Cassandra in the skies,
    For more adornment, a full thousand years;
She took their cream of Beauty's fairest dyes,
    And shap'd and tinted her above all Peers:
Meanwhile Love kept her dearly with his wings,
    And underneath their shadow fill'd her eyes
With such a richness that the cloudy Kings
    Of high Olympus utter'd slavish sighs.
When from the Heavens I saw her first descend,
    My heart took fire, and only burning pains,
They were my pleasures—they my Life's sad end;
    Love pour'd her beauty into my warm veins. . . .

"Poor Tom—that woman—and Poetry were ringing changes in my senses—now I am in comparison happy." Torn between anguish over Tom's growing weakness and this answering upsurge of sexual vitality, he had to escape. "I have relapsed into those abstractions which are my only life," he told Reynolds. This was important news. At last he had started to write *Hyperion*.

-»»-«««-

"Abstract" is the word Keats always used to describe *Hyperion* —a word full of meaning for this poem. Abstract, first, in the sense that the action takes place on a level far above the actualities of human life. Byron, Keats once said, "describes what he sees— I describe what I imagine—Mine is the hardest task." *Hyperion* is abstract also in seeming to follow no one source, but drawing on a few hints scattered through classical poetry of the primeval struggle between the Olympian gods and their forebears, the Titans.[11] It is abstract too in its apparent remoteness from the experiences that were pressing on him at the moment. But while most abstractions are fairly described as lifeless, this epic of the Titans, written at the bedside of his dying brother, became to Keats his "only life," a world of its own intense reality in which he could breathe freely again.

Deep in the shady sadness of a vale
Far sunken from the healthy breath of morn,
Far from the fiery noon, and eve's one star,
Sat gray-hair'd Saturn, quiet as a stone,
Still as the silence round about his lair;
Forest on forest hung above his head

Like cloud on cloud. No stir of air was there,
Not so much life as on a summer's day
Robs not one light seed from the feather'd grass,
But where the dead leaf fell, there did it rest.
A stream went voiceless by, still deadened more
By reason of his fallen divinity
Spreading a shade: the Naiad 'mid her reeds
Press'd her cold finger closer to her lips.

Along the margin-sand large foot-marks went,
No further than to where his feet had stray'd,
And slept there since. Upon the sodden ground
His old right hand lay nerveless, listless, dead,
Unsceptred; and his realmless eyes were closed;
While his bow'd head seem'd list'ning to the Earth,
His ancient mother, for some comfort yet.

From these first lines we are confronted with a mystery, a muta-
tion, what Auden once called "the strange event of qualitative
change." The chord that Keats struck for a moment in his "Ode
to Maia" is sounded again and again as the music goes gravely forward, sustained in every line. The emotion is severely controlled;
the poem seems to have been chiselled with great deliberation out
of pure imaginary experience. It is written not in Keats's earlier
fluent style but in what he later described as "an artful or rather
artist's humour," in an idiom carefully modelled on *Paradise Lost*.
But how can one account for a miracle? Keats had been reading
Milton closely for months, and much of the measured nobility
of his verse is echoed from his master. He had studied the Elgin
Marbles hour after hour till the silent eloquence of the Parthenon
friezes spoke through every gesture of his fallen gods. He had
tramped through the Lakes and the Highlands, and the rugged
grandeur of their mountains and cataracts shines out in the imagery of the poem. But perhaps the closest one can come to an
answer is to say that Keats had become a different person from the
man who had written *Endymion* a year ago; in fact the theme of
Hyperion is the struggle of spiritual growth itself.

This was the meaning that had been gathering round the original core of his story since the spring—"the grand march of intellect" which he had described to Reynolds, now projected into the
whole creation. In the second book of *Hyperion* the Titans debate
the reason for their fall, much as do Milton's rebel angels; and
Oceanus, the wisest, gives the answer which Keats seems to have

intended at the start. Growth is the law of life; and in the sum of time its direction is upward—from chaos to order, from darkness to light. The Titans, though fairer than their progenitors Earth and Heaven, who themselves sprang from Chaos and Darkness, are now challenged by a new generation of gods "more strong in beauty." In the contest the older gods have proved as frail as mortals, subject to all the human emotions of "fear, hope, and wrath." But for the higher forms of life to appear, the lower must be left behind, and the height of wisdom is to acquiesce in this progress, no matter what its cost to the individual:

> to bear all naked truths,
> And to envisage circumstance, all calm,
> That is the top of sovereignty.

But this conception had grown immensely complicated in the months since Keats began pondering his epic. Not the glory but the cost of the struggle preoccupied him now. Something had driven him off his course—Tom, with his exquisite love of life, dying before his eyes. The horror of undeserved suffering, of useless and degrading pain—the knowledge that made Keats fling at Bailey the reminder that women have cancers—broke through his plan and aligned him with the defeated. All the calm beauty of the new Olympian gods—Neptune scudding the waves in his chariot, young Apollo on Delos discovering his gift of song—could not justify the agonies of the supplanted Titans, too vivid to Keats in what Tom was enduring,

> pent in regions of laborious breath, . . .
> Heaving in pain, and horribly convuls'd
> With sanguine feverous boiling gurge of pulse.

Indeed, the keenest emotion recorded in the first two books is that flash of guilt the healthy person feels when he realizes that the ill person looking at him sees his own illness reflected in the other's eyes. As Hyperion, not yet overthrown, approaches the fallen Titans in all his original brightness, a light "made terrible" by the darkness in which they lie, he sees

> The misery his brilliance had betray'd
> To the most hateful seeing of itself.

So for Keats the hourly contact with his dying brother forced on him a new and painful self-awareness and with it a still more painful sense of self-division. Hyperion in his golden palace, gloomily previsioning his own downfall, recalls Keats the spring before, looking into the dark passages ahead of him; while Saturn in his overthrow, "smother'd up And buried from all godlike exercise," divided from "his strong identity, his real self," conveys the bewildering sense of loss of identity which assailed Keats that autumn when his own "godlike exercise" of poetry came to seem a crime.

This sense of being hemmed in and almost smothered recurs again and again in Keats's letters during these months.[12] At the time of starting *Hyperion* he confessed to Dilke that Tom's identity "pressed" on him so unremittingly that he had to go out or try writing "to ease myself of his countenance his voice and feebleness." He told George that Fanny's identity, being still unformed, did not "press" on him like his own. A letter to Woodhouse in October suggests the real pain the sensation caused him: "When I am in a room with People if I ever am free from speculating on creations of my own brain, then the identity of every one in the room begins so to press upon me that, I am in a very little time annihilated." His capacity for entering into the existence of others, once a delight to him, now became a suffocating weight on his consciousness, almost as heavy as his brother George pinning him down in their battles long ago at school. As Tom grew weaker Keats felt his own "real self" dissolving in his awareness of what his brother was enduring. This feeling is probably not a rare one, though rarely analysed—a sense of dissociation between one's familiar self and a new self, hardly yet one's own, emerging from troubled experience which the self has not yet assimilated; or between the inner self in this state of conflict and the social self habitually assumed in contact with the world. "There I am a child—there they do not know me not even my most intimate acquaintance," Keats wrote George, trying to describe his sensations in company. His frequent repetition of the word "identity" during this autumn suggests how deeply the conflict unsettled him. "Until we are sick, we understand not," he had remarked to Reynolds the spring before. Now he lived "in a continual fever" of spirit which, when it subsided some months later, was to leave him with an extraordinary insight into the struggle for identity; but meanwhile he had to endure a sense of alienation still keener than that he had felt in his year at medical school.

It would seem that in this autumn of 1818 the feeling of self-

hood which Keats had painfully achieved in the last two years—
that of the hopeful young poet of his first two volumes—was
broken down and the ground laid for the building of a new self.
Within himself, Keats had been thrown into a turmoil by Tom's
relapse. The approaching death of a member of one's family poses
a deep unconscious threat to the ego—the deeper for Keats because for years his sense of his own being had been bound up
intimately with Tom's.[13] It was a part of himself that was dying
before his eyes, at a time when he had begun to suspect that he
too had not long to live. His time for poetry was growing shorter;
yet Tom's illness made Keats feel it "a crime" even to think of the
ambition on which he had staked his whole being. Besides this
inner conflict, his sense of identity in the outer world also was
threatened. Months ago he had repudiated the youthful poet of
Endymion; now a caricature of that self mocked him from the
reviews and made him feel "little and rediculous in society." In
that world of drawing rooms George had always smoothed his way
and also helped keep young ladies at a safe distance; now his marriage and emigration knocked out the other chief prop to Keats's
security and raised the question of sexual commitment which he
had evaded before. More anxious than ever about his ability to
win a woman's love, he had been overwhelmed by Fanny Brawne
on their first meeting; yet on the point of declaring his love to her
he was—or so he thought—rebuffed. In her eyes he caught again
the reflection of "Mister John Keats five feet high." It was only
part of the truth about himself, he knew, but the one that mattered most in her presence.

It was a time to try all Keats's courage. Day after day he watched
at Tom's bedside, tending to his wasted body and doing what he
could to keep his spirits up; and day after day, in spite of all the
"interruptions to a train of feeling" around him—Tom's demands, the noisy Bentley children—he went on with *Hyperion.*
It was hard work and slower than anything he had ever done, demanding as much dogged endurance as tramping across Mull or
climbing Ben Nevis. The manuscript itself shows the many laborious "compositions and decompositions" it cost him.[14] For a
while he thought of giving it up and trying something easier and
more distracting, perhaps even in prose. But something in him
would not be distracted; for he was creating a new self, groping
his way out of "Purgatory blind," in the very act of writing *Hy-*

perion. And from week to week he grew more confident. On the day he began his epic he left the ranks of the "marvellous boys"; as he neared the end of the first book he remarked soberly in a letter to George, "I think I shall be among the English Poets after my death."

It was confidence wrested from something close to despair. For only a few days after Keats started *Hyperion* the *Quarterly* finally exploded with its review of *Endymion*. This was the verdict which would decide, as it had already done for Hazlitt, whether the "common place people" of the book-buying public would read his book or leave it to gather dust on Taylor and Hessey's shelves. The judgment was pronounced: *Endymion* had broken all the rules of poetry as the *Quarterly* thought the game should be played. "There is hardly a complete couplet enclosing a complete idea in the whole book," snorted John Croker—that "cobbling, carping, decasyllabic, finger-scanning criticaster," as Woodhouse called him. *Endymion* was damned as merely another effusion of Cockney verse—"which may be defined to consist of the most incongruous ideas in the most uncouth language"—and Keats was dismissed as "a copyist of Mr. Hunt," but "more unintelligible, almost as rugged, twice as diffuse, and ten times more tiresome and absurd than his prototype."

The *Blackwood's* attack could be shrugged off as beneath contempt, but the *Quarterly* was too powerful to be ignored. Keats's friends leaped to his defence. Hunt, who had not mentioned *Endymion* in *The Examiner*—whether out of tact or pique it is hard to say—immediately inserted a note on the front page congratulating Keats on the *Quarterly* notice as an "involuntary homage paid to his undoubted genius, in an article of grovelling abuse." Keats was touched by this gesture, coming as it did after a year of virtual estrangement. He called on Hunt shortly afterward and gave him the two best sonnets he had written since March to publish.[15] Meanwhile Reynolds in Devon wrote a counterblast to the *Quarterly* for a local paper, which Hunt later reprinted in *The Examiner* along with another defence of *Endymion* from *The Chester Guardian*. For a while it appeared that the *Quarterly* had cut its own throat, as Keats put it, by stirring up wider interest in *Endymion* than it would otherwise have received. A Devonshire admirer who signed himself "P. Fenbank, Teignmouth," sent Keats a laudatory sonnet, enclosing a twenty-five-pound note. Keats was amused by the sonnet's high-flown style—all "empyreal soarings" and "mild light and loveliness"—though rather galled by the gift; yet when he wrote a letter of thanks, hoping for a chance to return the money, no reply came.

Meanwhile two other anonymous admirers sent letters of protest to *The Morning Chronicle,* which Hessey, kindly and methodical as ever, forwarded to Well Walk. Keats's letter of thanks shows that, with his progress in *Hyperion,* he had already recovered his equanimity. "Praise or blame," he wrote, "has but a momentary effect on the man whose love of beauty in the abstract makes him a severe critic on his own Works. My own domestic criticism has given me pain without comparison beyond what Blackwood or the Quarterly could possibly inflict. and also when I feel I am right, no external praise can give me such a glow as my own solitary reperception & ratification of what is fine." So much for criticism; as for the writing of poetry itself, the *Quarterly* critic knew nothing about it. "The Genius of Poetry must work out its own salvation in a man: It cannot be matured by law & precept, but by sensation & watchfulness in itself—That which is creative must create itself."

It was a superb flash of insight into the meaning of his struggles, his discouragements, his exaltations. Six months before, Keats had seen little other reason for publishing *Endymion* than that he must put it behind him in order to move on. Now, though more aware than ever of its shortcomings, he saw more clearly what purpose the writing of it had served for him. This was well, for the reaction against the *Quarterly* article brought him an embarrassing reminder of his own reaction, several weeks earlier, to the *Blackwood's* review. Around the middle of October Woodhouse, who had been brooding over Keats's announcement in mid-September that he had given up poetry, saw the *Quarterly* review and was alarmed. He sat down in his rooms in the Temple and wrote Keats an impassioned letter, arguing that the poet has a responsibility even to the society that rejects him, and encouraging him to keep on undaunted. Keats, who by this time had nearly reached the middle of the second book of *Hyperion,*[16] must have felt a pang of remorse. Had he ever really said he would give up poetry—and meant it too? He could answer Woodhouse only by warning him not to place such faith in the poetic character—because, as he explained, essentially "it has no character," no settled view of things. "What shocks the virtuous philosopher, delights the camelion

Poet," he confessed—light and shade, fair and foul, one side of an argument as well as another. So the poet "is the most unpoetical of any thing in existence; because he has no Identity—he is continually informing and filling some other Body—The Sun, the Moon, the Sea and Men and Women who are creatures of impulse are poetical and have about them an unchangeable attribute—the poet has none. If then he has no self, and if I am a Poet," he continued, warming to his logic, "where is the Wonder that I should say I would write no more? Might I not at that very instant have been cogitating on the Characters of saturn and Ops?" But, he assured Woodhouse, he would continue writing "from the mere yearning and fondness I have for the Beautiful even if my night's labours should be burnt every morning and no eye ever shine upon them."

It was an important point he had reached. He had left the struggle to become a poet far behind, along with the lesser hopes of winning fame and fortune through his poems. Being a poet, he now realized, was no glorious thing in itself but merely a fact of his own nature. What alone mattered was the activity of writing, the kingdom of his own creation which he entered every time he sat down to work. Beside this solitary delight the world's applause or contempt meant nothing. He had not forgotten his ambition, which he mentioned to Woodhouse, "of doing the world some good"; but, perhaps from his long pondering of Milton's career, he saw that to write a poem that might in some way benefit the world would require many years of schooling his powers and gaining knowledge and experience—if he should live that long, he added thoughtfully. "In the interval," he concluded, "I will assay to reach to as high a summit in Poetry as the nerve bestowed upon me will suffer."

Fortunately, in this new abstracted state he met a "creature of impulse" whose poetical quality he felt free to relish as never before. Sometime near the middle of October, on one of his rare trips into town, he had dropped in at Little Britain—probably to see Reynolds, just back from Devon—and was introduced to a niece of Mrs. Reynolds who, as he had already heard, was visiting them during a falling-out with her grandfather and guardian.[17] Miss Jane Cox was a beauty of a kind that Keats did not often meet, an

Anglo-Indian heiress with "a rich eastern look," fine eyes and fine manners, who walked into a drawing room with the grace of a leopardess. Not quite a Cleopatra, Keats decided, but at least a Charmian. He recognized at once the self-absorbed and theatrical quality of her beauty, saw, too, that the Reynolds sisters hated her for it; yet he found pleasure in surrendering to her spell. "I always find myself more at ease with such a woman," he wrote George and Georgiana a few days later; "I am at such times too much occupied in admiring to be awkward or on a tremble. I forget myself entirely because I live in her." He also realized immediately that she was beyond his reach; she accepted his admiration gracefully because it meant nothing to her. "She is a fine thing speaking in a worldly way: for there are two distinct tempers of mind in which we judge of things—the worldly, theatrical and pantomimical; and the unearthly, spiritual and etherial—in the former Buonaparte, Lord Byron and this Charmian hold the first place in our Minds; in the latter John Howard, Bishop Hooker rocking his child's cradle and you my dear Sister are the conquering feelings. As a Man in the world I love the rich talk of a Charmian; as an eternal Being I love the thought of you. I should like her to ruin me, and I should like you to save me."

This contrast between two types of women—the good and the bad angel—raises some familiar echoes from the past; but it would also appear that Keats was gaining enough self-assurance to find the Jane Coxes of the world less a threat than a delight. His tenderness for Georgiana, however, was brimming over at the moment he wrote, for at last, in mid-October, the long-awaited letter from America had arrived. They had reached Philadelphia safely after a rough crossing. George had found a chance to play a game of cricket before they started on their westward journey; and Georgiana was already expecting a child. Their happiness was at the full, and they tried to persuade Keats he too should marry. But it was heavy news he had to send them in reply. He told them briefly of Tom's relapse and begged them to "bear up against any Calamity for my sake as I do for your's." He mentioned the adverse reviews only to dismiss them as "a mere matter of the moment," then went on to give them news of the Wylies and all their friends, talk about politics, recount his meeting with Jane Cox, and scribble some verses in prophecy that their child would be the first American poet. Though it would be several weeks before the next sailing to America, he promised to add a sheet of news—or, failing that, of his "Whims and Theories"—to his letter every day.

There was little to report for another week, however—a visit from Georgiana's brothers and small talk at Wentworth Place with Dilke and Brown, now back from Scotland at last, "of Euclid, of Metaphisics of the Bible, of Shakspeare of the horrid System and consequences of the fagging at great Schools." The next week Tom's condition improved somewhat; he seemed less nervous and slept better at night. This allowed Keats to get into town several times, where he dropped in on Taylor and Hessey and the Wylies and their cousins the Millars, walked with Hazlitt on his way to a game of racquets at Covent Garden, and called on Hunt, where unluckily he met Ollier. And on one of these days—October 24— he had an adventure. Walking down Theobald Road in an abstracted mood, he passed a lady, suddenly realized it was Isabella Jones, his acquaintance from Hastings, and turned back to greet her. She replied cordially and invited him to go with her to call on a friend of hers who had a boarding school in Islington. "As we went along, some times through shabby, sometimes through decent Streets I had my guessing at work, not knowing what it would be and prepared to meet any surprise," Keats wrote George. On leaving her friend's, he asked to accompany her home. "She consented and then again my thoughts were at work what it might lead to, tho' now they had received a sort of genteel hint from the Boarding School. Our Walk ended in 34 Gloucester Street Queen Square—not exactly so for we went up stairs into her sitting room —a very tasty sort of place with Books, Pictures a bronze statue of Buonaparte, Music, æolian Harp; a Parrot a Linnet—A Case of choice Liquers &c &c &. she behaved in the kindest manner—made me take home a Grouse for Tom's dinner—Asked for my address for the purpose of sending more game—As I had warmed with her before and kissed her—I thought it would be living backwards not to do so again—she had a better taste: she perceived how much a thing of course it was and shrunk from it—not in a prudish way but in as I say a good taste—She contrived to disappoint me in a way which made me feel more pleasure than a simple kiss could do —she said I should please her much more if I would only press her hand and go away. Whether she was in a different disposition when

I saw her before—or whether I have in fancy wrong'd her I cannot tell."

It was a tantalizing encounter: he was not sure what she wanted. "She has always been an enigma to me—she has ~~new~~ been in a Room with you and with Reynolds and wishes we should be acquainted without any of our common acquaintance knowing it." It was a curious suggestion, yet he met it at least halfway: "I expect to pass some pleasant hours with her now and then: in which I feel I shall be of service to her in matters of knowledge and taste: if I can I will—I have no libidinous thought about her—she and your George"—that is, Georgiana—"are the only women à peu près de mon age whom I would be content to know for their mind and friendship alone."

As with Charmian two weeks before, he tactfully refrained from referring to her by name; but the lady from Hastings evidently touched a deeper chord than Jane Cox had done. Charmian's beauty was "a passtime and an amuzement"; Isabella's charm added an intellectual attraction, and something more. It was not a simple matter of entering into her being and imaginatively "living in her"; clearly Mrs. Jones wished to enter his. Astute as she was, she must have sensed a change in Keats from the eager boy of two summers before; as a friend of Taylor's and a lady of liberal tastes, she would have read *Endymion* and formed a new opinion of its author. There is no doubt about her deftness in handling the occasion which presented itself so unexpectedly; however, there is much to wonder about in her situation at the time. Game, for instance, with which she seemed to be well stocked, could not be had legally in those days unless one was a landowner—or the friend of a landowner.[18] There was no visible evidence of "the jealous old Bald-pate" in her surroundings: was this in Keats's mind when he confessed that he may have wronged her in his imagination? He did not like to "think insults in a Lady's Company," yet he could not help sensing the ambiguity of the situation. Isabella Jones, a woman of some taste and wit and beauty, whose acquaintance (did Keats know it at the time?) was enjoyed by John Taylor, offered him her friendship and let a hint of other possibilities trouble the air. Nevertheless—and he must be credited with knowing his own feelings in the matter—Keats insisted that he had "no libidinous thought about her." [19] With Jane Cox also he had told George that he was not in love; she merely kept him awake one night "as a tune of Mozart's might do." Perhaps he instinctively sensed that neither woman could give him what he wanted: Jane Cox he could never possess, and Isabella Jones wished in some obscure way to possess him. But there was another reason, of which he was more fully aware. Poetry had conquered, for the third time in little more than a month: for him there could be no greater fulfilment. Since meeting Fanny Brawne he had probably written the first book of *Hyperion* and started the second, and he knew what they were worth.

And so he closed his account of this adventure by telling his brother and sister-in-law that, despite their recommendation, he hoped never to marry. "Though the most beautiful Creature were waiting for me at the end of a Journey or a Walk; though the carpet were of Silk, the Curtains of the morning Clouds; the chairs and Sofa stuffed with Cygnet's down; the food Manna, the Wine beyond Claret, the Window opening on Winander mere, I should not feel—or rather my Happiness would not be so fine, as my Solitude is sublime. Then instead of what I have described, there is a Sublimity to welcome me home—The roaring of the wind is my wife and the Stars through the window pane are my Children. The mighty abstract Idea I have of Beauty in all things stifles the more divided and minute domestic happiness—an amiable wife and sweet Children I contemplate as a part of that Beauty. but I must have a thousand of those beautiful particles to fill up my heart." For the time being, at least, the world that sprang to life as he added line after line to *Hyperion* seemed a complete one. "I feel more and more every day, as my imagination strengthens, that I do not live in this world alone but in a thousand worlds—No sooner am I alone than shapes of epic greatness are stationed around me—then 'Tragedy with sceptr'd pall, comes sweeping by' According to my state of mind I am with Achilles shouting in the Trenches or with Theocritus in the Vales of Sicily. Or I throw my whole being into Troilus and repeating those lines, 'I wander, like a lost soul upon the stygian Banks staying for waftage,' I melt into the air with a voluptuousness so delicate that I am content to be alone." In such a mood the sensation of seeming someone other than himself which assailed him in the Dilkes' drawing room mattered little. "Some think me middling, others silly, others foolish—every one thinks he sees my weak side against my will;

when in truth it is with my will—I am content to be thought all this because I have in my own breast so great a resource."

By the end of October it was time to send his long journal-letter off to catch the Boston post. Keats closed with a few anxious words of advice to his brother and sister-in-law, who were by now crossing the Alleghenies: George, the young pioneer fresh from a counting-house stool; and Georgiana, carrying her first child as their wagon jounced through the wilderness. "Take it calmly—and let your health be the prime consideration," he begged them. He thought for a moment of asking Tom for a message to send them, then decided against it. "Tom is still so nervous that I cannot speak to him of these Matters—I did not like to write before him a Letter he knew was to reach your hands—his heart speaks to you—Be as happy as you can." As he signed the letter he realized what day of the month it was—something he rarely remembered—and added a postscript: "This day is my Birth day." He was now twenty-three years old.

-»» ««-

The month of November 1818 would be a blank in the narrative except for three short letters—one to Rice on a broken engagement, one to Mrs. Davenport, a Hampstead neighbour who had asked after Tom's health, and a hopeless little note to his sister. Three calls on Abbey in the City had not persuaded him to allow Fanny more visits to Well Walk, and Tom was too ill for Keats to leave him for a trip to Walthamstow. Perhaps one more visit before Christmas—that was the best they could hope for. He made one or two trips into town to see Reynolds and probably several short calls a week at Wentworth Place; more we do not know. After his rally at the end of October, Tom took another turn for the worse: this one, it seemed, would be the last. Keats was with him almost constantly now, nursing him through the crises of his fever, watching his body grow more helpless, his features more shrunken each day, searching for words to nerve him for what lay ahead. George's old friend Haslam, who came regularly to help, was alarmed at how haggard Keats appeared. He told Severn privately that he had heard that a person who took care of a dying consumptive often came down with the same disease afterward.[20] But he could not persuade Keats to move into other lodgings, or even to let him take his place for more than an hour or two at a time. "Poor Tom looks upon me as his only comfort," Keats had told George. Day and night he watched without hope, remembering—could he have helped it?—the long nights, nine years before, when he fought off despair at his mother's bedside. On November 18 Tom had his nineteenth birthday; on December 1, early in the morning, he died.

Keats's first act after Tom's death was to write a note to his sister. The one visit she was to have been allowed before Christmas, Keats had put off through November because he knew it would be too painful for both Fanny and Tom. Now he wrote only to tell her briefly that Tom was much worse, to prepare her for the news he would bring her himself, and begged her to keep up her spirits for his sake. He took the letter to the post, then turned down the hill to Wentworth Place in the half-light of the winter morning. Brown was still asleep; he awoke to find Keats standing at his bedside. Keats took his hand, unable to speak, but Brown knew why he had come. After a few minutes he broke the silence: Keats must come and live with him at Wentworth Place. Keats agreed, glad to put Well Walk and its memories behind him at last. Brown at once stepped in to write his friends the news and shoulder other burdens. Haslam took over the task of writing George. On every side his friends stood by ready to help.

"The last days of poor Tom were of the most distressing nature," Keats wrote to George two weeks later; "but his last moments were not so painful, and his very last was without a pang—I will not enter into any parsonic comments on death"—the adjective suggests that an old wound had been opened and probed that fortnight—"yet the common observations of the commonest people on death are as true as their proverbs. I have scarce a doubt of immortality of some nature or other—neither had Tom." It seems a hope as wan as the English sun in December. A deep primitive need to believe that Tom lived on struggled against his dogged rejection of the formulas of Christianity. As the bells tolled in St. Stephen's the day Tom was laid beside his father and mother and grandparents, did Keats remember the angry sonnet he had written two years ago when they were living within the sound of those bells? Tom was dead—Tom with all his joy in life, Tom who, George said, "understood Keats better than any other human being."

The thought of his brother's death was to haunt Keats for months afterward, but he did not allow himself to give way openly to sorrow, even in writing to George. Two days before Tom's funeral, in fact, he drove down to Crawley Hurst in Sussex with Reynolds and all the sporting crowd to see the prizefight of the decade, the great battle in which Jack Randall defeated Ned Turner after thirty-four bare-fisted rounds.[21] And immediately after the funeral on December 7, he plunged into a round of activity to clear his mind of the memory of the last three months. It was the healthiest antidote to grief; and a week or so was all he needed. "I have been every where," he told George and Georgiana in mid-December: to call on the Reynoldses, the Dilkes, the Wylies, the Millars; to see Hunt, Haydon, Novello, Martin, and Lamb; even to meet up with Kirkman and Archer, friends from the Mathew days. Mrs. Dilke went with him to see Fanny at the Abbeys'. The following Sunday he walked with Haslam over the ten frozen miles to Walthamstow for another visit to his sister, then back into London with his friend. Dilke took him shooting on the Heath one morning—a rare pleasure for Keats, though all he bagged was a tomtit. With Brown he went to see Kean play Brutus in top style in a "very bad" new tragedy—his first trip to the theatre since George's departure. One of his pleasantest trips into town was a call on Hazlitt in his bare untidy rooms at 19 York Street, a house that had once been Milton's, from which Keats carried away the manuscript of the lectures on the English comic writers which he had missed in November. At least one other time, though he did not mention it to George, he paid a visit to Isabella Jones for a few hours' good conversation and perhaps a glass or two of her prize Farentosh whisky.

A less amusing occasion was a party at the Novellos', which Hunt induced him to attend with Brown. With Hunt's knack for "making fine things petty and beautiful things hateful," even Mozart seemed tiresome for once, and Keats agreed with Brown never to get trapped into another such affair. Then Woodhouse forwarded him an invitation that must have tempted him for a moment at least. Mary Frogley—it turned out that Woodhouse was her cousin —had loaned her copy of *Endymion* to the Misses Porter, two of the most successful novelists of the day, and through her Keats was offered an introduction to their set. He was wryly amused that his "meretricious romance verse" should appeal to those lady romancers; he must also have wondered whether Mary Frogley—who, Woodhouse discreetly hinted, was engaged—was still as lovely as ever. But, on the point of accepting, he suddenly changed his mind. "Look here Woodhouse," he wrote, "I have a new leaf to turn over —I must work—I must read—I must write—I am unable to affrod time for new acquaintances—I am scarcely able to do my duty to those I have."

For after a week or two of distraction he was ready to pick up and start forward again. In fact he was beginning to feel stifled in drawing-room crowds by a sense of "everlasting restraint"—"because I feel my impulses given way to would too much amaze them." So it was a relief at last to start his long-deferred letter to George and Georgiana on December 16. A sentence or two was all he could write about Tom's death; a few more about the closeness he felt to them across the Atlantic. "There you are with Birkbeck —here I am with brown—sometimes I fancy an immense separation, and sometimes, as at present, a direct communication of spirit with you. That will be one of the grandeurs of immortality— there will be no space and consequently the only commerce between spirits will be by their intelligence of each other—when they will completely understand each other." He suggested they each read a passage of Shakespeare every Sunday at ten o'clock—"and we shall be as near each other as blind bodies can be in the same room."

The next morning, clear, cold and quiet, he found himself alone at Wentworth Place and suddenly anxious to start writing again. The Dilkes were away; Brown had taken a pair of visiting nephews to see the lions at the Tower; and his old landlord Bentley had just brought him a clothes basket full of books from Well Walk. Yet he found it impossible to pick up where he had left off with *Hyperion*. He opened one of his books, a copy of Beaumont and Fletcher, inscribed "Geo. Keats to his affectionate Brother John"; read a little; then with the thought of "immortality of some nature or other" and the "direct communication of spirit" springing to his mind again, he worked out a little poem on "the double immortality of Poets." [22]

> Bards of Passion and of Mirth,
> Ye have left your souls on earth!
> Have ye souls in heaven too,
> Double-lived in regions new?

It fell into a new form, a kind of free-running "rondeau" which pleased him; he tried another. Hunt had just given him a copy of his latest production, a little Christmas gift-book, half diary and half anthology, in which he had printed the two sonnets Keats had given him in the autumn. "Full of the most sickening stuff you can imagine," Keats had decided after a glance at the twelve descriptive essays which Hunt himself had contributed, one for each month of the year. Yet evidently they started the theme of the seasons turning over in his head,[23] and this, compounded with his idea of the immortality of the imagination, rhymed itself into a second poem, an Ode on "Fancy," full of the fluent joy he felt at his new freedom to write again.

Yet his thoughts were veering in another direction that bright winter noon, away from an ideal season of the imagination to an ideal companion:

> Let, then, winged Fancy find
> Thee a mistress to thy mind:
> Dulcet-eyed as Ceres' daughter,
> Ere the God of Torment taught her
> How to frown and how to chide;
> With a waist and with a side
> White as Hebe's, when her zone
> Slipt its golden clasp, and down
> Fell her kirtle to her feet,
> While she held the goblet sweet,
> And Jove grew languid. Mistress fair!
> Thou shalt have that tressed hair
> Adonis tangled all for spite,
> And the mouth he would not kiss,
> And the treasure he would miss;
> And the hand he would not press,
> And the warmth he would distress.

One wonders whether there was a model for this "mistress of the mind" who emerges through Proserpina's petulance and Venus's abashment by a no less petulant Adonis. Perhaps a clue to her identity—and Adonis's as well—may be found in a passage which Keats added to his journal-letter only the day before. Here at last

he broke his three months' silence about Fanny Brawne by introducing her, a little awkwardly, to George and Georgiana, along
with her mother. "We have a little tiff now and then," he immediately added, "and she behaves a little better, or I must have sheered
off." At once he did sheer off in his letter, Adonis-like, to report
that he had been invited to a birthday dance by the much sought-
after Miss Mary Millar, to which he planned to go as a complete
dandy, "purple Hat and all—with a list of the beauties I have conquered embroidered round my Calves." He could mention Fanny
only while denying the effect she had on him.

> Break the mesh
> Of the Fancy's silken leash;
> Where she's tethered to the heart. . . .

Some kind of leash had begun to tug at him, and already he was
straining away from it.

In spite of his three months' silence on the subject of the
Brawnes, Keats had met them at least several times at the Dilkes'
after Brown's return in October, when they moved into a house
nearby at Downshire Hill. How much Fanny had driven him to
insist to George that he hoped he would never marry, we cannot
know. Quite clearly his first encounter with her had troubled him
too much to let him record it with the keen but detached interest
with which he described his meetings with Charmian and the lady
from Hastings. It is probably also significant that, once he did mention Fanny to George, he felt it necessary to introduce her by name:
she was a real person, not a character in an imaginary drama. Two
days later he ventured a little further: "Shall I give you Miss
Brawn? She is about my height—with a fine style of countenance
of the lengthen'd sort—she wants sentiment in every feature—she
manages to make her hair look well—her nostrills are fine—though
a little painful—her mouth is bad and good—her Profil is better
than her full-face which indeed is not full but pale and thin without showing any bone—Her shape is very graceful and so are her
movements—her Arms are good her hands badish—her feet toler-
able—she is not seventeen—but she is ignorant—monstrous in her
behaviour flying out in all directions, calling people such names—
that I was forced lately to make use of the term *Minx*—this is I
think not from any innate vice but from a penchant she has for

acting stylishly. I am however tired of such style and shall decline any more of it."

There are several things worth noting here. First, and significantly: "She is about my height." Again, he was a year and a half off in estimating her age. Like her mother, who had married a man six years younger than herself, Fanny appeared younger than she was. This suggests that her sense of style did not damp down an energy and spontaneity unusual in most young ladies of her day. She was no Charmian; she was far closer to Juliet. Evidently she felt no need to restrain her impulses for fear of amazing her company, and Keats evidently felt this impulsiveness as a challenge. It succeeded in freeing him from his usual constraint long enough to call her "Minx" to her face, and this "little tiff" seems to have startled them both into a new relationship. "She behaves a little better," Keats noted with satisfaction: on her, as not on Charmian, he could have some effect. Finally, "she wants sentiment in every feature." To an anti-sentimentalist, this was a recommendation. It is clear that, for all his offhandedness, he was being drawn again to Fanny by the same deep attraction he had felt on first meeting her. That it should have flared up with new intensity so soon after Tom's death is no surprise. For over three months his own vital impulses had been held in check with the long ebbing of Tom's life; now they flooded back as through a breaking dam.

Yet it was a desire for life in all its fullness—the "thousand particles" of beauty—that surged up in him. An afternoon or two with Haydon was enough to remind him of the plans for the future which he had put out of his mind during Tom's illness—the kingdoms of the earth and the glories thereof. At one of these meetings Haydon showed him a letter from the young explorer Ritchie, now in Tripoli, "among Camels, Turbans, Palm Trees and sands"; and Keats thought with pleasure of one copy of *Endymion* travelling westward into the wilds of America, another going eastward into the Sahara on a camel's back. Together he and Haydon talked of literary matters and the cartoons of Raphael, which Haydon was then arranging to have exhibited in London for the first time; and Keats looked through a book of prints of the frescoes by Bennozzo in the Campo Santo at Pisa. This first glimpse of early Italian art, so different from the sentimental Guido Reni then in fashion, filled Keats with astonished delight, as it did the young Pre-

Raphaelites thirty years later: "finer to me than more accomplish'd works—as there was left so much room for Imagination."

Haydon, however, was burdened with his usual problems and hinted he was so deep in debt that he must sell some of his drawings to keep going. Keats protested heatedly against this idea, then wrote Haydon impulsively the next morning to offer him more positive assistance. He must have known how endless his friend's demands were, set beside his own resources. But he was concerned about Haydon's recurrent eye trouble, which made it necessary for him to stop painting for weeks at a time; and unwisely he alluded to a fact which Haydon must have suspected, that some money would be coming to him from Tom's estate. This was in fact money which he had been lending Tom out of his own funds for some time, and which he was now counting on to tide him over for three or four more years of "study and travel," even if his own poems brought him nothing.[24] Yet once he was in funds again, Keats could think only of sharing his money with a friend: "Believe me Haydon I have that sort of fire in my Heart that would sacrifice every thing I have to your service—but let me be the last stay—ask the rich lovers of art first—Try the long purses."

The future was opening out before him once again; yet still the silken leash was pulling him another way. In mid-December he had been invited to go down to Hampshire with Brown on his annual Christmas visit to Dilke's brother-in-law, John Snook. Keats accepted tentatively, wishing rather to stay home and write; then, a few days before Christmas, he seized on the excuse of his recurrent sore throat to put off the visit. This involved him in a slight awkwardness with the Reynolds family, whose invitation to Christmas dinner he had declined in good faith the previous week. Mrs. Reynolds renewed her invitation, and Keats wrote her an embarrassed note to decline again. For in the meantime he had accepted a third invitation, which he was determined to keep a secret, and which may have been his real reason for postponing his trip to Hampshire. On Christmas Day he went to dine at Elm Cottage, Mrs. Brawne's house on Downshire Hill.

What happened that day is something of a mystery. Keats never mentioned the occasion, even to George and Georgiana. In fact he let a week go by without picking up his journal to America, then resumed it with no explanation for the lapse—though a few days later he unguardedly confessed, "I never forget you except after seeing now and then some beautiful woman." So the events of that day must be left mostly to the imagination. Yet there are a few tangible pieces of evidence. Sometime during these weeks he presented Fanny Brawne with *The Literary Pocket Book,* the little red leather poetic diary for 1819 which Hunt had given him, and no time seems likelier than Christmas Day. Whatever Keats may have thought of Hunt's sentimental prose, the book was a charming gift for a young lady whose mother had invited him to Christmas dinner, and, still better, it contained the only poetry of his own that had been published since *Endymion.* Fanny seems to have been pleased, for she signed her name in it forthwith and noted some birthdays in the diary spaces. It also seems very probable that she gave Keats a present in return that pleased him still more. For, immediately after Christmas, Keats began sealing his letters with a device he had never used before—a Greek lyre with half its strings broken, circled by the motto "Qui me néglige me désole." [25] This was one of the famous "Tassie gems," then in high fashion, and one which seems especially appropriate for a flirtatious young lady to pick out for a standoffish young man—though in another two years the device was to take on a very different meaning for Keats.

But what else happened that day? The surest clue, though still tantalizing, is Fanny Brawne's remark to Fanny Keats, three years later, that the Christmas of 1818 was the happiest day of her life up to that time. It is impossible not to conclude that somehow or other that day the distance between Keats and Fanny Brawne was bridged: he told her that he loved her and learned that she loved him in return.[26] It is significant, then, that a few weeks after this day Keats began a long poem in celebration of young love, set against a background of good food and music, revelry and rich attire, in which the lovers steal away from a midwinter festivity to reveal their love to each other. *The Eve of St. Agnes* is Keats's commentary on the hidden drama of his life at this time. In the terms of his allegory of human existence, he had emerged at last from the dark passages into the Third Chamber of life, stored with the bread of friendship and the wine of love.

Chapter Nine

>>>——————————————————————————————<<<

The Melancholy Storm

ON January 1 Keats dined again at the Brawnes', this time
with Mr. and Mrs. Dilke. He still kept silent about Christmas and mentioned this New Year's visit to George only to comment, "Nothing particular passed." On Sunday, the third, he
dined with the Dilkes and was invited (since Brown was still away)
to join them for tea that evening. The next morning he closed his
long letter to America with a brief note on that event: "When the
tray came up Mrs Dilke and I had a battle with celery stalks." This
poses a problem: from now on Keats's letters, even to George, record the trivia rather than the significant facts of his experience.
From the time Fanny Brawne claimed the centre of the stage, a
curtain of secrecy drops around the central situation of Keats's
life, and only a few stray facts and random observations in his letters, and the still more cryptic record of the poems, give a hint of
the drama behind. The last few pages of his journal to George are
filled with a barrage of small talk, ranging from an account of a
newly discovered kingdom in Africa to the plight of Caroline
Mathew, who had just been left high and dry by their old friend
Archibald Archer after a two-year courtship. Keats even went so
far as to ask his brother what topics he should discuss in his letters:
"Whether the affairs of Europe are more or less interesting to you
—whether you would like to hear of the Theatre's—of the bear
Garden—of the Boxers—the Painters—The Lecturers—the Dress
—The Progress of Dandyism—The Progress of Courtship—or the
fate of Mary Millar—being a full true and très particular account
of Miss M's ten Suitors."

Certainly the outward surface of his life during the first few weeks of January seemed placid enough. Hampstead now provided all the company he wanted; after another return of his "plaguy sore throat" he made few visits to London. One or two parties in town at holiday time were not even dull enough to keep him awake, as he complained to George: "All the evening's amusement consists in saying your good health, *your* good health, and YOUR good health—and (o I beg you pardon) your's Miss ——. Let my eyes be fed or I'll never go out to dinner any where." His new quarters at Wentworth Place pleased him immensely, especially his comfortable sitting room lined with bookshelves, and French windows opening out on the garden shared with the Dilkes. From Brown's upstairs bedroom one could see clear across the Heath to Highgate; and the basement was fitted up with a large brick-binned well-stocked wine cellar. For a few weeks Keats must have been glad to be alone, untroubled by Brown's misogynous presence, free to read and work as he pleased, to call at the Brawnes' and look each day for a letter from George and Georgiana. As he told them, it was only "seeing now and then some beautiful woman" that could put them out of his mind, "but that is a fever—the thought of you both is a passion with me but for the most part a calm one."

Fanny Brawne, then—alternately a feast and a fever—is the key to these first quiet weeks of January. Was she such a beauty as Keats implies? Some of his friends seem not to have thought so. Keats later wrote her, "I cannot conceive any beginning of such love as I have for you but Beauty"; but the casualness of his first appraisal—"beautiful I think"—leaves it an open question. The only portrait of her that survives—a miniature done in her early thirties, regarded as an almost worthless likeness by her family [1]— shows a face too long and thin, a nose too aquiline for a conventional beauty; a childhood ailment—asthma, perhaps—had made her habitually pale, and the oversensitive nostrils and the changeable mouth which Keats described to George in December suggest a bewildering variety of expression. It is interesting to put beside this first catalogue of her points, good and bad, in his letter to George, a later portrait of a woman drawn from the same model:

> Deep blue eyes, semi-shaded in white lids,
> Finish'd with lashes fine for more soft shade,
> Completed by her twin-arch'd ebon brows;

White temples of exactest elegance,
Of even mould, felicitous and smooth;
Cheeks fashion'd tenderly on either side,
So perfect, so divine, that our poor eyes
Are dazzled with the sweet proportioning,
And wonder that 'tis so,—the magic chance!
Her nostrils, small, fragrant, faery-delicate;
Her lips—I swear no human bones e'er wore
So taking a disguise. . . .*

Fanny Brawne's beauty differed from the self-possessed "unchange-able attribute" of a Charmian's, which left less room for the imagination to work on; it was more like love itself, as Keats once described it—"semireal," requiring "a greeting of the Spirit," some meeting of imagination or sympathy between subject and object, to make it wholly exist.

What, then, was the spirit that greeted Keats from under those enigmatic white lids? "Elegant, graceful, silly, fashionable and strange"; impulsive as well as beautiful—"flying out in all directions"; yet the nickname which Keats gave Fanny was not Juliet (that would have revealed too much) but Millamant. It was her wit and gaiety and sense of style that dazzled him at first, and other young men as well. Fanny Brawne had received the upbringing of a young lady of good family and had the intelligence to carry it off. Her father's ancestors had been knights and lawyers and abbots for more than five centuries. Her grandfather, Samuel Brawne, who like John Jennings had prospered in the coaching business, was an early believer in women's independence, for he left apprenticeship fees to his daughters so that they could learn trades in case of need. Her forebears on her mother's side had served in government and acquired considerable property in London and Kent. Fanny's mother—"a very nice woman," to Keats's mind—had married for love without her parents' approval, like Keats's own mother. There were other points of resemblance: Mrs. Brawne spoiled her children (according to her daughter), enjoyed merry company, and had a warm, hospitable nature. Her sister had married Lord North's secretary, William Brummell, who gave Fanny an unusually stylish cousin, George—the famous Beau Brummell; and a great-aunt and great-uncle had acted with Garrick at Drury Lane.[2] This heritage helps to explain Fanny's "penchant for acting

---

* *Otho the Great,* V. v. 61 ff.

stylishly" and her keen sense of comedy. It may also account for an unusual degree of feminine initiative. Jane Austen's Elizabeth Bennet incurred the scorn of the neighbouring ladies by walking three miles in muddy weather, but Fanny Brawne used to walk five or six miles into town alone to meet her brother at the theatre, and home again with him at night when they ran through their quarter's allowance and could not afford the coach.[3]

The theatre was one of Fanny's passions; another was costume, and in later years she became a skilful and inventive dressmaker. She also came to be known as a lively and intelligent conversation-alist, keenly interested in politics as well as literature.[4] But her occupations at eighteen were only what one would expect of a modish young lady: singing, waltzing, reading "trumpery novels," chatting in French with the *émigrés* of the Hampstead colony, flirting with the officers from the barracks in St. John's Wood. She once described herself as "not at all bashful and hardly modest," but she was too realistic to be vain. Knowing that "a person must be a great beauty to look well without them," she set great store by "dress manners and carriage," accomplishments which she believed were "within the reach of anybody of understanding." Hardly a romantic heroine; certainly a Regency one. Keats may have given her a Restoration nickname because she wore her hair in an original style copied with some care from the age of Charles II.[5]

His nickname "Millamant" suggests another side to Fanny's character, or rather the stage of development she had reached when Keats met her. Fanny at eighteen, at the height of her youthful vivacity, enjoyed the life of a Hampstead belle to the full. Elm Cottage was a favourite meeting place of the Dilke set, and Keats could have been only one among many callers there. He was also, as he must have suspected, one of the least eligible—an unsuccessful young poet with unconventional manners and no money, often moody and silent in company, handsome enough but too short and self-conscious to cut a figure on a ballroom floor. That Fanny did fall in love with him suggests unexpected depths in her nature, even though Keats had as yet only begun to trouble them. Privately she thought most men rather stupid, and it is significant that she was first impressed by Keats's conversation—"in the highest degree interesting," she later recalled.[6] Her mind was keen enough to recognize Keats's for what it was worth. But the real attraction went deeper: in Keats's own phrase, she had "a fire in her heart" like the one that burned in his, some superabundant vitality answering to his own hunger for life in all its fullness. But she was still only eighteen; she had some silliness to outgrow, and much frivolous experience that, like any pretty young woman, she wanted to live through.

Even these first few weeks of their affair cannot have been mere tranquil happiness, then. Nor could they quite blot out Keats's usual worries. At the end of December he had loaned Haydon thirty pounds as a stopgap [7]—borrowed, as usual, from Taylor; but now, when he went to Abbey to raise the large amount he had promised Haydon, he began to run into difficulties. *Hyperion* also was giving him trouble. "I have been writing a little now and then lately," he told Haydon on January 12, "but nothing to speak off—being discontented and as it were moulting." His "new Phoenix wings" of the autumn before were failing him, leaving him for a while only to recopy and revise what he had already written.[8] "I see by little and little more of what is to be done, and how it is to be done, should I ever be able to do it," he added despondently to Haydon. What was lacking was the right spirit. He had returned to *Hyperion* in mid-December, the evening after he had finished "Fancy," and at that time the joyous mood of his ode spilled over into the beginning of the third book. A correction in the eighth line, describing the Titans—"Many a fallen old divinity"—reveals something of his difficulty. What Keats wrote in December was first "lonely," then "mateless" [9]—a clue to his state of mind at the time which he immediately struck out. Still his thoughts kept running away from his theme, and after a few weeks' struggle he decided to give up *Hyperion* for a while. It seemed a good time to make his long-postponed visit to Hampshire. So on January 18 [10] he boarded the coach for Chichester to join Brown at Dilke's parents', where he had been staying several days, then round out his fortnight with a visit at the Snooks' in Bedhampton, ten miles away.

Chichester pleased him more than he expected. A prosperous city of graceful Georgian houses, it was full of reminders of its medieval past—the old walls which still enclosed the town, the eight-sided Gothic cross which marked the central square, the ancient buildings which lined the cobblestoned streets around the twelfth-century cathedral. Keats's elderly hosts, Mr. and Mrs.

Charles Dilke, Senior, had been warned by their daughter-in-law that they would find him "a very odd young man, but good-tempered and very clever indeed." They were eager to provide entertainment, chiefly in the form of "old Dowager card parties." Brown, with his bachelor's knack for charming old ladies, had already won the dowagers' hearts, or so he found it amusing to believe; and Keats had to sit through two evenings of their fooling. Miss Mullins, the leader of the card-playing set, managed to persuade Brown to shave off his whiskers at last. Keats took advantage of Brown's transformation to effect one himself—to start wearing his neckerchief in the accepted style, "up to my eyes," as he put it; and this change, probably due to Fanny, is the last we hear of his Byronic habits of dress. If his Chichester evenings were dull, in the daytime he was free to explore the old city and the cathedral, feasting his eyes on stone carving and stained glass, buttress and pillar and arch. When a letter came from Fanny Brawne shortly after his arrival, he took it to read walking up and down the aisles during the service in the choir, to his great and secret delight.

On Saturday, the twenty-third, he and Brown said their good-byes and walked the ten miles to Bedhampton on a fine windy morning. The Snook household was a livelier one than the senior Dilkes'; Keats had been promised he would be very much amused there. John Snook was a stout, cheerful country squire who lived with his hospitable wife and two sons in a charming old millhouse overlooking a quiet pond. The Snooks' larder was well stocked with game, and their cellar (we may assume) with wine; Keats, Brown noted, was now rationing himself to two glasses a meal. Together they spent Sunday morning chaffing Mrs. Snook and filling up a joint letter to the young Mrs. Dilke with a series of risqué puns. Keats rounded off his portion of the letter with a note in the margin: "Remember me to Wentworth Place and Elm Cottage—not forgetting Millamant."

On Monday he and Brown with young John Snook took a carriage and went on a strange excursion for two freethinkers—to attend the consecration of a chapel. Lewis Way, a wealthy eccentric, had recently bought up Stansted, one of the show places of Hampshire, and turned it into a College for the Conversion of the Jews. The house, originally a medieval structure, had been lavishly rebuilt by a seventeenth-century earl; the new chapel was

furnished with stained-glass windows designed by Way himself
to illustrate the unity of the Jewish Law and the Christian Gospel. Keats was bored by the visit. After a five-mile journey uphill
behind an obstinate horse in stormy weather, they arrived late
and got poor seats. The ceremony, led by "the two Big-wigs of
Gloucester & St Davids," lasted two or three hours and was "not
amusing." Yet as Keats's attention wandered around the neo-
Gothic chapel, there was much to catch his gaze. The side windows, high above him, were triple-arched and diamond-paned,
set with stained-glass scutcheons of the arms of Fitzalan and
Arundel, the early proprietors of Stansted. The sun, flashing out
from behind the wind-driven clouds, cast pools of light, blue,
amber, and blood-red, on the white lawn of the attendant priests.
After the consecration he and Brown and the boy paid a call at
Stansted House, now "crammed with Clergy," for whom a sumptuous feast had been laid. Keats did not enjoy the company, but
the house itself roused his imagination. Wide stairways and long
halls with panelling of oak carved in fruits and flowers by Grinling
Gibbons, Arras tapestries and gold-embroidered chairs, fringed
carpets and gold and silver service—it was a banquet for the eye.[11]

The first apparent result of this wet and windy expedition was
a return of Keats's sore throat. After Brown left for London the
next morning, Keats remained for another week at Bedhampton
without going beyond the garden gate. His hosts left him to his
own devices, and Keats came to "like them very much." In the evenings they talked religion and politics, and John Snook, who was
much interested in George's venture, offered to write up "all the
best part of his experience in farming" to send on to America.
During the day Keats was free to work. He had brought down
some thin paper which Haslam had given him for his long letters
to America, but he still found it impossible to begin his new journal. Instead his thoughts turned finally in the direction toward
which they had been veering ever since Christmas. On Haslam's
"thin genteel sheets" he drafted a poem into which he poured all
the feelings and sensations of the last month. From his impressions
of Chichester and Stansted—light and shadow, sumptuous colour
and texture and intricate architectural line—he built up a great
dusky-galleried house in which two young lovers, beset by a dark
and hostile world, meet and escape to their freedom together.

The Eve of St. Agnes is Keats's "Epithalamion" in narrative

form, celebrating the joys of a first love fulfilled in a runaway marriage. The abstract tone and superhuman drama of *Hyperion* are exchanged for a medieval world, remote enough for romance but as real as the cathedral and cloisters of Chichester, and peopled with beings of flesh and blood—the Beadsman telling his rosary with numb fingers, the dim-sighted Angela groping for the balustrade, Madeline unclasping the warm jewels from her white throat. The actual germ of the story seems to have been a recent suggestion of Isabella Jones's—the superstition that a maiden would see her future husband in a dream if she fasted on St. Agnes' Eve. And if one listens for them, echoes of the whole gamut of Keats's reading may be heard throughout the poem, from Spenser and Shakespeare and Milton to Boccaccio and Mrs. Radcliffe and the Arabian Nights. Still, these are not the real sources of the poem. What matters in *The Eve of St. Agnes,* as in all Keats's other work, is the poetic intention at the front of his mind which called up the words and images from his memory—the felt emotion, the actual experience, the sense of reality which he wished to express. We can only surmise his adventure with Fanny Brawne, though we know something of the actual circumstances of these weeks, from which he could not as yet disentangle his feelings: the frozen fields and the Christmas festivities at Hampstead; his elderly companions and medieval surroundings in Chichester; the baroque splendour of Stansted and the remote quiet of Bedhampton. And yet these very circumstances of warmth and cold, youth and age, sound and silence, all counterpointed against each other, perfectly project the emotion he felt at the unexpected birth of a new love in his time of sorrow after Tom's death. *The Eve of St. Agnes* is Keats's first great achievement in what he later called "the knowledge of contrast, feeling for light and shade" which he thought essential to a poem: the stillness of Madeline's room, "silken, hush'd, and chaste," balanced against the noisy celebrations in the hall below; the warmth of her bed contrasted with the chilly night; the pallid moon outside the triple-arched window casting soft amethyst and rose on Madeline's breast as she knelt in prayer. The light almost without shade of *Endymion* and the deep shadows of *Hyperion* here vivify and brighten each other. It is significant that *Romeo and Juliet* is the source echoed most frequently in this poem—knowing what symbolic value Keats set on Juliet. Yet the contrast between the fever heat of midsummer Verona and the aching cold of Keats's castle is striking, for he chose to intensify the passion of his story by an almost Spenserian insistence on its purity. In the authentic feeling of his first master, this is a "song made in lieu of many ornaments" in honour of his love.

→» «←

With *The Eve of St. Agnes* completed, Keats returned to London on February 2 and settled down prosaically to nurse his sore throat. He was determined this time to shake it off, and for ten days he kept to Hampstead. On the thirteenth he went into town, ran into Woodhouse scowling nearsightedly into a bookshop window, dropped in on Taylor, and met half a dozen other people "from all parts and of all sets." This gave him enough news to start his long-deferred letter to George the next morning. On the seventeenth he went into town again on business and had an uncomfortable interview with Abbey. On the eighteenth he wrote to Haydon to apologize for the delay in sending him the money he had promised; on the nineteenth he resumed his letter to America.

From the beginning this journal sounds a strange new note, stiff and impersonal, especially for a letter to George, with none of the usual play of Keats's "whims and theories." Rather it gives a dry, almost frozen account of his doings, and as the letter goes on an extraordinary note of bitterness creeps in. He states he is "almost tired of Men and things"; he refers to Chichester and Bedhampton only to insist that "nothing worth speaking of happened at either place"—a comment repeated on several other occasions; he mentions old friends either to give bad news or to say he has not seen them; he speaks with distaste of an essay on Valentine's Day which Lamb had just published in *The Examiner,* but quotes with pleasure a grotesque tale of a witch and the Devil that Brown was writing; he admits that he has not been in a mood for poetry lately and mockingly describes the titles of his two latest poems as "fine mother Radcliff names." All this within two weeks of his return from Hampshire; and the same tone holds for the month that followed, through an unflattering description of Henry Wylie's fiancée, an acid comment on Miss Millar's birthday dance, a satirical account of the London theatres, a catalogue of his literary dislikes, and several diatribes against parsons. One phrase of self-characterization which he quotes from Hazlitt and marks approvingly sums up this new mood—"a sour mal content." Nothing could be further from the gusto with which he reported the trivia of life at Wentworth Place and the small talk of London in his last letter, or strung together a series of puns on "bed" to send Mrs. Dilke from Bedhampton. The change must be accounted for.

There were enough worries nagging at Keats in February to bring on his old "blue devils." After two months of expecting a letter from George, he began to fear something had gone wrong in America. He was also concerned about his sister. The Abbeys had decided to take her out of school this winter, to her great distress. Subdued and delicate, backward in her manner and tastes for a girl of fifteen, Fanny needed the stimulus of schoolmates, and Keats hated to think of her mewed up alone in the gloomy household at Walthamstow. His expostulations were useless, however—though when Abbey tried to forbid visits or even letters, Keats protested angrily enough to win the concession of a letter every fortnight. His own affairs with his guardian were also at a crisis. In January, when he tried to persuade Abbey to turn over more of his capital to him for the loan to Haydon, the old man became suspicious. Keats's plan necessitated a close look into his financial affairs, for evidently he had promised to lend Haydon five hundred pounds for two years—which, he figured, would leave him just enough from his patrimony to live on in the interval.[12] But Abbey soon produced a stumbling block. The money owing Keats from Tom's estate, on which he had been counting for the loan, could not be touched till Fanny came of age. This was alarming news, for it meant that Keats's "moderate two years subsistence" mut now do for almost six. "Should it be so I must incontinently take to Corderoy Trowsers," he wrote to Haydon on February 18; "but I am nearly confident 't is all a Bam." He refused to accept Abbey's construction of the will and began a number of weary trips into town to wrestle with his lawyers. The only immediate outcome of these visits, however, was a mock petition which he drew up in his journal, addressed in the best legal language to the Governors of Saint Luke's, a charity hospital for lunatics, asking to be admitted as a confirmed poet and signed the "Count de Cockaigne."

Keats's use of Lockhart's nickname for Hampstead—Cockneyland—is another straw in the wind. The campaign of abuse in

Blackwood's had shown no signs of letting up since the fall. The *Quarterly* was silent, but now that the flurry of interest aroused by its attack on *Endymion* had died down it was clear that it had stopped his sales as effectively as it had Hazlitt's. Cowden Clarke, who paid an unexpected visit to Hampstead at this time, remembered Keats's talking angrily for half the night about the injustice of the review.[13] He managed to put on a brave face about it in his letter to America, however, admitting the poem had failed but resolving to try again for George's and Fanny's sake—though, he added, "in a selfish point of view I should suffer my pride and my contempt of public opinion to hold me silent." Yet he could not keep his bitterness from slipping out in several hits at Byron, whose latest canto of *Childe Harold,* he learned, had had an advance sale of four thousand copies. One of these hits suggests that another angry nerve had recently been touched. Mrs. Brawne had evidently been asking discreet questions about him, and his neighbour Mr. Lewis had described him to her as "quite the little Poet" —an unfortunate remark which soon got back to Keats. "Now this is abominable," he burst out to George, "you might as well say Buonaparte is quite the little Soldier—You see what it is to be under six foot and not a lord." As for the reviews, he complained, they had stopped men from thinking for themselves. Readers of the *Quarterly* "are like the spectators at the Westminster cock-pit —they like the battle and do not care who wins or who looses."

Yet Keats cannot have been surprised at the outcome of the attacks, and he had refused to be cast down when they first appeared. "Difficulties nerve the Spirit of a Man," he had remarked when starting *Endymion,* then proved it by finishing the poem in the very teeth of discouragement. Something else must have happened to cause his extraordinary change of mood in February and March. Something, it appears, had gone wrong in his relations with Fanny Brawne. Nothing else can quite account for his profound depression during these months, his inability to write, his increasing concern about money. He even began thinking—and this is significant—of giving up poetry and going to Edinburgh to complete his training as a physician. The idea did not appeal to him, but, as he remarked savagely to George, "it is not worse than writing poems, & hanging them up to be flyblown on the Reviewshambles." What exactly occurred between him and Fanny can only be guessed, however—something which, in his usual secrecy about his deepest feelings, Keats never directly mentioned in his letters.

This could have taken many forms. The most obvious one is that he now realized that their love could be kept a secret no longer, and that he must make some kind of proposal. His comment on Archer's "abominable behaviour" to Caroline Mathew shows that he was well aware of his responsibilities in such a situation. But what in fact could he do? His unlucky offer of a loan to Haydon had revealed that his funds were too low for him to marry unless he changed his whole way of life. He was facing the dilemma which Eliza Drewe had forced on John Reynolds, a choice between poetry and marriage. Mrs. Brawne, in spite of her amiability, had all the usual mother's ideas about a daughter's happiness. Her remark to her neighbour Mrs. Rodd, that Keats was "a mad boy," [14] shows what little encouragement she could have given him. Keats's gloomy remark about Edinburgh also implies that returning to medicine would cause him far deeper conflict than turning to the law had done for Reynolds. All the plans which he had confided to Haydon three days before Christmas—a life dedicated to writing and travel, unhampered by the need to earn a living—were now threatened. So he apparently began to wonder, uncomfortably, whether poetry would not always be more important to him than marriage, even to Fanny Brawne. Fanny's beauty was also beginning to stir up a familiar anxiety—the deep-seated conviction that no woman could ever love him for himself. A few months later, in the midst of praising her beauty, he confessed this galling sense of his physical insignificance: "I hold that place among Men which snub-nos'd brunettes with meeting eyebrows do among women." Now an anguished jealousy assailed him whenever in her old lighthearted way she smiled or even glanced at another man.

Still, what happened to produce an estrangement between them is a matter of speculation. Brown's presence at Wentworth Place may well have been disquieting. He resented several of Keats's close friendships with other men and, it seems clear, with women still more. Against young ladies he devised a characteristic stratagem to prevent their borrowing his books of manuscript copies of Keats's poems: he took to writing indecent verses and inserting them among the transcripts.[15] It seems that he quickly took a dislike to Fanny Brawne, which he did not conceal from Keats, and which he expressed in an attitude of amused contempt thinly disguised as flirting. A set of mocking valentine verses which he wrote to her in mid-February, though they amused her, must have exacerbated Keats, and were perhaps intended to do so. By an unlucky coincidence the Reynolds sisters came to spend a week with the Dilkes at just this time. "All very dull," Keats commented. But they, on the lookout as usual, evidently noticed the tension between Keats and Fanny and Brown and at once decided she was "an artful bad-hearted girl," [16] an opinion which they passed on to many of Keats's friends. Fanny at eighteen was undeniably a flirt, perhaps even less ready for marriage than Keats. She can hardly have guessed the emotion she had kindled in him, born of deep loneliness and the experience of death as well as his passionate adoration of beauty. Keats himself was unprepared for the surge of possessiveness which she had stirred up in him—a possessiveness which, it seems, some thoughtless word or act of hers now touched off into a jealous mistrust that was never afterward quite extinguished. But all that is certain is that Fanny, who had started copying his poems into the diary he had given her for Christmas, now suddenly stopped; and Keats remarked to George on Valentine's Day that he and Fanny had "every now and then a chat and a tiff." And with that she disappeared completely from his letters to America.

But February brought Keats still another disillusionment. During the Reynolds sisters' visit to Wentworth Place he learned some news of Bailey which was to estrange him permanently from Keats and his friends. At last Bailey had become engaged. From Thomasine Leigh to John Martin's sister (quite without Keats's knowing it), from Miss Martin to Mariane Reynolds (whom he had asked, the summer before, to take time to think over his proposal), his affections had winged and finally alighted—on Miss Hamilton Gleig, the sister of his college friend and daughter of the Bishop of Brechin. Once accepted, he broke off his London connections with a brusque note to Mrs. Reynolds and, after showing Mariane's letters to Gleig, asked her to return his own to him. "The great thing to be considered," Keats remarked soberly to George on February 19, "is—whether it is want of delicacy and principle or want of Knowledge and polite experience— And again Weakness—yes that is it—and the want of a Wife—yes that is it—Marians obstinacy is some excuse—but his so quickly taking to miss Gleig can have no excuse—except that of a Ploughmans who wants a wife." Bailey, the metaphysician and moralist, come to this! But it also appears from a number of signs that Keats now knew something at least of Bailey's part in the *Blackwood's* affair.[17] Out of pride or some not-quite-extinguished loyalty, he did not mention this incident to George; but his friendship with Bailey was over. "I begin to hate Parsons," he confessed to George a few days earlier while describing his visit to Stansted. As for Bailey, he had not written Keats since his conversation with Lockhart, though from his references to the incident in his subsequent letters to Taylor it appears that he was struggling to maintain a good opinion of himself. As Keats observed to George, the need to keep up an appearance of righteousness makes a parson "fester in himself"— "his features get a peculiar diabolical self sufficient iron stupid expression—He is continually acting—He must be either a Knave or an Ideot."

Yet he cannot have missed the irony of the situation: not only the Reynoldses' adulation of Bailey—"noble fellow—fine fellow! was always in their mouths"—but his own admiration. This was the friend in whom he had confided most openly, with whom he had shared his most searching speculations on the mystery of things. And it is on such a note of speculation that Keats ended his comment on Bailey and the Reynolds girls: "This may teach them that the man who redicules romance is the most romantic of Men—that he who abuses women and slights them—loves them the most—and above all that they are very shallow people who take every thing literal." Then, suddenly soaring away from his shabby story, he added, "A Man's life of any worth is a continual allegory—and very few eyes can see the Mystery of his life—a life like the scriptures, figurative—Lord Byron cuts a figure—but he is not figurative—Shakspeare led a life of Allegory; his works are the comments on it." It is a fine statement of a truth that his own life was proving: that the most significant experiences are often revealed in haphazard and trivial circumstance, and that it requires all the energy of the imagination to grasp their meaning and translate it into poetry.

Yet at just this moment a new friend stepped forward, a man whose first motive for seeking Keats's friendship was his own sense of the allegorical drama underlying Keats's work. Richard Woodhouse has remained in the background of Keats's acquaintance up till now—a scholarly and self-effacing young lawyer, slight, red-haired, and nearsighted. He had been impressed by Keats's con-versation at Hessey's dinner in September and still more by the letter Keats wrote him in October on the character of the poet. "Such a genius, I verily believe, has not appeared since Shakspeare & Milton," he wrote to his cousin Mary Frogley shortly afterward, "and if his Endymion be compared with Shakspeare's earliest work (his Venus & Adonis) written about the same age, Keats's poem will be found to contain more beauties, more poetry (and that of a higher order) less conceit & bad taste and in a word much more promise of excellence than are to be found in Shakspeare's work." With this, Woodhouse quietly decided to become Keats's Boswell. Again with Shakespeare in mind and the riddle of the Sonnets, he started to compile a set of notes to Keats's poems. "There is a great deal of reality about all that Keats writes," he observed, "and there must be many allusions to particular Circumstances, in his poems: which would add to their beauty and interest, if properly under-stood." He ordered copies of the *Poems* and *Endymion* interleaved for annotating, and began gathering Keats's unpublished poetry into a notebook, starting with some early verses culled from Mary Frogley's album.[18] His meeting with Keats on February 13 was a lucky coincidence; he carried him off to his coffeehouse, ordered a bottle of claret, and tactfully persuaded him to talk.

Evidently Keats responded good-naturedly to Woodhouse's prompting, for he gave him information about some of his early poems—those relating to his grandmother and the mysterious Vauxhall lady—which he had never confided to anyone. Certainly he enjoyed the claret. He mentioned the bottle, though not the boswellizing, in his journal to America on February 19, and at this point the gloom of his letter lifted for a moment and his prose took wings. "Now I like Claret whenever I can have Claret I must drink it.—'t is the only palate affair that I am at all sensual in. For really 't is so fine—it fills the mouth with a gushing freshness —then goes down cool and feverless—and the more ethereal Part of it mounts into the brain, not assaulting the cerebral apartments like a bully in a bad house looking for his trul and hurrying from door to door bouncing against the waistcoat *; but rather walks

---

* Keats seems to have intended "wainscot.'

like Aladin about his own enchanted palace so gently that you do not feel his step—Other wines of a heavy and spirituous nature transform a Man to a Silenus; this makes him a Hermes—and gives a Woman the soul and imortality of Ariadne." His prose ran on; one thing led inescapably to another. "I said this same Claret is the only palate-passion I have I forgot game I must plead guilty to the breast of a Partridge, the back of a hare, the backbone of a grouse, the wing and side of a Pheasant and a Woodcock *passim.*" He hesitated, thought of a pun, and went on: "Talking of game (I wish I could make it) the Lady whom I met at Hastings and of whom I said something in my last I think, has lately made me many presents of game, and enabled me to make as many—She made me take home a Pheasant the other day which I gave to Mrs Dilke—The next I intend for your Mother."

The association of ideas is significant; so is the information which he let slip out. On that busy February 13 he had gone to call on Isabella Jones.[19] A sudden impulse to see her at this time is understandable, and moreover he had a reason for calling. There can be little doubt that he took *The Eve of St. Agnes* to show her, and that she was delighted by the unexpected outcome of her suggestion. It is quite possible that she then told him a second legend to use as the framework of another poem.[20] It is certain that she sent him back to Hampstead with a pheasant, and that on that same evening he began what he described to George as "a little thing call'd the 'eve of St Mark.' "

It is an enchanting fragment of a poem, a series of vignettes as brightly coloured and lovingly detailed as a fifteenth-century Book of the Hours. "I think it will give you the sensation of walking about an old county Town in a coolish evening," Keats told George when he copied it for him some months later. The first half of the poem gives the rain-washed streets of a medieval city—Chichester, perhaps—filled with pious folk on their way to evensong, the bells ringing and the rooks wheeling above the elms behind the cathedral square, where a bright-haired girl sits reading alone in her room till the light fails. As the scene shifts to the interior of her house, the poem itself moves from the Middle Ages to the early nineteenth century, from Chichester to London—to what seems to be Mrs. Jones's square-panelled room in Gloucester Street with its firescreen and parrot cage.[21] The heroine herself, reading till her eyes ached, leaning forward to stir the fire with her shadow dancing on the wall behind, may indeed have been drawn from life. Yet a few lines further on, just as it is well begun, the poem breaks off abruptly—at the same time that all mention of Isabella ceases in Keats's journals. From the reference to the game he intended to give Mrs. Wylie, it is clear that Keats planned to see Mrs. Jones again. Yet with this brief hint of another visit, she drops from sight as suddenly as Fanny Brawne—the one on a note of anticipated pleasure, the other with "a chat and a tiff."

After the February 19 entry, Keats dropped his letter to America for two weeks. One is left wondering why he also broke off *The Eve of St. Mark* after such a promising start. It has been suggested that he was seized with foreboding by the legend itself— the superstition that whoever watches all night by the church door on St. Mark's Eve will see the ghosts of those who are to die the next year. It seems more likely that he felt both *The Eve of St. Agnes* and *The Eve of St. Mark* were distractions from the real task of *Hyperion,* for he referred to each of them as "little" things and, once having dropped the new poem on February 17, he felt no incentive to go back. What probably interrupted him that day was Abbey's announcement that the money due him from Tom's estate could not be touched for six years. With this alarming glimpse into the future, Keats must have realized that if he were to salvage his reputation as a poet he must get on with *Hyperion* and lose no time. The next entry in his letter to George, on March 3, gives only a stream of rather acid small talk, and when this ran dry he copied out whole pages of Hazlitt's "Letter to William Gifford Esq."—his superbly abusive counter-blast to the *Quarterly's* attack on his *Characters*—for George's amusement. Looking back over February, Keats could not recall anything worth writing about, even though, the week before, he had spent two or three days in town with Taylor, calling on friends and seeing a few plays as well as arguing with his lawyers about family finances. On March 8 he wrote Haydon to assure him he had not forgotten his promise about the loan and to apologize for not having come to see him since his return from Chichester. "I am mostly at Hampstead, and about nothing; being in a sort of qui bono temper, not exactly on the road to an epic poem." Five days later he wrote his sister to tell her his life was as dull as hers. His letter to America went on for a few days, describing a state of "uneasy indolence" rare for Keats—sleeping late, seeing none of his old friends, letting whole days slip by with nothing to show for them; then the journal broke off till mid-April.

The two months from mid-February to mid-April are the blankest and most puzzling period of Keats's creative life. It must be remembered that the record of his letters is often fragmentary and undependable, and so, though almost nothing seems to have happened all this while, even this is uncertain. Moreover, there are times in a man's life when his most important activity is to sit in a chair and think. This two months' blank would matter little, were it not that, looking back on this time from the months that followed, one can catch glimpses of a silent but far-reaching spiritual struggle taking place. Outwardly Keats seems to have sunk into the deepest of all his depressions. Several possible causes of this "qui bono temper" have been described; one effect appears certain—that from mid-February to mid-March he wrote not a single line of poetry. Another result seems to have been a long stretch of sleepless nights. Still another is hinted at here and there in his letters: that Keats now began drinking fairly heavily for the first time in his life. His rhapsody on claret, his attempt to ration himself to two or three glasses a meal, his getting tipsy at a claret feast for Dilke in March—all support Haydon's statement that Keats, in his depression after Tom's death, "flew to dissipation as a relief." One further expression of his "what's-the-use" mood is more speculative—that he began visiting Isabella Jones at this time more regularly than before.

These visits, if in fact they occurred, may be at the center of the mystery of these months; but this is far from certain.[22] There is no real evidence for the theory that Keats carried on a secret love affair with Isabella this winter, though it is likely that she took an interest in him which he can hardly have helped reciprocating. The only tangible proof of this, however, is a flirtatious note she wrote to John Taylor in May from Tunbridge Wells, begging him to write her and to go look at her portrait in the Royal Academy exhibition. In this letter she mentioned with a slightly proprietary air "*our* favourite *Endymion*"; but in the same breath she referred to a more fashionable young poet with the pointed inquiry "Who is Barry Cornwall?"[23] Evidently Mrs. Jones enjoyed collecting young men of literary promise, and for a while this winter she seems to have collected Keats. They were well

enough acquainted for Taylor to send her news of Keats in his
last illness, and for Brown to give her one of Keats's books after
his death. But a close attachment between them is another question. Even Taylor, who occupied a special place in Isabella's drawing room for several years, in the end grew tired of her provoca-
tive charm. She elicited two sonnets from him, one pondering her
motives in sending him a bust of Cupid, the other reproaching her
for surrounding herself with so many admirers.[24] Keats's reactions
to her gatherings may be inferred from the fact that he developed
a distaste for "hateful literary chit-chat" at about this time. "Conversation is not a search after knowledge but an endeavour at
effect," he remarked to Haydon early in March. "I will not mix
with that most vulgar of all crowds the literary." It may well have
been Mrs. Jones he had in mind in a later hit at women who
"would like to be married to a Poem and given away by a Novel."

Perhaps, then, his disenchantment with "the beautiful Mrs.
Jones," or the conflict of his feelings over both Isabella and Fanny
Brawne, had something to do with Keats's dark mood at this time.
This conflict, as has been suggested, may have been the origin of
a mysterious daydream he had one March morning, of "three figures on a greek vase," a man and two women, which he described
to George but refused to elucidate.[25] But there is another possible
cause for his depression—the steady company of Charles Brown.
When Keats at last started writing poetry again in the middle of
April, one of his first productions was an impromptu satire on his
friend. This little poem, an elaborate private joke, catalogues
Brown's traits by listing their opposites, in a mock-Spenserian
style which is itself a joking comment on this full-blooded Regency
gentleman. The last stanza hits off to perfection the slang and the
entertainment to be found in the "obscured purlieus" of London
where Brown went dodging the watchmen in search of damsels
"hoarse and rouge of cheek," or

> curled Jewesses with ankles neat,
> Who as they walk abroad make tinkling with their feet.

These stanzas, taken with his portrait of the "bully in a bad
house," give at least a hint that Keats may have kept him company
on these adventures. Perhaps, then, the note of self-digust that begins to appear in his letters at this time was Keats's unacknowl-
edged reaction to the friend who had by now replaced Haydon and

Bailey and Reynolds and his brothers at the centre of his life.

But there is another clue to the inner drama of these months: the sore throat which Keats told his sister in February had haunted him "at intervals nearly a twelvemonth." After his return from Bedhampton it lingered on for several more weeks, even though he was taking strict care of himself all this time under Sawrey's orders. His health did not improve during March; instead, he began feeling inexplicably fatigued. On Sunday, March 14, he dined with his neighbours the Davenports in Church Row, and came home to take a nap afterward. "I cannot bare a day anhilated in that manner," he wrote George—"to have nothing to do, and to be surrounded with unpleasant human identities; who press upon one just enough to prevent one getting into a lazy position; and not enough to interest or rouse one." Far better to sit at home alone, with his own speculations, "even of an unpleasant colour." "I do not know what I did on monday," he continued, "nothing —nothing—nothing. I wish this was any thing extraordinary." On Tuesday he roused himself sufficiently to go into town to see Abbey on business, walked back to Hampstead for dinner with Taylor and the painter Hilton, smoked a cigar after dinner, and walked back with his guests as far as Camden Town. These eight or nine miles exhausted him so much that he slept late the next morning, Wednesday the seventeenth, and did little with the rest of the day but read a play of Beaumont and Fletcher's and add a desultory page to his journal. The next day he played a game of cricket, got a black eye, and lay abed the next morning till eleven. This lassitude in an energetic young man of twenty-three is suspicious, especially when combined with certain other symptoms which Keats was showing at this time—chronic hoarseness, general irritability, insomnia, inability to concentrate. Today they would be recognized as early signs of tuberculosis.[26]

There can be no doubt that, whether he knew it or not, Keats had contracted the disease. In close hourly contact with Tom during the spring and fall of 1818, he could have escaped infection only by a miracle—if indeed he had not already been infected through nursing his mother years before. The depression and inertia of May and June 1818 may have been an early warning of this infection; certainly the loss of weight, high fever, and ulcerated throat of August 1818 showed something badly wrong. Yet no doctor in Keats's time could diagnose the onset of tuberculosis with any certainty, lacking thermometers, stethoscopes, X-rays, even the simplest technique of auscultation. In fact the first symptom then recognized was a cough, a sign of an advanced stage of the disease, and this was regarded not as a symptom but as a cause. As treatment various remedies were prescribed to allay the cough; wearing warm clothes and keeping out of cold damp air were recommended, as well as moderate exercise, a vegetable diet, and a sea voyage or a mild climate; while emotional agitation was to be avoided as much as possible.[27] From several remarks it is clear that Keats believed he was predisposed to tuberculosis by heredity and constitution and even temperament, given as he was to emotional extremes. The regime he was following this winter—treating his sore throat and avoiding the night air—shows that he at least suspected that he might be developing what he called "the family disease" and was doing what he could to scotch it. Even more significant is a plan he considered later in the spring, of becoming a ship's surgeon on an Indiaman—a sea voyage in southern waters. He could not have regarded his ulcerated throat as a doctor would today, as a secondary symptom showing tuberculosis of the lungs already well advanced. Yet from the fall of 1818 on Keats frequently mentioned an uncomfortable sense of pressure in his chest, almost like suffocation, in moments of anxiety—"the violence of my temperament continually smothered down," as he once described it—which indicates some constricted functioning of the lungs.[28] He also began keeping close watch on his young sister. Fanny was growing up thin and listless, more and more resembling Tom; and Keats's regular questions about her health show that he feared she too might be a consumptive type.[29]

These, then, were the "speculations of an unpleasant colour" from which he tried to escape in drink or sleep or sex or meaningless sociability, but which still waited for him at home at the end of each day. The vital tide that had lifted him up in December had ebbed again, and he was left contemplating what was still the most intense experience of his life up to that point—Tom's death, drawn out over three and a half months of suffering which Keats had shared with him day by day. The middle of March brought him to a crisis: the accumulated nothingness of his existence become intolerable. A few hours spent with people like the Davenports, "who have no light and shade," had come to seem an annihilation of life to which any reality, however painful, was preferable.

On March 17, after one of these evenings, he wrote a sonnet, his first poetry for a month.[30] It is not one of his good sonnets, but it is a revealing one. It asks the same question that posed itself on Ben Nevis the summer before, but in a mood far closer to despair:

> Why did I laugh tonight? No voice will tell:
>   No God, no Demon of severe response,
> Deigns to reply from Heaven or from Hell.
>   Then to my human heart I turn at once.
> Heart! Thou and I are here sad and alone;
>   I say, why did I laugh? O mortal pain!
> O Darkness! Darkness! ever must I moan,
>   To question Heaven and Hell and Heart in vain.
> Why did I laugh? I know this Being's lease,
>   My fancy to its utmost blisses spreads;
> Yet would I on this very midnight cease,
>   And the world's gaudy ensigns see in shreds;
> Verse, Fame, and Beauty are intense indeed,
> But Death intenser—Death is Life's high meed.

Once again the sickening suspicion overwhelmed him that nowhere in the world would he find an answer in his search for some meaning in existence—not even, for the moment, one summoned up from within his own consciousness. Yet in the very act of confronting this suspicion he managed to stare it down. As he told George, "I went to bed, and enjoyed an uninterrupted sleep— Sane I went to bed and sane I arose."

But Keats wrote with a meaning, not merely to rid himself of a mood. As he described it when copying the sonnet for George, "it was written with no Agony but that of ignorance; with no thirst of any thing but knowledge when pushed to the point though the first steps to it were through my human passions." This agony—an overwhelming doubt of the purpose of his life in the face of death—was "a great darkness" to him, in which he wrote "at random—straining at particles of light—without knowing the bearing of any one assertion of any one opinion." The thought of death, it seems, had momentarily paralysed his drive toward "Verse, Fame, and Beauty," the three great impulses of his nature. Yet he was renewing the struggle in another direction: "Give me this credit," he asked George, "Do you not think I strive—to know myself?" From the beginning his poetry had been shaped by his attempt somehow to escape from the realization of death; now he was finally relinquishing the attempt as meaningless. If the pros-

pect of death was faced squarely, he saw, it could be not the nega-
tion of all the struggles of life but the supreme experience, "in-
tenser" than all the others, in calling out all a man's heroism to
meet it. More than this, it might become "life's high meed," the
resolution of all those doubts which can never be settled in life
itself. Intensity—which he had described a year ago as a degree of
imagination in which "disagreeables evaporate" by being brought
into relationship with "Beauty and Truth"—he now saw could
not be attained except by admitting these disagreeables; and a life
without intensity, without light and shade, was hardly worth living. Darkness itself was preferable, the darkness of his own unanswered questions in which he still groped toward the light which
he still believed was there.

-»» «««-

Discouragement, lassitude, disillusionment, the ever-growing
conviction that time was running out—all had acted to silence
Keats's poetry during these weeks; yet he had another reason for
not writing. By January he had reached a crucial point in his epic,
where Apollo was to emerge as the new god of poetry in Hyperion's place. This brought Keats up against the central question
of his life—the making of a poet—at a time when he felt his greatest doubts about his own purposes. His theme is one of the largest
he could have set himself, and one that since his time has become
a central preoccupation of literature: the nature of the artist, the
validity of his insight, and the purpose his art serves in society.
In the English poetry of his time it was only beginning to emerge
as a theme for the poet himself to explore; yet it is characteristic
of Keats to have sensed immediately the central problem of his
age and attempted to solve it in his work even as he was grappling
with it in his own experience. "I would sooner fail than not be
among the greatest," he had said of the failure of *Endymion* at
the time he started *Hyperion*. Now, half a year later, he decided
to write no more till the answer to his own question became clearer
to him.

So he announced to Haydon, early in March, that he had resolved "never to write for the sake of writing, or making a poem,
but from running over with any little knowlege and experience
which many years of reflection may perhaps give me—otherwise

I will be dumb." This was more than a resolution, it was a defiance; for Haydon never saw Keats or wrote to him without urging him on with *Hyperion*. Yet the more Keats struggled with his
poem, the more he realized that great poetry could not be written
out of mere great ambition or even some gift of noble language,
but only out of a knowledge of life which he had not yet achieved.
He had enough to do for the present, he told Haydon, with "looking upon myself, and trying myself at lifting mental weights, as
it were." "I am three and twenty," he added, "with little knowledge and middling intellect. It is true that in the height of enthusiasm I have been cheated into some fine passages, but that is
not the thing."

The thing was evidently philosophy. It seems that, as he pondered his theme of "the grand march of intellect" in *Hyperion,*
Keats was turning with new interest to the philosophic classics,
those mental weights he tried lifting in these otherwise idle
months. Quoting Milton's line "How charming is divine Philosophy!" he explained to George that he now appreciated it as never
before; and his journal at this time shows a new concern with
the perennial questions of the nature of the good, the limits of
reason, and even the pre-existence of the soul. A discussion at
Taylor's evidently fired his interest in Plato again. The Socratic
motto "Know thyself" echoes in his letters during March; perhaps the Socratic paradox that the goal of the true philosopher
is death helped shape his line "Death is Life's high meed." His
imagination had been captured by the character of Socrates, who,
it now appeared to him, embodied the supreme virtue of disinterestedness more completely than any other men in history except
Jesus. And this led him off onto another train of thought. "What
I heard Taylor observe with respect to Socrates, may be said of
Jesus," he remarked to George, "—That he was so great a man
that though he transmitted no writing of his own to posterity, we
have his Mind and his sayings and his greatness handed to us by
others. It is to be lamented that the history of the latter was written and revised by Men interested in the pious frauds of Religion.
Yet through all this I see his splendour."

Inevitably his reading of philosophy led him back to the problems of religious faith—or his lack of it. Perhaps, on closer study
of *Paradise Lost*, he was revising his earlier judgment that Milton's theology could be grasped by one "not much advanced in

years." He was trying at any rate to extend his knowledge of religion, for he began reading Church history in March; and it may have been at this time that the works of Bishop Beveridge and Saint Ambrose and a folio Prayer Book found their way onto his shelves.[31] These excursions into theology did not lessen his distaste for Christian dogma; yet, along with a glance at earlier religions, Zoroastrian and Hindu, they helped widen the range of his speculation.

The year before, Keats had thought of Hazlitt as his guide along "the metaphysical road," and during this winter his admiration for Hazlitt's incisive mind reached its height. It seems likely that his recurrent concern with the idea of disinterestedness owed much to his reading of Hazlitt's early essay on *The Principles of Human Action* at this time. Yet Hazlitt's recent debate with the editor of the *Quarterly,* some of which Keats had copied out for George, struck him more forcibly. The essay raised a troubling question, however. In it Hazlitt maintained, citing Shakespeare's *Coriolanus* as an example, that the poet naturally leans to the aristocratic, or "arbitrary," side of the question rather than to the democratic, because it appeals more to the imagination, even though it may violate our rational and moral sense. Not "the cause of the people," he argued, but "the triumphant progress of the conquerors and mighty Hunters of mankind" provides poetry with its greatest themes. This idea implied a conflict between Keats's political convictions and a view of poetry which he found hard to refute; it also posed a dilemma for *Hyperion.* How could he reconcile Hazlitt's defense of the "poetry of power" with his own epic theme of the "general and gregarious advance" of mankind? It was his aim, as he remarked half-mockingly to George, to "tell truth unto the men of this generation, & eke to the women"; but Hazlitt seemed to force him into the position that "poetry is not so fine a thing as philosophy—For the same reason that an eagle is not so fine a thing as a truth."

The problem was not one to be solved by logic. A few days after copying the passage from Hazlitt on March 13, Keats wrote the sonnet "Why did I laugh tonight?" in his "Agony of ignorance"; then on March 19 he resumed his letter to George. He had just heard from Haslam that his father was on the point of death, and resolved to go to town the next day to see him. "This is the world," he mused. "Circumstances are like Clouds continually gathering and bursting—While we are laughing the seed of some trouble is put into the wide arable land of events—while we are laughing it sprouts it grows and suddenly bears a poison fruit which we must pluck—Even so," he added, "we have leisure to reason on the misfortunes of our friends; our own touch us too nearly for words." He realized how far he fell short of truly disinterested sympathy for his friend, and yet, he reflected, there was in the very intensity of most men's absorption in their immediate feelings a kind of "essential beauty." "The greater part of Men make their way with the same instinctiveness, the same animal eagerness as the Hawk—The Hawk wants a Mate, so does the Man—look at them both they set about it and procure one in the same manner. I go among the Feilds and catch a glimpse of a stoat or a field-mouse peeping out of the withered grass—the creature hath a purpose and its eyes are bright with it—I go amongst the buildings of a city and I see a Man hurrying along—to what? The Creature has a purpose and his eyes are bright with it." In another flash of detachment he saw himself as he sat writing, "pursueing the same instinctive course as the veriest human animal you can think of. May there not," he wondered, "be superior beings amused with any graceful, though instinctive attitude my mind may fall into, as I am entertained with the alertness of a Stoat or the anxiety of a Deer? Though a quarrel in the streets is a thing to be hated, the energies displayed in it are fine. By a superior being our reasonings may take the same tone—though erroneous they may be fine—This is the very thing in which consists poetry." This was the problem Hazlitt had posed; but as Keats pondered it the dilemma seemed to dissolve. Perhaps an eagle is not so fine a thing as a truth; yet the eagle, the lion, the hawk—all agents of the "eternal fierce destruction" that had sickened him to contemplate a year before—had the beauty of intensity to the mind that could see it, and this was the wellspring of poetry.

At this point, it seems, Keats turned back to *Hyperion*. By some mysterious force his long creative paralysis was broken at last. The lines he added to *Hyperion* sometime near the end of March, depicting the young Apollo's birth into godhead, describe the same struggle against darkness, the same mood of agonized questioning, as his sonnet of mid-March;[32] but now they are resolved. Where Keats had shown Hyperion—his younger self—waiting for his overthrow with dread, uncomprehending, unconsenting, he now made Apollo seek out the ordeal of his transformation. Alone on Delos, he has found its unshadowed beauty turning into "painful vile oblivion." The self-engrossed delights of the days of his first discovery of song, when he was content merely to sing his own name over and over in wonderment, now seem meaningless: he "aches" with his ignorance of the universe of which he is now aware. In answer to his distress, Mnemosyne appears to him—the mysterious goddess of Memory, repository of all the experience of the human race. Apollo has known her before as in a dream; now he is ready to confront the reality of knowledge she represents. At first she gives no answer to his troubled questions; but at the height of his anguish he finds he can read "a wondrous lesson" in her silent face. In an electric flash of insight he learns all he lacked before, and his despair yields to exultation:

> "Knowledge enormous makes a God of me.
> Names, deeds, gray legends, dire events, rebellions,
> Majesties, sovran voices, agonies,
> Creations and destroyings, all at once
> Pour into the wide hollows of my brain,
> And deify me. . . ."

This is no knowledge that philosophy could teach, but the wisdom born of the fullness of experience—the awareness of all the sufferings of mankind, the acceptance of "creations and destroyings" together. And as he receives this wisdom of Mnemosyne, Apollo undergoes a change almost beyond description. Keats's search for a metaphor to express this transformation is revealing:

> Soon wild commotions shook him, and made flush
> All the immortal fairness of his limbs
> Into a hue more roseate than sweet pain
> Gives to a ravish'd Nymph when her warm tears
> Gush luscious with no sob. Or more severe,—
> More like the struggle at the gate of death;
> Or liker still to one who should take leave
> Of pale immortal death, and with a pang
> As hot as death's is chill, with fierce convulse
> Die into life: so young Apollo anguish'd.[33]

All the most self-annulling experiences of life—the crises of sexuality, both masculine and feminine, of birth and ecstasy and death —are seized on here to convey an experience beyond themselves which in the end he could only describe literally as "dying into life."

> At length
> Apollo shriek'd;—and lo! from all his limbs
> Celestial Glory dawn'd: he was a god! [34]

Here Keats laid his poem down again. The long passage on Apollo's deification, as he later told Woodhouse, had seemed to come to him from some unknown source outside himself—"as it were something given to him." [35] Once the astonishing flow had ceased, there was nothing more to say, at least for the present. But these lines marked the end of a long struggle for Keats. The annihilation of his old identity was complete. The solitary youthful singer had emerged from the ordeal of innocence into the fullness of life at last, to become "the Father of all verse," a god of poetry indeed.

Chapter Ten

The Temple of Delight

AFTER this continuation of *Hyperion*, Keats lapsed into silence again. Following the long meditative entry of March 19, his journal shows a blank for four weeks; only a few brief letters and a single sonnet fill the interval. As he wrote his sister on April 12, idleness was becoming a habit with him that would be hard to break. Yet the only reason he would give was his worry over not hearing from George. Everything seemed at a standstill; only the season moved on. As the days grew warmer he started tramping over the Heath again, but evidently still made little effort to see his friends in town. With Rice in poorer health than usual, the card-playing set had fallen apart. Haslam was on the brink of marriage. Reynolds was completely "limed in the law," as Keats noted—not only reconciled to it but making a hobby-horse of it. His visits to his sister at Walthamstow were still strictly rationed, but he made a point of sending her a little present from town every week or so—Goldsmith's poems, a Tassie seal, drawing paper, seeds for her garden, and, since she was about to be confirmed, a brief treatise on the Catechism. When Fanny wrote him a long list of questions which the curate had put to her, he answered them with a flourish of his new theological knowledge and signed himself, wryly amused, "Your affectionate Parson John." In another letter he gave her a fanciful portrait of himself in his favourite pose, sunk in an armchair by a globe of gold-fish, staring out of a window shaded with japonica: "I should like the window to open onto the Lake of Geneva—and there I'd sit and read all day like the picture of somebody reading."

Outwardly this unproductive interval seems one of those fallow periods of "delicious diligent indolence" which Keats himself realized were the necessary prelude to intense creative effort. Yet from several signs it appears closer to the uneasy inaction of his continued depression. One clue, though a baffling one, is the hint of a crisis in his financial affairs at this time. After three months of wrangling with Abbey and the lawyers, it seems that at last he received some definite statement on his funds. It was worse even than he had feared. His grandmother's bequest had mysteriously dwindled down to almost nothing. His generosity in lending money to friends had cost him over two hundred pounds, a sum which he knew there was small chance of being repaid. When these loans were reckoned up with still larger ones to his brothers, his medical school expenses, lawyers' fees, and his drafts on his principal, he was left with little more than the hundred-odd pounds remaining in his cash account. Of the five hundred pounds he had deposited at Abbey's the preceding June, nearly half had vanished in loans to Tom and George that summer and a large withdrawal in March evidently to settle Tom's bills. The five hundred pounds, more or less, which he had been expecting from Tom's estate would, it now finally appeared, be withheld till his sister reached twenty-one. This meant that his supply of money had virtually run dry, and for more than five years he could count on nothing but what he could beg from Abbey. Keats must have been staggered. Abbey himself had nothing more constructive to suggest than that Keats enter a hatters' firm in which he had an interest; and he managed to convince him that he had only his own negligence to blame for the situation. Grimly Keats resolved to keep more careful accounts in the future. It did not occur to him that Abbey—as now seems probable—had quietly borrowed his ward's capital for his own use; for this is the only possible explanation of his failure to make over or even mention to Keats some seven or eight hundred pounds still due him from his grandfather's estate.[1] Not till four years later was the existence of these funds discovered, and Abbey's handling of his trust investigated by the Court of Chancery;[2] but by then it was too late.

Why Keats reacted to this revelation by drawing out the £106 remaining in his cash account on April 3 is not clear. But now at last he realized he could not meet his promise to Haydon. The painter, who had been pressing him for the loan all through March,

replied to this announcement on April 12 with a letter reproaching Keats for deceiving him and thus preventing him from obtain-
ing money elsewhere. At this, remembering all the trips to town,
the harangues, the worry, the time wasted, Keats flared up in sudden anger. He had acted in good faith, he told Haydon, and gone
to far more trouble than he would have done for himself. "I cannot
do two things at once," he retorted heatedly, "and thus this affair
has stopped my pursuits in every way. Now you have maimed me
again; I was whole I had began reading again—when your note
came I was engaged in a Book—I dread as much as a Plague the
idle fever of two months more without any fruit." The unexpected
note of petulance in these accusations suggests a deeper strain on
their relationship than either man would have admitted, similar
perhaps to that which had undermined Keats's friendship with
Hunt. Yet for Keats this was only a momentary flash of irritation.
Already his financial predicament seems to have jolted him out of
the doldrums into a new determination to act. His money would
last, he figured, for another six months. So, he decided, when
Brown went off for the summer he would take cheap lodgings in
Westminster, close to a good supply of books in the Abbey Library,
and try to finish *Hyperion*. Then, as he announced to George on
April 15, he would see what he could do "without poetry." It
seems he was thinking of earning his living by journalism, as
Reynolds had done; but if worse came to worst, he could always go
back to medicine. "I have no doubt of making by some means a
little to help on or," he added sardonically, "I shall be left in the
Lurch—with the burden of a little Pride." [3]

There was more to this decision, however, than the low ebb of
his funds. For more than a month he had known that his pleasant
life at Wentworth Place would soon be over, and not just for the
length of Brown's vacation. Ever since mid-February the Dilkes
had been planning to leave Hampstead. Dilke, like a true Godwin-
ian, was giving much anxious thought to his child's education.
Though Charley at nine was quite old enough to be sent away to
school, his father wanted to watch over his schooling himself and
so decided to move into town and send his son to Westminster as
a day pupil. This extravagance of concern first amused then irritated Keats; Dilke will ruin the boy with too much care, he
thought to himself. But he must have heard the sequel to this plan
with a rush of emotion. Mrs. Brawne, it now appears, had decided

to buy the Dilkes' half of Wentworth Place and move in after they left at the beginning of April. Immediately Keats realized this would be the end of his comfortable arrangement with Brown. He made up his mind apparently at once to leave Wentworth Place by the first of May, when Brown planned to rent his house for the summer as he usually did to eke out his income; but for some time Keats could not decide where to go. First Edinburgh occurred to him, then Westminster; then, for another few months, his mind was to run all over the world looking for a place.[4] Only one thing seemed certain: he could not live and work in peace with Fanny Brawne next door.

So matters stood on April 3, when the Dilkes left for Westminster and the Brawnes moved in [5]—a move which, significantly, Keats never mentioned to George. The next day, a Sunday, Mrs. Brawne invited him to dinner. Keats must have accepted with some uneasiness, but he managed at the same time to forget that he had asked his brothers-in-law Charles and Henry Wylie a few weeks before to dine with him that afternoon. When he remembered and tried to excuse himself, Mrs. Brawne insisted that they all come; and so a new chapter of his life at Wentworth Place began. As on New Year's Day, Keats noted in his journal only the mere fact of dining at the Brawnes'; so, as with his Christmas dinner at Elm Cottage, we are left to surmises. Did Fanny set out to dazzle the two good-looking young Wylies, or did she play Millamant to Keats's reluctant Mirabel? Or did she look a little paler than usual? Keats did not record even the impression that "Nothing particular passed"; but that something extraordinary did happen appears from the sonnet he wrote a few days later—the first since the troubled outburst of "Why did I laugh tonight?"

This sonnet sprang not out of the sleepless anxiety of mid-March but from a dream so beautiful that, as he exclaimed in his journal, he wished he could dream it every night. The dream itself was touched off by his rereading the fifth canto of the *Inferno*, where Francesca describes the fateful day she and Paolo read the story of Launcelot together and he "kissed her mouth all trembling." "I had passed many days in rather a low state of mind," Keats wrote to George, "and in the midst of them I dreamt of being in that region of Hell. The dream was one of the most delightful enjoyments I ever had in my life—I floated about the whirling atmosphere as it is described with a beautiful figure to whose lips

mine were joined as it seem'd for an age—and in the midst of all
this cold and darkness I was warm—even flowery tree tops sprung
up and we rested on them sometimes with the lightness of a cloud
till the wind blew us away again—I tried a Sonnet upon it—there
are fourteen lines but nothing of what I felt in it—"

> As Hermes once took to his feathers light,
>   When lulled Argus, baffled, swoon'd and slept,
> So on a Delphic reed, my idle spright
>   So play'd, so charm'd, so conquer'd, so bereft
> The dragon-world of all its hundred eyes;
>   And, seeing it asleep, so fled away,
> Not to pure Ida with its snow-cold skies,
>   Nor unto Tempe, where Jove griev'd that day;
> But to that second circle of sad hell,
>   Where in the gust, the whirlwind, and the flaw
> Of rain and hail-stones, lovers need not tell
>   Their sorrows,—pale were the sweet lips I saw,
> Pale were the lips I kiss'd, and fair the form
> I floated with, about that melancholy storm.

A sense of mysterious release and reunion is evoked so delicately
in these lines that one hesitates to link them to any actual experience. Still there are strange echoes in this sonnet, of the calm
beyond despair Keats had described in the Cave of Quietude and
the warmth of love in Madeline's chilly room, and others far more
remote—recollections of a pale and beautiful woman found in a
shadowy world of faithless lovers, of a nameless "fair form" to
which he remained joined in endless mute satisfaction. Some of
these overtones can have sounded only faintly in Keats's mind;
but, out of the wordless depths of feeling, the dream must have
spoken unmistakably to him of one desire which he had struggled
for months to deny. Fanny Brawne had returned after her mysterious disappearance, the hundred-eyed world had been lulled into
heedlessness, and his long winter was yielding to spring.

This realization was born in another uneventful week at Wentworth Place, in which, for all we know, Keats did nothing but
read and dig in the garden. On Saturday, April 10, Hunt and
Burridge Davenport, his Hampstead neighbour, came for dinner;
and Davenport, in an effort to impress Hunt, "never ceased talking and boaring," while Keats sat on the sidelines watching with
amusement Brown's irritation and Hunt's pleasure at the compliment. On Sunday he took a long walk over the Heath and met his

anatomy demonstrator from Guy's, Joseph Green, strolling with a portly middle-aged gentleman with a strange gleam in his eye—that "archangel a little damaged" whom he recognized at once as Samuel Taylor Coleridge. Keats joined them for two miles of leisurely conversation in which they discussed everything from nightingales and "a dream accompanied by a sense of touch"—was this Keats's contribution?—to mermaids and metaphysics. Two days later he wrote his angry reply to Haydon's reproaches about the loan; two days after that, on April 15, he started up his journal to America again after his month's lapse. And almost at once his letter records an extraordinary change of mood. In a sudden spurt of energy he had begun going into town again, six times within eight days—dining here and calling there, visiting the newly opened Leicester Gallery with Hunt, attending a rout where he talked with a dazzlingly pretty girl, inspecting a panorama of a polar expedition in Leicester Square, spending an entire pleasant Sunday at Taylor's with Woodhouse, going to "a new dull and half damnd opera" with three of his cronies, and all with evident enjoyment. On Monday, the nineteenth, he invited Taylor, Woodhouse, and Reynolds out to Hampstead for dinner, and, when a storm came up to keep them from returning, they played cards till daylight. Tuesday, he was "not worth a sixpence," but the next day he picked up his letter to America again to report a magnificent hoax which he was helping Reynolds perpetrate. Hearing that Wordsworth was about to publish another long-winded rustic narrative called "Peter Bell," Reynolds had written a parody of it, sight unseen, in a five-hour stretch, which he had persuaded Taylor to print under the same title a few days before Wordsworth's own was to appear. Keats, delighted, agreed to crown the joke by reviewing the pretended "Peter Bell" for *The Examiner,* and on Wednesday he roughed out a notice of it in his journal for George's amusement.

A number of things could have spurred him to this burst of activity—a return of good health with the good weather, a visit from Brown's two nephews with "little voices like wasps stings" which made him anxious to escape the house, or perhaps the disturbing new presence next door. But it is also possible that his sudden high spirits resulted from a reprieve on his departure from Wentworth Place. Evidently about this time Brown decided not to let his house till the end of June, and evidently this change of plan pleased Keats more than he would admit. Whatever it was that roused him out of his depression, it also tapped a new spring of poetry. "I am still at a stand in versifying—I cannot do it yet with any pleasure," he told George in starting up his journal on April 15. Yet as he wrote on, late into the evening, with the house quiet at last, his pen began running away with him; three pages of nonsense verse, full of private family jokes, came tumbling out. The next morning, after the nephews left, he went on filling up his letter with gossip for Georgiana and added the mock-Spenserian stanzas lampooning Brown. The following week he drafted a little ballad into his journal; a few days later he wrote a "Chorus of Four Faeries," one for each of the four elements. Then he did a series of experimental sonnets, one on sleep, two on fame, a sonnet on the sonnet itself—all written within a week and ringing unexpected new changes on the form. Nothing could be farther from the bitter satisfaction he had described to Haydon, early in March, "of having great conceptions without the toil of sonnetteering." He had given up his struggle with *Hyperion*, for the present at least, and now found himself absorbed in problems of craft with a delight he had never felt before.

Yet the most unexpected poetry of these two weeks sprang from a strange and troubling adventure. On April 15 Keats called at the Bentleys' to collect the last of the belongings he had left at Well Walk, including some of Tom's papers. Here he found something that brought back his young brother, pale and miserable, with almost unbearable vividness. It was a packet of love letters from the mysterious Amena, written supposedly at the dictation of Tom's friend Charles Wells, and strange letters they were too —such a mixture of high-flown sentiment and downright vulgarity that it is hard to believe that Tom could have taken them seriously, even at sixteen. "It is a wretched business," Keats wrote George that evening; "I do not know the rights of it—but what I do know would I am sure affect you so much that I am in two Minds whether I will tell you any thing about it." The next day, as he reread them, it dawned on him that Tom had been not simply jilted but hoaxed: Amena had never existed, and Tom's visit to France to meet her had been a wild-goose chase—"a cruel deception on a sanguine Temperament, with every show of friendship." Whether Keats caught some overtones of parody of his own early poetry in the letters is another question; [6] but he grew almost incoherent with

anger against Wells as he wrote: "I do not think death too bad
for the villain. I will hang over his head like a sword by a hair.
He is a rat and he shall have ratsbane to his vanity—I will harm
him all I possibly can." This rage seems excessive unless we remember what Keats and all his contemporaries believed—that emotional agitation, especially that of an unhappy love, could bring
on consumption.[7] Wells's hoax, it now appeared, had helped to
kill his brother. The thought of Tom, racked by a passion that was
not only hopeless but unreal, was almost too painful to bear. Keats
turned at once to something else—to copying the sonnet "On a
Dream" into his letter.

The sonnet and the adventure reappear, strangely linked, in
the little ballad that Keats wrote down in his journal five days later
—"La Belle Dame sans Merci." One hesitates to press this poem
for any meaning beyond itself, for it is poetry of a kind that, as
Keats said of his favourite passage in Shakespeare, "One's very
breath while leaning over these pages is held for fear of blowing
these lines away." [8] Yet it seems to have sprung from two recent
experiences, miraculously transformed: his own dream encounter
wth a beautiful woman in a sorrowful world of pale-lipped lovers,
and his discovery of his brother's miserable secret. Keats's corrections in the draft suggest all too clearly how the image of the
knight "palely loitering" by the wintry lake, "so haggard and so
woe-begone," sprang from his painful reminder of Tom the week
before:

> a
> I see death's lilly on thy brow,
>   With anguish moist and fever dew,
>   a
> And on thy cheeks death's fading rose
>   Fast withereth too.

The link between the beautiful lady the knight meets in a flower-
strewn meadow and the "beautiful figure" Keats dreamed of floating with in magical blossoming warmth is more delicate but still
perceptible. What matters, of course, is not Keats's actual dream or
recollection but his reshaping of it in the poem. For when the
knight falls asleep in the "elfin grot" he dreams not of love and
warmth but of betrayal and death:

> I saw pale kings and princes too,
>   Pale warriors, death-pale were they all;

They cried—'La Belle Dame sans Merci
        Hath thee in thrall!'

The dream has changed significantly since early in April; it has
turned into a "horrid warning" and comes to an abrupt end. The
Knight awakes to find himself alone "on the cold hill side"; the
lady herself, he realizes, was a delusion.

So Tom had been deluded and died; so Keats himself had loitered through the winter. And it is hard not to believe that the
lady who appeared and then vanished into the wintry air was not
also partly real:

> I met a lady in the meads,
>   Full beautiful—a faery's child,
> Her hair was long, her foot was light,
>   And her eyes were wild.

Fanny Brawne on one of her walks across the Heath has been
caught up in the process—vision or waking dream—which made
this poem.

> She took me to her elfin grot,
>   And there she wept, and sigh'd full sore,
> And there I shut her wild wild eyes
>   With kisses four.

Of course the poem gives no account of what actually happened in
that uncertain April, and it is immeasurably better than any literal
record of his experience Keats could have left. Still it is a fact
that somehow, sometime this month, he and Fanny met and broke
through the barrier that had separated them since February; and
it is hard not to listen for even a faint echo of that encounter. Was
it Fanny herself who made the first move? Two statements which
she wrung from Keats a few months later may be taken as comments on their reconciliation if not on the poem itself. "Ask yourself my love whether you are not very cruel to have so entrammelled
me, so destroyed my freedom," he wrote Fanny on the first of
July. He was enthralled, then, by a lovely lady without mercy—
a fate he had reason to fear. A week later he exclaimed, "I never
knew before, what such a love as you have made me feel, was; I
did not believe in it; my Fancy was affraid of it, lest it should burn
me up." He was torn between doubt that such a feeling could be
real and dread that it would be his undoing; yet its intensity was
such that he could no longer deny it. As Fanny later complained,

he had "been an age" in letting her take possession of him; now at last he gave himself up to loving her, though with a foreboding of what might follow—the pale fever, the dream of death, the lonely awakening on a cold hillside.

Yet the poems that began pouring forth a few days after "La Belle Dame sans Merci" show none of his lingering fear of involvement. The "Chorus of Four Faeries" celebrates the joys of a delicate and fanciful sensuality, while the two sonnets on fame mock his own long struggle to win a name with a great poem. The first sonnet, in stating that fame comes only to the man who has learned to be indifferent to it, paints a curious picture of two young lovers at cross purposes:

> Fame, like a wayward girl, will still be coy
>   To those who woo her with too slavish knees,
> But makes surrender to some thoughtless boy,
>   And dotes the more upon a heart at ease. . . .

It also implies an ironically happy ending in the advice to "lovesick Bards" to "repay her scorn for scorn":

> Make your best bow to her and bid adieu,
> Then, if she likes it, she will follow you.

The second sonnet, which Keats dashed off one morning while Brown was copying out some of his earlier poems, suggests another view of himself at this time. Fame he calls a "fierce miscreed" of salvation, a fever and vexation, from which he turns toward the serenity of growing things: a rose unfolding, a plum ripening with no thought of being plucked or tasted. These images of unforced growth recall his former axiom, "If Poetry comes not as naturally as the Leaves to a tree it had better not come at all"; but Keats was thinking here not of poetry but of life itself. In its full meaning— that all the conditions of growth must be accepted by a man as unconcernedly as a plant accepts them—the sonnet harks back to Keats's meditation on "animal eagerness" that had produced his addition to *Hyperion* toward the end of March; it also echoes the most richly reflective passage in all his letters, which Keats had written to George only a few days before the sonnet.[9]

For the end of April brought a rare moment of calm in which Keats once again could "look upon his mortal days with temperate blood." His poetry, his ambition, his love, and all the contingencies that hedged them about, now fell into a perspective suddenly intelligible and acceptable. At last he felt he could meet the challenges of life squarely on all fronts, without trying to rise above them in the privileged role of poet or taking refuge from them in philosophic abstraction. All his reading and thinking this spring had served only to sharpen his own conception of existence, wrested from his own bitter experience. The vision of "creations and destroyings" which had made the young Apollo into a god of poetry he now saw as giving meaning and value to all human experience, not merely the poet's—just as he now saw himself as a man who must suffer and act, not merely a poet who creates. This sense of things emerges in his journal to George as one evening he let his mind play over two very different books he had recently been reading—Robertson's *History of America* and Voltaire's *Age of Louis XIV*. From Peru to Versailles, he saw, the record of history everywhere refutes the fashionable belief in perfectibility, Shelley's youthful faith that the advance of civilization will eventually eliminate human suffering. "The nature of the world will not admit of it," Keats mused; first "let the fish philosophise the ice away from the Rivers in winter time." The inhabitants of the world will correspond to itself, he saw; and yet his awareness of the limitations on human possibility imposed by man's inescapable link to nature did not preclude a belief in something by which man rises above mere "animal eagerness" and approaches disinterestedness. Even while glimpsing the beauty of destructive animal vitality, Keats recognized "an ellectric fire in human nature tending to purify." [10] So the inevitability of human suffering was no argument against a carefully qualified faith in spiritual progress—such benefit to mankind as might result from "the persevering endeavours of a seldom appearing Socrates." Still less was it a proof of the Christian belief that this world is a vale of tears which will be redeemed by the joys of heaven. No, there was another reason for suffering, a positive value to be realized in this very world.

"Call the world if you Please 'The vale of Soul-making,'" he wrote to George. "Then you will find out the use of the world. I say '*Soul making*' Soul as distinguished from an Intelligence— There may be intelligences or sparks of the divinity in millions —but they are not Souls till they acquire identities, till each one is personally itself." It is significant that, after once viewing the lack of identity as the special exemption of the poet, Keats now saw the achievement of identity as the highest goal of human development. It was a new "system of salvation" he was trying to describe, a process of "Spirit-creation" from "three grand materials acting the one upon the other for a series of years"—the intelligence, the heart, and the "world of Circumstances." How, then, he asked, are souls to be made, to have identity given to them, "but by the medium of a world like this? I can scarcely express what I but dimly perceive," he confessed, "—that you may judge the more clearly I will put it in the most homely form possible—I will call the *world* a School instituted for the purpose of teaching little children to read—I will call the *human heart* the *horn Book* used in that School—and I will call the *Child able to read, the Soul* made from that *school* and its *hornbook*. Do you not see how necessary a World of Pains and troubles is to school an Intelligence and make it a soul? A Place where the heart must feel and suffer in a thousand diverse ways! Not merely is the Heart a Hornbook, It is the Minds Bible, it is the Minds experience, it is the teat from which the Mind or intelligence sucks its identity."

This last image is supremely characteristic of Keats in implying that the assimilation of experience beyond all conscious endeavour is what makes wisdom in the end.[11] The identity or "identical soul," as he now calls it, is not formed by taking thought: for it is the intelligence that must be sent to school, not the heart—the intelligence which must be "fortified and altered" by submitting itself to the world of circumstances and its lesson of perplexity and pain and death. Keats here moves beyond the Platonic idea of soul-making which seems to have tempted him at least briefly— the belief that with death the soul will slough off the imperfect knowledge of bodily life for the perfect knowledge of the intellect. Wisdom, like good, must be attained in this life if it is to be attained at all; and it is won by slow perfection not in knowledge but in experience. "As various as the Lives of Men are—so various become their souls," he concluded; and in the end the achievement of identity is good, however much suffering it entails, because—he can appeal only to experience—it brings "a bliss peculiar to each ones individual existence," the acceptance of one's self and one's destiny as the very condition of being. Whatever experience had brought him to this insight, one thing seems clear:

from his struggle with the world of circumstance, heart and mind together, he had emerged at last, altered and fortified, with the firm sense of his own identity which had eluded him so long.

>>> <<<

The last week of April and the first week or two of May seemed lifted out of time. The fine weather in mid-April had hurried the season forward; then for a few days the spring seemed to stand still. "This is the 3ᵈ of May & everything is in delightful forwardness," Keats wrote before closing his journal to George; "the violets are not withered, before the peeping of the first rose." He had another month at Wentworth Place to enjoy his pleasant sitting room opening on the garden, the garden itself coming into full bloom, the cellar under the garden path—and now the sight of Fanny strolling over the grass plot, and the chance of a meeting with her stolen from a walk on the Heath. For this little while the future must wait. "O there is nothing like fine weather, and health, and Books," he exclaimed in a letter to his sister, "and a fine country, and a contented Mind, and Diligent-habit of reading and thinking, and an amulet against the ennui—and, please heaven, a little claret-wine cool out of a cellar a mile deep."

After closing his journal to America on May 3, Keats wrote no real letter till May 31. Several friends came out from town to visit him, but he apparently remained rooted to Hampstead all this while. He was making a close study of Dryden's poetry and walking daily on the Heath with Fanny Brawne; otherwise we know nothing of his life during this month but what can be read from the four Odes of May—"On Indolence," "On a Grecian Urn," "To a Nightingale," and "On Melancholy"—to which should be added his "Ode to Psyche," written in the last week of April. In these odes Keats reached his own full ripeness as a poet at last. With the resolution of his struggle to understand himself, both as the poet represented in Apollo and as the human being of achieved identity, he was now free to express his own inner experience through his poetry with a sense of speaking for all mankind. At the same time his long discipleship to Shakespeare and Milton, masters of the concentrated phrase and long line, had brought him to the command of a new lyrical form, longer than the sonnet but as deliberately wrought—as "interwoven and complete," as he put it—in which every syllable carries its freight of meaning. The order in which the odes were composed is largely conjectural; [12] but even if their dates could be fixed, it is not so much they which cast light on Keats's life this spring, as all of Keats's life that illuminates the odes. For these few weeks he stood at a point of perfect balance, confident in his ability to meet the future, able to contemplate his past with calm, and rejoicing in the beauty of the season, the joy of an answered love, the delight of a mastered craft—the themes of the odes as well as his incentives to writing them.

The "Ode to Psyche" is the first product and the happiest in mood of this interval of peace. Keats told George as he copied it into his journal that it was the first poem with which he had taken "even moderate pains—I have for the most part dash'd off my lines in a hurry," he added. "This I have done leisurely—I think it reads the more richly for it." This comment is curious, for at first sight this ode seems an improvisation. Yet closer study reveals a highly conscious experimentation with stanzaic patterns: like the "Sonnet on the Sonnet," written during the same week, it evolves a form of its own that eludes all traditional symmetries. And while the sonnet takes as its theme the pattern-making faculty that gives a poem form, the ode is concerned with the imagination itself, the visionary faculty that provides its substance. Keats had been reading Apuleius's story of Cupid and Psyche in an Elizabethan translation of *The Golden Asse,* a tale of young love set in a magic palace in an enchanted valley, which blended with the images of spring outside his window, the

> hush'd, cool-rooted flowers, fragrant-eyed,
> Blue, silver-white, and budded Tyrian, . . .

the actual flowers he loved and the human beauty they inevitably suggested. But Psyche, he knew, was also the goddess of the soul in late classical legend, who had been deified too late to receive her proper worship in antiquity. As Keats mused over her story, she became the figure "of all Olympus' faded hierarchy" who held most meaning for the modern world, in which nature was no longer god-haunted. The sacred region was now, as Wordsworth had seen, the mind of man, and the poet its self-appointed priest; Psyche, as a woman who had had to submit to the trials of "a world of Circumstances" before her own soul was formed, was its tutelary goddess.[13] Only a few days earlier Keats had sketched out his own system of salvation in his theory of soul-making; now in this ode he described the ritual of his worship of the imagination. From the opening vision of the two legendary lovers asleep in a forest, the poem circles away to an imaginary woodland altar where Psyche is worshipped as a goddess in a sacred grove which is in fact the poet's own "working brain," which Keats touched in with a skilful suggestion of the physiology of the brain recalled from his days at Guy's.[14] The last few lines, while returning to the legend, bring the poem back to the here and now:

> And there shall be for thee all soft delight
> That shadowy thought can win,
> A bright torch, and a casement ope at night,
> To let the warm Love in!

Out of the meetings of these lovers in the dark mysterious palace, Keats has evoked a lighted window seen from a garden outside— no part of Apuleius's story—and his own longing to enter it. For a brief moment the joys of reality and imagination strike a balance: perhaps because his happiness still lay in a future of anticipated delight.

Keats copied the "Ode to Psyche" out in his journal just before closing it on May 3 and hurrying off to Walthamstow to collect his sister's letter to George. One of Birkbeck's sons was leaving for Illinois shortly and would carry their letters direct. As he jumbled the sheets together, Keats's eye was evidently caught by his description of the daydream he had had one lazy morning in March. "Neither Poetry, nor Ambition, nor Love have any alertness of countenance as they pass by me," he had written; "they seem rather like three figures on a greek vase—a Man and two women —whom no one but myself could distinguish in their disguisement." The image struck him as he looked at it again, and he tried working it out in another ode. The result, the "Ode on Indolence," [15] was not a success. His original idea had cooled for almost two months and could no longer give vital shape to the poem [16] or significance to the allegorical figures, who merely appear and reappear in a vain effort to rouse him from his daydreaming; and the conclusion, in which he dismisses Love and Poetry as well as Ambition, seems to ring false to his change of mood in the interval. Still the image haunted him, and he tried working it into

another poem. When the vision first came to him in March, the
immobility of the three figures had seemed a kind of reproach,
an image of the paralysis which had overtaken the three central
impulses of his life; in the first ode he tried, he was still separated
from the figures—now slowly moving, but with averted glance—
by his own determined indolence. Now, in the "Ode on a Grecian
Urn," they are quickened into new life as Keats the perceiver
becomes one with the thing perceived. As he questions the figures
on the urn and seeks to enter into their existence, allegory becomes symbol and the vase takes on a meaning of its own—the relation between the imagination and its creations, the illusions
and realities of art and life together.

The ode begins with a topic which Keats had debated many
times at Hunt's and Haydon's, the contrast between the visual
arts and poetry. In one of his most extraordinary metaphors—
"Thou still unravish'd bride of quietness"—Keats invokes not only
the immortal freshness of all great art, but also the enigmatic silence of the urn, which still can tell its tale "more sweetly than our
rhyme," and the serenity it preserves amid the scene of Bacchic
frenzy it depicts. These antinomies at once suggest another para-
doxical aspect of pictorial art, its representation of movement
through action arrested at its most dynamic moment. As the bride
of quietness reaches the fullness of her beauty while "still unravish'd," the bold lover is most passionate while "winning near
the goal." At first the poet finds the unenacted desire of the youth
on the urn an incompletion, for which he must console him:

> do not grieve;
> She cannot fade, though thou hast not thy bliss,
> For ever wilt thou love, and she be fair!

Immediately he realizes that by this very arrest of impulse the
lovers achieve a perfect bliss, "All breathing human passion far
above," which escapes the satiety implicit in all fulfilment. Yet
even this unchanging perfection of art—that of the unwearied
melodist "for ever piping songs for ever new"—is realized, paradoxically, for only a brief moment. In the fourth stanza, as the
poet turns to another scene, the eternity becomes a desolation.
As his wondering imagination follows the procession to the woodland altar, it suddenly calls up the town they have forever deserted,
its streets forever silent; the beauty immortalized at one point now

implies an emptiness perpetuated at some other. At the farthest
limits of this timeless world of art—that

> little town by river or sea shore,
> Or mountain-built with peaceful citadel, . . .

which is not even represented on the urn [17]—his enraptured contemplation is suddenly chilled by this discovery of the antinomies
of experience. The timeless perfection of art, he now sees, contains
its own imperfection, its immortality is in fact lifelessness—just
as truly as the converse that joy may be won in the world of time
only at the cost of the sorrow which time also brings in its revolu-
tions. With this insight, the illusion of the urn's vital existence
begins to collapse. The vase is only a vase, he remembers at last
—a shape, an attitude, a form empty of meaning till the imagination fills it; and the human imagination cannot rest even in a
dream of endless bliss. But at this moment, as he turns wearily
back to the world of time, the urn breaks its silence with a message
of consolation for him:

> Beauty is Truth,—Truth Beauty,—that is all
> Ye know on earth, and all ye need to know.*

With this dramatic reversal of the dialogue, the illusory nature
of the poet's own quest is finally revealed. He began by seeking in
the world of art that perfect happiness and unshadowed beauty
which Keats had long before rejected as a goal of life; and in exploring this world he finds in the end the joy and sorrow, the
"light and shade" together that make up the world of actual experience. So at last he is ready to hear the enigmatic message of the
urn and understand it for the first time. The imaginary world of
art and the real world of experience, which he tried at first to dis-
join, are in fact complementary and necessary to each other, for
each serves to reveal the value of the other. If the real or "true"
world is viewed as intensely and disinterestedly as the poet contemplates the imaginary world of the urn, it yields up its own
beauty; if the beauty of art is searched to the very depths of speculation, truth will be found there. The true beauty is not the merely
beautiful beauty of "an endless bliss," but the difficult beauty of
light and shade; so also the truth that this is "a World of Pains

---

* Following Keats's original punctuation, as given in all four contemporary
transcripts (see Alvin Whitley, "The Message of the Grecian Urn," *Keats-Shelley
Memorial Bulletin*, V [1953], 1–3).

and troubles" becomes beautiful when it is recognized as not merely necessary but desirable, as the truth that this world is also a "vale of Soul-making." So the urn's message is not, as it has often been called, a meaningless tautology, or, at best, a needless appendage to the poem, but rather its dramatic fulfilment and reason for being, a glimpse of the "knowledge enormous" which made the young Apollo a god of poetry, the wisdom of Keats's own widest experience of life.

The "Ode on a Grecian Urn" seems to have been written at that precarious moment of fulfilment conveyed through its own images of the bride, the lover, the melodist. The mood could not last: in the two remaining odes the shade overbalances the light. From the very beginning of May, Keats knew that he must start "buffeting it" again in another month; in the middle of May he received a poignant reminder of all the contingent world outside the garden of Wentworth Place. On May 13 the letter from America for which he had been waiting ever since December arrived at last. It contained unexpected news—only "tolerably" good. George and Georgiana, far gone in her pregnancy, had reached the end of their long and fatiguing journey by horse and wagon as far as Pittsburgh, then by boat down the Ohio to Henderson, Kentucky.[18] What troubled Keats was George's decision not to take a farm in Birkbeck's colony but to put his money into a Mississippi steamboat. George had great hopes for a quick return on his investment; but Keats, with his habit of "suspecting everybody," had misgivings about the backwoods *entrepreneur* and itinerant painter who had talked George into the plan—one John James Audubon. He took the letter to Mrs. Wylie and tried to put his doubts out of his mind, but the clouds of circumstance were beginning to gather again.

The garden at Wentworth Place was still enchanted, however; a pair of nightingales had built their nest there, and the May nights were flooded with music. One morning after breakfast Keats took his chair out into the garden and sat writing under the plum tree for two or three hours. When he returned to the house Brown noticed him thrusting several sheets of note paper among his books and asked to see what he had written. It was another ode, "To a Nightingale," written in a flow of song as sustained and almost as unfaltering as the nightingale's itself.[19] The poem has often been contrasted with the "Ode on a Grecian Urn," but the similarities are more significant. In each the poet attempts to escape the limitations of actuality by projecting himself into an essence outside him, the nightingale's song or the scenes on the urn; but at the farthest limit of this imaginary world he meets a reminder of the unhappiness he is trying to forget; the spell of identification is broken, and he returns to reality again. At last he realizes that the joy he seems to find in this other world is the product of his own imaginative activity: the lovers turn cold as marble, the happy nightingale's song becomes plaintive. This turning point is marked in each poem by a poignant image of desolation—the empty-streeted town, Ruth standing in tears "amid the alien corn," or the

> magic casements, opening on the foam
> Of perilous seas, in faery lands forlorn.

This last image casts a spell. It calls up one of Keats's favourite paintings, "The Enchanted Castle" of Claude Lorrain, which he had described in his "Epistle to Reynolds" in the spring of 1818; and the view of Windermere from Wordsworth's study window that summer—a sight which moved Keats so deeply that twice afterward he described his idea of perfect happiness as reading in a window looking out on a lake.[20] Behind this image loom two others—the lake and island of his first poem, and Keats himself sunk in the window-seat of his medical-school lodgings, staring moodily out into space. And if we note that "forlorn" means primarily "abandoned" or "lonely," and that Keats first described the seas not as "perilous" but as "keelless," [21] empty or unexplored, we catch another glimpse of Keats standing alone on the cliffs at Margate, gazing out over the ocean with the sense of embarking on a voyage of discovery. The sea has taken on many meanings for Keats in the three years since that summer, however; now, as it reappears in this frame of desolation and unreality, it suggests in the faintest of overtones that his quest may prove an illusion in the end.

In the "Ode on a Grecian Urn" for a brief moment the worlds of permanence and change were reconciled, the lifeless immortality of art balanced against the transitoriness of realized love; in the "Ode to a Nightingale" the balance is tipped. Beyond the knowledge that love and beauty must pass lies the awareness that they give way to misery insurmountable by joy:

> Where youth grows pale, and spectre-thin, and dies;
>   Where but to think is to be full of sorrow
>   And leaden-eyed despairs,
>   Where Beauty cannot keep her lustrous eyes,
>   Or new Love pine at them beyond to-morrow.

This ode is an effort not so much to reach a new awareness as to escape from awareness itself—a struggle inevitably doomed, as the very movement of Keats's stanzas seems to suggest.[22] For a moment the poet loses himself in the tranced beauty of the May night; then, as he realizes his own happiness, he longs for death at such a moment—an annulment of consciousness at a time when he would not be aware of it. But life exacts consciousness. Though the nightingale is hailed as deathless—immortal in the sense that its song recurs unchanged from generation to generation—its immortality, like that of the figures on the urn, is won at a price, not of life but of full human awareness. By imagination man can escape momentarily the burden of self-awareness; yet the same imagination causes him to look too far into the sea, as Keats had written Reynolds the year before:

>   It is a flaw
>   In happiness to see beyond our bourn—
>   It forces us in Summer skies to mourn:
>   It spoils the singing of the Nightingale.

The nightingale has no imagination, no individuality, and is doubtless happier for it; but, when pushed to the point, man would no sooner give up awareness or identity than life itself—nor, indeed, can he as long as he lives. So the poem returns to the real scene at the end, the meadows, the stream, the hillside; the poet comes to himself with a familiar sense of the unreality of his musings.

>   Was it a vision, or a waking dream?
>   Fled is that music:—Do I wake or sleep?

With the end of his flight, no such insight remains as at the end of the "Ode on a Grecian Urn"; only the weariness, the fever and the fret, to be faced once more.

For May was fast slipping by, and June would bring decisions to be made and acted on. The weather itself, so perfect earlier in the month, began to cloud over, and Keats had to put off a long-promised visit to Walthamstow for three weeks. His cash was too low for coach-hire, as he explained to Fanny, and he was unwilling to risk being caught in the rain by walking across the fields. These two hints of his recurrent worries about his health and his dwindling finances suggest the reason for an otherwise incomprehensible plan he began considering near the end of May. As he broached it to his sister, he was afraid he would be "forced to take a voyage or two" at the end of the summer, to take a post as ship's surgeon on an Indiaman or a South Sea whaler, or even to emigrate to South America. These are such extraordinary answers to the question of where he might live after leaving Wentworth Place that one cannot help wondering whether he consulted a doctor at this time about his troublesome sore throat and was advised to move to a warm climate for a while to shake it off. It was a choice of poisons, as he put it, even though the idea of becoming a ship's surgeon, which struck him as less appalling than the other, would have been a strange fulfilment of his two youthful ambitions. He could not agree to the suggestion, wherever it came from. The thought of leaving Fanny Brawne for such a length of time was evidently too much to face; but what could he do? The world was taking on "a quakerish look," he admitted—light and shade confounded in a landscape of greys.

This mood of dejected indecision underlies the ode—apparently the last of the five he wrote this spring—"On Melancholy." [23] An epitaph to the month of May, it carries the meditation of the two preceding odes to its ultimate conclusion. Beyond the awareness that all joy passes, and that life brings sorrow insurmountable by joy, this ode explores the thought not only that joy and sorrow are inextricable, but that the deepest joys hold the deepest sorrows. Where the "Grecian Urn" and the "Nightingale" odes recorded an attempt to transcend the world of circumstances, the "Ode on Melancholy" starts by condemning this attempt and turns to meet the consciousness of light and shade full-face, even to advance toward it. Only the melancholy man can fully savour the most poignant beauty—the morning rose, the rainbow in the breaking wave, the flash of anger in his mistress's eyes—because he alone realizes, in the very moment of seizing this beauty, that its perfection is "but a little moment." Melancholy is not only the result but the condition of the greatest intensity of experience:

> She dwells with Beauty—Beauty that must die;
> And Joy, whose hand is ever at his lips

> Bidding adieu; and aching Pleasure nigh,
>   Turning to poison while the bee-mouth sips. . . .

The honey of life, it seems, was turning bitter for Keats. It is easy
to guess that his longing for Fanny Brawne, so close and still ultimately denied to him by the confines of circumstance, had become unbearable after a month.

> Ay, in the very temple of Delight
>   Veil'd Melancholy has her sovran shrine,
>   Though seen of none save him whose strenuous tongue
> Can burst Joy's grape against his palate fine;
>   His soul shall taste the sadness of her might,
>   And be among her cloudy trophies hung.

Joy's grape—the sour-sweet fruit—is the final taste of life and the
conclusive image of the odes: a poignant beauty achieved through
a palpable act of possession, in which taste and touch, the most
intimate of the means of sensuous discovery, unite in the final
conquest. Yet at this moment of symbolic achievement the flush
of exultation chills, and the poet finds himself face to face with a
mysterious veiled figure waiting at the center of his experience.
Like the young Apollo at Mnemosyne's approach, he does not
recognize her at first; he knows only that there is "purport in her
looks for him," of a revelation still to come, some final experience
of her might. And so the odes, like the month which produced
them, end on a note of troubled foreboding.

On May 30 Keats began to prepare for leaving Wentworth Place
by sorting out books to be returned and burning old letters. Here
he turned up a forgotten bundle from the Jeffrey sisters in Teignmouth, their last letter unanswered since Tom's death. At once
Devon occurred to him as the alternative he was desperately
searching for, a mild climate in which he might give himself one
more chance to finish *Hyperion*. The next day he wrote to Sarah
Jeffrey, asking her to inquire for cheap lodgings in some nearby
village. After a painful apology for not sending her any news since
last autumn, he inquired politely after Marianne (who was now
married) and described the alternatives before him—serving as
ship's surgeon or "leading a fevrous life alone with Poetry." Be-

tween the two, he told her, "I would rather conquer my indolence and strain my nerves at some grand Poem—than be in a dunder-headed indiaman." Yet it was a question not of preference but necessity—the inescapable need to start earning his living by one means or another. "My Brother George always stood between me and any dealings with the world," he explained. "Now I find I must buffet it—I must take my stand upon some vantage ground and begin to fight—I must choose between despair & Energy—I choose the latter."

Sarah answered at once, arguing against the Indiaman and suggesting Bradley as a pleasant and inexpensive place to stay. But almost as suddenly as he had thought of Devon, Keats changed his mind. The memory of Tom which it stirred up was still too painful; and perhaps the very friendliness of Sarah's reply posed another problem. A lucky chance brought him a good excuse a few days later, when James Rice came out to Hampstead for a visit. Though they had seen little of each other all the previous year, Keats found Rice as droll and sensible as ever, despite his usual poor health. So when he suggested they spend part of the summer together on the Isle of Wight, Keats immediately agreed. He not only liked but admired Rice, who he knew had been extremely generous in helping Reynolds get started in the law, and whose fair-minded judgment on Bailey's engagement Keats had valued highly in forming his own. Rice assured him that Shanklin would fit their purses, and it struck Keats as just the thing for the present—and perhaps for next winter too. On June 9 he wrote Sarah Jeffrey again, explaining his change of mind with the candour which, whether he knew it or not, was his best defence against any charge of fickleness. By now he had given up the idea of the Indiaman; yet he insisted on defending it to her as a good one. Rather than deaden his abilities, as she feared, he thought it would strengthen them: "To be thrown among people who care not for you, with whom you have no sympathies forces the Mind upon its own resources, and leaves it free to make its speculations of the differences of human character and to class them with the calmness of a Botanist." England has produced the greatest writers in the world, he argued, because it has ill-treated them rather than honouring them while they were alive. Look at Ben Jonson, a common soldier in the Low Countries, who fought and killed a French trooper in single combat; look at Shakespeare, "a miserable and mighty Poet of the human Heart," whose own life was clouded over as much as Hamlet's. Yet once he stated his belief, Keats felt obliged to contradict it: "For all this I will not go on board an Indiaman, nor for examples sake run my head into dark alleys: I dare say my discipline is to come, and plenty of it too."

It came sooner than he expected. On settling his accounts with Brown the next week, Keats found he had run out of cash. On the sixteenth he went into town to ask Abbey for money for his trip to Shanklin. His guardian greeted him with two letters. One, from George, announced at last the birth of his child, a little girl; the other, from their aunt, Mrs. Midgley Jennings, notified them that she was filing a claim in Chancery against a disputed share in their grandfather's estate. The thin trickle of money that had been drying up for six months was now stopped at the source—or so Abbey maintained. So long as the suit was pending, he said, Keats could not touch even the small sum left from his own inheritance, and even if Mrs. Jennings lost her action there would be heavy legal expenses to pay. Here again it seems that Abbey was playing on Keats's ignorance of money matters for his own private reasons.[24] But by the time he reached Hampstead that evening, Keats had decided there was only one thing he could do: give up his summer plans and look for an apothecary's position at once.

At this news, Brown exploded. It was folly to give up now, he argued, with three long poems on hand that would fill up more than half a volume: *Isabella, The Eve of St. Agnes,* and *The Eve of St. Mark* if he would finish it. Keats should drop *Hyperion* for a while and work up a volume to catch the public's fancy, and Brown would lend him some money to help him through the summer. Keats was reluctant, for he had decided months ago not to publish anything till it could be above even the *Quarterly's* criticism; yet at another suggestion of Brown's, it seems, he caught fire. Brown had been reading Burton's *Anatomy of Melancholy,* a seventeenth-century miscellany of psychology, classical lore, and curious anecdote, perhaps with an eye for plots for his own satirical fairy tales. Evidently he pointed out several of these anecdotes to Keats on which he might base another verse narrative to round off his volume.[25] One immediately caught Keats's eye—the story of a young Greek philosopher named Lycius, who falls in love with a lamia, or vampire, who has taken the form of a beautiful woman and vanishes on their wedding day with her beautiful house, wedding feast and all, when his master, the philosopher Apollonius, penetrates her disguise. A strange tale, and likely to give the public the "sensation of some sort" which Keats was aiming at; strangely reminiscent, too, of the mysterious beauty who has appeared and disappeared in so many of his earlier poems.

The next day he wrote a number of friends to try to collect on his loans, as now seemed absolutely necessary—reluctantly including Haydon, who still owed him thirty pounds from December. "My purpose is now to make one more attempt in the Press," he announced; "if that fail, 'ye hear no more of me' as Chaucer says." A tactful misquotation: Chaucer had actually said, "Ye gete no more of me." He followed these with a letter to his sister telling her of his plan and regretting there would be no time for another visit before he left. But almost at once he postponed his departure with Rice, for Brown came up with a still better scheme. He proposed that he and Keats write a tragedy together, aimed at a Drury Lane production in the fall with Kean in the lead. He would provide the plot, and Keats would turn it into poetry. With one successful play to his credit, Brown could feel confident about another, and apparently it did not take much to persuade Keats. His old dream of making his "chief Attempt in the Drama" sprang to life again. If the play succeeded, it would send his new volume off to a flying start. Still, Keats was sober enough to realize that the reputation of his poems might spoil the play's chances, and he insisted that his part in it be kept a secret till after it was produced. For their subject they hit on the reign of Otto the Great, first of the Holy Roman Emperors and the scourge of the Hungarians, a period of history remote enough to give Keats full scope in a Shakespearian style. At once they set to work. Brown began sketching a plot of disguises and machinations and tragic misunderstandings, and Keats stayed on in Hampstead another week to wrestle over the scenario of the first act. They agreed that Brown would join Keats at Shanklin at the end of July, when Rice left, and they would continue the play together.

This plan to take both Drury Lane and Fleet Street by storm seems like a hopeless gamble, but Keats undertook it with remarkable coolness. It would demand the utmost of his energy and ability; yet of all the ways in which he might pull himself out of his financial difficulties, this was the one best suited to his talents. But there was far more to his decision than this. In finally giving up the plan of the Indiaman, whatever its recommendations, he appears also to have decided he could not separate himself so completely from Fanny Brawne. All through May they seem to have grown closer together; and now in June the prospect of his leaving Wentworth Place had evidently brought them at last to the point of discussing marriage. An engagement was still out of the question, for his situation needed to improve dramatically before Mrs. Brawne would give her consent. One can only wonder whether Keats sensed that Fanny herself was not yet ready for a binding commitment, or whether he, in the very intensity of his longing for her, hesitated at the idea of a long engagement. Their promises to each other were conditional: everything was staked on the summer. For him to win Fanny in the end, Keats realized, he must make a success of the new volume; and for that he must find the kind of solitude he always needed to work on a long poem, even if it meant exile from Fanny for the time being.

It was a difficult decision to make, and difficult to explain to Fanny herself. Both his pride and his love for her were involved. He felt he must warn her against "the unpromising morning" of his life; yet he wanted to offer her something better than the life of a small suburban doctor. "Do understand me, my love, in this," he wrote her from Shanklin a few weeks later. "I have so much of you in my heart that I must turn Mentor when I see a chance of harm beffaling you. I would never see any thing but Pleasure in your eyes, love on your lips, and Happiness in your steps. I would wish to see you among those amusements suitable to your inclinations and spirits; so that our loves might be a delight in the midst of Pleasures agreeable enough, rather than a resource from vexations and cares." It is a young man's dream of married love, perhaps, now joined to his earlier dream of a life of poetry and travel. "We might spend a pleasant Year at Berne or Zurich—if it should please Venus to hear my 'Beseech thee to hear us O Goddess.'" But he knew well enough what the odds against it were, and a day or two before he left Hampstead he discussed them soberly with her. He would not return to London, he told her, "if my Fate does not turn up Pam or at least a Court-card." In these circumstances she must continue with her usual life in Hampstead; for himself, he would "live upon hope and Chance."

Chapter Eleven

———————————————————————————————————————

Between Despair and Energy

O N a chilly Sunday, June 27, Keats left for the Isle of Wight at last. The day-long trip to Portsmouth was marked only by two small incidents, each in its way prophetic. His fellow passengers included some down-at-the-heel French refugees, one of them a woman, all courtly in their manner, despite their poor clothes. Once, when they climbed down from the coach to walk uphill, one of the Frenchmen picked a rose and gave it to the woman with a flourish—"Mam'selle, voilà une belle rose!" Keats was amused at the gesture of this ragged exile, "more gallant than ever I saw gentleman to Lady at a Ball," as he told his sister; and his amusement was tinged with a curious detachment. The second incident was a heavy shower of rain. Riding outside as usual, he caught cold again and arrived in Portsmouth with another sore throat, which was to hang on for the next two months.

The Isle of Wight was not as enchanting as he remembered it from the spring of 1817. Shanklin, the little fishing village overhanging the Chine, was now crowded with summer visitors; the hills behind it looked tame after the crags of Scotland. But the sandy beach below promised fine swimming, and beyond it the coast stretched for miles of walks along the rocks. He and Rice found a cottage in the village with a glimpse of the sea over the other rooftops. "We have Hill and Dale forest and Mead and plenty of Lobsters," Keats wrote his sister a few days later. Here, it seems, were the makings of a good summer. But Tuesday evening, the second night after his arrival, he was seized with such loneliness on going up to his narrow room that he could not keep from pouring out his feelings in a letter to Fanny Brawne which, he realized the next day, was too Rousseau-ish to send. On Thursday, July 1, he wrote her again in a more balanced mood, and with this, the first of Keats's letters to Fanny that has survived, the drama of their love affair emerges into our full gaze at last. "The morning," he said, "is the only proper time for me to write to a beautiful Girl whom I love so much: for at night, then believe me my passion gets entirely the sway, then I would not have you see those Rapsodies which I once thought it impossible I should ever give way to, and which I have often laughed at in another, for fear you should [think me] either too unhappy or perhaps a little mad." He begged her to send him a letter immediately. "Make it rich as a draught of poppies to intoxicate me—write the softest words and kiss them that I may at least touch my lips where yours have been." He was falling into another rhapsody: he immediately checked himself by reminding her of the task he must accomplish before returning to London. Yet for all his love and resolution, he could not keep a note of jealousy from creeping in at the end of his letter. Though he was trying to be as unselfish as he could about Fanny's happiness, the thought of a possible rival kept haunting him. "In case of the worst that can happen, I shall still love you," he told her—"but what hatred shall I have for another!"

In hope or despair, the thought of Fanny was a torment; only by plunging into work could he forget her and begin to resolve his dilemma. "When I am inclined I can do a great deal in a day," Keats once remarked to his sister; and the next ten days were probably the most concentrated working days of his life. By July 11 he had finished both the first act of *Otho* and the first part of *Lamia*—almost nine hundred lines.[1] When he first sat down to work, it struck him as odd that he was writing for money and not out of the sheer superabundance of poetry within him. But, as he wrote to Reynolds, "The very corn which is now so beautiful, as if it had only took to ripening yesterday, is for the market: So, why shoᵈ I be delicate?" He was sure he would succeed, too, for he now wrote more deliberately than before, with as much judgment as imagination. He had traded the wings of inspiration for "a pair of patient sublunary legs."

Yet from the beginning circumstances seemed to be against him. Mists drifted in from the sea and stayed bottled up in their valley for days; the air became stifling. His sore throat kept him from swimming and tethered him to a few miles' walk along the coast. Then, though he struggled against it, he began to find Rice a melancholy companion. Whatever Rice's chronic illness was— probably an arrested case of tuberculosis—he had always appeared to be surmounting it cheerfully; but now, living at close quarters with him, Keats realized how much of his humour was a courageous bluff. On July 6 disturbing news came from George. His partner wanted him to put still more money into the steamboat venture, for which he must sell what remained of his holdings. With the Chancery suit pending, this posed difficulties. Keats immediately despatched letters to his stockbroker and to Abbey and Sandell, his other guardian, in Holland, asking for power of attorney,[2] then wrote George as reassuring a reply as he could. George, it appears, was reproaching himself for his failure to make both their fortunes at once. So Keats reminded him that if worse came to worst he would always turn apothecary again. It was a cheerless prospect, but, as he said, he had "spent too many thoughtful days & moralized thro' too many nights" to let it dishearten him. Of course he would not mention his own thoughts of marriage to George; better let him think the only stakes he was playing for were books, travel, and the leisure to write. And, for the time being, his hopes were high.

The mails were slow at Shanklin, and Fanny Brawne's answer to his first letter did not reach him till the following Thursday, July 8. At once his passion flared up again. "All my thoughts," he wrote immediately in reply, "my unhappiest days and nights have I find not at all cured me of my love of Beauty, but made it so intense that I am miserable that you are not with me: or rather breathe in that dull sort of patience that cannot be called Life." Fanny, like many another young belle, wanted to be loved for something other than her beauty, and had reproached him accordingly; but, he answered, how else could he have loved her to begin with? "There may be a sort of love for which, without the least sneer at it, I have the highest respect, and can admire it in others: but it has not the richness, the bloom, the full form, the enchantment of love after my own heart." She had also asked him, with a hint of petulance, whether certain "horrid people" would keep him from seeing her again—perhaps Brown, perhaps Abbey —and wondered whether he might think she did not love him because she had agreed to their separation. It was a gambit, and he

accepted it with fervour: "In saying this you make me ache the
more to be near you," he exclaimed. As for her love for him, he
told her, "I love you the more in that I believe you have liked me
for my own sake and for nothing else." Keats could have paid her
no greater tribute than this. Fanny's love had helped him surmount, for the time being at least, the last barrier to self-acceptance
—his old doubt that he could ever be loved as a man rather than
a poet.

Desire and determination were balanced in this second letter;
with his work going well, he could afford to dwell on the thought
of his love. Yet in the following week he had to slack off against
his will. With the first act finished, *Otho* had to be laid aside till
Brown came; and for some reason Keats decided not to go on
with *Lamia* for a while. Instead he turned back to the other poems
he had brought with him to work up for publication and mulled
over them for a few days. But a feverish restlessness soon took
hold of him—"an irritable state of health," he called it—which
made it difficult to work. His daily contact with Rice was stirring
up all the irrational aversion to illness which he had never succeeded in conquering. Then after two short weeks he found he
was tired of Shanklin. The cottages covered with honeysuckle and
roses seemed like settings for a sentimental opera; even the wild
beauty of the Chine was spoiled by the tourists with spyglasses who
came "hunting after the picturesque like beagles."

Some of this restlessness comes out in his third letter to Fanny,
on July 15, which he wrote, against his own resolution, late in the
evening. Her letter the day before hinted she had been ill; he
guessed that she missed him and could not help feeling a little
glad of it. That night, in a fit of loverlike behaviour, he put her
letter under his pillow; in the morning he found the wax had
softened, obliterating her seal—a bad omen. Yet even as he laughed
at himself he realized it was a bad habit of his "to bode ill like the
raven," to suspect everyone and everything. He had been reading
a melancholy story from a collection of Oriental tales, curiously
like his own "Belle Dame sans Merci," about a beautiful lady
who, seen once, vanishes, to leave her lovers disconsolate ever
afterward, and he could not help thinking of it as symbolic of his
own apprehensive love for Fanny. A sudden desire to see her overwhelmed him. She had been pressing him to visit Hampstead,
perhaps for her birthday on August 9, and rashly he suggested he

might steal a brief visit sometime within the next month. The thought of London and its "hateful literary chitchat" made him uneasy, but still more did her absence. He begged her to write again at once—"for your letters keep me alive. My sweet Girl I cannot speak my love for you. Good night!"

The next day he shook himself out of this mood by writing a stiff note to Abbey, asking why he had not replied to his letter about George's affairs, then went off for a ramble about the island. On his return, it seems, he picked up not *Lamia* but his long-neglected *Hyperion*. He was growing dissatisfied with the poem as well as uncertain how to continue it. Just as with *Endymion*, it appears, his idea of it was changing even as he wrote: his epic of human progress was beginning to express his intensified awareness of the necessity of suffering. Yet with this shift in the meaning of the action, his hero Apollo—who receives the gift of poetry not by actual experience of suffering but through a godlike flash of insight—came to seem no more satisfactory a protagonist than the shadowy Hyperion, who is broken by his knowledge. For a few days Keats evidently pondered whether to go on with his original conception or rewrite the poem completely, as he had once thought of doing with *Endymion*.[3] Then on the twenty-second he was interrupted by Brown's arrival with Reynolds' old friend, the jocular Johnny Martin. In their wake came Martin's sister and three of her friends, who took the cottage opposite theirs for a short house-party. Between dining with the young ladies and playing cards with the men far into the night, Keats found no time for work or even a letter to Fanny. Not till Sunday evening, the twenty-fifth, after Rice and the visitors had left for London, did he sit down in his narrow coffin of a room, looking out over the sea, to write her at last.

In his fourth letter, the hidden battle between his longing and his resolution finally broke out into the open. "Forgive me if I wander a little this evening," he began, "for I have been all day employ'd in a very abstract Poem and I am in deep love with you —two things which must excuse me." He was troubled not only by the alien world which had intruded on his solitude but also by her last letter, which had come three or four days before. Fanny, it seems, was pretending not to be convinced by his reasons for going into exile, and reproached him for having taken so long to fall in love with her that winter. Keats could only reply in anguish that he had been the first to fall in love. Evidently she had mentioned that unlucky meeting with Severn, the gay and good-looking, almost a year ago; and though she said that she had admired him more than Severn even then, at once Keats lost faith in what he had begun to believe—that she loved him for his own sake. "I cannot be admired, I am not a thing to be admired," he insisted. "You are, I love you; all I can bring you is a swooning admiration of your Beauty." She had thrown him into a turmoil: "You absorb me in spite of myself—you alone," he burst out: "for I look not forward with any pleasure to what is call'd being settled in the world; I tremble at domestic cares—yet for you I would meet them." His mind seemed to swarm with a thousand anxieties, in which only two thoughts could bring him peace. "I have two luxuries to brood over in my walks, your Loveliness and the hour of my death. O that I could have possession of them both in the same minute." It was getting late, and, as he looked outside his window, a planet was growing bright against the sky. For a moment he was lifted out of himself as he had been on his first view of Windermere. Doubt and distraction left him: it was only beauty, Fanny's and the star's, that mattered. He closed his letter with the farewell: "I will imagine you Venus tonight and pray, pray, pray to your star like a Hethen. Your's ever, fair Star, John Keats."

From this moment a sonnet was born,[4] of a beauty so serene that for a while at least no other thought but poetry could have possessed him:

> Bright star! would I were steadfast as thou art—
>   Not in lone splendour hung aloft the night
> And watching, with eternal lids apart,
>   Like nature's patient, sleepless Eremite,
> The moving waters at their priestlike task
>   Of pure ablution round earth's human shores,
> Or gazing on the new soft fallen mask
>   Of snow upon the mountains and the moors—
> No—yet still steadfast, still unchangeable,
>   Pillow'd upon my fair love's ripening breast,
> To feel for ever its soft fall and swell,
>   Awake for ever in a sweet unrest,
> To hear, to feel her tender-taken breath,
> Half-passionless, and so swoon on to death.*

---

* Quoting the final version, except for the last two lines, which are left in their original form; see p. 379.

All the conflicts expressed in his letter to Fanny—the passion which absorbed him against his will, the longing to be assured of her love yet untroubled by the anxieties of marriage—are projected and momentarily resolved in the imagery of the sonnet. The contrasts so precariously balanced in the odes—between the timeless but unreal perfection of art and the time-bound realizations of life, between the unselfconscious joy of natural existence and the self-awareness of human experience—are repeated in a key of passionate urgency and pushed toward a synthesis of contradictions, an eternal calm within perfect sensuality, the ideal moment made actual. Knowing his desire was unattainable, yet still driven by it, Keats tried to resolve his dilemma not by finally submitting to the claims of consciousness, as in the odes, but by eluding them in a vision of death at the moment of supreme happiness. Yet metaphorically he did surmount his dilemma in the first half of his sonnet, which creates, in the imagination at least, an eternal joy.

This joy—a timeless disinterested contemplation of a tranquil unconscious beauty—is a state of being for which all his poetry had groped for an adequate symbol. The contemplating conciousness here imaged in the star, the abstract calm of some "superior being" looking down on the vicissitudes of earth, is implicit in all Keats's most searching remarks on poetry—on negative capability, the poetic identity, the ultimate vision in which truth and beauty become one. Again, the object of this contemplation—all the changes of nature which take place apart from human notice—is a special kind of beauty which had preoccupied him from his earliest poems: the blossoming of unseen flowers, the silent leafing of trees, the sweetening of fruit within its own skin, the ebb and flow of tides on deserted shores. The attempt to magically arrest this changing beauty through the self-annihilating intensity of his contemplation is the theme underlying and unifying the odes of May. But each of the odes turns on the dilemma that the human observer is capable only of brief and intermittent moments of self-transcending awareness. Not until this sonnet of July did Keats find an image for this consciousness which fuses it unchangeably with the object of its contemplation. [The star looking down on the sea through all time thus becomes his supreme metaphor, the formula of a state of awareness toward which his own life moved by successive stages of "annulling self."]

In tracing his steps toward this image, we may note that even in Keats's earliest poetry the heavens are not remote from human affairs but a vast field in which he searches for a lost but benevolent presence. In the Chapman sonnet the new planet embodies the beauty of the unobserved natural identity only to lose it immediately in the astronomer's triumphant discovery of its existence —a discovery so tremendous that his own identity, like that of Cortez staring at the Pacific, is momentarily annihilated. Yet gradually this "speculation of the stars" changes direction: the stars are no longer watched but become the watchers. The mortal who tries to read the "huge cloudy symbols" upon "the night's starr'd face" sees no such wonders as the stars themselves have seen in gazing eternally upon the earth, as Keats describes them—remote yet absorbed, patient or smiling, throbbing with joy or holding their breath in excitement. The image of the stars' unblinking contemplation first occurred to Keats in his letter from Windermere, as a symbol of the poetic insight he hoped to gain on his trip—the refinement of his "sensual vision" into "a sort of north star" watching "open-lidded and stedfast over the wonders of the great Power"; and the "lone splendour" of this vision is what he momentarily found in his sublime solitude when he began *Hyperion*.

But the vision, to be complete, requires its own perfect object. The sea which the star contemplates,

> The moving waters at their priestlike task
> Of pure ablution round earth's human shores, . . .

is the climactic metaphor of the sonnet, the unpremeditated leap across the void which every new metaphor must take. In Keats's earlier descriptions of the sea, there was always Keats himself, the solitary watcher on the cliffs, gazing out at this vast symbol of his own poetic enterprise or, later, of the unfathomable cruelty of life. Now the scene is empty; there is only the sea with the star looking down—the sea-in-itself as nearly as it can be imagined. And yet from this vision beyond all human notice an extraordinary humanity emerges. Keats no longer projects his own thoughts and feelings into the sea; yet he senses a vital interchange between sea and shore as only the star can observe it, along thousands of solitary miles—a relationship which is somehow human, even benevolent, in its priestlike act of purification. "Everything we see is blessed," Yeats concluded of one of his triumphant moments of insight; but this is the real triumph of the disinterested vision, a universe that does not require the blessing of human awareness for its perfection.

Yet things fall apart as the sonnet moves toward the end. The delicate links by which Keats tried to bind the star and the lover, each in his own rapt contemplation, are snapped in the final ✝ plunge toward unconsciousness. [His fair love's breast, as white and soft as new-fallen snow, rising and falling like the sea, holds only an illusion of calm.] The sonnet in fact implies a turning point in Keats's own direction. He had gone to Shanklin to write a volume of poetry whose success would make it possible for him to marry Fanny Brawne; now he realized he could accomplish this only by somehow stifling his passion for her. "You absorb me in spite of myself!" he had cried in his letter. In the sestet of the sonnet the human observer reappears, and at this the disinterested vision falters. The object it contemplates, the breathing body of the beloved woman, is the one in all the world most inimical to the vision; in the relinquishment which inevitably follows possession, Keats could imagine no return to the sustaining reality of the concrete world such as he found at the end of the odes. His momentary longing in May "to cease upon the midnight with no pain" now seemed the logical completion of his desire. To surrender to his longing for Fanny meant, in imagination at least, turning toward death; rather than succumb to despair, he chose energy.

⇒》》 《《⇐

The day after writing Fanny, Keats was hitched again to the dogcart, as he called *Otho,* with Brown pulling in the lead. Sitting across the table from Keats, Brown gave him a synopsis of each scene as they came to it; then Keats, after some questions, arguments, and wisecracks, turned the outline into verse without knowing what was to follow. Little wonder that the result reads like an improvisation, and hardly an improvisation of genius. Brown's plot is a jumble of mislaid letters, mistaken identities, and characters who never quite come to life—a father who unjustly suspects his son, a lover who mistakenly trusts his mistress, a villain who repents too late. Yet every now and then an authentic feeling flashes through Keats's lines, most often in those he gave to the betrayed lover Ludolph. "The Lover is madder than I am," he told Fanny: "he has a figure like the Statue of Maleager and double distilled fire in his heart." This was the role he was tailoring to Kean, the part which would make or break the play, and as he went on, Keats poured more and more of himself into the character. Many of Ludolph's speeches echo phrases of letters describing his own feelings that summer.[5] His imagination was catching fire, and he completed three more acts in less than three weeks.

Brown was a welcome change of company from Rice. Away from the disquieting presence at Wentworth Place, their friendship was mellowing into a deeply congenial companionship in which Keats came to accept a certain dependence on Brown in much the same way as he had with George; and their common interest in poetry provided a mutual stimulus. Brown, always full of projects, helped Keats begin his study of Italian, in which he himself was proficient, then dragged him out on painting expeditions in the intervals of their work on *Otho*. "The Art of Poetry is not sufficient for us," Keats reported to Dilke after a morning of sketching Shanklin Church, "and if we get on in that as well as we do in painting we shall by next winter crush the Reviews and the royal Academy." Brown was an expert draftsman, and could draw a head as well as a church. To judge from a set of seventy-two miniature portraits copied from Hogarth, now at Wentworth Place, he was a literal copyist. But this is the very reason for valuing so highly the drawing of Keats in profile, brawny fist to cheek, which Brown made this summer *—the closest likeness of all Keats's portraits, far closer than Severn's sentimental miniature. The two men also trudged over the island together as far as Steephill; but whether Keats kept Brown company on other expeditions there is room to wonder. Within a week of arriving in Shanklin, Brown had taken up with a young woman of the town named Jenny Jacobs. "Open daylight! he don't care," Keats remarked dryly to Dilke on July 31. "I am afraid there will be some more feet for little stockings." "Of Keats' making. (I mean the feet.)," Brown put in. The wit was lame enough. But from signs that appear a few weeks later it seems that Brown's roughshod approach to sex was beginning to batter down Keats's hard-won self-restraint.

Eleven days after his passionate and melancholy letter of July

---

* Reproduced as Plate IX.

25, Keats wrote Fanny Brawne again, and his tone was greatly changed. She had answered his letter by saying he must not write any more like the last; he promised to be obstinate and run the other way. "I am not idle enough for proper downright love-letters," he countered. "Thank God for my diligence! were it not for that I should be miserable." He was utterly absorbed by *Otho*, and told her so; he already regretted his promise of a visit some-time in August. "I shall keep it with as much sorrow as gladness," he remarked, "for I am not one of the Paladins of old who livd upon water grass and smiles for years together." These were brutal words to a girl in Fanny's situation, and more is needed to account for them than an intense physical longing constantly aroused and its satisfaction indefinitely postponed. His smouldering jealousy had flared up at a hint in her letter that she had gone to a dance in his absence: "Late hours will do you great harm," he reproved her. "What fairing is it?" But his churlishness may also be a disguised form of self-reproach if, as seems possible, he had already suc-cumbed to Brown's example of self-indulgence. Some mysterious poison was combining with all his other irritations and anxieties to make the very purpose of his summer's labours turn sour in his imagination. To wander through Europe with Fanny, spend a year in Switzerland—this had been his dream of marriage; but now the reality of living in Hampstead began to seem a kind of life im-prisonment. "God forbid we should what people call, *settle*," he exclaimed in his letter, "turn into a pond, a stagnant Lethe—a vile crescent, row or buildings. Open my Mouth at the Street door like the Lion's head at Venice to receive hateful cards Letters messages. Go out and wither at tea parties; freeze at dinners; bake at dances, simmer at routs. No my love, trust yourself to me and I will find you nobler amusements; fortune favouring."

Yet fortune did not seem to be favouring. Brown's funds were running low; Keats had received no answers to the letters he had written in June to collect on his debts. He wrote again, and still no reply—except from Haydon, who refused with such seeming unconcern that Keats angrily concluded that their friendship was ended. All summer he had not risked swimming because of his throat; now he became convinced that the mists of Shanklin were as unhealthy for him as the London smoke. Little things began to irritate him beyond measure—the shrill voice of the old lady across the way, the stolid unchanging face of a neighbouring fisherman.

the very names and doorposts of the cottages. When Brown returned from a few days' hike round the island, his presence broke "like a Thunderbolt" on Keats's comfortable solitude. At last he persuaded Brown they should move. They needed to settle some points of history in *Otho,* and Shanklin had no library. So they decided to go to Winchester—Keats's choice, not only for the books but also for the peace of a cathedral town.

The trip back on August 12 was an adventure after six dull weeks at Shanklin. When they took the ferry at Cowes they found that the Regent's yacht had anchored off the mainland opposite, and the entire fleet of the island was sailing out to meet it. Keats was enchanted by the silent gracefulness of the regatta, circling and tacking in every direction. But in the crowded channel they had an accident. As a small naval sloop cut across their bows, the top of its mast was caught in their bowlines and snapped off close by the board—luckily, for if the mast had been stouter the boat would have overturned. "In so trifling an event I could not help admiring our seamen," Keats wrote to Fanny four days later. "Neither Officer nor man in the whole Boat moved a Muscle—they scarcely notic'd it even with words." A trifling event, but one to compare with the incident on his trip down in the Portsmouth coach. There he had been amused by the Frenchmen's gallantry; now he found the Englishmen's imperturbability something to admire. And in the weeks to come the images of his letters show him time after time half-consciously casting himself in the role of a naval officer as he tried to summon up all his resolution for his work.

He liked Winchester at once, with its wide-windowed cathedral and quiet streets filled with old timbered houses: "A respectable, ancient aristocratical place," he described it to George, with "not one loom or any thing like manufacturing beyond bread & butter in the whole City." The capital of England before the Conquest, Winchester echoed with great names of the past—Sir Walter Raleigh, William of Wykeham, William the Conqueror, Alfred the Great, and the still more legendary Arthur. Keats and Brown found lodgings near the cathedral that were entirely satisfactory except for the fiddling of the landlady's son. Keats now had a room large enough to stroll in and a view of "a beautiful—blank side of a house," which for some reason pleased him immensely. On his walks through the city he discovered Winchester College, a Roman Catholic school, a nunnery, a chapel, and, half a mile outside the city gate, the ancient charitable foundation of St. Cross, where bread and ale were still doled out to passers-by. The air blowing across the downs was worth sixpence a pint after Shanklin, he wrote Taylor, and the clear chalk-bedded streams interlacing the meadows were the most beautiful he had ever seen.

After clearing the decks by writing another batch of irksome letters—including a very belated one to Bailey congratulating him awkwardly on his marriage—Keats turned back to *Otho* again. At once he objected that Brown's plans for the fifth act were too melodramatic and insisted on completing the play himself. Within eight or nine days the act was finished. It is hard to imagine how Brown's ending could have been more melodramatic than the one Keats actually wrote; it is still harder to understand why Keats apparently found greater satisfaction in writing the last act of *Otho* than in composing any of his other poems. As he confessed to Bailey, he hoped to "make as great a revolution in modern dramatic writing as Kean has done in acting"; and with each scene he felt more certain he would succeed. Day by day he became more convinced that "fine writing is next to fine doing the top thing in the world." This alone mattered to him now; this was the identity he had achieved. "My own being which I know to be," he wrote Reynolds exultantly the day after finishing *Otho*, "becomes of more consequence to me than the crowds of Shadows in the Shape of Man and women that inhabit a kingdom. The Soul is a world of itself." Yet for once Keats was completely mistaken about his work. *Otho* is a lumbering failure of a play, and in the last act the dramatic machinery breaks down completely. While the other actors stand helplessly by, the mad prince Ludolph plots to kill his faithless bride at his wedding banquet; Auranthe foils his plan by killing herself first, and he dies broken-hearted. All Keats's poetry could not redeem the hysteria of this ending, which provides an alarming clue to his own state of mind at the time.

On August 16, a day or two after starting the last act, Keats had written Fanny Brawne again. She had evidently answered his previous letter at once and in some pique, denying that she wanted to force him to a visit and telling him he could do as he pleased. To his question about her late hours, she apparently replied that she had attended a ball given by the Royal Artillery Mess at Woolwich—one of the most popular parties of the London summer season.[6] With the shock of this news, Keats could not bring himself to answer her letter for four or five days. When at last he did, a familiar numbness had settled down over his feelings, like a fog from the sea. She appeared to him now through a mist, he wrote, growing strangely unreal to him as he became more absorbed in the imaginary world of *Otho.* He refused to return to Hampstead now. "I would feign, as my sails are set, sail on without an interruption for a Brace of Months longer," he explained; "I am in complete cue—in the fever; and shall in these four months do an immense deal." Moreover, he retorted, he could not do what he pleased, for he was living on borrowed money. All this was most unloverlike and ungallant, but he could not help it: "I am no officer in yawning quarters; no Parson-romeo. My heart seems now made of iron. I can no more use soothing words to you than if I were at this moment engaged in a charge of Cavalry." It was a flint-worded letter, he admitted, and he begged her to forgive him. "Even as I leave off—it seems to me that a few more moments thought of you would uncrystallize and dissolve me—I must not give way to it—but turn to my writing again—if I fail I shall die hard." And with this, his correspondence with Fanny apparently broke off for four long weeks.*

"My heart seems now made of iron": so Ludolph makes his tongue "iron-stern" to denounce Auranthe, and so Keats now steeled himself against Fanny Brawne. Driven to choose between love and ambition, he flung himself into his work with all the intensity of his passion. "I look upon fine Phrases like a Lover," he confessed to Bailey on starting the last act of *Otho,* and on finishing it he told Reynolds that "Poetry is all I care for, all I live for." It is an extraordinary reversal, and cannot be explained simply by the fact that his longing for Fanny had become an unbearable distraction from a task which required all his energies. The stresses of their separation were bringing out all Fanny's wilfulness and all Keats's still unresolved ambivalence toward women. Probably Brown also helped to persuade Keats that, as he wrote not long afterward, "A Man in love cuts the sorryest figure in the world,"

---

* This break may well be apparent and not real, however, for there is no indication of a long silence between them in Keats's next letter to Fanny in mid-September. In reading these love letters it must be realized that the series is certainly incomplete, for around 1878 Sir Charles Dilke (Dilke's grandson) bought the letters from Fanny's son and burned a number of them (*More Letters and Papers of the Keats Circle,* ed. H. E. Rollins [1958], p. 102 n. 2)—presumably the most angry and passionate ones.

as well as convincing him that he was not one to live "upon water grass and smiles for years together." After a month in Brown's company, Keats began to describe his summer's work as fagging "to buy Pleasure"—a significant phrase, which he used twice again before the summer was over.[7] Yet degrading love in his mind to a pleasure to be bought and sold also degraded his poetry to the coin with which to buy it. So even as he became convinced that his work would win a popular success, Keats found himself filled with contempt for the reading public. Writing to Taylor on the day he finished *Otho,* he exploded: "I equally dislike the favour of the public with the love of a woman—they are both a cloying treacle to the wings of independence." It was a hateful situation to be caught in, and he confessed he was "a man fill'd with hatreds." But, he insisted, "this Pride and egotism will enable me to write finer things than any thing else could."

Keats himself realized this hatred was irrational and begged Taylor to forgive him "for hammering instead of writing." But he was gripped by forces he could not understand. In view of the extraordinary satisfaction he found in writing the last act of *Otho,* one wonders how much he unconsciously felt the killing of Auranthe as a symbolic revenge on Fanny Brawne. Yet it seems clear that this emotional disturbance had a physical cause as well: the silent spread of disease within him. Phrase after phrase in his letters this summer suggests his symptoms: the fever of his excitement about *Otho,* the ache of his longing for Fanny, the hammering of his quickened pulse, the taste of poison in his mouth, the giddy rise and fall of his emotions, with boundless confidence in his work followed by irritability and depression once he put it down. A year later Keats became convinced that "the too great excitement" of his writing had undermined his constitution. Rather it seems that his amazing productivity this summer was fueled by the low-burning fever of early tuberculosis, which often has the effect of heightening ambition, intensifying sensation, and releasing subconscious creative processes. Perhaps Keats was describing literally his own fevered perceptions in Ludolph's ravings at his bright-lit banquet in *Otho:*

> This is darkness,—when I close
> These lids, I see far fiercer brilliances,—
> Skies full of splendid moons, and shooting stars,
> And spouting exhalations, diamond fires,

> And panting fountains quivering with deep glows!
> Yes—this is dark—is it not dark?

As he told Reynolds near the end of August, his whole life had become "a history of sensations, and day-night mares."

It was in a mood of feverish optimism that Keats finished *Otho* and then, swept along by his own elation, decided to write another tragedy. Brown had been reading an account of the reign of Stephen, the hapless grandson of William the Conqueror, and was struck by its dramatic possibilities. He was starting to sketch a scenario when Keats stopped him: this play he would write for himself. He saw at once that Stephen would make a superb part for Kean, even better than the hysterical Ludolph—a role combining the energy of Richard III with the eloquence of Richard II. In three days he completed three scenes.[8] They make a brilliant beginning, full of bold strokes of character and powerful verse; Keats, it seems, had already far outdistanced Brown in dramatic construction. But on August 27 or 28 they heard news that threatened to cancel half the summer's work in a single stroke: Kean was planning to leave Drury Lane for a winter's tour of America. No other actor in England, Keats was convinced, could play the part of Ludolph; their work was thrown away. Brown, the practical, suggested sending the play in to Covent Garden; but Keats thought the Covent Garden company "ranting, coxcombical, tasteless" and was sure that *Otho* would be damned if put on there. It was useless to go on with *King Stephen;* everything, he realized, now depended on the volume of poetry which he had neglected for over a month. And time was running out, as well as money. Keats had sent Taylor a bombastic letter the week before, asking for a loan on his expectations of *Otho,* but no reply came. Suddenly sobered, he despatched another request in a more level-headed vein and turned resolutely back to *Lamia.*

In the second book of *Lamia,* Keats displayed the most remarkable poetic stamina of the whole remarkable summer. He completed it in about six days against staggering odds of ill health, worry, and discouragement, and in it he accomplished two miracles—transmuting history into poetry and magic into reality. From a musty volume of Greek archaeology [9] he brought ancient Corinth to life again in all its sounds and smells, its perfumed temples and crowded colonnades, its banquets and garlands and torches and the shuffling of sandals over its marble pavements in the cool hours of night. At the same time he turned Burton's tale of demonic influence into a drama of love and disenchantment that poses a riddling allegory of sexual passion. Is love a fatal illusion or a vital reality without which we cannot live? The question is left unanswered in the poem, perhaps because Keats intended the riddle as part of his poetic effect, perhaps because in his own mind he found no answer. The question is, in fact, the dilemma which he had tried all summer to solve—his longing for Fanny Brawne and his struggle to escape.

The extent to which *Lamia* reflects Keats's own predicament becomes clear in his additions to Burton's story. Keats made the philosopher Apollonius not merely one of the wedding guests, as in Burton, but Lycius's friend and teacher. In Keats's poem it is not Lamia herself but Lycius who tries to silence Apollonius, and —most significant of all Keats's changes—dies when Lamia vanishes. Lycius is caught, in fact, between the perilous enchantment of Lamia and the inhuman rationalism of Apollonius, just as Keats was torn between Fanny's beauty and Brown's cynicism.[10] But then is Lycius's death the result of heeding Apollonius's wisdom or of denying it? of loving Lamia or of losing her? Or perhaps of Keats's own despair of resolving his contradictory feelings about both Brown and Fanny? The equation of Lycius, Lamia, and Apollonius with Keats, Fanny, and Brown is too tidy; the poem is much more of a riddle than this. For one thing, Keats chose his subject and wrote the first part of *Lamia* a month before Brown joined him in Shanklin and the tension appeared in his letters to Fanny; it seems he cannot have intended this meaning at the start. Yet the poem contains some surprising links with Keats's previous work. The parallel with *Otho* is striking: in both the play and the poem there is a father-figure who tries to win the infatuated lover back to the truth; in both the woman deceives her lover and is punished by death; and in both the man dies on his wedding night, broken-hearted at the exposure of his bride's falsity. But this pattern of warning, betrayal, and death also resembles that of "La Belle Dame sans Merci," though there the knight is merely brought to the edge of death by the lady's betrayal and is warned by "Kings and princes" from beyond the grave. Auranthe's suicide in *Otho* is not directly presented; but Lamia is shown horribly transformed under Apollonius's stare in a kind of living death.

While the underlying situation remains the same, the terror of the climax mounts from poem to poem.

But there is another set of parallels which reach close to the very springs of Keats's creativity. It has been pointed out that in all three of these poems the revelation of the woman's falsity is prefaced by a scene of feasting and music—a scene anticipated, in far happier tones, in *The Eve of St. Agnes,* where Porphyro sets a banquet and plays the lute before revealing himself to Madeline.[11] But this same scene occurs several times in Keats's earlier poetry and may be traced back to still earlier events in his life; and the elements are not two but four: first sleep, then awakening, followed by a union of lovers and a feast with wine and music. In this, their original order, the experience is a joyful and health-giving one—as in *The Eve of St. Agnes* and, with a significant reversal of roles, in the second book of *Endymion,* where Venus wakens the sleeping Adonis from his winter sleep to the music of lyres in a chamber stocked with fruit and wine. A similar scene occurs in the third book of *Endymion,* when Scylla is revived by Glaucus and a celebration ensues, recalling the conclusion of "I Stood Tiptoe"—the earlier *Endymion*—in which the sick are wakened to health and reunited with the watchers by their bedside in a joyous festival on the eve of Cynthia's wedding. It is significant that all through his poetry Keats uses images of feasting —on honey, fruit, wine, even milk—as metaphorical equivalents of love. "Gorge the honey of life," he had advised Reynolds on his engagement; and "the very 'yes' and 'no' " of a beautiful woman's lips, he told George, were "a Banquet" to him. Two unabashed images from *Endymion* describing sexual pleasure as feeding at the breast suggest the origin of the metaphor, which also occurs in his letters to Fanny Brawne when Keats twice speaks of trying to wean himself from her.[12] This identification of food with love is rooted in our biological nature, of course; but its constant recurrence in Keats's poetry suggests that the biological process had an unusually deep significance for him. Keats's mother, a woman fond of eating and drinking and a "doting parent" who, we are told, loved and indulged him even more than she did her other children, had withdrawn her love from him in a shocking way shortly after his father's death. When she later returned home, he had reaffirmed his love for her by nursing her in her illness—feeding her, reading to her, watching at her bedside as she slept. This never-to-be-forgotten experience of his boyhood seems clearly to be the origin of the feast scenes in *The Eve of St. Agnes* and his earlier poems.

But the feast of love was followed in reality not by the happy awakening to new life which Keats had dreamed of, but by the disaster of his mother's death. And gradually, during the spring and summer of 1819, the scene changes in Keats's imagination. The feast and the love-making are followed, not preceded, by sleep, which is now not health-giving but deathlike, or filled with ominous dreams. The man, who provided the feast in the earlier scenes, is now fed by the woman, and dies afterward; she too dies or disappears or, more terrifying still, turns into a dying woman before his eyes, cold, blank of sight, and horribly pale. This recurrent image suggests the early fear of a surrender to love, from which Keats had not yet successfully freed himself; and the resurgence of this fear must underlie the transformation of the love feast that takes place between *The Eve of St. Agnes,* written in the first confident flush of his love for Fanny Brawne, and the later poems, produced in a period of intense anxiety and jealousy. Love, as Keats had once learned, is the prelude to death; and the death following the moment of possession, for which he had longed in the Bright Star sonnet, now seemed to him not so much the only assurance of unchanging love he could imagine as the consequence of a love that is inevitably an illusion or betrayal.

→»«←

Keats finished *Lamia* on the first or second of September with a surge of elation. As he wrote to Reynolds the week before, "I feel it in my power to become a popular writer—I feel it in my strength to refuse the poisonous suffrage of a public." *Lamia* proved this power. Looking it over afterward, he decided with satisfaction that it had "that sort of fire in it which must take hold of people in some way—give them either pleasant or unpleasant sensation." But even now there was no letting up: on he went, like so many strokes of a hammer. There were his earlier poems to revise; he turned back to them and decided at once they would not do. He was determined not to publish anything which could be laughed at again, and *Isabella* now seemed to show too much innocence of life—" 'A weak-sided Poem' with an amusing sober-sadness about it," he called it. There was almost the same objection to *The Eve of St. Agnes,* but this could be remedied. Adding a stanza, rewriting a few verses at the climax, Keats made it clear that his two young lovers became lovers in fact during the magic storm, then changed the ending to describe the Beadsman's death in grotesque detail. The poem now suited his new mood: it too would give people a "sensation of some sort."

But by now he and Brown were down to their last shillings, and still no money was in sight. No letters had been forwarded to them since Shanklin, not even a newspaper to confirm the rumor of Kean's trip to America. With their credit running out, the Winchester jail loomed up as a menacing possibility. Then, on September 5, in the nick of time, help arrived in a deluge—£30 from Hessey for Keats, another £30 from a friend of Brown's, and a £40 repayment from Keats's absent-minded friend Haslam, who had sent it to Chichester by mistake, along with a note from Taylor. They were jubilant. Keats dashed off a note of thanks to Hessey, adding, "To be a complete Midas I suppose some one will send me a pair of asses ears by the waggon." He may have wondered why Taylor had delayed in writing; he could not have guessed that Taylor, piqued by the arrogance of his first request for a loan, had sent it on to Woodhouse for his opinion. Keats's would-be biographer had risen loyally to his defence: "I wonder how he came to stumble upon that deep truth that 'people are debtors to him for his verses & not he to them for admiration.'—Methinks such a conviction on any one's mind is enough to make half a Milton of him." Then, digging down into his own pocket, Woodhouse came up with £50 which he sent to Taylor to be used for Keats's benefit. "Whatever People regret that they could not do for Shakespeare or Chatterton, because he did not live in their time, that I would embody into a Rational principle, and (with due regard to certain expediencies) do for Keats."

With his pockets full, Brown went off for several weeks to visit at Bedhampton, and Keats found himself alone again. Almost two months remained of the four he had allowed himself, and if he continued working at his summer's rate he would, as he promised Fanny, accomplish "an immense deal." The clear weather held unbroken, and his health began to improve. "I adore fine Weather as the greatest blessing I can have," he wrote his sister. "Give me

Books, fruit, french wine and fine whether and a little music out of doors, played by somebody I do not know—and I can pass a summer very quietly without caring much about Fat Louis, fat Regent or the Duke of Wellington." What or even whether Fanny Brawne replied to his flint-worded letter of August 16 we do not know; but it apparently had the effect of cancelling the understanding they had reached in June.[13] Yet, once the turmoil of this break subsided, Keats turned to his solitude with relief. In the midst of the world he lived as quietly as a hermit, he told George, content merely to write, study Italian, and walk a mile or two after dinner each day. If during his morning's work he found himself getting vaporish, he got up, doused his head in cold water, put on a clean shirt, brushed his hair, retied his shoes, "and in fact adonize as I were going out—then all clean and comfortable I sit down to write."

Yet Keats was no real hermit; this peace was brought at a price. A clue to his state of mind during these quiet weeks in September may be found in the book he was reading at the time—that farrago of donnish ribaldry and learning which Brown had given him in June, *The Anatomy of Melancholy*. Keats read it, as with other books that fascinated him, underscoring and annotating as he went, and the marginal jottings in his Burton form a curious private journal of these weeks, the only real diary he apparently ever kept.[14] At first his notes were mainly literary reminiscences, but as he went on they became more and more personal. For instance, beside a passage describing precious stones as a remedy against a melancholy, he noted wryly, "A valuable diamond would effectively cure mine." The section that drew his closest attention, however, was Burton's long penultimate discourse on Love-Melancholy, one of the most erudite, detailed, and scathing attacks on women ever penned. Keats was so delighted by the Rabelaisan gusto of a long description of an ugly woman that he copied out the entire page for George, adding a few flourishes of his own. But at the beginning of this section, where Burton describes the intellectual love which men share with God and the angels, Keats's marginal comment suddenly lays bare the real anguish of the summer. "Here is the old plague spot: the pestilence, the raw scrofula," he wrote in despair. "I mean that there is nothing disgraces me in my own eyes so much as being one of a race of eyes, nose and mouth beings in a planet called the earth who all from Plato to Wesley have always mingled goatish, winnyish, lustful love with the abstract adoration of the deity. I don't understand greek—is the Love of God and the Love of women expressed by the same word in Greek? I hope my little mind is wrong—if not I could—Has Plato separated these loves?" Hurrying on to the next page, where Burton introduces a distinction between them, he exclaimed, "Ha! I see how they endeavour to divide—but there appears to be a horrid relationship."

What crisis wrung these words from Keats we shall never really know—a moment of self-disgust so naked that we instinctively turn our eyes away. The physiological metaphor of "the old plague spot" somehow links this outburst with his sexual misadventure of two years before, and its recrudescence seems also somehow linked with his alienation from Fanny Brawne since mid-August. Another revealing annotation occurs farther on in Burton, beside some verses of Ausonius, where Keats misquoted a line of Tasso in the margin, *"Cogliam la rosa d'amore"*—an echo of Spenser's "Gather the rose of love"—then added and underscored the Latin word *ubique,* "everywhere." The only possible interpretation of this cryptic addition is that Keats had in fact followed Spenser's advice and joined Brown on his sexual expeditions in August. Certainly remorse for such a lapse would help account for his diatribe against "goatish, winnyish, lustful love"—a remorse which he had felt before, but never so keenly as now. Yet even this mood gave way to cynicism as he read further in *The Anatomy.* Page after page he went on, as Burton added detail to detail of his monstrous indictment. From Keats's approving comments—"Good!" "Aye, aye!" "Extraordinary!"—gradually emerges a portrait of "a man fill'd with hatreds" indeed, hatred of sex, of self, seemingly of all that he had felt and believed before.

Yet from this mood of morbid self-dissatisfaction an important resolution was born. He decided at last to give up *Hyperion,* to which he had devoted most of his thought and effort for over a year—not to discard it completely, but rather to rewrite it from the start on a new plan.[15] By now it seems he clearly saw that the conflict between his first optimistic theme and his increasingly tragic view of the individual's destiny could no longer be resolved in the character of Apollo. But he was also growing restless under his long tutelage to Milton as his own intentions clarified. "Miltonic verse cannot be written but in an artful or rather artist's humour," he explained to Reynolds in telling him later of his decision. "I wish to give myself up to other sensations." One of these sensations was the grave and disciplined clarity of Dante's verse.[16] During August, Keats had gone back to reading the *Inferno* in translation, while also attempting a few lines in the original as his Italian progressed—an effort "well worth the while," as he remarked to George. Dante's austere music echoes in the prologue to the new version of his poem, which he now entitled *The Fall of Hyperion—A Dream;* more than this, Dante's allegorical plan suggested a solution to his structural problem. To recast his epic as a vision in which he himself appeared as the poet witnessing the fall of the Titans, as Dante himself had wandered through the kingdoms of the dead—this would give scope both to his own bitter meditations and to Apollo's struggle for godhead.

> Fanatics have their dreams, wherewith they weave
> A paradise for a sect; the savage too
> From forth the loftiest fashion of his sleep
> Guesses at Heaven: pity these have not
> Trac'd upon vellum or wild indian leaf
> The shadows of melodious utterance.
> But bare of laurel they live, dream and die;
> For Poesy alone can tell her dreams,
> With the fine spell of words alone can save
> Imagination from the sable charm
> And dumb enchantment. Who alive can say
> 'Thou art no Poet; mayst not tell thy dreams?'
> Since every man whose soul is not a clod
> Hath visions, and would speak, if he had lov'd
> And been well nurtured in his mother tongue.
> Whether the dream now purposed to rehearse
> Be Poet's or Fanatic's will be known
> When this warm scribe my hand is in the grave.

So he began; and the poem moved serenely on, into the garden and the temple of his vision, with a terse and sober grace he had never achieved before.

For three or four days he continued; then his solitude was interrupted again. On September 10 a desperate letter came from George. Business had taken a bad turn throughout America. Pressed for credit, he had discovered that his partner was already deep in debt, contrary to the impression of prosperity he had originally given; in fact, Audubon was being sued by five creditors at the time he had persuaded George to invest in the steamboat.

With his cash run out, George's entire investment was threatened unless the rest of his holdings could be sold and the money forwarded at once.[17] Keats now found his worst suspicions of Audubon's honesty confirmed. All summer long Abbey had done nothing about their affairs; Sandell had not yet replied from Holland; the Chancery suit still blocked the road. At once Keats decided to go up to London to extricate George's money and try if he could to get an advance on his new volume of poems. For a moment he thought of approaching Byron's publisher, Murray, then decided that his stock stood too low in the literary market. He would appeal to Taylor and Hessey, even though he sensed they would be unwilling to take another gamble on him. Hastily he gathered up his manuscripts and set off for London in the night coach.

Going straight to Pancras Lane the next morning, a Saturday, Keats found Abbey about to leave for Walthamstow for the weekend and had to put off their interview till Monday evening. In Fleet Street he learned that Taylor was still not back from vacation and had to face the cautious Hessey instead. Hessey listened to his plan to bring out the new volume in time for Christmas, then told him it would not do. The final decision rested with Taylor, of course; but Hessey as business manager could remind Keats that the firm was over a hundred pounds out of pocket on *Endymion*. This was a third blow to his hopes, coming hard on the heels of George's misfortune and the news of Kean's departure. Keats took his leave and wandered up Fleet Street. Suddenly he felt he was in a foreign city, a stranger among the anonymous hurrying crowd. A year ago London had been the battlefield of his struggle for fame; now he was filled with bitterness toward the unseen enemies who had thwarted him. I am a weaver-boy to them, he thought— one of the cotton-spinners who struck for higher wages only to be starved into submission. He made a few calls and found nobody at home; Reynolds and Dilke, he knew, were still away in the country. He tried not to think of Hampstead: that would be venturing into a fire. For hours he drifted about the streets, trying to shake off the sensation of strangeness, then luckily found Rice in at Poland Street, where he managed to round off the day pleasantly enough.

Sunday morning Keats breakfasted at the Temple with Woodhouse, who had dropped in at Hessey's the morning before and was leaving for a holiday in Bath that afternoon. Woodhouse gave him a warmer welcome than Hessey had. He was full of a new discovery, Provençal poetry, and even had a plan for taking Keats with him on a prospecting tour of Provence next summer.[18] He also wanted to hear the new poem. Keats read *Lamia* aloud to him, rather badly, as Woodhouse thought: he sensed its drama but was puzzled about its meaning. Why, for instance, did Lamia consent to marry Lycius when she would thereby lose her immortality? Because, Keats answered, "Women love to be forced to do a thing, by a fine fellow." Still less could Woodhouse understand why Keats refused to include *Isabella* in the projected volume. He thought its simple pathos would have a strong appeal, but Keats insisted it was too mawkish to print. But when he produced the revised version of *The Eve of St. Agnes,* Woodhouse abused it "a full hour by the *Temple* clock." As publisher's reader, he saw at once that turning the dream marriage into a reality made the poem "unfit for ladies." Keats replied heatedly that he wrote not for ladies but for men. As Woodhouse reported with some amusement to Taylor, "he sh^d despise a man who would be such an eunuch in sentiment as to leave a maid, with that Character about her, in such a situation: & sho^d despise himself to write about it &c &c &c— and all this sort of Keats-like rhodomontade." Still, Keats knew what he was up against and probably appreciated the irony of Woodhouse's position. As they walked from the lawyer's rooms to the coachyard together, Keats begged him to write him in Winchester. Woodhouse agreed, then added, "All the reciprocity should not be on one side." Keats laughed; they shook hands at the coach door with a warm sense of fellowship, then Woodhouse rolled off on his journey, mulling over their conversation.

Keats went on to dine at the Wylies' with an uncomfortable sense of constraint. He could not show them George's latest letter, though Mrs. Wylie was full of news from Georgiana, who had just sent her a lock of the new baby's hair and her exact measurements— "the little span-long elf." So Keats joined Charles and Henry in the usual "quizzing"—of Mrs. Wylie's new gown, of Charles's whiskers, of Henry's fiancée, of their fat, smiling new cook, even of the passers-by in the street; but he was glad to escape at last. Monday morning the question he had evaded for two days became insistent. Would he go out to Hampstead? Would he even let Fanny know he had come to London? His equanimity began to collapse; quickly he wrote to explain why he could not come. "If I were to see you to day it would destroy the half comfortable sullenness I enjoy at present into downright perplexities. Knowing well that my life must be passed in fatigue and trouble, I have been endeavouring to wean myself from you: for to myself alone what can be much of a misery? I am a Coward, I cannot bear the pain of being happy." Even then he could not bring himself to mail the letter. He stuffed it into his pocket and took a coach out to Walthamstow to see his sister, putting Hampstead a dozen miles out of reach.

Back on Monday afternoon, he found the city in a hubbub of excitement. Henry Hunt, the Radical orator, was returning to London from Manchester for trial. A month before, a meeting for Parliamentary reform led by Hunt at St. Peter's Fields near Manchester had turned into a massacre when the local cavalry, sent to arrest him for disturbing the peace, charged the crowd with drawn sabres. Eleven men and women were killed and four hundred wounded. A cry of outrage went up from the Liberal press, which the Government answered by passing the infamous "Six Acts." It was the pattern of 1817—misery, protest, violence, repression—repeated in still darker tones. These were the events which added the word "Peterloo" to the English vocabulary; they also inspired Shelley in Italy to write his stirring "Mask of Anarchy," with the refrain

> Rise like Lions after slumber
> In unvanquishable number—
> Shake your chains to earth like dew
> Which in sleep had fallen on you—
> Ye are many—they are few . . .

which Leigh Hunt, in London, put off publishing till 1832. When Henry Hunt reached London in the afternoon of September 13, a crowd of nearly three hundred thousand lined the street from Islington to the Strand to greet him in the greatest triumphal entry the city had seen. At the head of the procession came chariots and barouches drawn by red-ribboned bay horses with red-cockaded outriders, followed by bands playing, men bearing oak branches, a red flag with the motto "Universal Suffrage," a blue flag reading "A Free Press," a white flag emblazoned "Trial by Jury," and rank after rank of marchers; then at last, riding in a landaulet with a banner proclaiming "Liberty or Death," came Hunt himself, looking pale and tired, bowing gravely to the throngs.[19] Somewhere

in the clapping, cheering, handkerchief-waving crowd Keats wandered, caught up in the surge of revolutionary ardour. This was
an hour to make him forget the sense of estrangement that had
gnawed at him since his arrival in London on Saturday, even to
cancel out the cynicism and despair of weeks past. Some things in
the world were real after all. Weeks later, deep in discouragement
again, he was to remember this day: "I have no cause to complain,"
he wrote Haydon, "because I am certain any thing really fine will
in these days be felt. I have no doubt that if I had written Othello
I should have been cheered by as good a Mob as Hunt."

Monday evening Abbey received him with unexpected good
humour and offered him tea. He looked grave at George's news
and promised to do everything possible: send George a remittance
immediately and press the lawyers to get rid of Mrs. Jennings' suit.
But when Keats hinted he needed money himself, Abbey was less
sympathetic. The sober truth had to be faced that Keats had now
anticipated most of the small sum remaining from his inheritance
by his borrowings over the summer. Abbey ended their interview
with a well-aimed dig. After blowing up Byron's poetry, he added
slyly, "The fellow does say true things now and then," and picked
up a magazine to read a stanza from Don Juan hitting at the folly
of literary ambition. Keats said good-bye, started aimlessly up
Cheapside, then decided to mail the letter to Fanny Brawne which
he had been carrying around all day and turned back toward the
Lombard Street post office. In Bucklersbury he met Abbey again.
As they walked down the Poultry together, Abbey hinted, to
Keats's surprise, that he could have a position in his hatter's shop
for the asking. Despite his discouragement, Keats saw the humour
of it. Abbey was trying to help in the only way he knew; as for
himself, he told George, "I do believe if I could be a hatter I might
be one."

Tuesday he called on Haslam, whom he found completely absorbed in new business and his approaching marriage—much to
Keats's amusement. From Severn's portrait of his fiancée, Keats
decided she was "though not very cunning, too cunning for him."
"Nothing," he exclaimed in his letter to George, "strikes me so
forcibly with a sense of the rediculous as love." That evening he
had nothing better to do than go to the second half of the program
at Covent Garden, where he met Abbey's junior partner Hodg-

kinson, George's old enemy, who, Keats noted with amusement, treated him with deference now he had become an author. On Wednesday he returned to Winchester at last. George's fate still hung in the balance, and his own prospects looked even blanker than they had three months before. He tried to pick up his work, but for a day or so his anxiety got the better of him. Then on Friday he pulled himself up short: rather than waste any more time in fretting, he would begin another long letter to George, as encouraging as he could make it. There was no blinking the mess they were in, he wrote—for "mess it is as far as it regards our Pockets." Yet, he added, "I assure you you shall more than share what I can get, whilst I am still young—the time may come when age will make me more selfish." It was a difficult promise to make, since it implied giving up all hope of marriage for the time being. But with George in need, there was nothing else he could do. As for himself, he admitted, he knew of no one whose friends were more generous—though, unfortunately, none of them could well afford their generosity. So he promised George he would send him what he could—if not hundreds, then tens; if not tens, then ones. "I have forgot how to lay plans for enjoyment of any Pleasure," he added. "I feel I can bear any thing, any misery, even imprisonment —so long as I have neither wife nor child."

The next morning his spirits began to rise. He reread *Lamia* and realized that in spite of Hessey's hedging and Woodhouse's bewilderment it was certain to succeed if ever he could get it published. He went back to his letter, rambling on with news, copying out Burton to amuse George, then embarked on the subject that was smouldering in his mind—the recent turn of political events. Trying to put Peterloo in the long perspective of the English struggle for liberty, he began to see hopeful signs in the dark record of the last few years. Henry Hunt's defiance of the Ministry, the solidarity of the London crowd that cheered him, the courage of the Radical pamphleteers and publishers such as Richard Carlile, whom the Government had indicted more than a dozen times but still feared to prosecute—all these were tokens of a new spirit of freedom stirred up by the Tories, which must come to good in the end. Of Carlile he exclaimed, "They are affraid of his defence: it would be published in all the papers all over the Empire: they shudder at this: the Trials would light a flame they could not extinguish." In his excitement the great words of the martyred Latimer facing death at the stake went ringing through his head.* There were still blows to be struck for freedom; the future was still full of possibility.

Yet even as he wrote, his mind was turning backward. Looking through some old papers that morning, he had turned up two reminders of the past: one of his letters from Scotland, describing his trip to Iona and Staffa; and a page from his journal of March which he had overlooked in sending it off in May. Rereading them, Keats was struck by the immense amount of time he had lived through since George had left. From the wonder and expectancy of his summer in Scotland through the paralysed despair of the following spring to his present state of frustrated indecision, the distance seemed almost incalculable. How differently things turn out from one's expectations, he mused, how often had he acted against his own resolves, how rarely did he speak in his letters of the things he thought of and felt most deeply. Uneasily he realized that George must have changed as much as he in the last fifteen months. "Every man does—Our bodies every seven years are completely fresh-materiald," he wrote, remembering in a flash the angry boy who seven years ago had clenched his fist against Hammond. On the edge of an unpredictable future, he realized his youth was drawing to a close. The abundance of energy without responsibility which he had squandered so heedlessly was running out with his hopes and his money. The loss was irrecoverable; but was there no gain as well? "Some think I have lost that poetic ardour and fire 't is said I once had—the fact is perhaps I have: but instead of that I hope I shall substitute a more thoughtful and quiet power. I am more frequently, now, contented to read and think—but now & then, haunted with ambitious thoughts. Quieter in my pulse, improved in my digestion; exerting myself against vexing speculations— scarcely content to write the best verses for the fever they leave behind. I want to compose without this fever. I hope I one day shall."

The season itself was retrospective. The walk which he took

---

* "Be of good comfort, Master Ridley, and play the man, we shall this day light such a candle, by God's grace, in England, as I trust shall never be put out." (John Foxe, *The Book of Martyrs;* see *The Letters of John Keats,* ed. H. E. Rollins [1958], II, 194 n.)

every day before his solitary dinner led him out past empty fields that a month before had been thick with full-grown wheat. At the beginning of the summer he had reflected ironically that his poetry was destined for the market, like the grain; for weeks he had watched it ripening while he went on with his own work. Now, with the harvest in, he felt a profound satisfaction. In his imagery, gold was always the colour of poetry, autumn the season of fulfilment; now, as he wandered through the mellow countryside, he could forget the uncertainties of his own summer's labour in the serenity of the harvest landscape. "How beautiful the season is now," he wrote Reynolds on the twenty-first, "How fine the air. A temperate sharpness about it. Really, without joking, chaste weather—Dian skies—I never lik'd stubble fields so much as now —Aye better than the chilly green of the spring. Somehow a stubble plain looks warm—in the same way that some pictures look warm—this struck me so much in my sunday's walk that I composed upon it."

What he wrote that Sunday afternoon was his most perfect and untroubled poem:

> Season of mists and mellow fruitfulness,
>   Close bosom-friend of the maturing sun;
> Conspiring with him how to load and bless
>   With fruit the vines that round the thatch-eves run;
> To bend with apples the moss'd cottage-trees,
>   And fill all fruit with ripeness to the core;
>   To swell the gourd, and plump the hazel shells
> With a sweet kernel; to set budding more,
>   And still more, later flowers for the bees,
>   Until they think warm days will never cease,
>   For Summer has o'er-brimm'd their clammy cells.
>
> Who hath not seen thee oft amid thy store?
>   Sometimes whoever seeks abroad may find
> Thee sitting careless on a granary floor,
>   Thy hair soft-lifted by the winnowing wind;
> Or on a half-reap'd furrow sound asleep,
>   Drows'd with the fume of poppies, while thy hook
>   Spares the next swath and all its twined flowers:
> And sometimes like a gleaner thou dost keep
>   Steady thy laden head across a brook;
>   Or by a cyder-press, with patient look,
>   Thou watchest the last oozings hours by hours.

Where are the songs of Spring? Ay, where are they?
  Think not of them, thou hast thy music too,—
While barred clouds bloom the soft-dying day,
  And touch the stubble-plains with rosy hue;
Then in a wailful choir the small gnats mourn
  Among the river shallows, borne aloft
    Or sinking as the light wind lives or dies;
And full-grown lambs loud bleat from hilly bourn;
  Hedge-crickets sing; and now with treble soft
  The red-breast whistles from a garden-croft;
    And gathering swallows twitter in the skies.

It is Keats's most characteristic because most impersonal poem. The poet himself is completely lost in his images, and the images are presented as meaning simply themselves: Keats's richest utterance is the barest of metaphor. The fullness of life, the joy of completion which the poem celebrates emerge directly from what he once called the rise, the progress, the setting of the imagery, as natural and magnificent as the sun's. All the hours of an autumn day are implied in this progression—misty morning, drowsy noon, and chilly sunset; all the characters, properties, and stages of the autumnal drama, in a scene that slowly widens from cottage yard to neighbouring fields and distant hills and skies; all the senses by which it is apprehended; all its varieties of action—motionless growth, unhurried toil, langour after harvest, restless stirring before flight. The poem is a garnering of perception, a summary of achievement, a half-conscious gesture of farewell.

The premonition of departure that concludes the poem, the hint of darker and colder days to come, was prophetic. For a day Keats went on, absorbed in his work, picking up *The Eve of St. Mark*—that little poem begun seven months before "quite in the spirit of Town quietude," as he described it to George—and adding a dozen lines or so.[20] Monday evening he filled up another long sheet in his journal with jokes and gossip, including some astonishing news of Severn. "I have to make use of the word Mum! before I tell you that Severn has got a little Baby—all his own let us hope—He told Brown he had given up painting and had turn'd modeller. I hope sincerely tis not a party concern; that no M͏ʳ—— or **** is the real *Pinxit* and Severn the poor *Sculpsit* to this work of art—You know he has long studied in the Life-Academy." Tuesday morning he continued in a more sober mood, with a hint of uneasiness under the surface. He could not wait much longer for the fate of his play and his poems to be decided. The question he had put off since spring must now be faced. If he could earn nothing from his writing, what should he do with his life? Restlessly he started a letter to Reynolds, then, after announcing that he had given up *Hyperion,* broke off impatiently. He needed time to think; he decided to go for a late-afternoon walk.

His usual route took him out the back gate of his house into the cathedral yard, past the cathedral, through two collegiate squares, then out the city gate and over the meadows to St. Cross. As he cut through the fields he came to a rail fence and absent-mindedly stooped under it. At once he asked himself why he had not climbed over it instead, and answered, "Because no one wanted to force you under." He was amused at the thought of his own wilfulness, yet, as he walked on, a mood of self-dissatisfaction dogged him. It was a selfish life he had led for the past two or three years, he mused, swept this way and that, anchored to nothing. All of a sudden he felt the lack of a purpose outside himself, of a meridian to measure his course by. Devoting himself selfishly to poetry had meant drifting with the tide of his own moods; now both he and George faced shipwreck unless he changed course. Should he head back toward a safe profession, as Reynolds had done? Three months before, he had been ready to return to medicine when it seemed the only way to marriage; but now, with that hope apparently abandoned, what would he gain? As he walked back along the river after sunset, an autumnal chill was in the air. At the edge of town the clangour and warmth of a blacksmith's shop stopped him. He stood for a while at the open door, watching almost with envy the free, unanxious energy of the men swinging their hammers at the anvil, then returned to his room to finish the letter to Reynolds. His purpose was forged.

The next day he wrote three letters—to Brown, Woodhouse, and Dilke—to announce his decision. He must start earning his living, like everyone else, he told them; but still he would not be sidetracked into medicine. Since he could no longer hope for success with *Otho,* he would return to London to take lodgings and try "prosing for awhile in periodical works." He would speak to Hazlitt, who might recommend him to the *Edinburgh Review* as he had Reynolds; meanwhile he would try to get the theatre reviews of a newspaper. He knew well enough that his friends would regard such hack work as a prostitution of his talents, even if only temporary; but he did not care. "Yea I will trafic. Any thing but Mortgage my Brain to Blackwood," he remarked cynically to Dilke. Yet, from his statement to Brown that he would write "on the liberal side of the question" for whoever would pay him, it is clear that Keats's decision had an idealistic motive as well as a practical one. For the present, poetry would have to wait. "When I can afford to compose deliberate poems I will," he told Brown, and they would be the better for the discipline he imposed upon himself. At the end of another year, he promised, "you shall applaud me,—not for verses, but for conduct."

His plan meant giving up not only poetry but his close relationship to Brown, and announcing it stirred Keats for a moment out of his usual reticence about his deepest feelings. He told Brown that he must break his vicious habit of looking toward him "as a help in all difficulties" and leave him free for the pleasures which, Keats assured him, it was his duty to procure while still in the prime of life. Brown's happiness was one of his chief anxieties: "I wish you could see my heart towards you," he added, apologizing for the word which he never used except in poetry. As for himself, he insisted he was as far from being unhappy about the turn of events as possible. "Imaginary grievances have always been more my torment than real ones," he admitted; real ones only roused him up to action. Journalism was no great calling like poetry; yet in days like these it could serve a great cause, the very one for which Henry Hunt was fighting. The example of Hazlitt stood before him, and the image—which he would not mention directly even to Brown—of Milton laying down the first sketches of his epic to become pamphleteer for the Puritans. "I hope sincerely," he wrote in all earnestness to Dilke, "I shall be able to put a Mite of help to the Liberal side of the Question before I die."

Chapter Twelve

Unmeridian'd and Objectless

T H E day of decision was followed by over a week of inaction. Keats did not plan to start for London till he heard from Brown. But when Brown replied from Bedhampton on the twenty-third, he told Keats to do nothing till he rejoined him in Winchester, and in a sudden return of irresolution Keats decided not to send his impulsive letter announcing his decision to Dilke. He resumed waiting for word from Abbey to send to George; but none came. He added a few pages to his journal, teasing Georgiana, describing a wildly successful practical joke he had played on Brown's summer tenant and another played on himself and the young wife of an elderly major in the next apartment at Winchester, but saying nothing of his new plan. George would suspect that it was his own setbacks that had forced Keats to the decision, and this he wished to avoid. On the twenty-seventh another urgent appeal came from George, who was growing desperate at the delay. Keats wound up his letter to send off immediately, adding a bit of good news of his own: he had heard that Kean might not go to America after all. If the rumour was true, there was some hope for *Otho*. He was still surrounded by "uncertainties east west, north, and south," but he would not admit it to George.

The only real record of his uneasy frame of mind at this time is found in *The Fall of Hyperion*. It is impossible to tell just where Keats laid it down when he hurried up to London on September 10, but the most probable point is at the dreamer's entry into the temple of Saturn. His ensuing conversation with the mysterious goddess Moneta appears to have been written after Keats's return, for it is a striking echo of the disillusionment with poetry Keats expressed in his letters all through the following weeks.[1] He told Dilke that he marvelled that people read as much poetry as they did, and remarked even more cynically to Haydon that he had done nothing with his life so far "except for the amusement of a few people who refine upon their feelings till anything in the unun-derstandable way will go down with them." This section of *The Fall of Hyperion* thus seems clearly a comment on his resolution to give up writing poetry: now, if never before, Keats was writing a deliberate allegory of his inner life. The dreamer's progress from the garden into the temple corresponds to the poet's growth from unreflective delight in all the beauty of the world to his first aware-ness of the misery which life holds for the sentient man—the de-velopment which Keats previsioned in "Sleep and Poetry" and *Endymion* and underwent in reality with Tom's last illness. What the dreamer sees in the temple of Saturn are, literally, the relics of the wars of the Titans, but in their vastness and antiquity they suggest the whole sum of human experience environing his span of years. His journey through this temple of consciousness is also symbolic; for he moves not from west to east, as through a Chris-tian cathedral, but from east to west, in the direction of earthly time itself. Near the altar he meets the veiled priestess who is to be the Beatrice of his journey—Moneta, the Roman goddess of admonition, sometimes identified with the Greek goddess Mne-mosyne who appeared to Apollo in the first *Hyperion*. She bids him ascend the steps to her side or die at once at the altar's foot. He starts to climb, but it costs him an agony as great as death itself:

> Suddenly a palsied chill
> Struck from the paved level up my limbs,
> And was ascending quick to put cold grasp
> Upon those streams that pulse beside the throat:
> I shriek'd; and the sharp anguish of my shriek
> Stung my own ears—I strove hard to escape
> The numbness; strove to gain the lowest step.
> Slow, heavy, deadly was my pace: the cold
> Grew stifling, suffocating, at the heart;
> And when I clasp'd my hands I felt them not.

But miraculously, "one minute before death," he sets foot on the lowest step and finds strength to climb the stairs to Moneta's side. There he begs her to tell him why he should have been saved, and she answers that he has already learned "What 'tis to die and live again before Thy fated hour." The reward of such an experience —the "dying into life" of *Hyperion*—is insight into human suffering: and, she explains,

> "None can usurp this height, . . .
> But those to whom the miseries of the world
> Are misery, and will not let them rest.
> All else who find a haven in the world,
> Where they may thoughtless sleep away their days,
> If by a chance into this fane they come,
> Rot on the pavement where thou rotted'st half."

Astonished, he then asks why he should be there alone, for surely there are thousands of his fellow beings in the world who not merely "feel the giant agony of the world" but also "labour for mortal good." The priestess explains that he is different from these "slaves to poor humanity":

> "They are no dreamers weak,
> They seek no wonder but the human face;
> No music but a happy-noted voice—
> They come not here, they have no thought to come—
> And thou art here, for thou art less than they—
> What benefit canst thou do, or all thy tribe,
> To the great world?"

The poet differs from ordinary "thoughtless" mortals, then, since he at least can share imaginatively the suffering of others; yet he also differs from the truly disinterested, who not only "love their fellows even to the death" but work effectively to relieve their suffering, as the poet does not. At this the dreamer protests that not all poetry is useless: is not the poet "a sage, A humanist, Physician to all men?" Moneta's answer implies that this is true of a few great poets, but certainly not of himself:

> "Art thou not of the dreamer tribe?
> The poet and the dreamer are distinct,
> Diverse, sheer opposite, antipodes.
> The one pours out a balm upon the world,
> The other vexes it."

Apparently Keats later cancelled these lines and made a fresh start; but, it is important to note, he left unqualified his original dismissal of most poetry as useless and of himself as "a dreaming thing," whose imagination merely "venoms all his days." [2] Like Dante, then, who began his spiritual journey aware of how far he had fallen from the good, Keats started *The Fall of Hyperion* with a devastating indictment of his own previous achievement in poetry as well as of the selfish passivity and indulgence in "imaginary woes" which his life as a poet had encouraged.

The comparison he draws here between the true poet and the physician is especially significant, for it shows this aspect of Keats's identity once more emerging into consciousness at a time of crisis. Images of sickness, it is not surprising to note, are scattered everywhere in *Otho the Great,* and do much to establish its tone of fevered frenzy; but in *The Fall of Hyperion* illness is used not simply as a metaphor for various emotional states but as a symbol of the poet's own consciousness. "Until we are sick, we understand not," Keats had written Reynolds over a year before; but there is more to it than that. The dreamer is a sick man, "a fever of himself," when he enters the temple, but in his encounter with Moneta he looks for health:

> "By such propitious parley medicin'd
> In sickness not ignoble, I rejoice."

The self-cured physician here becomes Keats's image of redemption through poetry. By confronting his own sickness, Keats implies, the dreamer may at last surmount it, become a true poet who does not "vex" mankind with dreams of unreal happiness but heals it through his own understanding of "the giant agony of the world." But his debate with Moneta also illuminates Keats's decision to turn to journalism till he was ready for this kind of poetry. The "ambition to do the world some good" which had dogged him ever since he had given up medicine was now to be translated into action; by writing on the liberal side Keats hoped humbly to join the ranks of those who "labour for mortal good."

By the end of September, Brown had returned to Winchester. At once, it appears, he tried to persuade Keats to give up his plan. The prospects for *Otho* looked bright again; why not wait till Elliston, the manager of Drury Lane, read the play and passed judgment? At this Keats may have wavered, but on one point he was adamant. He would not go back to live at Wentworth Place. "I like Miss Brawne and I cannot help it," he was driven to admit. Two weeks before, he had realized that even a short visit to Fanny would disrupt his plans to remain hard at work in Winchester till his four months were up. Living next door to her through the winter was unthinkable: any resolution would be shattered. Accordingly, on October 1 he wrote another letter to Dilke, asking him to find cheap lodgings for him in Westminster, where he would be "in reach of books"; then, two days later, to Haydon, requesting that he get him another ticket to the British Museum Reading Room —without, however, mentioning to either his plan for trying journalism. On October 8 he packed up and returned to town. The lodgings which Dilke had found for him at 25 College Street, near his own house in Great Smith Street and the Westminster Library, were a pleasant set of rooms with a view of the Abbey gardens, as cloistered and quiet as Winchester itself. With his books and pictures moved in, Keats could settle down in complete comfort. Accordingly, on Sunday the tenth, summoning up all his courage, he went out to Wentworth Place to collect his belongings and make his farewells. He took one backward look—and all was lost.

It was a new Fanny who awaited him, as beautiful in his eyes as ever, but schooled to a new tenderness. In the last two months she must have learned much she had never known before—stung pride, bewildered anger, then the long ache of loss. This time she was the one to fear the withdrawal of love, and evidently she welcomed Keats with a passion newly wakened by uncertainty. Keats was overwhelmed, dazzled, driven almost speechless. The old unassuageable desire gripped him again, and the subtler torture of a lingering doubt. Was it true? Could he believe in her kindness? Fanny remained self-possessed enough to threaten to "be cruel" if he ever again allowed his work to come between them, and Keats was helpless. He returned to Westminster in a turmoil. His promise to George, his peace of mind, his plans for the future were threatened. He struggled to blot out her image for an hour—the light of her glance, the touch of her lips, the warmth of her breath on his cheek: it was no use. He tried to steady himself by writing; the tumultuous "Lines to Fanny" were the result.[3]

> What can I do to drive away
> Remembrance from my eyes? for they have seen,
> Aye, an hour ago, my brilliant Queen!
> Touch has a memory. O say, love, say,
> What can I do to kill it and be free
> In my old liberty? . . .

The next morning, against his will, each scene of the day before played itself over and over in his head. There was nothing to do but to write Fanny confessing he was at her mercy, begging her to find a day they could pass alone together.

Two days went by while Keats tried to put his resolution into effect. It seems altogether likely that he went to York Street to ask Hazlitt's advice about entering journalism, though there is no record of such a visit. But if we can assume that the interview took place, we can also infer that it was a discouraging one. Hazlitt was facing a depressing crisis of his own that fall, with the final break-down of his miserable marriage, a new low in his finances, and the apparent collapse of his own career.[4] Keats, whose first glimpse of York Street the year before had left him with a vivid impression of Hazlitt's son as a "little Nero," may well have been daunted by a closer view of Hazlitt's private life at this time—his contempt for his wife, his unconcealed promiscuity, the sordid bleakness of his living habits—and still more by his despair over what he called "this trade of authorship." Though Hazlitt had become a top-ranking journalist a few years after starting, he had been muzzled, libelled, underpaid, and unceremoniously dismissed every step of the way. And in the fall of 1819, he hardly needed to remind Keats, the rewards of writing "on the liberal side of the question" were not a modest livelihood but the possibility of indictment for sedition. Perhaps he tried to persuade Keats to "try the press once more" with his poems, for only a month later he complimented his work by quoting "Sleep and Poetry" in the first of his new series of lectures. But Hazlitt later recorded his opinion of Keats as a poet lacking "masculine energy" and "hardy spirit";[5] one wonders whether this impression sprang from a glimpse of Keats's desperate conflict at this time.

One friend, as we do know, came to visit Keats in Westminster this week—Severn, full of excitement at his own latest project. He had entered the Royal Academy competition for historical paint-ing, in spite of his lack of experience in this genre, and by now he had nearly finished his canvas on the subject set, the scene at the "Cave of Despair" in *The Faerie Queene*. Keats quoted from mem-ory the central stanza of the episode, to Severn's delight; he then read *Lamia* to him and talked about his other poems, though with no mention of journalism. Yet Severn was troubled by Keats's appearance. Four months in the country had evidently not improved his health. Under an air of confident resolve his friend sensed a deep uneasiness.

By Wednesday, Keats's indecision had become more than he could bear. He could not write; he could not even keep his mind on the drudgery of copying what he had already written. At last he started a letter to Fanny. "The time is passed when I had power to advise and warn you against the unpromising morning of my Life. I am forgetful of every thing but seeing you again—my Life seems to stop there—I see no further. You have absorb'd me. My sweet Fanny, will your heart never change? My love, will it?" At this moment her note of reply to his Monday letter arrived. She assured him she loved him; she had threatened to "be cruel" only in jest. His love flowed over: "I have been astonished that Men could die Martyrs for religion—I have shudder'd at it—I shudder no more—I could be martyr'd for my Religion—Love is my religion." For a moment he had a sensation of dissolving; his resolution was giving way. "You have ravish'd me away by a Power I cannot resist; and yet I could resist till I saw you; and even since I have seen you I have endeavoured often 'to reason against the reasons of my Love'. I can do that no more—the pain would be too great—My Love is selfish—I cannot breathe without you."

The sequel to this letter was another visit to Wentworth Place. On Friday the fifteenth Keats went out to Hampstead to spend three days at Brown's, once more under the same roof with Fanny, surrendering completely to her fascination. One would like to think that for these three days Keats tasted for once in his life the "unalloyed happiness" of the ordinary thoughtless man. Yet from the sonnet "The day is gone," which he probably wrote over this weekend, it appears that even while drugged with joy in his love he ached with the sense of its incompleteness:

> Faded the sight of beauty from my eyes,
> Faded the shape of beauty from my arms,
>   Faded the voice, warmth, whiteness, paradise—
> Vanish'd unseasonably at shut of eve,
>   When the dusk holiday—or holinight
> Of fragrant-curtain'd love begins to weave
>   The woof of darkness thick, for hid delight. . . .

"Only the dreamer venoms all his days," Moneta had warned him; and when he woke from his "three days dream" on Monday to face the consequences of his decision, it was with "a cry to dream again."

What followed was a sudden reversal of his plans. All at once he gave up his rooms in College Street and went to stay with the Dilkes for a few days. He had decided to return to live in Hampstead, even if it meant giving up the idea of journalism. The acutely physical anguish that separation from Fanny now caused him—"I cannot breathe without you"—had grown too great. Dilke was evidently astonished at the sudden collapse of an intention which he must have heartily endorsed. Yet Keats could not explain his behaviour to anyone's satisfaction without betraying the secret of his love; much worse, even to himself he could not justify it. For one miserable night he considered what he had done—the responsibilities shirked, the new distraction risked. The next morning, Tuesday the nineteenth, he wrote Fanny to announce his decision: "I must be busy, or try to be so. I must impose chains upon myself—I shall be able to do nothing—I shold like to cast the die for Love or death—if you ever intend to be cruel to me as you say in jest now but perhaps may sometimes be in earnest be so now—and I will—my mind is in a tremble, I cannot tell what I am writing." *

On Wednesday he returned to Hampstead and the die was cast for love. Mrs. Brawne was finally persuaded to consent to their engagement. As she confided to Mrs. Dilke, she had done all she could to prevent it, and agreed at last in the hope it would "go off." [6] With Keats's prospects still so uncertain, no date for the marriage could even be considered. The engagement was therefore to be kept a secret. Probably at this time Keats gave Fanny a garnet ring that may have belonged to his mother, but she did not wear it openly as a sign of their betrothal till a year and a half later.[7] Keats did not even tell Brown his secret for many months,[8] and with other friends he formed the habit of never mentioning Fanny's name. His deepest joys, like his deepest sorrows, were beyond confiding.

-»»««-

Back at Wentworth Place, as an act of imposing chains upon himself, Keats gave the script of *Otho* a final polishing before submitting it to Drury Lane. This provided at least a shadow of an excuse for returning to his old quarters with Brown, though Keats's

---

* The complete letter is reproduced as Plate XIII.

part in the tragedy was still an official secret. In the hope of gaining a fair reading, the play was to be sent in signed only by Brown. Keats's plan for a new volume of poetry seems to have been shelved, perhaps when he learned of Taylor's reactions to his changes in *The Eve of St. Agnes*. Writing to Woodhouse in reply to his report on the revisions, Taylor had exploded against Keats's "preposterous conceit" and "stupid folly" in "flying in the face of all decency and discretion." "If he will not so far concede to my wishes as to leave the Passage as it originally stood," the publisher concluded grimly, "I must be content to admire his Poems with some other Imprint." Keats met this rejection by turning back to *King Stephen* after finishing the revision of *Otho*. Yet, after adding one more scene,[9] he laid it down in discouragement. Aimlessly he picked up his history books, searching Holinshed for another subject for a play, starting an index to his copy of Selden, then putting it aside after making two entries.[10]

One reason for his restlessness was the long-standing excuse of George's affairs. At the beginning of November he finally received the power of attorney for which he had been waiting since July. By this time also the lawyers had evidently got far enough along in their efforts to dismiss Mrs. Jennings' claim that the sale of George's stocks could begin. This was a tedious business, involving Keats in frequent trips to town, and a discouraging one as well. The market was very low, and Abbey kept advising him to wait. By this time Keats had run through Hessey's loan and had to borrow £30 from Haslam. When he told Abbey of his own financial straits, the tea-broker met him with another well-meant suggestion—that he turn bookseller. Meanwhile the weeks went by and no word came from Drury Lane. It was a vicious circle of frustration: he could not marry without money, he could not earn money except by writing, he found it harder and harder to write with all the anxiety pressing on him. The nautical imagery which keeps recurring in his letters this fall describes well his sense of helpless drifting, without a meridian, compass, or rudder, lost in a mist after the confident course he had been steering two months before. On November 12 he sent a letter to George, explaining the long delay in forwarding him his money, then burst out against the worries that had nagged at him ever since his unlucky promise of help to Haydon the previous December. "Nothing," he exclaimed, "could have in all its circumstances fallen out worse for me than the last year has done, or could be more damping to my poetical talent."

It is an extraordinary indictment of a year of extraordinary achievement—the year in which he produced almost all of his enduring poetry. Yet this November it seemed Keats's old hardihood in meeting adverse circumstance was flagging. His friends began noticing a change in him. He seemed to be losing his old gift of easy friendship, growing more secretive, given over to unpredictable moods. Severn on a visit to Hampstead found him veering between feverish gaiety and apathetic dejection. Despite his frequent trips to town on George's business, he could not summon up the energy to attend Hazlitt's new lectures at the Surrey Institution, and when Severn invited him to see his painting hung at the Royal Academy, Keats put him off with a joke. "I wish you to return the Compliment by going with me to see a Poem I have hung up for the Prize in the Lecture Room of the surry Institution. You had best," he added, "put me into your Cave of despair." Even Taylor was concerned. On November 15 he invited Keats to dinner and evidently questioned him about his work, for two days later Keats wrote him to say that he had decided not to publish any of the poems he now had ready. His one ambition when he felt ambitious—"I am sorry to say that is very seldom"— was to write "a few fine Plays"; and for that, he was now convinced, he would not be ready for some years yet. Nevertheless, he told Taylor, he planned to bring out a poem before long—"and that I hope to make a fine one."

The new work to which Keats referred so cryptically may have been *The Fall of Hyperion,* on which he was still working sporadically, or perhaps another project which Brown had encouraged him to start not long before. Brown, seeing Keats at closer hand than any of his friends, was the most troubled by his depression. After a chance conversation one day on an idea he had for "a comic faery poem," he urged Keats to try working it out himself as a relaxation from his other labours. The subject was the royal scandal which had been rocking the kingdom since August—the Regent's threat to bring Princess Caroline to trial for adultery; the style indicated was Brown's own blend of Byronic satire and Ariostonic fantasy. Brown suggested entitling this jest at royalty *The Cap and Bells;* Keats preferred to call it *The Jealousies.* Evidently the idea chimed with his mood at the moment, for he began turning out ten or twelve stanzas a morning, and soon his imagination began running away with the original theme. Here and there the poem showed flashes of a real satiric gift, as in the description of nightfall in the City end of his fairy capital—the one glimpse of Pancras Lane we get in all Keats's poetry:

> It was the time when wholesale houses close
> Their shutters with a moody sense of wealth,
> But retail dealers, diligent, let loose
> The gas (objected to on score of health),
> Convey'd in little solder'd pipes by stealth,
> And make it flare in many a brilliant form. . . .*

But the strained relations between the elfin monarch and his unwilling bride began to echo strangely of Byron's scandalous break with the unhappy Annabella Milbanke, while the courtiers took on suspicious resemblances to figures of literary London.[11] Brown had doubts about where the poem was really headed, but Keats assured him that all the confusions would be ironed out in the end and went gaily ahead.

Yet this new interest soon flagged. The fairy machinery began to creak and after eighty-eight stanzas broke down completely; but long before that the poem lost all sense of direction. For no apparent reason Keats began throwing in material from his earlier poems, chiefly *The Eve of St. Mark,* and his satire ends like a parody of the poet he had been. His elation gave way to another depression. Then Brown made an alarming discovery: Keats was taking laudanum. At once Brown intervened. Keats should know better than anyone else, he argued, that he risked ruining his health, and Keats agreed not to touch the drug again.

This is the point he had reached within a month or two of his engagement to Fanny; and the account Brown gives of him this fall is not the picture of a happy man. The paralysis of February and March was now compounded with the bitterness of August; and yet this time Keats was neither estranged nor separated from Fanny Brawne but living as her fiancé under the same roof with her. Part of his depression may have had a very simple cause—the

---

* This stanza should be set beside Shaw's comment on Keats as "the sort of youth who calls a window a casement": "If Keats had ever described a process so remote from Parnassus as the taking down and putting up of the shop shutters, he would have described them in terms of a radiant sunrise and a voluptuous sunset, with the red and green [apothecary] bottles as heavenly bodies and the medicines as Arabian Balsams" (*The John Keats Memorial Volume* [1921], p. 174).

physical strain which any man of twenty-four would have felt in his situation; another part, the blow to his pride which the situation itself represented. He had failed to achieve the decisive success by which he had hoped to claim Fanny as his own; he had broken a deeply considered resolution in returning to her; and he had accepted an indefinite postponement of their marriage for reasons of prudence and respectability which were antithetical to his whole nature. Yet none of this quite accounts for the form which his frustrated desire took at this time—a jealousy inflamed rather than allayed by Fanny's constant presence.

Here we are as much in the dark about their relations as any of Keats's friends. No record remains from the autumn of 1819, beyond two or three tortured poems, to suggest whether his jealousy had any real foundation. Indeed, the only clear insight we have into Fanny Brawne's nature and behaviour—for Keats's letters and poems hardly give us that—comes from the long series of letters she began writing to Fanny Keats a year later. These reveal her as a warmhearted, humorous, fair-minded, and straightforward young woman gifted with great control over her own feelings as well as insight into others'. It was the experiences of the coming year that were to prove her as a person; yet the girl of nineteen cannot have been fundamentally different from the young woman she became at twenty. Fanny at eighteen was no doubt a minx, as giddy and lighthearted as any girl of her position was expected to be; Fanny at nineteen had at least started to grow a character. Love is a great educator, and Fanny must have learned much from her first year of involvement with Keats. After the estrangement of the summer, when she might well have been reduced to bewilderment or mere injured vanity, she not only received him with new love but also succeeded in overcoming her mother's opposition to their engagement. It is hard to believe that she did not feel her commitment to Keats with all the intensity of her nature. Yet from the jealous outburst in the "Ode to Fanny," which he wrote probably this November or December,[12] it appears that Fanny continued going to dances even when Keats was not well enough to go himself. Perhaps this shows too great a love of pleasure on her part, or a lingering trace of girlish self-absorption; but with Keats's insistence that their engagement be kept a secret, Fanny can hardly have been expected to withdraw from Hampstead society. And the agonized mistrust of the "Ode to Fanny" seems to have sprung from one of those "imaginary grievances" which Keats admitted were more his torment than real ones. "He doesn't like anyone to look at or speak to her," Mrs. Dilke noted apprehensively around this time. At a word, a smile, a glance between Fanny and another man, his old tendency to "suspect everybody"—the lingering effect of his mother's faithlessness years before—returned with new virulence.

But this suspicion apparently concealed another more devastating jealousy, born of his sense of the contrast between Fanny's radiant health and his own failing energy, between her gaiety and the hatred of the world growing like a cancer within him. Behind his doubt of Fanny's fidelity was gathering a far more terrible uncertainty—the sensation of "dissolving" as a personality which he mentioned in his letter of October 13. In the sonnet to Fanny beginning "I cry your mercy—pity—love!" which he probably wrote soon after the "Ode," Keats cried out to be reassured not simply of her love but also of his own continuing identity:

> Yourself—your soul—in pity give me all,
>   Withhold no atom's atom or I die,
> Or living on perhaps, your wretched thrall,
>   Forget, in the mist of idle misery,
> Life's purposes,—the palate of my mind
> Losing its gust, and my ambition blind! *

Such reassurance—that he remain the person and the poet he was before disease had started to undermine his very existence—was impossible for anyone to give him, even Fanny herself, at least under the conditions of their engagement. Yet, from a few lines written one morning in the midst of his work on *The Cap and Bells*, it appears that it was now not love but life itself which he demanded of Fanny Brawne:

> This living hand, now warm and capable
> Of earnest grasping, would, if it were cold
> And in the icy silence of the tomb,
> So haunt thy days and chill thy dreaming nights
> That thou wouldst wish thine own heart dry of blood
> So in my veins red life might stream again,
> And thou be conscience-calm'd—see here it is—
> I hold it towards you.

---

* Following De Selincourt's reading of "without" as "withhold" in line 2 (*Poems of John Keats,* ed. Ernest de Selincourt, 5th ed., revised [1926], p.287).

Only one thing can finally explain this despair—that Keats was now convinced that he was succumbing to tuberculosis. After his brief spell of good health in September, all the feverish sensations of the summer returned with new force. As yet, it seems, there was no dramatic proof of illness requiring drastic remedy. Yet on October 20, the very day that he moved back to Wentworth Place, Keats dropped a hint of his fear in a letter to his sister. He announced that he had "left off animal food that my brains may never henceforth be in a greater mist than is theirs by nature." The explanation is a joke, of course. He could have had only one conceivable reason for giving up meat—that a milk and vegetable diet was recommended to bring down a consumptive fever.[13] A month or two later he had a warm greatcoat and a pair of thick shoes made for him at his doctor's advice. When these items are added to the list of all the steps he had taken during the previous year to shake off his sore throat—staying at home in wet or cold, refraining from swimming all summer long, leaving Shanklin for more healthful air, even considering a move to a warm climate—one suddenly realizes that Keats had followed every detail of the treatment then prescribed for the early stages of consumption.[14] In the four months after his return from Winchester he felt strong enough for only one visit to Walthamstow. One wonders whether his sudden abandonment in October of his plan to become a journalist was motivated not only by his longing to be near Fanny again but also by a premonition that he was not well enough to carry the plan through—though this makes it seem half-suicidal for him to have risked another winter in London, apparently against his doctor's recommendation.

As he felt himself drifting toward illness in spite of all his efforts, Keats's whole life became the kind of "day-night mare" he mentioned to Reynolds in August. Little of this is directly expressed in the few letters he wrote during this fall, except for one or two outbursts of macabre humour. Later, however, he told Rice that every day since the end of July had been a battle against a kind of angry gloom or passionate longing—"or if I turn'd to versify that acerbated the poison of either sensation." Yet all during the fall he kept up the struggle and even managed to make supreme poetry from his profoundest despair. Evening after evening, alone in his sitting room, Keats pored over the manuscript of *The Fall of Hyperion,* weaving fragments of the first version into the new poem, adding line to line with the greatest difficulty. Something of his own battle against inertia may be read in the dreamer's struggle to climb the altar steps in the very grip of death. As the poem goes on it turns from an indictment of his own earlier poetry into what seems a record of the almost superhuman effort it cost him to continue writing at all—as when the dreamer watches with Moneta the grief-stricken Thea kneeling before Saturn:

> Without stay or prop
> But my own weak mortality, I bore
> The load of this eternal quietude,
> The unchanging gloom, and the three fixed shapes
> Ponderous upon my senses a whole moon.
> For by my burning brain I measured sure
> Her silver seasons shedded on the night
> And ever day by day methought I grew
> More gaunt and ghostly—Oftentimes I pray'd
> Intense, that Death would take me from the vale
> And all its burthens—Gasping with despair
> Of change, hour after hour I curs'd myself.

With this consciousness, as crushing as that which made a god of Apollo, the dreamer has at last become a poet with "power of enormous ken, To see as a god sees"; what Keats himself seems to have struggled to express in these lines was the final realization of his own mortality.

Yet this revelation came to him in an image overpowering in its beauty as well as its terror, the most compelling image in all his poetry, in which Keats summoned up all that remained of his poetic energy. The veiled priestess promises the dreamer a vision of the primeval warfare between the Titans and the rebel gods— the vision which will make him a poet. Yet he is too overwhelmed to speak in his terror of her presence,

> And chiefly of the veils, that from her brow
> Hung pale, and curtain'd her in mysteries
> That made my heart too small to hold its blood.

Seeing this, Moneta parts her veils to reassure him:

> Then saw I a wan face,
> Not pin'd by human sorrows, but bright blanch'd
> By an immortal sickness which kills not;
> It works a constant change, which happy death
> Can put no end to; deathwards progressing
> To no death was that visage; it had pass'd

The lily and the snow; and beyond these
I must not think now, though I saw that face—
But for her eyes I should have fled away.
They held me back, with a benignant light,
Soft-mitigated by divinest lids
Half closed, and visionless entire they seem'd
Of all external things—they saw me not,
But in blank splendor beam'd like the mild moon,
Who comforts those she sees not, who knows not
What eyes are upward cast.

It is still the face of the Goddess of Memory, who has gazed for ages with infinite compassion on the sufferings of the world; it is also the Goddess of Melancholy whom he had met, still mysteriously veiled, in the Temple of Delight. Yet it is also the pale lady of the disastrous wedding feast, La Belle Dame, Auranthe with eyes "semi-shaded in white lids," Lamia staring at her lover without recognition—though now her visage is softened to benignance; it is the open-lidded star and the moon "floating through space with ever-loving eye" that presided over his earlier poetry, but whose gaze is now recognized at last and forever as sightless. In the end it is the face of death itself, in the most beautiful and terrifying aspect in which Keats had met it—the face of his dead mother, shrouded for her coffin. It is the ultimate image of Keats's poetry, that "one scene, one adventure, one picture" which Yeats called the image of man's secret life, which, "if he would but brood over it his life long," would bring him in the end to an understanding of all his experience.[15] It is the very foundation of Keats's poetic structure, the metamorphoses recurrent throughout his poetry of the "Beauty that must die" and the dead miraculously brought to life again; it suggests the driving force behind the metamorphoses of his own identity. The boy whose heroic assertiveness was formed in protest against his mother's faithlessness, the adolescent who became a doctor in half-conscious expiation of his failure to save her from death, the young man who first turned to poetry to escape the memory of her suffering but became a true poet in facing and accepting the burdens of his own identity—now at last in his fullest self he confronts the experience that so greatly shaped him and regards it with love and pity, not with terror. In his discovery of beauty in the face of death Keats emerged as the poet who is "Physician to all men." Here he finally proved himself capable of the poetry he had dreamed of writing; yet these were almost the last lines he ever wrote.

≫≫≪≪

In the second week of December, when Keats's hopes were at their lowest ebb, suddenly the tide turned. After almost two months' silence word came from Drury Lane: *Otho* was accepted. This must have lifted Keats high out of his gloom: at last he had proved to all his doubting friends that he could write an actable play. Still the news was only semi-good, for Elliston would not promise to put it on before next season. In thus accepting *Otho* for performance the following year, he unwittingly balked Keats's main purpose in writing it—to shore up his sinking reputation as a poet and bring in some money at once. Brown voted to withdraw the play and send it to Covent Garden instead, but Keats still objected. Elliston's postponement was not final; and, better yet, Kean had evidently been pleased with the role of Ludolph. So they decided to force the manager's hand by threatening to submit the script to Covent Garden unless he would commit himself to an immediate production. This was a gamble, but it seemed worth taking. Meanwhile Keats set to work revising the play once more, in case Elliston should call their bluff.

A few days later he had another stroke of luck. Taylor, evidently impressed by Elliston's approval of the tragedy, decided to take the risk of bringing out the new collection of poems after all. This time poet and publisher reached a satisfactory understanding. *Lamia* was to be included, substantially revised,[16] along with *Isabella* and *The Eve of St. Agnes,* which Keats agreed to let stand in its original and respectable version. The volume was scheduled for the spring, to coincide, if all went well, with the production of *Otho* at Drury Lane. Now the success which had eluded Keats for months looked near enough to grasp. And within the same week two other events seemed to show the tide running steadily in the right direction. The first was Severn's unexpected success. To his own surprise, and his friends' as well, his painting won the Gold Medal at the Academy. This was a special distinction, since in twelve previous competitions no painting had been judged good enough for the award. The second good omen was another proposition from Abbey, that Keats become a tea-broker. Keats, leaping to the conclusion that Abbey meant to offer him the brokerage of his own firm, replied that he might be interested. The work could be done with little trouble and good profit, he decided to himself, and he might be able to turn it over to George afterward. In the rush of his new confidence, everything seemed possible. Yet a few days later, when he questioned Abbey about the business, his enthusiasm veered round. Abbey described the responsibilities of the position in detail, and Keats realized it was more work than he had bargained for.

Christmas drew near in a season of close, muggy weather. Keats had promised his sister a holiday visit but had to renege in the end. His new greatcoat and thick shoes made no difference: after even a short walk in the cold his throat burned with fever. Moreover, he was hard at work on revisions and begrudged the time for the trip after so many weeks of idleness. For Christmas Day he accepted an invitation to dine at the Dilkes' with Brown, Reynolds, Rice, and Taylor. No doubt Mrs. Dilke and her five bachelors made as merry as ever, though Keats on this occasion remained in the background. Dilke and Brown got into an argument over fairy tales, with Dilke, the rationalist, maintaining they were nonsense that anyone could write, whereupon Brown challenged him to a contest. When their tales were read a few weeks later, however, Dilke's won the wager, and Brown had to pay up as promised—a punch-and-beefsteak supper for the whole set.

So far all seemed to be well. But shortly after Christmas two setbacks came in quick succession. First Elliston refused Brown's gambit. *Otho,* he decided at last, could not be put on this season. There was nothing to do but try patching it up again and submitting it to Covent Garden. This was a bitter disappointment. Keats tried hopefully to visualize Macready—whom he once thought "execrable"—playing Ludolph instead of Kean: "I am *not* afraid it will be damn'd in the Garden," he insisted, but he was whistling in the dark. The second disaster came in a letter from George, announcing that he was on his way back to England. He was close to bankruptcy and needed to raise capital immediately.[17] He had not even waited for Abbey's September remittance to reach him but had borrowed some money from a Kentucky neighbour and set out for London, determined to pry loose the remainder of his inheritance without further delay.

Hard on the heels of his own letter, George arrived at the end of the first week of January. The brothers' meeting must have been a strange one. In spite of their happiness at seeing each other again, the unspoken contrast of this reunion with their hopeful leavetaking a year and a half before must have sharpened in each of them an awareness that the other had changed. Even at first glance, there was a difference: George was balder, John thinner and less energetic. George had become disillusioned about America, but bragged endlessly about his baby girl, impervious to his friends' teasing; Keats, by contrast, was reserved and sarcastic as George had never known him. In each the experience of defeat was accentuating certain traits previously held in check: in George, a ruthless energy of purpose; in John, a moody secretiveness. Another irritant was a budding antagonism between George and Brown, who, it must have appeared to George, had taken his place in his brother's confidence. But for the first week these differences were submerged in a round of parties for the returned pioneer, including a family reunion at the Wylies', a trip to the theatre, dinner at Taylor's, "a pianoforte hop" at the Dilkes', a visit to Haslam's fiancée at Deptford, which Keats managed to shirk, and a gathering of their old set at Wentworth Place.

Yet George must have noticed that Keats showed none of his old gaiety at these occasions. At the Dilkes' he sat on the sidelines. bored or ill-tempered. "There was very little amusement in the room but a Scotchman to hate," he reported in a letter to Georgiana back in Kentucky. "Threepenny parties, halfpenny Dances," the theatre, even the company of his friends, now filled him with unconquerable ennui. "I know the different Styles of talk in different places: what subjects will be started how it will proceed, like an acted play, from the first to the last Act—If I go to Hunt's I run my head into many-times heard puns and music. To Haydon's worn out discourses of poetry and painting: the Miss Reynolds I am affraid to speak to for fear of some sickly reiteration of Phrase or Sentiment. At Dilkes I fall foul of Politics. All I can say is that standing at Charing cross and looking east west north and south I can see nothing but dullness." Then, with almost a pang of revulsion, he added, "I hope now soon to come to the time when I shall never be forc'd to walk through the City and hate as I walk."

With the parties over, the brothers turned to business, and at once it became clear how far apart they had drifted. What had been a tangle in their finances two years ago was now a hopeless snarl of miscalculations and misunderstandings. George evidently succeeded in cutting through the legal difficulties which Keats had found impenetrable, for he persuaded Abbey to give him not only the rest of his own inheritance but his share of Tom's estate as well—something around £300. But he needed more than this and therefore asked Keats to lend him the money which he was to inherit from Tom.[18] On the surface, George's request was reasonable. Keats still had *Otho* to count on, which he had told George would be "a bank" to him if it were produced, and *The Cap and Bells,* which all his friends believed would score a great success when finished, even if the new volume of poems did not.[19] George himself was confident that he could repay at least half of the loan by the next summer. But Keats was caught in a dilemma. He had offered to help George at a time when he had no hope of marrying Fanny and when his health seemed good enough for him to turn to medicine or even journalism if he failed with poetry. Now all this was changed. He was gloomy about *Otho*'s prospects at Covent Garden; he was in debt to several of his friends; he could not tell George of his fears for his health, and he would not tell him of his commitment to Fanny Brawne. Even this put another barrier between them, for George, sensing some strain in Keats's behaviour toward Fanny, accepted the Reynoldses' opinion of her as "an artful, bad-hearted girl." But if Keats could no longer confide in his brother as he used to do, he could not yet break a promise. With the superior strength of insensitivity, George had pinned him to the ground, as he had done time and again in their school-days. Only to Fanny could Keats hint at his resentment, remarking that "having a family to provide for makes a man selfish." [20]

The long journal-letter to Georgiana which he started during George's visit gives only an intimation of this conflict. It is the wittiest letter Keats ever wrote, affectionate and full of fun—"and if Scandal happens to be fun," he noted, "that is no fault of ours." Georgiana's disenchantment with America seems to have drawn them closer together. To prove that London was as dull as Louisville could possibly be, he drew a gallery of satirical sketches of their acquaintance, lit up with flashes of Shandean nonsense. Haslam's fiancée at Deptford, for instance, filled him with something livelier than mere ennui—a magnetic repulsion that drove him metaphorically across the whole map of southeastern England. He dashed off a comparison of the three greatest wits of his acquaint-ance—Rice, Reynolds, and Richards—in a parody of Hazlitt's "fine discriminating criticism" of Swift, Voltaire, and Rabelais which had delighted him two winters ago, then capped it with an account of the three greatest bores he knew, then blew it all up with an anatomy of nonsense stretching around the globe. "Upon the whole I dislike Mankind," he concluded; "whatever people on the other side of the question may advance they cannot deny that they are always surprised at hearing of a good action and never of a bad one." "Thank God," he said, "there are a great many who will sacrifice their worldly interest for a friend: I wish there were more who would sacrifice their passions. The worst of Men are those whose self interests are their passion—the next those whose passions are their self-interest." It is a curious distinction. One wonders whom Keats would have chosen to illustrate the first class. The second class seems to be as near as he could come to criticizing George to his sister-in-law.

So Keats began to smoulder with suppressed rage at the world; but only once during these weeks did he let it blaze out. One afternoon he was invited to dine in town at Hilton's, the painter and friend of Taylor. The party was made up mostly of other painters, and the talk soon turned to the recent Academy award of the Gold Medal. None of the Academy set had ever heard of Severn before, and none of them liked his painting. The general critical comment, as a matter of fact, had been fairly scathing: Haydon's own magazine, *The Annals of the Fine Arts,* described it as a "humble mediocrity." One of Hilton's guests came up with the tale that Severn was an elderly incompetent who had tried for the prize so many times that the council gave it to him in the end out of pity. Keats sat glowering while the others laughed at the story, waiting for Hilton to deny it. But Hilton said nothing. Keats then rose from his seat in one of those rages that made him look like a tall man. It was a lie, he shouted. Severn was a young painter who had never tried for the prize before; he knew the man himself and admired the painting. And he would not sit at the same table with men willing to believe such falsehoods. Then he stalked out of the house.[21]

So January passed and George's visit drew to a close. On the twenty-eighth Keats dashed off one last page to Georgiana before posting his letter in a hurry to catch up with George, who had left

London for Liverpool at six that morning. This postscript adds a few jokes and gives one piece of news. Keats was planning once again to move away from Hampstead into the country. Whether it was the state of his pockets or of his health that persuaded him, he gave no hint, nor did he say anything of George's departure. That had been no joking matter. George, who set out in too great a hurry to say good-bye to Fanny in Walthamstow, carried with him the remainder of his brother's inheritance—all except a few pounds to tide Keats over till he started repaying the loan. His visit had been a success, for he managed to raise some £700 in all. Yet, as he said good-bye, George wondered whether he should have pressed his brother so hard. He tried to reassure himself out loud: after all, John had many friends to fall back on. His words must have echoed ironically in Keats's ears, for they were the very reassurance he had given George in his letter from Winchester. They parted at the inn-yard in the chilly gloom of the January morning, and Keats returned to Hampstead with the anger swelling inside him. When at last he reached Wentworth Place he pulled out of his pocket a bundle of notes and handed it to Brown. It was all the money he had left in the world. Brown counted it over at once: it came to £60. After subtracting his borrowings and unpaid bills, Keats was worse than penniless: George had left him £20 in debt.[22]

"Brown—he ought not to have asked me." So Brown reported Keats's words—his first open criticism of his brother.[23] In astonishment, Brown asked Keats why he had agreed to the loan. The story of his unlucky promise to George came out. Brown was indignant that Keats had kept the promise a secret from him, but Keats merely replied that he knew Brown would have opposed the loan if he had told him about it. It was too late to argue, but it was time enough to regret Keats's act. A few days later [24] *Otho* was sent back from Covent Garden with a note of rejection in a boy's handwriting. Brown suspected that the manuscript had not even been opened. Now there was nothing to hope from the tragedy for the time being at least—and thus little from the new volume of poems.

A few days after George's departure a long spell of cold snowy weather broke and a thaw set in. On February 3 Keats went into town for the day without his greatcoat, the weather had turned so warm. When he came to take the evening coach back to Hampstead, it was frosty again. As usual, he could afford only an outside seat, and, riding back full against the wind, he was chilled to the bone. All day long he had felt fevered; now, as he walked down Pond Street, his head whirled. When Brown saw him come staggering into Wentworth Place he thought at first that Keats was drunk. At second glance he saw he was seriously ill, flushed and trembling, hardly able to speak. Immediately Brown told him to go to bed. As Keats groped his way up the cold staircase and climbed into bed, a fit of coughing seized him. Brown, who followed him with a glass of spirits, heard him gasp, "That is blood from my mouth."

As Brown hurried to his side, Keats hitched himself up on the pillows and told him to bring the candle close. In the wan circle of light Brown saw a spot of blood on the sheet, bright red against the white. Keats muttered, "This is unfortunate." Then, according to Brown's account, he looked very steadily up into his friend's face and said, "I know the colour of that blood. It's arterial blood. There's no mistaking that colour." As calmly as he could, he added, "That blood is my death-warrant. I must die."

➤➤➤———————————————————————⧫⧫⧫

Chapter Thirteen

A Wrecked Life

I T had come at last, the proof of the suspicion that had been
growing within him for months. And when it came, his only
thought was of Fanny Brawne. The blood rushed up in his lungs
so violently that for a few minutes he felt almost suffocated; as
it seethed within him, he was sure he was dying and could think
only that if he died he lost Fanny forever. Slowly the tide ebbed,
and still he thought of her. The first minute he could leave him,
Brown ran for Mr. Rodd, the Hampstead surgeon, and, according
to the best medical practice of the day, Keats was bled. Hour after
hour he lay awake, while Brown watched anxiously by his bedside;
then toward morning he fell asleep at last. The next day his first
request was to see Fanny. Brown told him that she had gone to
town. Keats insisted on writing a note to send as soon as she returned, begging her to come to see him. The hours crawled by.
All afternoon Keats lay straining for a glimpse of the London
coach through the window or studying the pattern of the bed
curtains. At last Brown admitted he had been telling a tale: the
Brawnes had been at home all the time.

One hopes that Fanny was allowed to come that evening, as
she did almost every day in the weeks that followed. Her visit at
the end of the afternoon became the centre of his day, her existence his reason for fighting his way back to health. At first he made
good progress. On February 6, the third day after the attack, he
was well enough to receive a few visitors and sit up to read the
papers—full of news of the death of George III—and write a
letter to his sister. His own illness filled him with new anxiety for

her. He dropped a hint of this to Fanny Brawne, "My Sister would be glad of my company a little longer"; but to Fanny herself he could speak only of his concern for her health. "You must be careful always to wear warm cloathing not only in frost but in a Thaw," he warned her. He made light of his own illness, blaming it on the treacherous weather; then, for lack of news, described the view out of his window. "The half built houses opposite us stand just as they were and seem dying of old age before they are brought up. The grass looks very dingy, the Celery is all gone, and there is nothing to enliven one but a few Cabbage Staks that seem fix'd on the superanuated List." Two days later he was well enough to go downstairs, supported by Brown and their Irish housekeeper, to sit wrapped up in blankets on the sofa in the front parlour. In high spirits, he wrote Fanny again, sketching the passers-by: a pot-boy with the one-o'clock beer, colliers and brick-makers and gipsies, a fellow with a wooden clock under his arm, the old French emigrant "whith his hands joined behind on his hips, and his face full of political schemes," and two old ladies from Well Walk, coaxing their fat little dog along with an ivory-tipped cane.

Like most invalids in the first days of recovery, he saw every-thing around him shining with a new light. "How astonishingly does the chance of leaving the world impress a sense of its natural beauties on us," he wrote to Rice on the fourteenth. "Like poor Falstaff, though I do not babble, I think of green fields. I muse with the greatest affection on every flower I have known from my infancy—their shapes and coulours are as new to me as if I had just created them with a superhuman fancy." Rice had written Keats to warn him against the "haunting and deformed thoughts and feelings" that often assailed him after one of his own relapses. Yet to Keats his illness seemed to have the opposite effect. "As far as I can judge in so short a time," he wrote, "it has relieved my Mind of a load of deceptive thoughts and images and makes me perceive things in a truer light." There can be no doubt that he was thinking of Fanny Brawne. The brooding jealousies of the previous months had lifted like a mist. For the time being he could demand of her only what she could fully and gladly give— a wave of her hand from the garden, a half-hour of chatter at the end of the afternoon, a kiss at parting, a good-night note each evening before he slept. But for Fanny also the shock of his illness must have marked the end of thoughtless girlhood at last and the start of her own soul-making. For weeks she refused to leave Wentworth Place, in order to be there whenever he wanted her. Brown, jealous of his position as head nurse, objected to her calls and had them cut down to a few minutes at a time; but still she stood by. The summer before, Keats remembered, she had complained that he loved her only for her beauty; now he could prove he had other reasons. "Do not I see a heart naturally furnish'd with wings imprison itself with me?" She convinced him of her love all over again by this tribute; as he exclaimed, "I could build an Altar to you for it."

Yet after the first week his recovery slowed down to a discouraging pace. On the tenth the morning was mild enough for a walk in the garden; but this experiment was not repeated for quite a while. For one thing, the weather turned cold and raw again; for another, his strength was not returning at the rate he hoped. Keats blamed it on the diet ordered for him, so little food that "a mouse would starve upon it." Then the medicine he was taking began to set his nerves on edge. Brown, while sitting with Keats, amused himself by copying grotesque heads from his collection of Hogarth prints; and one of these—"a damn'd melancholy picture" of a Methodist meeting—gave Keats "a psalm singing nightmare" which made him almost faint away in his sleep. Yet when Mr. Rodd examined him at the end of the second week he found no signs of injury to the lungs. "Quietness of mind and fine weather," he told his patient, were all he needed to cure him.

To an extent this prescription was right, for there is little doubt that Keat's first haemorrhage had been brought on largely by the crisis of his anger against George.[1] Yet, as he told Fanny, his mind had always been "the most discontented and restless one that ever was put into a body too small for it." And knowing as much about his disease as his doctor did, and how little could really be done for it, he could not be cheered by Rodd's encouragement. As the weeks went by and the weight and tightness in his chest did not lift, he became certain that his lungs had been damaged. As for quietness of mind, he was now ordered to give up the two things that mattered most in the world—poetry and his love. "My dearest Girl," he wrote to Fanny in dejection, "According to all appearances I am to be separated from you as much as possible. I am reccommended not even to read poetry much less write it. I wish

I had even a little hope. I cannot say forget me—but I would mention that there are impossibilities in the world."

This oblique reference to "impossibilities" was as close as he could come to saying what he realized must be said, once the first shock of his illness had passed. He must release Fanny from their engagement. At this her love and pride and suspicion flared up all at once. Evidently she sensed this was not so much Keats's idea as someone else's suggestion; but she also took Keats's gesture of renunciation half childishly as a rejection. "My dearest Girl," he replied in distress, "how could it ever have been my wish to forget you? The utmost stretch my mind has been capable of was to endeavour to forget you for your own sake. Believe too my Love that our friends think and speak for the best, and if their best is not our best it is not their fault." Who these friends were is a guess—perhaps Brown or possibly Reynolds, who came to see Keats around this time. Fanny evidently accepted his explanation and promised him she would wait for as long as was necessary. This reassurance was "as much a wonder to me as a delight," [2] he told her, not quite able to believe it entirely. Soon afterward she gave him a ring, engraved in true-love style with both their names inside, and for a day he was as happy as illness would let him be. "Health is my expected heaven," he wrote her, "and you are the Houri—this word I believe is both singular and plural—if only plural, never mind—you are a thousand of them."

Yet there was one thought of surpassing bitterness that even the assurance of Fanny's love could not drive from Keats's mind. He had lost his gamble against time; he was now convinced that he had failed to win the immortality as a poet on which he had staked his whole life. The new volume of poems was still not ready to send off to the printer; but even if he got back his strength to complete the revisions, it would be a poor thing beside what he had aimed at achieving. For with *Hyperion* still only half started, all the work of the last two years went for nothing. "I must make myself as good a Philosopher as possible," he told Fanny, and this conviction of failure called out all his stoicism. Night after night he lay awake, looking back over his life and trying to sum it up in some fashion he could accept. " 'If I should die,' said I to myself, 'I have left no immortal work behind me—nothing to make my friends proud of my memory—but I have lov'd the principle of beauty in all things, and if I had had time I would have made myself remember'd.' " It was a noble assertion of identity, a moment of recognition such as is demanded of the great tragic hero in his hour of defeat. Yet in the same breath Keats asked Fanny to forgive him for thinking of fame instead of herself alone, and the words of Milton nerving himself against the possibility of an early death flashed across his memory. "Thoughts like these," he wrote her, "came very feebly whilst I was in health and every pulse beat for you—now you divide with this (may *I* say it?) 'last infirmity of noble minds' all my reflection."

So February went by, a silent battle for peace of mind waged amid the trivialities of an invalid existence. Friends came out from London to call; Hampstead ladies showered him with jam and black currant jelly, which he spilled on Brown's Ben Jonson; Fanny kept him stocked with oranges. Hunt, who had recently moved to nearby Kentish Town, walked over several times, bringing with him the fashionable poet "Barry Cornwall"—Bryan Waller Procter, who brought Keats his latest books. Keats must have been ironically entertained by his *Sicilian Story*, for Procter had also taken Hazlitt's recommendation and retold the tale of Isabella and her pot of basil in a sentimental and decorous version that immediately became popular. His milksop diet of reading also included some of Rousseau's correspondence with lady friends, which it amused him to compare with his own and Fanny's. Otherwise there was little more to mark one day from another than the first thrush singing over the fields, the news of Cobbett's campaign for election to Parliament, an occasional good night's sleep, and a glimpse of Fanny as she went walking over the Heath.

Early in March he took an unexpected turn for the worse. His rapid pulse and starvation diet combined to bring on an attack of palpitations which left him so shaken that for several days he could not endure the sound of an unexpected voice or the sight of a newly arrived letter. On March 8 Mr. Rodd decided to call in Dr. Robert Bree from London for consultation. Bree was a Fellow of the Royal College of Physicians, one of the country's leading respiratory specialists, and doctor to one of the royal dukes. Yet after examining Keats he merely repeated Rodd's verdict that there was "no pulmonary affection and no organic defect whatever" and told Keats that his disease was all "on his mind." He cautioned him against worrying and recommended a more robust diet as well as a little fresh air and exercise. Accordingly Keats was walking in the garden a few days later and picking up the revision of his poems. On the fourteenth he made an ill-advised trip into town to dine with Taylor, and the next day the palpitations returned. More than a week later he was still too upset to write more than a scrap of a letter to his sister. He could not trust Bree's diagnosis. To Fanny Brawne he wrote, "God alone knows whether I am destined to taste of happiness with you: at all events I myself know thus much, that I consider it no mean Happiness to have lov'd you thus far—if it is to be no further I shall not be unthankful—if I am to recover, the day of my recovery shall see me by your side from which nothing shall separate me."

But Brown, hovering in the background, took Dr. Bree's pronouncement at face value. Two days after the physician's visit, he wrote jubilantly to Taylor that Keats was now "perfectly out of danger"—even though he was still too nervous to read his mail—and began talking with Keats about their making a trip to Hampshire together. With the unconscious insensitivity of many robust people, Brown seemed unwilling to admit that Keats was seriously ill. It was unfortunate, this illness, but Brown was also beginning to find it inconvenient. To his credit it must be said that he had nursed Keats faithfully for over a month; but now, as he began to think ahead to the summer, he must have wondered how much more would be required of him. Furthermore, he had problems of his own to concern him—those pleasures which, as Keats had told him in September, it was his duty to procure while still in the prime of life. This pursuit of duty was bearing unexpected fruit, for sometime during the autumn Abby, the Irish housekeeper, had become pregnant.

Just how much of a problem this posed to Brown is uncertain. He had been taken with Abby's lively humour and robust good looks, but he apparently had no intention of becoming involved with her. In his eyes a mistress was as much of an encumbrance as a wife,[3] and he wanted neither; besides, Abby was an ignorant peasant girl and a fanatical Catholic. Nor did Brown seem at this point to have any interest in a child as such, even though years later the son himself testified that Brown had deliberately seduced Abby "for the sake of the offspring." [4] If this story is true, as seems doubtful, Brown's way of providing himself with an heir is curious, to say the least. It was an age in which illegitimacy was an accepted fact of life, and Keats's comment on Severn's by-blow shows that he and his friends took it in their stride. Brown seems to have been concerned this spring mainly with getting Abby out of sight to bear her child and with being at a safe distance himself when the time came.[5] For this he must convince Keats that he was getting well—well enough, at least, to spend the summer away from Wentworth Place, for Brown also needed the money which his summer rental always brought in.

Keats's own reaction to Brown's situation is also uncertain. Several months later the thought of Brown living next door to Fanny "with his indecencies" became too bitter for him to stomach; but during the spring his loyalty to Brown remained unshaken. When Brown learned from Sam Brawne, Fanny's brother, that a neighbour of theirs was spreading malicious gossip about his behaviour in another matter, Keats begged Fanny to tell him what she had heard, for he felt "the least attaint on the disinterested character of Brown very deeply." Yet for whatever cause, the old tension between Brown and Fanny began to be felt again. Between Brown's scorn of women in general or jealousy of Fanny in particular and Fanny's habit of rising gaily to every occasion, Keats was caught once more in an exacerbating conflict. In his own depressed moods, the sight of Fanny good-humouredly meeting Brown's over-hearty badinage began to rasp his nerves unendurably. "To see you happy and in high spirits is a great consolation to me," he wrote with unexpected coolness one day; "still let me believe that you are not half so happy as my restoration would make you." The best he could do was try to keep them apart; so one morning he stiffly suggested to Fanny that she wait till Brown went out before coming to see him. She took this as a reproach, and once again he capitulated in anguish. "Sweetest Fanny," he wrote back, "You fear, sometimes, I do not love you so much as you wish? My dear Girl I love you ever and ever and without reserve. In every way—even my jealousies have been agonies of Love. I have vex'd you too much. But for Love! Can I help it?"[6] She found this argument unanswerable, but for several weeks they kept up the stratagem: she waited till she saw Brown disappearing down the lane, then slipped next door for her visit.

Toward the end of March it seemed Keats had reached firm ground at last. Day by day his chest felt freer, his pulse steadier;

his short walks in the garden became more regular. His spirits picked up; he began to suspect that he had worried too much about his illness. Now one visit with Fanny a day was not enough. "I imagine you now sitting in your new black dress which I like so much," he wrote at the end of one afternoon, "and if I were a little less selfish and more enthusiastic I should run round and surprise you with a knock at the door. I fear I am too prudent for a dying kind of Lover. Yet, there is a great difference between going off in warm blood like Romeo, and making one's exit like a frog in a frost." Best of all, perhaps, he could now pick up his poems where he had left off revising them. He still had to take it slowly, but the task heartened him as nothing else could do. "Let me have another oportunity of years before me," he wrote, "and I will not die without being remember'd."

On the twenty-fifth he made his first public appearance at a long-awaited occasion. Haydon had at last finished "Christ's Triumphal Entry into Jerusalem" and was exhibiting it, complete with a frame weighing six hundred pounds, at the Egyptian Hall. The word had already got around that the painting was a masterpiece; and on the afternoon of the opening Piccadilly was blocked with carriages. Ministers, ambassadors, bishops, beauties, all crowded into the great hall to see and be seen. For a while the verdict was uncertain. The weak yet unconventional portrayal of Christ riding an ass puzzled some and displeased others. One sardonic Academician, James Northcote, quipped, "Mr. Haydon, the ass is the Saviour of your picture." But the day was saved for Haydon when Mrs. Siddons swept in at her most majestic. Suddenly silencing the room, she stared at the painting for a minute, then "in her solemn and sublime tone" declared, "It is perfect!" [7] From this moment Haydon's fame was secure, and for a while his fortunes too: the exhibition brought him almost £1800. Keats, caught in the kind of crowd he hated most, retreated to a corner, where he found Hazlitt, who was present as art critic for *The Edinburgh Review*. It was the first time in months that they had seen each other, and for Keats the day was made.

A few days later, at Keats's request, Brown wrote to George, whom Keats had decided not to send any news of his illness till it could be good news. Brown had reasons of his own for pretending that Keats was making better progress than he was, and gave George far too rosy a picture of his brother's health—that he was eating, drinking, and sleeping as well as ever and walking five miles without fatigue. This letter was not written at Keats's dictation, for it mentioned a matter about which he knew nothing. Dr. Bree had recommended that Keats be sent to Italy in the fall. This was a standard prescription for English consumptives, but with Keats's finances in the state they were, it also posed a problem. So Brown reminded George of his promise to repay his brother £200 by the summer. It is odd, however, that he did not discuss the matter with Keats himself.[8] The inference seems plain—that Brown suspected Keats would ask him to go to Italy with him, and that he had no intention of doing so. Accordingly he kept the proposal a secret and proceeded with his own plans.

So April started for Keats with the prospect of returning health, of walks on the Heath with Fanny and a visit to his sister in Walthamstow. He could work more steadily now at preparing his poems for the press. The weather turned fine; his spirits rose; then suddenly the spring clouded over. Brown announced that he must rent his house again and had found a tenant to take it from early May to late October. With his usual single-mindedness, he had decided to go on another walking trip in Scotland for the summer, leaving Abby to bear her child in July alone in London, and Keats to fend for himself through the summer. Though Keats could not have been completely unprepared for this announcement, he was badly shaken by it nevertheless. He realized he could not ask Brown to stay on in Hampstead for his sake, but he could not talk or even think of leaving Wentworth Place without becoming unbearably anxious. Yet his depression merely confirmed the doctor's opinion that he needed a change of scene—perhaps the voyage up to Scotland with Brown and then back. "The Doctor assures me," he wrote gloomily to his sister on April 21, "that there is nothing the matter with me except nervous irritability and a general weakness of the whole system which has proceeded from my anxiety of mind of late years and the too great excitement of poetry—Mr Brown is going to Scotland by the Smack, and I am advised for change of exercise and air to accompany him. They tell me," he added, "I must study lines and tangents and squares and circles to put a little Ballast into my mind."

Geometry and sea air—it is a pitiful prescription. Yet Keats considered the voyage with Brown for over a week before deciding he could not bear so great a separation from Hampstead. As he told his sister, he was endeavouring to avoid all melancholy or anxious thoughts as "pernicious to health." He tried not to think of George, who had not written him since his good-bye note from Liverpool. But he could not help worrying about Fanny in her imprisonment at the Abbeys'. They had forbidden her to visit him all spring; they made her give away her spaniel and kept her short of pocket-money, then nagged at her for ingratitude. Mrs. Abbey even hinted that she was living on their charity, a remark which drove Fanny to ask Keats to look into her financial affairs. He sent her some money which he could hardly spare, for he was now running hopelessly into debt. On paying his doctors' bills and settling accounts with Brown at the beginning of May, Keats found his obligations added up to £25 more than he possessed— not including his previous debts or allowing for the immediate future.[9] As a last service to his friend before leaving, Brown borrowed £50 at interest from his lawyer to tide Keats over the summer. On May 6 Keats sailed with him down the Thames as far as Gravesend, then got off the Smack with the pilot. No doubt Brown was as jocular as ever as they said good-bye, for he urged Keats to finish *The Cap and Bells;* Keats was more constrained. One wonders whether it occurred to either man that he might not see the other again.

⇨⇨ ⇦⇦

Keats had decided to spend the summer in Kentish Town, a pleasant little village on the edge of the Heath about two miles from Hampstead. This was close enough for frequent visits to and from Wentworth Place, though one wonders why he did not choose lodgings in Hampstead, where he could see Fanny every day. Still, in Kentish Town he would have Hunt as a neighbour. The spring had brought a renewal of their friendship, on terms very different from the old uneasy relationship of master and disciple. Keats on his side had grown far beyond the intolerance of untried youth for the failures of its elders. He had learned something of defeat and betrayal since his break with Hunt, and could value the older man's warmth and generosity more truly than before. Hunt was still struggling cheerfully under the burdens of debt, poor health, a large family, and an ailing wife. But he now gladly accepted Keats as an equal and evidently suspected nothing

of the younger man's battle against his domination three years
before. As a gesture of friendship Keats gave him some of the
shorter poems which he had not included in his new volume, and
Hunt immediately published "La Belle Dame" in his new literary
weekly *The Indicator*. And it was Hunt who found lodgings for
Keats in May, a set of quiet, airy rooms in Wesleyan Place, only
a few doors from his own house in Mortimer Terrace.

Here Keats was comfortable enough, though hardly happy, and
May went by without event. "I am well enough to extract much
more pleasure than pain out of the summer, even though I should
get no better," he wrote Brown after moving into his new quarters.
Reading the proofs of the new volume kept him busy for a while.
He did not yet feel equal to going ahead with *The Cap and Bells*,
however—"being willing," as he explained, "in case of a relapse,
to have nothing to reproach myself with." Still he was well enough
to go walking alone, though unexpected showers kept him dodging from shelter to shelter. Several times he journeyed into town
to visit friends, and for daily companionship he could always drop
in at Hunt's. There he would have found the same set-tos of
punning and music as before, the same picnics on the Heath complete with cold ham, salad, ginger beer, children, and poetry.
Though he remained a rather silent spectator on these occasions,
they kept him from real loneliness. At Hunt's too he found a
shelf of the Waverley Novels, which provided him with hours of
good reading. And one especially fine summer afternoon Hunt's
stockbroker friend Horace Smith invited him to dinner at his
country house in Fulham with his literary cronies. They ate early,
sitting out under the trees, and—perhaps in honour of Keats's
forthcoming book—drank a dozen bottles of his favourite Château
Margaux.

Yet slowly isolation from Fanny began to have its poisonous
effect on Keats again. At the end of his occasional visits to Hampstead he found parting from her almost more than he could bear.
Day after day, as May wore into June, he remained alone in his
rooms, thinking back over the happiness they had shared, racked
with longing for what was still denied him. "I see you come down
in the morning," he wrote her, "I see you meet me at the Window
—I see every thing over again eternally that I ever have seen."
For one whole day he was haunted by a memory of Fanny in a
moment of triumph, wearing a shepherdess dress at some costume

ball. Yet these images led inexorably to others—Fanny as gay and brilliant as ever in his absence, beautiful to other eyes than his own. Without the daily reassurance of her presence, she became to him more and more the projected image of his old irrational suspicion of the beloved woman. Three months before, he had begged her not to remain at home for his sake; now the news that she had gone to a party at the Dilkes' filled him with savage possessiveness. "Do not live as if I was not existing," he burst out when he learned she had gone into town alone, *"promise me you will not for some time, till I get better."* It was unreasonable, he knew; but he could be convinced of her love only if she was as unhappy as he. "You must be so if you love me—upon my Soul I can be contented with nothing else," he stormed. "If you can smile in peoples faces, and wish them to admire you *now,* you never have nor ever will love me. You must be mine to die upon the rack if I want you."

It was a terrible letter, and one which can be understood only as the outcry of a man of twenty-four against the slow approach of death. He was in a state of mind, as he wrote his sister, that "makes one envy Scavengers and Cinder-sifters." As week after week dragged by with no further improvement in his health, Keats began to lose faith—in his own eventual recovery, in Fanny's love if he should recover, even in a life after death if he should not. This last doubt was to grow more terrifying as the months went by. "I long to believe in immortality," he wrote Fanny in despair in mid-June. "I shall never be able to bid you an entire farewell. If I am destined to be happy with you here— how short is the longest Life—I wish to believe in immortality— I wish to live with you for ever." This was an anguish which Fanny, with her simple religious faith, could understand even less than his jealous rages. Stunned by his previous letter, she had written back to protest that he had wronged her "in word thought and deed." He replied in a rush of remorse: "If I have been cruel and injust I swear my love has ever been greater than my cruelty which lasts but a minute whereas my Love come what will shall last for ever. Do muse it over again and see into my heart," he added; "my Love to you is 'true as truth's simplicity and simpler than the infancy of truth.' "

Yet it was not as simple as all that; for, in echoing the words of Shakespeare's Troilus, Keats implied again the suspicion which, in February, he told her he had "dismissed utterly"—"of you being a little inclined to the Cressid." His copy of Shakespeare's Sonnets gives a revealing glimpse into his mind during these lonely weeks, for he was rereading them with the same brooding intensity with which he had read and marked his *Anatomy of Melancholy* the autumn before. The theme of all his markings now was "the pangs of dispriz'd love"—remorse, reproach, doubt, jealousy, weariness, despair, all the welter of his feelings about Fanny:

> If that be fair whereon my false eyes dote,
>   What means the world to say it is not so?
> If it be not, then love doth well denote
>   Love's eye is not so true as all men's: no,
> How can it? O, how can Love's eye be true,
>   That is so vex'd with watching and with tears? . . .*

And in the turmoil of his distrust of Fanny he began to be consumed with another suspicion—that his friends were spying on their attachment and trying to come between them. It is possible that Mrs. Dilke began inviting Fanny to parties in town out of real concern for her future; it is likely that the Reynolds girls were discussing their affairs behind his back. Whatever happened, Keats was driven to fury. "My friends laugh at you!" he exploded. "I know some of them—when I know them all I shall never think of them again as friends or even acquaintance." His long-smouldering resentment against the Reynolds girls—"these Laughers, who do not like you, who envy you for your Beauty, who were plying me with disencouragements with respect to you eternally"— now flamed out in the open. "Do not let my name ever pass between you and those laughers," he begged Fanny. "Your name never passes my Lips—do not let mine pass yours."

This suspicion evidently provoked some kind of outburst at the Dilkes' on one of his visits around the middle of June. Writing to Brown shortly afterward, Keats alluded to the incident but refused to apologize for it.[10] "I know that they are more happy and comfortable than I am; therefore why should I trouble myself about it? I foresee I shall know very few people in the course of a year or two," he commented acidly. Going on to tell Brown about an exhibition of portraits he had recently seen in Pall Mall, he betrayed his mood by picking out only the unpleasant faces to

---

* Sonnet CXLVIII, marked by Keats in his copy of Shakespeare's *Poetical Works*, in the Keats House at Hampstead.

describe. "There is James the first,—whose appearance would disgrace a 'Society for the suppression of women;' there is old Lord Burleigh, who has the appearance of a Pharisee just rebuffed by a gospel bon-mot. Then, there is George the second, very like an unintellectual Voltaire, troubled with the gout and a bad temper." To Brown himself he was curiously cool in his letter, ending with a brusque "Good morning to you" very different from his usual affectionate closing. But he gave one clue to what was going on in his mind: "My book is coming out with very low hopes, though not spirits on my part. This shall be my last trial; not succeeding, I shall try what I can do in the Apothecary line."

The new volume was due to appear at last toward the end of June, and already he was convinced it would fail. Taylor kept fretting over the conclusion of *Lamia* and asking Keats to bowdlerize it here and there; [11] he also insisted on including *Hyperion* —the two and a half books of the original version. Keats had protested vehemently against printing the poem in its unfinished state, but without success. Now, he realized, the work by which he had hoped to be remembered would stand forever as an abortive fragment, falling even further short of his intentions than *Endymion*. And, try as he might, he could not keep from worrying about the reviews to come. On June 22, the day before the book was expected to appear, a note arrived from his sister, begging him to come see her. Evidently her affairs at the Abbeys' had reached a crisis. Keats started out at once but turned back a few minutes later. He had begun to cough again, and his mouth was filled with the rusty taste of blood.

It was not a haemorrhage but only a premonition of one that pulled him up short. He returned to his rooms to spend the rest of the day alone. At the end of the afternoon he pulled himself together to go to the Hunts' for tea, where he found they had guests —a Mr. and Mrs. William Gisborne, friends of the Shelleys in Italy. Keats said nothing of his attack but remained pale and silent while the conversation ran on. The talk soon turned to singing, an interest which Mrs. Gisborne shared with Hunt. She described the great Italian tenor Farinelli, who had the art of holding a note almost indefinitely while taking imperceptible breaths. At this Keats was evidently overwhelmed by his recurrent nightmare of suffocation. In a voice so low he could hardly be heard, he observed that it must be as painful to listen to this prolonged note as to wait for a diver who has disappeared into the depths of the sea to emerge above the surface at last. Mrs. Gisborne at first had not believed that this insignificant-looking young man was the author of *Endymion;* but she was so struck by this remark that she wrote it down in her journal that night. Tea over, Keats dragged himself back to his lonely rooms, and there, a few hours later, a real haemorrhage set in.

Dr. Lambe, the local physician, was called and found Keats's condition so serious that Hunt insisted he be moved into Mortimer Terrace the next day. The house was small and untidy, overrun with five dirty, ill-disciplined children, but it offered Hunt's companionship and Mrs. Hunt's care. Keats could do nothing but agree. On the twenty-third he was settled in an upstairs room, where he lay with Fanny Brawne's ring on his finger and some flowers she had sent on the table, hardly speaking, struggling to be patient. And so began a seven-week imprisonment during which he never once saw Fanny, a period which he could not remember afterward without shuddering. A spell of stifling heat set in on the twenty-fourth. The cries of ballad singers and street venders drifted up from the road below, while the children shouted and scuffled through the house. Hunt, though unwell himself, did his best to take Keats's mind off his illness, getting him to help in writing an essay on the hot weather for that week's *Indicator,* and dedicating his newest volume, a translation of Tasso's *Amyntas,* to him. Yet, as the sun beat mercilessly down on the roof over his room, Keats's blood-spitting continued. Soon Lambe found it necessary to call in Dr. George Darling, a well-known London physician who had attended Taylor, Haydon, and a number of Keats's other friends, and under their combined care Keats began to regain strength. He ordered a copy of Spenser to give to Fanny and went through it, marking his favourite passages for her. For another week he continued to mend; then he learned something which at once destroyed the little hope he had left for the future. Darling and Lambe had prescribed the final remedy, a voyage to Italy. The news was broken to Keats on July 5. He must leave England at the end of the summer.

To Keats this meant one thing only. "They talk of my going to Italy," he wrote Fanny shortly afterward. " 'Tis certain I shall never recover if I am to be so long separate from you." Now at last he was convinced that he would die. He became so nervous that having to speak to a stranger half choked him. Severn came out to see him and was shocked by the change in Keats's appearance. Emaciated, dejected, he had begun to look startlingly like Tom in his last months. His hands already resembled an old man's, the colour faded, the veins swollen. When the Gisbornes next called, Hunt drew Gisborne aside and asked him to write Shelley asking him to befriend Keats in Italy. Keats was aware of this well-intentioned plotting but too numb with hopelessness to protest. It was not merely that he felt he could not survive the separation from Fanny: he could not convince himself that she would be faithful to him in his absence. Yet to explain to Hunt why he could not go to Italy would mean confiding the secret of his engagement. So he put off consenting to the plan, though every morning the thought of it woke him up at dawn and haunted him throughout the day.

Hunt was quick to sense that Keats was deeply disturbed and guessed that he was worrying about the fate of the new volume. This was certainly one reason for Keats's depression.[12] The book had finally appeared on July 1 with an "Advertisement" which roused him to fury. Without consulting him, Taylor had apologized for the unfinished *Hyperion* by explaining that it was printed "contrary to the wish of the author" and that it was "intended to have been of equal length with *Endymion,* but the reception given to that work discouraged him from proceeding." In the first copy that came to hand, Keats savagely crossed out the entire Advertisement and wrote above it "I had no part in this; I was ill at the time." Beneath the statement that he had given up *Hyperion* because of the adverse reviews of *Endymion,* he scrawled "This is a lie." Yet in his growing despondency the lie began to appear a truth. Since February he had gradually come to believe with his doctors that anxiety and disappointment were the real causes of his illness;[13] now his hatred of the reviewers who had killed his hopes brimmed over. Thanks to them, he would be remembered as a failure, his works a mockery; Lockhart's sneers had doomed his chances not only of worldly success but even of marriage, of life itself—or so he began to think. And for the first six weeks after the new book's appearance, it seemed it might receive the same treatment as *Endymion.* Except for two enthusiastic reviews by Lamb and Hunt and a favourable notice in *The Sun,* it was either damned with faint praise or dismissed as another Cockney effusion, "a nosegay of enigmas." [14] Week by week Keats's anger smouldered till in a letter to Brown in mid-August he exclaimed in a moment of scalding bitterness, "If I die you must ruin Lockhart." *

Yet it was the thought of Brown himself and Fanny that drove Keats to the edge of sanity in these weeks at Hunt's. In his obsession with keeping their love a secret, he forbade Fanny to come to visit him in Mortimer Terrace. His letters to her were addressed to her mother to avert all notice; he even waited till he reached the end of one of his letters before writing the salutation "My dearest Girl" at the top—"that no eye may catch it." Day after day he sat looking toward Hampstead, waiting for Fanny's letters to come, or surrendering in desperation to the fantasies that now raged uncontrollably across his mind. The thought of the last two years became an acutely physical sensation—the taste of brass on his palate. "I cannot forget what has pass'd," he wrote her in agony. "When you were in the habit of flirting with Brown you would have left off, could your own heart have felt one half of one pang mine did. Brown is a good sort of Man—he did not know he was doing me to death by inches. Though I know his love and friendship for me, though at this moment I should be without pence were it not for his assistance, I will never see or speak to him until we are both old men, if we are to be." Then in a great eruption of fury he blazed out, "How have you pass'd this month? Who have you smil'd with? I appeal to you by the blood of that Christ you believe in: Do not write to me if you have done anything this month which it would have pained me to have seen. Be serious! Love is not a plaything—I would sooner die for want of you than—"

And so the letter broke off in an anguish beyond expressing. Beyond answering too, perhaps. Yet Fanny by now had apparently passed beyond indignation at his injustice. Years later she stated that even in the worst of his illness Keats "never could have addressed an unkind expression, much less a violent one, to any human being" [15]—a loyal transcendence of the truth. Eventually, it seems, she learned from these letters to understand his violence

---

* This remark, recorded by Woodhouse in his Commonplace Book (Claude Lee Finney, *The Evolution of Keats's Poetry* [1936], II, 746), evidently belongs in the letter of August 14, 1820, to Brown, who discreetly truncated this sentence in transcribing it (cf. *The Letters of John Keats*, ed. H. E. Rollins [1958], II, 321).

toward her as only a kind of delirium brought on by his fever. On his side Keats maintained his own queer loyalty still, by refusing to speak of Fanny to anyone. Yet in the end he was driven from this position. One afternoon Hunt saw him looking out the window with "a manner more alarming than usual" and suggested a drive to distract him. Keats agreed, and they took a coach over the country roads for an hour. Reaching Hampstead, they stopped at the end of Well Walk and sat down on the bench where Keats used to lounge with Tom in the spring of 1818. Suddenly rocked with the memory of Tom and all his grief, Keats buried his face in his handkerchief. After a few minutes he raised it again, his eyes full of tears, and told Hunt he was dying of a broken heart. He did not mention Fanny's name, but Hunt, in his tact, could guess it. Yet he was amazed by Keats's breakdown. "He must have been wonderfully excited to make such a confession," Hunt wrote afterward, "for his spirit was lofty to a degree of pride." [16]

After this, Keats seemed approaching the exhaustion of despair. In one last letter to Fanny in early August, he wrote, "Every hour I am more and more concentrated in you; every thing else tastes like chaff in my Mouth. I hate men and women more. I see nothing but thorns for the future—wherever I may be next winter in Italy or nowhere Brown will be living near you with his indecencies— I see no prospect of any rest. I am glad there is such a thing as the grave." To think of her merely as living apart from him, smiling with friends, going about her own pursuits, was intolerable. Seared with jealousy, he exclaimed, "Hamlet's heart was full of such Misery as mine is when he said to Ophelia 'Go to a Nunnery, go, go!' " He sent the letter off with a passage from one of her letters which he asked her to express less coldly and resumed his waiting at Hunt's window.

A day went by, then another; no reply came. On the third day young Thornton Hunt produced a letter with the seal broken. It had arrived two evenings before, but the maid instead of taking it up to Keats had maliciously kept the letter back and read it. According to Mrs. Hunt, it contained "not a word of the least consequence"; but it was from Fanny. When she gave it to Keats he broke down completely. He wept for several hours, then pulled himself together and announced he must leave. All Hunt's entreaties could not shake him. That evening he started back to

Hampstead, determined to live in Well Walk again. But halfway up the long hill to Hampstead, drawn by a force he could not withstand, he turned off toward Wentworth Place.

≫≪

Mrs. Brawne must have been overcome by the sight of his wretchedness when he appeared on her doorstep that evening, for she drew him in and insisted that he stay with them. Keats had come home at last. His remaining days in England were to be spent at Wentworth Place under her nursing, and for this brief spell he was secure in the motherly tenderness he had lacked so long. Fanny later wrote that Keats and her mother became deeply attached in these weeks; to Severn he seemed like a child in his surrender to her care. As for Fanny, the nightmare of the summer was over. She was now simply and truly herself to him again, his young love, his beauty, his own, no longer a figure of bale. From this time on, every word Keats wrote or spoke of her turned on one thought alone—that she had been life to him and parting from her now would be death. For now he finally admitted the necessity which he could not bear to face at Hunt's. He realized at last that he must agree to the plan for sending him to Italy.

The plan itself had been taking shape behind his back all during July. Shelley had been alerted; inquiries were made about doctors and bankers in Rome. Taylor, still confident that the new volume would succeed, agreed to advance money for the passage to Italy and back.[17] Brown's loan was running out by now; at this point, it seems, Haslam stepped forward with another.[18] All Keats's friends apparently believed with the doctors that the Italian climate would save him, and that the change would do his spirits good too. Jane Reynolds, whom he had suspected of gossiping about Fanny, wrote to Maria Dilke that she hoped his absence from England would "weaken, if not break off a connexion that has been a most unhappy one for him." [19] Keats found himself "cheveaux-de-frised with benefits," trapped by the good intentions of his friends. In the end it was the thought of Fanny that decided him. It would be better for her if he went; she must be spared the experience of his death.[20] Two months before, he had grasped at her like a drowning man—"You must be mine to die upon the rack if I want you." Now, convinced that his death was inevitable, he turned to meet it with all the soldierly courage he still possessed. He would go to Italy, he told Taylor, "though it be with the sensation of marching up against a Batterry."

The image is revealing, and it occurs twice in the letters in which he announced his decision, a day or two after his return to Wentworth Place. His nerves were still badly shaken; with each line he penned, the tightening in his chest increased. In a brief note to his sister he broke the news as gently as he could: " 'T is not yet Consumption I believe, but it would be were I to remain in this climate all the Winter." To Hunt he sent an apology for leaving his house as he did, thanking him for his "many sympathies." Then Keats wrote to Taylor, asking him to find out the cost of the journey and a year's residence in Italy. The next day he added a postscript, a scrap of paper containing his will. "All my estate real and personal consists in the hopes of the sale of books publish'd or unpublish'd. Now I wish *Brown* and you to be the first paid Creditors—the rest is in nubibus—but in case it should shower pay my Taylor the few pounds I owe him. My Chest of Books divide among my friends." It was a declaration of worldly bankruptcy. Four years had been enough to run through his inheritance and his hopes of success. In the same spirit of casting his accounts and facing his failure, he wrote to Shelley two days later.

Shelley had invited Keats to spend the winter with him in Pisa in a letter combining tact and grace with the unconscious patronage that had stung Keats's pride at their first meeting.[21] The offer was generous; yet Shelley managed to add some double-edged praise of *Endymion* while recommending his own tragedy *The Cenci,* which he had lately sent to Keats, and *Prometheus Unbound,* which had just been published. The two men's careers had run curiously parallel ever since 1817, with each matching the other in romantic narrative, Elizabethan-style tragedy, allegorical epic, and satirical extravaganza. Keats now had to watch Shelley pull ahead of him in the race for fame, with the four splendid acts of *Prometheus* forever towering above his unfinished *Hyperion.* So Shelley's tribute—"I feel persuaded that you are capable of the greatest things, so you but will"—must have rankled cruelly. He answered the invitation to Pisa circumspectly, for he was still undecided where to go. But he met Shelley's implied criticism of *Endymion* squarely with a trenchant comment on Shelley's own work. "There is only one part of it I am judge of; the Poetry, and dramatic effect, which by many spirits now a days is considered the mammon. A modern work it is said must have a purpose, which may be the God—*an artist* must serve Mammon—he must have 'self concentration' selfishness perhaps. You I am sure will forgive me for sincerely remarking that you might curb your magnanimity and be more of an artist, and 'load every rift' of your subject with ore." It is telling criticism of Shelley's hortatory bent; yet Keats, remembering their first conversation three and a half years before, was also struck with the irony of it. "I remember you advising me not to publish my first-blights"—his first fruits—"on Hampstead heath," he added. "And is not this extraordinary talk for the writer of Endymion? whose mind was like a pack of scattered cards— I am pick'd up and sorted to a pip."

The cards were dealt, he had picked up a good hand—and suddenly, for no reason, the game was called off. Only a hint of the injustice of it all escapes in a remark to Haydon who, as he heard, had started a new painting: "Go on—I am affraid I shall pop off just when my mind is able to run alone." Yet even as Keats wrote, another ironic twist was being given to his destiny. Critical opinion was beginning to turn in his favour. In mid-August at long last the *Edinburgh Review* spoke out. The mighty Jeffrey himself wrote a lengthy critique of *Endymion*—so long, in fact, that he had little space to discuss the *Lamia* volume; but he praised the earlier poem, two years too late, as the surest touchstone of "a native relish for poetry." Shortly afterward the *Edinburgh Magazine* followed suit with another belated appreciation of *Endymion*, concluding "If this be not poetry, we do not know what it is." Their highly favourable notice of the *Lamia* volume did not appear till October, but by that time most of the other reviews had fallen into line. Even the Tory critics were to retract some of their earlier ridicule. The *Quarterly* remained silent, but *Blackwood's* conceded, still with some mockery, that there was much merit in the new volume. But for all this the book sold very slowly—only a few hundred copies by the end of the summer. It did not do nearly as well as the poems of Taylor's latest protégé, the peasant poet John Clare, or Barry Cornwall's newest work, *Marcian Colonna*. The timing was bad, for one thing. The royal scandal had erupted in full view with George IV's indictment of Queen Caroline before Parliament, and for several months pamphlets and lampoons on this subject elbowed other books out of the public's attention.[22]

And here is the final irony; for if Keats had ever finished *The Cap and Bells* he might have made some money as well as a name for himself.

As things now stood, he depended completely on his friends for support. No word had yet come from George. Abbey had promised Keats to lend him some money if George did not remit, but when Keats asked him for it he replied with chilly self-righteousness that he had warned Keats not to lend his money to George and that he himself was harassed by bad debts and could spare nothing. Except for Taylor's generosity, Keats could not have left for Italy at all. Early in September the publisher made a liberal settlement of their accounts which, reckoning all Keats's borrowings against the assignment of the three copyrights, left him with enough money at least to pay for his passage to Italy. Then, though Taylor was short of cash himself and still some £200 out of pocket on both *Endymion* and *Lamia*,[23] he arranged a credit of £150 for Keats's expenses abroad, counting rather doubtfully on George to reimburse him. He also arranged—since Keats had now decided not to go to Pisa—an introduction to Dr. James Clark in Rome, a young English physician with an excellent reputation as a specialist in phthisis.

All Keats needed now was a travelling companion. On August 14 he had written Brown an urgent letter in which he broke the news of his relapse and evidently asked him to return before he left for Italy, adding the secret of his engagement to Fanny and the savage request to "ruin Lockhart." A few days later, having decided against going to Shelley's, he wrote again more anxiously, begging Brown to accompany him on the trip. With luck he might have a reply in eight or ten days, but none ever came. According to Brown, the letters were misdirected and never reached him till September 9 at Dunkeld, whereupon he promptly returned to England. But it is strange that Brown deleted this and subsequent requests from Keats's letters when he later transcribed them into his *Life of Keats*,[24] and that he returned to England at last by the slowest rather than the fastest means available. It is hard not to suspect that he was dodging the issue. Knowing that Keats's physician had recommended he be sent to Italy in the fall, Brown had, as it seems, arranged to be conveniently out of the way when Keats would leave. He had stood by Keats in the spring, it is true, but now clearly wished to do so no longer. Keats, however, put off his departure several weeks in the vain hope that Brown would return in time to go with him. But as September drew on with no word from Scotland, he had to face the prospect of going to a strange country alone, convinced that he would die there. In desperation he asked Mrs. Brawne to accompany him. For a while she wavered; then Fanny begged to go too. It was unthinkable. He withdrew his request, and it was agreed that if he was well enough to return in the spring they would be married at last.[25] It was the dimmest of all hopes; but Keats must have resolved that Fanny at least should have something to hope for.

Under this mounting anxiety he had another haemorrhage on August 30. It was clear that his leaving could not be postponed much longer. Summer was over; a spell of chilly rain set in, and the winds were turning cold toward evening. Taylor got passage for him on the brig *Maria Crowther,* which was to sail from London for Naples around the middle of September, and Keats's friends began to pay their farewells. Haydon came out to the Brawnes' to find him in bed, fevered and irritable. "He seemed to be going out of Life with a contempt for this world and no hopes of the other," Haydon recorded. Evidently he tried to console him with thoughts of the life after death—the last thing in the world Keats wanted to hear about. Angrily he muttered that if he did not get well soon he would kill himself. Haydon tried to argue with him, then left, "deeply affected" by what seemed to him Keats's spiritual disintegration—the result, he thought, of Hunt's renewed influence.[26] Keats's despairing mood seems to have had a similar effect on Reynolds, who was not on hand to bid a final farewell. After his departure, Reynolds wrote Taylor with misplaced facetiousness that he was glad to hear that Keats had escaped the "vain and heartless" company of Leigh Hunt and had left for "a better Lungland," "so comfortably, so cheerfully, so sensibly." As for leaving Fanny, Reynolds chose to believe that Keats could only benefit by "absence from that poor idle Thing of Womankind to whom he has so unaccountably attached himself." [27]

The old circle was breaking up. From a remote parish in Northamptonshire, Bailey wrote Taylor his grave doubts about Keats's character and chances of literary success. By keeping the wrong society, Keats had picked up mistaken notions of morals and religion which, Bailey feared, would prevent him from realizing his promise as a poet. When Taylor replied that he disagreed,

Bailey answered some months later that he found a few traces of intellectual progress in the *Lamia* volume, and sent his kindest remembrances. For himself, Bailey admitted that his literary interests were waning; he still hoped to get something published in the Tory *New Monthly Magazine,* but "if they espouse any freethinking notions I have done with them." A stranger in Scotland, however, one John Aitken, who had admired the *Lamia* volume and been distressed to read in *The Indicator* of Keats's illness, wrote inviting him to come and stay at his country house, offering a good library and freedom in which to write. Of all Keats's friends in London, it was Haslam who, just as two years before, stood by him most faithfully, writing George when Keats could not, and making most of the arrangements for the voyage.

Yet none of these partings mattered to Keats in the face of his separation from Fanny. His whole existence was now concentrated in her. They had never been closer; yet his longing for her, now never to be slaked, had never been more painful. Weeks later it wrung from him a confession of pure despair in a letter to Brown: "I should have had her when I was in health, and I should have remained well. I can bear to die—I cannot bear to leave her." After his haemorrhage at the end of August he could hardly keep up the deception that he might recover in Italy, though Fanny herself accepted the doctors' assurances, like everyone else. He still struggled, however, against his growing conviction that death would be the final and irreversible parting. "Some of the phrases she was in the habit of using during my last nursing at Wentworth place ring in my ears," he wrote Brown at the end of September. "Is there another Life? Shall I awake and find all this a dream? There must be we cannot be created for this sort of suffering." With his whole being he longed to share Fanny's simple faith in immortality, yet the anguish of his incommunicable doubt continued.

The date of his sailing approached with still no companion in sight. No word had yet come from Brown, and all Keats's other friends were bound to England by their families or their work. Yet Haslam, though he could not go himself, was determined that Keats should not go alone. On Tuesday, September 12, the day before Keats was to leave Hampstead, Haslam thought of asking Severn. He was hardly the man for the responsibility, a cheerful young fellow but naïve and inexperienced; still, his company would be better than none. Severn himself was taken aback by the idea. A trip to Italy meant leaving his adoring mother and sisters and a secure career as a miniature painter, all on the shortest possible notice. Yet he could see a possible advantage in accompanying Keats. As the winner of a Royal Academy Gold Medal, he was eligible to apply for its travelling fellowship, which carried a comfortable three years' income; and after a winter of study in Rome he would have a better painting to submit to the jury next summer than if he remained drudging away in England. While Severn puzzled over his decision, Haslam hurried out to spend Tuesday night in Hampstead. His suggestion was a great relief to Keats, whose only plan had been to spend some time in Naples, waiting for Brown to catch up with him. He still expected that Brown would follow him to Rome as soon as he returned from Scotland, and now he would have a companion for the voyage. It was with a courageous show of calm that he made his farewells and set out to town with Haslam the next morning.

After the closeness of the weeks before, there could have been little left for Keats and Fanny to say to each other. She recorded the event simply in her diary with the note, "Mr. Keats left Hampstead." As his final gifts Keats had presented her with his miniature by Severn and his most treasured books—Dante, Spenser, and his Folio Shakespeare. They exchanged locks of hair, after the sentimental custom of the time; each still wore the other's ring. Fanny had lined his travelling cap with silk and given him a new pocket diary and a penknife. To her younger sister Margaret, Keats gave an amethyst brooch [28]—perhaps the last of his mother's relics. To his own sister he sent a last message, dictated to Fanny Brawne. She had been forbidden to visit him up to the very end. Keats had dreaded the thought of their final parting and was relieved to be spared it; yet he was haunted by the thought of her unhappiness with the Abbeys. He asked Fanny Brawne to write to her regularly and do everything she could for the younger girl. In his last letter he reassured her about his health as best he could; then after it was sealed he thought of one word more, which he asked Fanny Brawne to send her. She must avoid chills and coughs and remember never to go out into the cold air from the warmth of the greenhouse. As he later wrote to Brown, she "walks about my imagination like a ghost—she is so like Tom."

In town Wednesday morning Keats went to Taylor's while Haslam hurried off to get Severn's final word. At noon the message arrived: Severn had agreed to go. He had a busy time ahead of him, packing for the voyage, getting his passport, visiting his family, and collecting £25 due him for a miniature—all the cash he had to start the trip on. Fortunately, they learned Wednesday noon, the *Maria Crowther* would not sail till Sunday morning, though for Keats this meant only a few more weary days of farewells, which he had done all he could to avoid.[29] One and all, his friends re-assured him that he would return the next year, miraculously re-covered, to pick up his interrupted work. If anyone had a suspicion to the contrary, he succeeded in hiding it from the others. Yet each man revealed something of himself in his manner of farewell: not only Reynolds with his ill-concealed pleasure that Keats was escap-ing from the bondage of his engagement, and Haydon in his re-criminations against Keats's failure of nerve, but Taylor with his kindness carefully spelled out in business terms, and Woodhouse, the most self-effacing of all in his generosity. Saturday night he sat down in his rooms and wrote an affectionate letter to give to Keats the next day with his last handshake. Without mentioning his anonymous loan the summer before, he explained a little awk-wardly that he was glad to know that Keats was well supplied with money for the time being, since his own funds were low at present. In about six months, however, he promised they would have re-covered enough to answer any draft that Keats might make on them. Then, quoting from the sonnet which Keats's mysterious benefactor "P. Fenbank" had sent him from Teignmouth two years before and which Woodhouse had duly copied into his Keats scrap-book, he signed himself

> —one, whose hand will never scant
> From his poor store of fruits all *thou* canst want.

Leigh Hunt also wrote a letter of farewell to Keats, to be published in *The Indicator* the week after he left. Sentimental, even flam-boyant, still it did what only Hunt could do—remind a still in-different public of its loss. "Thou shalt return with thy friend the nightingale, and make all thy other friends as happy with thy voice as they are sorrowful to miss it," he ended. "Farewell for awhile: thy heart is in our fields: and thou wilt soon be back to rejoin it." [30]

Chapter Fourteen

>>>———————————————————————————<<<

End of the Voyage

IT dawned pale and chilly on Sunday the seventeenth as a little
group gathered at the London docks near the Tower to see Keats
off. Taylor, Woodhouse, and Haslam planned to sail down the
river to Gravesend with him; a young assistant of Taylor's and
one or two other friends made up the rest. Severn arrived late, wan
and shaken from parting with his family, for his father in one of
his overbearing rages had tried forcibly to prevent his leaving in
the end. Keats looked feverish and dejected but made his good-
byes with apparent calm. Their trunks were loaded, the last hand-
shakes exchanged, and Keats boarded the ship with his four companions to wait the turn of the tide. By mid-morning it reached its
height, and they cast off. With the sights and sounds of the Thames
traffic and the fresh air of the river, Keats's spirits soon picked
up. Suddenly Severn realized he had forgotten his passport. Luckily
they were to stop over for a day at Gravesend, where Haslam promised to have it sent. They reached Gravesend early in the afternoon
and dropped the pilot. Haslam drew Severn aside to beg him to
keep a regular journal of the trip, while Keats asked Taylor to
send his sister an account of his departure. Taylor gave him a Greek
and Latin Testament in parting,[1] and Woodhouse took a lock of
his hair. Then at last they were gone.

Taylor wrote Fanny at once that Keats was comfortably settled
and looking forward to an agreeable month's voyage, but this was
putting a cheerful front on the affair. The *Maria Crowther* was
small, a two-masted brig of less than 130 tons, built for coasting on
the Cardiff-Liverpool run; she turned out to be cramped as well

as poorly provisioned for a journey of over 2600 miles. There was one cabin of six berths for the captain and the passengers. Two of their fellow voyagers were women—Mrs. Pidgeon, a robust middle-aged lady who seemed affable enough on first acquaintance, and a Miss Cotterell, who was to get on at Gravesend the next day. Captain Walsh was a good fellow, anxious to please, but his resources were limited. Severn, who had recently had a bout with his liver and was a poor sailor, began to look melancholy, but Keats was determined to make the best of a bad situation. At tea in the cabin he cracked one joke after another, amusing Mrs. Pidgeon and bringing Severn round again. That night Severn kept waking up in his narrow berth, unable to think where he was—once, it seemed, in a shoemaker's shop, another time in a wine-cellar; then, restless and upset, he lay awake, listening to the others' snores, while the ship gently rocked and creaked around him. Outside in the quiet river a smack from Dundee drew up and anchored nearby. She carried another sleeping passenger, Charles Brown. At dawn, as the tide turned, she weighed anchor and started up-river for London.

The next morning Severn was alarmed by Keats's low voice; but he ate a good breakfast, as if to prove he was well. When the captain invited Severn to go ashore with him to help lay in his last supplies, Keats gave him a list of medicines to buy at the apothecary's. Included was a bottle of laudanum, a standard remedy for seasickness at that time. Severn obligingly returned with all his commissions and an extra supply of apples and biscuits. That afternoon at dinner Keats was "full of his waggery," by Severn's report. At six the missing passport arrived, and Miss Cotterell soon after. Keats was brought up short at the sight of her. Young, pretty, with gentle manners, she was obviously in an advanced stage of consumption, and a winter in Italy had been prescribed as a last resort. She had a brother in business in Naples, whom she would join there, but she was desolate at the thought of the long journey ahead. Keats, who had never conquered his uneasiness in the presence of illness, was now to be faced with a living image of his own disease for the whole voyage. But at once he tried cheering Miss Cotterell up, dragging Severn along with him in a wild rush of badinage. Severn suspected nothing of her effect on his friend; instead he was struck by the fact that each invalid confided to him that he was in much better health than the other. Severn himself was still feeling "done up" and evidently showed it, for a lady companion of Miss Cotterell asked as she left, a little too audibly, which was the dying man.

Late that night they sailed. Tuesday, Severn rose to watch the sunrise, then had to walk up and down with Miss Cotterell, who was already upset by the roll and pitch of the ship as it reached the Channel. At breakfast Severn himself began to feel "a waltzing in the stomach"; at once he groped his way to the deck, followed by Miss Cotterell and shortly by Keats, who was sick, according to Severn, "in a most gentlemanly manner." Mrs. Pidgeon stayed behind, laughing at them, but a few minutes later joined them at the rail; then Miss Cotterell fainted. This was only the first of many times. Keats helped her below and brought her round, after which all four passengers took to their bunks. There they remained all day as the ship went bucking through the Strait of Dover, and the air in the small cabin became stifling. But they were too shaken even to get out of their clothes that night. Mrs. Pidgeon turned surly and uncooperative; Miss Cotterell became ill again and again, and Keats, showing only a pale profile from his upper berth, dictated instructions to Severn to assist her. Wednesday morning was fair enough for breakfast on deck, but by early afternoon they ran straight into a gale. Once that evening Severn managed to get up on deck, where he watched the ship staggering from crest to trough of the waves, and clambering up again, the sea flooding across the foredeck with each plunge. He groped his way back to the cabin to find their trunks sliding over the floor and water seeping through the planks. The women were terrified, but Keats remained cool enough to joke with Severn about it. For hours they lay in the dark, listening to the groan of the pumps, the shouts of the crew, and the crash of the waves outside; then at last the captain decided to abandon their course and make for shelter.

For another day they hugged the coast of Kent, tacking slowly forward, but soon the wind died down into a mere breeze. On the twenty-first they put in at Dungeness, where Severn and Keats were glad to get ashore and stretch their legs. Then they returned to another week of contrary winds, and Keats's patience began to wear thin. Seasickness brought on fever, and once or twice the terrifying thought crossed Severn's mind that Keats might die on the voyage. At the week's end Captain Walsh decided to anchor at

Portsmouth till the wind changed, and on September 28 Keats and Severn went ashore again to spend the night. Keats, realizing that Bedhampton was only seven miles away, was seized with an impulse to drive over with Severn to surprise his friends the Snooks with a visit. They were delighted to see him and hear him abuse the captain's seamanship and Mrs. Pidgeon's manners in a fine show of cheerfulness. But they had bitter news for him. Brown had returned from Scotland and come down to Hampshire for a month's visit; he was at the senior Dilkes' in Chichester that very day. Keats must have been thunderstruck to realize not only that Brown had reached London only a day after he left but, still more, that he seemed to have no plans to follow him to Italy. Twenty miles to Chichester and back—the distance was too great for the time he had before returning to Portsmouth. All at once his resolution cracked; he was ready to give the voyage up and return to London. He almost persuaded Severn, then with a great effort got himself in hand again. Next morning they drove back to the ship and started off with a favouring breeze. But soon the wind changed, and they found themselves becalmed off Yarmouth.

After almost a fortnight at sea they had gone barely two hundred miles. Severn was disturbed to see Keats's dogged gaiety give way to silent brooding. This was hardly remarkable, for both captain and passengers were bad-tempered and weary after their ordeal with the weather. But Severn had no inkling of Keats's real thoughts. He had never been one of his intimates, and he was not a perceptive young man; it seems he literally believed all the assurances he heard that Keats would recover in Italy. As the voyage wore on and his first resolution flagged, Keats began to withdraw more into himself, to turn over and over in his mind the anguish of his parting with Fanny, his growing doubt that Brown would join him, his terrible conviction that he would die in Italy. He had put off writing Brown till he might send him good news of his health; but now it struck him as useless to wait any longer. On the morning of the thirtieth he started a letter to him in a collected spirit, expressing his disappointment at missing him in Bedhampton. "I should have delighted in setting off for London for the sensation merely," he added; "for what should I do there? I could not leave my lungs or stomach or other worse things behind me." At this his wild longing for Fanny broke through at last. "The very thing which I want to live most for will be a great occasion of my death," he exclaimed. "Were I in health it would make me ill, and how can I bear it in my state? I wish for death every day and night to deliver me from these pains, and then I wish death away, for death would destroy even those pains which are better than nothing. Land and Sea, weakness and decline are great seperators, but death is the great divorcer for ever."

He had fought to put Fanny out of his mind, but failed completely. For the last two weeks he had been able to think of no one else, not even his sister, or George and Georgiana: only Fanny, whom he had lost forever, as from the first he had dreaded he might. "The thought of leaving Miss Brawne is beyond every thing horrible," he confessed to Brown—"the sense of darkness coming over me—I eternally see her figure eternally vanishing." The irrational suspicions of the summer had receded into the past, but he could not forget the hostility which still divided the two people he loved the most, or what he in his weakness had done to add to it. "I think without my mentioning it for my sake you would be a friend to Miss Brawne when I am dead," he begged Brown. "You think she has many faults—but, for my sake, think she has not one —if there is any thing you can do for her by word or deed I know you will do it." For himself he could not even ask whether Brown intended to come to Italy. "I will say nothing about our friendship or rather yours to me more than that as you deserve to escape you will never be so unhappy as I am." A bitter truth was concealed in this remark, which Brown probably did not recognize. Gloomily Keats concluded, "I feel as if I was closing my last letter to you."

Keats had resolved to write Fanny that day but could not find the courage; he could not even bring himself to send his letter to Brown, so naked in despair, but put it back in his writing case.[2] Next morning there was still no wind in sight, and the captain decided to put in at Lulworth Cove, where Keats and Severn went ashore again. As they rambled along the rugged coast, Keats's spirits rose, and for a few hours he seemed to Severn his old self once more. Memories of Margate and Devon and the Isle of Wight must have come flooding back—those days when he had watched and listened endlessly to the sea in all its tones and colours and changes of mood. It was a beautiful evening when they returned to the ship, at the hour Keats had always liked best, with "a few white Clouds about and a few stars blinking—the waters ebbing and the Horison a Mystery." Back on board he got out his copy of Shakespeare's *Poems* and turned over the leaves till he found a blank page. There, opposite Shakespeare's boldly printed title "A Lover's Complaint," he wrote down a sonnet. It was the final version of the one he had written at Shanklin the summer before, wrought from the same elements of sea and evening and longing for Fanny, but with the last two lines reshaped to a more dramatic ending:

> Still, still to hear her tender-taken breath,
> And so live ever—or else swoon to death.

No longer the mingling of love and death in a half-drugged confusion of their separate natures, but all too clear a sense of their tragic antithesis—this was the final meaning he wrung from the contrast between the eternal calm watchfulness of the star and his own eternal restlessness, and in effect his final message to Fanny. And to the end of his life Severn thought that "Bright Star" was the last poem Keats ever wrote.[3]

It was their last evening in England, at any rate. Next morning the wind freshened and shifted, and soon they were scudding across the Channel. After rounding the tip of Brittany and turning into the Bay of Biscay, they ran into another severe storm. With her constant seasickness, Miss Cotterell grew weaker every day. When the portholes were closed, she fainted continually from lack of air; but when they were opened Keats began to cough uncontrollably. Slowly it began to dawn on Severn that he had taken charge of a desperately ill man. More and more he noticed "a starved haunting expression" on Keats's face that bewildered him. As for himself, Severn was proving a good enough sailor to spend most of the time on deck, wrapped in his greatcoat and watching the sea with delight. When the wind dropped again off Cape St. Vincent he made water-colour sketches or leaned over the side, watching strange fish circle below. Together he and Keats read *Don Juan* aloud; but Keats soon grew annoyed with Byron's unflagging cynicism and tossed the book aside. Once they saw a whale shoulder through the placid surface of the sea. Another time they sighted a few warships. To their alarm a four-decker approached them and fired a shot to bring the *Maria Crowther* about. It was a ticklish moment, for pirates still prowled in these waters; but the commander claimed he was a Portuguese admiral and only wanted information about rebel privateers. Captain Walsh had none to give him, and slowly the huge ship, its decks swarming with ragged sailors, drifted off. Later in the day they learned from an English naval sloop that the Portuguese fleet was supporting the Carlist rebellion in Spain and trying to intercept loyal shipping.

By mid-October they reached Gibraltar. They passed through the straits early in the morning and saw the Rock lit up by the first rays of the sun, glowing like a vast topaz, as Severn described it. He sketched while Keats lay watching, glad to have passed this milestone in their journey. Hopeful as always, Severn decided that the Mediterranean air was working a miracle, for Keats was showing signs of recovery. But a day or two later he took an unexpected turn for the worse and began to vomit blood. Severn was terrified. Luckily the vomiting soon ceased, but for several days his fever hung on, with violent sweating at night. Yet as they sailed along through perfect weather and Keats's fever subsided, Severn's optimism returned. It was easy enough to blame any illness on the bad weather, poor food, and lack of exercise, their airless cabin and damp beds, the distressing sight of Miss Cotterell day in and day out. And they were approaching the end of the journey. On October 21 they entered the Bay of Naples at sunrise. Italy at last, most glorious of all the kingdoms of the earth Keats had dreamed of seeing. Around them in a vast semicircle, flanked by islands like cliffs floating in light, rose the shadowed hills of Campania. Before them the white villas of Naples gleamed in the dawn, with terraced vineyards and olive orchards, bronze-green and grey-green, climbing tier on tier over the slopes behind. From the summit of Vesuvius drifted a long purplish cloud of smoke, edged with the gold of the rising sun; to the southeast the cliffs of Sorrento shone like lapis lazuli. As the morning advanced, the blue of the sea deepened to an intensity Severn had never seen before, catching and concentrating the light of the sky like an immense sapphire.

For an hour at least all memory of the surly Atlantic was blotted out in the radiance of the scene. But as they entered the harbour of Naples they learned they could not land for another ten days. There had been a epidemic of typhus when they left London, and they were required to round out the six weeks of quarantine. After more than a month at sea, this was a maddening disappointment. Yet for the first day the stir and bustle of the port provided endless amusement. The *Maria Crowther* anchored off the tiny island of the Castel dell' Ovo, once the site of the villa of Lucullus, now of a stolid Norman fortress. Here they could watch ships of all rigs and sizes coming and going, the fishing boats returning with their catch, little skiffs loaded with supplies weaving between the larger craft. Keats sat looking at it, half in a dream. In his mind's eye he could see the harbour as it had been two thousand years ago, crowded with Greek galleys and Tyrrhenian sloops carrying merchants or colonists with their wares and their legends from the East. But the reality was as good as the imagination. Boatloads of singers, sunburnt and gaily dressed, rowed out to greet them, and pedlars came by with wine in straw-covered bottles and flowers and baskets of fruit piled to their gunwales—melons, peaches, figs, and grapes. The air rang with the singsong of the hawkers, the tinkling of guitars, and ceaseless Neapolitan laughter.

The adventure soon turned into a nightmare. Out in the Bay a British naval squadron lay anchored, standing guard against the recent liberal uprising in Naples; and shortly a young lieutenant was sent to make inquiries of the British arrival. Instead of remaining alongside the *Maria Crowther,* he blundered aboard with his six men, and there they had to stay till the quarantine was up. Their quarters, close enough before, became unspeakably crowded when after the first day it began to rain, driving them all into the cabin. Soon the air was almost too foul to breathe. Miss Cotterell became pitiably ill, and Keats suffered more from bad air and poor digestion than he had during the entire voyage. Severn, for all of his gaiety and good health, once broke into tears under the strain. Before the week was up, Miss Cotterell's affable brother joined them on board. Though his coming left them still shorter of space, Cotterell's good humour helped speed the time. He flung jokes back and forth with the boatmen swarming around them, persuaded them to sing, and translated their gibes for the passengers' benefit. And Keats, out of the energy of despair, summoned up more puns in a week—so he wrote Brown—than in any year of his life.

While they were penned up Keats wrote a letter to Mrs. Brawne which, when compared to the gloomy note Severn scribbled to Haslam at the same time, is a triumph of cheerfulness. "I would always wish you to think me a little worse than I really am," he remarked; "if I do not recover your regret will be softened if I do your pleasure will be doubled.—Yet you must not believe I am so ill as this Letter may look," he added, "for if ever there was a person born without the faculty of hoping I am he." He tried to write a message to Fanny but failed: "I dare not fix my Mind upon Fanny. I have not dared to think of her," he continued to Mrs. Brawne. "The only comfort I have had that way has been in thinking for hours together of having the knife she gave me put in a silver-case—the hair in a Locket—and the Pocket Book in a gold net—Show her this." He began to describe the life around them and was overwhelmed by a sense of unreality. "There is enough in this Port of Naples to fill a quire of Paper—but it looks like a dream—every man who can row his boat and walk and talk seems a different being from myself. O what an account I could give you if I could once more feel myself a Citizen of this world— O what a misery it is to have an intellect in splints!" He sent messages to all at Wentworth Place, to Brown and the Dilkes as well. "Tell Tootts [Fanny's younger sister] I wish I could pitch her a basket of grapes—and tell Sam the fellows catch here with a line a little fish much like an anchovy, pull them up fast." He closed his letter affectionately to Mrs. Brawne, then, just before sealing it to go, added a postscript in a small and very ragged hand: "Good bye Fanny! god bless you." [4] These were his last words to her.

≫≫⋘⋘

At last their term in quarantine was up. On October 31—his twenty-fifth birthday—Keats stepped ashore with Severn in a cold driving rain. The fresh air revived them a little, but the first encounter with the smells and squalor and confusion of Naples was overwhelming—beggars and ballad-singers elbowing each other in the crowded streets, fish-pedlars and macaroni-venders shouting their wares, women washing and cooking in the doorways of their houses, and children swarming everywhere in the filthy gutters. Cotterell took them to the Villa di Londra and gave them a good dinner; but, in spite of comfortable rooms with a superb view of Mount Vesuvius, both Keats and Severn were depressed. All night the shouts and singing and clatter in the streets below made it impossible to sleep.

The next morning they hurried off some letters to catch the English courier. To Brown, Keats wrote what he hoped would be a short calm letter; but after two sentences describing their quarantine, the compulsion to speak of Fanny swept him off his course again. "As I have gone thus far into it, I must go on a little," he apologized cryptically; "perhaps it may relieve the load of WRETCHEDNESS which presses upon me. The persuasion that I shall see her no more will kill me. I cannot q—" He broke off, unable to finish the sentence or even the word; then the flood of his emotion carried him on. "Oh, God! God! God! Every thing I have in my trunks that reminds me of her goes through me like a spear. The silk lining she put in my travelling cap scalds my head. My imagination is horribly vivid about her—I see her—I hear her. There is nothing in the world of sufficient interest to divert me from her a moment. This was the case when I was in England; then there was a good hope of seeing her again—Now!—O that I could be buried near where she lives!" He hardly dared think of the exile ahead of him and could barely bring himself to remind Brown of his still unanswered request.[5] "If I were in better health I should urge your coming to Rome," he remarked; but even that seemed useless. "I fear there is no one can give me any comfort." After asking about his brother and sister, he begged Brown to let Fanny Brawne know somehow that he did not forget her, and to promise for his sake to "be her advocate for ever."

That night at last Keats broke down and told Severn something of his misery. Severn wrote Haslam the next day that he had persuaded Keats to talk to him about "a heavy grief that may tend more than anything to be fatal"; but what Keats actually said Severn did not make clear. Years later Severn recalled that Keats insisted his greatest misfortune in leaving England was "being cut off from the world of poetry"; but it seems likelier that this time Keats told him, as he told Hunt, of some thwarted love which he left nameless. The one thing certain is that in his stubborn pride he never mentioned Fanny's name. Severn knew of Keats's close friendship with the Brawnes, and even that Fanny was "Keats's favourite" in the family; and from several hints in Brown's letters he might easily have guessed the real relationship between them. But Keats himself never let Severn suspect he was engaged to Fanny.[6] Whatever it was that he confided to Severn that evening, however, it did Keats good; he went to bed much calmer and slept till nearly ten the next morning.

The next day Keats's spirits picked up again: Severn took it as a hopeful sign that he made an Italian pun. They decided to take

a week to rest up for the difficult journey to Rome and began en-
joying a cordial reception from the little English colony in Naples.
Cotterell, in his gratitude for their care of his sister, could not do
enough for them. He took them driving to see the sights of the
city, then out into the country through the vineyards to Capo di
Monte and the Ponte Rossi. It was still glorious autumn; the sun
was warm, and late roses bloomed in front of the cottages by the
road. The last of the grapes were being harvested, and the sight
of heavy-laden carts lumbering off to the presses and the fragrance
of the air must have been a joy to Keats. On their way back to the
city he stopped the carriage at the Capuan Gate to watch a group
of workmen standing around a cauldron, eating spaghetti by immense handfuls without knives or forks. The unrestrained vitality
of the peasants delighted him, but he was unimpressed by the
Neapolitan troops whom they saw in grand review the day they
landed. "No backbone," he commented to Severn, and events soon
proved him right. The very week of their visit, the King of Naples
was conspiring with Metternich to betray the newly established
constitutional government to the Austrians, and four months later
the Army was to surrender without a fight.[7] When Keats and
Severn went to the opera they found sentinels standing under the
proscenium arch, whom they took as part of the scenic effect until
they realized they were real soldiers, posted there to quell any
disturbance. At this symbol of submission to tyranny Keats flared
into anger. The air of Naples suddenly became stifling; he wanted
to leave at once. A letter came from Shelley in Pisa, full of advice
about diet and climate, urging him to come to Pisa but not repeating his earlier invitation to stay at his own house.[8] But Keats
by now had set his mind on Rome. There Severn would find the
opportunities for study that were his reason for the trip, and Keats
himself was anxious to make contact with his new physician, Dr.
Clark. So they collected their visas and, on the morning of November 8, set out for the Papal States.

The journey to Rome, a distance of a hundred and forty miles
over rough country, usually took two or three days. The little carriage which Keats and Severn hired for the trip stretched it out to
eight. The inns at the regular stopping-places were poor enough,
but in the primitive villages where Keats and Severn were forced
to spend the nights they were "villainously coarse" by Severn's
account. The vile food followed by hours of jolting over bad roads

left Keats continually queasy. Severn, however, was enchanted with the flower-strewn hillsides, the festooned vineyards, and the lucent blue of the Mediterranean in the distance. It was a good thing that, as Keats had written Mrs. Brawne two weeks before, Severn's nerves were "too strong to be hurt by other peoples illnesses." He walked alongside the crawling *vettura* for most of the way, which put him in excellent health by the end of the trip, and he managed to cheer Keats up by bringing him armfuls of wild flowers. After Terracina, the midpoint of their route, they entered the vast malarial wasteland of the Campagna, where the only sights were an occasional goatherd with his flock, a few skeletons of horses by the road, a stretch of ruined aqueduct, and, impaled on posts along the way, the shrunken arms and legs of bandits, who still infested the roads. Once they passed a red-cloaked cardinal out shooting songbirds, with an owl tied to a stick with a mirror round its neck used as lure; as Severn observed, the real sport was in not shooting the owl.

After this unexpected adventure came the unimaginable actuality of Rome itself. On November 15 at last they caught sight of the crumbling mass of the Aurelian Wall looming up before them; then entered the city by the Lateran Gate and drove past the Colosseum and the Forum to the Piazza di Spagna, which even at that time was a center for English visitors. Keats went at once to call on Dr. Clark, who had been anxiously awaiting his arrival. Clark had already found them an apartment immediately across the square from his own, in a house at the foot of the wide marble stairs leading up dozen by dozen to the tawny-coloured church of Santa Trinità dei Monti. The rooms were narrow but neat and comfortably furnished. The windows facing south and west looked down two stories to the steps and the square below, where the Barcaccia, Bernini's boat-shaped fountain, splashed in the sun. The piazza itself was an endless spectacle. Lined with the shops of print-sellers and artisans in mosaic, it was crowded with loungers and flower-venders and artists' models, who gathered for hire on the steps in their costumes. Flocks of goats or cattle jostled with the passers-by over the cobblestones, and carriages of English "milords" which were too large for the dank mews below the square stood drawn up in the open. Their landlady, Anna Angeletti, was a lively, smart little woman with two well-brought-up daughters.[9] She asked nearly five pounds a month for the apart ment—a price at which Keats apparently demurred, for one of the first things that struck Clark was his uneasiness about money matters. But prices were high in Rome, at least for English visitors,[10] and there was nothing to do but give in.

Dr. Clark turned out to be as good a friend and neighbour as he was a physician. Unknown to Keats, he wrote to England shortly after his arrival to urge that Keats's friends reassure him about his financial situation. "I wish I were rich enough that his living here should cost him nothing," he added. "I feel very much interested in him." He not only called on Keats at least twice every day but also watched the English magazines for reviews of *Lamia* and got his wife to cook special dishes for the patient. Clark's bedside manner, which was later to recommend him to the King of the Belgians and Queen Victoria, sprang from a genuine warmth of heart. A personable young Scot in his early thirties, he had served as a surgeon in the Royal Navy and trained as a physician at Edinburgh. He gave Keats the most skilful and devoted care that was obtainable at the time, even though by present-day standards his diagnosis was tragically inadequate. On first examining Keats he was cautiously hopeful. He had only a suspicion that Keats's lungs were affected and perhaps also his heart; the chief trouble, he thought, was his stomach. There is no doubt that the tubercular infection had now spread to Keats's digestive tract, but it still seems incredible that Clark, a specialist in phthisis, was not overly concerned about his lungs. As for the cause of the disease, Clark laid it to his "mental exertions." Fresh air, moderate exercise, and avoidance of worry above all were his prescription: relieve Keats's anxiety and "throw medicine to the dogs." Accordingly he recommended that Keats go riding and hired a horse for him—at six pounds a month, to Severn's indignation. When Keats said he wanted music and Severn rented a piano (for another thirty shillings a month), Clark loaned him a number of volumes of music, including a prized set of Haydn's sonatas.

So for a few weeks all ran smoothly. Keats really appeared to be convalescing, as Severn wrote in a hopeful letter to Haslam.[11] They settled down into a comfortable round of activity, dull for Severn, Keats feared, but within the limits of his own strength. They began to explore the city, loitered along the Corso or strolled up the fashionable Pincian Hill. Here they met another young English consumptive, one Lieutenant Elton, who kept Keats company

11 GEORGE KEATS

From a miniature by Joseph Severn,
Keats-Shelley Memorial House, Rome

TOM KEATS

a drawing by Joseph Severn,
s-Shelley Memorial House, Rome

IV BENJAMIN ROBERT HAYDON

From the 1828 portrait by Georgiana
Margaretta Zornlin, National Portrait
Gallery, London

V LEIGH HUNT

From the 1821 portrait by B. R. Haydon, National Portrait Gallery, London

Seymour Kirkup A.
Rome 1822

VI JOSEPH SEVERN

From an engraving after a pencil drawing by Seymour Kirkup, 1822, reproduced in William Sharp's *Life and Letters of Joseph Severn* (1892)

CHARLES BROWN

m the 1828 bust by Andrew Wilson,
ts Memorial House, Hampstead

PHOTOGRAPH BY
CHRISTOPHER OXFORD

viii JOHN KEATS, 1816

From a drawing by Joseph Severn, Victoria and
Albert Museum, London
CROWN COPYRIGHT

ix JOHN KEATS, 1819

From a drawing by Charles Brown, National Portrait Gallery, London

On the first looking into Chapman's Homer

Much have I travell'd in the Realms of Gold,
And many goodly states, and Kingdoms seen;
Round many Western islands have I been,
Which Bards in fealty to Apollo hold.
Of one wide expanse had I been told,
Which deep brow'd Homer ruled as his Demesne:
Yet could I never judge what Men could mean,
Till I heard Chapman speak out loud and bold:—
Then felt I like some Watcher of the Skies—
When a new Planet swims into his Ken,
Or like stout Cortez when with wond'ring eyes
He star'd at the Pacific, and all his Men
Look'd at each other with a wild surmise—
Silent upon a Peak in Darien—

XI FANNY BRAWNE

From a silhouette cut by Auguste Edouard, reproduced
in H. B. Forman's edition of *Letters of John Keats to
Fanny Brawne* (1878)

XII WENTWORTH PLACE, HAMPSTEAD

Great Smith Street
Tuesday Morn

My sweet Fanny,

On awakening from my three days dream
("I cry to dream again") I find one and another astonish'd
at my idleness and thoughtlessness. I was miserable
last night. the morning is always restorative. I
must be busy, or try to be so. I have several things
to speak to you of tomorrow morning. Mrs Dilke
I should think will tell you that I purpose living at
Hampstead. I must impose chains upon myself. I shall
be able to do nothing. I should like to cast the die for
Love or death. I have no patience with any thing
else. If you ever intend to be cruel to me as you
say in jest now but perhaps may sometimes be
in earnest be so now. and I will. my mind is
in a tremble, I cannot tell what I am writing.

Ever my love yours

John Keats

PHOTOGRAPH BY THE AUTHOR

while Severn went off to sketch the ruins or study the Raphaels in the Vatican. Elton was tall and good-looking and soon caught the eye of a famous beauty among the promenaders—Pauline Bonaparte, the Princess Borghese, a sister of Napoleon. Her languorous stares irritated Keats so keenly that they gave up walking on the Pincio thereafter. But when the three young Englishmen went to see Canova's notorious statue of the princess lying half nude on a sofa, propped on one elbow, with an apple in the other hand, Keats gave it a nickname, "The Aeolian Harp," which has stuck ever since. Evenings at home Keats read while Severn sketched or played the piano. The Haydn sonatas delighted Keats: he told Severn that Haydn was like a child, "for there is no knowing what he will do next." They practised Italian together, and Keats went on studying Italian poetry. Their one real complaint against Rome was the abominable food sent up from a *trattoria* in the square, at four shillings a dinner. Though Keats's Italian was still far from fluent, he soon found an effective way of protesting. One evening when their meal appeared, tasteless as ever, Keats sniffed the dishes, then emptied them one by one out the window—fowl, cauliflower, macaroni, pudding—and motioned to the porter to take the basket away. The man laughed and returned fifteen minutes later with an excellent dinner, at no extra charge. From that time on they ate well.

Severn had good reason to think Keats was on the mend, for he started talking about poetry again. The idea had come to him of writing a long poem on the story of Sabrina, the river-nymph of Milton's *Comus* and tutelary goddess of the Severn—no doubt as a gesture of thanks to his friend. Thoughts of Milton and English legend and Spenser's lovely Una ran together in his mind as he discussed it—and perhaps also of Fanny, whose faith had endured as many trials as Una's. Keats also encouraged Severn to get to work on his painting for the Academy fellowship, uneasily remembering the gossip about him at Hilton's the winter before. At his urging Severn went and presented his letters of introduction and soon made some valued acquaintances among the connoisseurs and a crowd of young English architects and painters of good family. Severn seems to have had a good eye for the main chance; he had started on the trip thinking that Keats's company in Rome would prove a solid advantage to him, and he later promised his family never to know anyone who was not his superior in talent or fortune or position so that he would be constantly "raising myself and improving." [12] Yet he was so ingenuous in his eagerness to get on with people that no one could dislike him, and he did not resent the fact that his new friends took a greater interest in Keats than in himself.

It was a good show that Keats put on, and in the first month he faltered only once. One day he started reading a copy of Alfieri's tragedies, but at the second page unexpectedly broke down and threw the book aside. The lines

> *Misera me! sollievo à me non resta*
> *Altro che'il pianto, ed il pianto è delitto* *

had touched the nerve which he had managed till then to guard. Severn was upset; he still could not guess the anguish that underlay Keats's resolute control. Even in his last letter to Brown on November 30—the last he ever wrote—Keats kept carefully to the surface of things. "My dear Brown," he began, " 'Tis the most difficult thing in the world to me to write a letter. My stomach continues so bad, that I feel it worse on opening any book,—yet I am much better than I was in Quarantine. I have an habitual feeling of my real life having past, and that I am leading a posthumous existence. God knows how it would have been—" he hesitated, thinking if only Brown had come with him; [13] started again, "but it appears to me—however, I will not speak of that subject." Grasping at calm, he tried instead to speak of some of the matters which Brown had mentioned in a letter that had recently arrived from him, but found he could not even look at the letter again: "I am so weak (in mind) that I cannot bear the sight of any hand writing of a friend I love so much as I do you." He tried to give a little news of himself, but there was nothing worth saying. "There is one thought enough to kill me—I have been well, healthy, alert &c., walking with her —and now—the knowledge of contrast, feeling for light and shade, all that information (primitive sense) necessary for a poem are great enemies to the recovery of the stomach." For one perilous moment he nearly lost his balance, then recovered it. "There, you rogue, I put you to the torture,—but you must bring your philosophy to bear—as I do mine, really—or how should I be able to live?" He added a few messages to friends in London, explaining his

---

* *Filippo*, I.i.19 f.: "Unhappy me! No solace remains for me but weeping, and weeping is a crime."

failure to call before leaving England or promising to write before the next post. The farewell to Brown was almost too much. "I can scarcely bid you good bye even in a letter," he ended. "I always made an awkward bow."

Partly by Keats's fortitude, partly by Brown's careful deletions, the letter conceals Keats's sickening realization that he would probably never see his friend again. The letter of Brown to which he was replying, written from Chichester during Brown's visit there at the end of September, has not survived; but in it he no doubt explained his delay in returning from Scotland by the accidents of the mails and told Keats of the unlucky coincidence of their ships passing at Gravesend. Apparently he also rationalized his refusal to start for Italy by praising Severn's rather doubtful virtues as a companion and by insisting that Keats would be well enough to return in the spring.[14] How much he said of his real preoccupation this fall can of course only be guessed. But it must have been about this time that Brown decided to acknowledge Abby's child as his own son and heir. In order to conciliate Abby, it would be necessary to go through the formality of a Roman Catholic marriage—which, as Brown knew, had no legal force in England at that time—and take her back under his roof.* Once he gained safe possession of the boy, however, he evidently planned to get rid of the mother and go his own way as usual.[15]

Whatever the content of Brown's letter from Chichester, its tone may be gauged by the jocularity of a later letter which has survived, written from Wentworth Place in reply to Keats's "posthumous" letter of November 30. On December 21 Brown wrote a long screed of gossip about their friends, a new literary feud, a lucrative evening of poker—and Abby and the child. "O, I must tell you Abby is living with me again, but not in the same capacity,—she keeps to her own bed, & I keep myself continent. Any more nonsense of the former kind would put me in an awkward predicament with her." These arrangements, he assured Keats, "prevent the affair from giving pain next door." As for the child,

---

* The objections of Brown's friends to his behaviour are an interesting reflection of the double standard of the time. According to Brown, Rice later told him that "As for getting the woman with child, there was no harm in it; but there is harm in taking the child into your own house," if only because Brown was "pretending to have more feeling" than his neighbours while in fact ruffling their sensibilities. (Charles Brown, *Some Letters and a Miscellanea*, ed. M. B. Forman [1937], p. 26.)

he was thriving gloriously—"but between you and me, I think an infant is disagreeable,—it is all gut and squall."

Once again he refused Keats's request that he join him in Rome, pleading the heavy extra expense—an expense which, it may be noted, he afforded without difficulty two years later when the trip was not necessary.[16] It is significant that Brown later deleted this request when he transcribed Keats's November 30 letter for publication. He similarly omitted without indication Keats's offer to meet the costs of his trip out of George's expected remittance— an offer which Brown indignantly refused even though the sum was clearly owing to him. At the end of September a much-delayed letter, written in mid-June, had come from George, who in response to the news of his brother's illness promised to sell the steamboat and send him the expected £200 in a few weeks. If Keats ever read this letter, he would have learned from it the astonishing fact that Brown had written to George without his knowledge about sending him to Italy as long ago as March. But it seems clear that Brown opened it in Chichester and decided merely to summarize it in his own letter to Keats rather than forward it.[17] Yet this fact may also help to explain the inward uneasiness that drove Brown to insist in a letter to Taylor that "the indulgence of his friends" had actually harmed Keats and that the bad weather and company and accommodations of the voyage were "good physic" to his mind, as well as to impel him to tamper with the record of this chapter in Keats's life when he came to write it years later. Brown then rationalized his refusal by stating that he was "preparing to follow [Keats to Italy] very early in the spring, and not return, should he prefer to live there"; but he nowhere mentioned this plan in any of his letters during this winter.[18] Yet this is the friend whom Keats told that he would think of him in his dying moments.

Keats's "posthumous existence" dated from the receipt of Brown's letter from Chichester, and not long afterward it turned in the inevitable direction. On December 10 Severn went out for his early-morning walk and posted some letters; when he returned, Keats was awake and ready for breakfast, in good spirits. Then, without warning, a fit of coughing seized him. Gasping for breath, he vomited nearly two cupfuls of blood. Severn, in terror, ran downstairs and across the square for Dr. Clark, who came at once and took another cupful of blood from Keats's arm to arrest the haemorrhage. Faint with bleeding, Keats lapsed back into bed;

but as soon as Severn left the room he staggered out and began groping among his belongings for the bottle of laudanum which Severn had unsuspectingly bought for him at Gravesend. Severn returned a moment later and in a flash of comprehension snatched the bottle away. Keats pleaded, then flew into a rage, but it was no use. Back in bed, with Severn watching him with a new and startled anxiety, he stared in blank despair at the prospect before him. Only the last painful stage of disease lay ahead—the steady sapping of each vital power, the slow breaking of the spirit. He had gone each step of the way with Tom, and before he left England he had resolved to kill himself rather than accept this final defeat. Now once more he found himself trapped by his friends, impaled on their very kindness.

The next morning he had another attack as violent as the first, then three more in one terrible week. Between the haemorrhages and the blood-letting, all his carefully hoarded strength ebbed away. His fever soared, his eyes turned glassy and staring; but worse still was the hunger he suffered. His power of digestion was nearly gone, and Dr. Clark ordered him onto a starvation diet, as little as one anchovy and a piece of toast a day, to keep down the bleeding. Day after day he begged the anguished Severn for more food; night after night he could not sleep. By the end of the week all his courage and self-control had been battered down. He talked for hours in a delirium of discomfort—about Brown and the Brawnes, George and Fanny and most of all Tom, with every memory or foreboding twisted by his despair; of the friends whose hopes he had disappointed and the enemies who had ruined his career. In his extremity, it seems, he suspected that someone in London had poisoned him.[19] Severn feared Keats was losing his mind. Day and night he watched by his bed, hardly leaving him to sleep. The servants refused to wait on them any longer, out of the Italian superstition that consumption was contagious. "Little did I dream on THIS when I left London," Severn exclaimed to Brown in horror. Yet now he manfully shouldered all the burdens of lighting fires, cooking meals, sweeping and washing up, tending to Keats's bodily needs, then reading to him for hours from *Don Quixote* and Maria Edgeworth, old favourites which Keats had brought with him as convalescent reading.

Two weeks later the crisis subsided, leaving them to face the wreckage of their hopes. Dr. Clark told Severn privately that consumption would set in soon and that Keats could never return to England—indeed, that he should never have left it. Yet not until an Italian physician was called in on consultation did he decide that Keats's lungs were affected as well as his stomach. Meanwhile Clark's kindness to Keats was unflagging. He now called on his patient four or five times a day; once he went all over Rome looking for a special kind of fish which he could eat. Mrs. Clark prepared all Keats's food herself and baked mince pies for Severn. His new acquaintances called regularly, though the sight of a strange face usually made Keats miserable. One of them, the young sculptor William Ewing, spelled Severn at the invalid's bedside and searched the city for ice jellies when they were recommended for Keats.[20]

But once Keats's fever abated he settled down into an unshakable depression which frightened Severn still more. On Christmas morning, when he saw Severn writing to Taylor, he joked, "Tell Taylor I'll soon be out in a second edition—in sheets—and cold press." It was a bad joke. His relapse had brought back his old longing to believe in immortality with a still wilder despair, and Severn, who was a simple believing Christian, found the sight of Keats "dying in horror" unspeakably painful. He tried to convince Keats there would be some kind of reward for his suffering, but Keats was only exacerbated by the piety he could not accept. Yet he desperately wished to believe in something—not the Christian faith, which he found impossible, but in some philosophy that would ease the task of dying for him. In anguish he made Severn write down a list of books—Jeremy Taylor's *Holy Living and Holy Dying, Pilgrim's Progress,* and Madame Dacier's translation of Plato. His mind was turning back to the old arguments with Bailey, and to the noble example of Socrates, who had led him to grapple for his own system of soul-making. Yet none of these books could be found. In his anguish he groaned against the "malignant being" which denied him faith—that "last cheap comfort, which every rogue and fool may have," as Severn was appalled to hear him call it.

Christmas for Severn, his first away from home, was "the strangest and saddest" he ever spent. Yet the day was lightened by a shower of letters from England. Three came for Keats—one from Hessey, another from Brown, which "gravely answered" Keats's despairing letter from Naples with, no doubt, the familiar advice to "keep your mind easy, my dear fellow, and no fear of your body." The third was from Fanny Brawne. The sight of that slender slanting hand was too much. Keats, "affected most bitterly," handed the letters back to Severn, the one from Fanny still unopened, and said, "No more letters for me." By now the pattern of the events of the last year must have been clear to him. The voyage to Italy had been useless from the start, as he had suspected all along; the friend whom he held dearest had intended all along not to go with him; and he would die now cut off both from the woman he loved and from the friend on whose loyalty he had counted to the end. In the weeks ahead, as Severn recalled, it was "the kindness of his friends" that Keats brooded over with the greatest bitterness.[21] Later on Christmas Day, in a desperate gesture of self-destruction, he asked Severn as his last request that his death not be mentioned in the newspapers and that no engraving be made from any picture of him. In his last days in England, Fanny Brawne recalled, "his most ardent desire was to live to redeem his name from the obloquy cast upon it." [22] Now, in what seemed to him the failure of everything for which he had hoped in life, he wanted the record to be wiped clean, his very name forgotten. Only the thought of annihilation could give him peace.

Back in England the members of Keats's circle went each his own way, each one concerned with Keats's progress in his own fashion. Hessey, kindly and conscientious, copied out almost every letter from Rome to send around to Keats's friends, while Brown took his own next door to read to the Brawnes with discreet omissions. Meanwhile he was dickering with John Scott to publish his journal of the Scottish trip and waiting with rising irritation for George to send the promised £200. But George's hopes for selling the steamboat had been dashed when the purchaser disappeared; his only news this fall was the completion of his lumber mill and the birth of his second daughter. In a dejected letter to his brother in November, he suggested "Marriage might do you good," then offered to send Miss Brawne "an India crape dress or merino shawl or something scarce with you but cheap with us." Haslam, whom Brown had already persuaded that George was responsible for all Keats's worries, wrote Severn in deep anxiety never to mention George to Keats but to urge him to unburden his mind.[23] He still counted on the Italian spring to work a miracle, for he could not bear the thought of losing his friend: "If I know what it is to love,

I truly love John Keats." Only Haslam was allowed to call on Fanny Keats at Walthamstow with news of her brother; Mrs. Dilke and Mrs. Brawne were still refused. Yet Fanny Brawne started writing her regularly the day after Keats sailed—tactful, affectionate letters which the girl managed to hide from the terrible eye of Mrs. Abbey. The news which Fanny sent was never bright, for she was more convinced by Keats's hoplessness about his condition than any of his friends. She tried not to expect to hear from Keats herself for a long time—knowing what an effort each letter cost him. Yet two months went by with no word except the "God bless you!" he sent her from quarantine; then a third. "If I have a right guess, a certain person next door is a little disappointed at not receiving a letter from you," Brown observed in mid-December, "but not a word has dropped." Fanny kept her proud silence up; even to Fanny Keats she was no more than her brother's next-door neighbour. At the end of December she was rewarded, briefly, with the good report Severn had sent Haslam from Rome at the beginning of the month.

The three or four weeks that lapsed between the sending and receiving of letters made Fanny very impatient, as she once confessed; [24] they also make for ironic discrepancies in the narrative of these months. The dark December in Rome was a time of rising hopes in London; then early in January, just as the news of Keats's relapse reached Hampstead, Severn was watching a change in Keats which gave him a flicker of hope. A new calm succeeded the black despair of the weeks before. Severn sensed that Keats had at last given up not only the thought but even the desire of recovery. Yet it seemed that this quietude relieved him as no medicine had done. Accordingly on January 11 Severn wrote Mrs. Brawne that he now hoped to bring Keats back to England in the spring; for "if anything will recover him it is this absence of himself."

Outside their window the Roman spring was already starting; in the mild sunshine the fruit trees opened their blossoms to the delicate air. The day before Keats had seemed well enough to get up. Severn put fresh clothes on him and helped him into the sitting room, where he stretched out on the sofa and began to talk with Severn about his own concerns. Keats was anxious about Severn's health, and kept prescribing medicines, rest, exercise, even change of air for his friend. "He is my doctor," Severn told Taylor. [25] But especially since his relapse Keats had worried that Severn would lose his precious chance of the R.A. fellowship by taking care of him. For a month Severn had found hardly an hour or two together for sketching in the back room, but Keats managed to rouse him up to write Sir Thomas Lawrence about his progress. That evening, as he finished his letter to Mrs. Brawne, Severn looked in at Keats: he was sleeping peacefully, looking more like himself than he had for weeks. From somewhere, for a while at least, he had got his courage back, his hard-won sense of identity. The poet was dead in him, the discontented, restless, and eloquent self who had fought for an immortal name and failed. Yet at this crisis his other earlier selves reappeared and buoyed his spirit up: the doctor who, mastering his own distress, sought patiently to do some good for others; and the proud image of his boyhood, the young officer who faced death with wordless fortitude.

⇒≫ �≪⇐

By January 15 this brief respite was over, and Keats turned into the last stage of his journey. There were no more haemorrhages, only the relentless advance of the final symptoms: a high fever and a hammering pulse; cold sweats at night that set his teeth chattering; a constant dry cough, with the noose inside his chest slipping a little tighter each time; a thicker and thicker expectoration of mucus, clay-coloured and blood-streaked. By the end of January his digestion had failed and he could live only on milk. The flesh began wasting away from his limbs, his knees growing knobbled, his hands shrinking to a ghastly thinness which once brought him to tears to look on. And each step in this slow destruction of the athletic body in which he had once taken such delight, Keats recognized with dreadful clarity. At last Severn acknowledged there was no hope: Keats's death was only two or three weeks away.

It was a terrible time for Severn. Besides his daily sharing of Keats's sufferings, which bound him closer to his friend every day, he now had several growing anxieties. At the end of December he learned that the landlady had reported Keats's illness to the police. Under Roman law Severn was threatened with heavy additional expenses—not only an autopsy but also a complete refurbishing of every room Keats had entered, in which everything would be destroyed down to the paper on the walls and the varnish on the floor. With his English conviction that this fear of contagion was nonsense, Severn was enraged, but also alarmed: Keats's books, his own painting materials, even the hired piano would be sacrificed. Another anxious secret he had to keep from Keats was a sudden crisis in their finances. In December, on the advice of his banker, Torlonia, Keats had drawn the entire remaining sum in his letter of credit to deposit in Rome, not realizing that the London bankers would not honour drafts above a certain small figure. When the bill for £120 was presented in London, it was promptly returned; and, early in January, Severn found their credit refused at Torlonia's and his supply of cash reduced to a few crowns. Dr. Clark immediately loaned him some money and wrote an explanation to London, but several weeks went by before the misunderstanding was cleared up. Severn meanwhile was paralysed with frustration: he could easily earn money by going out to paint miniatures, but Keats was too nervous to endure a strange face at his bedside. Gallantly he continued his day-and-night watch, performing all the most menial tasks, reading to Keats until, dizzy with fatigue, he hardly understood the words he uttered. Many nights he sat up with him almost till dawn, writing letters or sketching Keats's head on the pillow to keep himself awake,* and stringing the candles together with thread to keep one lit if he fell asleep. His letters to his family were always resolutely cheerful; only to Haslam and Brown did he confide his troubles. Inevitably he fell ill himself, toward the end of January. Keats insisted that a nurse be found to give Severn a respite. Luckily Dr. Clark found an English nurse whom Keats seemed to like, and for two hours every other day Severn had a little precious freedom.

Under this testing, Severn's thoughtless gaiety and simpleminded piety were being transmuted into a resilient and self-effacing devotion that none of his friends in England could have predicted. It was sorely tried in these last weeks of January as Keats's irritability became uncontrollable. He would ask for food, then refuse it when Severn prepared it for him, five or six times a day. For a while he was too nervous even to be read to; then a great desire for books came on him, and Severn read steadily for three days. The longing for some faith in a life after death still

---

* Severn's sketch, with the inscription "28th Jan. 3 o'clock Mg. Drawn to keep me awake—a deadly sweat was on him all this night," is reproduced among the illustrations as Plate XIV.

tormented him. By good fortune Severn located a copy of *Holy Living and Holy Dying,* but it did not bring Keats the solace he hoped for. Instead, as the weary days and restless nights wore on, he began to accuse Severn of the blackest cruelty in thwarting his attempt at suicide. He could think only of the long sleep of death with any comfort. "He talks of it with delight," Severn wrote Taylor in wonder, "the strangeness of his mind every day surprises me—no one feeling or one notion like any other being." One morning on his early walk Severn saw the first roses blooming and reported them to Keats when he awoke. To Severn's dismay, Keats wept at the news. He had always been able to escape from suffering, he told Severn, in watching the silent growth of flowers; now —he had hoped to be dead before the spring came round again.

Since Christmas, when the mere sight of Fanny Brawne's handwriting had been too much for him, Keats had not been able to read any of his letters from England. Early in February a letter arrived from Hampstead, addressed in Brown's robust hand, and Keats summoned up the courage to open it. In a searing flash of recognition he saw the letter inside was from Fanny Brawne. His nerves, already taut as fiddle strings, now must have snapped. "The effects were on him for many days," Severn noted. When he could bring himself to mention it again, Keats asked Severn to put the letter in his coffin, along with his sister's, after his death. In a day or two he changed his mind and told Severn that only his sister's letters should be buried with him. One last fit of anger choked him at the thought of the desire forever unfulfilled. "He found many causes of his illness in the exciting and thwarting of his passions," Severn wrote Brown in mystification, "but I persuaded him to feel otherwise on this delicate point." But the greatest torment in these last weeks was the thought of the nameless friends who had sent him to a lonely death in Rome. Severn, always unsuspecting, wrote Brown that Keats was dying a martyr to "these infernal scoundrels," "a thousand miles from his dear home, without one comfort but me when—" then broke off in anguish. "I cannot bear to think of it." Neither, apparently, could Brown, for he later deleted this passage in transcribing Severn's letter for publication.[26]

Meanwhile the news of Keats's relapse had reached England, shattering at once all the cheerful expectations of the autumn before. Brown, who first heard it, was stunned almost to speechlessness. For a week he could not bring himself to write Severn, haunted as he was by a vision of Keats constantly at his side, looking intently into his face. "So much as I have loved him," he cried out, "I never knew how closely he was wound about my heart." But at once he defended himself by leaping to the attack. Keats's disease, he reminded Severn, was all in the mind, all the result of George's cruelty—an accusation which he repeated not only to Haslam but also to Taylor and Hessey. "I sit planning schemes of vengeance upon his head," he wrote—that "canting, selfish, heartless swindler—who will have to answer for the death of his brother." Yet two weeks later he was compelled to confess to Severn his remorse that "I did not, at all hazards, and in spite of apparent difficulties, follow you both to Italy, and relieve you in your distressing attentions." [27] Taylor, on learning the news, wrote Severn to read the Book of Job to comfort Keats; then, after sending George a stiff letter demanding to be reimbursed for the £150 letter of credit, he began raising a second fund to meet Keats's further needs. Reynolds informed Taylor that he had already sent £50 to Keats, though it turned out a few months later that he had only intended to and never did in fact. Another friend sent a £50 credit to a banker in Florence for Keats to use there in the summer—Woodhouse, perhaps, honouring a little belatedly his farewell promise. Hessey, deeply concerned for Keats's spiritual welfare, urged Severn to convince Keats of God's forgiveness through Christ and "pray with him—pray by him—pray for him." [28] Bailey, in a letter of literary chit-chat to Taylor, found some consoling "dispensation of a kind Providence" in the thought that Keats would be spared many inevitable disappointments by his death. "Poor Fellow," he added, "my heart bleeds for him; but human sorrow is very unavailing." Leigh Hunt, from whom Bailey thought Keats had learned the "fatal error" of irreligion, sent Severn a letter whose tenderness redeems all that Keats or his friends could ever blame him for. Hunt begged Severn to remind Keats that recovery was still possible if he would only hope steadfastly for it; but if he was beyond all hope, Hunt wrote, "tell him that we shall all bear his memory in the most precious part of our hearts, and that the world shall bow their heads to it, as our loves do. Tell him," he added, "that the most sceptical of us has faith enough in the high things that nature puts into our heads, to think that all who are of one accord in mind and heart, are journeying to one and the same place, and shall unite somehow or other again face to face, mutually conscious, mutually delighted. Tell him he is only before us on the road, as he was in everything else, and that we are coming after him." [29]

The greatest anxiety among Keats's friends was borne in the greatest silence. Fanny Brawne took care, as she later told Fanny Keats, "never to trouble them with any feelings of mine"; and Brown himself wondered at her firmness. Mrs. Brawne tried to soften the blow of the bad news, but Fanny replied, "I know he must die soon: when you hear of his death, tell me immediately—I am not a fool." [30] For a while she tried to shield Fanny Keats from the news, writing her a collected letter saying nothing of her brother's relapse; then, on February 21, she decided she must be told. Yet, as she wrote, her emotion began to break through, half against her will. For months she had silently watched Brown, next door, playing the part of Keats's dearest friend while dodging the responsibility which she had expected from the first he would fulfil, of following Keats to Italy. Now the news that Keats no longer wished to live overwhelmed her: he was being killed, she wrote Fanny Keats, not only by the malignity of an indifferent world but also by "want of feeling in those who ought above all to have felt for him." [31] Driven by her grief, she started to take Fanny into her confidence. "And now my dear Girl, my dear Sister for so I feel you to be, forgive me if I have not sufficiently softened this wretched news. Indeed I am not now able to contrive words that would appear less harsh—if I am to lose him I lose everything, and then you, after my mother, will be the only person I shall feel interest or attachment for—I feel that I love his sister as my own."

By the middle of February, Keats had fallen back into the calm of sheer exhaustion. Slowly his body was relaxing its hold in its unconscious wrestling against death, and his mind lapsed into a new peace. He now could talk easily to Severn for hours, and at night he fell into comfortable sleep. Even his dreams were pleasant. The fresh milk on which he was subsisting came to seem beautiful to him—its sight and smell and taste. He began to tell Severn of his last wishes, one by one. Severn was to have his seven-volume set of Shakespeare's plays and his treasured volume of Shakespeare's *Poems*. The purse which Fanny Keats had made for him as a final gift was to be placed in his coffin, along with all his unopened letters and a lock of hair—Fanny Brawne's, though Severn did not know it. And on his gravestone he asked that no name or date should be written, only the legend "HERE LIES ONE WHOSE NAME WAS WRIT IN WATER." Above it was to be carved a Greek lyre with four of its eight strings broken—"to show his Classical Genius cut off by death before its maturity," as Severn later interpreted it. He knew that Keats had had this thought for a long time, for in Hampstead the spring before he had asked Severn to sketch the lyre for him, without telling him the reason. But there was more in Keats's mind than Severn guessed. The lyre was the device of the Tassie gem which Fanny Brawne had evidently given him that Christmas Day of 1818. Not his name, then, but her seal was to mark his resting place.[32]

After making these requests, Keats lay quietly in bed for several days, staring up at the white cross-beams of the ceiling with its yellow rosettes set in blue squares, shifting from one hand to another a white carnelian—Fanny's seal, though Severn did not recognize it.[33] Outside his window the Roman artillery rumbled through the streets; Rome lay in the path of the Neapolitan advance against the Austrians, and it was feared that the city might be ransacked. But Keats hardly noticed the disturbance. He was thinking of the open meadow outside the Aurelian Wall near the Pyramid of Caius Cestius, where a few Protestant graves were scattered between the cypresses in the long grass. Severn had visited the cemetery at his request and returned to tell him of the flocks of sheep that grazed there, with their tinkling bells the only sound to break the silence, and the early daisies and violets already in bloom.

Meanwhile Keats's Roman friends stood by as best they could. Dr. Clark called as regularly as ever and now tried to steady Severn against the event to come. William Ewing also came to help out from time to time. Once he brought a handsome young Spanish gentleman, a romantic novelist and revolutionary-in-exile named Valentine Llanos Guiterez, whose brief meeting with Keats was to be a turning point in his life. But for Keats now it was only Severn's presence that mattered. For long hours he slept as Severn dozed at his bedside by a solitary candle. Sometimes Keats would wake in a moment of terror, wondering where he was or who was with him; then his eyes wandered over the dim room till they fell on Severn and closed again in sleep.

Around February 19 or 20 Clark told Severn to expect Keats's death any day. His face now showed the same emaciation as his body, the cheeks hollowed, the nose beaked, the ridges of the forehead jutting out over the eyes, which still glittered with fever. Yet for all his longing for death, his body fought stubbornly against it up to the end, holding out weeks after Clark thought it possible. Even out of his despair Keats managed to make a joke: he greeted Clark one morning with the question, "How long will this posthumous life of mine last?" His mind still stood over and above the ruin that was overtaking his body, and in two of his last conversations with Severn he was thinking only of his friend. Still fearful that Severn might lose his fellowship, Keats now thought that Hilton should request an extension for him at the Royal Academy—if only for Keats's sake. He made Severn promise to write to Taylor and ask him to take up the matter with Hilton; Severn agreed, and Keats was satisfied.[34] But one more subject had to be discussed, the most painful of all. It took all that was left of the hero in Keats to tell Severn what, as a doctor, he knew his friend must be prepared for. With a calmness that astonished Severn, he asked him if he had ever seen anyone die. Severn answered no; then Keats replied, "Well then I pity you— poor Severn, what trouble and danger you have got into for me." But he must be firm, Keats told him, for it would not last long, and he did not think he would be convulsed at the end. He must have been remembering Tom's last moments, which—so at least he had told George—were "not so painful"; and the very last was "without a pang." So much hope, at least, Keats tried to hold out to his friend.

On the night of February 21 Severn thought the end had come. Keats breathed with such pain that Severn had to prop him up on the pillows, where, hour after hour, he struggled against suffocation; yet he was still alive when the windows turned pale with dawn. Another day and night Severn watched while Keats coughed the breath in and out of his body. On the twenty-third the English nurse came and stayed all day while Severn snatched a little sleep. The nurse left, and the afternoon sank toward evening; then Keats gasped out to his friend, "Severn—I—lift me up—I am dying." Severn took him in his arms and held him close, but Keats broke out into a sweat and cried, "Don't breathe on me—it comes like ice." The phlegm was boiling in his throat, and he gripped Severn's hand very hard as he fought for breath. He was face to face with death, but even at this moment he did not lose his awareness of his friend. Clinging to Severn, he whispered, "Don't be frightened—I shall die easy—be firm, and thank God it has come!"

He did not die easy: for seven hours he fought against slow drowning. Severn listened to the mucus gurgling in his throat as slowly Keats lost the strength to cough. Still he kept his eyes fixed on Severn, watching him with fierce wordless consciousness but seemingly without pain. Toward eleven o'clock the struggle grew quieter; Severn thought he had fallen asleep. Then he realized that Keats was dead.

Epilogue

THE next day Dr. Clark took the shattered Severn over to his house to begin a long recovery from grief and fatigue. Then the machinery of death was put in motion. Casts were taken of Keats's face, hand, and foot. The following day an autopsy was performed. Keats's lungs were entirely destroyed; it was the worst consumption Clark had ever seen, and a miracle that he had lived so long. The third day, Monday, February 26, Keats was buried at dawn, with the last gifts and unopened letters of Fanny Brawne and Fanny Keats sealed in his coffin. The English chaplain at Rome and eight mourners followed his body to the grave, which lay near that of Shelley's third child, within the shadow of the Pyramid of Caius Cestius. When the service was over Dr. Clark and his friends heaped turfs of daisies on the grave. Immediately afterward the police took charge of the apartment at the Piazza di Spagna, burning all the furniture, scraping the walls and floors and even making new doors and windows. Severn, though still too shaken to be left alone for almost a fortnight after Keats's death, wrote a brief letter to Brown on February 27 to break the news.

For weeks Brown had tried to pretend he wished Keats's sufferings at an end, but as each letter came from Rome he read it "in a horror" lest his wish had been realized. Now, when the news reached Hampstead on March 17, he was overcome. The next day he sent off four or five notes to pass on the word, then went next door to tell the Brawnes. Writing Severn a few days later, he could not describe the first shock of his announcement, but merely reported that Fanny was "now pretty well,—and thro' out she has shown a firmness of mind which I little expected from one so young." At once she and her family went into mourning. The reactions of Keats's other friends are not recorded. Each man grieved in his own way, then sooner or later returned to his inevitable preoccupations. Haslam broke the news to Fanny Keats. Taylor sent the obituary notices to the papers, then began laying plans to write a biography of Keats and trying once again to collect from George and Abbey some of the funds which he himself had raised for Keats. Bailey, on hearing the news, wrote Taylor that Keats's death seemed a visitation of Providence—"a merciful severity." Haydon recorded Keats's death in his diary almost as an afterthought to that of his friend the journalist John Scott, who had just been killed in a duel arising from a quarrel with the *Blackwood's* set; a month later he wrote Miss Mitford that Keats died a victim of "want of nerve" to bear abuse.[1] Brown in July executed Keats's will by dividing his books among his friends, carefully omitting any gift to George. In Rome, Severn slowly climbed back to health and returned to his painting. In May he wrote Haslam that Keats's grave was now overgrown with daisies, and that he often visited it "with a most delicious melancholy."

But Fanny Brawne, after steeling herself so long against the news of Keats's death, broke down a few weeks after its arrival. She fell ill and her hair was cut short; after her recovery she took to wearing a widow's cap and weeds. Grown alarmingly thin, she shut herself up in her room to pore over Keats's letters, or wandered alone over the Heath day after day and often far into the night, so the watchmen had to be sent with lanterns to find her.[2] As she wrote to Fanny Keats near the end of May, "All his friends have forgotten him, they have got over the first shock, and that with them is all. They think I have done the same, but I have not got over it and never shall—it's better for me that I should not forget him, but not for you."

From the first, it was only to Keats's sister that Fanny Brawne unburdened herself. "For myself, I am patient, resigned, very resigned," she wrote her a week after receiving the news of his death. "I know my Keats is happy, happier a thousand times than he could have been here, for Fanny, you do not, you never can know how much he has suffered. All that grieves me now is that I was not with him, and so near it as I was. And yet it was a great deal through his kindness for me for he foresaw what would happen, he at least was never deceived about his complaint." Once again she was overwhelmed by the thought of his being sent to "that wretched country" to die when his recovery was impossible "and he might have died here with so many friends to soothe him and me *me* with him." With this she broke through her reticence at last and told Fanny the secret: "Had he returned I should have been his wife and he would have lived with us. All now in vain— could we have foreseen—but he did foresee and everyone thought it was only his habit of looking for the worst." Then, remembering Keats's dread of gossip, she begged Fanny never to mention her name in connection with his, and told her she allowed no one to speak of him to her. A month later, reading *As You Like It* in Keats's folio Shakespeare, she pencilled the words "Fanny April 17 1821" beside the FINIS at the end.[3]

→》》 《《←

Keats's friends had not forgotten him that spring, as Fanny thought; but even then his memory and reputation were entering a long eclipse. At the end of March, Taylor had made a public announcement of his intention of writing Keats's biography and began gathering the manuscripts of his poems and letters from Woodhouse, Bailey, and Keats's other friends. But Brown immediately opposed the idea, thinking Taylor "a mere bookseller," and persuaded Severn to send all of Keats's papers to him instead. Thus began a long many-sided rivalry among Keats's friends— including Reynolds, Cowden Clarke, and even Shelley—for the honour of being his biographer, which only served to hasten the breakup of his circle, while the life remained unwritten. Meanwhile, in Rome, Severn worried about the gravestone. He was uncertain whether to use the bitter inscription which Keats had dictated to him, and had to write Brown several times asking his advice in the matter.[4] He also had to nudge Brown to send him the sketch of the lyre he had made in Brown's copy of *Endymion* the year before at Keats's request. Not till a year and a half later did work begin according to his design; then, over two years after Keats's death, the gravestone was erected at last, at Severn's expense. His friends honoured Keats's dying wish that his grave be nameless, but Brown thought that his inscription should be prefaced by an explanation.[5]

This Grave
contains all that was Mortal
of a
YOUNG ENGLISH POET
Who
on his Death Bed,
in the Bitterness of his Heart
at the Malicious Power of his Enemies,
Desired
these Words to be engraven on his Tomb Stone
"Here lies One
Whose Name was writ in Water"

The first real memorial to Keats was Shelley's elegy *Adonais*, published in June 1821—the most enduring and yet in some ways the most misleading of all the tributes to him. Shelley had picked up a few hints from Hunt about Keats's brooding over the reviews during his illness at his house the previous summer, and, smarting as he was over his own treatment by the Tory critics, decided that the *Quarterly* article had actually brought on Keats's fatal haemorrhage.[6] As a living poet, Keats mattered little to Shelley; as a martyr to Tory injustice and a symbol of neglected genius, he inspired some of Shelley's most fervent lines.

> He has outsoared the shadow of our night;
> Envy and calumny and hate and pain,
> And that unrest which men miscall delight,
> Can touch him not and torture not again;
> From the contagion of the world's slow stain
> He is secure. . . .

Though Shelley did much to rescue Keats from Lockhart's caricature of the Cockney bardling, "the amiable Mister Keats," he succeeded only by substituting another distorted picture, the poet of fragile, almost feminine sensibility who could not face adverse criticism. This in turn provoked some deserved ridicule from Byron in *Don Juan*, along with a little grudging appreciation of the promise shown in *Hyperion*:

> John Keats, who was killed off by one critique
> Just as he really promised something great
> If not intelligible, without Greek
> Contrived to talk about the gods of late
> Much as they might have been supposed to speak.
> Poor fellow! His was an untoward fate;

'Tis strange the mind, that fiery particle,
Should let itself be snuffed out by an article.

Yet for many years the myth of Adonais was the only alternative
to Lockhart's gibes. Even many of his friends who knew Keats in
health as well as in sickness repeated Shelley's story in one form
or another, out of their own varying needs to blame the tragedy
of his death on someone. Hazlitt, who had his own reasons for
attacking the Tory critics, described Keats again and again as " 'a
bud bit by an envious worm,' " "a little western flower" on which
the reviews had dropped their poison.[7] Hunt, writing the first real
memoir of Keats in 1828 in a sketch included in his volume of
reminiscences of Byron, helped fix this impression of his weakness
even while trying to correct the Lockhart portrait. He managed
also to hint at Keats's dependence on Brown and himself in a way
that enraged George Keats, and described his morbidity during his
illness in detail that distressed both Brown and Fanny Brawne; [8]
but Keats's other friends either would not or could not refute these
implications.

For some years it seemed that Keats's own despairing wish to be
forgotten might well be realized. Almost all his friends took him
at his own final estimate—that he had left "no immortal work"
behind him, though he would have made himself remembered
if he had lived. Even the most sympathetic reviewers of the *Lamia*
volume saw it as full of poetic promise rather than achievement.
Long after 1820 most readers remained puzzled or offended by
Keats's innovations—his original use of mythology, his complex
and concentrated imagery, his range through the whole spectrum
of the English language. In 1846 De Quincey spoke with a heavy
weight of critical authority in protesting that "upon his mother
tongue, upon this English language, has Keats trampled as with
the hoofs of a buffalo." [9] The year before, Taylor had sold all his
copyrights of Keats's poems and rights in his unpublished manuscripts for a mere fifty pounds. The firm of Taylor and Hessey
had long since failed and dissolved; there was no demand for a
reprint of Keats's works in England until 1840, and when one
appeared that year it was soon remaindered.[10] In 1836, when Severn
suggested that a monument be raised to Keats in England, Brown
replied that his fame was not great enough to warrant it.[11]

Meanwhile the years had moved on, carrying each of his friends, as Keats had foreseen, farther in his own separate direction. There is a tragic fitness in the fact that the first and indeed the only one to escape the touch of "the world's slow stain" with him was Shelley. A year after writing *Adonais*, Shelley was drowned in a shipwreck in the Bay of Spezia after sailing to Leghorn to welcome Leigh Hunt to Italy. When his body was washed ashore near Viareggio, a sea-soaked copy of *Lamia* was found doubled back and thrust into a pocket of his jacket.[12] Hunt himself was to subside comfortably into the Victorian age, his foibles smiled away, his old critical rallying-cries accepted as articles of poetic belief. Yet he continued to do good service to Keats's memory by discussing and occasionally reprinting his poetry in his literary journals. Haydon, who had reached the height of his ambition and prosperity at the time of Keats's death, married soon afterward and found, to his disgust, that he must turn portrait-painter to support his wife and family. In and out of debtors' prison, his reputation declining, he stubbornly continued to paint larger and larger canvases,[13] for which there was less and less room in Victorian England. Finally, at the age of sixty, after the failure of an exhibition of two huge paintings at the Egyptian Hall, where the famous Tom Thumb was drawing crowds of a hundred thousand to Haydon's hundred, he lost his nerve, as he once accused Keats of doing, and shot himself. John Reynolds married the beautiful Eliza Drewe at last, in 1822, but could not give up playing the gay blade in the London clubs and theatres and magazines, even though his law career suffered as a result. They had one child, whom they lost, much to Reynolds' grief. Ten years after his marriage he was in financial straits, with a reputation for hard drinking and sharp card-playing. After slowly losing ground, he ended as an assistant clerk at County Court in the Isle of Wight and died at fifty-two, a broken and forgotten man.

Jane Reynolds, the serious and sentimental, eventually married Thomas Hood the wit—to the surprise of George Keats, who wondered how she ever "captivated so facetious a genius." The cheerful but ailing James Rice took Reynolds into partnership and with his aid mismanaged Fanny and George Keats's legal affairs for a while before dying after a long lingering, in his mid-thirties. The self-effacing Haslam lived out the rest of his days in obscurity and hard work. Woodhouse continued to help Taylor to collect materials for his life of Keats; then he too developed consumption.

His last good deed for Keats was to visit Brown, by then living in Italy, shortly before his death in 1834 and make him promise to start his much-delayed memoir. Hessey turned schoolmaster after failing as a bookseller, and Taylor pursued a long career as editor and scholar. Dilke had as long and more noteworthy a career as a man of letters, while also looking after the interests of Fanny Brawne and George and Fanny Keats. This involved him in a painful quarrel with his old friend Charles Brown when Brown, in gathering materials for his biography of Keats, tried to pin the blame for much of Keats's suffering on George's selfishness. Dilke at once came to George's defence, and the friendship finally ended with bitter words on both sides. Brown, after some difficulty in gaining possession of his boy from "his obstinate mother," went to Italy a year and a half after Keats's death and remained there for twelve years, occupying himself pleasantly in journalism. Having returned to England, he finally wrote his biographical sketch of Keats under curious emotional stress, oppressed by headaches or weeping like a child, haunted by the image of Keats watching him as he wrote. The life was given a public reading in Plymouth at the end of 1836, but Brown could not find a publisher to take it. Five years later he emigrated with his son to New Zealand, where he died in 1842.

Meanwhile George Keats worked hard and prospered in Louisville, raising a large family, paying off his brother's debts, and trying without success to find someone to print Keats's unpublished poems with a brief memoir, for which he was willing to assume the publisher's losses. In his early forties he suffered another financial setback, developed consumption with startling suddenness, and died a few months later. Fanny Keats was the only member of the family to become—as John once promised he and she both should—fat and old "with triple chins and stumpy thumbs." She had to wait patiently for her release from the Abbeys at twenty-one, then go to law, with the help of Dilke, to wrest her inheritance from her guardian—"that consummate villain," as she came to regard him. These were the proceedings that revealed Abbey's mishandling of his trust, and from them Fanny emerged with a portion of £4500—of which about £1200 would have gone to Keats if he had been alive. A year later she married the romantic young Spaniard who had called on Keats a few days before his death, and lived more or less happily ever after as Señora Valentin

Llanos of Madrid. In her late fifties, on a visit to the Piazza di Spagna, she unexpectedly met Joseph Severn for the first time in the very house where Keats died. It was like a reunion of long-lost brother and sister; yet, as a friend of Severn's recalled, Señora Llanos had nothing to say of "her wizard brother," of whom she spoke "as a mystery." [14] But the most unforeseeable change wrought by the years was in Severn himself. Keats's dying advice, that he request Hilton to intercede with the Royal Academy for him, achieved its purpose; in spite of arriving in London three months late, his painting of "The Death of Alcibiades" won him the three-year fellowship as he had hoped. After Keats's death he was taken up by the leaders of the English colony in Rome, and seven years later he married the ward of his patroness, the Countess of Westmoreland. He lived long and happily, though without gaining any distinction as a painter, and in 1860 was appointed British Consul in Rome—a post in which he charmed everyone, according to John Ruskin, from the cardinals in council to the brightest English belles on picnics in the Campagna.

"What fools we mortals are," wrote George Keats on the squabbles over his brother's biography, "how we are straining for ever so small a niche in the temple of Fame." It was not his friends' failings, or lack of them, that mattered to Keats, but some quality that continued to draw him toward them after these failings were recognized; so also it is his gift for friendship that is remembered long after the friends themselves are forgotten. If they are remembered a century or more after their deaths, it is largely in the measure of their loyalty to Keats. Severn, who was honoured to the end of his life as Keats's devoted friend in his last hour, repeatedly acknowledged how much his career owed to this accident of their friendship. But Fanny Brawne, who kept the secret of her engagement for years, as Keats wished, received no such reward for her loyalty. When she recovered from her illness after Keats's death, her beauty had lost all its colour and freshness. She remained in mourning for several years and continued to wear Keats's ring till the end of her life. In 1829 a friend of Valentin Llanos described her as looking very thin and sadly worn, though dazzling in her manner despite her pale looks. She was the same Fanny still. She kept writing gay, affectionate letters to Keats's young sister during her long imprisonment in Walthamstow, full of gossip about books, clothes, their common acquaintances, and Fanny Keats's pet pigeons. When she began going to parties in Hampstead again, her wit was sharp as ever. Sometime after 1825 when she appeared at a ball in a dress trimmed with bugles, John Reynolds punned, "It's good to wear bugles and be heard wherever one goes"; whereupon Fanny Brawne retorted, "And it's good to be a brother-in-law of Tom Hood's and get your jokes for nothing." [15] Her life was darkened again when her brother died of tuberculosis in 1828 and her mother from burns in a tragic accident the following year. Finally in 1833, in her early thirties, she decided to marry, and there is poignant meaning in the fact that she chose a man who, twelve years younger than herself, was close to Keats's own age at the time she first met him in 1818. The rest of her sixty-five years she spent living quietly on the Continent with her husband, Louis Lindon, and their three children.

In 1829, however, four weeks after the death of her mother, Fanny received a disturbing letter from Charles Brown, asking permission to mention her affair with Keats—though not her name—in his projected biography and to quote some of Keats's last bitter poems and letters referring to her. Fanny's reply has often been cited against her to prove she never really loved Keats; yet it is an extraordinary revelation of her honesty and complexity of feeling.[16] Characteristically she said nothing to Brown about her mother's death nor even hinted her possible doubts as to his qualifications as Keats's biographer. After some hesitation she granted Brown's request to mention their story, realizing unhappily that many people both within and without her circle of acquaintance would blame her for a lack of womanly reticence. For herself, she admitted, she did not want to give away the key to her own feelings, or even be connected with all the old abuse of Keats; * and, remembering Keats's desire to be forgotten, she thought it would be kinder "to let him rest for ever in the obscurity to which unhappy circumstances have condemned him." Yet at the same time she hated the picture that had been given to the public—first by Shelley, then by Hazlitt and Hunt—of a "weakness of character that only belonged to his ill health." Though she feared nothing could be done to prove his unfulfilled

---

* Fanny crossed out this sentence in the draft; not, I think, because she feared Brown would think less of her for speaking so forthrightly (as she herself said, "I was more generous ten years ago"), but because on second thought she realized that by surrendering some of her privacy she might help in the vindication of Keats's name.

promise as a poet, she thought his character should be rescued from the misrepresentations of his friends as well as of his enemies. For that reason in the end she approved Brown's intention of telling the full truth of Keats's life; though for herself, she added, "Without claiming too much constancy I may truly say that he is well-remembered by me and that satisfied with that I could wish no one but myself knew he had ever existed."

⁓⟫⟪⁓

Fanny's wish was not to be realized. Unknown to her and to most of Keats's friends, a new generation was already springing up to whom his work spoke with the authentic voice of poetry. In the very month that Fanny Brawne wrote her troubled letter to Brown the Cambridge Union maintained in debate against Oxford that Shelley was a greater poet than Byron—sign of an undergraduate cult in which every ardent reader of *Adonais* was also a champion of Keats.[17] In 1834 Severn wrote Brown from Rome that a group of Cambridge men there wanted to perform *Otho*. Even as early as 1826 the discovery of Keats and Shelley fired the fourteen-year-old Robert Browning with the ambition to become a poet himself. Still it was very slowly that, as the age of George IV gave way to the age of Victoria, old battles were forgotten and new allegiances formed; it was largely the success of another Cambridge admirer and close student of Keats's poetry, young Alfred Tennyson, that won Keats a wide audience at last.

It was to Richard Monckton Milnes, the most brilliant of Keats's champions at Cambridge, that Brown eventually turned over his memoir and collection of Keats manuscripts in the hope of getting them published. After Brown's unexpected death, Milnes decided to write the biography of Keats himself—a task for which he was well fitted as poet, politician, and man of the world. He managed to conciliate all the rival biographers and collect their materials; and his *Life, Letters and Literary Remains,* published in 1848, at last presented Keats in something of his true stature, though heavily draped in Victorian respectability. Though Milnes himself thought the book—"the biography of a mere boy"—would rouse little interest, it scored a wide success, and from this time Keats began to be acknowledged as one of the greatest poets of his generation—or even greater. In the wild-eyed enthusiasm of the young Pre-Raphaelite poets he came to be ranked only one step below Shakespeare, in the immortal company of Homer, Dante, Chaucer, and Leonardo da Vinci.[18] A poignant echo of this sudden adulation of a near-forgotten genius is found in the epitaph inscribed on Reynolds's gravestone at his death in 1852—"The Friend of Keats."

Inevitably a new sentimental appreciation of Keats sprang up alongside the respectable. It was the sentimentalists who raised a fund to have Severn's body reinterred in 1881, two years after his death, by the side of Keats in Rome, with a matching gravestone commemorating his devotion. The respectable tradition received a severe jolt at this time, however, when Keats's letters to Fanny Brawne first appeared in print. Dilke's grandson, Sir Charles, had done all he could to prevent this by buying up and even burning an undisclosed number; and most Victorian readers regarded their publication as an outrage, a revelation of the great poet as a snivelling, sensuous, badly bred surgeon's apprentice. But the condemnation of Fanny Brawne that the letters stirred up was far more scathing. She was reviled as unlovely, unfaithful, totally unfitted to have been Keats's wife, and soon she took the place of Lockhart as the person whose cruelty had killed Keats—"as surely as ever any man was killed by love," [19] it was averred. Remembering the reticence of those two proud characters, no reader of Keats's letters to Fanny can help feeling a pang at some point over the violation of their privacy. Yet Fanny was right when she wrote Brown in 1829 that "if his life is to be published no part ought to be kept back." She was a century ahead of her time in her dedication to the whole truth, however, and, as she had never troubled people with her real feelings, she had to wait until 1936 for something of the real truth of her life to be told. Then, with the publication of her letters to Fanny Keats, she was at last allowed to speak for herself and quietly refute the legend that she was unworthy of Keats's love.

With the centenary of Keats's death in 1921, the tide of his reputation reached its flood. Since then he has received all the varieties of recognition that can be heaped on a poet today—from the publication of edition after edition of his work and volumes of critical analysis and biographical research to the dedication of his living places in Hampstead and Rome as memorials to his name; from translations of his poems into some twenty languages to fictionalizations and dramatizations of his life. Much of this activity would astonish if not also amuse him, one suspects, remembering his wry comment on receiving an invitation to a Shakespeare birthday party—"Shakespeare would stare to see me there." Yet the kind of tribute which would please him most—the comments of a fellow craftsman on his craft—has been the least frequent. In fact the spread of Keats's influence on Victorian poetry ended by making him a symbol of the poet which the new talents of the 1910's and 1920's were determined to repudiate. The Victorians had fastened on the more imitable and less valuable aspects of Keats's work, his sensuousness without his objectivity, his melancholy without his "knowledge of light and shade." Our sense of Keats has changed; yet what now seems most significant in his art—the sureness of ear and firmness of structure, the dialectic of imagery, the tragic vision of life—remains a lesson which every poet must learn for himself.

Nevertheless, Keats's work has survived better than that of any of his contemporaries the long devaluation of romantic poetry that began about the time of Auden's appearance on the scene. Eliot has paid tribute to the Shakespearean quality of Keats's greatness, especially as it appears in his letters; and his best poems have stood up well under the most rigorous analysis of recent criticism. When these critical assessments are added to the evaluations of Keats in recent scholarship—those focused on his interest in ideas, his concern with technique, his absorption in the whole range of the English language and the whole tradition of English poetry —his place in the tradition begins to be seen more clearly. Each new discovery about his life helps disprove Byron's quip that he was "snuffed out by an article," or indeed by anything else than tuberculosis, and to reveal him as a man uniquely gifted with the stamina needed to translate the vision of poetry into performance. And for all one's regret at the poems he never lived to write, every new critical insight into his actual accomplishment sets him further apart from "the inheritors of unfulfilled renown" with whom Shelley classed him.

Yet even the most generous assessment of Keats's stature implies another devaluation—an inversion in effect of Byron's joke about Keats's ignorance of Greek. To an extent it is true that, as Middleton Murry put it, what Keats achieved in four years against heavy disadvantages can only be described as a miracle—one greater even than Shakespeare's achievement, which has had so many doubters.[20] Yet it is more than a miracle. It is a fact of poetic growth which can be traced step by arduous step through Keats's poems and letters, where he may be watched laboriously reshaping the language and the sensibility he inherited into an instrument adequate to his own ideal of poetry and his own vision of human experience; it is a living proof of that continual interanimation of tradition and original talent which is the life force of poetry. In an age in which, by its best critics at least, originality was exalted far above tradition, Keats's special originality was his sense of dedication to the whole tradition of English poetry and his attempt to recover it for the use of poetry in his time. And, as Eliot has said, "Tradition cannot be inherited; if you want it you must obtain it by great labour." Keats earned his place in the tradition of English poetry by his courage to take the great dare of self-creation, his willingness to accept failure and move beyond it, his patience in learning his craft from those who could teach him. His sober prophecy as he started *Hyperion*—"I think I shall be among the English Poets after my death"—has been fulfilled; as Matthew Arnold confirmed it, sixty years later, "He is—he is with Shakespeare."

Notes

All references to Keats's poems are to the second Oxford edition, *The Poetical Works of John Keats* (1958), by H. W. Garrod, cited as *Works*. All references to Keats's letters are to the Harvard edition, *The Letters of John Keats* (2 vols., 1958), by Hyder Edward Rollins, cited as *Letters*. Where more than one item by a single author is cited, subsequent references are given with the initials of the title: thus, for a book, "Gittings, JKLY" stands for "Robert Gittings, *John Keats: The Living Year*"; for an article, "Gittings, 'KSR'" stands for "Robert Gittings, 'Keats's Sailor Relation,' TLS, 15 April 1960." In addition, the following abbreviations are used throughout:

Hampstead *The Poetical Works and Other Writings of John Keats,* ed. Harry Buxton Forman, revised by Maurice Buxton Forman (Hampstead Edition), 8 vols., 1938–1939.

HBF *The Poetical Works and Other Writings of John Keats,* ed. Harry Buxton Forman, 4 vols., 1883.

HLB *Harvard Library Bulletin.*

KC *The Keats Circle: Letters and Papers 1816–1878,* ed. Hyder Edward Rollins, 2 vols., 1948.

KHM *Keats House and Museum: Historical and Descriptive Guide,* 4th ed., Hampstead, n.d.

KSJ *Keats-Shelley Journal.*

KSMB *Keats-Shelley Memorial Bulletin.*

LFBFK *Letters of Fanny Brawne to Fanny Keats 1820–1824,* ed. Fred Edgcumbe, 1937.

LJKFB *Letters of John Keats to Fanny Brawne,* ed. Harry Buxton Forman, 1878.

MBF *The Letters of John Keats,* ed. Maurice Buxton Forman, 2nd ed., revised, 1935.

MLPKC *More Letters and Poems of the Keats Circle,* ed. Hyder Edward Rollins, 1955.

PMLA *Publications of the Modern Language Association.*

PQ *Philological Quarterly.*

SP *Studies in Philology.*

TLS *Times Literary Supplement.*

I. CLOSE TO THE SOURCE

1. Dorothy Hewlett, *A Life of John Keats* (2nd ed., revised, 1949), p. 21.

2. Richard Abbey: KC, I, 303. On Abbey's general reliability as a witness, see Rollins, KC, I, xli–xlii.

3. Garrod, *Works,* p. lxxix n.; H. E. Briggs, "The Birth and Death of John Keats," PMLA, LVI (1941), 593–94.

4. Jean Haynes, "John Jennings: Keats's Grandfather," KSMB, XIII (1962), 18.

5. Leigh Hunt: HBF, IV, 275.

6. Jean Haynes, "Elizabeth Keats," KSMB, IX (1958), 21.

7. KC, I, 305.

8. William Sharp, *The Life and Letters of Joseph Severn* (1892), p. 5 n.

9. Hewlett mentions this fact in her discussion of John Jennings' will (pp. 375–76) but does not comment on it.

10. HBF, IV, 276; KC, I, 309 and II, 208.

11. Edmund Blunden, *John Keats,* Supplement to *British Book News* (1950), p. 10.

12. Robert Gittings, "Keats's Sailor Relation," TLS, 15 April 1960, p. 245.

13. *The Autobiography and Journals of Benjamin Robert Haydon,* ed. Malcolm Elwin (1950), p. 10.

14. Gittings, "KSR," p. 245.

15. R. Y. Keers and B. G. Rigden, *Pulmonary Tuberculosis* (1953), p. 57.

16. *The Diary of Benjamin Robert Haydon,* ed. Willard Bissell Pope (1960), II, 107.

17. KC, I, 328; also II, 147 and 165.

18. Fourteen is the usual age for confirmation in England, as Keats himself noted in a letter showing a thorough knowledge of the catechism (*Letters,* II, 49).

19. The bearded man in a helmet (the seal which appears, e.g., on his letter to Taylor and Hessey of 21 March 1818) has been identified as King Alfred by Mr. A. W. Wheen, Keeper of the Library at the Victoria and Albert Museum.

20. *The Autobiography of Leigh Hunt,* ed. J. E. Morpurgo (1949), pp. 76–77, 98, and cf. Douglas Bush, *Mythology and the Romantic Tradition in English Poetry* (1937), p. 86 n. 5, which suggests that Keats shared Hunt's interest. Clarke in 1846 merely "suspected" that Keats's familiarity with classical mythology could "be traced" to his reading of Lemprière, Tooke, and Spence (KC, II, 147–48), though the two latter works are not listed among Keats's books; in 1861 Clarke, then seventy-three, recalled that Keats "appeared to learn" Lemprière by heart ("Recollections of Keats," *Atlantic Monthly,* VII [1861], 87). See Chapter IV, note 8 below.

21. Joanna Richardson, "New Light on Mr. Abbey," KSMB, V (1953), 26–31.

22. Gittings, "KSR," p. 245.

23. HBF, IV, 312; Charles W. Hagelman Jr., *John Keats and the Medical Profession,* unpublished dissertation, University of Texas (1956), pp. 11–18.

24. Ibid., pp. 21–26, 153.

25. Ibid., p. 21.

II. THE WIDENING STREAM

1. E. L. Woodward, *The Age of Reform, 1815–1870* (1938), p. 17.

2. A. S. Turberville, ed., *Johnson's England* (1933), II, 266–70.

3. KHM, nos. 16, 17.

4. Despite his later scorn for Pope's poetry, it is Pope's translation of Homer, not Chapman's, that Keats quotes in his letters (I, 354 n., 404 n.; II, 205 n.).

5. The statements to this effect by Clarke (HBF, IV, 338), Severn (KC, II, 132), and Bailey (ibid., 283; see also Hunt, A, pp. 79–80) are borne out by Ernest de Selincourt's study of the influences on the diction of Keats's early poetry (*The Poems of John Keats* [5th ed., 1926], pp. xxxii–xxxiii, 607 ff.).

6. Clarke's conventional tastes are indicated by Keats's "Epistle to Charles Cowden Clarke," ll. 53 ff. Clarke's own mentor, Leigh Hunt, was contemptuous of Wordsworth's poetry until 1814 (Edmund Blunden, *Leigh Hunt and His Circle* [1930], p. 67).

7. G. Pederson-Krag, " 'O Poesy! For Thee I Hold My Pen,' " in *Psychoanalysis and Culture: Essays in Honor of Géza Roheim,* ed. G. W. Wilbur and W. Muensterberger (1951), p. 445.

8. KC, II, 169, 177.

9. HBF, IV, 306.

10. Claude Lee Finney, *The Evolution of Keats's Poetry,* 2 vols. (1936), I, 36–38; George D. Stout, "The Political History of Leigh Hunt's *Examiner,*" *Washington University Studies* (New Series) *in Language and Literature,* no. 19 (1949), pp. 29–35. "Horrors," the reading of W³ (*Works,* p. 527; see Hampstead, IV, 17), not only makes better sense than "honours" but also echoes Hunt's editorial.

11. *Works,* p. 531. It is significant that in Mary Frogley's copy, evidently the only early transcript, the poem is dated 1816, not 1814.

12. As appears from the fact that the sonnets to Byron, Chatterton, and his grandmother and the stanzas "To Hope" were not transcribed at the time Keats wrote them, in contrast to other poems of 1814 and 1815, considerably lighter in tone, which were copied by his friends.

13. Neither autograph nor transcript of the sonnet survives; and when Hunt met Keats a year and a half later, he did not recall reading any of his poetry before that time (HBF, IV, 277).

14. The three sonnets "On Woman" have been attributed on very slender evidence to the spring of 1816 by Finney (I, 111); but Keats's grouping of them with his poems of 1814 and 1815 in his first volume and Mathew's praise of these sonnets in his review suggest that they belong to the previous year.

15. James R. Caldwell, "Woodhouse's Annotations in Keats's First Volume of Poems," PMLA, LXIII (1948), 759.

16. Quoted by Catherine MacDonald MacLean, *Born Under Saturn: A Biography of William Hazlitt* (1944), p. 325.

17. Stout, "PHLHE," p. 30.

18. The only indication of the date of this poem is Woodhouse's note, "Written probably when much in company with Leigh Hunt." The spring of 1815 seems far more likely than that of 1814, when Keats was celebrating constitutional monarchy in his sonnet "On Peace," or the spring of 1816, when he turned to non-political themes.

19. Hagelman, p. 59.

III. THE DARK CITY

1. Edward B. Hinckley, "On First Looking into Swedenborg's Philosophy," KSJ, IX (1960), 15–16.

2. On the probable date, see John Middleton Murry, *Studies in Keats* (1930), pp. 2–5.

3. Hagelman, pp. 148–52.

4. Ibid., pp. 155–56.

5. Mathew's recollections of Keats some thirty years later (KC, II, 184–88) contain several inconsistencies which evidently represent the several stages of their friendship from early 1815 to late 1816. An attempt is made to separate these stages in Chapters II, III, and IV.

6. George A. R. Winston, "John Keats and Joshua Waddington," *Guy's Hospital Reports*, XCII (1943), 101.

7. Hinckley, pp. 22–23.

8. KC, II, 206 n. 2.

9. Hagelman, pp. 130–31.

10. Ibid., p. 263 n. 117.

11. John Flint South, *Memorials* (1884), p. 52.

12. Ibid., p. 54.

13. Hagelman, p. 316.

14. Keats explicitly discussed his lack of identity in a number of later letters; in his early poems he expressed this feeling of "annihilation" as a sense of being "smothered" or "overwhelmed" or "borne along to nothingness" by experience (cf. e.g., "I Stood Tiptoe," 1. 132; "Sleep and Poetry," 1. 157; *Endymion* IV, 471 ff.). The term "identity" had some philosophic currency in Keats's time, going back as far as Locke (see *An Essay Concerning Human Understanding*, Book II, Chap. XXVII, especially sects. 9–10), and Keats probably met with it in Hazlitt's *Essay on the Principles of Human Action*. But for Hazlitt as for Locke the term "personal identity" meant primarily the continuing unchanging unique sameness of the individual consciousness, the product of the sum of his perceptions (*Works*, ed. P. P. Howe [1930–1934], I, 28–32; see also XII, 230–41; XVII, 264–75; XX, 171–86 and 376–86). It could also refer to the object of the individual's self-love, which serves to isolate him from other identities (XVII, 264); or to an "internal, original bias," physiologically given, which is born with him and not changed by experience (XVII, 23–34). Hazlitt's conception is thus very different from Keats's notion of a gradually developing sense of self which emerges as the individual matures, in reaction to the crises of his emotional experience and from imaginative interaction or identification with the identities of others. See Chapter X, pp. 276–78.

15. This count excludes purely platonic poems to young ladies, such as his sonnet to Georgiana Wylie; doggerel verses on sex, such as those he wrote in Devon; long narrative poems on love, which are not addressed to a real woman; and the sonnets written to the Vauxhall lady four years after their meeting. The "brief interlude" refers to a few short lyrics written probably in the summer of 1817 (see p. 124 above).

16. Woodhouse's note, quoted by Mabel A. E. Steele, "The Woodhouse Transcripts of the Poems of John Keats," HLB, III (1949), 242.

17. J. Burke Severs has suggested that it is a fairy speaking in this poem,

not a human being ("Keats's Fairy Sonnet," KSJ, VI [1957], 109–13). But this reading does not preclude Keats's use of the fairy imagery as a metaphor for his own feelings of inadequacy (on which Woodhouse commented in his note on the poem, quoted by Caldwell, p. 759); and in other poems written about this time Keats suggested a similar contrast between himself and a magnificent knight to whom he feels somehow inferior.

18. Preface to *Immaturity*, quoted by Erik H. Erikson, "The Problem of Ego Identity," *Journal of the American Psychoanalytic Association*, IV (1956), 58.

19. Haydon, D, II, 101; Winston, p. 105; Sir Benjamin Ward Richardson, *The Asclepiad* (1884), p. 142.

20. I. Peter Glauber, "A Deterrent in the Study and Practise of Medicine," *Psychoanalytic Quarterly*, XXII (1953), 382.

21. *Letters*, I, 245; II, 123, 126, 134, 349.

22. Haydon, D, II, 107.

23. Otto Rank, *Art and Artist: Creative Urge and Personality Development* (1932), pp. 43–50.

24. Ibid., 27–28, 41 ff.

25. HBF, IV, 321; and cf. p. 97 above.

26. Sharp, p. 20.

27. See *Works*, e.g., p. 3, l. 17; p. 8, l. 144; p. 12, l. 17; p. 45, "demesne—mean"; p. 41, "uproar"; and the last line of "To a Friend Who Sent Me Some Roses," p. 41, which in Tom Keats's copy book has not merely six feet (as do five or six of Keats's other sonnets) but seven.

28. There is no reason for thinking that Keats had the time or the motive for starting "Calidore" immediately after the appearance of Hunt's *Rimini* in February, as Sir Sidney Colvin suggests (*John Keats: His Life and Poetry, His Friends, Critics and After-Fame* [1917], p. 34). A more probable incentive was Hunt's publication of Keats's sonnet "O Solitude!" in May, as Keats implies in his "Induction," ll. 57 ff. Furthermore, several poems of the summer of 1816 indicate that he was working on a long poem in the style of *Rimini* at that time: "To one who has been long in city pent," ll. 7–8; "As late I rambled in the happy fields," ll. 3–4; "Epistle to My Brother George," ll. 15–18, 23–44; and "Epistle to Charles Cowden Clarke," ll. 42–48.

29. Sir William Hale-White, *Keats as Doctor and Patient* (1938), p. 31.

30. Pederson-Krag, p. 445.

31. Evidently not the two-volume third edition of the *Lyrical Ballads*, as Rollins suggests (KC, I, 253 n. 3), but the octavo *Poems in Two Volumes* of 1807, which contained all the poems of Wordsworth which influenced Keats most deeply, and whose section-headings Keats twice quoted in his letters (I, 263, 287).

32. "I Stood Tiptoe," ll. 114ab (*Works*, p. 7): lines which suggest the approximate point at which Keats picked up the poem at Margate, especially when it is noted that this section of the poem is written on a sheet of laid paper of a larger size than the wove paper on which Keats started and later finished the poem in London. No one has yet attempted to assign the various sections of this poem to the six months in which it was composed. But a close study of the deletions and insertions in the manuscript noted by Garrod (*Works*, pp. lxxxiv–lxxxviii) and of the paper on which various sections now in the Harvard University Library were written suggests that the first main section (ll. 1–60, 107–14) was written mostly in London and finished in Margate; then in the middle of page 5 (f. iii r.) Keats ran into difficulties, can-

celled some lines (missing in the MS. after 114b: recto of the draft of ll. 65–69), and decided to double back. Starting on the back of the same sheet, Keats then wrote a second section (ll. 61–106), which seems to be as far as he carried the poem at Margate. The third section (ll. 116 to probably 192) picks up in the middle of page 5 again and, after a number of false starts, modulates into a section on mythology influenced by Hunt or Words-worth, and probably written in October or November (see pp. 80–81 above). The fourth section (ll. 193 to the end), in which the poem begins to turn into "Endymion," was evidently written in several "attacks," as Keats de-scribed it, in early December (*Letters*, I, 121).

33. As George Keats, who was still living with Abbey, reported (KC, I, 277).

34. Hagelman shows (pp. 12–20) that Keats did not express his dislike of medicine to Clarke till the fall of 1816.

35. The closings of Keats's letters are a clue to the warmth of his friend-ships. He did not sign himself "Your affectionate friend" to Reynolds till fourteen months after their meeting, though he began using this or a similar intimate style almost at once with Haydon and Bailey (*Letters*, I, 190; 117, 145, 168, 175).

36. Following the autograph version in the Harvard Library, which, from the marginal guide-lines, the correction in l. 6, and the "wond'ring eyes" of l. 11, appears to be the first draft, rather than the copy in the Morgan Library as Garrod thinks (*Works*, p. 45).

IV. THE GREEN SHORE

1. Haydon, D, II, 107.

2. B. W. Procter ("Barry Cornwall"), *An Autobiographical Fragment* (1877), pp. 195–200.

3. Haydon, D, II, 136; see also W. B. Pope, "Leigh Hunt and His Com-panions," KSJ, VIII (1959), 90 n. 3.

4. HBF, IV, 376.

5. A. H. Beavan, *James and Horace Smith* (1899), p. 137.

6. See *Works*, p. 5, l. 64a; p. 406, xxxi, l. 9; p. 459, l. 13.

7. Edmund Blunden, *Keats's Publisher: A Memoir of John Taylor* (1936), pp. 40–41; G. D. Stout, "Leigh Hunt's Money Troubles: Some New Light," *Washington University Studies, Humanistic Series*, XII (1925), 223–26.

8. Keats's sudden new interest in Greek mythology in the fall of 1816 (see Chapter I, note 20 above) is evident from a study of his allusions. Up to this time, his references to classical legend are infrequent and perfunctory; in fact, his significant allusions are to an English tradition—King Lear, Calidore, the Red Cross Knight, "the sweet mountain nymph" Liberty, King Alfred, William Wallace, Robert Burns, Byron, Chatterton, Sydney, Russell, and Vane. Keats's absorption in Greek myth first appears in "Sleep and Poetry" and the second half of "I Stood Tiptoe," and was evidently due to Hunt's influence rather than to Wordsworth's, as usually stated, since it appears that Keats had barely started reading *The Excursion* at this time. Despite occasional echoes of *The Exucrsion*, IV, 847–87 in "I Stood Tiptoe," ll. 125–92, Keats's view of mythology in the fall of 1816 was far closer to that expressed by Hunt in his review of Keats's *Poems* in 1817—"lovely tales" (De Selincourt, p. 390)—or even in his preface to "The Nymphs" in *Foliage*, 1818—"embodied essences of all the grand and lovely qualities of nature"

(quoted by Bush, p. 175). For the transforming influence of *The Excursion* on Keats's work in 1817, see Chapter V, note 12 below.

9. James Augustus Hessey: MLPKC, p. 117.

10. KC, II, 281; W. B. Pope, "Haydon's Portraits," TLS, 25 January 1947, p. 51.

11. Clark Olney, *Benjamin Robert Haydon, Historical Painter* (1952), pp. 56, 85 n. 10. Haydon nowhere mentions Blake in his *Diary* or *Autobiography*.

12. Ibid., p. 46; A. H. Smith, *The Sculptures of the Parthenon* (1910), pl. 17, Fig. 29.

13. Eric George, *The Life and Death of Benjamin Robert Haydon* (1948), pp. 82–87.

14. *Letters*, I, 118 n. 4.

15. Haydon, D, II, 101; Henry Stephens, KC, II, 211–12.

16. Blunden, LHHC, pp. 57–58, 112.

17. Ian Jack, " 'The Realm of Flora' in Keats and Poussin," TLS, 10 April 1959, p. 212.

18. De Selincourt, p. xxxix.

19. The dash at the end of "I Stood Tiptoe" is noteworthy, for it indicates that Keats intended to let it stand as what J. M. Murry calls, in speaking of *Hyperion*, "a finished fragment" (*Keats and Shakespeare* [1925], p. 82). Compare the endings of "Calidore," "Imitation of Spenser," "Nature withheld Cassandra," "The Eve of St. Mark," and *Hyperion*, where the punctuation gives a similar indication of their fragmentary character.

20. Hampstead, I, 25 n.

21. Beavan, pp. 137–38.

22. *The Complete Works of Percy Bysshe Shelley*, ed. Roger Ingpen and W. E. Peck (1926–1930), IX, 211–13. On the veracity of this letter, which has sometimes been questioned, see Newman Ivey White, *Shelley* (1940), I, 484–85 and 723, n. 45 and 46.

23. HBF, IV, 296; Shelley, Preface to *Prometheus Unbound*.

24. This story evidently originated in Canon Dix's recollection of someone's statement, thirty years after the event, that Shelley visited Charles Richards in 1817 to ask about printing "a little volume" of Keats's poems (John Dix, *Pen and Ink Sketches* [1846], p. 144). The volume was evidently a pamphlet of his own (see White, I, 504, 515); as for Keats's poetry, Shelley either ignored or disparaged it while Keats was alive (HBF, IV, 247–50; White, II, 543) and apparently never read the 1817 volume (see *Letters of Mary W. Shelley*, ed. Frederick L. Jones [1944], II, 344 n. 11).

25. See Hewlett, pp. 24 and 375–77, where the wills of Alice and John Jennings are summarized. It appears that Keats should have received approximately £2000 from his grandmother, £250 from his grandfather, £415 from his mother, £125 from the estate of his great-aunt Mary Sweetingburgh, and some share of the estate of his uncle Midgley Jennings (this was later contested), not counting either the expenses of his medical training or the accumulation of interest. On what he actually received, see George Keats: KC, I, 277–78; also Marie Adami, *Fanny Keats* (1937), pp. 118–19.

26. Charles Brown, in a letter to C. W. Dilke of 6 September 1824 (KHM, no. 80), spoke of £200 as "a moderate two years' subsistence" for Keats. The record of his cash account at Abbey's shows that Keats was in the habit of drawing £20 every two months, £30 when travelling (*Letters*, I, 42–49).

27. Lawrence E. Tanner, "The Library and Muniment Room," *Westmin-*

ster Abbey Papers, no. 1 (1935), pp. 7–9. It should be noted that Keats thought of moving to Westminster several times for the express purpose of "being in the reach of books" (*Letters,* II, 52, 179, 225).

28. Edmund Blunden, *Shelley and Keats as They Struck Their Contemporaries* (1925), p. 87.

29. The draft of "I Stood Tiptoe," for instance, shows Keats eliminating such Huntisms as "gently," "gentlest," "little," "nestling," "embower," "dainties," "soft," "tender," "peep," "delicious," "swoonlike," and "elegance" (*Works,* pp. 3–11; Neville Rogers and Mabel A. E. Steele, " 'I Stood Tiptoe Upon a Little Hill': A Hitherto Uncollated Fragment," KSJ, X [1961], 13).

30. Thomas Medwin, *Life of Percy Bysshe Shelley,* ed. H. B. Forman (1913), pp. 178–79. Colvin questions this story (p. 73), but all the circumstantial evidence seems to corroborate it (see *Letters,* I, 170; *Endymion,* I, 39–57; and Shelley, *Works,* IX, 237). Both poems came to over 4000 lines, each far longer than any previous work by either poet.

31. Mr. W. R. LeFanu, Librarian of the Royal College of Surgeons, reports that Keats's name is not listed among any of the candidates who appeared for the monthly examinations of the college during the first half of 1817, and adds that the candidates must have reached the age of twenty-two to qualify for the examination.

32. Willard B. Pope, *Studies in the Keats Circle,* unpublished dissertation, Harvard University (1932), p. 237.

33. Sharp, p. 29.

34. Stephen A. Larrabee, *English Bards and Grecian Marbles* (1943), p. 213.

35. The December 1816 date usually assigned this sonnet is, as Garrod points out (*Works,* p. lxxxi), very doubtful. From its echoes of Keats's dedicatory sonnet it seems to have been written as a reply, and therefore at about the time of the *Poems'* appearance.

36. Keats's decision in mid-March to leave town in order to live alone in "the country" seems to refer not to his visit to the Isle of Wight (see Rollins, *Letters,* I, 125 n. 2) but to his move a few days later to Hampstead (which he repeatedly described as "country" in contrast to London or "town" [*Letters,* I, 172, 175 and II, 52, 56; cf. II, 37]). There is nothing to indicate that his brothers moved with him to Hampstead in March; it seems clear, however, that he decided to go to the Isle of Wight rather suddenly in mid-April, sometime after Hunt's departure for Marlow on April 6 (*Letters,* I, 137).

37. Finney (I, 180–81) dates this episode as occurring before the publication of Keats's *Poems* at the beginning of March. But his argument is not convincing, since it was not Keats himself but George Keats and Thomas Richards who transcribed Hunt's sonnets on the crowning episode into their presentation copies, obviously some time after receiving them. Keats's transcription of his own sonnets into Reynolds' copy (in the Harvard University Library) appears to have been made at a different and therefore later date than that of the inscription and the Elgin Marbles sonnets. The March 1 date on Hunt's autograph (*Works,* p. 529) also suggests that the crowning took place before the appearance of Keats's *Poems;* yet it seems unlikely that the event occurred during the Shelleys' stay at Hunt's from late January till mid-March (*Mary Shelley's Journal,* ed. F. L. Jones [1947], pp. 70–77).

38. See *Letters,* I, 137 and note. Nothing in the *Examiner's* account of the trial of R. G. Butt supports Rollins' inference that "Old Wood" was

Sir George Wood, the presiding judge in the case; and Keats's linking of the papers which Hunt requested him to destroy with "Receipts" suggests they were financial records.

39. Stout, "LHMT," pp. 226–28.

V. A LEAP INTO THE SEA

1. *Letters,* I, 169–70.

2. Hampstead, I, 129–36.

3. So listed in the London Post Office Directory for 1818; and the Olliers' letter of 29 April 1817 was addressed to George at 62 Bread Street, evidently his business address at the time (see MBF, p. 101 n. 3). On Keats's loan, see MLPKC, pp. 28–29. It seems improbable that Wilkinson was a lawyer (*Letters,* I, 129 n. 2); Keats never mentioned a law career for George, but did refer to his inability "to get on in trade" (I, 287). "C. Wilkinson," Keats's friend, may have been the son or younger brother of Thomas.

4. KC, II, 469; see also I, 253 n. 2 and 260 n. 68; Blunden, KPMJT, pp. 96–98; Garrod, *Works,* pp. xxxviii–xxxix n.; Joanna Richardson, *Fanny Brawne* (1952), pp. 20 and 172, where Mrs. Jones is identified as the lady from Hastings; and Robert Gittings, *John Keats: The Living Year* (1954), pp. 30–33, 59–60, and 230–35 (also Gittings, *The Mask of Keats* [1956], pp. 45–53).

5. Probably January 1818, not, as Mr. Gittings argues (JKLY, pp. 57–64), January 1819: see Aileen Ward, "Christmas Day, 1818," KSJ, X (1961), 17–20.

6. Even after his fair copy was sent to the printer in January 1818, Keats made numerous revisions in the text of Book I (Garrod, *Works,* pp. xxxi–xxxii).

7. MBF, pp. xvi–xvii; cf. *Letters,* I, 169.

8. These lyrics are usually assigned to November 1817 because the transcript of "Think not of it, sweet one, so" is dated "Nov. 11, 1817" by Reynolds (*Works,* p. 432), and the other lyrics appear to belong to the same period (Colvin, pp. 157–58). But the November dating is very doubtful, for several reasons. First, Reynolds usually dated his transcripts by the date on which he copied them, not the date of the poem itself (see *Works,* pp. 262, 264, 268, 481). Second, Woodhouse dated "Think not of it, sweet one, so" April 1817 in W¹: a date which he probably got from Keats himself two years later. Third, Reynolds quoted a line from "Unfelt, unheard, unseen" in *The Champion* of 17 August 1817 (Leonidas M. Jones, "Reynolds and Keats," KSJ, VII [1958], 48 n. 6), which shows that this poem and, presumably, the others must have been written some time before mid-August. On the connection with Mrs. Jones, see Finney, I, 191.

9. This Folio, which Keats acquired in 1817, seems most likely to be the volume which Keats later recalled reading with Reynolds (*Letters,* I, 274, 276).

10. Hewlett, p. 51.

11. KHM, no. 104.

12. *Endymion,* II, 827–53: the first clear parallel to *The Excursion* in all of Keats's writings (*Exc.,* IV, 631–41; cf. also 718–62, 846–87). The idea of the "legend-laden" wind—an epithet which especially pleased Keats (*Letters,* II, 171)—recurs in *The Fall of Hyperion,* II, 1–6. Other echoes worth noting are "the poor patient oyster" (*End.,* III, 66–68) with the "contented" mole (*Exc.,* IV, 428–30); the "Hymn to Pan" with *Exc.,* IV, 879–87; and "the lidless-eyed

train Of planets" (*End.*, I, 598–99) with "the polar star that never closed His steadfast eye" (*Exc.*, IV, 694–700)—the ultimate source, if one is needed, of Keats's recurrent image of the "open-lidded and stedfast" star (*Letters,* I, 299; *Hyperion,* I, 350–53; "Bright Star," ll. 1–3, and compare "the moving waters" of line 5 with *Exc.*, IX, 9). The full force of the influence of *The Excursion* was slow in appearing in Keats's work, but—as J. M. Murry amply proves (*Keats* [1955], Chapter IX)—it was of central and enduring importance.

13. MLPKC, p. 34.

14. *Leigh's New Picture of England and Wales* (1820), p. 520.

15. Letter of Charles Brown to C. W. Dilke, 20 January 1830 (KHM, no. 80).

16. B. W. Richardson, pp. 138–43; see Rollins, *Letters,* I, 186 n. 5. Miss Lowell's discussion (Amy Lowell, *John Keats* [1925], I, 512–14) overlooks Richardson's highly circumstantial account; and Hale-White's point (p. 46) that mercury was later prescribed for Keats's sore throat likewise fails to disprove it—in fact, a persistent sore throat is a secondary symptom of syphilis. If promptly recognized, syphilis could be cured "with a fair degree of success" in Keats's time with mercury compounds, though a two-year moratorium on marriage was strongly recommended (Morris Fishbein, *Modern Home Medicine Adviser* [1956], pp. 736–39).

17. *Letters,* I, 196 n. 6. With Keats's remark on "vicious beastliness" (I, 175), compare his later comment on being "sick of Venery" (I, 279); on the effect of this experience, see F. W. Bateson, *English Poetry: A Critical Introduction* (1950), p. 222 n.

18. Haydon, D, II, 463.

19. *Endymion,* IV, 496 to about 590, according to Miss Lowell (I, 527).

20. *Endymion,* III, 66–68; KC, I, 59.

21. See, e.g., De Selincourt, pp. xl, 428, 444, 566–67. The variety of goals which De Selincourt attributes to Endymion's quest ("self-realization," "beauty," "truth," "the ideal"), and the various means by which he is said to achieve his end (from a synthesis of opposites to an upward progression from lower to higher), suggest the difficulty in interpreting *Endymion* according to any coherent allegorical scheme.

22. KC, I, 54 and II, 270, 283. The disguise, which was passed over without comment by Hunt and Reynolds, was accepted by *Blackwood's* as a device "to vary the intrigue" (Hampstead, II, 252); Bailey described the ending as a "catastrophe" in the Aristotelian sense (Hampstead, II, 241), and defended its abruptness by comparing it to *Paradise Regained* (KC, I, 25). On Spenser, see *The Poets and Their Critics,* ed. H. S. Davies, Penguin Books (1943), pp. 49–54.

23. On Mrs. F. M. Owen's study, see Colvin, p. 544, and De Selincourt, pp. 566–67; for Jeffrey's praise, see Hampstead, II, 278; and Bailey's comment, KC, I, 35.

24. The original form of "fellowship with essence," *Endymion,* I, 778.

25. Two crucial lines near the end of Book IV are both capable of a double interpretation. In lines 957–58 Endymion may be renouncing either the Indian maid or his recent vow to lead a hermit's life; in lines 975–76 he may be either defying the fate which bars him from the maid or protesting against the fate of mortality which he has incurred through loving her.

26. On the much-discussed question of whether Keats borrowed the device of Phoebe's disguise from Drayton's *Endimion and Phoebe,* it will be noted here merely that Keats could without difficulty have had access to this extremely

rare book in the Westminster Abbey Library (see Chapter IV, note 27 above), and that the three important parallels between Keats's poem and Drayton's (which De Selincourt thinks "can hardly be mere coincidence," p. 568) are limited to Book IV of *Endymion*. It is at least possible, then, that Keats discovered Drayton's *Endimion* after returning from Oxford in a mood of dissatisfaction with his own poem and decided that Drayton's device would solve the problem of his own ending.

27. Lines 988–93 clearly imply that Endymion's "unlook'd for change" took place after his defiance of the "decrees of fate" in freeing Glaucus from his doom of endless age and Phoebe from her doom of eternal chastity (III, 1022 ff.; II, 776 ff.): that is, in Book IV, in which the action does in fact take an unexpected new direction.

VI. SOUNDINGS AND QUICKSANDS

1. Taylor's agreement with Keats in April mentioned "the refusal of his future works" (Blunden, KPMJT, p. 42); it seems clear that the manuscript was being read prior to its final acceptance and revisions.

2. Beavan, pp. 111–18.

3. See Aileen Ward, "Keats's Sonnet, 'Nebuchadnezzar's Dream,'" PQ, XXXIV (1955), 177–88. Keats's biting reference to habeas corpus in his review of "Edmund Kean as a Shakespearean Actor" (Hampstead, V, 227), written on December 19 or 20, suggests that the issue was much on his mind that week.

4. Hampstead, V, 227–30.

5. See Bailey's replies to Taylor's comments to him, KC, I, 11, 19, 25; also Taylor's letter to James Taylor of 14 June 1818 (KHM, no. 50): "Endymion does not by any means please me as I had expected."

6. See *Endymion*, I, 311, 315, 598 (*Works*, pp. 74, 83). Taylor's bowdlerizing may be seen in I, 157 and 777–80; II, 27–30, 67, 96, 271, 526–34, 948.

7. Hewlett, pp. 144–45; Colvin, p. 246; Clarke, p. 97; Lowell, I, 543.

8. Bernice Slote, *Keats and the Dramatic Principle* (1958), Chaps. 2, 3.

9. Garrod, *Works*, p. xxxii; for the cuts, see pp. 65, 76–81, 85–86.

10. KC, II, 143–44; Sharp, p. 33. On Wordsworth's presumed opinion of *Endymion* as a whole, see *Letters*, I, 270 n. 4.

11. For the original form of the passage, where "blending pleasurable" stood for "fellowship with essence," see *Works*, p. 88, and De Selincourt, p. 427. The original four lines were excised and patched over, evidently at Taylor's suggestion, in the copy sent to the printer on January 22, and the omission troubled Keats for a whole week before he restored them in revised form (*Letters*, I, 218). The fact that Keats was satisfied with the original version till Taylor deleted the lines in January shows that Keats had the idea of "blending pleasurable" in mind when he referred to his first book as an illustration of his idea of "essential beauty" created by passion in his letter to Bailey of 23 November 1817.

12. *Letters*, I, 184, 323 and II, 213.

13. P. P. Howe, *The Life of William Hazlitt* (Penguin Books, 1949), p. 96.

14. Ibid., p. 250.

15. Compare Keats's remarks on "composition and decomposition" (*Letters*, I, 265) with Hazlitt, *Lectures on the English Poets* (Everyman's Library, 1910), p. 51; on "subject" in poetry, *Letters*, I, 223–24 and *Lectures*, p. 53; on the poet's gusto for all experience and his lack of a proper character, *Letters*,

I, 387 and *Lectures,* p. 47. Still further echoes are found in the "Ode on a Grecian Urn" (III, 3–4; *Lectures,* p. 98), *Lamia* (II, 234; *Lectures,* p. 9); and Keats's description of "three witty people" in January 1820 (*Letters,* II, 245; *Lectures,* pp. 111–12).

16. John Hamilton Reynolds, *Poetry and Prose,* ed. George L. Marsh (1928), p. 94.

17. "To Spenser," ll. 11–12; see also *Letters,* I, 214, 232, 238, 288, and "When I have fears," ll. 3–4; and cf. *Endymion,* II, 40–41.

18. Quoting the original version of the last sentence, which was censored not by Keats (see Rollins, *Letters,* I, 252 n. 7) but evidently by Haydon himself, who bowdlerized many passages in his *Diary* and *Correspondence* (see a similar excision by Woodhouse's clerk, *Letters,* I, 263 n. 3). It should be noted that Haydon's paraphrase of the censored passage—"I should like him to damn me" keeps the meaning of Keats's original—"Damn me if I shouldn't like him to damn me."

19. *Letters,* I, 241 and II, 38.

20. KC, I, 7–8, 20 n. 6.

21. *Letters,* I, 242. The meaning of this sentence is badly tangled, as is frequently the case when Keats is embarrassed. The statement as it stands— "I do not think that nothing in this world is proveable"—contradicts the following assertion about his scepticism and the whole direction of his thought at this time. (See "Epistle to Reynolds," ll. 72–82, and *Letters,* I, 185, 193, 243.)

22. *The John Keats Memorial Volume* (1921), p. 175.

23. Hampstead, V, 292. The passage from *The Reason of Church Government* was quoted by Hazlitt in his lecture on Shakespeare and Milton (*Lectures,* pp. 57–58).

24. *Letters,* II, 193.

25. They left hastily, for Keats had written George only a few days before to send him his folio Shakespeare (*Letters,* I, 274); but it is improbable that they left because Tom had taken a turn for the worse, as Miss Lowell suggests (I, 631). The reason for their departure must then be the crystallization of George's plans.

26. Woodhouse's note, quoted by Finney, II, 746.

VII. MIST AND CRAG

1. Naomi J. Kirk, "Memoir of George Keats," Hampstead, I, lxxxv.

2. The January issue, which did not appear till early June (J. R. MacGillivray, *Keats: A Bibliography and Reference Guide with an Essay on Keats's Reputation* [1949], p. xxiv).

3. Hampstead, II, 239.

4. *Letters,* I, 281, 293 (three references), 325, 343, 387. Hunt stated in 1828 that "Keats felt that his disease was mortal, two or three years before he died" (HBF, IV, 293), echoing a similar statement by Keats to his sister (*Letters,* II, 309). See also his resolutions to take better care of his health at this time (I, 325, 343).

5. KC, II, 15.

6. Not on April 23, as Gittings suggests (JKLY, p. 204); but probably during the third week of June, when the programs of the English Opera House announce "Mr. Mathews At Home" (Harvard Theatre Collection).

7. Dilke's comment to this effect (KC, II, 104–105) is confirmed by Keats's

own letters, in which Brown is mentioned far less frequently and more casually than Dilke till he began sharing Brown's house in December 1818.

8. See *Letters,* I, 248, and Brown's letter to Dilke of 17 December 1829 (KHM, no. 80).

9. *Leigh's New Pocket Road Book of England and Wales* (1825), p. 184.

10. I have drawn freely on Brown's journal of the trip (KHM, no. 87, reprinted in part in *Letters,* I, 421-42) to supplement Keats's own account in the following pages.

11. Though Keats told Reynolds he had finished *Isabella* at the end of April 1818 (*Letters,* I, 274), the MS. draft indicates much reworking. There are numerous revisions, additions, and deletions, and the sections of the manuscript now in the Harvard University Library are written on two different kinds of paper; some sections appear to be a fair copy, others a first draft; and the stanzas are not numbered. This appearance lends support to Woodhouse's note "Finished about the latter end of 1818 or the beginning of 1819" (*Works,* p. 215).

12. *Prelude,* VI, 636-37; Prospectus to *The Excursion,* ll. 42-45 (Murry, K, p. 287).

13. George M. Harper, *William Wordsworth* (1916), II, 287.

14. *Letters,* II, 67.

15. Letter to Charles Brown, Jr., 22 September 1839 (KHM, no. 80).

16. See Brown's letters to his son regarding Dilke (15 March 1839) and a woman named Fanny whom his son apparently wished to marry (11 November 1838, 15 March 1839, 10 March 1840, and 16 April 1840; KHM, no. 80).

17. KC, I, lv.

18. From the synopsis of *Walter Hazlebourne,* inserted in the first MS. volume of the novel (KHM, no. 82) and cast in the first person. Brown's letter to his son of 27 January 1839 (KHM, no. 80) makes it clear that the novel is autobiographical in large part.

19. HBF, III, 354-59.

20. KC, II, 137.

VIII. THE SHORES OF DARKNESS

1. Not to the Brawnes' (Lowell, II, 126), since Fanny Keats did not know of their existence till September 1820 (LFBFK, p. 3), or to the Hunts' (Gittings, JKLY, p. 28), since they had moved away from Hampstead the year before (*Letters,* I, 168). Keats mentioned Mrs. Dilke in a letter he wrote Fanny soon after her visit (I, 386).

2. Brown protested to Dilke in a letter of 17 December 1829 (KHM, no. 80) that Hunt's account of Keats's origins—"of the humblest"—in *Lord Byron and Some of His Contemporaries* was "indecent."

3. Howe, pp. 266-68, 271-76, 262 and note.

4. Blunden, KPMJT, p. 56.

5. KC, I, 36.

6. Ibid., 246.

7. KC, II, 288, 299.

8. All the evidence points to a meeting in early September, rather than November or December as frequently stated. First, Dilke noted in his copy (now in the Morgan Library) of Richard Monckton Milnes's *Life, Letters, and Literary Remains of John Keats* (1848), with reference to Keats's letter to

Reynolds of 22 September 1818: "About this time, he met *Miss Brawne* for the first time at my house, . . . soon after his return from Teignmouth" (for "Scotland": I, 240–41). Dilke clearly links the letter to Fanny; there is no ground for H. B. Forman's inference that it refers instead to Jane Cox, or that Keats met Fanny "very soon after" writing it (MBF, p. 217 n.). Second, Fanny herself stated that she met Keats at "about the time" of his return from Scotland, and that his spirits were good "except when anxiety regarding his brother's health dejected them" (Medwin, p. 296)—a comment which can hardly refer to a first meeting in November. Gittings argues for a November meeting on the grounds of Severn's "typhoid" fever that fall (JKLY, p. 40). But Keats stated that Severn was ill not with typhoid but with "typhous" fever in October (*Letters*, I, 393), an affair of two or three weeks rather than five or six (cf. *Encyclopaedia Britannica*, 6th ed. [1823], "Medicine," XIII, 268); it is possible, therefore, that Severn visited the Brawnes with Keats during September.

9. *Letters*, II, 132; I, 132 and n. 5. There is no reason to link this letter to Jane Cox (see note 8 above), whom Keats met at the Reynoldses' sometime before the middle of October. His lengthy description of this meeting in his journal for October 14 (*Letters*, I, 394–95) suggests, first, that he did not actually meet her on his first call at the Reynoldses' after his return, in early September; and second, that he was describing a very recent encounter, since his account is cast in the present tense and given in fresh detail. It also seems unlikely that Keats would have mentioned meeting Jane Cox in a letter to Reynolds, who could all too easily have guessed her identity.

10. *Letters*, II, 133; LFBFK, p. 13.

11. So it has always been described by Keats's critics, from Woodhouse on (see De Selincourt, pp. 485–86). Keats did in fact draw on a wide range of reference to the story of the Titans, from Homer to Milton; but one source which has been overlooked in this connection gives extended treatment to the legend and brings together most of the details, such as proper names, mentioned by Keats in *Hyperion*. This is the *Pantheon* of William Godwin ("Edward Baldwin"), a compendium of classical mythology which Keats still possessed at his death (KC, I, 258) and which was probably the handbook which Clarke remembered his learning by heart. Its account of the wars of the Titans and Olympians in Chapters 6 and 7, together with the later war of the Giants, would then have long been familiar to Keats in general outline. It even suggests the theme of *Hyperion* as set forth in Oceanus's speech (II, 206 ff.), in the statement that Saturn was reconciled with his sons Jupiter, Neptune, and Pluto because he was "so struck with their beauty and hopeful qualities, that he forgave his wife [Cybele, who had saved them from being devoured by Saturn at birth] and took them into his favour" (*Pantheon* [1806], p. 45)—an interpretation not to be found in Keats's classical sources.

12. *Letters*, I, 369, 387, 392, and cf. Chapter IX, note 28 below.

13. That Keats identified much more closely with Tom than with George is seen in the fact that in his letters written to both his brothers he addressed Tom directly almost three times as often as George (compare *Letters*, I, 196, 197, 199, 200, 201, 214, and 217 with 129, 196, 235).

14. See Chapter IX, note 8 below.

15. "Ailsa Rock" and "The Human Seasons," which appeared in Hunt's *Literary Pocket Book* in December.

16. Compare his mention of Saturn and Ops on October 27 (*Letters*, I, 387) and *Hyperion*, II, 78, 113, 129 ff.

17. See notes 8 and 9 above.

18. David Thomson, *England in the Nineteenth Century* (1955), p. 17.

19. Gittings thinks otherwise (JKLY, pp. 25-36); but see Murry, K, pp. 116-23, and Aileen Ward, "The Date of Keats's 'Bright Star' Sonnet," SP, LII (1955), 82-84.

20. Sharp, p. 37.

21. Lowell, II, 121; H. D. Miles, *Pugilistica* (1906), I, 328-46.

22. The poem is drafted in Keats's copy of Beaumont and Fletcher (KHM, no. 21): perhaps suggested by Beaumont's song "Mirth," in *The Knight of the Burning Pestle*.

23. Gittings, JKLY, pp. 49-50. On the suggestion that "Fancy" was patterned on the introductory verses in Burton's *Anatomy of Melancholy*, and that Keats started reading Burton at this time, see Aileen Ward, "Keats and Burton: A Reappraisal," PQ, XL (1961), 539-40.

24. Between £400 and £500, according to Brown (letters to C. W. Dilke of 17 December 1829 and 20 January 1830. KHM, no. 80).

25. Ward, "CD1818," pp. 21-24. Miss Lowell reproduced the lyre seal on the title page of *John Keats* but failed to notice its significance.

26. Murry, K, pp. 33-36.

IX. THE MELANCHOLY STORM

1. H. B. Forman, LJKFB, p. lxvii.

2. J. Richardson, pp. 2-7; C. E. Baker, *Manuscript History of the Brawne Family* (KHM, no. 76).

3. LFBFK, p. 59.

4. H. B. Forman, LJKFB, p. lxvi.

5. MLPKC, pp. 30-31.

6. Medwin, p. 296.

7. See *Letters*, I, 417, II, 206, and note 12 below.

8. De Selincourt suggests (p. 494) that the autograph manuscript of *Hyperion* ("A" in Garrod's apparatus; cf. *Works*, pp. xli-xlii) was "intended to be a fair copy" of an earlier draft, and that Keats made "numerous alterations" on it "when he came to view his work a second time." The excellent quality of the paper, the flourish of the title, and the generally fair handwriting of the MS. (British Museum Add. 37000) support this inference. Evidently this "fair copy" or second draft, which contains many revisions made in the process of recopying, was made sometime between December 1818 and April 1819, when Keats gave it to Woodhouse to transcribe. The most likely date for these revisions is early January.

9. *Works*, p. 300. On the date of the first section of the third book, see Gittings, JKLY, pp. 46-47.

10. Not on January 21, as Gittings suggests (JKLY, p. 62): see H. E. Rollins, "Keats's Misdated Letters: Additional Notes," HLB, VIII (1954), 243-45, and Murry, K, pp. 132-33.

11. On Keats's visit to Stansted, see Gittings, JKLY, Chapters 7 and 8.

12. *Letters*, I, 415 and II, 31, 32, 39-40. Brown's letter to Dilke of 6 September 1824 (KHM, no. 80) describes the sum in question as £500.

13. MacGillivray, p. 101; KC, II, 151.

14. J. Richardson, p. 30.

15. KC, I, 98 and II, 103.

16. MLPKC, pp. 20, 23 n. 4; LFBFK, p. 49.

17. This seems indicated by the sudden break in their correspondence that fall, after Keats's extremely warm and confidential letter that summer (*Letters*, II, 7, 139; cf. I, 369), and by his repeated outbursts against "ideot Parsons" that winter; see also Brown's mention of Bailey's "guilt" and his harsh criticism of him (though not by name) in the draft of his *Life of Keats* (KC, II, 64). Bailey's behaviour to Mariane Reynolds could hardly have been sufficient reason to Keats for the rupture of their friendship.

18. Steele, "WTPJK," p. 244; KC, I, 65–66.

19. Not on February 17 (cf. Rollins, *Letters,* I, 48), which Keats described as a day of business (II, 66), and which on February 19 he referred to as "day before yesterday" in contrast to February 13, "the other day" (II, 64, 65)—which he described as a day of seeing many people.

20. Gittings, JKLY, p. 86.

21. Ibid., pp. 87–91.

22. See Gittings, JKLY, Chapters 3–10, and compare Murry, K, Chapter 3, and the articles by Ward cited above, Chapter V, note 5 and Chapter VIII, notes 19, 23.

23. Blunden, KPMJT, pp. 96–97.

24. Mabel A. E. Steele, "The Authorship of 'The Poet' and Other Sonnets," KSJ, V (1956), 75–76.

25. Gittings, JKLY, p. 102.

26. R. L. Cecil and R. F. Loeb, *A Textbook of Medicine* (1951), pp. 254 ff., 269 ff. Gittings' contention (JKLY, p. 4) that Keats was "in robust health during most of the year" from September 1818 to September 1819 is refuted by Keats's own frequent references to his poor health (especially his sore throat) during this time. Nor does Hale-White's account of Keats's health (pp. 69, 73, 79) bear out Gittings's statement; rather, it implies that Keat's pulmonary infection had already "progressed considerably" (p. 79).

27. *Encyclopaedia Britannica,* 6th ed. (1823), "Medicine," XIII, 225, 349–55.

28. See Chapter VIII, note 12 above; and *Letters,* II, 12, 77, 81. This sensation of weight and tightness in his chest became greatly intensified after his illness, especially in moments of anxiety (ibid., 264, 281, 283, 314, 315, 321). His most vivid expression of the sensation occurs in his marginal comment on *Paradise Lost,* IX, 179 ff., where Satan entered the body of the serpent "but his sleep Disturbed not": "Whose spirit does not ache at the smothering and confinement, the *waiting close?* No passage of poetry ever can give a greater pain of suffocation" (Hampstead, V, 305). A comparison with *Hyperion,* I, 259 ff., suggests this note was written in the fall of 1818.

29. Dilke's note in his copy of Milnes's *Life* (Morgan Library), I, 215; *Letters,* II, 42, 52, 77, 149 et seq.

30. The date of the sonnet is uncertain. It cannot have been written on the morning of March 19, when Keats copied it out fair and referred to it in the past tense (*Letters,* II, 81), and probably not on the evening of the eighteenth, when Keats was laid up with a black eye; the evening of the seventeenth is quite possible, however, and the sonnet fits the mood of utter negativism expressed in his journal for that day.

31. KC, I, 256, 258.

32. The parallelism between "Why did I laugh tonight?" and *Hyperion* III, 86–107 has been noted by Murry, KS, pp. 89 ff., and Gittings, JKLY, pp. 100–101.

33. The third, fourth, and fifth lines were omitted from the printed version, presumably on Woodhouse's initiative, for they were left uncancelled in Keats's

autograph but cancelled in pencil in Woodhouse's transcript, now in the Harvard University Library (cf. *Works,* pp. 304–305).

34. The ending pencilled by Woodhouse into his clerk's transcript (W[1], now in the Harvard University Library; cf. *Works,* p. 305): "probably a subsequent amendment," as Murry describes it (KS, p. 230). Keats's autograph draft (A) provides another ending, "Apollo shriek'd, and lo! he was the God!" The truncated ending of the printed version seems to have been devised to give the effect of "A Fragment," as Taylor and Hessey decided to publish it in 1820.

35. KC, I, 129.

X. THE TEMPLE OF DELIGHT

1. See Chapter IV, note 25, above, and Hewlett, pp. 255 and 340 n. 1.

2. Rollins, MLPKC, pp. 3–5.

3. *Letters,* II, 52, 84.

4. Ibid., 61 and 46; 70, 52, 83, 111, 113, 114, 115, 123.

5. Dilke's note in his copy of Milnes's *Life* (Morgan Library), I, 288.

6. Hewlett, p. 381; Gittings, JKLY, pp. 120–23.

7. See *Letters,* II, 257, 261, 285, 287, 288, 309, 330; also Keats's comment, recorded by Woodhouse, "Wells should have brothers and sicker than I even had" (Finney, II, 746).

8. Marginalia to *Troilus and Cressida,* I.III.316 ff., Hampstead, V, 271.

9. Rollins assigns "La Belle Dame," the "Chorus of Four Faeries," and the "vale of Soul-making" passage to a single evening, April 21 (*Letters,* II, 95–104). But the manuscript of the letter, now in the Harvard University Library, shows clear breaks after "La Belle Dame" and the "Chorus," suggesting that these three sections were written on three different occasions.

10. *Letters,* II, 80.

11. Compare this image of suckling *(Letters,* II, 103) with *Endymion,* II, 869 and III, 456; the sonnet "To Spenser," ll. 11–12; and *Letters,* I, 232.

12. Lowell arranges the odes according to a progression of mood (II, 244 ff.), Finney by the development of the ode stanza (II, 610 ff.), H. W. Garrod by the development of a single theme, the search for a transcendent joy (*Keats* [1926], pp. 97 ff.), and Gittings by their connection with Keats's reading, presumably of Burton (JKLY, pp. 136–46; but cf. Ward, "KBR," pp. 535–42). The following analysis draws on all these methods but departs from all the schemes cited above by putting the "Ode on Indolence" immediately after "Psyche" and before "On a Grecian Urn," for reasons noted below.

13. Robert Wagner, "Keats's 'Ode to Psyche' and the Second *Hyperion,*" forthcoming in KSJ.

14. H. J. Pettit, "Scientific Correlatives of Keats's 'Ode to Psyche,'" SP, XL (1943), 560–67; Charles W. Hagelman, Jr., "Keats's Medical Training and the Last Stanza of the 'Ode to Psyche,'" KSJ, XI (1962), 73–82.

15. The "Ode on Indolence" was probably not written early in June, for Keats referred to it then as written some indeterminate time ago and confessed also that he had been "very idle lately" (*Letters,* II, 116). More likely it was written early in May, since it closely echoes the March 19 section of the letter to George (ibid., pp. 78–79), which Keats probably reread before sending it off on May 3. It also echoes the two sonnets on Fame and the "Ode to Psyche," written at the end of April or beginning of May; and the last lines of "Indolence" closely parallel a sentence from *The Golden Asse*

(quoted by Colvin, p. 412 n. 1), which Keats was reading at the time he wrote "Psyche."

16. The order of the stanzas is a matter of dispute, and the versification lacks force: four stanzas (nos. 1, 2, 4, and 5 in *Works*, pp. 447-48) follow a pattern of almost monotonous regularity, which is then altered in the third and sixth stanzas for no discernible reason.

17. Cleanth Brooks, *The Well-Wrought Urn* (1947), p. 148.

18. HBF, IV, 387 ff.

19. Gittings dates the "Ode to a Nightingale" April 30 (JKLY, p. 132), but it is improbable that Keats wrote it on the same morning as his two sonnets "On Fame" and in the same week as the "Ode to Psyche." Stanza v gives the date as mid-May—the time when nightingales usually start nesting in the vicinity of London (H. F. Witherby, *Handbook of British Birds* [1949], II, 188).

20. *Letters*, I, 307, 403 and II, 46.

21. Newell F. Ford, "Keats's Romantic Seas: 'Ruthless' or 'Keelless'?" KSJ, I (1952), 11-22.

22. In contrast to the preponderantly regular versification of the "Ode on a Grecian Urn," the "Ode to a Nightingale" shows a great variety of irregular verses within the first seven lines of each stanza, subsiding, after the truncated eighth line, into two regular lines at the end. The greatest metrical irregularity is concentrated in the first line of each stanza, suggesting a violent effort to break out of the recurrent pattern confirmed in the last two lines.

23. The only clues to the date of the "Ode on Melancholy" are its similarity in mood to the letter of May 31 to Miss Jeffrey and its position as the last of the odes in the 1820 volume.

24. Hewlett, p. 255.

25. Ward, "KBR," pp. 542-43.

XI. BETWEEN DESPAIR AND ENERGY

1. Keats may have started *Lamia* in June at Hampstead, as De Selincourt suggests (p. 453), and possibly *Otho* as well; but the letter which De Selincourt cites (II, 128) is very inconclusive on this point. In any event, the long first scene of *Otho* was extensively rewritten (*Works*, pp. 312-18).

2. *Letters*, II, 228-29. The emendation of "Holland" to "Holt and" (n. 4) is unnecessary, for Brown speaks of "a trustee being in Holland at the time" (i.e. in the fall of 1819) in a letter to Dilke of 6 September 1824 (KHM, no. 80). Keats's handwriting frequently shows spaces between letters within a word.

3. Keats could not have begun the revised version at this time, as is usually suggested (*Letters*, II, 139 n. 3). Though he was working on "a very abstract Poem" on July 25, a day or two later he resumed writing *Otho* with Brown (ibid., p. 135), and evidently was completely occupied with Acts II–IV of *Otho* between July 26 and August 11 and with Act V of *Otho*, scenes i–iii of *King Stephen*, Part II of *Lamia*, and the revision of *The Eve of St. Agnes* between August 13 and September 5—a schedule which left no time for his epic. Therefore his reference to "writing parts of my Hyperion" on August 14 cannot be taken to mean he had started *The Fall of Hyperion* at this time—especially when it is noted that he was describing the work of the entire previous year in this letter to Bailey (ibid., p. 139). Furthermore, Keats gave up *Hyperion* because, as he stated on September 21, he was dissatisfied

with its Miltonic quality (ibid., p. 167); but several times during August he expressed fervent admiration for *Paradise Lost* (ibid., pp. 139, 146). All of this suggests that Keats was working on the original *Hyperion* at the end of July but did not decide to give it up till early September (see note 15 below).

4. On the date of this sonnet, see Ward, "DKBSS," pp. 75–85.

5. Compare *Otho*, I.III.115 and V.v.146 and *Letters*, II, 141 and 146; *Otho*, II.i.4 and *Letters*, II, 140; *Otho*, II.i.135 and *Letters*, II, 133; *Otho*, III.ii.98 and *Letters*, II, 141 and 144; *Otho*, IV.i.13 and *Letters*, II, 144; *Otho*, V.iv.26 and *Letters*, II, 113 and 142.

6. Colvin, pp. 330–31 n.; Gittings, JKLY, p. 162.

7. *Letters*, II, 144, 176–77, 179.

8. KC, II, 67; cf. Gittings, JKLY, p. 164. Scenes 1–3 of *King Stephen* come to 135 lines, but they are followed by a fourth scene 58 lines long: it therefore seems likely that Keats wrote the first three scenes in August, as Brown suggests (KC, II, 67), then added the fourth scene in November on learning that Kean had decided against going to America—when he told Taylor that his ambition was to write "a few fine Plays" (*Letters*, II, 234). This addition would account for the discrepancy between the August date in Brown's *Life* and the November date on his transcript.

9. Potter's *Archaeologia Graeca*: Douglas Bush, "Notes on Keats's Reading," PMLA, L (1935), 785–806.

10. Murry, KS, pp. 157 ff.

11. Gittings, JKLY, pp. 172–73.

12. *Endymion*, II, 868 and III, 456; *Letters*, II, 160 and 257; Chapter X, note 11 above.

13. Fanny Brawne stated that Keats "was not engaged to me" when he offered to lend George "any assistance or money in his power," in September 1819 (LFBFK, p. 25; *Letters*, II, 185, 210; and see note 17 below).

14. The annotations are reprinted in Hampstead, V, 306–20; on their date, see Ward, "KBR," pp. 543–48.

15. Keats's remark to this effect in his letter to Reynolds of 21 September is usually taken to refer to giving up *The Fall of Hyperion* (*Letters*, II, 167 n. 1), because in writing to Woodhouse on the same day he quoted a passage near the end of *The Fall of Hyperion* (De Selincourt, p. 582). Yet this evidence is not at all conclusive. The passage itself (II, 1–4, 6) may be only an isolated fragment which Keats later fitted into place, since it forms an abrupt transition from the preceding passage and is immediately followed by forty-two lines of unbroken quotation from the first *Hyperion* and, after a five-line interpolation, eight more lines from the first version, after which *The Fall* breaks off. Since Keats was working on *The Fall of Hyperion* in November and December (KC, II, 72), it seems unlikely that all his work then added merely five new lines (II, 49–53) to the poem. Several other considerations suggest that Keats in fact gave up the original, not the revised, *Hyperion* at this time. First, since he most probably did not start work on *The Fall* till early September (see note 3 above), he could hardly have written the entire First Canto—containing some of the most concentrated poetry in all his work—in the eight or nine working days between Brown's departure and Keats's letter to Woodhouse. Second, the Miltonic quality which Keats cited as his reason for "giving up Hyperion" is much more pronounced in the first than in the second version (as De Selincourt admits, pp. 519, 582). Third, the passages from *The Fall* which Keats quoted to Woodhouse were later

revised (ibid., p. 582), and Keats quoted them in a manner clearly indicating he was pleased with them (*Letters,* II, 171). Fourth, Keats told Reynolds to reread *Hyperion* and mark it (*Letters,* II, 167): but Reynolds could not yet have seen the revised version, though he had access to Woodhouse's copy of the original version at the time. Fifth, the central passage in *The Fall of Hyperion* (I, 147–210) echoes a disillusionment with poetry that Keats began to express in his letters near the end of September (See Chapter XII, note 2, below).

16. John Livingston Lowes, *"Hyperion* and the *Purgatorio,"* TLS, 11 January 1936, p. 35; Gittings, MK, pp. 33–44.

17. *Letters,* II, 185. None of George's three letters between May and September has survived, but their contents may be reconstructed from Keats's replies. In the letter which arrived in May, he told Keats of the steamboat scheme but expressed no need of money at this time (II, 228); Keats evidently replied to his in June in a lost letter (I, 11), congratulating him on the birth of his daughter (II, 121) and telling him of the Chancery suit (II, 217, 231). Keats next wrote from Shanklin in July in immediate reply to a second less optimistic letter from George, in which he asked Keats to sell his remaining holdings (II, 124–25, 128, 131–32). Not until September did his situation seem so precarious that Keats offered to lend him money of his own (II, 185, 210). Gittings' conjecture (JKLY, p. 138) that Keats offered to lend George money in a letter of May, which he later forgot having written, seems unwarranted. As for Audubon's unreliability, Miss Kirk points out that he ultimately bankrupted six business partners—though George's later belief that Audubon tricked him into investing in the steamboat after it had already sunk cannot be substantiated (Kirk, pp. lxxxvii–lxxxviii; cf. *Letters,* II, 185, 211).

18. KC, I, 88.

19. *The Times,* 14 September 1819; *The Examiner,* 19 September 1819.

20. It seems probable that the two Chaucerian passages were added in September from the fact that Keats copied out lines 1–98 for George on September 20 with the prefatory remark "I will give it [as] far as I have gone," and then added the second Chaucerian passage (ll. 99–114) after a distinct break (*Letters,* II, 201, 204), but did not include the first Chaucerian passage (ll. 98a–p; *Works,* p. 452), which was evidently added later, as were the last four lines (115–19). See also the references in his letters to Venice (II, 201) and to Chatterton (II, 167, 212) and the repetition of the phrase "kepen in solitarinesse" (II, 166, 209), all of which link the poem with this period. The appearance of the rough draft of "The Eve of St. Mark" in the British Museum (Egerton 2780) also suggests a similar break between the first 98 lines and the remaining portion.

XII. UNMERIDIAN'D AND OBJECTLESS

1. This conjecture is supported by the fact that when Reynolds made a copy of *The Fall of Hyperion* sometime after Keats's return to London, he transcribed only as far as I, 326—presumably the point which Keats had reached at that time.

2. Murry (K, pp. 238–46) and De Selincourt (pp. 517–19, 583–84) have disagreed as to whether the passage from which these lines are quoted (I, 187–210) should stand, since it was cancelled by Woodhouse in his two

transcripts with a pencil mark and a note (though not in the Reynolds transcript); they agree, however, that Keats's intention in this section of the poem was to glorify his own role as a "true poet." This writer disagrees with this interpretation. De Selincourt oversimplifies Keats's argument by reducing it to the Shelley-like contrast between the poet and "the practical unimaginative man" (p. 519), thus overlooking the higher type of the disinterested man of action who is Keats's true ideal. But Murry reads something into Keats's argument of which the text gives no hint if the disputed passage is dropped, as he recommends: that Keats counted himself "a true poet," one who had "utterly rejected dreams," and thus exempt from Moneta's condemnation (p. 242). Keats may have cancelled the disputed passage, not because he disagreed with Moneta's condemnation (which remains in ll. 166–70), but because in his temporary disillusionment with poetry he overstated his case and thus apparently nullified his intention in the poem as a whole. If the dreamer was eventually, like Apollo in *Hyperion,* to be transformed into a true poet, he must maintain his faith in this possibility, rather than accept Moneta's reproof as an irreversible indictment (as in ll. 202–10). When Keats returned to the poem later in the fall, he must have realized the inconsistency and, at least provisionally, cancelled the digression.

3. Murry, K, p. 50.

4. Herschel Baker, *William Hazlitt* (1962), pp. 260–63.

5. Ibid., p. 250.

6. Sir Charles W. Dilke, ed., *Papers of a Critic,* 2 vols. (1875), I, 11, where no date is given. Murry's conjecture that the formal engagement took place in October 1819 (K, pp. 33–36) best fits the few known facts of the matter.

7. KHM no. 67; J. Richardson, p. 87.

8. *Letters,* II, 321 n. 4.

9. See Chapter XI, note 8 above.

10. MBF, p. 513 n.

11. Gittings, MK, pp. 122–39.

12. Murry, K, pp. 51–52.

13. *Encyclopaedia Britannica,* 6th ed. (1823), "Medicine," XIII, 355; compare Keats's own recommendation of a light diet, *Letters,* II, 252.

14. See above, p. 258.

15. W. B. Yeats, *Collected Works* (1908), VI, 109–10.

16. KC, I, 97; *Works,* pp. xxxiv–xxxvi.

17. Not because of the supposed sinking of his steamboat (Hewlett, p. 269; Gittings, JKLY, p. 180), for George mentioned the steamboat twice in the following year (*Letters,* II, 295–96, 356; cf. II, 256–57).

18. Jack Stillinger states the facts of this transaction as clearly as they can be gathered in "The Brown-Dilke Controversy," KSJ, XI (1962), 39–45.

19. LFBFK, p. 34.

20. Ibid.

21. Sharp, pp. 65–66.

22. KC, I, 217; LFBFK, p. 33; Brown, letter to Dilke, 6 September 1824 (KHM, no. 80).

23. KC, II, 102 n. 3.

24. The date is conjectural: but *Otho* was submitted to Covent Garden soon after the middle of January (*Letters,* II, 241) and "speedily returned" (KC, II, 67), and it was evidently shelved by February 11 (MBF, pp. 461–62 n.).

XIII. A WRECKED LIFE

1. It is significant that George Keats, in whom tuberculosis was evidently latent for years, suffered his first haemorrhage at the time of a desperate financial crisis (KC, I, cviii).

2. This letter (No. 223) appears to follow rather than precede Nos. 225, 226, and 227, all of which refer to breaking the engagement, since Keats here alludes to the subject as closed. On Reynolds' disapproval of his engagement, see *Letters*, II, 258 n. and 292 n. and KC, I, 156.

3. Brown's unpublished letters (British Museum Add. 38109 *passim*) are full of expressions of his derogatory attitude toward women. Writing to Leigh Hunt on 28 November 1829, he commented that their friend Kirkup was "a lucky fellow" to have got rid of "two incumbrances" at the same time by the death of his wife and the marriage of his mistress to an actor (fol. 62).

4. KC, I, lxvii. Brown's rather casual suggestion about leaving the child with his friend Thomas Richards while he went abroad (*Some Letters and a Miscellanea*, ed. M. B. Forman [1937], p. 10) indicates his attitude.

5. On the probable date of Brown's illegal marriage to Abby, which is completely a matter of conjecture (see *Letters*, II, 159 n. 7), see Chapter XIV, note 15 below.

6. This letter (No. 244) seems linked fairly clearly with No. 238 by the mention of the prohibition against visiting when Brown was at home and Keat's allusion to watching when she went out for her walk on the Heath.

7. Haydon, D, II, 265; Baker, p. 238; Sharp, p. 34.

8. Keats evidently did not learn of this plan till July 5 (*Letters*, II, 305); and his report of his own health at the end of March is much less optimistic than Brown's (compare II, 295 and 283–84).

9. Brown's letter to Dilke of 2 May 1826 (KHM, no. 80).

10. The quarrel was evidently not with Bailey (see *Letters*, II, 298 n. 6), with whom Keats had not been reconciled, but probably with Dilke, who noted in his biographical sketch of Keats in his copy of *Endymion* (KHM, no. 47A), "The very kindness of friends was at this time felt to be oppressive to him."

11. *Works*, pp. xxxiv–xxxv.

12. Hunt spoke of Keats's suffering from "critical malignity" during his illness (HBF, II, 536); see also KC, I, 232 and II, 95 n. 77.

13. See Chapter X, note 7 above.

14. Hewlett, pp. 324–27.

15. Medwin, p. 297.

16. HBF, IV, 293–94; Lowell, II, 438.

17. Letter to James Taylor, 10 August 1820 (KHM, no. 50). The date shows that plans were being laid for the trip before Keats finally agreed to go.

18. The difference between his loan of £30 in November 1819 (*Letters*, II, 226) and Keats's debt of £50 at the time of his death (MLPKC, pp. 26–28).

19. Dilke, PC, I, 11.

20. HBF, IV, 294; LFBFK, pp. 25–26.

21. See also MBF, p. 506 n. 1, and compare p. 525 n. 1.

22. Hewlett, p. 306.

23. KC, I, 215.

24. *Letters*, II, 329 and n. 3; compare 321, 327, and see also II, 364 and 359–360.

25. LFBFK, pp. 25–28.
26. HBF, IV, 358–61.
27. KC, I, 155–56.
28. KHM, no. 74.
29. Dilke's note in his copy of *Endymion* (KHM, no. 47A).
30. HBF, IV, 200.

XIV. END OF THE VOYAGE

1. Blunden, KPMJT, p. 79.

2. *Letters,* II, 350. The letter was never sent (KC, II, 130); Severn evidently opened it after Keats's death and sent Brown a copy. A comparison of the autograph (now in the Harvard University Library) with Brown's transcript (KC, II, 80–82) reveals that Brown occasionally omitted entire sentences without indication (cf. *Letters,* II, 345 n. 2, 4).

3. As he told Milnes, who printed this account of the sonnet in his 1848 *Life* (I, 72)—even though, as M. B. Forman noted (Hampstead, IV, 235–36), he had seen and quoted the earlier version of the sonnet in Brown's transcript, which is clearly dated 1819. Severn's detailed reminiscences of the trip from London to Rome are printed in Sharp, pp. 58–64.

4. KHM, no. 14; cf. *The Keats Letters, Papers, and Other Relics Forming the Dilke Bequest in the Hampstead Public Library,* ed. George C. Williamson (1914), pl. XLVII.

5. Brown may have deleted a reminder, however, as he did in transcribing Keats's letter of 30 November (see note 13 below).

6. KC, II, 130; *Letters of Joseph Severn to H. B. Forman* (1933), pp. 7, 9, 11, 18–19.

7. Harold Acton, *The Bourbons of Naples* (1956), pp. 681–87.

8. MBF, p. 525 n. 1.

9. "Keats's Roman Landlady," from "A Correspondent," *The Times* (London), 2 February 1953.

10. KC, I, 183–84. Severn later found he could live on three shillings a day in Italy (ibid., p. 273). For his reminiscences of his stay with Keats in Rome, see Sharp, pp. 64 ff.

11. This letter has not survived, but its contents can be reconstructed from Fanny Brawne's recapitulation of it (LFBFK, p. 16); Severn evidently mailed it on December 9 (*Letters,* II, 363).

12. KC, I, cxxxiii.

13. These breaks may mark a deletion, since this letter was clearly censored: compare Keats's letter (as transcribed by Brown) and Brown's reply, *Letters,* II, 359–60 and 364.

14. See KC, II, 77, 80.

15. The date and place of Brown's marriage to Abby is conjectural *(Letters,* II, 159 n. 7). From all the contemporary references to Brown's relations with her, it appears to have taken place after the birth of the boy "Carlino," not before, as usually assumed; cf. Rice and other friends' protests to Brown that the boy's birth was "a heinous crime" (Brown, p. 26); Brown's description of his arrangements with Abby in December 1820 as recent (*Letters,* II, 365); and his reproach to Carlino for "wincing under the circumstances of [his] birth" (letter of 12 June 1840, KHM, no. 80). Brown always spoke of Abby "with the utmost callousness" (Rollins, KC, I, lxvii); he was estranged from

her six months after Carlino's birth, and separated finally from her a year later.

16. Rollins, *Letters,* II, 364 n. 2.

17. Since Brown opened and endorsed this letter (now in the Harvard University Library), he evidently withheld it from forwarding, as with George's letter of 8 November 1820 (cf. KC, I, 168 n. 1).

18. KC, II, 80. See also *Letters,* II, 329 n. 3; and KC, I, 159, 160, 173, 174, 186, 200 ff., 228 ff.; also Severn's letters to Brown, KC, I, 175 ff. and II, 90 ff. and 94 ff., which are silent on this point.

19. From a conjectured reading of Severn's mutilated letter in the Harvard University Library which appears necessary from the context and which fits into the gaps: "His dreadful state of mind turns to [per]secuti[on and some] times even murder—he is now under the [terrible de]lusion [that poison] was administered to him by an individual in London" (cf. KC, I, 180).

20. HBF, IV, 362.

21. KC, II, 92.

22. Medwin, p. 297.

23. Sharp, pp. 72–73; KC, I, 168, 201.

24. LFBFK, p. 17.

25. KC, I, 182.

26. Brown's omission may be found in Fanny Brawne's transcript of this letter (compare KC, II, 93 and HBF, IV, 214).

27. KC, I, 201, 207; Sharp, p. 76. It should be noted that Keats's last references to George in his letters were extremely affectionate.

28. MLPKC, p. 117.

29. HBF, IV, 221–22.

30. Sharp, p. 75.

31. LFBFK, p. 20. Fanny implies in a later letter to Fanny Keats that it was Keats's assurance that Brown would go to Rome that kept her from going herself (p. 25).

32. Ward, "CD1818," pp. 24–25. The lyre, as sketched by Severn in Brown's copy of *Endymion* (now in the Keats House at Hampstead), is reproduced in the device on the title page of this volume.

33. Ward, "CD1818," pp. 25–26; Sharp, pp. 91–93.

34. KC, I, 251; HBF, IV, 364.

EPILOGUE

1. HBF, IV, 358–59.

2. H. B. Forman, LJKFB, p. lxv.

3. Dorothy Hyde Bodurtha, KSJ, II (1953), 111.

4. HBF, IV, 366–68; Sharp, pp. 110–12.

5. Colvin, p. 524. On the actual date of Keats's death, incorrectly given on his tombstone as February 24, 1821, see KC, I, 226.

6. MacGillivray, pp. xxxii–xxxvi.

7. Baker, p. 250.

8. MBF, pp. lxi, lxiv; KC, I, 313–14, 326–27.

9. Colvin, p. 529.

10. Ibid., p. 528.

11. D. H. Bodurtha and Willard B. Pope, eds., *Life of John Keats by Charles Armitage Brown* (1937), p. 10.

12. Leslie A. Marchand notes that this is one of the few undoubted details amid the legends surrounding Shelley's death ("Trelawny on the Death of Shelley," KSMB, IV [1952], 17).

13. George, pp. 171-72; Haydon, D, II, 499.

14. Colvin, p. 536.

15. J. Richardson, p. 113.

16. Both letters are printed in MBF, lxi-lxiv.

17. MacGillivray, p. xlv.

18. Ibid., pp. lviii-lx.

19. Dilke, I, 7.

20. Murry, KS, p. 13.

Selective Bibliography

Adami, Marie. *Fanny Keats,* 1937.

Altick, Richard. *The Cowden Clarkes,* 1948.

Baker, Herschel. *William Hazlitt,* 1962.

Beavan, A. H. *James and Horace Smith,* 1899.

Beyer, Werner William. *Keats and the Daemon King,* 1947.

Blunden, Edmund. *John Keats.* Supplement to *British Book News,* 1950.

——. *Leigh Hunt and His Circle,* 1930.

——. *Keats's Publisher: A Memoir of John Taylor,* 1936.

——. *Votive Tablets,* 1931.

Brown, Charles. *Some Letters and a Miscellanea,* ed. M. B. Forman, 1937.

Bush, Douglas. *Mythology and the Romantic Tradition in English Poetry,* 1937.

Caldwell, James R. "Woodhouse's Annotations in Keats's First Volume of Poems," PMLA, LXIII (1948), 757–59.

Clarke, Charles Cowden. "Recollections of Keats," *Atlantic Monthly,* VII (1861), 86–100.

Colvin, Sir Sidney. *John Keats: His Life and Poetry, Friends, Critics, and After-Fame,* 1917.

Dilke, Sir Charles Wentworth, Bart., ed. *The Papers of a Critic,* 2 vols., 1875.

Encyclopaedia Britannica, 6th ed. (1823), art. "Medicine," XIII, 349 ff.

Erikson, Erik H. "The Problem of Ego Identity," *Journal of the American Psychoanalytic Association,* IV (1956), 56–121.

Finney, Claude Lee. *The Evolution of Keats's Poetry,* 2 vols., 1936.

George, Eric. *The Life and Death of Benjamin Robert Haydon,* 1948.

Gittings, Robert. *John Keats: The Living Year,* 1954.

——. "Keats's Sailor Relation," TLS, 15 April 1960, p. 245.

——. *The Mask of Keats,* 1956.

Hagelman, Charles W., Jr. *John Keats and the Medical Profession,* unpublished dissertation, University of Texas, 1956.

Hale-White, Sir William. *Keats as Doctor and Patient,* 1938.

Harper, George MacLean. *William Wordsworth,* 2 vols., 1916.

Haydon, Benjamin Robert. *Autobiography and Journals,* ed. Malcolm Elwin, 1950.

——. *Diary,* ed. Willard Bissell Pope, 2 vols., 1960.

Hazlitt, William. *Complete Works,* ed. P. P. Howe, 21 vols., 1930–1934.

——. *Lectures on the English Poets,* Everyman's Library, 1910.

Hewlett, Dorothy. *A Life of John Keats,* 2nd ed., revised, 1949.

Howe, P. P. *The Life of William Hazlitt,* Penguin Books, 1949.

Hunt, Leigh. *Autobiography,* ed. J. E. Morpurgo, 1949.

Keats House and Museum: A Historical and Descriptive Guide, 4th ed., revised; n.d.

Keats, John. *Anatomical and Physiological Notebook,* ed. Maurice Buxton Forman, 1934.

——. *Letters,* ed. Hyder Edward Rollins, 2 vols., 1958.

——. *Letters,* ed. Maurice Buxton Forman, 2nd ed., revised, 1935.

——. *Letters to Fanny Brawne,* ed. Harry Buxton Forman, 1878.

Keats, John. *Poems,* ed. Ernest de Selincourt, 5th ed., revised, 1926.
———. *Poems and Verses,* Edited and Arranged in Chronological Order by John Middleton Murry, 1930.
———. *The Poetical Works,* ed. H. W. Garrod, 2nd ed., 1958.
———. *The Poetical Works and Other Writings,* ed. Harry Buxton Forman, 4 vols., 1883.
———. *The Poetical Works and Other Writings,* ed. Harry Buxton Forman, revised by Maurice Buxton Forman, Hampstead Edition, 8 vols., 1938–1939.
Kirk, Naomi J. "Memoir of George Keats," in *The Poetical Works and Other Writings of John Keats,* ed. H. B. Forman and M. B. Forman, 1938–1939, I, lxxiii–xcviii.
Lindon, Fanny Brawne. *Letters to Fanny Keats, 1820–1824,* ed. Fred Edgcumbe, 1937.
Lowell, Amy. *John Keats,* 2 vols., 1925.
MacGillivray, J. R. *Keats: A Bibliography and Reference Guide,* 1949.
Medwin, Thomas. *Life of Percy Bysshe Shelley,* ed. H. B. Forman, 1913.
Milnes, Richard Monckton. *Life, Letters, and Literary Remains of John Keats,* 2 vols., 1848.
Murry, John Middleton. *Keats,* 1955.
———. *Keats and Shakespeare,* 1925.
———. *Studies in Keats,* 1930.
Olney, Clark. *Benjamin Robert Haydon, Historical Painter,* 1952.
Pederson-Krag, Geraldine. " 'O Poesy! For Thee I Hold My Pen,' " in *Psychoanalysis and Culture: Essays in Honor of Géza Roheim,* ed. G. W. Wilbur and W. Muensterberger, 1951, pp. 436–52.
Pope, Willard Bissell. *Studies on the Keats Circle,* unpublished dissertation, Harvard University, 1932.
Quennell, Peter. *Byron: The Years of Fame,* 1935.
Rank, Otto. *Art and Artist: Creative Urge and Personality Development,* 1932.
Reynolds, John Hamilton. *Poetry and Prose,* ed. George L. Marsh, 1928.
Richardson, Sir Benjamin Ward. *The Asclepiad,* 1884.
Richardson, Joanna. *Fanny Brawne,* 1952.
Ridley, Maurice Roy. *Keats's Craftsmanship,* 1933.
Rollins, Hyder Edward, ed. *The Keats Circle: Letters and Papers, 1816–1878,* 2 vols., 1948.
———. *More Letters and Papers of the Keats Circle,* 1955.
Severn, Joseph. *Letters to H. B. Forman,* 1933.
Sharp, William. *Life and Letters of Joseph Severn,* 1892.
Shelley, Percy Bysshe. *Complete Works,* ed. Roger Ingpen and W. E. Peck, 10 vols., 1926–1930.
Slote, Bernice. *Keats and the Dramatic Principle,* 1958.
South, John Flint. *Memorials,* 1884.
Spurgeon, Caroline. *Keats's Shakespeare,* 1929.
Steele, Mabel A. E. "The Woodhouse Transcripts of the Poems of John Keats," HLB, III (1949), 232–56.
Stout, George Dumas. "Leigh Hunt's Money Troubles: Some New Light," *Washington University Studies, Humanistic Series,* XII (1925), 221–32.
———. "The Political History of Leigh Hunt's *Examiner,*" *Washington University Studies (New Series) in Language and Literature,* no. 19, 1949.
Trilling, Lionel. "The Poet as Hero: Keats in His Letters," in *The Opposing Self,* 1955.
Ward, Aileen. "Christmas Day, 1818," KSJ, X (1961), 17–27.
———. "The Date of Keats's 'Bright Star' Sonnet," SP, LII (1955), 75–85.
———. "Keats and Burton: A Reappraisal," PQ, XL (1961), 535–52.
White, Newman Ivey. *Shelley,* 2 vols., 1940.

Index